Microsoft®
SQL Server™
7.0
Resource Guide

Microsoft Press

PUBLISHED BY
Microsoft Press
A Division of Microsoft Corporation
One Microsoft Way
Redmond, Washington 98052-6399

QA
76
.9
C 55
M 52
1999

Copyright © 1999 by Microsoft Corporation

Library of Congress Cataloging-in-Publication Data
Microsoft BackOffice 4.5 Resource Kit / Microsoft Corporation.
    p. cm.
  ISBN 0-7356-0583-1
  1. Microsoft BackOffice. 2. Client/server computing.
I. Microsoft Corporation.
QA76.9.C55M525 1999
005.7'1376--dc21   99-13771
                                        CIP

Printed and bound in the United States of America.

1 2 3 4 5 6 7 8 9 WCWC   4 3 2 1 0 9

Distributed in Canada by ITP Nelson, a division of Thomson Canada Limited.

A CIP catalogue record for this book is available from the British Library.

Microsoft Press books are available through booksellers and distributors worldwide. For further information about international editions, contact your local Microsoft Corporation office or contact Microsoft Press International directly at fax (425) 936-7329. Visit our Web site at mspress.microsoft.com.

Macintosh is a registered trademark of Apple Computer, Inc. Intel is a registered trademark of Intel Corporation. Active Desktop, ActiveX, Authenticode, BackOffice, Developer Studio, FoxPro, FrontPage, JScript, Microsoft, Microsoft Press, MSDN, MS-DOS, MSN, Outlook, PivotTable, PowerPoint, Visual Basic, Visual C++, Visual FoxPro, Visual InterDev, Visual J++, Visual Studio, Win32, Windows, and Windows NT are either registered trademarks or trademarks of Microsoft Corporation in the United States and/or other countries. Other product and company names mentioned herein may be the trademarks of their respective owners.

The example companies, organizations, products, people, and events depicted herein are fictitious. No association with any real company, organization, product, person, or event is intended or should be inferred.

Acquisitions Editor: Juliana Aldous
Project Editor: Maureen Williams Zimmerman

Part No. 097-0002191

Contents

Part 3   Deployment

Part 4   Performance Tuning

Part 7   Troubleshooting

Part 8   Disaster Recovery

Part 9   Architecture

Part 10   Security

Part 11   Upgrading and Migrating

Part 12   Programming

P A R T   1

Introduction

Part 1 introduces the *Microsoft SQL Server 7.0 Resource Guide*.

CHAPTER 1

Introducing the Microsoft SQL Server 7.0 Resource Guide

Welcome to the *Microsoft SQL Server 7.0 Resource Guide*. This guide is designed for people who are, or want to become, expert users of Microsoft SQL Server.

If you are responsible for designing a database solution, administering one or more SQL Server databases, or programming applications to streamline database activities, this guide is for you. It has been compiled largely from articles written by Microsoft staff to answer frequently asked questions and provide insights and ideas.

In addition to the information in this guide, various SQL Server tools and utilities are included on the *Microsoft BackOffice 4.5 Resource Kit* CD-ROM. Demonstrations of these product applications can be found on the CD-ROM. If you develop SQL Server database systems, you can pick up code samples from the CD-ROM. Also included on the CD-ROM are product add-ons and stand-alone applications you can use to simplify administering SQL Server.

Throughout the guide, you will learn about different uses for SQL Server. The *Microsoft SQL Server 7.0 Resource Guide* supplements SQL Server Books Online, included with the Microsoft SQL Server product, and does not replace the documentation as the source for learning how to use Microsoft SQL Server.

About the Resource Guide

Part 1, "Introduction"

Provides an overview of the *Microsoft SQL Server 7.0 Resource Guide* and resources for further information about SQL Server.

Part 2, "Planning"

Provides detailed information about planning the capacity of SQL Server, replication configurations, and heterogeneous data.

Part 3, "Deployment"

Provides comprehensive information for planning customized business applications.

Part 4, "Performance Tuning"

Provides valuable information for SQL Server tuning performance and SQL Server indexes.

Part 5, "Integration"

Provides an example of integrating SQL Server with another BackOffice application.

Part 6, "Tools and Utilities"

Describes SQL Server tools included on the *Microsoft BackOffice 4.5 Resource Kit* CD-ROM.

Part 7, "Troubleshooting"

Provides a useful reference for solving daily administrative and maintenance problems.

Part 8, "Disaster Recovery"

Provides valuable tips for backing up data and recovering from system failures.

Part 9, "Architecture"

Provides a detailed description of the internal structure of SQL Server, including the query processor and the storage engine.

Part 10, "Security"

Provides a description of SQL Server security configurations.

Part 11, "Upgrading and Migrating"

Provides detailed information for planning system upgrades and migrations, including information about Oracle, Sybase, and Btrieve migrations.

Part 12, "Programming"

Provides information for advanced programming, including English Query and OLE DB connectivity.

Additional Information

See these Web sites for up-to-date information about Microsoft SQL Server.

www.microsoft.com/sql/

The Microsoft SQL Server Web site contains information about Microsoft SQL Server and links to information about other Microsoft BackOffice products.

www.microsoft.com/support/

The Microsoft SQL Server Technical Support Web site gives you access to the Microsoft SQL Server Knowledge Base, support information, and frequently asked questions (FAQs).

www.microsoft.com/technet/

The Microsoft TechNet Web site contains information about subscribing to Microsoft TechNet. Microsoft TechNet provides in-depth technical information about Microsoft business products, including Microsoft SQL Server and other BackOffice products.

www.microsoft.com/train_cert/

The Microsoft Training and Certification Web site provides information about training options and the Microsoft Certified Professional Program.

www.microsoft.com/developer/

The Microsoft Developer Network Web site provides programming resources and information.

Conventions Used in This Guide

This table summarizes the typographical conventions used in this guide.

Convention	Description
bold	Menus and menu commands, command buttons, toolbar buttons, tab and dialog box titles and options, command-prompt commands, and portions of syntax that must be typed exactly as shown. Bold is also used for elements of a SQL Server database such as table, column, view, index, device, server names, data types, and configuration and database options as well as Transact-SQL stored procedures.
Initial capitals	Names of applications, file names, and directories in a path.
italic	Information you provide, terms that are being introduced, and book titles.
`monospace`	Example code, statements, and commands, program code and program output.

All Internet addresses (URLs) in this volume are correct at the time of publication. For more information about Microsoft products, see www.microsoft.com.

P A R T   2

Planning

The chapters in Part 2 provide a foundation for planning customized business strategies using SQL Server:

- Storage Engine Capacity Planning Tips
- Replication
- Heterogeneous Data

CHAPTER 2

Storage Engine Capacity Planning Tips

The I/O subsystem (storage engine) is a key component of any relational database management system (RDBMS). A successful RDBMS implementation requires careful planning at the early stages of the project. The storage engine comprises much of this planning, including what hardware to purchase, how to store data on the hardware, and how to set the configuration parameters appropriately. To accomplish these tasks requires an extensive understanding of the RDBMS architecture.

This chapter includes:

- Descriptions of the new dynamic features of SQL Server 7.0 and recommendations for when to use them.
- Descriptions of the architecture of the I/O subsystem, memory, processor threading, and utilities to improve capacity planning.
- Recommendations for setting system configurations to exploit resources more effectively.

SQL Server 7.0 Storage Engine Highlights

Microsoft SQL Server 7.0 reduces the configuration and tuning required to implement and run database applications. A major goal of SQL Server 7.0 is to minimize the need for database expertise. This is accomplished by new features, including but not limited to, on-demand memory, on-demand disk, and dynamic tuning of configuration parameters. Many users can now implement a database application successfully without knowledge about the internal architecture of the database system. (A small percentage of high-end applications always require more detailed knowledge.)

The table describes the changes and new features included in the Microsoft SQL Server 7.0 storage engine.

New features	Description
Performance improvements	Performance for both OLTP and decision support is improved by implementing new features and improving existing systems. New features include: ■ Fibers (lightweight threads scheduled within a single operating-system thread). ■ Larger I/O sizes. ■ Spinlock contention reduction. ■ Faster searches. ■ Parallel data access. ■ Faster utilities.
Complete row-level locking	The benefits of dynamic locking (choosing the right level of lock: row, key range, page, multiple pages, or table on the fly) are extended to all database operations: updates, deletes, and reads.

(continued)

New features	Description
Scalable storage, including VLDB support	The on-disk format and the storage subsystem can provide storage that is scalable from the very small database (fits on a floppy) to very large databases (VLDB). Specific changes include:
	▪ The ability to grow the database automatically within limits. The database administrator can set a maximum, but no longer has to preallocate space and manage extents.
	▪ Simplified mapping of database objects to files. On the small scale, this means a database, including metadata, can be in a single file, allowing a simple copy of the database. For large databases, database objects can be mapped to specific disks to load balance I/O.
	▪ More efficient space management including increasing page size from 2 KB to 8 KB, 64-KB I/O, rows that span pages, lifting of the column limit, variable length character fields up to 8 KB, and the ability to add and delete columns from existing tables without unloading or reloading the data.
	▪ Redesigned utilities to support terabyte-size databases efficiently.
Improved text and image support	SQL Server has complete content text query capability with new full-text search engine additions, which include full-text indexing.

Files and Filegroups

In Microsoft SQL Server version 6.5, devices and segments are used to physically allocate space for storing data, indexes, and logs. This can be cumbersome for applications with large amounts of data. In Microsoft SQL Server version 7.0, files and filegroups are used to allocate space for data, indexes, and logs, giving you many more choices for setting up data.

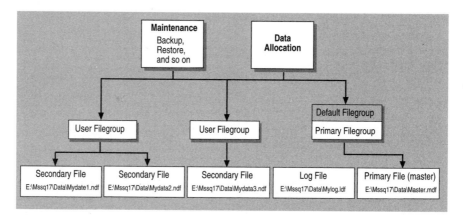

A file is a physical allocation of space and can be one of three types: primary, secondary, or log.

A primary file is the starting point of the database and contains the pointers to the rest of the files in the database. Every database has one primary data file. The recommended file extension for primary data files is .mdf (E:\Mssql7\Data\Master.mdf). Some databases may not have secondary data files, and others may have multiple secondary data files. The recommended file extension for secondary data files is .ndf (E:\Mssql7\Data\Mydata1.ndf). Log files hold all of the log information used to recover the database. There must be at least one log file for each database, although there can be more than one. The recommended file extension for log files is .ldf (E:\Mssql7\Data\Mylog.ldf).

Database objects can be grouped in filegroups for allocation, performance, and administration purposes. There are two types of filegroups: user-defined filegroups and the primary filegroup. The primary filegroup or any of the user filegroups can be the default filegroup. The primary file is assigned to the primary filegroup. (The preceding illustration shows a primary filegroup assigned as the default.) Secondary files can be assigned to user filegroups or the primary filegroup. Log files are never a part of a filegroup. Log space is managed separately from data space.

Care must be taken with the size of the primary filegroup, especially if it is also the default filegroup. Because the primary filegroup contains all the system tables, if it runs out of space, no new catalog information can be added to the system tables. In contrast, if a user-defined filegroup fills up, only the user tables specifically allocated to that filegroup are affected. The primary filegroup fills if the autogrow feature is off or if the disk holding the primary filegroup runs out of space. If either of these should occur, set autogrow on or move other files off the disk to free more space.

When creating objects such as tables and indexes, you can specify the filegroup to which the tables and indexes are assigned. A table can be assigned to one filegroup, and that table's index(es) can be assigned to a different filegroup. If you do not specify a filegroup, the table or index is assigned to the default filegroup.

Recommendations:

- Carefully plan the size of the primary filegroup or set it to autogrow to avoid running out of space.
- With large systems that use filegroups for administration and performance reasons, create a user-defined filegroup and make it the default filegroup. Create all of the secondary database files in user-defined filegroups so that user objects do not compete with system objects for space in the primary filegroup. This also facilitates the customization of maintenance for each filegroup.

Several questions that you may have about files and filegroups are:

- How many files should I create per filegroup?
- How many filegroups should I have for my database(s)?
- How should I place my data objects (tables/indexes) into filegroups?
- How should I set up my hardware to get the best performance from files and filegroups?
- Do I even need to worry about filegroups if I have a smaller database?

The answers to these questions depend on three factors:

- Maintenance requirements
- Performance requirements
- Hardware I/O layout

Assigning Files to Filegroups for Maintenance Reasons

Maintenance operations such as backup and restore can be performed at the file or filegroup level. It may be appropriate to perform some operations such as backup, restore, update statistics, or DBCC against some objects (tables) more often than others. By placing tables with similar maintenance requirements in the same filegroup, the maintenance operations can be executed against this specific filegroup.

Recommendations:

- Group tables and indexes with similar maintenance requirements into the same filegroups.

  An example of this is a data warehouse application with 50 tables. Assume three of the tables are modified or refreshed daily and the other 47 tables are modified or refreshed weekly.

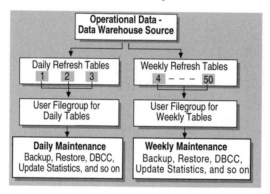

  By creating two filegroups and assigning tables to them, you can run daily maintenance tasks (backups, DBCC, update statistics, and so on) against the tables in the daily refreshes group and weekly maintenance tasks against the tables in the weekly refreshes group.

- Assign an individual high maintenance table to its own filegroup.

  For example, a specific table is updated frequently and may need to be recovered as an individual table. Because SQL Server can restore both files and filegroups, you can place a table in its own filegroup so you can restore only that table.

- When you work with small databases, using filegroups is not necessary. The primary filegroup can be used for easier administration of small databases.

The primary filegroup (the default, unless explicitly changed) contains the pages for all tables and indexes that are not assigned to a filegroup when they are created. In each database, only one filegroup at a time can be the default filegroup: a useful option for sites that have limited or no database administrator support. (Members of the **db_owner** fixed database role can switch the default filegroup from one filegroup to another.)

Assigning Files to Filegroups for Performance Reasons

Setting up database objects on files and filegroups for either maintenance or performance reasons is not necessarily mutually exclusive. You can set the database for maintenance and still exploit file setup for performance.

Considerations for files and filegroups include:

- A file or filegroup cannot be used by more than one database. For example, the files Sales.mdf and Sales.ndf, which contain data and objects from the **sales** database, cannot be used by any other database.
- A file can be a member of only one filegroup.
- Data and log information cannot be part of the same file. Data files and log files are always separate.
- Log files are never part of any filegroups. Log files are always separate.
- A file is a unit of parallelism.
- A file is the smallest unit of recovery.
- Filegroups are the mechanism for assigning objects to specific files.
- Tables cannot be moved between filegroups.
- Tables can only be assigned to one filegroup.

Multiple files can be created on separate disk drives and then assigned to the same filegroup. A table is then created and assigned to a filegroup. Filegroups use a proportional fill strategy across all the files within each filegroup. As data is written to the filegroup, an amount proportional to the free space in the file is written to each file within the filegroup, rather than writing all the data to the first file until it is full, and then proceeding to the next file. For example, if file 1 has 100 MB free, and file 2 has 200 MB free, one extent is allocated from file 1, and two extents from file 2, and so on. This way both files become full at about the same time and simple striping is achieved.

Each file is physically placed on a disk or set of disks (if the hardware disks are striped). SQL Server maintains a map of each file's location on the disk. If one file is created across a hardware stripe of four disks, one map points to the location of data on all four disks. If four files are created across a hardware stripe of four disks, four maps point to the location of the data on all four disks, one map in each file for each object in that file.

Whenever a data object (table) is accessed sequentially, a separate thread is created for each file in parallel. Therefore, a tablescan for a table that is assigned to a filegroup with four files uses four separate threads to read the data in parallel.

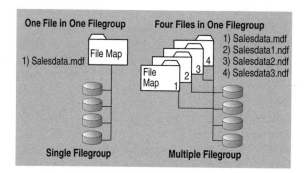

Due to the parallel data access from multiple files in a filegroup, a general rule is more files are better. Eventually, a saturation point is reached at which too many files are created, resulting in too many parallel threads and bottlenecks on the I/O subsystem. You can identify these bottlenecks by using Windows NT Performance Monitor to check the **Physical Disk** counter and **Counter Disk Queue Length**. If **Disk Queue** length is above 3, consider reducing the number of files. (**Counter Disk Queue** length can be affected by other things, such as insufficient physical disks or poor placement of data on disks.)

Recommendations:

- Create multiple files per filegroup. A good rule is to have one file per physical disk.

- Monitor disk activity to determine if too many or too few files have been created.

- Determine the number of filegroups by maintenance requirements rather than by performance, especially if you are using hardware striping.

Prior to the creation of RAID, a big performance boost was attained by physically separating data objects such as tables and indexes on disparate physical devices. SQL Server 7.0 accomplishes the same task with files and filegroups. A possible performance gain can be realized if you separate indexes from tables and read both objects in parallel.

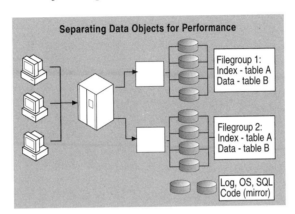

In the preceding illustration, Filegroup 1 is assigned to files on one stripe set with four disks and Filegroup 2 is assigned to files on another stripe set also with four disks. Table A is created and put in Filegroup 2 and the index for table A is put on Filegroup 1. If both table A and index A are being used for the same query, good performance results as both filegroups are being fully used with no contention. On the other hand, if only table A·is being scanned and index A is not being used, Filegroup 1 is used and Filegroup 2 is doing nothing. The best I/O performance comes from all disks being accessed at one time. If you cannot predict the type of access that will take place and when, it is a safer decision to place the objects across all disks as shown in the following illustration. This guarantees that all disks are being accessed because all data and indexes are spread evenly across all disks, no matter which way the data is accessed. This is also a simpler approach for database administrators.

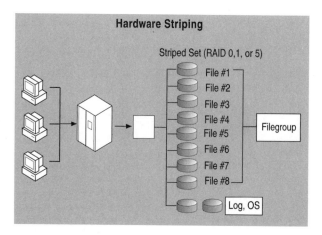

Separating tables and indexes into different filegroups can provide potential performance improvements, but spreading all objects across as many physical disks as possible is easier and more reliable. The preceding illustration can be shown with multiple filegroups and there would be no impact on read performance, because both filegroups are spread equally across all disks.

Recommendation:

- Use hardware striping to assign all objects to as many physical disks as possible rather than separating the data objects into different filegroups on different disks.

Hardware I/O Layout for Files and Filegroups

Spreading data across as many physical drives as possible is advantageous because it improves throughput by using parallel data access with multiple files. With hardware striping, all files are evenly spread across all disks in the stripe set. The data objects are assigned to a filegroup that proportionately fills each file.

This is an easy setup for the database administrator because it is one big logical drive. All files are created on the same large logical file, but physically they are spread across all disks.

In the previous section, the illustration of hardware striping shows one disk controller for all of the disks. Multiple disk controllers potentially can improve I/O throughput. The illustration of separating data objects for performance shows an I/O subsystem setup with multiple disk controllers. You can set up only one hardware stripe set per controller, therefore the illustration shows two separate stripe sets.

Spreading Data Across Multiple Controllers

To spread the data evenly across multiple controllers requires one of three options:

Option 1: Use hardware striping only (and/or Microsoft Windows NT striping). This configuration requires a Windows NT stripe on top of a hardware stripe for each controller to make it look like one logical drive. The illustration shows this configuration.

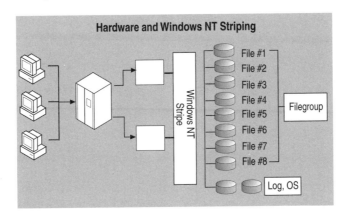

Option 2: Use SQL Server to stripe. The capabilities of SQL Server files and filegroups allow you to spread the data evenly across all disks without hardware striping. If a physical file is created on each disk and a filegroup is assigned to each of these files, SQL Server uses proportional fill to evenly distribute the data across all of the files and all of the disks. The following illustration shows this option. Some disadvantages of this configuration are:

- The database administrator has more work to do.

- The only option you have for hardware availability is RAID 1(mirroring), the most expensive option.

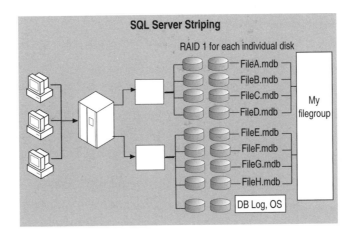

Because this configuration can be accomplished by using hardware striping with fewer disks and easier administration, this is not recommended.

Option 3: Use a combination of SQL Server and hardware striping. This configuration uses the best features of both options.

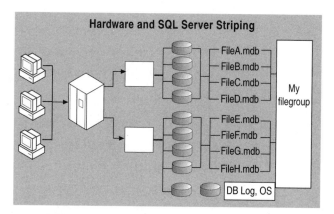

The illustration shows two controllers pointing to two hardware striped sets. An alternative to the Windows NT striping method that assigns data from all objects to all disks, a filegroup is assigned to all files on both stripe sets. This option spreads the data evenly across all disks while keeping administration simple, unlike options 1 and 2.

Recommendation:

- To spread data evenly across all disks, set up hardware striping and use filegroups to spread data across multiple hardware stripe sets.

Growing Data Files

One of the bigger challenges with SQL Server 6.5 and all other RDBMSs is the management of the physical space allocated to database objects such as tables and indexes. In SQL Server 6.5, if a database runs out of space, the database is inoperable until more space is added.

In SQL Server 7.0, files can grow automatically (autogrow) from their originally specified size. When you define a file, you can specify a growth increment. Each time the file fills, it increases its size by the growth increment set by the database creator. If there are multiple files in a filegroup, none of them grows automatically until all are full. Growth then occurs in a round-robin algorithm.

Each file can also have a specified maximum size. If a maximum size is not specified, the file continues to grow until it has used all available space on the disk. The lack of a maximum size is especially useful if a SQL Server database is embedded in an application for which no system administrator is readily accessible or if SQL Server is implemented in a distributed location without a database administrator. The files can grow automatically, reducing the administrative burden of monitoring the amount of free space in the database and of allocating additional space manually.

For example, a **Sales** database is created as a 50-MB data file. The autogrow feature is on, and it is set for 10 percent growth to a 500-MB maximum.

As soon as this database reaches 50 MB, 5 MB is added (50 MB + 50 MB*.10 = 55 MB). As soon as the database reaches 55 MB, 5.5 MB is added. This process continues until 500 MB is reached or until the database shrinks.

Performance degrades when a database must be altered to grow. If sufficient space is not initially assigned to a database, the database could grow continuously and performance would degrade slightly. The default autogrow setting is 10 percent of the size of the data file. For example, a database created at 1 MB with a maximum size of 500 MB requires multiple restarts of the autogrow feature if you add a large amount of new data. The database would start at 1 MB, grow to 1.1 MB, then grow to 1.22 MB, and then to 1.34 MB, and so on.

Although this method works, performance is improved if the initial file size and the percent growth are set to a reasonable size to avoid the frequent activation of the autogrow feature. In the previous example, a growth set to an increment of 5 MB would be better.

Recommendations:

- Leave the autogrow feature on at database creation time to avoid running out of space.

- Set the original size of the database to a reasonable size to avoid the premature activation of the autogrow feature.

- Set the autogrow increment to a reasonable size to avoid the frequent activation of the autogrow feature.

Shrinking Data Files

You must decide whether to implement the autoshrink feature or manually shrink your data. The autoshrink feature is on by default for the Desktop Edition of SQL Server 7.0 and off by default for the Standard and Enterprise editions. The autoshrink feature can be set by using the **sp_dboption** stored procedure. When autoshrink is on, it executes every 30 minutes and shrinks in increments of 25-percent free space.

When **sp_dboption** is used to shrink the database automatically (autoshrink), shrinking occurs whenever a significant amount of free space is available in the database. However, the free space to be removed automatically cannot be configured. To remove a certain amount of free space, such as only 50 percent of the current free space in the database, you must run either the DBCC SHRINKFILE statement or DBCC SHRINKDATABASE statement manually.

For example, to manually decrease the size of the files in the **UserDB** database to allow 10-percent free space in the files of **UserDB**, use:

```
DBCC SHRINKDATABASE (UserDB, 10)
GO
```

When the autoshrink feature or manual shrink is started, the best point to shrink to is calculated by using the free space setting as a guideline. The user cannot configure the point to shrink to when using the autoshrink feature. The shrinking task shrinks to the original or altered size of the created file only, although this can be overridden with the manual shrink file command. The following illustration shows the movement of each individual heap page (nonclustered index pages) row by row to create free space. B-tree nodes (for example, clustered index pages) are moved as a page to create free space. This shrinking task is a low priority background thread, but it can still affect performance on a busy system due to the movement and locking of pages. Avoid continuously autoshrinking and then autogrowing. Nonclustered index maintenance may be required to point to the new location of the data. Also, clustered indexes have the potential to fragment the clustered index pages, and you might consider reorganizing the clustered indexes periodically after shrinking.

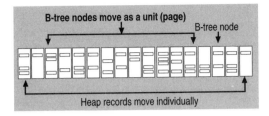

Recommendations:

- As the default, leave the autoshrink feature on for SQL Server Desktop Edition, and off for Standard and Enterprise editions.
- Set up SQL Server Agent tasks to shrink data and index files periodically during off-peak times.
- If you are shrinking the clustered index, periodically run a reorganization of the clustered index.
- When you shrink files, leave free space of at least 10 percent to avoid immediately autogrowing the next time you add new data.

Transaction Log

A Microsoft SQL Server database has at least one data file and one transaction log file. Data and transaction log information is never mixed on the same file, and individual files are used by only one database.

SQL Server uses the transaction log of each database to recover transactions. The transaction log is a serial record of all modifications that have occurred in the database, and which transaction performed each modification. The log records the start of each transaction, the changes made to the data, and enough information to undo the modifications, if necessary. The log grows continuously as logged operations occur in the database. For some large operations, such as CREATE INDEX, the log records the fact that the operation took place. The log records the allocation and deallocation of pages, and the commit or rollback of each transaction. This allows SQL Server either to restore or to back out of each transaction:

- A transaction is rolled back when SQL Server backs out of an incomplete transaction. SQL Server removes from the database all modifications that followed the BEGIN TRANSACTION statement. If SQL Server encounters log records that indicate a CREATE INDEX was performed, SQL Server reverses the statement. These operations are reversed from most recent to oldest.

- A transaction is rolled forward when a transaction log is restored. SQL Server copies to the database the image of the data that followed every modification or reruns statements such as CREATE INDEX. These actions are applied in the same sequence in which they originally occurred. At the end of this process, the database is in the same state as it was at the time the log was backed up.

At a checkpoint, SQL Server ensures that all log records and all database pages that have been modified are written to disk. During the recovery process of each database that occurs when SQL Server is restarted, a transaction must be rolled forward only when it is not known whether all the data modifications in the transaction were actually written from the SQL Server buffer cache to disk. Because a checkpoint forces all modified pages to disk, it represents the point at which the startup recovery must start rolling transactions forward. All pages that were modified before the checkpoint are guaranteed to be on disk, so there is no need to roll forward any transaction that was completed before the checkpoint.

Each log file is divided logically into smaller segments called virtual log files. Virtual log files are the unit of truncation for the transaction log. When a virtual log file no longer contains log records for active transactions, it can be truncated and the space becomes available to log new transactions.

The smallest size for a virtual log file is 256 KB. The minimum size for a transaction log is 512 KB, which provides two virtual log files of 256 KB each. The number and size of the virtual log files in a transaction log increase as the size of the log file increases. A small log file might have a small number of small virtual log files (for example, a 5-MB log file comprised of 5 virtual log files of 1 MB each). A very large log file has larger virtual log files (for example, a 500-MB log file comprised of 10 virtual log files of 50 MB each).

SQL Server avoids having many small virtual log files. When SQL Server recovers a database, it must read each virtual log file header. Each log file header costs one page I/O. The more virtual log files, the longer the time required for a database to start. Approximately 50 to 100 log files is acceptable; 1,000 log files may be too many. The number of virtual log files grows much more slowly than their respective sizes. If a log file grows in small increments, it tends to have many small virtual log files. If a log file grows in larger increments, SQL Server creates fewer larger virtual log files. For example, if the transaction log grows by 1-MB increments, the virtual log files are smaller and more numerous than those corresponding to a transaction log that grows at 50-MB increments.

By default, a log file automatically grows (autogrow) unless you specified otherwise when you created it. The log grows by the increment set at creation time. The increment can be a percentage of the file or a specific MB/GB value. Every time the autogrow feature activates, more virtual files are created. To avoid creating too many virtual files by preventing frequent activation of the autogrow feature, set the autogrow increment to a reasonable size. For example, if the log is 200 MB and grows to 400 MB daily, set the autogrow increment to 50 or 100 MB rather than to 1 MB.

The autogrow feature also stops the transaction log to allow for the addition of space. As a rough estimate, you can add 3 MB per second. As records are written to the log, the end of the log grows, moving from one virtual log file to the next. If there is more than one physical log file for a database, the end of the log grows, moving through each virtual log file in each physical file before it circles back to the first virtual log file in the first physical file. Only when all existing log files are full will the log begin to grow automatically.

The log can also be set to shrink automatically (autoshrink). By default, autoshrink is on for the SQL Server Desktop Edition and off for the Standard and Enterprise editions.

The autoshrink feature does not shrink logs smaller than their original sizes set by the database administrator. If the autoshrink feature is on, a calculation is performed every 30 minutes to determine how much of the log has been used. If the log size exceeds the original size, the log is marked for shrinkage, assuming available free space. The actual shrinking of the log takes place with the next log truncation or BACKUP TRANSACTION LOG statement. The shrinking of a log incurs a performance cost.

Recommendations:

- Set the original size of the transaction log to a reasonable size to avoid constant activation of the autogrow feature, which creates new virtual files and stops logging activity as space is added.

- Set the autogrow percent to a reasonable but small enough size to avoid frequent activation of the autogrow feature and to prevent stopping the log activity for too long a duration.

- Use manual shrinking rather than automatic shrinking.

Changes to sp_configure

In SQL Server 6.5, **sp_configure** options for improving the performance of the
I/O subsystem include: **max async IO**, **max lazywrite**, **RA cache hit limit**, **RA
cache miss limit**, **RA delay**, **RA prefetches**, **RA slots**, **RA worker threads**,
recovery interval, and **logwrite sleep**. SQL Server 7.0 minimizes the manual
tuning required of the database administrator when configuring a system. Most of
the system configuration options in SQL Server 7.0 are self-tuning.

	SQL Server 6.5		SQL Server 7.0	
Configuration options	Min.	Max	Min.	Max
max async IO	1	1,024	1	255
max lazywrite	1	1,024	N/A	N/A
RA cache hit limit	1	255	N/A	N/A
RA cache miss limit	1	255	N/A	N/A
RA delay	0	500	N/A	N/A
RA prefetches	1	1,000	N/A	N/A
RA slots	1	255	N/A	N/A
RA worker threads	0	255	N/A	N/A
recovery interval	1	32,767	0	32,767
logwrite sleep	1	500	N/A	N/A

In SQL Server 7.0, the **max lazywrite** option is no longer available. The
SQL Server memory manager calculates the right time to flush the data cache
based on free buffers and activity.

In SQL Server 7.0, **max async IO** is still available but has changed to represent
the maximum number of outstanding asynchronous disk input/output (I/O)
requests that the entire server can issue against a file (not database). Therefore,
you must know how many files are in the database. The default has changed from
8 in SQL Server 6.5 to 32 in SQL Server 7.0 because of the vast improvements in
hardware speeds. As in SQL Server 6.5, you should monitor disk activity to
determine if this parameter should be raised or lowered. If disk activity is low, this
parameter can be raised. If there are spikes in disk activity showing 100 disk time
and queue length greater than 3, consider lowering **max async IO**.

Recommendations:

- Leave **max async IO** at the default of 32. If you have a very sophisticated I/O
  subsystem with many disks and controllers, configure it to 64 or higher.
  Monitor disk write activity and watch for lazywrite spikes. If the spikes peak
  the I/O **%Disk Time**, lower this configuration value. If the I/O activity is low,
  raise the value.

- If you have many files, decrease **max async IO**.

Though read-ahead (RA), or prefetch, has been dramatically improved in SQL Server 7.0, all of its parameters have been removed. Read-ahead is tuned automatically based on data access. By using file maps, called Index Allocation Maps (IAM), each file is prefetched in parallel on sequential reads. Because the optimizer informs SQL Server when data needs to be scanned, SQL Server automatically activates read-ahead without tuning configuration parameters.

The **logwrite sleep** option has also been removed from SQL Server 7.0. **logwrite sleep** is rarely used in SQL Server 6.5, and it is recommended that the default remain unchanged. The **logwrite sleep** option delays the 16-KB buffer written from memory to the log to ensure that the buffer is being filled prior to writing to the log. In SQL Server 7.0, the log write operation has been improved dramatically; this configuration option is no longer necessary.

The **recovery interval** option controls when SQL Server issues a checkpoint to each database. Checkpoints are issued on a per database basis. At a checkpoint, SQL Server ensures all log information and all modified pages are flushed from memory to disk, reducing the time needed for recovery by limiting the number of transactions rolled forward. Modifications performed before the checkpoint must not be rolled forward because they have been flushed to disk at the checkpoint. The actual checkpoints are controlled by a combination of the **recovery interval** setting and how much data was written to the log during that interval. For example, if the **recovery interval** is set to 5 minutes and very little log activity has taken place after 5 minutes, the system checkpoint will not trigger.

In SQL Server 6.5, the default for **recovery interval** is 5 minutes. In SQL Server 7.0, the default is 0, which means SQL Server automatically configures the option. The recovery process is much quicker and the system checkpoint is less intrusive, therefore SQL Server may checkpoint more often to guarantee faster recovery upon a failure. Monitor the disk writes for the data to determine if this is the appropriate setting. If you see spikes of activity that is causing heavy use of the disk, you can change this parameter to checkpoint less often. If you are going to change this parameter, you may want to change it to 5 and continue monitoring.

Recommendations:

- Leave the **recovery interval** set to 0 so SQL Server determines the best time to run system checkpoints.
- Monitor disk-write activity on the data files, and if you see periodic spikes that send disk utilization to 100 percent you can change the **recovery interval** to a different value. (We suggest resetting to 5 and continue monitoring).

The tempdb Database

The **tempdb** database holds all temporary tables and work tables in queries and handles any other temporary storage needs such as sorting, joining, and aggregation of data for queries. The **tempdb** database is a global resource: The temporary tables and stored procedures for all users connected to the system are stored there. The **tempdb** database is re-created every time SQL Server starts so the system starts with a clean copy of the database. Because temporary tables and stored procedures are automatically dropped on disconnect, and no connections are active when the system is shut down, there is never anything in **tempdb** to be saved from one session of SQL Server to another.

Because of enhancements in the query processor, the **tempdb** database is used more often in SQL Server 7.0 than it is in earlier versions. As a guideline, expect the size of **tempdb** to be 25 to 50 percent larger, depending on the size and complexity of the queries.

Calculating an appropriate size for **tempdb** is challenging in SQL Server 6.5. When **tempdb** runs out of space, the active query requesting **tempdb** terminates. Therefore, you must make **tempdb** very large, even if only 1 to 5 percent of your activity requires a large database. SQL Server 7.0 addresses this issue with the autogrow feature of **tempdb**. The **tempdb** database automatically grows as needed. Each time the system is started, **tempdb** is reset to its default size. Automatically growing **tempdb** results in some performance degradation, just like automatically growing other user databases and logs. Set a reasonable size for **tempdb** and the autogrow increment to ensure that the autogrow feature is not frequently activated.

The **tempdb** database is on disk, therefore your disk configuration can affect performance. If **tempdb** is stored on a single physical disk and multiple requests are made for **tempdb** use, requests are quickly queued on that disk. A simple solution is to stripe **tempdb** across the same drives as the data and indexes. A larger stripe set with availability (either RAID 1 or RAID 5), results in adequate performance for **tempdb** unless the disks are already busy. The fastest performance for **tempdb** may result from storing **tempdb** alone on a separate set of RAID 0 disks. There is no contention and only one write because RAID 0 does not have a high availability feature. You can run **tempdb** with no availability because your current active transaction is lost only during a disk failure. **tempdb** is not persistent and is never recovered, therefore availability features on **tempdb** disks are not needed. The disadvantage is that if a physical drive fails, the whole server is inaccessible to users while you replace it. The trade-off is the availability of the server versus the performance of **tempdb**.

Recommendations:

- Leave the autogrow feature on for **tempdb** so that large queries are not terminated in the middle of execution.
- Size **tempdb** adequately to avoid **tempdb** automatically growing too often.
- Set an adequate **tempdb** autogrow increment to avoid **tempdb** automatically growing too often.
- Place **tempdb** on a fast I/O subsystem to get good performance and multiple files.

In SQL Server 7.0, individual **text**, **ntext**, and **image** pages are not limited to holding data for only one occurrence of a **text**, **ntext**, or **image** column. A **text**, **ntext**, or **image** page can hold data from multiple rows; the page can even have a mix of **text**, **ntext**, and **image** data. This feature along with larger page sizes (8 KB) helps to reduce the space requirements for storing **text** and **image** data. The illustration shows potential space savings.

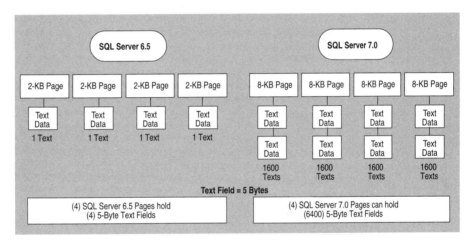

text, **ntext**, and **image** values are not stored as part of the data row but in a separate collection of pages. For each **text**, **ntext**, or **image** value, only a 16-byte pointer is stored in the data row. Each pointer indicates the location of the **text**, **ntext**, or **image** data. A row containing multiple **text**, **ntext**, or **image** columns has one pointer for each **text**, **ntext**, or **image** column.

Although you always work with **text**, **ntext**, and **image** data as if it were a single long string of bytes, the data is not stored in that format. The data is stored in a collection of 8-KB pages that are not necessarily located next to each other. In SQL Server 7.0, the pages are logically organized in a B-tree structure, and in earlier versions of SQL Server they are linked in a page chain. The advantage of the method used by SQL Server 7.0 is that operations starting in the middle of the string are more efficient. SQL Server 7.0 can quickly navigate the B-tree; earlier versions of SQL Server have to scan through the page chain. The structure of the B-tree differs slightly depending on whether there is less than 32 KB of data or more.

Although this B-tree storage method for **text** data may require more I/Os than a normal **char** or **varchar** data retrieval, it provides much faster text and content text search than in SQL Server 6.5.

Because SQL Server pages have increased from 2 KB to 8 KB, the **char** and **varchar** data types now allow up to 8,000 bytes of character data. If you have a text field with less than 8,000 bytes of data, you can use **varchar** instead of the **text** data type to improve query performance by avoiding traversing the text B-tree.

Recommendation:

- For faster data retrieval, consider using the data type **varchar** instead of **text** for text that is less than 8,000 bytes.

SQL Server Memory Planning

This section describes the architecture of Microsoft SQL Server memory algorithms. It makes recommendations for exploiting the new enhancements in memory, including: dynamic memory configuration, stored procedures, log, and other configuration settings.

The memory algorithms and use of memory by SQL Server objects are major changes in SQL Server 7.0 that improve the performance of the database and also minimize the work the database administrator must do to configure memory for good performance.

Memory Management in SQL Server 6.5

In Microsoft SQL Server 6.5, memory is segmented and manually managed. The database administrator must first determine how much memory SQL Server should use versus the operating system. For example, with 256 MB of memory, SQL Server may get 200 MB and leave 56 MB for the operating system. This in itself is an art, not a science. It is very difficult to plan how much the database alone needs, much less plan what the operating system and other applications, such as Web servers, running on the same computer might need. Use of memory is not stagnant; it is possible that SQL Server may need more memory from 8 A.M. to 5 P.M., and the operating system may need more memory from 5 P.M. to 8 A.M. to run nightly batch work. Changing the memory configuration requires a shutdown and startup of SQL Server 6.5.

After memory is allocated to SQL Server 6.5, it is segmented into four sections: static structures, data cache, stored procedure cache, and dynamic allocations (a subset of data cache).

Static structures are the preallocation of SQL Server memory to SQL Server components such as user connections, locks, open objects, and worker thread. The static structure memory is allocated upon SQL Server startup. The dynamic structures are allocations of memory for users, locks, and objects added above and beyond the static structure allocation and take memory away from the data cache. The rest of the memory is divided between the data cache and the stored procedure cache. The SQL Server 6.5 **procedure cache** configuration option sets the percentage of available memory for the procedure cache, and the remainder is assigned to data cache.

As an example of SQL Server 6.5 memory allocation, assume that the system has 256 MB. The SQL Server **memory** option allocates 200 MB to SQL Server, leaving 56 MB for Windows NT. Of the 200 MB of SQL Server memory, static structures require 10 MB, leaving 190 MB. The **procedure cache** is set to 30 percent; therefore, stored procedure memory receives 57 MB (190 * .3) and data cache receives 133 MB (190 - 57). Any further dynamic allocations are taken from the data cache.

SQL Server 6.5 memory manages data with a LRU (least recently used) and MRU (most recently used) link list. Data in memory that is active (being read or written to) links to the MRU part of the link list. Data in memory buffers that has not been accessed for a while is shuffled to the LRU part of the link list. The MRU/LRU link list is constantly being modified.

Memory Management in SQL Server 7.0

Microsoft SQL Server 7.0 has dramatically improved the way memory is allocated and accessed. Unlike SQL Server 6.5 in which memory is managed by the database administrator with configuration settings, SQL Server 7.0 has a memory manager to eliminate manual memory management.

SQL Server 6.5 has a **memory** configuration option that allocates a fixed amount of memory on startup. If the parameter is set too high, SQL Server cannot start. When SQL Server 7.0 starts, its dynamic memory allocation determines how much memory to allocate based on how much memory Windows NT and Windows NT applications are using. For example, assume that Windows NT has a total of 512 MB of memory. When SQL Server starts up, Windows NT and the applications running on Windows NT are using 72 MB of memory. SQL Server uses available memory, leaving 5 MB free. Therefore, SQL Server uses 435 MB of memory (512 MB total – 72 MB for active Windows NT – 5 MB of free memory = 435 SQL Server MB memory). If another Windows NT application is started and uses the 5 MB of free space, SQL Server proactively releases memory to ensure that 5 MB of free space always remains free. Conversely, if Windows NT releases memory so that the free memory is more than 5 MB, SQL Server uses that memory and uses it for database operations.

This dynamic memory algorithm has many advantages. You no longer need to guess the correct memory percentages for Windows NT, Windows NT applications, and SQL Server. You can also avoid Windows NT paging during times of heavy Windows NT usage, and you can use Windows NT free memory during times of light Windows NT usage.

The memory algorithm for SQL Server 7.0 Desktop Edition works differently. Rather than taking memory when it is free, it gives memory back to the operating system when it is not needed. This is because it is more likely that the Desktop Edition is running other applications.

min server memory Option

In SQL Server 7.0, the **min server memory** configuration option ensures that SQL Server starts with a minimum value and does not release memory below this value. SQL Server never goes below the **min server memory** value. If the value is set at 0, SQL Server memory manager manages this for you. The value of this option should be set based on the size and activity of the computer running SQL Server.

max server memory Option

The SQL Server 7.0 **max server memory** configuration option determines the maximum amount of memory SQL Server can allocate at startup and during execution. A **max server memory** value of 0 indicates that there is no maximum and enables dynamic memory to determine the value. If **max server memory** is set to a value, SQL Server does not allocate memory above that value. Set the **max server memory** option if multiple applications are running on Windows NT and you want to guarantee these applications the appropriate amount of memory.

Recommendations:

- Do not set the **min server memory** and **max server memory** options to the same value in order to revert to SQL Server 6.5 behavior. SQL Server 7.0 dynamic memory allocation gives you the best overall performance over time. If despite this recommendation, you still want to fix the memory allocation of SQL Server 7.0 as you did in SQL Server 6.5, set the **min server memory** and the **max server memory** parameters to the same value.

- When running multiple applications on the same Windows NT server with SQL Server, set the **min server memory** option to a reasonable value to ensure that Windows NT does not request too much memory, thus degrading SQL Server performance.

- Set the **max server memory** option only if you want to guarantee that Windows NT application running on the same server gets a specified amount of memory.

The SQL Server 7.0 data access method uses a clock algorithm. Unlike the MRU/LRU link list in which pages are constantly linked and relinked, SQL Server 7.0 sweeps through the buffers and keeps two values in each buffer: Last Touched and Last Checked. Last Checked is the last time the clock has checked on this buffer. Last Touched is the last time this buffer page was active. Pages are marked as part of the free buffer list when Last Touched has not changed in some time. If Last Touched has changed (for example, data was read or written to this buffer page), this page stays out of the free buffer list for a longer period of time. The reason the clock algorithm is superior to the SQL Server 6.5 LRU/MRU link list is that links do not have to be updated, only the Last Touched and Last Checked values.

Changes to sp_configure

Because SQL Server 6.5 does not have a true memory manager like SQL Server 7.0, you can set several **sp_configure** options in SQL Server 6.5 to improve memory performance. These configuration options include: **free buffers, hash buckets, locks, logLRU buffers, max lazywrite IO, max worker threads, memory, open databases, open objects, procedure cache, recovery interval, set working set size, sort pages**, and **tempdb in RAM**. SQL Server 7.0 minimizes the amount of tuning needed by the database administrator for system configurations. Most of the system configuration parameters in SQL Server 7.0 are self-tuning.

	SQL Server 6.5		SQL Server 7.0	
Configuration options	**Min.**	**Max**	**Min.**	**Max**
free buffers	20	524,288	N/A	N/A
hash buckets	4,999	65,003	N/A	N/A
locks	5,000	2,147,483,647	0	2,147,483,647
max lazywrite IO	1	1,024	N/A	N/A
max worker threads	10	1,024	10	1,024
memory	2,800	1,048,576	N/A	N/A
open databases	5	32,767	N/A	N/A
open objects	100	2,147,483,647	0	2,147,483,647
procedure cache	1	99	N/A	N/A
recovery interval	1	32,767	0	32,767
set working set size	0	1	0	1
sort pages	64	511	N/A	N/A
tempdb in RAM	0	2,044	N/A	N/A

In SQL Server 6.5, the **free buffers** option determines the size of the free buffer list, which is 5 percent of SQL Server memory by default. The **free buffers** option is no longer tunable in SQL Server 7.0. With dynamic memory set on and memory size changing dynamically, it would be difficult for any database administrator to estimate the right size for free buffers.

The value of the **hash buckets** option is a prime number used as input into a memory-hashing algorithm. The larger the memory allocation, the larger the **hash bucket** value should be. Because dynamic memory changes the size of SQL Server memory, this option is now set automatically by the memory manager and no longer appears as a configurable option in SQL Server 7.0.

Locks are a perfect example of the power of the SQL Server 7.0 memory manager. In SQL Server 6.5, you must specify enough locks to prevent running out. If you run out of locks, the active thread requesting locks terminates. If you specify too many locks, the memory is preallocated and wasted. Each lock requires approximately 30 to 60 bytes of memory. In SQL Server 7.0, you can specify the configured value as 0 to allow SQL Server to manage it. In the case of **locks** set to 0, SQL Server 7.0 memory manager ensures you never run out. It adds more locks as you need them.

Recommendation:

- Set the **locks** option to 0.

The **max lazywrite** option is set by the database administrator to help the SQL Server 6.5 memory determine how often to flush the cache. The SQL Server 7.0 memory manager manages the lazywrite process automatically, and the option has been removed from the **sp_configure** stored procedure.

The **max worker threads** option indicates the amount of internal SQL Server threads used by SQL Server connected users to get SQL Server resources. The default setting for this option is 255, slightly too high. Each worker thread that is allocated, but not active, uses unnecessary resources such as memory that can be used better by other operations. This configuration value should be similar to the concurrent user connections to SQL Server, but cannot exceed 1024.

In SQL Server 6.5, the **memory** option indicates a fixed allocation of memory for SQL Server. SQL Server 7.0 memory allocation is dynamic at start time. SQL Server allocates as much as memory as is available, reserving 5 MB as free memory.

The **open databases** option, specifying the number of active databases SQL Server allows at any one time, has been removed for SQL Server 7.0. There is no longer a limit.

The **open objects** option indicates the number of actively open objects SQL Server allows at any point in time. Open objects include all tables, views, stored procedures, extended stored procedures, triggers, rules, defaults, and constraints. If you run out of open objects, the active thread requesting an object terminates. In SQL Server 6.5, this option should be set high enough to avoid running out, but not so high as to waste preallocated memory for objects. Each object in SQL Server 6.5 uses 240 bytes of memory. In SQL Server 7.0, you can set **open objects** to 0 so that SQL Server manages objects for you and dynamically adds them when you need them.

Recommendation:

- Set the **open objects** option to 0.

In SQL Server 6.5, the **procedure cache** option indicates the amount of SQL Server memory that is reserved to store the active running stored procedures. You must ensure that you reserve enough memory for the stored procedure usage, but at the same time not so much as to waste memory. This option is no longer valid in SQL Server 7.0. Stored procedure memory shares the same buffer pool as data and is managed by the SQL Server memory manager.

Use the **set working set size** option to reserve physical memory space for SQL Server that is equal to the memory setting. The memory setting is automatically configured by SQL Server based on the workload and available resources. It dynamically varies between **min server memory** and **max server memory**. Setting the **set working set size** option means that Windows NT does not swap out SQL Server pages, even if they can be used more readily by another process when SQL Server is idle.

Do not set **set working set size** if you allow SQL Server to use memory dynamically. Before setting **set working set size** to 1, set both **min server memory** and **max server memory** to the same value, which is the amount of memory you want SQL Server to use. Dynamic memory is a powerful feature in SQL Server 7.0 and it is recommended that you use it in almost all cases.

Recommendation:

- Leave **set working set size** set to 0 to enable SQL Server to dynamically manage the memory allocation.

In SQL Server 6.5, the **sort pages** option indicates the amount of memory allocated per user for sorting operations. The larger the allocation, the faster the sort performs. This option was used for all sorting including query sorts and create index sorts. The query processor now manages queries, and index sorts are managed by the new **index create memory** configuration option. In SQL Server 7.0, the **sort pages** option is no longer valid .

All join and sort operations that are not performed in memory take place in the **tempdb** database. In SQL Server 6.5, you can move the entire **tempdb** into memory. Having the **tempdb** database in RAM is not a benefit because it takes away memory from other data access uses. Because SQL Server 6.5 memory allows only minimal size for sorting (64 2-KB pages to 511 2-KB pages), using the **tempdb in RAM** option is the only way to sort at RAM speeds. SQL Server 7.0 allows a much higher allocation of memory for sorting and the **tempdb in RAM** option is no longer a valid option.

New sp_configure Options

These new **sp_configure** options allow values to be set as memory configurations to determine minimum and maximum values:

- **extended memory size**
- **index create memory**
- **max server memory**
- **min server memory**
- **min memory per query**

The **extended memory size** option is only available for Microsoft SQL Server 7.0, Enterprise Edition running under future versions of Microsoft Windows NT, Enterprise Edition, on an Alpha platform. This option indicates the number of megabytes of memory to use as a disk cache in addition to the conventional buffer pool. For example, on a computer with 8 GB of memory, a reasonable value for extended memory size might be in the range of 5,000 to 6,000. This allows 2 GB of conventional memory usage for SQL Server and most of the rest for use as an extended memory cache.

When SQL Server Enterprise Edition is used on future versions of Windows NT, Enterprise Edition, if the system administrator has configured the 3-GB switch in Boot.ini (referred to in Windows NT as 4GT tuning), the conventional memory can be a maximum of 3 GB instead of 2 GB. In this situation, the default value of 0 (self-configuring) for **max server memory** would cause the server to use up to 3 GB of conventional memory. Therefore, the absolute upper end of the extended memory range (for the hypothetical 8-GB system) would be 5,000.

The **index create memory** option controls the amount of memory used by index creation sorts. If you build large indexes, you may want to experiment with increasing the value of this setting from its default. Memory sort allocations are controlled through the **min memory per query** option. Therefore, if you request 2,000 KB for **index create memory** and **min memory per query** is set to 2,000 KB, the create index operation waits to execute until it can get that much memory. On a large scale production server, creating indexes is not a frequent task. Most often it is a scheduled job at off-peak times because of the intrusiveness of the create index process. Therefore, if you are running create index operations infrequently and at off-peak hours, increase this number significantly. Remember to keep **min memory per query** at a lower number so the job will activate even if all the requested memory is not available.

Recommendations:

- Increase the **index create memory** option if you are creating infrequent large indexes.

- Keep **min memory per query** (KB) low enough to allow the CREATE INDEX statement to run even if all memory for index creation is not available at execution.

Use the **min memory per query** option to specify the minimum memory (in kilobytes) to be allocated for the execution of a query. For example, if **min memory per query** is set to 2,048 KB, the query is guaranteed to receive at least that much total memory. You can set the **min memory per query** option to any value from 0 to 2,147,483,647KB (2 GB). The default is 1,024 KB.

Increasing the value of query memory generally improves the performance of queries that use hashing or sorting operations, particularly when there is significant memory available and few concurrent queries. **min memory per query** includes memory allocated for sorting and replaces the sort pages option in earlier versions of Microsoft SQL Server. Do not set **min memory per query** too high, especially on very busy systems, because the query must wait until it can get the minimum memory requested or until the **query wait** setting is reached. (**query wait** is another **sp_configure** option that specifies how long to wait for resources before canceling the query altogether.)

Recommendations:

- Increase **min memory per query** if you are performing sorts and hash joins and you have enough memory to support these operations with the expected number of concurrent users.

- Do not set **min memory per query** too high on busy systems (systems with many active users) or your query must wait until the **min memory per query** value can be allocated.

- Consider setting **query wait**. The **query wait** value should be specific to user requirements.

SQL Server 7.0 Stored Procedure Cache

In SQL Server 6.5, stored procedure cache is a fixed segment of memory based on the **procedure cache** option of the **sp_configure** stored procedure. In SQL Server 7.0, this option has been eliminated. SQL Server 7.0 memory manager dynamically manages how much memory stored procedures require and allocates it to them.

How stored procedures are used in memory has also changed. In SQL Server 6.5, if 100 users want to use a precompiled stored procedure at the same time, SQL Server must bring up 100 copies of that stored procedure in memory. In SQL Server 7.0, only one instance of that stored procedure is in memory and is used by all 100 users. Stored procedures often get passed variables and these variables may affect the query plan. The SQL Server 7.0 memory manager determines when to recompile that stored procedure and bring in a new plan based on the input variables.

In this example, stored procedure A has two variables passed to it that are inserted into a SQL statement as part of an equal clause:

```
"SELECT * FROM Table WHERE field1=&variable1 AND field2=&variable2"
```

The plan remains the same because it follows an equal predicate and the cached stored procedure is used.

In this example, stored procedure A has two variables passed to it that are inserted into a BETWEEN clause:

```
"SELECT * FROM Table WHERE field1 BETWEEN &variable1 AND &variable2"
```

The stored procedure may have to be recompiled to get a new plan because the variables may dictate a new plan.

Dynamic Query Caching

Microsoft SQL Server 7.0 now caches the plan for dynamic Transact-SQL statements as well as static statements. This can be advantageous in an ad hoc environment in which many users are executing the same dynamic Transact-SQL statement. The memory manager gives a lower priority to dynamically cached Transact-SQL than it does to static Transact-SQL, such as stored procedures; therefore, the stored procedure stays in the buffer cache longer.

Monitoring Memory Efficiency

The **SQL Server: Buffer Manager** object in Windows NT Performance Monitor provides counters to monitor how SQL Server uses memory to store data pages and internal data structures. Monitoring the memory used by SQL Server can help determine whether bottlenecks exist due to a lack of available physical memory for storing frequently accessed data in cache, in which case SQL Server must retrieve the data from disk. By monitoring memory, you can determine if query performance can be improved by adding more memory, or making more memory available, to the data cache or SQL Server internal structures.

The table shows some of the **SQL Server: Buffer Manager** counters.

SQL Server: Buffer Manager counters	Description
Buffer Cache Hit Ratio	Percentage of pages that were found in the buffer cache without having to read from disk. This number is an accumulation from when SQL Server is started.
Committed Pages	Number of buffer pages committed.
ExtendedMem Cache Hit Ratio	Percentage of page requests that were satisfied from the extended memory cache.
ExtendedMem Cache Migrations	Number of pages migrated into the extended memory cache region.
ExtendedMem Requests	Number of requests for pages from large memory region.
Free Buffers	Number of free buffers available.
Lazy Writes	Number of buffers written by buffer manager's lazy writer.
Page Requests	Number of requests for buffer pages.
Readahead Pages	Number of requests to asynchronously prefetch pages before they are actually encountered.
Reserved Page Count	Number of buffer cache reserved pages.
Stolen Page Count	Number of buffer cache pages that have been stolen to satisfy other server memory requests.

SQL Server 7.0 Processor Planning

Microsoft SQL Server 7.0 uses multiple processors for single tasks such as queries, utilities, and scanning data. This section describes how SQL Server exploits hardware processors. It can help you determine the hardware processors you need to get the most out of SQL Server as well as describe the threading model and parameters that you can set to get the best possible performance.

SQL Server Threading

The threading model used by SQL Server affects how efficiently the processors are used. This includes how many concurrent users it can handle and how quickly each of the users gets processing power.

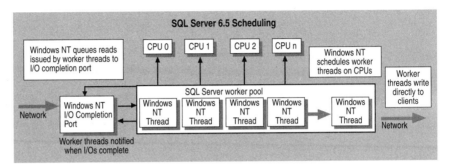

SQL Server 6.5 uses native Window NT threads. The Windows NT kernel uses its own scheduler to manage the SQL Server thread scheduling as well as synchronization services. Although this process has produced high concurrency on a small number of processors, it does have limitations. At high loads, the thread context switching has some overhead. (Although the implementation of I/O completion ports aided significantly here). Because SQL Server lets Windows NT manage the threads, it has little control over which threads are preempted on and off of the processor and how often. The Windows NT kernel scheduler and dispatch lock periodically sees contention with a large number of threads. Although this contention can exist, SQL Server 6.5 has achieved more than 5,000 concurrent users on a four-way processor in TPC-C testing.

SQL Server 7.0 has improved the threading model.

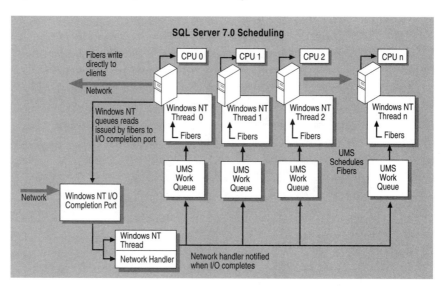

The most important enhancement is the replacement of the Windows NT kernel schedule with the Microsoft SQL Server scheduler called User Mode Schedulers (UMS). SQL Server has one UMS for every processor. This UMS controls the scheduling of fibers and/or thread requests.

Fibers are a new Windows NT feature exploited in SQL Server 7.0, and are useful on CPU-busy systems with high-context switching. Fibers are lightweight and run on top of native Windows NT threading as shown in the preceding illustration. SQL Server now uses only one Windows NT thread per processor and many lightweight fibers on top of that thread. Fibers automatically assume the identity of the Windows NT thread they are running on and are nonpreemptive with respect to other SQL Server threads running on the other processors. Fibers, called lightweight pooling, should be turned on only if CPU is 100 percent and context switching is high.

The most CPU-intensive database applications benefit from this added thread scheduling flexibility. You now have the ability to move to an even higher number of concurrent users and achieve greater transaction throughput.

Recommendation:

- Leave lightweight pooling off, unless CPUs are saturated (close to 100 percent busy) and you notice a consistently high level of context switching.

Parallel Query

The Microsoft SQL Server 7.0 query processor has been redesigned to support the large databases and complex queries found in decision support, data warehouse, and OLAP applications. The query processor includes several new execution strategies that can improve the performance of complex queries. One of the significant improvements is in the area of parallel queries.

SQL Server 7.0 supports parallel execution of a single query across multiple processors. A CPU-bound query that must examine a large number of rows often benefits if portions of its execution plan run in parallel. SQL Server 7.0 automatically determines which queries will benefit from parallelism and generates a parallel execution plan. If multiple processors are available when the query begins executing, the work is divided across the processors. Parallel query execution is enabled by default.

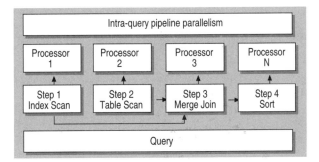

During query optimization, SQL Server looks for queries that might benefit from parallel execution. For these queries, SQL Server inserts exchange operators into the query execution plan to prepare the query for parallel execution. An exchange operator is an operator in a query execution plan that provides process management, data redistribution, and flow control. After exchange operators are inserted, a parallel query execution plan results. A parallel query execution plan can use more than one thread, whereas a serial execution plan, used by a nonparallel query, uses only a single thread for its execution. The actual number of threads used by a parallel query is determined at query plan execution and initialization and is called the degree of parallelism.

The advantage of the exchange operator is that parallel query is enabled for all aspects of query execution (insert, delete, and select operations), and is enabled in one place efficiently and reliably. This is more effective than implementing parallel query multiple times in multiple operations.

Performance results from parallel query speak for themselves.

Query	SQL 6.5 (sec)	SQL 7.0 (sec)	Comment
SELECT COUNT (*) FROM bench WHERE K2 = 2 AND K25 = 3	222.8	4.3	Merge join
SELECT SUM (K1K) FROM bench WHERE KSEQ (BETWEEN 4000000 AND 500000) AND K100 = 3	56.7	0.6	Index seeks with BETWEEN, AND, OR
SELECT B1.Unique2, B1.Unique1, B1 Onepercent, B1 String U1 INTO #TMP FROM tabbig B1 WHERE B1 UNIQUE BETWEEN 1001 AND 11000	33.8	1.2	Nonclustered index scan
SELECT KSEQ, K500K FROM bench WHERE ((K25 = 11 OR K25 = 19) AND (K100<41) (K1K BETWEEN 850 AND 950) AND (K10=7)	591	10.2	Parallel merge join

Degree of Parallelism

Microsoft SQL Server automatically detects the best degree of parallelism for each instance of a parallel query execution by considering the following:

- Is SQL Server running on a computer with more than one processor (an SMP computer)?

  Only computers with more than one processor can take advantage of parallel queries.

- What is the number of concurrent users active on the SQL Server?

  SQL Server monitors its CPU usage and adjusts the degree of parallelism at query startup time. Lower degrees of parallelism are chosen if the CPUs are already busy.

- Is there sufficient memory available for parallel query execution?

  Each query requires a certain amount of memory to execute. Executing a parallel query requires more memory than a nonparallel query. The amount of memory required for executing a parallel query increases with the degree of parallelism. If the memory requirement of the parallel plan for a given degree of parallelism cannot be satisfied, SQL Server automatically decreases the degree of parallelism or completely abandons the parallel plan for the query in the given workload context and executes the serial plan.

- What is the type of query being executed?

  Queries that ravenously consume CPU cycles are the best candidates for a parallel query, for example, joins of large tables, substantial aggregations, and sorting of large result sets. Simple queries, often found in transaction processing applications, illustrate that the additional coordination required to execute a query in parallel outweigh the potential performance boost. To distinguish between queries that benefit from parallelism and those that do not, SQL Server compares the estimated cost of executing the query with the **cost threshold for parallelism** value. Although not recommended, you can change the default value of 5 using **sp_configure**.

- Are a sufficient number of rows processed in the given stream?

  If the optimizer determines the number of rows in a stream is too low, it does not introduce exchange operators to distribute the stream. Consequently the operators in this stream are executed serially. Executing the operators in a serial plan avoids scenarios when the startup, distribution, and coordination cost exceeds the gains achieved by parallel operator execution.

Recommendations:

- Buy a multiprocessor computer if your query workload is of sufficient complexity and volume to take advantage of parallel query.
- Parallel query uses more memory than a query that runs nonparallel.

Parallel Data Scanning

Microsoft SQL Server 7.0 can read sequential data in parallel by using files and filegroups. Having multiple CPUs available to you allows execution of these parallel data scans to take place quickly.

Recommendation:

- Multiple processors allow quicker scheduling of parallel data scans.

Parallel Operations

Microsoft SQL Server 7.0 server operations, such as backup, restore, DBCC, bulk copy, and CREATE INDEX run much faster and have less impact on server operations. Performance for these operations has improved for two reasons: the way each of these operations uses the SQL Server 7.0 optimizer and the ability of SQL Server to run many of these operations in parallel.

Multiple backup devices can be used for backup and restore operations. This allows SQL Server to use parallel I/O to increase the speed of backup and restore operations because each backup device can be written to or read from concurrently with other backup devices. For example, if it takes four hours to back up a database to a single tape drive, then the backup speed when two tape drives are used is likely to be two hours. For enterprises with very large databases, using many backup devices can decrease the time required for backup and restore operations.

Multiple nonclustered indexes can be scheduled in parallel, significantly reducing the time it takes to create multiple nonclustered indexes on a single table. Multiple CPUs can help run these create index operations faster.

Recommendation:

- Multiple CPUs improve the speed of backup, restore, DBCCs, and CREATE INDEXES.

SQL Server 7.0 exploits multiple processors better than SQL Server 6.5. SQL Server 7.0 does not require you to upgrade your computers to more processors, but can achieve much better performance if multiple processors are available.

sp_configure Options

In SQL Server 7.0, three **sp_configure** stored procedure options that relate to processor use are:

- **affinity mask**
- **lightweight pooling**
- **priority boost**

In Windows NT, an activity or thread in a process can migrate from processor to processor, with each migration reloading the processor cache. Under heavy system loads, specifying which processor should run a specific thread can improve performance by reducing the number of times the processor cache is reloaded. The association between a processor and a thread is called processor affinity.

You can use the **affinity mask** option to increase performance on SMP systems with more than four microprocessors operating under heavy load. You can associate a thread with a specific processor and specify which processor(s) SQL Server will use. You can exclude SQL Server activity from processors that are given specific workload assignments by the Windows NT operating system.

Recommendations:

- If applications other than SQL Server are running on the server and you want to make sure SQL Server leaves processing power for them, set the **affinity mask** option.
- Set the **affinity mask** option for all processors to SQL Server to achieve improved performance on a complete high volume, high user workload.

The **lightweight pooling** option provides a means of reducing the system overhead associated with the excessive context switching sometimes seen in SMP environments. When excessive context switching is present, lightweight pooling may provide better throughput by performing the context switching inline, thus helping to reduce user/kernel ring transitions. You can find the **Context Switches/sec** counter in Windows NT Performance Monitor under the object thread.

Setting the **lightweight pooling** option to 1 causes SQL Server to switch to fiber mode scheduling. The default value for this option is 0, or threading.

Recommendation:

- Leave lightweight pooling at default 0 (which means threads not fibers) unless your %Processor Time is 100 percent and **Context Switches/sec** is high (estimate 8,000+).

The **priority boost** option is used to specify whether SQL Server should run at a higher Windows NT scheduling priority than other processes on the same computer. If you set this option to 1, SQL Server runs at a higher priority in the Windows NT scheduler. The default is 0 (run at priority base 7 on a single processor computer and at priority base 15 on an SMP computer). Setting the **priority boost** option to 1 changes the Windows NT priority base to 15 on a single processor computer and 24 on an SMP computer.

Although **priority boost** may seem like a useful option, it can cause more harm than good. By setting this option to 1 instead of 0, you increase the Windows NT priority for SQL Server threads over normal Windows NT user threads. This seems beneficial, but it can degrade the performance of users who are not SQL Server users.

If SQL Server is running on a computer with other applications and you want to ensure that all the applications get equal processor use, you can set the **affinity mask** option so that SQL Server gets only specific processors, and then set **priority boost** to 1, which will give SQL Server high priority on the specific processors and leave the other processors available for other applications.

Recommendation:

- For most applications, leave the **priority boost** option at 0.

When several applications are running on the same server, you can set the **affinity mask** option so SQL Server gets only specific processors, and leaves processors free for the other applications. In this case, set the **priority boost** option to 1.

C H A P T E R 3

Replication

Replication provides a fast and reliable way to disseminate corporate information to multiple locations in a distributed business environment, allowing organizations to move their data closer to knowledge workers in corporate, branch, or mobile offices. This chapter provides information about the replication capabilities of Microsoft SQL Server version 7.0, and how they can empower users, improve decision-making, and increase performance and reliability of existing systems by reducing dependencies on centralized data.

What Is Replication?

What do a data warehouse, a corporate intranet, and a sales force automation application have in common? Aside from relying on a database for their storage requirements, all three of these application types must move data quickly and reliably throughout an organization. For example, a data warehouse receives sales data from an order processing system; a corporate intranet application moves financial data from a site in New York to a site in Japan; and a sales force automation system replicates customer information to the laptop computer of a local sales representative.

Today, more and more business applications are being designed to run in distributed computing environments. In addition to distributing applications across a network of workstations, servers, and legacy mainframe systems, organizations are distributing applications from centralized corporate offices to regional and satellite offices, and increasingly, to mobile offices (employee laptop computers).

Distributed office locations and personnel demand 24-hour operations and elaborate tracking systems, along with higher data integrity requirements. Aggravating the issue, most organizations have acquired a mix of disparate networks and computing platforms. The ensuing challenge for today's administrator is determining the best way to distribute large amounts of data across heterogeneous systems in a timely fashion.

SQL Server enables customers to replicate data from one SQL Server database to others throughout the enterprise. SQL Server 7.0 replication goals include:

- Scalable replication solutions

  Providing a full range of scalable replication solutions to meet the complete spectrum of application requirements.

- Reduced complexity

  Helping to lower the cost and complexity of replicated environments by making replication easier to build, manage, and use.

- Heterogeneity and interoperability

  Enabling bidirectional replication capabilities to heterogeneous data sources and easy integration with third-party applications.

Replication Model

SQL Server version 7.0 replication builds on the "publish and subscribe" model introduced in SQL Server version 6.0. The model consists of Publishers, Subscribers and Distributors, publications and articles, and push and pull subscriptions. Four new intelligent agents—Snapshot Agent, Log Reader Agent, Distribution Agent, and Merge Agent—manage the SQL Server 7.0 replication process. All agents can run under the SQL Server Agent and can be fully administered using SQL Server Enterprise Manager. The Snapshot and Log Reader Agents execute on the Distributor server, while the Distribution and Merge Agents execute on the Distributor server for push subscriptions, and on the Subscriber server for pull subscriptions. SQL Server replication is built on OLE DB and ODBC, the industry standards for data access, providing rich interoperability with a wide variety of relational and nonrelational data sources.

Components of SQL Server Replication

These basic components comprise SQL Server's replication model.

Publisher

The Publisher is a server that makes data available for replication to other servers. In addition to identifying the data to replicate, the Publisher detects the data that has changed and maintains information about all publications on the server. Any given data element that is replicated has a single Publisher, even if the data can be updated by any number of Subscribers or published again by a Subscriber.

Subscribers

Subscribers are servers that store replicas and receive updates. In earlier versions of SQL Server, updates could be performed only at the Publisher. However, SQL Server 7.0 allows Subscribers to make updates to data, although a Subscriber making updates is not the same as a Publisher. A Subscriber can, in turn, also become a Publisher to other Subscribers .

Publication

The publication is a collection of one or more articles, and an article is a grouping of data to be replicated. An article can be an entire table, only certain columns (using a vertical filter), or only certain rows (using a horizontal filter), or even a stored procedure (in some types of replication).

Distributor

The distributor is a server that contains the distribution database. The exact role of the Distributor is different in each type of SQL Server replication.

Pull subscription

The pull subscription is one in which the Subscriber asks for periodic updates of all changes at the Publisher. Pull subscriptions are best for publications that have a large number of Subscribers (for example, Subscribers using the Internet). Pull subscriptions are also best for autonomous mobile users because they determine when the data changes are synchronized. A single publication can support a mixture of push and pull subscriptions.

Push subscription

The push subscription is one in which the Publisher propagates the changes to the Subscriber without a specific request from the Subscriber. Push subscriptions are used to propagate changes as they occur, or to set the schedule set by the Publisher.

Snapshot Agent

A Snapshot Agent prepares the schema and initial data files of published tables and stored procedures, stores the snapshot on the Distributor, and records information about the synchronization status in the distribution database. Each publication has its own Snapshot Agent that runs on the Distributor and connects to the Publisher.

Log Reader Agent

A log reader agent moves transactions marked for replication from the transaction log on the Publisher to the distribution database. Each database published using transactional replication has its own Log Reader Agent that runs on the Distributor and connects to the Publisher.

Distribution Agent

A Distribution Agent moves the transactions and snapshot jobs held in distribution database tables to Subscribers. Transactional and snapshot publications that are set up for immediate synchronization when a new subscription is created have their own Distribution Agent that runs on the Distributor and connects to the Subscriber. Transactional and snapshot publications not set up for immediate synchronization share a Distribution Agent across the Publisher/Subscriber pair that runs on the Distributor and connects to the Subscriber. Pull subscriptions to either snapshot or transactional publications have Distribution Agents that run on the Subscriber instead of the Distributor. The Distribution Agent typically runs under SQL Server Agent and can be administered directly using SQL Server Enterprise Manager.

Merge Agent

A Merge Agent moves and reconciles incremental data changes that occurred after the initial snapshot was created. In merge replication, data moves either in both directions (first from the Subscriber to the Publisher, and then from the Publisher to the Subscriber) or in one direction only. Each merge publication has its own Merge Agent that connects to both the Publisher and the Subscriber and updates them. Push subscriptions to merge publications have Merge Agents that run on the Publisher, while pull subscriptions to merge publications have Merge Agents that run on the Subscriber. Snapshot and transactional publications do not have Merge Agents. The Merge Agent can also be embedded and driven in an application using the Microsoft ActiveX control.

Two-phase commit

A two-phase commit is a process that ensures transactions that apply to more than one server are completed either on all servers or on none.

Scalable Replication Solutions

Replication is not a one-size-fits-all solution. Businesses have different application requirements, and SQL Server 7.0 delivers a broad range of replication solutions to meet them. Envision a spectrum of application requirements with site autonomy (all sites operating in a disconnected state) at one end, and transactional consistency (all sites are guaranteed to have the same data values at the same time) at the opposite end.

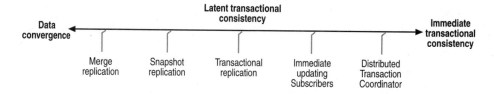

An application's position along the range of requirements determines the appropriate replication solution. For example, contrast the requirements of a sales force automation system with those of an accounts receivable system. Both applications use replication for distributing data. However, the company's mobile sales force can take customer orders on laptop computers while disconnected from the central office network. The lack of a network connection (and an accurate report of inventory) must not prevent the salesperson from taking and submitting the order. Thus, the need for autonomy in the sales application outweighs the risk of taking orders for out-of-stock items (back orders are allowed). In contrast, the invoices sent out by the accounts receivable department must be completely accurate and current for auditing purposes. In this case, transactional consistency outweighs the need for employee autonomy.

SQL Server provides three types of replication you can use as you design your applications:

- Snapshot replication
- Transactional replication
- Merge replication

Each of these types provides different capabilities and different attributes to satisfy the needs for site autonomy and transaction consistency. However, these are not mutually exclusive technologies. It is common for the same application to use multiple replication types.

Snapshot Replication

As its name implies, snapshot replication takes a picture, or snapshot, of the published data in the database at one moment in time. Snapshot replication is the simplest type of replication, and it guarantees latent consistency between the Publisher and Subscriber. Snapshot replication is most appropriate in read-only application scenarios such as look-up or code tables, or in decision support systems in which data latency requirements are not strict and data volumes are not excessive. Snapshots can occur either on a scheduled basis or on demand.

Snapshot replication requires less processor overhead than transactional replication because it does not require continuous monitoring of data changes on source servers. Instead of copying INSERT, UPDATE, and DELETE statements (characteristic of transactional replication), or data modifications (characteristic of merge replication), Subscribers are updated by a total refresh of the data set. Therefore, snapshot replication sends all the data to the Subscriber instead of sending the changes only. If the article is large, it can require substantial network resources to transmit. In deciding if snapshot replication is appropriate, you must balance the size of the entire data set against the volatility of change to the data.

Snapshot replication offers strong site autonomy when updates are not made to Subscriber data. If updates are required, snapshot replication provides little site autonomy, limiting its usefulness in a disconnected environment: the higher the update frequency, the more limited the solution. In either case, loose transactional consistency is maintained.

Transactional Replication

The second mode of replication is called transactional replication. Transactional replication monitors changes to the publishing server at the transaction level: insert, update or delete operations. Changes made to the Publisher flow continuously or at scheduled intervals to one or more subscribing servers. Changes are propagated in near real time; typically, with a latency of seconds. With transactional replication, changes must be made at the publishing site to avoid conflicts and guaranteeing transactional consistency.

Only committed transactions are sent to subscribing servers, and in the guaranteed order in which they were committed at the Publisher. This guarantees loose transactional consistency: ultimately all the subscribing sites will achieve the same values as those at the Publisher. The data at any participating site will be the same as it would be had all operations been performed at a single site.

If Subscribers need near-real-time propagation of data changes, they will need a network connection to the Publisher. Transactional replication in a well-networked environment can provide low latency to Subscribers. Push Subscribers would often receive changes within 5 or 10 seconds of when they occurred at the Publisher, provided the network link remains available.

Because transactional replication relies on a given data element having only a single Publisher, it is most commonly used in application scenarios that allow for logical partitioning of data and data ownership. A branch system with centralized reporting (corporate rollup) is an appropriate use of transactional replication. In this scenario, data ownership is maintained at the branch level and is published to a centralized server for read-only reporting. Transactional replication is also an appropriate solution for periodic downloads of read-only data in either a well-connected or disconnected scenario. For example, every night from a hotel room, a mobile salesperson pulls down the incremental changes to a price list, which is modified only at the corporate office.

Immediate Updating Subscribers Option

In their simplest form, both snapshot and transactional replication are based on a model of one-way replication, in which data is modified only at the Publisher and flows downstream to a Subscriber. However, some applications require the ability to update data at subscribing servers and have those changes flow upstream. The **Immediate Updating Subscribers** option, available with either snapshot or transactional replication, allows data to be updated at subscribing sites.

This option is set when the article is created and allows a Subscriber to update the copy of its local data, as long as that update can be immediately reflected to the Publisher with the two-phase commit (2PC) protocol. If the update can be performed successfully between the Subscriber and the Publisher, the Publisher propagates those changes to all other Subscribers during the next distribution. Because the Subscriber making the update already has the data changes reflected locally, the user can continue working with the updated data secure in the guarantee that the Publisher data also reflects the change.

The **Immediate Updating Subscribers** option is most appropriate for use with well-connected and reliable networks where application contention for data is relatively low. For example, a distributed ticketing system maintains local replicas of the ticketing database so that available seating can be accessed quickly. However, a seat can be sold only once, so it is critical that the local transaction (for example, the ticket sale) is updated immediately and committed to the central server, the Publisher. The transaction can then be replicated to all other local ticket offices in the next distribution, and any attempt to sell the same seat will be prohibited.

How Immediate Updating Subscribers Works

When a publication is enabled to support the **Immediate Updating Subscribers** option, a Subscriber site can modify replicated data if the transaction can be performed using 2PC with the Publisher. This approach provides latent guaranteed consistency to other Subscribers without requiring that updates be made only at the publishing site. The 2PC transaction with the Publisher is done automatically so that an application can be written as though it is updating just one site. This approach does not have the availability constraint of doing full 2PC to all participating sites because only the Publisher must be available. After the change is made at the Publisher, it is published to all other Subscribers to the publication, thereby maintaining latent guaranteed consistency.

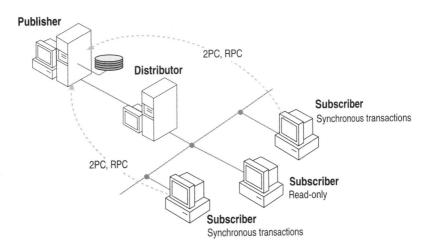

With this option, applications are not required to be written to perform data modification operations at the Publisher and read operations at the Subscriber. The application works with data at one site, and the 2PC transaction is performed automatically. The application should be equipped to deal with a failure in the transaction, just as it would in a nonreplication environment. If the transaction is successful, the Subscriber can work with the changed values immediately, as the update has been accepted at the Publisher without conflict and will eventually be replicated to every subscription of the publication. A Subscriber performing updates does not have full autonomy because the Publisher must be available at the time of the update. Nevertheless, autonomy is much higher than it would be with the full 2PC case in which every site must be available for any site to perform changes.

Merge Replication

Merge replication provides the highest level of autonomy for any replication solution. Publishers and Subscribers can work independently and reconnect periodically to merge their results. If a conflict is created by changes being made to the same data element at multiple sites, those changes are resolved automatically. These characteristics make merge replication an ideal solution for applications, such as sales force automation, in which users need full read/write access to local replicas of data in a highly disconnected environment.

When conflicts occur (more than one site updated the same data values), merge replication provides automatic conflict resolution. The winner of the conflict can be resolved based on assigned priorities, who first submitted the change, or a combination of the two. Data values are replicated and applied to other sites only when the reconciliation process occurs, which might be hours, days, or even weeks apart. Conflicts can be detected and resolved at the row level, or at a specific column in a row.

The Snapshot Agent and Merge Agent perform merge replication. The Snapshot Agent prepares snapshot files containing schema and data of published tables, stores the files on the Distributor, and records synchronization jobs in the publication database. The Merge Agent applies to the Subscriber the initial snapshot jobs held in the distribution database tables. It also merges incremental data changes that occurred after the initial snapshot was created, and reconciles conflicts according to rules you configure, or using a custom resolver you create.

How Merge Replication Works

When a table is published with merge replication, SQL Server makes three important changes to the schema of the database. First, SQL Server identifies a unique column for each row in the table being replicated. This allows the row to be uniquely identified across multiple copies of the table. If the base table already contains a unique identifier column (**rowguid**) with the ROWGUIDCOL property, SQL Server uses that column as the row identifier for that replicated table automatically. Otherwise, SQL Server adds the column **rowguid** (with the ROWGUIDCOL property) to the base table. SQL Server also adds an index on the **rowguid** column to the base table.

Second, SQL Server installs triggers that track changes to the data in each row or (optionally) each column. These triggers capture changes made to the base table and record these changes in merge system tables. Different triggers are generated for articles that track changes at the row level or the column level. Because SQL Server supports multiple triggers of the same type on the base table, merge replication triggers do not interfere with the application-defined triggers; that is, application-defined triggers and merge replication triggers can coexist.

Third, SQL Server adds several system tables to the database to support data tracking; efficient synchronization; and conflict detection, resolution, and reporting. The **msmerge_contents** and **msmerge_tombstone** tables track the updates, inserts, and deletes to the data within a publication. They use the unique identifier column **rowguid** to join to the base table. The **generation** column acts as a logical clock indicating when a row was last updated at a given site. Actual timestamps are not used for marking when changes occur, or for deciding conflicts, and there is no dependence on synchronized clocks between sites. At a given site, the generation numbers correspond to the order in which changes were performed by the Merge Agent or by a user at that site.

Priority-based Conflict Resolution

Under priority-based conflict resolution, every publication is assigned a priority number, 0 being the lowest and 100 the highest. The following diagram represents the simplest case. In this scenario, all three sites agree that Site A created version one of the row, and no subsequent updates occurred. If Sites A and B both update the row, the Site A update is the conflict winner because it has the higher priority.

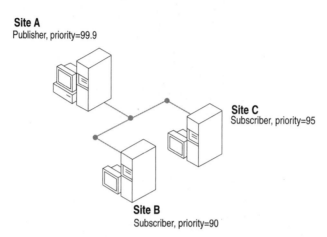

Site A
Publisher, priority=99.9

Site C
Subscriber, priority=95

Site B
Subscriber, priority=90

In a more complex scenario, if multiple changes have occurred to the same row since the last merge, the maximum site priority for a change that was made to the common version is used to determine the conflict winner. For example, Site A makes version two, and sends it to Site B, which makes version three. Site B then sends version three back to Site A. In the meantime, Site C also made a version two and attempts to reconcile it with A. The maximum site priority for the changes that occurred to the common version is 100 (Site A's priority). Site A and B's joint changes are thus the priority winner, so Site A is the conflict winner.

Custom Conflict Resolution

Merge replication is designed to handle an application's need for flexible conflict resolution schemes. An application can override the default, priority-based resolution by providing its own custom resolver. Custom resolvers are COM-objects or stored procedures that are written to the public resolver interface and invoked during reconciliation by the Merge Agent to support business rules.

For example, suppose multiple sites participate in monitoring a chemical process and record the low and high temperatures achieved in a test. A priority-based or first-wins strategy would not deliver the "lowest low" and the "highest high" values. Design templates and code samples help you create a custom resolver to solve such a business case.

Merge replication is a great solution for disconnected applications that require very high site autonomy, can be partitioned, or do not need transactional consistency. Merge replication is not the right choice for applications that require transactional consistency and cannot supply an assurance of integrity by using partitioning. Transactional consistency refers to strict adherence to the ACID (Atomicity, Consistency, Isolation, Durability) properties, specifically durability. Any replication solution that allows conflicts cannot, by definition, achieve the ACID properties. Any time conflicts are resolved, a transaction that had been committed is undone, breaking the rule for durability.

Lower Complexity

One of the primary design goals of SQL Server 7.0 replication was to make it easier to build, manage, and use. Microsoft has achieved this goal through a combination of wizards and sophisticated design and monitoring tools. SQL Server Enterprise Manager introduces several new wizards to simplify the installation and maintenance of replication. From a single server or workstation that has SQL Server installed, you can use SQL Server Enterprise Manager to set up a complete replication environment spanning as many servers as necessary across your enterprise. Replication Monitor enables users to view and modify the replication properties and to troubleshoot replication activity.

Replication Wizards

SQL Server includes various replication wizards and numerous dialog boxes to simplify the steps necessary to build and manage replication.

- The Configure Publishing and Distribution Wizard helps you specify a server to use as a Distributor and other replication components you may need.

- The Create Publication Wizard helps you create a publication from the data in your database.

- The Disable Publishing and Distribution Wizard helps you disable publishing, distribution, or both, on a server.

- The Pull Subscription Wizard helps you "pull" a subscription to a publication on one server into a database on another server.

- The Push Subscription Wizard helps you "push" a subscription from a publication on one server to one or more servers or server groups.

- The Replication Conflict Viewer helps you review the manner in which conflicts were resolved and make changes to these resolutions.

After you have used the wizards to configure replication initially and create publications and articles, you can change most of the initial settings through dialog boxes.

Replication Monitor

Use Replication Monitor to view the status of replication agents and troubleshoot potential problems at a Distributor. Replication Monitor is activated as a component of a server in SQL Server Enterprise Manager only when the server is enabled as a Distributor and the current user is a member of the **sysadmin** fixed server role. All replication agents must be scheduled through SQL Server Agent. Replication and Replication Monitor will not work unless SQL Server Agent is running.

You can use Replication Monitor in SQL Server Enterprise Manager to:

- View a list of Publishers, publications, and subscriptions to the publications that are supported by the Distributor.
- View scheduled replication agents and monitor real-time "heartbeat" status and history for each agent.
- Set up and monitor alerts related to replication events. If an event occurs, SQL Server responds automatically, either by executing a task that you have defined or by sending an e-mail or a pager message to an operator that you have specified.

Monitoring Publishers, Publications, and Subscriptions

Replication Monitor is a powerful tool for getting detailed information about Publishers, publications, and subscriptions. For example, Replication Monitor provides a list of all of the Publishers that use the server as a Distributor, display all of the publications for a particular Publisher, or identify all subscriptions to a particular publication.

Monitoring Replication Agents

For troubleshooting purposes, Replication Monitor graphically monitors the activity of all replication agents: Snapshot, Log Reader, Distribution, and Merge Agents. To display the four agents, select a Distributor, and then click **Replication Monitor**. To expose the detailed activity and the task history for that agent, expand the node of a specific agent.

Monitoring Replication Alerts

Replication Monitor and the SQL Server Agent provide a powerful mechanism for setting up lights-out management for a replication environment. SQL Server Agent monitors the Windows NT application log, watching for an event that qualifies as one of the defined alerts. If such an event occurs, SQL Server Agent responds automatically, either by executing a task that you have defined or by sending an e-mail or a pager message to an operator that you have specified.

You can select a Distributor and use Replication Monitor to display a list of all replication-related alerts on the server.

Windows NT Application Log

To view the Windows NT application log, use the Windows NT Event Viewer. If you are part of the **Windows NT Administrators** group, you can also view remote event logs. The Windows NT application log contains SQL Server error messages as well as messages for all activities on the computer. When you use the Windows NT application log, each SQL Server session writes new events to an existing log; you can filter the log for specific events. Unlike the SQL Server error log, a new Windows NT application log is not created each time you start SQL Server; however, you can specify how long logged events are retained.

Heterogeneous Interoperability

Many distributed applications require interoperability with custom solutions and multiple data stores. SQL Server 7.0 addresses this requirement in two ways. First, all replication programming interfaces are exposed and documented, allowing software developers to integrate applications tightly with SQL Server replication. For example, independent software vendors (ISVs) who specialize in replication solutions can easily layer their functionality on top of SQL Server replication to support replication to and from multiple data stores. Sales force automation vendors can easily build SQL Server replication directly into their applications, creating a seamless solution for customers. Second, SQL Server 7.0 replication is built on OLE DB and ODBC, the primary standards for data access, which provide built-in heterogeneous replication capabilities.

Replicating to Heterogeneous Data Sources

SQL Server supports replication to heterogeneous data sources that provide 32-bit ODBC or OLE DB drivers on the Microsoft Windows NT and Microsoft Windows 95 and Windows 98 operating systems. Out of the box, SQL Server supports Microsoft Access, Pocket Access, Oracle, and DB2 with the Microsoft BackOffice family of products as heterogeneous subscribers. In addition, SQL Server 7.0 supports any other database server that complies with ODBC or OLE DB Subscriber requirements.

The most straight forward way to publish data to a Subscriber that is not running SQL Server is to use ODBC/OLE DB and create a push subscription from the Publisher to the ODBC/OLE DB Subscriber. Alternately, you can create a publication, and then create an application with an embedded distribution control. The embedded control implements the pull subscription from the Subscriber to the Publisher. For ODBC/OLE DB Subscribers, the subscribing database has no administrative control over the replication being performed.

Replicating from Heterogeneous Data Sources

SQL Server enables heterogeneous data sources to become Publishers within the SQL Server replication framework. Microsoft has exposed and published the replication interfaces, allowing a developer to use all the transaction replication tools of SQL Server.

The replication tools available to heterogeneous data sources include:

- Programmable SQL-DMO replication objects for administering and monitoring replication.
- Replication distributor interface for storing replicated transactions.
- Distribution Agent to forward the transactions to Subscribers.
- SQL Server Enterprise Manager to administer and monitor replication graphically.

The following diagram illustrates how a heterogeneous data source is integrated into the replication framework as a Publisher.

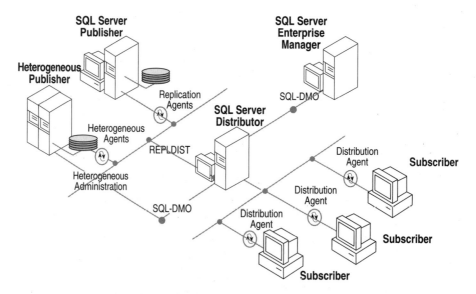

Microsoft has been actively promoting the Distributor Agent interfaces to the developer community to help ensure that ISVs are able to integrate their heterogeneous replication solutions tightly with SQL Server 7.0. Several vendors, including Platinum and Praxis, are building applications to the distributor interfaces, allowing them to drop publications from third-party databases directly into the SQL Server replication framework. After a heterogeneous publication is dropped into the distribution process, it can be monitored directly from third-party tools that support SQL-DMO replication objects.

Application Design Considerations

Data replication is a complex technology, and SQL Server replication developers recognize that a single solution is not right for all applications. Unlike other replication products that promote a single "update-anywhere-anytime" approach, SQL Server provides a variety of replication technologies that can be tailored to your application's specific requirements. Each technology provides different benefits and satisfies requirements across three important dimensions:

- Transactional consistency
- Site autonomy
- Partitioning data to avoid conflicts

Transactional Consistency

Transactional consistency, with respect to replication, means that the data at any participating site will be the same as it would be had all operations been performed at a single site. That is, the act of replicating the data does not in itself change the data in ways that would not occur if replication were not used. When working with distributed applications that modify data, there are three basic levels of transactional consistency:

- Immediate guaranteed consistency
- Latent guaranteed consistency
- Convergence

Immediate Guaranteed Consistency

With immediate guaranteed consistency (called tight consistency in SQL Server version 6.x), all participating sites are guaranteed to have the same data values at the same time, and the data is in the state that would have been achieved had all the work been done at the publishing site. The only way to achieve immediate guaranteed consistency in a distributed update environment (in which updates can be made to the same data at any location) is with the use of a two-phase commit (2PC) between all participating sites. Each site must simultaneously commit every change, or no site can commit the change. Such a solution is obviously not feasible for large numbers of sites because of unforeseen conditions, such as network outages.

Latent Guaranteed Consistency

With latent guaranteed consistency (called loose consistency in SQL Server version 6.x), all participating sites are guaranteed to have the same data values that were achieved at the publishing site at some point in time. There can be a delay in the data values being reflected at the Subscriber sites, so that at any instant in time, the sites are not assured of having the same data values. If all data modification could be paused long enough to allow every site to catch up and have every change applied, all sites would have the same data values. However, having the same value is not sufficient for latent guaranteed consistency. In addition, the data must be in the state that would have been achieved had all the work been done at one site. The difference between immediate and latent guaranteed consistency is whether the values are consistent at the same instant in time. If the system were allowed to catch up, the values would be identical regardless of whether the system is based on immediate or latent guaranteed consistency.

Convergence

With convergence, all the sites may end up with the same values, but not necessarily the values that would have resulted had all the work been done at only one site. All sites may work freely in a disconnected manner, and when all the nodes have synchronized, all sites converge to the same values. Lotus Notes is an example of a convergence product used to build useful distributed applications, yet it provides neither atomic transactions nor any model of guaranteed consistency.

Database vendors that support atomic transactions at a single site promote "update anywhere" replication solutions. Most database vendors offer the ability to resolve conflicts by discarding or changing the effects of one transaction because of another competing transaction performed at another node. These solutions are promoted as providing complete site autonomy. However, it is not well promoted that the act of conflict resolution means there is no guaranteed transactional consistency.

Example of Transactional Consistency

Three sites are participating in a replication scenario. Site 3 submits five transactions: T1, T2, T3, T4, and T5 for synchronization with the other two sites. Transactions T1 and T2 have no conflicts and are accepted. But transaction T3 has a conflict, and the reconciliation mechanism discards the transaction. Transactions T4 and T5 must also be discarded because these transactions may have read, and depended on, data that transaction T3 had modified. Because transaction T3 was subsequently discarded, it logically never existed. T4 and T5 are also in doubt. If they had been accepted, the results may have differed from the result that would have been obtained had all updates been done at a single site, thereby breaking the rules of transactional consistency.

Even a compensating transaction (for example, a delete if an insert had been accepted) is not sufficient to guarantee transactional consistency. Subsequent transactions may have applied changes to the transient data that resulted from the transaction that was resolved away. To remain in a state in which transactional consistency is guaranteed, not only must transaction T3 be discarded, but all subsequent work performed at that site, including T4 and T5, must be discarded as well.

Site Autonomy

Site autonomy refers to whether the operations of one site are affected seriously by those of another. There is complete site autonomy if one site's ability to do its work is independent of its connectivity to another site, and the state of operations at that site. For example, the use of 2PC makes every change to data dependent on whether every other participating site is able to accept the transaction successfully and immediately. If one site is unavailable, no work can proceed. At the other end of the spectrum, in merge replication, every site works independently and can be completely disconnected from all other sites. Merge replication has high site autonomy but not guaranteed consistency. 2PC has guaranteed tight consistency but a total absence of site autonomy. Other solutions are somewhere between both dimensions.

Partitioning Data to Avoid Conflicts

You can segregate data at multiple sites to provide your guarantee of transactional consistency. The absence of guaranteed transactional consistency does not imply guaranteed transactional inconsistency. If you can design your application so that each participating site works with data that is strictly segregated (or partitioned) from other sites, you can maintain transactional consistency. For example, to ensure that orders never will conflict, design your order entry system so that a given salesperson has a unique, known territory.

Partitioning adds a crucial third dimension to consider when designing and deploying distributed applications. While some of the SQL Server replication technologies allow for detection and resolution of conflicts, partitioning enables avoidance of conflicts. When possible, it is better to avoid conflicts before the update rather than to resolve them afterward. Conflict resolution always results in some site's work being overwritten or rolled back, and the loss of guaranteed transactional consistency. A high number of conflicts requires substantial processing to resolve, is more difficult to administer, and can result in data states that are entirely unpredictable and are not auditable. As a practical matter, if you choose a distributed technology that does not guarantee transactional integrity, you should be certain that your application and deployment will not produce many conflicts. Conflicts should be the exception rather than the rule, and reconciliation can be used to resolve these exceptions.

Other Distributed Technologies

SQL Server 7.0 replication provides powerful technologies for building and supporting a wide range of distributed applications. However, there are applications for which replication may not be the best solution. For these applications, SQL Server introduces several other distributed database technologies:

- Heterogeneous distributed queries
- Microsoft Distributed Transaction Coordinator (MS DTC)
- Data Transformation Services (DTS)

These SQL Server technologies can be used either in conjunction with, or in place of replication, depending upon the requirements for your application.

Heterogeneous Distributed Queries

Based on OLE DB, the distributed query technology for SQL Server 7.0 enables queries to heterogeneous data sources. Any data source supported by ODBC/OLE can participate in a distributed query. For example, an international company has eight regional offices, each using a different database product to store sales data (Oracle, Microsoft Access, Microsoft Excel, SQL Server, and so on). The sales manager uses distributed queries to read the data from each data source and prepare a quarterly report showing the sales, salary, and commission results for the last three years.

SQL Server allows a single SELECT statement to be issued to databases to the data sources, tapping into all the power of SQL, including heterogeneous joins and subqueries. If an application does require access to distributed data, but the use of a particular piece of data is infrequent, distributed queries may be a better choice than replication.

Microsoft Distributed Transaction Coordinator

Microsoft Distributed Transaction Coordinator (MS DTC) supports distributed updates in an application. This is the only way to guarantee tight consistency (all copies of your data always have the exact same data values at the exact same time) and that the data is in a state that would have been achieved had all the work been done at one site. SQL Server ships with the MSDTC service, which allows for this tight consistency, with real-time updates.

Data Transformation Services

Data Transformation Services (DTS) makes it easy to import, export, and transform data between multiple heterogeneous data sources using an OLE DB-based architecture. DTS allows you to move and transform data to and from:

- Native OLE DB providers such as SQL Server, Excel, Microsoft Works, and Access.
- ODBC data sources such as Access, Oracle, and DB2 using the OLE DB Provider for ODBC.
- ASCII fixed-field length text files and ASCII-delimited text files.

C H A P T E R 4

Heterogeneous Data

Enterprise business applications are designed more frequently to run in a distributed computing environment. In addition to distributing applications across a network of workstations, servers, and legacy mainframe systems, organizations are distributing applications across geographic boundaries, time zones, and divisions. As organizations evolve and grow, they also often acquire a heterogeneous collection of computers, networks, and databases.

These organizations need access to information and data from diverse enterprise business applications. For example, an organization might need to access the data residing on a UNIX workstation or an Oracle database in a way that is transparent to the end users. Transparent access is essential to developing powerful distributed solutions that allow an organization to be responsive to the marketplace. The Microsoft solution is the Universal Data Access (UDA) architecture as shown in this illustration.

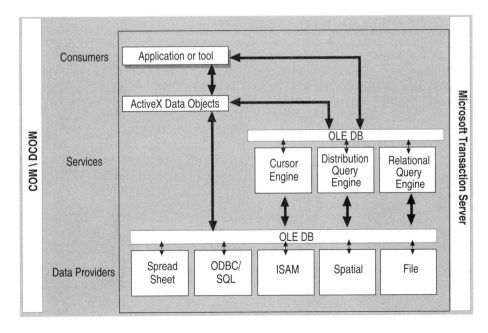

This chapter addresses the strategies and techniques for transparently accessing data in a heterogeneous environment. Microsoft SQL Server 7.0 is based on the UDA architecture, which is implemented by means of OLE DB. OLE DB is an interface specification that provides for distributed data access without regard to the data's source or format. Oracle, in contrast, takes a universal server approach, in which all data must exist in a single repository and must be accessed using a single access language.

The primary goal of SQL Server 7.0 is to take advantage of the capabilities offered through the UDA architecture, which allows data to exist in multiple formats and to be accessed using many different methods. With the release of SQL Server 7.0, Microsoft provides a more powerful relational database management system (RDBMS), and a mechanism for gathering disparate information stores and for presenting data in a consistent and useful manner without having to migrate or convert heterogeneous data to a single data store.

In addition to support for UDA, SQL Server 7.0 provides these new technologies for working with data in a heterogeneous environment:

- Data Transformation Services (DTS)

  SQL Server 7.0 allows the import, export, and transformation of data from heterogeneous data sources without any additional software investment. Any OLE DB provider can use DTS, including Oracle, Informix, and Microsoft Excel.

- Support for distributed queries

  SQL Server 7.0 allows linking remote servers (using any OLE DB provider) and using data in queries that come from heterogeneous sources. This action is transparent to the client program, which sees the tables as if they were native SQL Server tables, and improves network traffic because the query engine tries to execute as much work as possible at the remote computer. In addition, data does not need to be moved; it remains in its native store.

- Heterogeneous replication

  Any Open Database Connectivity (ODBC) driver or OLE DB data provider can participate in SQL Server 7.0 replication.

- Integrated support for data warehousing

   Data warehouses or data marts can be created easily from a variety of relational databases, including SQL Server, Oracle, and Informix.

All this functionality comes as part of SQL Server 7.0 at no additional cost. In addition, wizards make it easier for the user to build heterogeneous solutions using SQL Server.

The following scenarios explore situations in which SQL Server and Oracle would need to coexist.

Scenario A: Oracle as a Legacy Database

In this scenario, a bookstore uses Oracle to track book orders and inventory. The bookstore is introducing an online ordering system through the Internet and is considering using the built-in Web server for Windows NT Server, Internet Information Services (IIS) version 4.0, and SQL Server 7.0 to receive and process orders. Unless SQL Server is given the functionality to handle the orders and inventory, the two systems must coexist.

Online orders processed by SQL Server are published to Oracle. This is achieved without the use of any add-ons because the Oracle OLE DB driver provided with SQL Server 7.0 supports Oracle as a Subscriber in a SQL Server publication. Also, inventory can be directly accessed or modified in Oracle from SQL Server using linked remote servers and stored procedures. Reports can be built that access Oracle and SQL Server databases using the heterogeneous query support provided in SQL Server 7.0.

Given the proliferation of Windows NT and IIS and the ease of maintenance of Microsoft products, existing customers with Oracle databases can use a Microsoft Internet solution if they can easily access their legacy Oracle data.

Scenario B: SQL Server and Oracle as Peer Databases

In this scenario, a company uses both Oracle and SQL Server. The company purchased Oracle in a package. SQL Server was implemented to solve a divisional computing need. In this scenario, the divisional system has grown in size and complexity and houses important data useful to both the division and the enterprise. The Oracle system can be modified to provide enterprise data for the growing departmental needs, or the departmental systems data can be migrated to a central data store. Either option is a large undertaking that might result in little if any increased functionality.

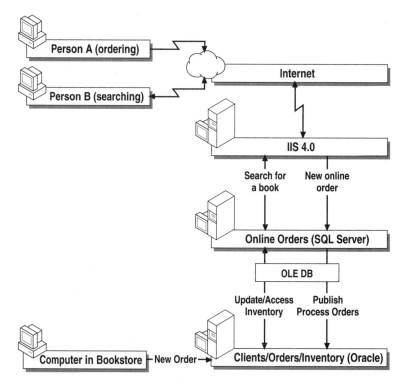

Another approach is for the two systems to share data in a peer-to-peer relationship. For example, consider the case of a training company whose contact management, classes, students, and orders are stored in a SQL Server 7.0 database, and its financial data is stored in an Oracle database. When a new order is created in SQL Server, an invoice must be produced from the Oracle database.

By using Microsoft Transaction Server (MTS), part of Windows NT Server, the appropriate entries are created in the Oracle database. And, if an order is canceled, an MTS transaction can update both the SQL Server and the Oracle databases.

A middle tier must be created to define the business rules and procedures, and care must be taken that all clients use it to perform business functions.

This peer approach leaves existing data in place, does not disrupt existing systems, and allows developers to focus efforts on enhancing functionality rather than reorganizing data.

SQL Server 7.0 for the Heterogeneous Environment

To respond to the demands of key distributed business applications, enterprise planners, administrators, and programmers must determine the best way to distribute large amounts of data so that it is in the right place at the right time. Microsoft SQL Server 7.0 provides several alternatives for processing distributed data in a heterogeneous environment:

- Replication
- Data Transformation Services (DTS)
- Heterogeneous distributed queries
- Microsoft Distributed Transaction Coordinator (MS DTC)

Replication

By using SQL Server 7.0 , you can easily replicate data from one database to another throughout the enterprise. The SQL Server replication technology copies data, moves these copies to different locations, and synchronizes the data so that all copies have the same data values. Other options allow you to selectively designate data from your tables to be replicated from a source database to a destination database. Replication can also be implemented between databases on the same server or on different servers connected by local area networks (LANs), wide area networks (WANs), or the Internet.

SQL Server 7.0 supports:

- Replication to heterogeneous databases using ODBC and OLE DB.

  SQL Server includes an ODBC driver that supports Oracle subscriptions to SQL Server on Intel-based computers. Other databases that provide 32-bit ODBC drivers on Windows NT, such as Sybase and Informix, can be part of the replication design.

- Programmatic interfaces for replicating data from heterogeneous databases.

  The Replication Distribution Interface (RDI) allows replication of data from heterogeneous data sources such as Microsoft Access or Oracle. Replication ActiveX controls provide a means of programmatically controlling Merge Agent and Distribution Agent activity at a Subscriber that has a pull subscription.

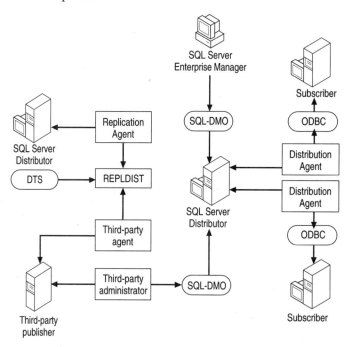

A company using Oracle is often concerned about using other databases because the information in the new database may not be accessible at the enterprise level. Using the previous example of a training company that has a central Oracle database system running Oracle financials, the environment is one in which the information technology (IT) staff is well-versed in Oracle and its development tools. When a department decided to purchase a SQL Server system, IT was concerned about how the SQL Server system would be supported and how it would integrate with the Oracle database.

In this case, all of the transactional inputs are maintained at the department level; however, some of the data in the departmental system is needed periodically for centralized reporting. Replication services are employed, allowing replication of the required data in the Oracle database, creating a planned, off-time window of network activity to move the data to the central database immediately prior to the scheduled report runs. This allows the two systems to coexist, giving the department the system they required, and still satisfying the need of central IT for data access.

SQL Server 7.0 provides a variety of replication options to choose from when considering replication between a variety of Publishers and Subscribers, including:

- Transactional replication

  Transactional replication is the original SQL Server Publisher/Subscriber model. It uses the transaction log to monitor changes to data. Changes are queued and then sent and applied to Subscribers.

- Snapshot replication

  Snapshot replication takes a picture, or snapshot, of the published data in the database at one moment in time. Snapshot replication requires less constant processor overhead than transactional replication because it does not require continuous monitoring of data changes on source servers.

- Merge replication

  Merge is a new replication model in which users work freely and independently. At a later time, the work is combined into a single, uniform result. This model is ideal for offline or disconnected applications.

In addition, the overall replication architecture in SQL Server 7.0 has been enhanced and includes:

- Stored procedure (functional) replication.
- Improved monitoring, ease of use, and troubleshooting capabilities.
- Scripting for easier mass deployment.
- Support for SQL Server 6.*x* Publishers and Subscribers.
- Improved Internet support.
- Improved SQL Server replication graphical user interface.
- Support for multisite updates.

For more information about the replication capabilities in SQL Server 7.0, see "Replication" earlier in this volume.

Data Transformation Services

Data Transformation Services (DTS) facilitates the import, export, and transformation of heterogeneous data. It supports transformations between source and target data using an OLE DB–based architecture. This allows you to move and transform data between the following data sources:

- Native OLE DB providers such as SQL Server, Microsoft Excel, Microsoft Works, Microsoft Access, and Oracle.
- ODBC data sources such as Sybase and Informix using the OLE DB Provider for ODBC.
- ASCII fixed-field length text files and ASCII delimited text files.

For example, consider a training company with four regional offices, each responsible for a predefined geographical region. The company is using a central SQL Server to store sales data. At the beginning of each quarter, each regional manager populates an Excel spreadsheet with sales targets for every salesperson. These spreadsheets are imported to the central database using the DTS Wizard. At the end of each quarter, the DTS Wizard is used to create a regional spreadsheet that contains target versus actual sales figures for each region.

DTS also can move data from a variety of data sources into data marts or data warehouses. Currently, data warehouse products are high-end, complex add-ons. As companies move toward more data warehousing and decision processing systems, the low cost and ease of configuration of SQL Server 7.0 makes it an attractive choice. For many, the fact that much of the legacy data to be analyzed may be housed in an Oracle system will focus their attention on finding the most cost-effective way to retrieve that data. With DTS, moving and massaging the data from Oracle to SQL Server is less complex and can be completely automated.

DTS introduces the concept of a *package*, which is a series of tasks performed as a part of a transformation. DTS has its own in-process component object model (COM) server engine that can be used independent of SQL Server and that supports scripting for each column using Visual Basic and JScript development software. Each transformation can include data quality checks and validation, aggregation, and duplicate elimination. You can also combine multiple columns into a single column, or build multiple rows from a single input.

Using the DTS Wizard, you can:

- Specify any custom settings used by the OLD DB provider to connect to the data source or destination.

- Copy an entire table, or the results of an SQL query, such as those involving joins of multiple tables or distributed queries. DTS also can copy schema and data between relational databases. However, DTS does not copy indexes, stored procedures, or referential integrity constraints.

- Build a query using the DTS Query Builder Wizard. This allows users inexperienced with the SQL language to build queries interactively.

- Change the name, data type, size, precision, scale, and nullability of a column when copying from the source to the destination, where a valid data type conversion applies.

- Specify transformation rules that govern how data is copied between columns of different data types, sizes, precisions, scales, and nullabilities.

- Execute an ActiveX script (Visual Basic or JScript) that can modify (transform) the data when copied from the source to the destination. Or you can perform any operation supported by Visual Basic or JScript development software.

- Save the DTS package to the SQL Server **msdb** database, Microsoft Repository, or a COM-structured storage file.

- Schedule the DTS package for later execution.

After the package is executed, DTS checks for the destination table and then gives you the option of dropping and re-creating the destination table. If the DTS Wizard does not properly create the destination table, you can verify that the column mappings are correct, select a different data type mapping, or create the table manually and then copy the data.

Each database defines its own data types and column and object naming conventions. DTS attempts to define the best possible data type matches between a source and a destination. However, you can override DTS mappings and specify a different destination data type, size, precision, and scale properties in the **Transform** dialog box.

Each source and destination may have binary large object (BLOB) limitations. For example, if the destination is ODBC, then a destination table can contain only one BLOB column and it must have a unique index before data can be imported. For more information, see the OLE DB for ODBC driver documentation.

Note DTS functionality may be limited by the capabilities of specific database management system (DBMS) or OLE DB drivers.

DTS uses the source object's name as a default. However, you can also add double quote marks (" ") or square brackets ([ ])around multiword table and column names if this is supported by your DBMS.

Data Warehousing and OLAP

DTS can function independent of SQL Server and can be used as a stand-alone tool to transfer data from Oracle to any other ODBC or OLE DB–compliant database. Accordingly, DTS can extract data from operational databases for inclusion in a data warehouse or data mart for query and analysis.

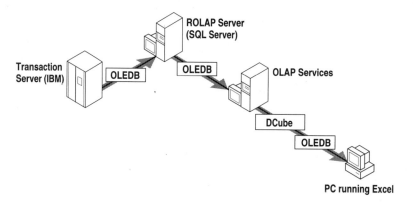

In the illustration, the transaction data resides on an IBM DB2 transaction server. A package is created using DTS to transfer and clean the data from the DB2 transaction server and to move it into the data warehouse or data mart. In this example, the relational database server is SQL Server 7.0, and the data warehouse is using OLAP Services to provide analytical capabilities. Client programs (such as Excel) access the OLAP Services server using the OLE DB for OLAP interface, which is exposed through a client-side component called Microsoft PivotTable service. Client programs using PivotTable service can manipulate data in the OLAP server and can even change individual cells.

SQL Server OLAP Services is a flexible, scalable OLAP solution, providing high-performance access to information in the data warehouse. OLAP Services supports all implementations of OLAP equally well: multidimensional OLAP (MOLAP), relational OLAP (ROLAP), and a hybrid (HOLAP). OLAP Services addresses the most significant challenges in scalability through partial preaggregation, smart client/server caching, virtual cubes, and partitioning.

DTS and OLAP Services offer an attractive and cost-effective solution. Data warehousing and OLAP solutions using DTS and OLAP Services are developed with point-and-click graphical tools that are tightly integrated and easy to use. Furthermore, because the PivotTable service client is using OLE DB, the interface is more open to access by a variety of client applications.

Issues for Oracle Versions 7.3 and 8.0

Oracle does not support more than one BLOB data type per table. This prevents copying SQL Server tables that contain multiple text and image data types with modification. You can map one or more BLOBs to the **varchar** data type and allow truncation, or split a source table into multiple tables. Oracle returns numeric data types such as **precision = 38** and **scale = 0**, even when there are digits to the right of the decimal point. If you copy this information, it is truncated to integer values. If mapped to SQL Server, the precision is reduced to a maximum of 28 digits.

The Oracle ODBC driver is not compatible with DTS and is not supported by Microsoft. A Microsoft Oracle ODBC driver is provided with SQL Server. When exporting BLOB data to Oracle using ODBC, the destination table must have an existing unique primary key.

Heterogeneous Distributed Queries

Distributed queries access data currently stored in SQL Server (homogeneous data) and also data traditionally stored in a data store other than SQL Server (heterogeneous data). Distributed queries behave as if all data were stored in SQL Server. SQL Server 7.0 supports distributed queries by taking advantage of the UDA architecture (OLE DB) to access heterogeneous data sources, as shown in this illustration.

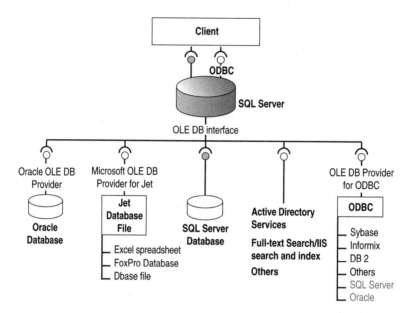

The advantages of heterogeneous distributed queries include:

- Working with providers at various levels.
- SQL query access against non-SQL data sources.
- Dialect independence, meaning Transact-SQL against everyone.
- The same mechanism for distributed RDBMS and heterogeneous nonrelational data.
- Minimizing network traffic by executing as much as possible remotely.

Issues for Oracle Versions 7.*x* and 8.0

Oracle supports heterogeneous distributed queries with SQL Server through the use of gateways. The SQL Server gateway is not included with Oracle; it must be purchased separately. SQL Server is more cost effective because heterogeneous distributed queries are provided with SQL Server 7.0. Because it uses OLE DB, you can access a wider spectrum of heterogeneous relational databases and nonrelational data providers.

Microsoft Distributed Transaction Coordinator

MS DTC was first released as part of SQL Server 6.5 and is included as a component in the MTS. MS DTC implements a transparent two-phase commit protocol that ensures that the transaction outcome (either commit or abort) is consistent across all resource managers involved in a transaction. The MS DTC ensures atomicity, regardless of failures, race conditions, or availability.

MS DTC supports resource managers that implement either the OLE transaction protocol or the X/Open XA specification for Distributed Transaction Processing.

SQL Server 7.0 in an Oracle Environment

Disparate databases exist in the same environment for many reasons. Oracle provides several products that facilitate connectivity and coexistence with Microsoft SQL Server.

Oracle Transparent Gateway

The Oracle transparent gateway allows Oracle client applications to access SQL Server. The gateway, in conjunction with an Oracle server, creates the appearance of all data residing on a local Oracle server, even though the data might be widely distributed. The Oracle transparent gateway provides:

- Transparent access to data.
- Heterogeneous transactions.
- Two-phase commit.
- Application portability.

The gateway accesses SQL Server data. Oracle client applications do not connect directly to the gateway, but connect indirectly to an Oracle server. The Oracle server communicates with the gateway by using SQL*Net. The gateway is started as a Windows NT–based service.

Client Applications

Client applications and Oracle tools, such as Oracle Forms, access the gateway through the Oracle server. When a client application queries a SQL Server database through the gateway, the query triggers the following sequence of events:

1. Client application sends a query to the Oracle server.
2. Oracle server sends the query to the gateway.
3. For the first transaction in a session, the gateway logs into SQL Server using a username and password that is valid in the SQL Server database.
4. Gateway converts the Oracle PL/SQL statement to a Transact-SQL statement understood by SQL Server.
5. Gateway retrieves the data using a Transact-SQL statement.
6. Gateway converts the retrieved data to a format compatible with Oracle.
7. Gateway returns the query results to the Oracle server.
8. Oracle server returns the query results to the client application.

Oracle Server

The Oracle server connects directly to the gateway, allowing heterogeneous queries against Oracle and SQL Server data. The Oracle server also post-processes Oracle SQL functions not supported by SQL Server. Definitions of database links for the SQL Server database are stored in the Oracle server.

SQL*Net

SQL*Net version 2.0 provides client-to-server and server-to-server communication. This allows a client to communicate with the Oracle server, and the Oracle server to communicate with the gateway.

The Oracle server and the gateway work together to present the appearance to the client of a single Oracle database.

Heterogeneous Database Integration

The Oracle server can accept an SQL statement that queries data stored in several different databases. The Oracle server passes the appropriate SQL statement directly to other Oracle databases and through gateways to other databases. The Oracle server then combines the results and returns them to the client, allowing a query to be processed that spans SQL Server and local and remote Oracle data.

Oracle Replication Services

Oracle offers a suite of additional products called Replication Services, which replicate SQL Server data into Oracle. By using Replication Services, either incremental row changes made to the SQL Server data or a full refresh can be propagated into Oracle.

Replicating data with Oracle transparent gateway provides both a synchronous and an asynchronous means for maintaining Oracle and SQL Server copies of data. When updates are made to Oracle, synchronous copies of Oracle and SQL Server data can be maintained automatically by using Oracle database triggers. For gateways that provide two-phase commit functionality, an Oracle trigger can be developed to fire every time an update is made to the Oracle data. The two-phase commit feature supported by the transparent gateways ensures that transaction consistency is maintained.

Synchronous technology ensures application integrity, but requires communication between Oracle and SQL Server to complete a transaction. By ensuring that all updates are made before a transaction is complete, all copies are synchronized at a single point in time.

Replication in a mixed database environment using asynchronous technology allows applications to complete transactions without requiring access to the replicated copies of the data. Updates made to the source are committed, and updates to the replicated targets are deferred until a later time. If a system is not available, then the operation is delayed until the system becomes available. Eventually, all copies will be identical, but there may be differences in the various copies of the data at any single point in time.

Oracle transparent gateway also provides asynchronous capabilities for replicating data. Oracle transparent gateway uses the Oracle snapshot replication feature to automatically and asynchronously replicate SQL Server data into Oracle. Snapshot replication can be used with any Oracle transparent gateway, thereby providing a simple method for automatically replicating data from the data stores.

Oracle/OLE Integration

Oracle Objects for OLE provides Oracle data access without using native database APIs or external data drivers. Using OLE2 technology, it provides a programmatic interface for Visual Basic, C++, and OLE 2.0 scripting applications to access Oracle data.

Integration with Windows Applications

For Visual Basic or other 4GL development, Oracle Objects for OLE uses an OLE in-process server that supports Oracle functionality in Windows–based applications.

Access to Oracle Functionality

Oracle Objects for OLE provides native access to Oracle so you can obtain features, such as shared SQL, PL/SQL, stored procedures, array processing, and server-side query parsing. Client-side features include bidirectional and scrollable cursors, find and move, customizable local data cache, commit/rollback, and row-level locking.

Data Access

Microsoft has developed the UDA architecture based on COM, which is a binary standard for objects that defines how an object should present itself to the system after it has been compiled from its target language into machine code. Defining a standard allows objects to be compatible regardless of their source languages. The UDA architecture allows applications to efficiently access data where it resides without replication, transformation, or conversion.

The strategy behind implementing distributed connectivity is to assure open, integrated, standards-based access to all types of data (SQL, non-SQL, and unstructured) across a wide variety of applications, from traditional client/server to the Web. Under UDA architecture, ActiveX Data Objects (ADO) is the high-level interface that most applications developers use. OLE DB providers are the data-access engines or services, as well as the business logic components, that these applications can use in a highly interoperable, component-based environment.

The two fundamental components of UDA architecture are the ODBC standard and the OLE DB standard. ODBC unifies access to relational data from heterogeneous systems. Any application that supports ODBC can access information stored in any database that houses relational data, including Oracle. If all of the data were stored in relational databases, integration could be solved by using ODBC only. However, much data is nonrelational, or unstructured (for example, audio and video clips, and e-mail messages). To simplify integration of unstructured data across the enterprise, Microsoft offers OLE DB.

OLE DB is a set of OLE interfaces that provides applications with uniform access to unstructured data regardless of type or location on the network. Developers can write applications that connect to any OLE DB provider, whether a file system, Oracle database, Microsoft Excel spreadsheet, or DB2 database, and can allow end users running Windows-based desktop applications to share and manipulate data stored there.

OLE DB is based on COM and provides:

- The ability to expose all types of data through a set of standard interfaces.
- Seamless integration between consumer applications and controls, data providers, and data sources.
- Plug-and-play usage of service providers, such as query processors and cursor engines. Query processors compatible with OLE DB can be smoothly integrated into the data access environment and can serve multiple consumer applications and data providers.

Connectivity Options

Microsoft products provide several data access connectivity options that are illustrated in the following diagram and summarized in the following discussion.

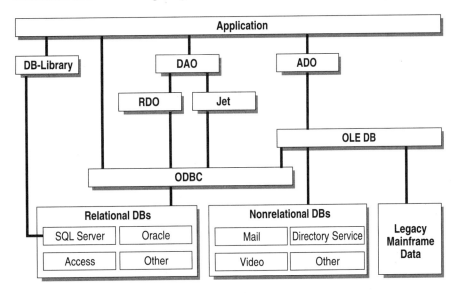

Open Database Connectivity

ODBC, a C/C++ API, is designed to target different sources from the same source code by substituting different drivers. It provides access to server-specific extensions, and developers can write code to query which extensions are available.

Microsoft developed the ODBC interface to provide applications with a single API through which to access data stored in a wide variety of DBMSs. Prior to ODBC, applications written to access data stored in a DBMS had to use the proprietary interface specific to that database. If application developers wanted to provide their users with heterogeneous data access, they had to code to the interface of each data source. Applications written in this manner are difficult to code, maintain, and extend. ODBC was created to overcome these difficulties.

Data Access Object

Data Access Object (DAO), which is designed for desktop access to data, is based on the Microsoft Jet database engine technology and uses Jet to gain access to other sources. Jet supports heterogeneous queries by using linked tables. This solution, however, is inefficient because the query processor does not attempt to optimize the query.

Remote Data Objects

Remote Data Objects (RDO) is an object interface to ODBC that is similar to DAO in its programming techniques. RDO is a thin OLE layer on top of ODBC specifically optimized for SQL Server and Oracle databases. It provides a less complex programming model than ODBC, and it is tuned for SQL Server and Oracle access.

ODBCDirect

ODBCDirect integrates RDO methods directly into DAO, bypassing the Jet engine and thus improving performance. ODBCDirect provides similar features as RDO, but it uses the DAO object model. It offers an easy path to upscale Microsoft Access applications for SQL Server and Oracle.

OLE DB

OLE DB is the foundation of the UDA architecture. It is a specification for a set of COM-based data-access interfaces that encapsulate various data management services, allowing an application to access data without regard to its source. This abstraction of the data-access method provides a more flexible development environment and allows developers to focus their efforts on the application rather than the data. To become an OLE DB provider, you can implement OLE DB components from the OLE DB interfaces for the level of OLE DB support you want. This component-based model allows you to work with data sources in a unified manner and allows for future extensibility.

OLE DB components can be separated into three categories: data providers, data consumers, and service components. A data provider owns the data it exposes to the outside world. Although each OLE DB provider handles implementation details independently, all OLE DB providers expose their data in a tabular format through virtual tables.

A data consumer is any component, whether it be system or application code, that must access data from the OLE DB provider. Development tools, programming languages, and many sophisticated applications fit into this category.

A service component is a logical object that encapsulates a piece of DBMS functionality (such as query processors, cursor engines, or transaction managers). One of the design goals of OLE DB is to implement service components as standalone products that can be plugged in when needed.

ActiveX Data Objects

ADO is an application-level programming interface to data and information. ADO supports a variety of development needs, including front-end database clients and middle-tier business objects using applications, tools, languages, or browsers. Remote Data Services (RDS), previously known as Active Data Connector, is a client-side component that interfaces with ADO and provides cursors, remote object invocation, and explicit and implicit remote recordset functionality such as fetch and update. OLE DB provides the low-level interface to data across the enterprise.

While ADO interfaces with OLE DB behind the scenes, applications can still access OLE DB directly. And ADO includes the ODBC components that have become the standard for working with relational databases. Although the emphasis in the UDA architecture is on OLE DB native providers, ODBC remains a backward-compatible solution.

Remote Data Services

RDS is responsible for client-side services such as caching and updating data and binding data to controls. RDS controls use ADO as their data source, and then the cursor engine in RDS communicates with ADO using OLE DB. RDS is a valuable component of the UDA architecture because it is responsible for improving client-side performance and flexibility in the Windows Distributed interNet Applications (DNA) architecture.

DB-Library

The Microsoft DB-Library, a C API, is a set of functions used to create client applications that interact with SQL Server. DB-Library offers the best performance because it is designed to communicate directly with SQL Server, bypassing ODBC and OLE DB. DB-Library is backward-compatible, but it is not the recommended way of connecting to SQL Server.

For more information about connectivity, see the Microsoft Interactive Developer article on Universal Data Access at www.microsoft.com/mind/0498/uda/uda.htm.

Third-Party and Middleware Connectivity Options

Several independent software vendors (ISVs) have incorporated OLE DB as the data-access technology in their products. The ISVs, in turn, are making commitments to market OLE DB technology. Intersolv and ISG are two examples of ISVs that provide OLE DB–based solutions and that produce OLE DB components such as providers and service providers. For more information about ISVs building OLE DB providers, see www.microsoft.com/data/oledb/.

Data-access middleware based on OLE DB provides a data access tier, which buffers an application from the native interface of the data source, the location of the data source, and the data model. To the client application, the middleware presents a transparent interface and data model, regardless of the type and number of data sources.

Data-access middleware processes application requests for data from a variety of database types. It packages the requests and transports them to a specific server system, which handles the request. After processing the request, the middleware returns the data to the application.

The following are examples of the current middleware and third-party products available for data access.

ISG Navigator

ISG Navigator is universal data access middleware that provides access and manipulation of data residing on Windows and platforms other than Windows (such as OpenVMS and UNIX). ISG Navigator is OLE DB compliant, providing access to data sources such as hierarchical databases, indexed sequential files, simple files, personal databases, spreadsheets, and mail folders. By using ISG Navigator, nonrelational data can be accessed in the same way as relational data, that is, by using standard SQL.

ISG Navigator also allows heterogeneous queries, in where data from relational and nonrelational data sources can be integrated in a single query. ISG Navigator provides access to multiple data sources including SQL Server and Oracle.

Although ISG Navigator is designed natively for OLE DB, it also provides an ODBC interface so that application programs accessing data through ODBC can readily benefit from ISG Navigator. In other words, ISG Navigator appears to the application as an ODBC data source but, unlike other ODCB data sources, ISG Navigator encapsulates as one many data sources on multiple platforms. The ISG Navigator OLE DB query processor for Windows NT, together with its ODBC interface, is included in the Microsoft OLE DB software development kit (SDK) as ODBC Bridge.

Intersolv

Intersolv provides full support for the OLE DB initiative through its full-function ODBC solutions. The Intersolv DataDirect ODBC Drivers version 3.0 contains optimizations for use in the OLE DB environment. Intersolv is developing a series of OLE DB service providers and data providers.

Sequiter Software

Sequiter Software is developing an OLE DB provider for Xbase databases such as dBASE and Microsoft FoxPro. The Metawise Computing OLE DB providers, which use the IBM data access Distributed Data Management (DDM) protocol, work with AS/400 and virtual storage access method (VSAM) on Multiple Virtual Storage (MVS). These providers are included as part of the base system, with no host code required. MapInfo is releasing a client product with an OLE DB interface.

Component Object Model

COM arose out of the need for an efficient method of interprocess communication. COM provides a group of conventions and supporting libraries that allow interaction between different pieces of software in a consistent, object-oriented way. COM objects can be written in many languages, including C++, Java, and Visual Basic, and they can be implemented in dynamic link libraries (DLLs) or in their own executables, running as distinct processes.

A client using a COM object need not be aware of either what language the object is written in or whether it is running in a DLL or a separate process. This functionality is achieved because COM defines an object concept known as an *interface*, which is a collection of methods that a client application can call. Interfaces are assembled and exposed to the system in the same way, regardless of the language used to create the object. This design provides a system whereby any COM-based component can communicate with any other existing or future COM-compliant component. These components can be created and accessed both on local and remote computers.

Distributed COM (DCOM) allows objects to be created and accessed on remote computers. DCOM provides a standard protocol that can sit on top of any standard networking protocol. If connectivity is established between computers at the network layer, DCOM-based communications can occur.

DCOM runs on top of these network protocols:

- TCP/IP
- IPX/SPX
- UDP
- NetBIOS
- HTTP

DCOM communications also work between dissimilar computer hardware platforms and operating systems. If DCOM has been implemented on both ends of a communication, it does not matter to either the client or the component which operating system is executing the other.

These platforms currently support DCOM, or will support it in the future:

- Windows NT
- Windows 95/98
- Sun Solaris
- AIX
- MVS
- Unixware (SCO)
- Linux
- Macintosh (Apple)

Developing DCOM servers capable of processing a few clients is manageable. However, developing servers capable of processing thousands of transactions can be daunting. In an effort to facilitate the development of scalable DCOM servers, Microsoft has developed and released MTS, which is designed to insulate developers from complex system-oriented tasks, such as process and thread management, and from involvement in development-intensive activities, such as directory management. MTS handles all of the applications' infrastructure, allowing developers to focus on business logic. Support is provided for accessing SQL Server and Oracle databases within MTS.

Microsoft Transaction Server

Microsoft Transaction Server (MTS) provides a run-time environment executing under Windows NT, which uses the COM interface mechanism to provide a flexible application development environment. MTS is suited for creating multitier client/server and Web-based applications. MTS is based on proven transaction processing methods, but its significance transcends the domain of transaction processing monitors. It defines a simple programming model and execution environment for distributed, component-based server applications.

MTS applications are composed of ActiveX components that provide the business-application function. These components are developed as if for a single user. By installing these components to execute within the MTS environment, the server application automatically scales to support many concurrent clients with high performance and reliability. MTS is specifically designed to allow server applications to scale over a wide range of users, from single-user systems to high-volume Internet servers. MTS provides the robustness and integrity traditionally associated with high-end transaction processing systems.

Server Infrastructure

Servers require a sophisticated infrastructure. Building a network application server from scratch is a complex task. Implementing the business function is a small fraction of the work. In fact, most of the work involves building a sophisticated infrastructure to attain acceptable levels of performance and scale.

Application server developers usually must develop much of the infrastructure themselves. For example, even with the rich services provided by remote procedure call (RPC) systems, developers must:

- Develop server-process executables to host the business function.
- Register servers with the directory system.
- Manage server process pools and thread pools. Ultimately, rather than dedicating a thread to work on behalf of a single client, servers must manage thread pools for servicing multiple client requests.
- Synchronize access to shared data and resources across concurrent requests from clients. This requires sophisticated locking protocols that must account for deadlocks, race conditions, starvation, and other performance issues.
- Manage client context, including database connections and per-user data structures (or objects).
- Cache state on the client for improved latency across slow networks.
- Implement security to ensure that business functions and objects are available only to those authorized to use them.
- Implement management and configuration tools to allow remote installation and administration of the servers.

MTS provides the application-server infrastructure that satisfies these requirements and allows the developer to focus on creating the business logic.

Application Integrity

It is critical that business systems accurately maintain the state of the business. For example, an online bookstore must track orders reliably. If it does not, revenue and customers can be lost.

Maintaining the integrity of business systems has never been easy. While computers are becoming increasingly reliable, systems are becoming increasingly unreliable. Failures are common with systems that are composed of multiple desktop computers connected through intranets and the Internet to multiple server computers.

The problem is compounded by the demand for distributed applications. Business transactions increasingly involve multiple servers. Credit must be verified, inventory must be shipped and managed, and customers must be billed. As a result, updates must occur in multiple databases on multiple servers. Developers of distributed applications must anticipate that some parts of the application will continue to run even after other parts have failed. These failure scenarios are orders of magnitude more complicated than those of monolithic applications, which fail as a whole. Business applications are frequently required to coordinate multiple pieces of work as part of a single transaction. Coordinating the work so that it all happens, or none of it happens, is difficult without system support. By using multiple components, which by design hide their implementations, problems are compounded.

Applications must provide consistent behavior when multiple clients are accessing a component. Concurrent orders of the same item should not result in attempting to send a single item to two customers. Unless the application is properly written, race conditions eventually will cause inconsistencies. These problems are difficult and expensive to resolve, and are more likely to occur as volume and concurrency increase. Again, multiple components compound the problem.

MTS integrates transactions with component-based programming so that you can develop robust, distributed, component-based applications.

Issues for Oracle Versions 7.*x* and 8.0

Because Oracle is XA-compliant and supports the Microsoft Oracle ODBC driver, Oracle databases can participate in MTS transactions. Oracle 7.3.3 is the first release of Oracle that supports MTS transactions. MTS also works with Oracle 8.0, but you must access Oracle 8.0 using the Oracle 7.3.3 client. MTS does not currently support Oracle 8.0 clients. It does work with Oracle Parallel Server.

The table outlines the data access methods that work with Oracle.

Data access method	Comments
ADO	Provides an object-oriented programming interface for accessing OLE DB data sources. ADO permits a collection of records to be passed between clients and servers in the form of a recordset. A recordset can be used to pass a query result from the server to the client, and to pass updated records from the client to the server.
Java Database Connectivity (JDBC)	Allows Java components to invoke ODBC databases.

(continued)

Data access method	Comments
OLE DB	Provides a standard interface to any tabular data source. ADO/OLE DB currently only supports transactions through the ODBC to OLE DB provider. The Microsoft OLE DB Provider for Oracle supports transactions when it becomes available. You cannot call OLE DB interfaces directly from Visual Basic because OLE DB is a pointer-based interface. A Visual Basic-based client can access an OLE DB data source through ADO.
ODBC	Provides a standard interface to relational data sources.
RDO	Provides an object-oriented programming interface for accessing ODBC data sources.

New Features of SQL Server 7.0

This section provides a summary of the new features in Microsoft SQL Server 7.0.

Database Architecture

One of the strengths of Microsoft SQL Server 7.0 is its universal accessibility. The SQL Server database architecture has been refined to include a query processor that supports parallel execution, the ability to query both ODBC and OLE DB, and other enhancements such as increased size limits for pages, rows, and tables, and support for row-level locking.

Query Processor

The SQL Server 7.0 query processor supports large databases and complex queries by using hash join, merge join, and hash aggregation techniques. The query processor uses fast sampling to extract and gather statistics. It also supports parallel execution of a single query over multiple processors, which allows SQL Server to perform query execution.

OLE DB

SQL Server 7.0 uses OLE DB technology to perform distributed queries to access data in multiple SQL Servers, heterogeneous databases, file systems, and other network sources.

Improved I/O

SQL Server 7.0 has enhanced I/O capability in database page size. Page size has been increased from 2 KB to 8 KB, with a maximum of 8,060 bytes per row. Other enhancements change the character data type limit from 255 bytes to 8,000 bytes and the columns per table limit from 250 columns to 1,024 columns. These changes allow SQL Server to handle much larger databases.

Enterprise System Support

SQL Server 7.0 can handle larger enterprise systems. SQL Server 6.5 was limited to approximately 100 gigabytes (GB) for high-availability online transaction processing (OLTP) applications. In contrast, SQL Server 7.0 supports terabyte-size applications, increasing earlier version capabilities by a factor of 10.

Backup Utilities

SQL Server 7.0 backup utilities can perform incremental backups capturing only the pages that have changed since the last database backup.

SQL Server 7.0 backup restoration automatically creates the database and all necessary files, enhancing the restoration procedure. SQL Server 7.0 supports the Microsoft Tape Format so that backup files can be stored on the same media as other backup files.

Oracle Integration

SQL Server 7.0 includes an OLE DB driver for Oracle, which facilitates the migration and movement of data and tables to and from Oracle servers to SQL Server 7.0 servers. DTS is one method that can be implemented to migrate and transform data. Data also can be migrated from one Oracle table to another using SQL Server 7.0 and DTS. The OLE DB driver for Oracle provided with SQL Server 7.0 allows an Oracle database to be a Subscriber in a SQL Server 7.0 Publisher without using a third-party product. In contrast, Oracle requires a SQL Server gateway for SQL Server to participate in Oracle replication.

Replication APIs

SQL Server 6.5 can replicate to any ODBC-compliant database, but replication to SQL Server 6.5 from a database other than SQL Server requires a custom solution. With SQL Server 7.0, replication APIs are publicly available so that ISVs can implement bidirectional replication solutions.

Expanded Database

The database size has expanded from 1 terabyte in SQL Server 6.5 to 1,048,516 terabytes in SQL Server 7.0. SQL Server 7.0 can shrink or grow databases automatically.

Enhanced SQL Server Enterprise Manager

The SQL Server Enterprise Manager provides wizards for common tasks that database administrators perform, including creation of databases, tables, views, indexes, jobs, alerts, and stored procedures. The Index Tuning Wizard examines a server activity capture file and then analyzes submitted queries against a database's index configuration, suggesting new indexes. The Maintenance Plan Wizard schedules table reorganizations to add fill-factor space, updates statistics, checks table and index integrity, and runs backups.

Self-Tuning Engine

SQL Server 7.0 dynamically allocates memory and disk space based on system resources and current workload. Devices that shrink dynamically are a feature that helps optimize resource use. Disk devices have been modified to become operating-system files, thus avoiding the overhead that SQL Server 6.5 imposes with database-specific devices.

Comparison of SQL Server and Oracle Features

This section compares and contrasts Microsoft SQL Server 7.0 and Oracle features.

System Administration

SQL Server Enterprise Manager is a plug-in to Microsoft Management Console (MMC), the standard user interface for all Microsoft BackOffice family products. This provides consistency and usability with all other Microsoft server products.

SQL Server 7.0 provides more than 25 wizards that significantly simplify system administration. In addition, more than 100 prewritten scripts can be used to administer the database. Oracle does not offer either the wizards or the prewritten scripts. However, Oracle has many system tables that can provide the information required.

SQL Server 7.0 uses autotuning of parameters, thus reducing the number of parameters that the administrator must set to optimize the server.

SQL Server 7.0 handles memory management automatically. To increase the performance of an application in Oracle, the database administrator must alter the buffer cache and memory pool parameters in the Init.ora file. The amount of space allocated varies by system and is constrained by the amount of memory on the server and the resources required by the shared pool.

Development

Oracle and SQL Server use standard SQL, with extensions provided by each database server. Oracle uses PL/SQL to extend its SQL usage with developers, and SQL Server uses Transact-SQL. Stored procedures can be used in both environments.

Both SQL Server and Oracle come with a battery of utilities that allow developers to manipulate data within the database as well as to import and export. Users can take advantage of transactions, foreign key constraints, and triggers.

A difference between Oracle and SQL Server is that SQL Server works almost transparently with other development tools, and it can be accessed by either ODBC or OLE DB. Oracle works best with other Oracle products. To access an Oracle database using ODBC, the client computer must have SQL*Net installed.

Backup and Recovery

Oracle and SQL Server use different backup and recovery terminology but the results are the same. All transactions can be logged, archived, and recovered as needed, and backups can be performed without degradation to server performance.

Although there are many similarities, the greatest difference is administration time. Oracle can require a longer continuous period of time to administer than does SQL Server.

Components

SQL Server does not use conventions of schemas and instances; Oracle does. In SQL Server, each database is an autonomous application hosted within SQL Server. The database is a logical definition that associates the objects within the database, and then identifies the level of access granted to users and groups.

The defined structure for SQL Server and for the data systems it is hosting, is kept in a set of system tables that are roughly equivalent to data dictionaries in Oracle. The illustration shows the SQL Server defined structure.

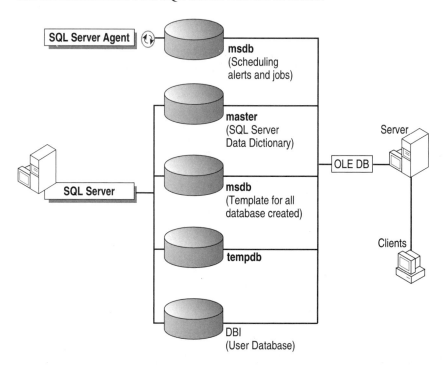

- The **master** database records all of the system-level information for the SQL Server system. It records all login accounts and all system configuration settings. **master** records the existence of all other databases and the location of the primary files that contain the initialization information for SQL Server and user databases.

- The **model** database is used as the template for all the databases created on the system. When a CREATE DATABASE statement is issued, the first part of the database is created by copying in the context of the **model** database.

- The **tempdb** database is the temporary storage area used by all databases. It serves the same function as the Oracle "system global area."

- The **msdb** database is used by the SQL Server Agent component for scheduling alerts and jobs.

In addition to the logical constructs maintained within SQL Server, there are a number of system services that are implemented. Unlike Oracle, which implements a set of system services for each instance, SQL Server initiates only one set of system services for all instances. The **MSSQLServer** service is the primary service responsible for SQL Server. The **SQLServerAgent** service is the service responsible for the SQL Server Agent component and manages alerts and scheduled jobs.

Security

The SQL Server 7.0 security system architecture is based on users and groups of users, called *security principals*. The following illustration shows how Windows NT–based users and groups can map to security accounts in SQL Server, and how SQL Server can handle security accounts independent of Windows NT–based accounts.

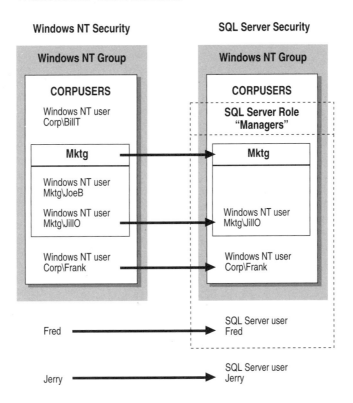

SQL Server provides security at the database level by using individual application security. SQL Server operates in one of two security (authentication) modes:

- Windows NT Authentication Mode (Windows NT Authentication)
- Mixed Mode (Windows NT Authentication and SQL Server Authentication)

Mixed Mode allows users to connect using Windows NT Authentication or SQL Server Authentication. Users who connect through a Windows NT–based user account can make use of trusted connections in either Windows NT Authentication Mode or Mixed Mode. After successful connection to SQL Server, the security mechanism for both modes is the same.

Security systems based on SQL Server logins and passwords can be easier to manage than security systems based on Windows NT user and group accounts, especially for nonsensitive, noncritical databases and applications. For example, a single SQL Server login and password can be created for all users of an application, rather than creating all the necessary Windows NT user and group accounts. However, this eliminates the ability to track and control the activities of individual users.

The security environment in Windows NT and SQL Server is stored, managed, and enforced through a hierarchical system of users. To simplify the administration of many users, Windows NT and SQL Server use *groups* and *roles*. A group is an administrative unit within the Windows NT operating system that contains Windows NT users or other groups. A role is an administrative unit within SQL Server that contains SQL Server logins, Windows NT logins, groups, or other roles. Arranging users into groups and roles makes it easier to grant or deny permissions to many users at one time. The security settings defined for a group are applied to all members of that group. When a group is a member of a higher-level group, all members of the group inherit the security settings of the higher-level group, in addition to the security settings defined for the group or the user accounts.

The organizational chart of a security system commonly corresponds to the organizational chart of a company, as demonstrated in this illustration.

Sample Company Organization

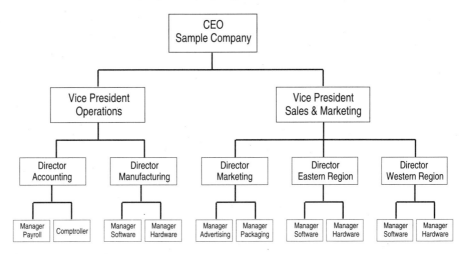

Sample Company Windows NT Security Groups

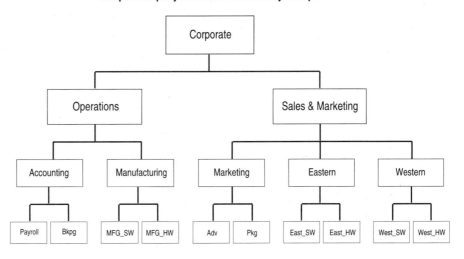

The organizational chart for a company is a good model for the security system of a company, but there is one rule for a company's organizational hierarchy that does not apply to the security model. Common business practice usually dictates that an individual reports to only one manager. This implies that an employee can fall under only one branch of the organizational hierarchy.

The needs of a database security system go beyond this limitation because employees commonly need to belong to security groups that do not fall within the strict organizational hierarchy of the company. Certain staff members, such as administrators, can exist in every branch of the company and require security permissions regardless of organizational position. To support this broader model, the Windows NT and SQL Server security system allows groups to be defined across the hierarchy. An administrative group can be created to contain administrative employees for every branch of the company, from corporate to payroll.

This hierarchical security system simplifies management of security settings, and it allows security settings to be applied collectively to all group members without having to be defined redundantly for each person. The hierarchical model also accommodates security settings applied to only one user.

PART 3

Deployment

Part 3 describes the deployment of mobile business applications using SQL Server.

C H A P T E R   5

Developing Mobile Applications

Changing demographics and the popularity of laptop computers are fueling an explosive growth in mobile applications. Many organizations are decentralizing parts of their companies to save money and provide employees with a more flexible work environment. In addition, workers increasingly use computers when away from the office. According to Dataquest *1998 Mobile Computing Forecast* (gartner12.gartnerweb.com/dq/), the mobile computing market is expected to grow more than 18 percent per year by 2002.

Increasingly, people use computers when they are on the road. For example, sales personnel might use a computer to enter orders, update customer information, or manipulate financial information. When they reconnect to the network, new or updated information must be merged into the enterprise databases. Similarly, any changes made to the enterprise databases while the user was offline must be copied to the user's computer. The application logic that is required to synchronize the multiple databases can be complex. For example, the application must resolve conflicts if two remote users update the same information independently while offline.

This chapter describes why Microsoft SQL Server version 7.0 offers a compelling database and development architecture for implementation and administration of mobile applications. It also compares SQL Server 7.0 functionality with that of another product for mobile applications, Sybase Adaptive Server Anywhere 6.0.

Evaluating Mobile Database Solutions

For many users, developing, deploying, and administering mobile applications can be challenging without the right tools and the appropriate infrastructure. Many enterprise-class relational database management systems (RDBMSs) were designed for client/server–based computing. Client/server applications typically assume that the user has a permanent connection to a server. For this reason, there is no local data store and no facility for working offline. A traditional client/server application can be modified to work in a mobile environment, but the code required to ensure that data on the client and server remains synchronized is considerable.

To develop scalable mobile applications, you must rely on services in the operating system and RDBMS to distribute and synchronize updates made on either the mobile client or the central database. The operating system and RDBMS should provide these basic features for developing a mobile database application:

- An RDBMS engine that can run on both the client and the server and that can synchronize updates easily on either the client or the server.
- Administration tools that allow database administrators to deploy client code and data easily, as well as manage synchronization between many clients and servers.
- Tools that allow developers to migrate existing client/server applications easily to applications that support mobile clients.

RDBMS Client and Server Engines

When evaluating database applications for mobile clients, you should ask these questions about the RDBMS client and server engines:

- Does the vendor offer a single RDBMS engine that scales from a mobile client to an enterprise-class server?
- Do the local and central RDBMS engines support atomic transactions?
- Does the RDBMS engine support two-way merge replication, which guarantees delivery of data in a disconnected environment?
- Does the RDBMS engine support heterogeneous replication to other RDBMS engines?
- Will the RDBMS engine scale to support multiple mobile clients?
- What are the system requirements for running the database engine and replication engine on the client?

Administration and Total Cost of Ownership

When evaluating database applications for mobile clients, you should ask these questions about administration and total cost of ownership:

- How easy is it to manage security for multiple mobile clients?

- What tools and built-in functions are provided for resolving conflicts when users independently update the same record with different information?

- Can the administration tools be customized easily to meet the specific needs of an organization?

- Do the tools take advantage of existing skill sets, or will the database administrator need to learn new procedures and programming languages to administer the database efficiently?

- Can the database administrator manage a multiple clients as a single logical group?

- How well are the administration and system-monitoring tools integrated into the operating system?

- How easy is it to deploy both the database engine and the databases on the client?

Cost-Effective Application Development

When evaluating database applications for mobile clients, you should ask these questions about the tools for developing mobile applications:

- How easy is it to convert an existing client/server application to a mobile application?

- What tools are available for upsizing tables, schemas, data, and referential-integrity information from a desktop database such as Microsoft Access or Microsoft FoxPro to an RDBMS engine that supports multiple mobile clients?

- What tools are available for building best-of-breed, three-tiered applications?

Supporting Mobile Applications with SQL Server 7.0

Microsoft SQL Server 7.0 is a full-featured, enterprise-class RDBMS that runs on Microsoft Windows NT, Windows NT Server, Enterprise Edition, Microsoft Windows 95, and Microsoft Windows 98 operating systems.

Scalability and Performance

Customer questions about scalability and performance can include the following:

- How easily can the application move from a laptop to an enterprise-class server?

- How many concurrent clients can a single server support for a given online transaction processing (OLTP) or decision-support scenario?

- What is the response time for executing complex queries on large databases?

- Is the RDBMS designed to support backup, restore, and maintenance of very large databases?

An important benefit that SQL Server offers for mobile applications development is that applications written for SQL Server run unchanged from Windows 95 or Windows 98 laptops to Windows NT Server, Enterprise Edition, multiprocessor clusters. SQL Server 7.0 is the first RDBMS engine to provide a single codebase that can scale from a mobile client to a high-end enterprise-class server.

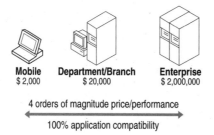

Mobile   Department/Branch   Enterprise
$ 2,000 $ 20,000 $ 2,000,000

4 orders of magnitude price/performance

100% application compatibility

SQL Server 7.0 handles the needs of both small and large organizations. Recent benchmarks from the Transaction Processing Performance Council (TPC) show that SQL Server 7.0 is among the best-performing RDBMSs available for the Windows NT operating system. For more information about TPC benchmarks, see www.tpc.org.

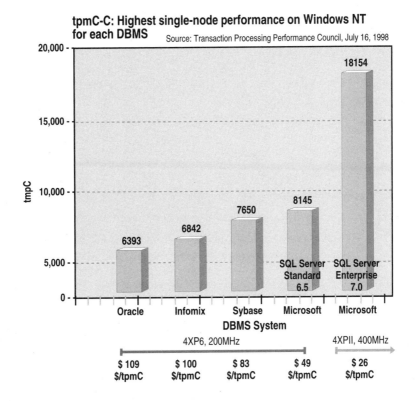

tpmC-C: Highest single-node performance on Windows NT for each DBMS   Source: Transaction Processing Performance Council, July 16, 1998

Support for Smaller Databases

SQL Server 7.0 includes the following support features for smaller databases located on either a mobile client or a workgroup server. In these environments, ease of management is the primary concern.

Dynamic memory

   Dynamic memory improves performance by optimizing memory allocation and usage. The simplified design minimizes contention with other resource managers. This feature simplifies management of SQL Server on the Windows 95 or Windows 98 and Windows NT Workstation operating systems because administrators do not need to predefine the cache size for particular databases.

Dynamic space management

   The database can grow and shrink automatically within configurable limits, minimizing the need for intervention by the database administrator. It is not necessary to preallocate space and manage data structures. Dynamic space management also simplifies administration of mobile clients.

Automatic statistics maintenance
 SQL Server maintains statistics on data distribution to improve query
 performance. This means that application developers can rely on the query
 optimizer for the latest statistics rather than overriding the query optimizer
 with specific hints in their Transact-SQL statements.

Scalable storage
 The disk format and storage subsystem provides storage that is scalable from
 very small to very large databases. Specific changes include:

 - Simple mapping of database objects to files.

   This provides less complex management and more tuning flexibility by
   mapping database objects to specific disks to balance I/O load.

 - Efficient space management.

   Page sizes have increased from 2 KB to 8 KB, 64 KB I/O, column limits
   have lifted, variable-length character fields have increased to 8 KB, and the
   ability to add and delete columns from existing tables without unloading
   and reloading the data has been added.

 - Support for terabyte-size databases.

   Redesigned utilities support large databases efficiently.

Support for Large Databases

SQL Server 7.0 includes the following features to support very large databases
that are typically located in a managed-server environment. In this environment,
efficiency and performance are the primary concerns.

Hash joins and merge joins
 Hash, merge, and nested loops joins are available for processing complex
 queries. Multiple join types can be used within a single query. The query
 optimizer supports specialized join operations, such as star schema joins.

Superior cache management
 In general, larger I/O sizes support higher throughput rates. In SQL Server 7.0,
 the page size is 8 KB, extents are 64 KB, and most I/O operations use 64 KB
 blocks. Smart I/O is the key to enhancing performance. More efficient read
 aheads, physical row-order scans, and parallel I/O also improve performance.

Parallel queries
 SQL Server 7.0 provides intraquery parallel execution across multiple
 processors. Steps in a single query are executed in parallel, delivering the
 optimum response time. Users can take advantage of symmetric
 multiprocessing (SMP) hardware for complex analysis.

Dynamic row-level locking
> Full row-level locking is implemented for both data rows and index entries. Dynamic locking automatically chooses the optimal level of lock (row, page, multiple page, table) for all database operations. This feature provides optimal concurrency levels.

Large memory support
> SQL Server 7.0, Enterprise Edition, supports memory addressing greater than 4 gigabytes (GB) with Alpha processor-based systems running the Windows NT Server 4.0 operating system.

Read-ahead
> Smart read-ahead logic improves performance and eliminates the need for manual tuning.

Backup and restore
> The parallel backup and restore utilities in SQL Server 7.0 are limited only by device speeds. Very high server transaction processing rates are maintained during full online backups.

Bulk copy program (BCP)
> The **bcp** utility offers fast import and export transfer capabilities. The **bcp** utility uses OLE DB and works in conjunction with the query processor to load and unload data quickly.

Sybase Scalability and Performance

Sybase SQL Anywhere Studio is a family of RDBMS server products from Sybase, Inc., that includes the Adaptive Server Enterprise and Adaptive Server Anywhere 6.0 server engines. Both server engines have similar architectures but are based on different code bases. This means that applications written for Sybase Adaptive Server Enterprise may not be compatible with Sybase Adaptive Server Anywhere, and vice versa. The result is additional development, testing, and administration to assure application compatibility when using both database products.

The Sybase Adaptive Server Anywhere 6.0 server engine is not primarily offered as an enterprise-class database, so there are no TPC benchmarks available. Organizations would need to upsize to Sybase Adaptive Server Enterprise to obtain a comparison. For a comparison of Microsoft SQL Server and Sybase Adaptive Server Enterprise benchmarks, see the TPC Web site at www.tpc.org/.

Sybase Adaptive Server Anywhere 6.0 does not support dynamic memory allocation. Typically, a database in a mobile or disconnected environment requires additional memory only for short periods of time to process queries. Sybase Adaptive Server Anywhere 6.0 requires a fixed amount of memory while the application is running. There also is an administrative overhead because the cache size on the client must be preassigned by using startup parameters.

Sybase claims that Adaptive Server Anywhere 6.0 can run in as little as 1 megabyte (MB) of memory. However, this figure does not take the following factors into consideration:

- A 2-MB cache size, which is required for any meaningful work.

- If you use Java, the Java Virtual Machine requires an additional 2 MB per database, and the database memory cache must be increased to use Java in the database. This memory cannot be reallocated.

- A default memory requirement of 2 MB for the SQL remote synchronization engine.

In a real-world application, Sybase Adaptive Server Anywhere 6.0 users need from 6 MB through 8 MB of memory on a client computer, about the same as for SQL Server 7.0. Because mobile clients are running all the code on the client, Windows 95 or Windows 98–based users need at least 32 MB of memory, and Windows NT Workstation users need at least 48 MB. These figures may vary depending on the number and size of applications running on the client.

Advanced Replication Functionality

SQL Server 7.0 offers three types of replication:

- Snapshot

  The replication agent copies an entire view of data to another computer. The destination database view is overwritten with the new version.

- Transactional

  Transactions (INSERT, UPDATE, or DELETE statements) executed on one computer are replicated to another computer.

- Merge

  Updates on any computer are replicated to another computer at a later time.

For applications with disconnected users, merge replication is the most frequently used form of replication. Merge replication maintains consistency between mobile clients and the central server. It supports bidirectional updates, meaning that during the synchronization process, new or updated records on the mobile client are copied to the server, and vice versa, to ensure that both copies remain synchronized. If two mobile clients change the same data, SQL Server applies criteria that you established to resolve the conflict on the central database automatically.

SQL Server 7.0 uses a publish and subscribe metaphor to set up and administer replication. A Publisher offers publications, which contain articles (tables or views), to which other SQL Server databases or Open Database Connectivity (ODBC) data sources can subscribe. A Subscriber receives publications. A distributor retrieves and stores modified data from the Publisher and sends the data to the Subscriber. In the case of merge replication, the Subscriber can be either another SQL Server database or a Microsoft Access 2000 database.

When a subscription is initiated, the Publisher sends the Subscriber an initial snapshot of the publication. This creates the necessary database objects (schemas and data) for the Subscriber. This customizable script is generated automatically by SQL Server.

After the initial snapshot is set up, only changes made on the Publisher (not the entire publication) are sent to the Subscriber. Each time a record is added, modified, or deleted, SQL Server detects the changes and sends the appropriate Transact-SQL statement to a distribution server. If many clients are subscribing to a single SQL Server database, an administrator may assign the role of distribution server to another instance of SQL Server to improve performance. The distribution engine can send updates to Subscribers, either on demand or as scheduled. The Subscriber also can initiate merge replication.

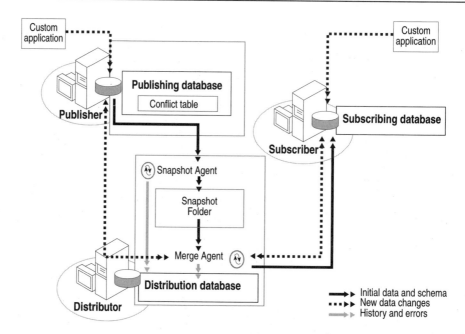

SQL Server 7.0 allows you to publish a subset of rows and columns from a table. For example, sales representatives typically cover a specific geographic territory. In this case, you would replicate only the data relevant to each sales representative. SQL Server allows you pass parameters to publications, which simplifies the process of supporting many subscribers. For example, an administrator may want to pass the username and computer name to a publication as a parameter so that each sales representative receives data about their sales region only.

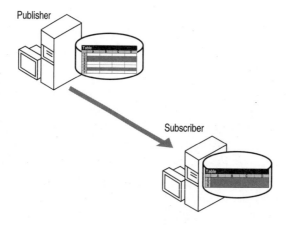

The architecture required to support merge replication may vary significantly depending on these factors:

- The number of users the system must support
- Whether users will be dialing in over phone lines or ISDN lines, or connecting directly to the local area network (LAN) when synchronizing
- The size and number of tables that require synchronization
- The anticipated frequency of updates (daily, weekly, or other)

A carefully considered architecture and rigorous operational procedures are key to the successful implementation of a mobile application. For example, it is not practical to have multiple clients simultaneously trying to synchronize with a single database. This not only strains the physical resources of the network, but it also means that updates to the central database occur so frequently that nobody has an up-to-date version of the data.

To solve this problem, the central database should be partitioned over several servers that are located as geographically close as possible to the mobile client. The following diagram demonstrates how a database might be partitioned to support multiple clients.

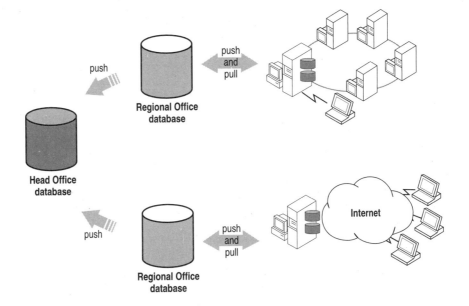

Performance and scalability of merge replication can be greatly enhanced by:

- Scheduling replication between client and server databases for off-peak times.
- Refreshing look-up tables on mobile clients only when needed.
- Replicating only the rows and columns specifically required by each mobile client.
- Implementing procedures that avoid simultaneous synchronizing by multiple clients.
- Using anonymous subscriptions.

SQL Server 7.0 uses a variety of communication methods to synchronize updates:

- Remote Access Services (RAS), to provide native connectivity to a LAN
- A standard Internet connection (FTP)

SQL Server 7.0 assures delivery of updates regardless of the communication protocol. For more information about network library support, see SQL Server Books Online.

Sybase Merge Replication

Sybase Adaptive Server Anywhere 6.0 uses a message-based replication system called SQL Remote to synchronize updates between a client and the server. Sybase SQL Remote uses the File, FTP, MAPI, SMTP, and VIM message-based protocols.

There are several problems inherent to relying on message-based protocols:

- The user must have e-mail installed and configured.
- If you choose SMTP or VIM, messages generated by Sybase Adaptive Server Anywhere 6.0 can appear in the user's inbox. Users might delete messages generated by SQL Remote and cause synchronization to fail.
- The File protocol is a file-sharing system that can be difficult to manage and administer.
- The administrator must enter each user's messaging address separately.

Replication with Heterogeneous Databases

Many organizations must support databases from a wide range of vendors. SQL Server 7.0 supports replication to and from heterogeneous data sources using ODBC or OLE DB. For example, Microsoft Access 2000 supports bidirectional merge replication natively. SQL Server 7.0 supports transactional replication to any heterogeneous Subscriber. Heterogeneous Publishers, however, must support the SQL Merge Agent application programming interface (API) to participate in bidirectional merge replication. For more information about bidirectional merge replication, see SQL Server Books Online.

SQL Server 7.0 includes a SQL Merge control object that manages heterogeneous replication. The SQL Merge control object provides the functionality of the Merge Agent and is used in conjunction with subscriptions to merge publications. The same properties that can be set by invoking the SQL Merge control object are available using the replication Merge Agent utility.

The following illustration shows a heterogeneous replication scenario. In this example, a heterogeneous Publisher is configured to exchange updates with a central SQL Server database. The central SQL Server Publisher then synchronizes changes to the three client Subscribers. All of these Publishers and Subscribers are managed by SQL Server Enterprise Manager using SQL Distributed Management Objects (SQL-DMO).

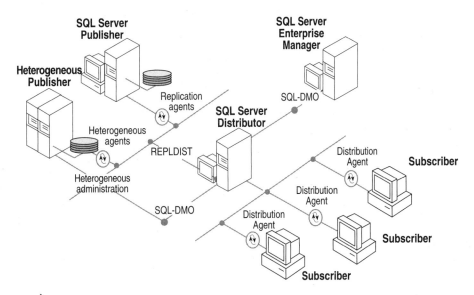

Sybase Interoperability

Sybase Adaptive Server Anywhere 6.0 supports heterogeneous replication through the Sybase Open Client Interface. However, you must use the Sybase Replication Server to gain access to heterogeneous data sources. If you want Replication Server to be a Subscriber to Sybase Adaptive Server Anywhere 6.0, you must use the Replication Agent for Sybase Adaptive Server Enterprise.

Choosing a Development Architecture for Mobile Applications

Choosing the appropriate architecture and best-of-breed tools is essential to the success of any application, and the Microsoft Windows Distributed interNet Applications (DNA) architecture is a key tool for developing mobile applications.

Windows DNA

Most companies are turning to distributed computing and the Internet to provide users with fast access to information. Windows DNA is a framework for building a new generation of computing solutions that brings together the worlds of personal computing and the Internet. Windows DNA is the first application architecture that fully embraces and integrates both the Web and client/server models of application development.

By using the Windows DNA architecture, developers can build scalable, multitier business applications that can be delivered over any network, provide open access to diverse data sources across different platforms, and be freely accessed by any client computing platform. Windows DNA allows organizations to develop cross-platform applications that can access data sources on any server environment including Windows NT, Unix, and Systems Network Architecture (SNA)–based systems. By using Windows DNA architecture, organizations can capitalize on their existing technology infrastructure while also adopting new technologies (such as the Internet and World Wide Web) to meet new requirements.

The Windows DNA architecture has three tiers:

- User interface and navigation

    This layer is the user interface plus basic validation code. Typically, this is a Web browser or a full-featured front-end client.

- Business process

    This layer, which includes middleware components and system services, handles application logic.

- Integrated storage

    This layer is the database or another unstructured storage layer.

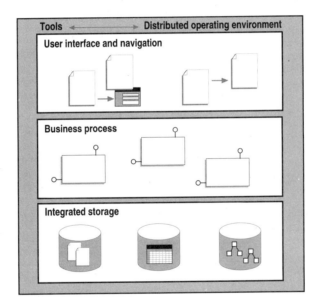

For more information about Microsoft Windows DNA, see www.microsoft.com/dna/.

In a mobile computing environment, the business process and integrated storage layers also must reside on the client. The Microsoft Component Object Model (COM) and Distributed COM (DCOM) components provide the foundation for component integration in a distributed environment. This offers several advantages when developing mobile applications:

- If designed properly, a COM component can run on either a Windows operating-system client or server without modification. This means that mobile clients can share the same code as LAN-based clients.
- Microsoft Visual Studio 6.0 (which includes Microsoft Visual C++, Microsoft Visual Basic, Microsoft Visual J++, and Microsoft Visual FoxPro) is the complete development tools suite for building enterprise applications for the Windows DNA framework. Developers can also choose from third-party development tools to create Microsoft SQL Server applications.
- Microsoft ActiveX Data Objects (ADO), an API for OLE DB, provides an object-based interface to a wide range of data sources, on both the client and the server.

Sybase Applications

Sybase Adaptive Server Anywhere 6.0 can participate in multitiered applications. However, heterogeneous joins are not supported without using Sybase OmniConnect.

Sybase Adaptive Server Anywhere 6.0 supports Java in the database engine. In theory, Java code that is written to run in the database server can be moved to run elsewhere. However, the code relies heavily on Java extensions that make sense only in the context of the database server. Moving the code to another location could break it.

Web-based Solutions

Using a Web browser for mobile applications presents special challenges for the developer. If the Web application interacts with a database or uses server-side scripting, you must install Microsoft Personal Web Server (PWS) on the client to provide offline functionality. PWS is included with the Windows 98 operating system and can be installed from the Windows 95 and Windows NT Workstation Web sites. Unattended installation of PWS is supported. Applications written for the Windows NT Server built-in Web server, Internet Information Services (IIS) version 4.0, should run unchanged on PWS as long as there are no references to server-specific APIs.

IIS 4.0 is a fully programmable Web server that offers developers the following basic features:

- Active Server Pages

  You can write server-based scripts in Visual Basic, Scripting Edition; Microsoft JScript; or PerlScript.

- ADO

  You can access any OLE DB or ODBC data source through the ADO object model by using any of the Visual Studio tools.

- COM and Microsoft Transaction Server

  You can reference COM components, including those in Microsoft Transaction Server (MTS), part of Windows NT Server, written in a variety of languages by using Visual Studio tools.

- Transactional Web page support

  You can call MTS-supported databases by using ASP scripts.

- Session management

  You can use session-level or user-level variables on the server to store user-specific information.

Client-Side and Server-Side Debugging

By using Visual J++ 6.0 and Visual InterDev 6.0 (included in the Microsoft Visual Studio development system), developers delivering Web-based applications can take advantage of COM components and SQL Server. By including Microsoft FrontPage, the Web-based developer has a consistent and easy-to-use tool set for Rapid Application Development (RAD) that provides both component and site creation ability and content development ability. Visual J++ 6.0 and Visual InterDev 6.0 both support rich server and client-side debugging. By using either tool, a developer can debug from the client-side script through the ASP page and into the COM and MTS components.

Sybase Web-based Solutions

Sybase Adaptive Server Anywhere 6.0 comes with an offline Web server called Sybase PowerDynamo, which includes tools for deploying Web pages to clients. PowerDynamo uses a superset of JScript for building server-side scripts. Database access and data formatting are provided by extensions to JScript.

PowerDynamo provides the basic functionality for developing a Web application and accessing it offline. However:

- Programmers must learn proprietary extensions to JScript for connecting to a database and formatting data.

- PowerDynamo does not support COM components or calls to external programs, which limits application functionality, compatibility, and extensibility.

- Although Sybase Adaptive Server Anywhere 6.0 provides transaction support, developers cannot define a Web page as a single transaction.

Conversion of Existing Applications to Support Mobile Clients

In many cases, organizations will convert existing client/server applications or file-sharing applications to support mobile clients. Client/server applications based on SQL Server 7.0 should not require significant changes. For example, developers might add refresh or synchronize features to an application that initiates the synchronization process with the central SQL Server database.

To take advantage of SQL Server's built-in merge replication features and scalability from the desktop to the enterprise, you should convert your application to SQL Server 7.0.

Migrating Data

Microsoft provides resources (tools, services, and documentation) to guide you in your migration of data to SQL Server 7.0. For more information about migrating data to Microsoft SQL Server 7.0, see www.microsoft.com/sql.

Microsoft SQL Server 7.0 Data Transformation Services (DTS) dynamically imports or exports data to and from any ODBC or OLE DB data source. DTS includes a graphical tool for scripting data transformations. This feature can be used for moving data to SQL Server or for performing regularly scheduled data transformation operations.

Microsoft Access 2000 will provide direct support for the Jet engine and the Microsoft Database Engine (MSDE). MSDE, which will ship with Microsoft Office 2000, shares the same code base as SQL Server 7.0. Developers can use Access 2000 to upsize existing Access applications to SQL Server or to develop new applications. The Access 2000 upsizing tool will move not only all the tables and data to SQL Server but also will migrate the referential integrity, Access views, and index definitions to SQL Server.

By using Microsoft Visual FoxPro 5.0, applications can be moved to SQL Server. The SQL Server Upsizing Wizard (part of Visual FoxPro) moves all the tables, views, referential integrity, index definitions, and data to SQL Server.

Migrating Applications

If your application currently runs on another database, only ODBC or OLE DB connectivity is required to move the data using DTS. For more information about migrating applications to run on Microsoft SQL Server 7.0, see www.microsoft.com/sql.

Administering Mobile Applications

Mobile applications can require more administration than LAN-based applications. In environments that need to support thousands of mobile clients, there can be an increase in administrative tasks, including:

- Installing the client database engine, databases, and application code. If offline Web access is required, you might need to install Microsoft PWS.
- Establishing security for users.
- Configuring and monitoring merge replication.
- Managing conflict resolution.
- Backing up remote databases.

Installation

Microsoft Systems Management Server (SMS) is the preferred solution for installing SQL Server 7.0, PWS, and client application code on multiple clients. Among other features, SMS offers unattended software distribution of off-the-shelf programs and in-house applications. For more information about Microsoft SMS, see www.microsoft.com/smsmgmt/.

An alternative to using SMS is to perform an unattended installation and configuration of SQL Server and PWS. Applications created with Visual Studio also can be configured for unattended installation.

Do not preload the SQL Server databases for the application, because the SQL Server Snapshot Agent does this automatically when you set up replication.

Administration Tools Architecture

SQL Server Enterprise Manager is a snap-in component for the Microsoft Management Console (MMC), a universal tool for managing the Microsoft BackOffice family of products and third-party server products. MMC, which is supported on the Windows 95 and Windows 98 and Windows NT operating systems, is a COM-based component that can be controlled from any programming tool that supports COM, such as Visual Basic, Visual C++, PowerBuilder, or Delphi.

SQL Server also offers COM components that can be used to write customized applications to fully administer a SQL Server database: SQL-DMO, SQL-Namespace (SQL NS), SQL-DTS, and replication components. These objects are so robust that they were used by Microsoft to build SQL Server Enterprise Manager, the primary tool for performing administrative tasks on SQL Server 7.0.

Any number of SQL Servers can be centrally administered, either by using a graphical tool such as SQL Server Enterprise Manager or by using a COM-based interface such as SQL-DMO. You can write SQL-DMO scripts in any programming language that supports COM, including Windows Scripting Host (WSH) for Windows 98 and Windows NT, Microsoft Visual Studio, Microsoft Office Visual Basic for Applications (VBA), IIS 4.0 ASP, PowerSoft PowerBuilder, and any third-party tools that support COM; for example:

- Graph a database size across a group of servers by using Microsoft Excel with SQL-DMO.
- Create a program that backs up a database by using Visual Basic with SQL-DMO.
- Create an ASP application that sets up replication based on input from an administrator.

By using SQL-DMO, a programmer can write a few lines of code to back up an entire group of registered servers running SQL Server databases. The SQL-DMO object hierarchy and sample code is included with SQL Server 7.0, Microsoft Developers Network (MSDN), and the Microsoft Knowledge Base.

SQL Server provides dynamic self-management, which allows the server to monitor and manage itself and minimize repetitive tasks. SQL Server 7.0 also offers more than 40 wizards, as well as task pads, to help database administrators.

Multiserver Administration Features

Many database administration tasks can be repetitive and time-consuming. SQL Server 7.0 allows administrators to manage a group of servers as a single entity. In a multiserver environment, the master SQL Server server distributes jobs and receives events (notification of job success or failure) from the target SQL Server server. The master server stores the central copy of all jobs to be executed on the target servers. For example, you can write a single backup task that applies to all servers in your organization.

All jobs are managed by SQL Server Agent, which helps database administrators schedule maintenance functions such as backups, SQL Server programs, or external programs. It can maintain a list of database administrators and their work schedules and provides appropriate notification by pager or e-mail regarding the success or failure of a particular task. SQL Server notifies operators when an unexpected error occurs on the server, or starts a program that can take corrective action.

These features provide organizations with proactive management tools that reduce the cost of administering multiple SQL Servers.

Sybase Administration Tools

Sybase Adaptive Server Anywhere 6.0, PowerDynamo, and Adaptive Server Enterprise can be administered from Sybase Central, which is similar to MMC, but has some significant differences:

- There is no published API or COM interface for extending Sybase Central; therefore, database administrators cannot automate the administration of Sybase Central from other applications.

- Database administrators must use Watcom SQL scripting to automate tasks. Watcom SQL, like Transact-SQL, is a proprietary language. Watcom SQL requires more code than SQL-DMO does to perform similar tasks. Additionally, the choice of programming tools for Watcom SQL is limited.

- There is no support for debugging Watcom SQL from Sybase.

Sybase Adaptive Server Anywhere 6.0 has no built-in scheduling capabilities and no alert notification. Proactive management of a server is not possible using this product alone.

Security

The SQL Server 7.0 security model supports Windows NT–based users and groups and supports SQL Server users and roles.

By improving integration with Windows NT, SQL Server 7.0 provides increased flexibility. Database permissions can be assigned directly to Windows NT users or groups, and you can define SQL Server roles to include Windows NT users and groups and SQL Server users and roles.

A SQL Server user can be a member of multiple SQL Server roles. This allows database administrators to manage SQL Server permissions through Windows NT groups or SQL Server roles, rather than directly through individual user accounts. System-defined server and database roles such as the **dbcreator**, **securityadmin**, and **sysadmin** fixed server roles provide flexibility and improved security.

A user passes through two security stages when working in SQL Server 7.0: authentication and permissions validation. The authentication stage identifies the user accessing a login account and verifies only the ability of the user to connect with SQL Server. If authentication is successful, the user connects to SQL Server. The user then receives permissions to access databases on the server by using an account in each database mapped to the user's login. The permissions validation stage controls the activities the user is allowed to perform in the SQL Server database. You can bypass this account mapping by granting permissions directly to Windows NT groups or users.

When users connect to SQL Server, the activities they can perform are determined by the permissions granted to their security accounts, Windows NT groups, or role hierarchies to which their security accounts belong. The user must have the appropriate permissions to perform any activity. The ability to assign logins and specify permissions is provided by SQL Server Enterprise Manager, Transact-SQL, and SQL-DMO.

Sybase Security

Sybase Adaptive Server Anywhere 6.0 provides limited support for Windows NT–based integrated security. Although login rights can be granted to Windows NT users, they cannot be granted to a Windows NT user group. This means that every user must be entered individually, regardless of whether database security or integrated security is used.

In addition, Sybase Adaptive Server Anywhere 6.0 does not support database security roles, which makes it more difficult to set up an application's administration infrastructure.

Merge Replication

The following steps are needed to configure merge replication for a remote user:

1. Set up the merge publications and articles on the central database to which the mobile client will receive a subscription.

2. Register the mobile client in SQL Server Enterprise Manager.

3. Subscribe the mobile client to the publications.

If possible, set up an anonymous subscription from the client. For normal subscriptions, detailed information about each Subscriber is stored at the Publisher, and performance information about each Subscriber is kept at the Distributor. However, this information is not stored about an anonymous Subscriber.

If you have multiple Subscribers or do not want the overhead of maintaining detailed information, you can allow anonymous subscriptions. Additionally, this can be useful if you want to allow Subscribers using anonymous FTP over the Internet.

Many organizations partition a database by user. For example, a sales representative needs to see accounts only in his territory. One way to do this is to set up a separate publication for each user so that each publication receives only the appropriate data. SQL Server simplifies this process by allowing you to pass the username and computer name as a parameter to the Publisher, so one publication can handle many users.

If you have multiple clients that require customized publications, you should consider automating the procedure with SQL-DMO, which eliminates the time-consuming task of setting up clients one by one.

After replication is enabled between the central database and mobile client, you might want to monitor replication activities. SQL Server Enterprise Manager includes a replication monitor that logs, by Subscriber (unless they are anonymous), the success or failure of all replication activities. Because this information is stored in SQL Server tables, you can generate reports of replication activities easily.

Windows NT is the preferred operating system for your management console because it supports the Windows NT application event log and performance monitor. You also can set up alerts that provide notification by e-mail or pager when problems occur. For information about alert messages, see SQL Server Books Online.

Sybase Merge Replication

Sybase Adaptive Server Anywhere 6.0 uses a separate module called SQL Remote for managing mobile clients. For each remote user, the database administrator must specify a username, a transport protocol, and an address, rather than relying on the operating system for this information.

Sybase Adaptive Server Anywhere 6.0 also requires administrators to install the initial snapshot to the mobile client. SQL Server 7.0 executes the initial snapshot automatically.

Conflict Resolution

Replication conflicts are minimal if the data is partitioned correctly. By assigning ownership of data, you can minimize synchronization conflicts. For example, you might not want to allow sales representatives to change data in other sales representatives' territories. However, you do want to allow a sales manager to change data in several territories. SQL Server 7.0 provides a flexible approach to handling conflict resolution by managing conflicts automatically using built-in rules or custom rules.

By default, SQL Server 7.0 uses priority-based conflict resolution. Every Subscriber and Publisher is assigned a number between 0 and 100. Whenever a conflict occurs, the changes made by the client with the highest priority rating win.

Site A
Publisher, priority=99.9

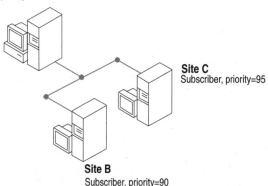

Site C
Subscriber, priority=95

Site B
Subscriber, priority=90

A benefit of this priority rule is that the conflict-resolution mechanism will not undo changes made by the highest priority user. It does not prevent lower priority clients from making subsequent changes to the rows; however, when a conflict occurs, high priority rated replicas always win.

In the event that the priority rule results in a tie, then the change at the central database server wins. For all synchronizations, one site always acts as the central database server.

If you do not want to use a priority-based approach, you can use SQL-DMO to create your own conflict-resolution agent. You can use Visual Studio, C++, or any other language that supports COM, to write the conflict-resolution agent.

Sybase Conflict Resolution

Sybase Adaptive Server Anywhere 6.0 supports conflict resolution with table triggers. However, you must write a conflict-resolution script for every published table. There is no support for priority-based resolution, and there are no defaults. Writing a reliable conflict-resolution script is difficult without priority-based resolution.

Watcom SQL is the only language supported for resolving conflicts in Sybase Adaptive Server Anywhere 6.0.

Backup

It may not be necessary to back up remote databases because the data was replicated from a central database. If local backups are required, administrators can create a simple backup script to perform the backup (or restore). A backup or restore script can be executed either by SQL Server Agent at a predefined time or from an application using the SQL-DMO interface. Other database administration tasks can be managed in a similar way. SQL Server includes a database administration wizard that generates maintenance scripts for you.

Specifications

The following table outlines the differences between Microsoft SQL Server 7.0 and Sybase Adaptive Server Anywhere 6.0.

Topic	Microsoft SQL Server 7.0	Sybase Adaptive Server Anywhere 6.0*
Client Hardware Requirements		
IBM PC or compatible	Yes	Yes
DEC Alpha	Yes	No
RAM (total system)	32 MB	32 MB[1]
Disk space (without help/samples)	66 MB (41 MB if shared components already installed)[2]	50 MB

(continued)

Topic	Microsoft SQL Server 7.0	Sybase Adaptive Server Anywhere 6.0*
Operating System Platforms[3]		
Windows 95 or Windows 98	Yes	Yes
Windows 3.1	No	Yes
Windows NT	Yes	Yes
Novell Netware	No	Yes
Network Support		
Named pipes (Windows NT only)	Yes	No
TCP/IP sockets	Yes	Yes
Novell Netware IPX	Yes	Yes
Appletalk	Yes	No
Banyan VINES	Yes	No
Shared memory (local only)	Yes	No
NetBIOS	No	Yes
SQL Compliance	SQL-92	SQL-92
Database Features		
Transaction processing	Yes	Yes
INSERT, UPDATE, DELETE triggers	Yes	Yes
Stored procedures	Yes	Yes
Extended stored procedures (dynamic link libraries)	Yes	Yes
Bidirectional and scrollable cursors	Yes	Yes
Row-level locking	Yes	Yes
Cost-based query analyzer	Yes	Yes
Parallel query	Yes	No
Heterogeneous joins	Yes	No
Online backup and recovery	Yes	Yes
Binary large object (BLOB) support	Yes	Yes
Symmetric multiprocessing (SMP) support	Yes	Yes
Embedded SQL support	Yes	Yes
Unicode support	Yes	Yes

(continued)

Topic	Microsoft SQL Server 7.0	Sybase Adaptive Server Anywhere 6.0*
Import/export	Any ODBC data source	xBASE, ASCII, Lotus, DIF
Microsoft Distributed Transaction Coordinator (MS DTC)	Yes	No
Database Statistics		
Databases per server	32,767	255
Index types	Clustered and nonclustered	Nonclustered
Maximum database size	1,048,516 terabytes	12 terabytes
Columns per index	16	999
Object name length (in characters)	128	128
Table Statistics		
Indexes per table	249	32,767
Maximum table size	Limited to database size	1,024 GB
Tables per query	256	32,767
Tables per database	2 billion	32,767
Columns per table	1,024	999
Row size	8,060 bytes	2 GB
BLOB size per column	2 GB	32,767 bytes
Rows per table	Limited to database size	Maximum table size
Security		
Integrated Windows NT security	Yes	Yes
Support for Windows NT groups	Yes	No
Roles-based security	Yes	No
Replication[4]		
Transactional (near real time)	Yes	No
Merge (two-way)	Yes	Yes
Snapshot	Yes	No
Homogeneous	Yes	No

(continued)

Topic	Microsoft SQL Server 7.0	Sybase Adaptive Server Anywhere 6.0*
Administration Tools		
Central management console	Yes	Yes
Programmable management console	Yes	No
Group management	Yes	No
DTS	Yes	No
Performance monitoring	Yes (Windows NT)	Yes
Query analyzer	Yes	Yes
Query profiler for tracing SQL network traffic	Yes	No
Wizards	Yes	Yes
Alert notification	Yes	No

⋆ **Source: Sybase Adaptive Server Anywhere Reviewer's Guide**

1 Sybase documentation states from 8 MB through 16 MB. This does not include the operating system.

2 The Microsoft SQL Server figure includes the master system database.

3 Sybase Central, PowerDynamo, and other tools require the Windows NT, Windows 95 or Windows 98 operating systems.

4 Sybase recommends Replication Server for robust replication.

P A R T   4

Performance Tuning

The chapters in Part 4 provide information to help you tune your SQL Server database:

- Performance Tuning
- Index Tuning Wizard

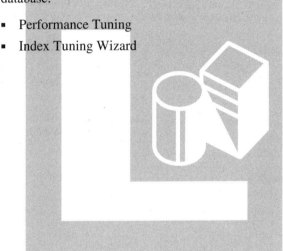

C H A P T E R   6

Performance Tuning

This chapter provides information to help you configure Microsoft SQL Server 7.0 for maximum performance and to help you determine the cause of poor performance in a SQL Server environment. This chapter also provides information about using SQL Server indexes and SQL Server tools for analyzing the I/O performance efficiency of SQL Server queries.

Performance Tuning Comparison

The table compares SQL Server version 7.0 behaviors with behaviors of earlier versions of SQL Server.

SQL 6.x considerations	SQL Server 7.0 enhancements and philosophies
There are many configuration options to consider during performance tuning.	The database engine has become self-configuring, self-tuning, and self-managing. The lazy writer and Read Ahead Manager are self-tuning. The **max async IO** option is the only **sp_configure** option that must be configured initially, and then only when you are working with servers with large amounts of storage. This reduction in tuning requirements saves valuable administrative time, which can be applied to other tasks.

(continued)

SQL 6.x considerations	SQL Server 7.0 enhancements and philosophies
	There are fewer **sp_configure** options that you must adjust manually to achieve good SQL Server performance. Although it is still possible to manually configure and adjust many of the **sp_configure** options available in earlier versions of SQL Server, it is recommended that you allow SQL Server to automatically configure and tune all **sp_configure** options for which SQL Server provides defaults. This allows SQL Server to adjust automatically the configuration of the database server as factors affecting the server change, such as RAM and CPU utilization for SQL Server and other applications running on the database server.
Manual tuning of lazy writer is sometimes necessary.	Unlike earlier versions of Microsoft SQL Server, Microsoft SQL Server 7.0 automatically configures and tunes the lazy writer. You no longer need to manually tune **free buffer** and **max lazywrite IO**. Free buffer and lazy writer I/O activity still can be monitored with SQL Server 7.0 Performance Monitor objects.
Manual tuning of checkpoint is sometimes necessary.	In earlier versions of Microsoft SQL Server, the **recovery interval** option also was used to tune the checkpoint process. When the **recovery interval** option is set to the default of 0, Microsoft SQL Server 7.0 automatically monitors and tunes the recovery interval. The default setting maintains recovery times of less than one minute for all databases, as long as there are no exceptionally long-running transactions present on the system. For more information, see SQL Server Books Online.
SQL Server 6.x log pages share RAM cache with data pages. Manual tuning of the log manager is sometimes necessary.	The SQL Server log manager has changed significantly. The SQL Server 7.0 log manager manages its own log cache. SQL Server no longer depends on the **syslogs** table as it does in earlier versions of SQL Server. Separating the log file management from the data cache management brings enhanced performance for both components.
	SQL Server log manager also is capable of performing disk I/O in larger block sizes than in earlier versions. Larger I/O size and the sequential I/O aids logging performance. SQL Server 7.0 automatically tunes the performance of SQL Server log manager. It is no longer necessary to manually tune the **sp_configure** option **logwrite sleep**, which has been removed from SQL Server 7.0. For more information, see SQL Server Books Online.

(continued)

SQL 6.x considerations	SQL Server 7.0 enhancements and philosophies
Page splitting is costly to a database server operation.	In earlier versions of Microsoft SQL Server, B-tree index pages were high maintenance due to significant row pointer recalculation necessary on the index pages during page splits (page splits occur as insert rows fill a data or index page). This issue has been minimized with the SQL Server 7.0 storage structures. Nonclustered index pages now use either Fixed RID (Row ID) for tables with no clustered index (these tables are called *heaps*) or a Clustering Key for tables with a clustered index. B-tree maintenance activities during inserts and page splits have been dramatically reduced. The overall effect is that index maintenance is much faster, which means that more nonclustered indexes can be created on a table with less impact on data modification performance. For more information, see SQL Server Books Online.
SQL Trace	SQL Server Profiler replaces the SQL Trace utility in SQL Server 6.5. SQL Server Profiler provides similar but significantly enhanced functionality.
ISQL/W	SQL Server Query Analyzer replaces ISQL/W from earlier versions of SQL Server.
Devices and segments	Files and filegroups replace the device and segment model used in earlier versions. Files and filegroups provide a more convenient method for spreading data proportionately across disk drives or RAID arrays. For more information, see SQL Server Books Online.

Principles for Performance Tuning SQL Server

Microsoft SQL Server 7.0 introduces and enhances methods and tools to tune SQL Server for optimum performance. Keep these principles in mind when you are tuning SQL Server:

- Let SQL Server do most of the tuning.

  Microsoft SQL Server has been enhanced to create an auto-configuring and self-tuning database server. Take advantage of the auto-tuning settings available with SQL Server. These settings help SQL Server run at peak performance even as user load and queries change over time.

- RAM is a limited resource.

An integral feature of the database server environment is the management of RAM buffer cache. Access to data in RAM cache is much faster than access to the same information from disk, but RAM is a limited resource. If database I/O can be reduced to the minimum required set of data and index pages, these pages will stay in RAM longer. Too much unneeded data and index information flowing into buffer cache quickly push out valuable pages. The focus of performance tuning is to reduce I/O so that buffer cache is best utilized.

- Pick good indexes.

A key factor in maintaining minimum I/O for all database queries is to ensure that good indexes are created and maintained.

- Evaluate disk I/O subsystem performance.

The physical disk subsystem must provide a database server with sufficient I/O processing power for the database server to run without disk queuing. Disk queuing results in poor performance. For more information, see "Disk I/O Performance" later in this chapter.

- Tune applications and queries.

Tuning your applications and queries becomes especially important when a database server will service requests from hundreds or thousands of connections by way of a given application. Because applications typically determine the SQL queries that will be executed on a database server, application developers must understand SQL Server architectural basics and how to take full advantage of SQL Server indexes to minimize I/O.

- Take advantage of SQL Server Profiler and Index Tuning Wizard.

SQL Server Profiler can be used to monitor and log a SQL Server workload, which can then be submitted to the Index Tuning Wizard to tune indexes for better performance. Regular use of SQL Server Profiler and the Index Tuning Wizard helps you optimize the indexes, allowing SQL Server to perform well with changing query workloads.

- Take advantage of SQL Server Performance Monitor.

SQL Server 7.0 provides a revised set of Performance Monitor objects and counters, which are designed to provide helpful information for monitoring and analyzing the operations of SQL Server. For more information, see "Key Performance Monitor Counters" later in this chapter.

- Take advantage of graphical showplan and SQL Server Query Analyzer.

SQL Server 7.0 Query Analyzer introduces Graphical Showplan, an enhancement to help analyze problematic Transact-SQL queries. SQL Server Query Analyzer also includes STATISTICS IO, another important tool option for tuning queries.

Review the max async IO Option During Configuration

The **max async IO** option should be reviewed and adjusted if necessary during your initial configuration of Microsoft SQL Server 7.0.

The **max async IO** option default of 32 is sufficient for lower-end disk subsystems. With a higher-end RAID storage subsystem attached to a database server that is capable of high disk I/O transfer rates, the setting of 32 may be inadequate because the RAID subsystem is capable of completing many more simultaneous disk transfer requests than 32. If the SQL Server write activity also dictates the need for more disk transfer capability, the **max async IO** option should be set higher.

An appropriate value for the **max async IO** option is one that allows checkpoint to finish before another checkpoint is needed (based upon desired recovery characteristics), but not to finish so fast that the system is seriously stressed by the event. For more information, see "Lazy Writer" and "Checkpoint" later in this chapter.

A general rule to follow for setting the **max async IO** option for SQL Servers running on large disk subsystems is to multiply by two or three the number of physical drives available to do simultaneous I/O. Then watch Performance Monitor for signs of disk activity or queuing issues. The negative impact of setting this configuration option too high is that it may cause checkpoint to monopolize disk subsystem bandwidth that is required by other SQL Server I/O operations such as reads.

To set the **max async IO** option value, execute this command in SQL Server Query Analyzer:

sp_configure 'max async io', *value*

value is expressed as the number of simultaneous disk I/O requests that SQL Server system can submit to the Windows operating system during a checkpoint operation, which in turn submits the requests to the physical disk subsystem. For more information, see "Disk I/O Tuning Performance" later in this chapter. This configuration option is dynamic and does not require a stop and restart of SQL Server to take effect.

For more information, see SQL Server Books Online.

Components that Consume CPU and Disk I/O Resources

You can optimize SQL Server performance with some careful attention to Microsoft SQL Server components that can consume resources.

Worker Threads

Microsoft SQL Server maintains a pool of Windows operating-system threads to service batches of SQL Server commands submitted to the database server. The total of these threads (called *worker threads*) available to service all incoming command batches is dictated by the setting for the **sp_configure** option **max worker threads**. If the number of connections actively submitting batches is greater than the number specified for **max worker threads**, the worker threads are shared among connections actively submitting batches. The default setting of 255 works well for many installations.

Worker threads write out most of the dirty 8-KB pages from the SQL Server buffer cache. I/O operations are scheduled by worker threads asynchronously for maximum performance.

For more information, see SQL Server Books Online.

Lazy Writer

SQL Server lazy writer helps produce free buffers, which are 8-KB data cache pages without any data contained in them. As lazy writer flushes each 8-KB cache buffer out to disk, it initializes the cache page identity so that other data can be written into the free buffer. Lazy writer produces free buffers during periods of low disk I/O, so disk I/O resources are readily available for use and there is minimal impact on other SQL Server operations.

SQL Server 7.0 automatically configures and manages the level of free buffers. Monitor the **SQL Server: Buffer Manager - Free Buffers** object to ensure that the free buffer level remains steady. Lazy writer ensures that the level of free buffers keeps up with the user demand for free buffers. The **SQL Server: Buffer Manager - Free Buffers** object should not drop to 0 because this indicates there were times the user load demanded a higher level of free buffers than the SQL Server lazy writer was able to provide.

If the lazy writer cannot keep the free buffer steady, or at least above 0, it might mean the disk subsystem cannot provide lazy writer with the disk I/O performance that it needs to maintain the free buffer level (compare drops in free buffer level to any disk queuing to confirm there is a disk subsystem problem). One solution to the disk queuing problem is to add more physical disk drives (also called *spindles*) to the database server disk subsystem to provide more disk I/O processing power. The **SQL Server: Buffer Manager – Lazy Writes/sec** object indicates the number of 8-KB pages written to disk by lazy writer.

Monitor the current level of disk queuing in Performance Monitor by looking at the counters for (logical or physical) **Disk: Average Disk Queue** or **Current Disk Queue** and ensure the disk queue is at a level less than 2 for each physical drive associated with any SQL Server activity. For database servers that employ hardware RAID controllers and disk arrays, divide the number reported by (logical or physical) disk counters by the number of actual hard disk drives associated with that logical drive letter or physical hard disk drive number reported by the Windows NT Disk Administrator program. Windows and SQL Server are unaware of the actual number of physical hard disk drives attached to a RAID controller. You should know the number of drives associated with RAID array controller to interpret the disk queue numbers Performance Monitor reports.

Adjust lazy writer disk I/O request behavior with the **max async IO** option, which controls the number of 8-KB disk write requests that SQL Server (including requests coming in from lazy writer, checkpoint, and the worker threads) can simultaneously submit to the Windows operating system and in turn, to the disk I/O subsystem. If disk queuing occurs at unacceptable levels, decrease the level of the **max async IO** option. If the currently configured level of the **max async IO** option must be maintained, add more disks to the disk subsystem until disk queuing reaches acceptable levels.

For more information, see SQL Server Books Online.

Checkpoint

Checkpoint writes out dirty pages to the SQL Server data files. Dirty pages are any buffer cache pages that have been modified since being brought into the buffer cache. A buffer written to disk by checkpoint still contains the page, and users can read or update it without rereading it from disk, which is not the case for free buffers created by lazy writer.

Checkpoint allows worker threads and lazy writer to do most of the work writing out dirty pages by waiting an extra checkpoint before writing out a dirty page. This gives the worker threads and lazy writer more time to write out the dirty pages. The conditions under which this extra wait time occurs are explained in your SQL Server documentation. Checkpoint evens out SQL Server disk I/O activity over a longer time period with an extra checkpoint wait.

To make checkpoint more efficient when there are many pages to flush out of cache, SQL Server sorts the data pages to be flushed in the order the pages appear on disk. This sorting helps minimize disk arm movement during cache flush and potentially allows checkpoint to take advantage of sequential disk I/O. Checkpoint also submits 8-KB disk I/O requests asynchronously to the disk subsystem. This allows SQL Server to finish submitting required disk I/O requests faster because checkpoint does not wait for the disk subsystem to report back that the data actually has been written to disk.

You should watch disk queuing on hard disk drives associated with SQL Server data files to notice if SQL Server is sending down more disk I/O requests than the disk(s) can handle. If it is, then more disk I/O capacity must be added to the disk subsystem to handle the load.

Adjust the checkpoint dirty page flushing behavior by using the **max async IO** option. The **sp_configure** option **max async IO** controls the number of 8-KB cache flushes that checkpoint can submit simultaneously to the Windows operating system and in turn, to the disk I/O subsystem. If disk queuing occurs at unacceptable levels, decrease the **max async IO** option. If SQL Server must maintain the currently configured level of the **max async IO** option, add more disks to the disk subsystem until disk queuing decreases to acceptable levels.

If you must increase the speed with which SQL Server executes checkpoint and the disk subsystem is powerful enough to handle the increased disk I/O while avoiding disk queuing, then increase the **max async IO** option to allow SQL Server to send more asynchronous disk I/O requests. Observe the disk queuing counters carefully after you change the **max async IO** option. Be sure to watch disk read queuing in addition to disk write queuing. If the **max async IO** option is set too high for a disk subsystem, checkpoint may queue up many disk write I/O requests, which can cause SQL Server read activity to be blocked. Physical disk and logical disk objects in Performance Monitor provide the **Average Disk Read Queue Length** counter, which can be used to monitor queued disk read I/O requests. If disk read queuing is caused by checkpoint, you either can decrease the **max async IO** option or add more hard disk drives so the checkpoint and read requests can be handled simultaneously.

Log Manager

Like other major RDBMS products, SQL Server ensures that all write activity (inserts, updates, and deletes) performed on the database is not lost if something interrupts the SQL Server online status (for example, power failure, disk drive failure, fire in the data center, and so on). The SQL Server logging process helps guarantee recoverability. Before any implicit (single Transact-SQL query) or explicit (transaction that issues BEGIN TRANSACTION, COMMIT, or ROLLBACK statements) transactions can be completed, the SQL Server log manager must receive a signal from the disk subsystem that all data changes associated with the transaction have been written successfully to the associated log file. This rule guarantees the transaction log can be read and reapplied in SQL Server when the server is turned on after an abrupt shut down during which the transactions written into the data cache are not yet flushed to the data files. Flushing data buffers are checkpoint or lazy writer responsibility. Reading the transaction log and applying the transactions to SQL Server after a server stoppage is referred to as *recovery*.

Because SQL Server must wait for the disk subsystem to complete I/O to SQL Server log files as each transaction is completed, disks containing SQL Server log files must have sufficient disk I/O handling capacity for the anticipated transaction load.

The method for monitoring disk queuing is not the same for SQL Server log files and for SQL Server database files. You can use the Performance Monitor counters **SQL Server: Databases** *database instance* **: Log Flush Waits Times** and **SQL Server: Databases** *database instance* **: Log Flush Waits/sec** to view log writer requests waiting on the disk subsystem for completion.

For highest performance, you can use a caching controller for SQL Server log files if the controller guarantees that data entrusted to it is written to disk eventually, even if the power fails. For more information about caching controllers, see "Effect of On-board Cache of Hardware RAID Controllers" later in this chapter and SQL Server Books Online.

Read Ahead Manager

The Microsoft SQL Server 7.0 Read Ahead Manager is completely self-configuring and self-tuning. Read Ahead Manager is tightly integrated with the operations of SQL Server query processor. SQL Server query processor identifies and communicates situations that will benefit from read-ahead scans to the Read Ahead Manager. Large table scans, large index range scans, and probes into clustered and nonclustered index B-trees are situations that would benefit from a read-ahead. Read-ahead reads occur with 64-KB I/Os, which provide higher disk throughput potential for the disk subsystem than 8-KB I/Os do. When a large amount of data must be retrieved from SQL Server, read-ahead is the best way to do it.

Read Ahead Manager benefits from the simpler and more efficient Index Allocation Map (IAM) storage structure. The IAM is the SQL Server 7.0 method of recording the location of extents (eight pages of SQL Server data or index information for a total of 64 KB of information per extent). The IAM is an 8-KB page that tightly packs information through a bitmap about which extents within the range of extents covered by the IAM contain required data. The compact IAM pages are fast to read and tend to keep regularly used IAM pages in buffer cache.

The Read Ahead Manager can construct multiple sequential read requests by combining the query information from query processor and quickly retrieving the location of all extents that must be read from the IAM page(s). Sequential 64-KB disk reads provide excellent disk I/O performance.

Read-ahead activity is monitored by the **SQL Server: Buffer Manager - Readahead Pages** counter. You can find more information about read-ahead activity by executing the DBCC PERFMON (IOSTATS) statement. Some of the information provided is RA Pages Found in Cache and RA Pages Placed in Cache. If the page is already hashed (the application read it in first and read-ahead wasted a read), it is a page found in cache. If the page is not already hashed (a successful read-ahead), it is a page placed in cache.

Too much read-ahead can be detrimental to overall performance because it can fill cache with unnecessary pages, requiring additional I/O and CPU that could have been used for other purposes. The solution is a performance tuning goal that all Transact-SQL queries are tuned so a minimal number of pages are brought into buffer cache. This includes using the right index for the right job. Save clustered indexes for efficient range scans and define nonclustered indexes to help locate single rows or smaller rowsets quickly.

For more information, see SQL Server Books Online.

Disk I/O Performance

When you configure a SQL Server that contains only a few gigabytes of data and does not sustain heavy read or write activity, you are not as concerned with disk I/O and balancing SQL Server I/O activity across hard disk drives for maximum performance. If you build larger SQL Server databases, however, that contain hundreds of gigabytes of data and/or will sustain heavy read and/or write activity, you must configure SQL Server to maximize disk I/O performance by load-balancing across multiple hard disk drives.

Advertised Disk Transfer Rates and SQL Server

An important aspect of database performance tuning is I/O performance tuning. Unless SQL Server is running on a computer with enough RAM to hold the entire database, I/O performance is dictated by how fast reads and writes of SQL Server data can be processed by the disk I/O subsystem.

The typical hard disk drive is capable of providing the Windows operating system and SQL Server with about 75 nonsequential (random) and 150 sequential I/O operations per second. Advertised transfer rates for these hard disk drives are around 40 megabytes (MB) per second. It is much more likely for a database server to be constrained by the 75/150 I/O transfers per second than the 40-MB per second transfer rate. This is illustrated by these calculations:

(75 random I/O operations per second) x (8-KB transfer) = 600 KB per second

This calculation indicates that by doing strictly random single-page read and write operations on a hard disk drive, you can expect at most 600 KB (0.6 MB) per second I/O processing capability from that hard disk drive. This is much lower than the advertised 40 MB per second I/O handling capacity of the drive. SQL Server worker threads, checkpoint, and lazy writer perform I/O in 8-KB transfer sizes.

(150 sequential I/O operations per second) x (8-KB transfer) = 1200 KB per second

This calculation indicates by doing strictly sequential single-page read and write operations on a hard disk drive, it is reasonable to expect at most 1200 KB (1.2 MB) per second I/O processing capability from the hard disk drive.

(75 random I/O operations per second) x (64-KB transfer) = 4800 KB (4.8 MB) per second

This calculation illustrates a worst-case scenario for read-aheads, assuming all random I/O. Even in the completely random situation, the 64-KB transfer size provides much better disk I/O transfer rate from disk (4.8 MB per second) than the single-page transfer rates (0.6 and 1.2 MB per second):

(150 sequential I/O operations per second) x (64-KB transfer) = 9600 KB (9.6 MB) per second

This calculation indicates that by doing strictly sequential read or write operations on a hard disk drive, you can expect at most 9.6 MB per second I/O processing capability from that hard disk drive. This is much better than the random I/O case. SQL Server Read Ahead Manager performs disk I/O in the 64-KB transfer rate and attempts to arrange reads so read-ahead scans are done sequentially (often referred to as *serially* or *in disk order*). Although Read Ahead Manager performs I/O operations sequentially, page splitting tends to cause extents to be read nonsequentially rather than sequentially. This is one reason to eliminate and prevent page splitting.

Log manager writes sequentially to log files up to 32 KB.

Sequential vs. Nonsequential Disk I/O Operations

The terms sequential and nonsequential (random) have been used to refer to hard disk drive operations. A single hard disk drive consists of a set of drive platters, each of which provides services for read and write operations with a set of arms with read and write heads that can move across the platters and read information from the drive platter or write data onto the platters. Remember these points about hard disk drives and SQL Server:

- Using sequential I/O is good for SQL Server performance.

  The read/write heads and associated disk arms must move to find and operate on the location of the hard disk drive platter that SQL Server and the Windows operating system requested. If the data is located on nonsequential locations on the hard disk drive platter, it takes significantly more time for the hard disk drive to move the disk arm and read/write head to all of the necessary hard disk drive platter locations. This contrasts with the sequential case, in which all of the required data is located on one continuous physical section of the hard disk drive platter, so that the disk arm and read/write heads move a minimal amount to perform the necessary disk I/O operations. The time difference between the nonsequential versus sequential case is significant, about 50 milliseconds per nonsequential seek versus approximately 2 to 3 milliseconds for sequential seeks. These times are rough estimates and will vary based on how far apart the nonsequential data is spread on the disk, how fast the hard disk platters can spin (RPM), and other physical attributes of the hard disk drive.

- Using Read Ahead Manager and separating SQL Server log files from other nonsequentially accessed files can improve SQL Server performance.

A typical hard disk drive supports about 75 nonsequential and 150 sequential I/Os per second. It takes almost as much time to read or write 8 KB as it does to read or write 64 KB. Within the range of 8 KB to about 64 KB the disk arm and read/write head movement account for most of the time of a single disk I/O transfer operation. Perform 64-KB disk transfers as often as possible when more than 64 KB of SQL data must be transferred, because a 64-KB transfer is fast as an 8-KB transfer and eight times the amount of SQL Server data is processed for each transfer. Read Ahead Manager does disk operations in 64-KB chunks (referred to as a *SQL Server extent*). Log manager also performs sequential writes in larger I/O sizes.

Disk I/O Transfer Rates and PCI Bus Bandwidth

A typical hard disk provides a maximum transfer rate of about 40 MB per second or 75 nonsequential/150 sequential disk transfers per second. Typical RAID controllers have an advertised transfer rate of about 40 MB per second or approximately 2,000 disk transfers per second. PCI buses have an advertised transfer rate of about 133 MB per second and higher. The actual transfer rates achievable for a device usually differ from the advertised rate. You should understand how to use these transfer rates as a starting point for determining the number of hard disk drives to associate with each RAID controller and in turn, how many drives and RAID controllers can be attached to a PCI bus without I/O bottlenecks.

The maximum amount of SQL Server data that can be read from or written to a hard disk drive per second is 9.6 MB. Assuming a RAID controller can handle 40 MB per second, you can calculate the number of hard disk drives that should be associated with one RAID controller by dividing 40 by 9.6 to get about 4. This means that at most 4 drives should be associated with that one controller when SQL Server is doing nothing but sequential I/O of 64 KB. Similarly, with all nonsequential I/O of 64 KB, the maximum data sent from the hard disk drive to the controller is 4.8 MB per second. Dividing 40 MB per second by 4.8 MB per second gives approximately 8 as the result. This means that at most 8 hard disk drives should be associated with the single controller in the nonsequential 64-KB scenario. The random 8-KB data transfer scenario requires the most drives. Divide 40 by 0.6 to determine that about 66 drives are needed to saturate a RAID controller doing 100 percent random 8-KB reads and writes. This is not a realistic scenario because read-ahead and log-writing use transfer sizes greater than 8-KB and it is unlikely that a SQL Server will perform 100 percent random I/O.

You can also determine how many drives should be associated with a RAID controller by looking at disk transfers per second instead of looking at the megabytes per second. If a hard disk drive is capable of 75 nonsequential (random) I/Os per second, then about 26 hard disk drives working together could theoretically produce 2,000 nonsequential I/Os per second, or enough to hit the maximum I/O handling capacity of a single RAID controller. Alternately, it takes only about 13 hard disk drives working together to produce 2,000 sequential I/Os per second and keep the RAID controller running at maximum throughput because a single hard disk drive can sustain 150 sequential I/Os per second.

RAID controller and PCI bus bottlenecks are not as common as I/O bottlenecks related to hard disk drives. For example, assume a set of hard disk drives associated with a RAID controller is busy enough to push 40 MB per second of throughput through the controller. The next consideration is how many RAID controllers can be attached safely to the PCI bus without risking a PCI bus I/O bottleneck. To make an estimate, divide the I/O processing capacity of the PCI bus by the I/O processing capacity of the RAID controller: 133 MB/sec divided by 40 MB/sec results in approximately three RAID controllers that can be attached to a single PCI bus. Most large servers come with more than one PCI bus, which increases the number of RAID controllers that can be installed in a single server.

These calculations illustrate the relationship of the transfer rates of the components that comprise a disk I/O subsystem (hard disk drives, RAID controllers, PCI bus) and are not literal figures. These calculations assume all sequential or all nonsequential data access, which is not likely in a production database server environment. In reality, a mixture of sequential, nonsequential, 8-KB and 64-KB I/O occurs. Additional factors influence how many I/O operations can be pushed through a set of hard disk drives at one time. On-board read/write caching available for RAID controllers increases the amount of I/O that a set of drives can effectively produce. How much more is difficult to estimate for the same reason that it is difficult to determine an exact number an 8-KB versus a 64-KB I/O SQL Server environment needs.

RAID

When scaling databases more than a few gigabytes (GB), it is important to have at least a basic understanding of RAID (Redundant Array of Inexpensive Disks) technology and how it relates to database performance.

These are the benefits of RAID:

- Performance

  Hardware RAID controllers divide read/writes of all data from Windows and applications such as Microsoft SQL Server into slices (usually 16 KB to 128 KB) that are spread across all disks participating in the RAID array. Splitting data across physical drives distributes the read/write I/O workload evenly across all physical hard disk drives participating in the RAID array. This increases disk I/O performance because the hard disks participating in the RAID array are all kept equally busy, instead of some disks becoming a bottleneck due to uneven distribution of I/O requests.

- Fault tolerance

  RAID provides protection from hard disk failure and accompanying data loss with two methods: mirroring and parity.

Mirroring

Mirroring is implemented by writing information onto two sets of drives, one on each side of the mirrored pairs of drives. If there is a drive loss with mirroring in place, the data for the lost drive can be rebuilt by replacing the failed drive and rebuilding the data from the failed drive's matching drive. Most RAID controllers can provide a failed drive replacement and rebuild from the other side of the mirrored pair while Windows and SQL Server are online (referred to as "Hot Plug" capable drives). Mirroring is the best performing RAID option when fault tolerance is required. Each SQL Server write in the mirroring situation costs two disk I/O operations, one to each side of the mirrorset. Mirroring also provides more fault tolerance than parity RAID implementations. Mirroring can sustain at least one failed drive and may be able to survive failure of up to half of the drives in the mirrorset without forcing the system administrator to shut down the server and recover from file backup. The disadvantage of mirroring is cost. The disk cost of mirroring is one drive for each drive of data. RAID 1 and its hybrid, RAID 0+1 are implemented through mirroring.

Parity

Parity is implemented by calculating recovery information about data written to disk and writing this parity information on the other drives that form the RAID array. If a drive fails, a new drive is inserted into the RAID array and the data on that failed drive is recovered by taking the recovery information (parity) written on the other drives and using this information to regenerate the data from the failed drive. RAID 5 and its hybrids are implemented through parity. The advantage of parity is low cost. To protect any number of drives with RAID 5, only one additional drive is required. Parity information is evenly distributed among all drives participating in the RAID 5 array. The disadvantages of parity are performance and fault tolerance. Due to the additional costs associated with calculating and writing parity, RAID 5 requires four disk I/O operations for each Windows NT and SQL Server write as compared to two disk I/O operations for mirroring. Read I/O operation costs are the same for mirroring and parity. Also, RAID 5 can sustain only one failed drive before the array must be taken offline and recovery from backup media must be performed to restore data.

A general rule is to stripe across as many disks as necessary to achieve solid disk I/O performance. Performance Monitor indicates whether there is a disk I/O bottleneck on a particular RAID array. Be ready to add disks and redistribute data across RAID arrays and/or SCSI channels as necessary to balance disk I/O and maximize performance.

Effect of On-board Cache of Hardware RAID Controllers

Many hardware RAID controllers have some form of read and/or write caching. Take advantage of this available caching with SQL Server because it can enhance the effective I/O handling capacity of the disk subsystem. The principle of these controller-based caching mechanisms is to gather smaller and potentially nonsequential I/O requests coming in from the host server (hence SQL Server) and try to batch them with other I/O requests so the batched I/Os can form larger (32 KB to 128 KB) and maybe sequential I/O requests to send to the hard disk drives. This helps produce more disk I/O throughput given the fixed number of I/Os that hard disks can provide to the RAID controller. The RAID controller cache arranges incoming I/O requests by making the best use of the hard disks' underlying I/O processing ability.

RAID controllers usually protect their caching mechanisms with a form of backup power. The backup power can preserve the data written in cache for a period of time (perhaps days) in case of a power outage. And in production environments, the backup power can provide the database server greater protection by providing adequate UPS protection to the server to flush data to disk if power to the server is disrupted.

RAID Levels

RAID 1 and RAID 0+1 offer the best data protections and best performance among RAID levels but costs more required disks. When cost of hard disks is not a limiting factor, RAID 1 or RAID 0+1 are the best RAID choices for performance and fault tolerance.

RAID 5 provides fault tolerance at the best cost but has half the write performance of RAID 1 and 0+1 because of the additional I/O that RAID 5 must do reading and writing parity information onto disk. RAID 5 is not as fault tolerant as RAID 1 and 0+1.

The best disk I/O performance is achieved with RAID 0 (disk striping with no fault tolerance protection), but because there is no fault tolerance with RAID 0, this RAID level typically can be used only for development database servers or other testing environments.

Many RAID array controllers provide the option of RAID 0+1 (also referred to as RAID 1/0 and RAID 10) over physical hard disk drives. RAID 0+1 is a hybrid RAID solution. On the lower level, it mirrors all data, like RAID 1. On the upper level, the controller stripes data across all of the drives, like RAID 0. Thus, RAID 0+1 provides maximum protection (mirroring) with high performance (striping). These mirroring and striping operations are transparent to Windows NT and SQL Server because they are managed by the RAID controller. The difference between RAID 1 and RAID 0+1 is on the hardware controller level. RAID 1 and RAID 0+1 require the same number of drives for a given amount of storage. For more specifics about RAID 0+1 implementation of specific RAID controllers, contact the hardware vendor that produced the controller.

This illustration compares RAID 0, RAID 1, RAID 5, and RAID 0+1. To hold four disks of data, RAID 1 (and RAID 0+1) needs eight disks, whereas Raid 5 needs five disks. Be sure to involve the appropriate hardware vendors to learn more about RAID implementation specific to the hardware running the database server.

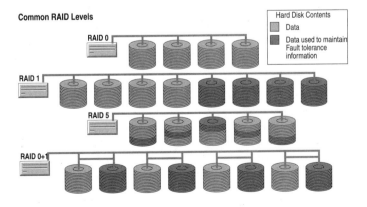

Online RAID Expansion

Online RAID expansion is a feature that allows disks to be added dynamically to a physical RAID array while SQL Server is online, as long as there are hot-plug slots available. Many hardware vendors offer hardware RAID controllers capable of providing this functionality. Data is automatically restriped across all drives evenly, including the newly added drive, and there is no need to shut down SQL Server or Windows. You can take advantage of this functionality by leaving hot-plug hard disk drive slots free in the disk array cages. Thus, if SQL Server is regularly over-taxing a RAID array with I/O requests (this is indicated by disk queue length for the Windows logical drive letter associated with that RAID array), you can install one or more new hard disk drives into the hot-plug slot while SQL Server is still running. The RAID controller redistributes some existing SQL data to these new drives so that SQL data is evenly distributed across all drives in the RAID array. Then, the I/O processing capacity of the new drives (75 nonsequential/150 sequential I/Os per second, per drive) is added to the overall I/O processing capacity of the RAID array.

Performance Monitor and RAID

In Windows NT Performance Monitor, logical and physical disk objects provide the same information. The difference is that logical disks in Performance Monitor are associated with what Windows NT interprets as a logical drive letter. Physical disks in Performance Monitor are associated with what Windows NT interprets as a single physical hard disk.

To enable Performance Monitor counters, use the command **diskperf.exe** from the command line of the command-prompt window. Use **diskperf –y** so that Performance Monitor reports logical and physical disk counters when using hard disk drives or sets of hard disk drives and RAID controllers, without the use of Windows NT software RAID.

When running Windows NT software RAID, use **diskperf –ye** so that Performance Monitor correctly reports physical counters across the Windows NT stripe sets. When **diskperf –ye** is used in conjunction with Windows NT stripe sets, logical counters do not report correct information and must be disregarded. If logical disk counter information is required in conjunction with Windows NT stripe sets, use **diskperf –y** instead. With **diskperf -y** and Windows NT stripe sets, logical disk counters are reported correctly but physical disk counters do not report correct information and should be disregarded.

The effects of the **diskperf -y** command do not occur until Windows NT has been restarted.

Hardware RAID controllers present multiple physical hard disk drives that compose a single RAID mirror set or stripe set to the Windows operating system, as one single physical. The Windows NT Disk Administrator application is used to associate logical drive letters to the single physical disk and does not need to know how many hard disks are actually associated with the single hard physical that the RAID controller has presented to it.

You should know how many physical hard disk drives are associated with a RAID array so you can determine the number of disk I/O requests that the Windows operating system and SQL Server send to each physical hard disk drive. Divide the number of disk I/O requests that Performance Monitor reports as associated with a hard disk drive by the number of actual physical hard disk drives known to be in the RAID array.

To estimate I/O activity per hard disk drive in a RAID array, multiply the number of disk write I/Os reported by Performance Monitor by either 2 (RAID 1 and 0+1) or 4 (RAID 5). This accurately accounts for the number of I/O requests being sent to the physical hard disk drives. It is at this physical level that the I/O capacity for hard disk drives apply (75 nonsequential and 150 sequential per drive). But do not expect to calculate exactly how much I/O is hitting the hard disk drives when the hardware RAID controller is using caching, because caching can change the amount of I/O that is hitting the hard disk drives.

It is best to monitor on disk queuing unless I/O is causing a problem. The Windows operating system cannot see the number of physical drives in a RAID array, so to assess disk queuing per physical disk accurately, you must divide the disk queue length by the number of physical drives participating in the hardware RAID disk array that contains the logical drive being observed. Keep this number under two for hard disk drives containing SQL Server files.

For more information about SQL Server and RAID, see SQL Server Books Online.

Windows NT Software RAID

Windows NT provides fault tolerance to hard disk failure by providing mirror sets and stripe sets (with or without fault tolerance) through the Windows NT operating system, instead of through a hardware RAID controller. The Windows NT Disk Administrator application is used to define either mirror sets (RAID 1) or stripe sets with parity (RAID 5). Windows NT Disk Administrator also allows the definition of stripe sets with no fault tolerance (RAID 0).

Software RAID uses more CPU resources because Windows NT is the component managing the RAID operations, versus the hardware RAID controller. Thus, performance with the same number of disk drives and Windows NT software RAID may be a few percent less than the hardware RAID solution if the system processors are near 100 percent utilized. But Windows NT software RAID generally helps a set of drives to service SQL Server I/O better than those drives would have been able to do separately. This can reduce the potential for an I/O bottleneck, leading to higher CPU utilization by SQL Server and better throughput. Windows NT software RAID can provide a better-cost solution for providing fault tolerance to a set of hard disk drives.

For more information about configuring Windows NT software RAID, see Online Help for Windows NT and SQL Server Books Online.

Disk I/O Parallelism

With smaller SQL Server databases located on a few disk drives, disk I/O parallelism is not a likely performance factor. But with large SQL Server databases stored on many disk drives, performance is enhanced by using disk I/O parallelism to make optimal use of the I/O processing power of the disk subsystem.

Microsoft SQL Server 7.0 introduces files and filegroups, which replace the device and segment model of earlier versions of SQL Server. The files and filegroups provide a more convenient method for spreading data proportionately across disk drives or RAID arrays. For more information, see SQL Server Books Online.

A technique for creating disk I/O parallelism is to create a single "pool of drives" that serves all SQL Server database files, excluding transaction log files. The pool can be a single RAID array that is represented in Windows NT as a single physical disk drive. Or a larger pool can be set up using multiple RAID arrays and SQL Server files/filegroups. A SQL Server file can be associated with each RAID array, and the files can be combined into a SQL Server filegroup. Then a database can be built on the filegroup so that the data is spread evenly across all of the drives and RAID controllers. The drive pool methodology depends on RAID to divide data across all physical disk drives to help ensure parallel access to the data during database server operations.

The pool methodology simplifies SQL Server I/O performance tuning because there is only one physical location to create database objects. The single pool of drives can be watched for disk queuing and, if necessary, more hard disk drives can be added to the pool to prevent disk queuing. This technique helps optimize for the common case, in which it is not known which parts of databases will see the most use. Do not segregate part of available I/O capacity on another disk partition because SQL Server might do I/O to it 5 percent of the time. The single pool of drives methodology can make all available I/O capacity available for SQL Server operations.

SQL Server log files should always be physically separated onto different hard disk drives from all other SQL Server database files. For SQL Servers with busy databases, transaction log files should be physically separated from each other. Transaction logging is primarily sequential write I/O. Separating transaction logging activity from other nonsequential disk I/O activity can result in I/O performance benefits. That allows the hard disk drives containing the log files to concentrate on sequential I/O. There are times when the transaction log must be read as part of SQL Server operations such as replication, rollbacks, and deferred updates. If you administer SQL Servers that participate in replication, make sure all transaction log files have sufficient disk I/O processing power because of the reads that must occur.

Physically separating SQL Server objects from the rest of their associated database through SQL Server files and filegroups requires additional administration. Separating the objects can be worthwhile to investigate active tables and indexes. By separating table or index from all other database objects, accurate assessments can be made of the object I/O requirements. This is not as easy to do when all database objects are placed within one drive pool. Physical I/O separation can be appropriate during database development and benchmarking so that database I/O information can be gathered and applied to capacity planning for the production database server environment.

These are the areas of SQL Server activity that can be separated across different hard disk drives, RAID controllers, PCI channels, or combinations of the three:

- Transaction log files
- **tempdb**
- Database files
- Tables associated with considerable query or write activity
- Nonclustered indexes associated with considerable query or write activity

The physical separation of SQL Server I/O activities is made convenient by using hardware RAID controllers, RAID hot plug drives, and online RAID expansion. The approach that provides the most flexibility consists of arranging the RAID controllers so that a separate RAID SCSI channel is provided for each database activity. Each RAID SCSI channel should be attached to a separate RAID hot plug cabinet to take full advantage of online RAID expansion (if it is available through the RAID controller). Windows logical drive letters are associated with each RAID array and SQL Server files can be separated between distinct RAID arrays based on known I/O usage patterns.

With this configuration you can relate disk queuing to a distinct RAID SCSI channel and its drive cabinet as Performance Monitor reports the queuing behavior during load testing or heavy production loads. If a RAID controller and drive array cabinet support online RAID expansion and if slots for hot-plug hard disk drives are available in the cabinet, disk queuing on that RAID array is resolved by adding more drives to the RAID array until Performance Monitor reports that disk queuing for that RAID array has reached acceptable levels (less than 2 for SQL Server files.) This can be accomplished while SQL Server is online.

The **tempdb** database is created by SQL Server to be a shared working area for a variety of activities, including temporary tables, sorting, subqueries and aggregates with GROUP BY or ORDER BY, queries using DISTINCT (temporary worktables must be created to remove duplicate rows), cursors, and hash joins. You should enable the **tempdb** database I/O operations to occur in parallel to the I/O operations of related transactions. Because **tempdb** is a scratch area and update-intensive, RAID 5 is not as good a choice for **tempdb** as RAID 1 or 0+1. The **tempdb** database is rebuilt every time the database server is restarted; therefore, RAID 0 is a possibility for **tempdb** on production SQL Server computers. RAID 0 provides the best RAID performance for the **tempdb** database with the least physical drives. The concern with using RAID 0 for **tempdb** in a production environment is that SQL Server must be stopped and restarted if physical drive failure occurs in the RAID 0 array—this does not necessarily occur if **tempdb** is placed on a RAID 1 or 0+1 array.

To move the **tempdb** database, use the ALTER DATABASE statement to change the physical file location of the SQL Server logical file name associated with the **tempdb** database. For example, to move the **tempdb** database and its associated log to the new file locations E:\Mssql7 and C:\Temp, use these statements:

```
ALTER DATABASE tempdb MODIFY FILE (NAME ='tempdev',FILENAME=
'e:\mssql7\tempnew_location.mDF')
ALTER DATABASE tempdb MODIFY FILE (NAME ='templog',FILENAME=
'c:\temp\tempnew_loglocation.LDF')
```

The **master**, **msdb**, and **model** databases are not used much during production compared to user databases, so they are not typically a consideration in I/O performance tuning. The **master** database is used only for adding new logins, databases, and other system objects.

Nonclustered indexes reside in B-tree structures that can be separated from their related database tables with the ALTER DATABASE statement. In this example, the first ALTER DATABASE creates a filegroup. The second ALTER DATABASE creates a file with a separate physical location associated with the filegroup. At this point, indexes can be created on the filegroup as illustrated by creating the index called **index1**. The **sp_helpfile** stored procedure reports files and filegroups present for a given database. The **sp_help** *tablename* has a section in its output that provides information about the table indexes and filegroup relationships.

```
ALTER DATABASE testdb ADD FILEGROUP testgroup1
ALTER DATABASE testdb ADD FILE (NAME = 'testfile',
    FILENAME = 'e:\mssql7\test1.ndf') TO FILEGROUP testgroup1
CREATE TABLE test1(col1 char(8))
CREATE INDEX index1 ON test1(col1) ON testgroup1

sp_helpfile
sp_help test1
```

For more information, see SQL Server Books Online.

SQL Server Indexes

This section contains information about how SQL Server data and index structures are physically placed on disk drives and how these structures apply to disk I/O performance.

SQL Server data and index pages are 8 KB each. SQL Server data pages contain all of the data associated with the rows of a table, except **text** and **image** data. For **text** and **image** data, the SQL Server data page, which contains the row associated with the **text** or **image** column, contains a pointer to a B-tree structure of one or more 8-KB pages.

SQL Server index pages contain only data from columns that comprise a particular index; therefore, an 8-KB index page contains much more information than an 8-KB data page because it compresses information associated with many more rows. If the columns picked to be part of an index form a low percentage of the row size of the table, information about more rows can be compressed in an 8-KB index page, which has performance benefits. When an SQL query requests a set of rows from a table in which columns in the query match values in the rows, SQL Server can save I/O operations by reading the index pages for the values and then accessing only the rows in the table required to satisfy the query. Therefore, SQL Server does not have to perform I/O operations to scan all rows in the table to locate the required rows.

SQL Server indexes are built upon B-tree structures formed out of 8-KB index pages. The difference between clustered and nonclustered indexes is at the bottom of the B-tree structures (referred to as *leaf level*). The upper parts of index B-tree structures are referred to as nonleaf levels of the index. A B-tree structure is built for every single index defined on a SQL Server table.

In a nonclustered index, the leaf-level nodes contain only the data that participates in the index. In the nonclusterered index leaf-level nodes, index rows contain pointers to the remaining row data on the associated data page. At worst, each row access from the nonclustered index requires an additional nonsequential disk I/O to retrieve the row data. At best, many of the required rows will be on the same data page and thus allow retrieval of several required rows with each data page fetched.

In the clustered index, the leaf-level nodes of the index are the actual data rows for the table. Therefore, no bookmark lookups are required for retrieval of table data. Range scans based on clustered indexes perform well because the leaf level of the clustered index (and hence all rows of that table) is physically ordered on disk by the columns that comprise the clustered index, and will perform I/O in 64-KB extents. These 64-KB I/Os are physically sequential if there is not much page splitting on the clustered index B-tree (nonleaf and leaf levels). The dotted lines indicate there are other 8-KB pages present in the B-tree structures but they are not shown. The illustration shows the structural difference between nonclustered and clustered indexes.

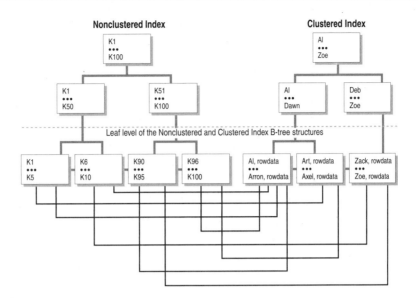

Clustered Indexes

There can be only one clustered index per table because, while the upper parts of the clustered index B-tree structure are organized like the nonclustered index B-tree structures, the bottom level of the clustered index B-tree consists of the actual 8-KB data pages associated with the table. There are performance implications:

- Retrieval of SQL data based on key search with a clustered index requires no bookmark lookup (and a likely nonsequential change of location on the hard disk) to get to the associated data page, because the leaf level of the clustered index is already the associated data page.

- The leaf level of the clustered index is sorted by the columns that comprise the clustered index. Because the leaf level of the clustered index contains the actual 8-KB data pages of the table, the row data of the entire table is physically arranged on the disk drive in the order determined by the clustered index. This provides a potential I/O performance advantage when fetching a significant number of rows from tables greater than 64-KB based on the value of the clustered index, because sequential disk I/O is being used unless page splitting is occurring on this table. For more information about page-splitting, see "FILLFACTOR and PAD_INDEX" later in this chapter. You should pick the clustered index on a table based on a column that is used to perform range scans to retrieve a large number of rows.

Nonclustered Indexes

Nonclustered indexes are most useful for fetching few rows with good selectivity from large SQL Server tables based on a key value. Nonclustered indexes are B-trees formed out of 8-KB index pages. The bottom or leaf level of the B-tree of index pages contains all the data from the columns that comprised that index. When a nonclustered index is used to retrieve information from a table based on a match with the key value, the index B-tree is traversed until a key match is found at the leaf level of the index. A bookmark lookup is made if columns from the table are needed that did not form part of the index. This bookmark lookup will likely require a nonsequential I/O operation on the disk. It even might require the data to be read from another disk if the table and its accompanying index B-tree(s) are large. If multiple bookmark lookups lead to the same 8-KB data page, there is less I/O performance penalty because it is necessary to read the page into data cache only once. For each row returned for a SQL query that involves searching with a nonclustered index, one bookmark lookup is required. These bookmark lookups are the reason that nonclustered indexes are better suited for SQL queries that return only one or a few rows from the table. Queries that require many rows to be returned are better served with a clustered index.

For more information, see SQL Server Books Online.

Covering Indexes

A special situation that occurs with nonclustered indexes is called the *covering index*. A covering index is a nonclustered index built upon all of the columns required to satisfy an SQL query, both in the selection criteria and in the WHERE clause. Covering indexes can save I/O and improve query performance. But you must balance the costs of creating a new index (with its associated B-tree index structure maintenance) with the I/O performance gain the covering index will bring. If a covering index will benefit a query or a set of queries that run often on SQL Server, creating the covering index may be worthwhile, for example:

```
SELECT col1,col3 FROM table1 WHERE col2 = 'value'
    CREATE INDEX indexname1 ON table1(col2,col1,col3)
```

Or from SQL Server Enterprise Manager, use the Create Index Wizard.

The **indexname1** index in the preceding example is a covering index because it includes all columns from the SELECT statement and the WHERE clause. During the execution of this query, SQL Server does not need to access the data pages associated with **table1**. SQL Server can obtain all of the information required to satisfy the query by using the index called **indexname1**. When SQL Server has traversed the B-tree associated with **indexname1** and has found the range of index keys where **col2** is equal to value, SQL Server fetches all required data (**col1,col2,col3**) from the leaf level of the covering index. This improves I/O performance in two ways:

- SQL Server obtains all required data from an index page, not a data page; therefore, the data is more compressed and SQL Server saves disk I/O operations.

- The covering index organizes all of the required data by col2 physically on the disk. The hard disk drives return all of the index rows associated with the WHERE clause (col2 = value) in sequential order, which gives better I/O performance. From a disk I/O standpoint, a covering index becomes a clustered index for this query and any other query that can be satisfied completely by the columns in the covering index.

If the number of bytes from all the columns in the index is small compared to the number of bytes in a single row of that table, and you are certain the query taking advantage of the covered index will be executed frequently, then it makes sense to use a covering index. But, before building many covered indexes, consider how SQL Server 7.0 can effectively and automatically create covered indexes for queries on the fly.

Automatic Covering Indexes or Covered Queries

The Microsoft SQL Server 7.0 query processor provides index intersection. Index intersection allows the query processor to consider multiple indexes from a given table, build a hash table based on those multiple indexes, and use the hash table to reduce I/O for a query. The hash table that results from the index intersection becomes a covering index and provides the same I/O performance benefits that covering indexes do. Index intersection provides greater flexibility for database user environments in which it is difficult to determine all of the queries that will run against the database. A good strategy in this case is to define single column, nonclustered indexes on all columns that will be queried frequently, and let index intersection handle situations in which a covered index is needed; for example:

```
SELECT col3 FROM table1 WHERE col2 = 'value'
    CREATE INDEX indexname1 ON table1(col2)
    CREATE INDEX indexname2 ON table1(col3)
```

Or from SQL Server Enterprise Manager, use the Create Index Wizard.

In the preceding example, **indexname1** and **indexname2** are nonclustered, single column indexes created on the SQL Server table called **table1**. When the query executes, the query processor recognizes that index intersection using the two indexes is advantageous. The query optimizer automatically hashes the two indexes together to save I/O while executing the query. No query hints were required. Queries handled by covering indexes (whether by explicitly declared covering indexes or index intersection) are called *covered queries*.

For more information, see SQL Server Books Online.

Index Selection

How indexes are chosen significantly affects the amount of disk I/O generated and, subsequently, performance. Nonclustered indexes are appropriate for retrieving a few rows and clustered indexes are good for range scans. In addition, you should try to keep indexes compact (few columns and bytes). This is especially true for clustered indexes because nonclustered indexes use the clustered index to locate row data. For more information, see SQL Server Books Online.

Consider selectivity for nonclustered indexes because, if a nonclustered index is created on a large table with only a few unique values, use of that nonclustered index does not save I/O during data retrieval. In fact, using the index causes much more I/O than a sequential table scan of the table. Possible candidates for a nonclustered index include invoice numbers, unique customer numbers, social security numbers, and telephone numbers.

Clustered indexes are much better than nonclustered indexes for queries that match columns or search for ranges of columns that do not have many unique values, because the clustered index physically orders the table data and allows for sequential 64-KB I/O on the key values. Possible candidates for a clustered index include states, company branches, date of sale, zip codes, and customer district. Defining a clustered index on the columns that have unique values is not beneficial unless typical queries on the system fetch large sequential ranges of the unique values. To pick the best column on each table to create the clustered index, ask if there will be many queries that must fetch many rows based on the order of this column. The answer is very specific to each user environment. One company may do more queries based on ranges of dates, whereas another company may do many queries based on ranges of bank branches.

These are examples of WHERE clauses that benefit from clustered indexes:

WHERE *column_name* >*some_value*

WHERE *column_name* BETWEEN *some_value* AND *some_value*

WHERE *column_name* < *some_value*

Clustered Index Selection

Clustered index selection involves two major steps: First, determine the column of the table that will benefit most from the clustered index by providing sequential I/O for range scans, and second, use the clustered index to affect the physical placement of table data while avoiding hot spots. A hot spot occurs when data is placed on hard disk drives so that, as a result, many queries try to read or write data in the same area of the disk(s) at the same time. This creates a disk I/O bottleneck because more concurrent disk I/O requests are received by the hard disk than it can handle. The solution is either to stop fetching as much data from this disk or to spread the data across multiple disks to support the I/O demand. This consideration for the physical placement of data can be critical for good concurrent access to data among hundreds or thousands of SQL Server users.

These two decisions often conflict with one another, and the best decision is to balance the two. In high user-load environments, improved concurrency (by avoiding hot spots) can be more valuable than the performance benefit gained by placing the clustered index on that column.

With SQL Server 7.0, nonclustered indexes use the clustered index to locate data rows if there is a clustered index present on the table. Because all nonclustered indexes must hold the clustered keys within their B-tree structures, it is better for performance to keep the overall byte size of the clustered index keys as small as possible. Keep the number of columns in the clustered index to a minimum and carefully consider the byte size of each of the columns chosen to be included in a clustered index. This helps reduce the size of the clustered index and subsequently, all nonclustered indexes on a table. Smaller index B-tree structures can be read more quickly and help improve performance. For more information, see SQL Server Books Online.

In earlier versions of SQL Server, tables without clustered indexes insert rows at the end of the table stored on the disk. This can create a hot spot at the end of a busy table. The SQL Server 7.0 storage management algorithms provide free space management that removes this behavior. When rows are inserted in heaps, SQL Server uses the Page Free Space (PFS) pages to quickly locate available free space in the table in which the row is inserted. PFS pages find free space throughout the table, which recovers deleted space and avoids insertion hot spots. Free space management affects clustered index selection. Because clustered indexes affect physical data placement, hot spots can occur when a clustered index physically sequences based on a column in which many concurrent inserts occur at the highest column value and are at the same physical disk location. For columns with monotonically increasing values, a clustered index sequentially orders data rows on disk by that column. By placing the clustered index on another column or by not including a clustered index on the table, this sequential data placement moves to another column or does not occur at all.

Another way to think about hot spots is within the context of selects. If many users select data with key values that are very close to but are not in the same rows, most disk I/O activity occurs within the same physical region of the disk I/O subsystem. This disk I/O activity can be spread out more evenly by defining the clustered index for this table on a column that spreads these key values evenly across the disk. If all selects are using the same unique key value, then using a clustered index does not help balance the disk I/O activity of this table. By using RAID (either hardware or software), you can alleviate this problem by spreading the I/O across many disk drives. This behavior can be described as disk access contention. It is not locking contention.

Clustered Index Selection Scenario

A scenario can illustrate clustered index selection. For example, a table contains an invoice date column, a unique invoice number column, and other data. About 10,000 new records are inserted into this table every day, and the SQL queries often search this table for all records for one week of data. Many users have concurrent access to this table. The invoice number is not a candidate for the clustered index. The invoice number is unique, and users do not usually search on ranges of invoice numbers; therefore, placing invoice numbers physically in sequential order on disk is not appropriate. Next, the values for invoice number increase monotonically (1001,1002,1003, and so on). If the clustered index is placed on invoice number, inserts of new rows into this table occur at the end of the table beside the highest invoice number on the same physical disk location, and create a hot spot.

Consider the invoice date column. To maximize sequential I/O, the invoice date column is a candidate for a clustered index because users often search for one week of data (about 70,000 rows). But for concurrency, the invoice date column may not be a candidate for the clustered index. If the clustered index is placed on an invoice date, all data tends to be inserted at the end of the table, and a hot spot can occur on the hard disk that holds the end of the table. The insertions at the end of the table are offset by the 10,000 rows that are inserted for the same date, therefore, invoice date is less likely to create a hot spot than invoice number. Also, a hardware RAID controller helps spread out the 10,000 rows across multiple disks, which can minimize the possibility of an insertion hot spot.

There is no perfect answer to this scenario. You can place the clustered index on invoice date to speed up queries involving invoice date ranges, even at the risk of hot spots. In this case, you should monitor disk queuing on the disks associated with this table for possible hot spots. It is recommended that you define the clustered index on invoice date because of the benefit to range scans based on invoice date and so that invoice numbers are not physically sequential on disk.

In this example, a table consists of the invoice number, invoice date, invoice amount, sales office where the sale originated, and other data. Suppose 10,000 records are inserted into this table every day, and users often query invoice amounts based on sales office. Sales office should be the column on which the clustered index is created because that is the range on which scans are based. Newly inserted rows will have a mix of sales offices; inserts should be spread evenly across the table and across the disks on which the table is located.

In some cases, range scans may not be an issue. For example, a very large employee table has employee number, social security number, and other data. As rows are inserted, employee number is incremented. There are 100,000 retrievals from this table every day and each retrieval is a single record fetch based on social security number. A nonclustered index created on social security number provides excellent query performance in this scenario. A clustered index on social security number provides slightly better query performance than the nonclustered index, but may be excessive because range scans are not involved. If there will be only one index on this table, place the clustered index on the social security number column. The question then is whether to define a clustered index on this table. In earlier versions of SQL Server, it is important to define a clustered index on a table even if it is not required for queries, because it helps with deleted row space recovery. This is not an issue with the SQL Server 7.0 space allocation algorithms and storage structures.

The recommendation in this example is to create the clustered index on social security number, because the social security number has data distributed so it does not follow the sequential pattern of employee number, and social security number tends to have an even distribution. If a clustered index is created on this evenly distributed column data, the employee records are evenly distributed on disk. This distribution, in conjunction with FILLFACTOR and PAD_INDEX, provides open data page areas throughout the table to insert data. Assuming that newly inserted employee records have an even distribution of social security numbers, the employee table fills evenly and page splitting is avoided. If a column with even distribution does not exist on the table, it is worthwhile to create an integer column on the table and populate the column with values that are evenly distributed and then create the clustered index column. This "filler" or "dummy" column with a clustered index defined on it is not being used to query, but to distribute data I/O across disk drives evenly to improve table access concurrency and overall I/O performance. This can be an effective methodology with large and heavily accessed SQL tables.

Another possible solution in this example is to refrain from creating a clustered index on this table. In this case, SQL Server 7.0 manages all aspects of space management. SQL Server finds a free space to insert the row, reuses space from deleted rows, and automatically reorganizes physical ordering of data pages on disk when it makes sense (to allow greater amounts of sequential I/O). The reorganization of data pages happens during database file autoshrink operations. For more information, see SQL Server Books Online.

FILLFACTOR and PAD_INDEX

If a SQL Server database is experiencing a large amount of insert activity, you should plan to provide and maintain open space on index and data pages to prevent page splitting. Page splitting occurs when an index page or data page can no longer hold any new rows and a row must be inserted into the page because of the logical ordering of data defined in that page. When this occurs, SQL Server must divide the data on the full page and move about half of the data to a new page so that both pages have some open space. This consumes system resources and time.

When indexes are built initially, SQL Server places the index B-tree structures on contiguous physical pages, which supports optimal I/O performance by scanning the index pages with sequential I/O. When page splitting occurs and new pages must be inserted into the logical B-tree structure of the index, SQL Server must allocate new 8-KB index pages somewhere. This occurs elsewhere on the hard disk drive and breaks up the physically sequential index pages, which switches I/O operations from sequential to nonsequential and cuts performance in half. Excessive page splitting should be resolved by rebuilding the index to restore the physically sequential order of the index pages. This same behavior can be encountered on the leaf level of the clustered index, which affects the data pages of the table.

Use Performance Monitor to watch the **SQL Server: Access Methods - Page Splits** counter. Nonzero values for this counter indicate page splitting. Further analysis should be done with the DBCC SHOWCONTIG statement. For more information about how to use this statement, see SQL Server Books Online.

The DBCC SHOWCONTIG statement can reveal excessive page splitting on a table. Scan Density, a key indicator that DBCC SHOWCONTIG provides, should be a value as close to 100 percent as possible. If this value is below 100 percent, rebuild the clustered index on that table by using the DROP_EXISTING option to defragment the table. The DROP_EXISTING option of the CREATE INDEX statement permits re-creating existing indexes and provides better index rebuild performance than dropping and re-creating the index. For more information, see SQL Server Books Online.

The FILLFACTOR option on the CREATE INDEX and DBCC DBREINDEX statements provides a way to specify the percentage of open space to leave on index and data pages. The PAD_INDEX option for CREATE INDEX applies what has been specified for FILLFACTOR on the nonleaf-level index pages. Without the PAD_INDEX option, FILLFACTOR mainly affects the leaf-level index pages of the clustered index. You should use the PAD_INDEX option with FILLFACTOR. For more information, see SQL Server Books Online.

The optimal value to specify for FILLFACTOR depends on how much new data is inserted into an 8-KB index and data page within a given time frame. Keep in mind that SQL Server index pages typically contain many more rows than data pages because index pages contain only the data for columns associated with that index, whereas data pages hold the data for the entire row. Also consider how often there will be a maintenance window that permits the rebuilding of indexes to avoid page splitting. Strive to rebuild the indexes only as the majority of the index and data pages have become filled with data by properly selecting clustered index for a table. If the clustered index distributes data evenly so that new row inserts into the table occur across all of the data pages associated with the table, then the data pages will fill evenly. This provides time before page splitting occurs and forces you to rebuild the clustered index. FILLFACTOR should be selected based partly on the estimated number of rows that will be inserted within the key range of an 8-KB page in a certain time frame, and partly by how often scheduled index rebuilds can occur on the system.

You must make a decision based on the performance trade-offs between leaving a lot of open space on pages and page splitting. A small specified percentage for FILLFACTOR leaves large open spaces on the index and data pages, which helps avoid page splitting but also negates some performance gained by compressing data onto a page. SQL Server performs faster if more data is compressed on index and data pages because it can fetch more data with fewer pages and I/Os. Specifying too high a FILLFACTOR may leave too little open space on pages and can allow pages to overflow too quickly, which causes page splitting.

Before using FILLFACTOR and PAD_INDEX, remember that reads tend to outnumber writes, even in an online transaction processing (OLTP) system. Using FILLFACTOR slows down all reads, because it spreads tables over a wider area (reduction of data compression). Before using FILLFACTOR and PAD_INDEX, you should use Performance Monitor to compare SQL Server reads to SQL Server writes and use these options only if writes are more than 30 percent of reads.

If writes are a substantial percentage of reads, the best approach in a busy OLTP system is to specify as high a FILLFACTOR as will leave a minimal amount of free space per 8-KB page and still prevent page splitting and allow SQL Server to reach the next available time window for rebuilding the index. This method balances tuning I/O performance (keeping the pages as full as possible) and avoiding page splits (not letting pages overflow). You can experiment by rebuilding the index with varying FILLFACTOR values and then simulating load activity on the table to validate an optimal value for FILLFACTOR. After the optimal FILLFACTOR value has been determined, automate the scheduled rebuilding of the index as a SQL Server task. For more information, see SQL Server Books Online.

SQL Server Performance Tuning Tools

Microsoft SQL Server version 7.0 includes several tools that can assist database administrators with performance tuning.

Sample Data and Workload

This example shows how to use SQL Server performance tools. First, the table is constructed:

```
CREATE TABLE testtable (nkey1 int IDENTITY, col2 char(300) DEFAULT
'abc', ckey1 char(1))
```

Next, the table is loaded with 10,000 rows of test data:

```
DECLARE @counter int
SET @counter = 1
WHILE (@counter <= 2000)
BEGIN
    INSERT testtable (ckey1) VALUES ('a')
    INSERT testtable (ckey1) VALUES ('b')
    INSERT testtable (ckey1) VALUES ('c')
    INSERT testtable (ckey1) VALUES ('d')
    INSERT testtable (ckey1) VALUES ('e')
    SET @counter = @counter + 1
END
```

These queries comprise the database server workload:

```
SELECT ckey1,col2 FROM testtable WHERE ckey1 = 'a'
select nkey1,col2 FROM testtable WHERE nkey1 = 5000
```

SQL Server Profiler

SQL Server Profiler records detailed information about activity occurring on the database server. SQL Server Profiler can be configured to watch and record one or many users executing queries on SQL Server and to provide a widely configurable amount of performance information, including I/O statistics, CPU statistics, locking requests, Transact-SQL and RPC statistics, index and table scans, warnings and errors raised, database object create/drop, connection connect/disconnects, stored procedure operations, cursor operation, and more. For more information about what SQL Server Profiler can record, see SQL Server Books Online.

Using SQL Server Profiler with Index Tuning Wizard

SQL Server Profiler and Index Tuning Wizard can be used together to help database administrators create proper indexes on tables. SQL Server Profiler records resource consumption for queries into a .trc file. The .trc file can be read by Index Tuning Wizard, which evaluates the .trc information and the database tables, and then provides recommendations for indexes that should be created. Index Tuning Wizard can either automatically create the proper indexes for the database by scheduling the automatic index creation or generate a Transact-SQL script that can be reviewed and executed later.

These are the steps for analyzing a query load:

▶ **To set up SQL Server Profiler (Enterprise Manager)**

1. On the **Tools** menu, click **SQL Server Profiler**.

2. On the **File** menu, point to **New**, and then click **Trace**.

3. Type a name for the trace.

4. Select **Capture to file**, then select a **.trc** file to which to output the SQL Server Profiler information.

▶ **To run the workload (Enterprise Manager)**

1. On the **Tools** menu, click **SQL Server Query Analyzer**.

2. Connect to SQL Server and set the current database to be where the table was created.

3. Enter these queries into the query window of SQL Server Query Analyzer:

```
SELECT ckey1,col2 FROM testtable WHERE ckey1 = 'a'
SELECT nkey1,col2 FROM testtable WHERE nkey1 = 5000
```

4. On the Query menu, click **Execute**.

▶ **To stop SQL Server Profiler**

1. On the **File** menu, click **Stop Traces**.

2. In the **Stop Selected Traces** dialog box, choose the traces to stop.

▶ **To load the .trc file into the Index Tuning Wizard (SQL Server Profiler)**

1. On the **Tools** menu, click **Index Tuning Wizard**, and then click **Next**.

2. Select the database to analyze, and then click **Next**.

3. Make sure **I have a saved workload file** is selected, and then click **Next**.

4. Select **My workload file**, locate the .trc file created with SQL Server Profiler, click **OK**, and then click **Next**.

5. In **Select Tables to Tune**, select the tables, and then click **Next**.

6. In **Index Recommendations**, select the indexes to create, and then click **Next**.

7. Select the preferred option, and then click **Next**.

8. Click **Finish**.

This is the Transact-SQL generated by Index Tuning Wizard for the sample database and workload:

```
/* Created by: Index Tuning Wizard   */
/* Date: 9/7/98          */
/* Time: 6:42:00 PM          */
/* Server: HENRYLNT2          */
/* Database : test        */
/* Workload file : E:\Mssql7\Binn\Profiler_load.sql */

USE [test]
BEGIN TRANSACTION
CREATE CLUSTERED INDEX [testtable2] ON [dbo].[testtable] ([ckey1])
if (@@error <> 0) rollback transaction
CREATE NONCLUSTERED INDEX [testtable1] ON [dbo].[testtable] ([nkey1])
if (@@error <> 0) rollback transaction
COMMIT TRANSACTION
```

The indexes recommended by Index Tuning Wizard for the sample table and data are expected. There are only five unique values for **ckey1** and 2,000 rows of each value. Because one of the sample queries (SELECT **ckey1**, **col2** FROM **testtable** WHERE **ckey1** = a) requires retrieval from the table based on one of the values in **ckey1**, it is appropriate to create a clustered index on the **ckey1** column. The second query (SELECT **nkey1**, **col2** FROM **testtable** WHERE **nkey1** = 5000) fetches one row based on the value of the column **nkey1**. **nkey1** is unique, and there are 10,000 rows; therefore, it is appropriate to create a nonclustered index on this column.

SQL Server Profiler and Index Tuning Wizard are powerful tools in database server environments in which there are many tables and queries. Use SQL Server Profiler to record a .trc file while the database server is experiencing a representative set of queries. Then load the .trc file into Index Tuning Wizard to determine the proper indexes to build. Follow the prompts in Index Tuning Wizard to automatically generate and schedule index creation jobs to run at off-peak times. Run SQL Server Profiler and Index Tuning Wizard regularly (perhaps weekly) to see if queries executed on the database server have changed significantly, thus possibly requiring different indexes. Regular use of SQL Server Profiler and Index Tuning Wizard can keep SQL Server running in top form as query workloads change and database size increase over time.

For more information, see SQL Server Books Online.

Analyzing SQL Server Profiler Information

SQL Server Profiler provides an option to log information into a SQL Server table. When it is complete, the table can be queried to determine if specific queries are using excessive resources.

▶ **To log SQL Server Profiler information into a SQL Server table (Enterprise Manager)**

1. On the **Tools** menu, click **SQL Server Profiler**.
2. On the **File** menu, point to **New**, and then click **Trace**.
3. Type a name for the trace, then select **Capture to Table**.
4. In the **Capture to Table** dialog box, enter a SQL Server table name to which to output the SQL Server Profiler information. Click **OK**.
5. On the **File** menu, click **Stop Traces**.
6. In the **Stop Traces** dialog box, choose the traces to stop.

For more information, see SQL Server Books Online.

SQL Server Query Analyzer

After the information is recorded into the SQL Server table, you can use SQL Server Query Analyzer to determine which queries on the system are consuming the most resources, and database administrators can concentrate on improving the queries that need the most help. For example, this query is typical of the analysis performed on data recorded from SQL Server Profiler into a SQL Server table:

```
SELECT TOP 3 TextData,CPU,Reads,Writes,Duration FROM profiler_out_table
ORDER BY cpu desc
```

The query retrieves the top three consumers of CPU resources on the database server. Read and write I/O information, along with the duration of the queries in milliseconds is returned. If a large amount of information is recorded with the SQL Server Profiler, you should create indexes on the table to help speed analysis queries. For example, if CPU is going to be an important criteria for analyzing this table, you should create a nonclustered index on CPU column.

Statistics I/O

SQL Server Query Analyzer provides a **Show stats I/O** option under the **General** tab of the **Connections Options** dialog box. Select this checkbox for information about how much I/O is being consumed for the query just executed in SQL Server Query Analyzer.

For example, the query SELECT **ckey1**, **col2** FROM **testtable** WHERE **ckey1** = a returns this I/O information in addition to the result set when the **Show stats I/O** connection option is selected:

```
Table 'testtable'. Scan count 1, logical reads 400, physical reads 382,
read-ahead reads 400.
```

Similarly, the query SELECT **nkey1**, **col2** FROM **testtable** WHERE **nkey1** = 5000 returns this I/O information in addition to the result set when the **Show stats I/O** connection option is selected:

```
Table 'testtable'. Scan count 1, logical reads 400, physical reads 282,
read-ahead reads 400.
```

Using STATISTICS I/O is a good way to monitor the effect of query tuning. For example, create the two indexes on this sample table as recommended by Index Tuning Wizard and then run the queries again.

In the query SELECT **ckey1**, **col2** FROM **testtable** WHERE **ckey1** = a, the clustered index improved performance as indicated below. The query must fetch 20 percent of the table; therefore, the performance improvement is reasonable.

```
Table 'testtable'. Scan count 1, logical reads 91, physical reads 5,
read-ahead reads 32.
```

In the query SELECT **nkey1**, **col2** FROM **testtable** WHERE **nkey1** = 5000, the creation of the nonclustered index had a dramatic effect on the performance of the query. Because only one row of the 10,000 row table must be retrieved for this query, the performance improvement with the nonclustered index is reasonable.

```
Table 'testtable'. Scan count 1, logical reads 5, physical reads 0,
read-ahead reads 0.
```

Showplan

Showplan can be used to display detailed information about what the query optimizer is doing. SQL Server 7.0 provides text and graphical versions of Showplan. Graphical Showplan output can be displayed in the Results pane of SQL Server Query Analyzer by executing a Transact-SQL query with **Ctrl+L**. Icons indicate the operations that the query optimizer will perform if it executes the query. Arrows indicate the direction of data flow for the query. Details about each operation can be shown by holding the mouse pointer over the operation icon. The equivalent information can be returned in text-based showplan by executing SET SHOWPLAN_ALL ON. To reduce the query optimizer operation details from text-based showplan, execute SET SHOWPLAN_TEXT ON.

For more information, see SQL Server Books Online.

Examples of Showplan Output

This section shows sample showplan plan output using the following example queries and the **set showplan_text on** option in SQL Server Query Analyzer.

Query:

```
SELECT ckey1,col2 FROM testtable WHERE ckey1 = 'a'
```

Text-based showplan output:

```
|--Clustered Index Seek(OBJECT:([test].[dbo].[testtable].[testtable2]),
SEEK:([testtable].[ckey1]='a') ORDERED)
```

This query takes advantage of the clustered index on column **ckey1**, as indicated by Clustered Index Seek.

The illustration shows equivalent graphical showplan output.

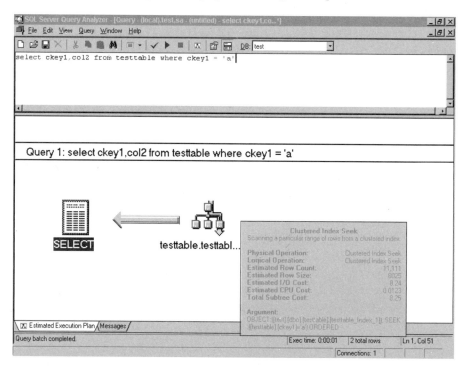

If the clustered index is removed from the table, the query must use a table scan. The showplan output below indicates the change in behavior.

Text-based showplan output:

```
|--Table Scan(OBJECT:([test].[dbo].[testtable]),
WHERE:([testtable].[ckey1]='a'))
```

The illustration shows equivalent graphical showplan output.

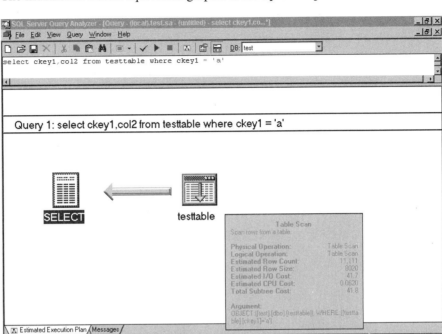

Table scans are the most efficient way to retrieve information from small tables. But on larger tables, table scans indicated by showplan are a warning that the table may need better indexes or that the existing indexes must have their statistics updated (by using the UPDATE STATISTICS statement). SQL Server 7.0 provides automatically updating indexes. You should let SQL Server automatically maintain index statistics because the maintenance helps guarantee queries will always work with good index statistics.

Query:

```
SELECT nkey1,col2 FROM testtable WHERE nkey1 = 5000
```

Text-based showplan output:

```
|--Bookmark Lookup(BOOKMARK:([Bmk1000]),
OBJECT:([test].[dbo].[testtable]))
     |--Index Seek(OBJECT:([test].[dbo].[testtable].[testtable1]),
SEEK:([testtable].[nkey1]=5000) ORDERED)
```

The illustration shows equivalent graphical showplan output.

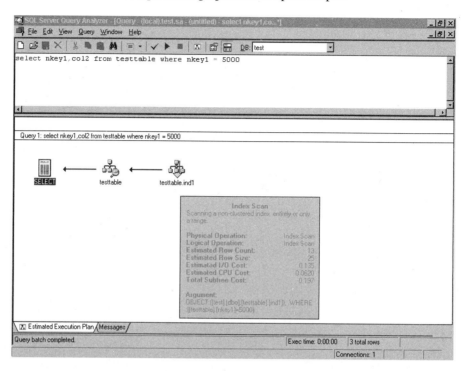

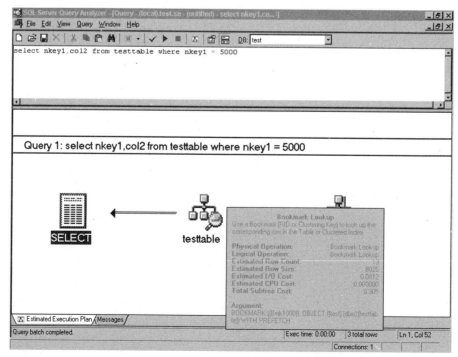

This query uses the nonclustered index on the column **nkey1**, which is indicated by the Index Seek operation on the column **nkey1**. The Bookmark Lookup operation indicates that SQL Server must perform a bookmark lookup from the index page to the data page of the table to retrieve the requested data. The bookmark lookup was required because the query asked for the column **col2**, which was not part of the nonclustered index.

Query:

```
SELECT nkey1 FROM testtable WHERE nkey1 = 5000
```

Text-based showplan output:

```
|--Index Seek(OBJECT:([test].[dbo].[testtable].[testtable1]),
SEEK:([testtable].[nkey1]=[@1]) ORDERED)
```

The illustration shows equivalent graphical showplan output.

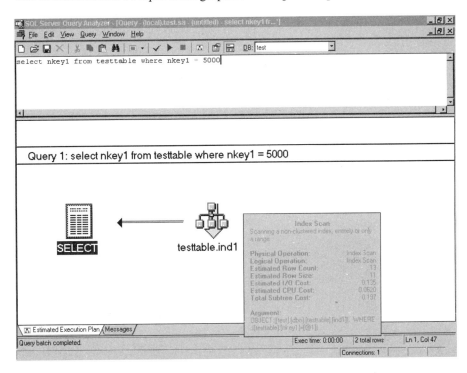

This query uses the nonclustered index on **nkey1** as a covering index. No bookmark lookup operation was needed for this query because all of the information required for the query (both SELECT and WHERE clauses) is provided by the nonclustered index. A bookmark lookup to the data pages is not required from the nonclustered index pages. I/O is reduced compared to the case in which a bookmark lookup was required.

Performance Monitor

Windows NT Performance Monitor provides information about Windows and SQL Server operations occurring on the database server. For SQL Server specific counters, see SQL Server Books Online.

In Performance Monitor graph mode, note the Max and Min values. Do not emphasize the average because polarized data points can affect this value. Study the graph shape and compare to Min and Max to gather an accurate understanding of the behavior. Use BACKSPACE to highlight counters.

You can use Performance Monitor to log all available Windows NT and SQL Server performance monitor objects and counters in a log file and also to view Performance Monitor interactively in chart mode. Setting a sampling interval determines how quickly the log file grows. Log files can get big fast (for example, 100 MG in one hour with all counters turned on and a sampling interval of 15 seconds). The test server should have a couple of gigabytes free to store these files. But if conserving space is important, try running with a large log interval of 30 or 60 seconds. By doing so, Performance Monitor does not sample the system as often, and all of the counters are resampled with reasonable frequency, but a smaller log file size is maintained.

Performance Monitor also consumes some CPU and Disk I/O resources. If a system does not have much disk I/O and/or CPU to spare, consider running Performance Monitor from another computer to monitor the server running SQL Server over the network. This applies to Performance Monitor graph mode only. When using log mode, it is more efficient to log Performance Monitor information locally on the server running SQL Server. If you must use log mode over the network, then consider reducing the logging to only the most critical counters.

You should log all counters available during performance test runs into a file for analysis later. Configure Performance Monitor to log all counters into a log file and at the same time monitor the most interesting counters in one of the other modes, such as graph mode. This way, all of the information is recorded, but the most interesting counters are presented in an uncluttered Performance Monitor graph while the performance run is taking place.

▶ **To start the logging feature (Performance Monitor)**

1. On the **View** menu, click **Log**.

2. Click (**+**).

3. In the **Add to Log** dialog box, select the counters to add to the log.

4. Click **Add**, and then click **Done**.

5. On the **Options** menu, click **Log**.

6. In **File Name**, enter the name of the file into which the performance information will be logged.

7. Click **Start Log**.

▶ **To stop the logging feature (Performance Monitor)**

1. On the **Options** menu, click **Log**.

2. Click **Stop Log**.

▶ **To load the logged information into Performance Monitor (Performance Monitor)**

1. On the **View** menu, click **Log**.

2. On the **Options** menu, click **Data From**, and then select **Log File**.

3. Click browse (**...**), then double-click the file.

4. In the **Data From** dialog box, click **OK**.

5. On the **View** menu, click **Chart**, and then click (**+**).

6. Click the (**+**) button.

7. In the **Add to Chart** dialog box, add desired counters to the graphical display by highlighting the object/counter combination, and then click **Add**.

▶ **To relate Performance Monitor logged events back to a point in time**

1. Follow the steps for How to load information into Performance Monitor.

2. On the **Edit** menu, click **Time Window**.

3. In the **Input Log File Timeframe** dialog box, you can adjust the start and stop time window of the logged data by clicking and holding down the mouse button on the slidebars.

4. Click **OK** to reset the chart to display only data logged for the selected time window.

Key Performance Monitor Counters

You can observe several Performance Monitor disk counters. To enable these counters, run the **diskperf –y** command from a Windows NT command window and restart Windows NT. The **diskperf -y** command consumes some resources on the database server, but it is worthwhile to run the **diskperf -y** command on all production SQL Server servers. As a result, disk queuing problems can be confirmed immediately and all Performance Monitor counters are immediately available to diagnose disk I/O issues. If disk I/O counters are required, the **diskperf -y** command must be executed, and Windows NT must be restarted before the disk I/O counters will report data in Performance Monitor.

(Physical or Logical) Disk Queue > 2

Physical hard disk drives that experience disk queuing hold back disk I/O requests while they catch up on I/O processing. SQL Server response time is degraded for these drives, which costs query execution time.

If you use RAID, you must know how many physical hard disk drives are associated with each drive array that Windows NT interprets as a single physical drive so you can calculate disk queuing per physical drive. A hardware expert can explain the SCSI channel and physical drive distribution to help you understand how SQL Server data is held by each physical drive and how much SQL Server data is distributed on each SCSI channel.

There are several choices for viewing disk queuing in Performance Monitor. Logical disk counters are associated with the logical drive letters assigned by the Windows NT Disk Administrator, whereas physical disk counters are associated with what Windows NT Disk Administrator interprets as a single physical disk device. What looks like a single physical device to the Windows NT Disk Administrator may be either a single hard disk drive or a RAID array, which consists of several hard disk drives. The **Current Disk Queue** counter is an instantaneous measure of disk queuing, whereas the **Average Disk Queue** counter averages the disk queuing measurement over the Performance Monitor sampling period. Take note of any counter in which **Logical Disk: Average Disk Queue** is greater than 2, **Physical Disk: Average Disk Queue** is greater than 2, **Logical Disk: Current Disk Queue** is greater than 2, or **Physical Disk: Average Disk Queue** is greater than 2.

These recommended measurements are specified per physical hard disk drive. If a RAID array is associated with a disk queue measurement, the measurement must be divided by the number of physical hard disk drives in the RAID array to determine the disk queuing per physical hard disk drive.

On physical hard disk drives or RAID arrays that hold SQL Server log files, disk queuing is not a useful measure because SQL Server log manager does not queue more than a single I/O request to SQL Server log file(s). For more information, see SQL Server Books Online.

System: Processor Queue Length > 2 (per CPU)

When the **System: Processor Queue Length** counter is greater than 2, the server processors are receiving more work requests than they can handle as a group; therefore, Windows must place these requests in a queue.

Some processor queuing can be an indicator of good SQL Server I/O performance. If there is no processor queuing and if CPU use is low, it can be an indication of a performance bottleneck somewhere in the system, and most likely in the disk subsystem. A reasonable amount of work in the processor queue means that the CPUs are not idle and the rest of the system is keeping pace with the CPUs.

A general rule for determining an optimal processor queue number is to multiply the number of CPUs on the database server by 2.

Processor queuing significantly above 2 per CPU should be investigated. Excessive processor queuing costs query execution time. Eliminating hard and soft paging can help save CPU resources. Other methods that help reduce processor queuing include tuning SQL queries, picking better SQL indexes to reduce disk I/O (and hence CPU), or adding more CPUs (processors) to the system.

Hard Paging - Memory: Pages/Sec > 0
or Memory: Page Reads/Sec > 5

Memory: Pages/Sec greater than 0 or **Memory: Page Reads/Sec** greater than 5 means that Windows is going to disk to resolve memory references (hard page fault), which costs disk I/O and CPU resources. The **Memory: Pages/Sec** counter is a good indicator of the amount of paging that Windows is performing and the adequacy of the database server RAM configuration. A subset of the hard paging information in Performance Monitor is the number of times per second Windows had to read from the paging file to resolve memory references, which is represented by the **Memory: Pages Reads/Sec** counter. A value of **Memory: Pages Reads/Sec** greater than 5 is bad for performance.

Automatic SQL Server memory tuning adjusts SQL Server memory use dynamically so that paging is avoided. A small number of pages per second is normal but excessive paging requires corrective action.

If SQL Server is automatically tuning memory, then adding more RAM or removing other applications from the database server are options to help bring the **Memory: Pages/Sec** counter to a reasonable level.

If SQL Server memory is being configured manually on the database server, it may be necessary to reduce memory given to SQL Server, remove other applications from the database server, or add more RAM to the database server.

Keeping **Memory: Pages/Sec** at or close to 0 helps database server performance because Windows and all its applications (including SQL Server) are not going to the paging file to satisfy any data in memory requests; therefore, the amount of RAM on the server is sufficient. A **Pages/Sec** value slightly greater than 0 is not critical, but a relatively high performance penalty (Disk I/O) is paid every time data is retrieved from the paging file rather than from RAM.

You should understand the difference between the **Memory: Pages Input/sec** counter and the **Memory: Pages Reads/sec** counter. The **Memory: Pages Input/sec** counter indicates the actual number of Windows 4-KB pages being brought from disk to satisfy page faults. The **Memory: Pages Reads/sec** counter indicates how many disk I/O requests are made per second to satisfy page faults, which provides a slightly different point of view. A single page read can contain several Windows 4-KB pages. Disk I/O performs better as the packet size of data increases (64 KB or more), so it can be worthwhile to consider these counters at the same time. For a hard disk drive, completing a single read or write of 4 KB costs almost as much time as a single read or write of 64 KB. Consider this situation: 200 page reads consisting of eight 4-KB pages per read could finish faster than 300 page reads consisting of one 4-KB page. And we are comparing 1600 4-KB page reads finishing faster than 300 4-KB page reads. The key to all disk I/O analysis is to watch not only the number of disk bytes/sec but also the disk transfers/sec. For more information, see "Disk I/O Counters" and "The EMC Disk I/O Tuning Scenario" later in this chapter.

It is useful to compare the **Memory: Page Input/sec** counter to the **Logical Disk: Disk Reads/sec** counter across all drives associated with the Windows NT paging file, and the **Memory: Page Output/sec** counter to the **Logical Disk: Disk Writes/sec** counter across all drives associated with the Windows paging file. They provide a measure of how much disk I/O is strictly related to paging as opposed to other applications, such as SQL Server. Another way to isolate paging file I/O activity is to ensure the paging file is located on a separate set of drives from all other SQL Server files. Separating the paging file from the SQL Server files also can help disk I/O performance, because disk I/O associated with paging can be performed in parallel to disk I/O associated with SQL Server.

Soft Paging - Memory: Pages Faults/Sec > 0

A **Memory: Pages Faults/Sec** counter greater than 2 indicates that Windows NT is paging but includes hard and soft paging within the counter. Soft paging means that there are application(s) on the database server that requests memory pages still inside RAM but outside of the application's Working Set. The **Memory: Page Faults/Sec** counter is helpful for deriving the amount of soft paging that occurs. There is no counter called soft faults per second. Instead, calculate the number of soft faults happening per second this way:

Memory: Pages Faults/sec - Memory: Pages Input/sec = Soft Page Faults per Second

To determine if SQL Server is causing excessive paging, monitor the **Process: Page Faults/sec** counter for the SQL Server process and note whether the number of page faults per second for Sqlservr.exe is similar to the number of pages per second.

Because soft faults consume CPU resources and hard faults consume disk I/O resources, soft faults are better than hard faults for performance. The best environment for performance is to have no faulting of any kind.

Until SQL Server accesses all of its data cache pages for the first time, the initial access to each page causes a soft fault, so do not be concerned if soft faulting occurs under these circumstances. For more information, see "Monitoring Processors" later in this chapter.

For more information on memory tuning, see SQL Server Books Online.

Monitoring Processors

Keep all server processors busy enough to maximize performance but not so busy that processor bottlenecks occur. The performance tuning challenge is to determine the source of the bottleneck. If CPU is not the bottleneck, then a primary candidate is the disk subsystem, and the CPU is being wasted. CPU is the most difficult resource to expand above a specific configuration level, such as four or eight on many current systems, so it is a good sign when CPU utilization is above 95 percent. In addition, the response time of transactions should be monitored. Greater than 95 percent CPU use can mean that the workload is too much for the available CPU resources and either the CPU must be increased or the workload must be reduced or tuned.

Monitor the **Processor: Processor Time %** counter to ensure all processors are consistently below 95 percent utilization on each CPU. The **System: Processor Queue** counter is the processor queue for all CPUs on a Windows NT–based system. If the **System: Processor Queue** counter value is greater than 2 per CPU, there is a CPU bottleneck, and it is necessary to either add processors to the server or reduce the workload on the system. Reducing workload can be accomplished by query tuning or improving indexes to reduce I/O and subsequently CPU usage.

Another counter to monitor when a CPU bottleneck is suspected is **System: Context Switches/sec** because it indicates the number of times per second that Windows NT and SQL Server had to change from executing on one thread to executing on another. Context switching is a normal component of a multithreaded, multiprocessor environment, but excessive context switching slows down a system. Only be concerned about context switching if there is processor queuing. If processor queuing is observed, use the level of context switching as a gauge when you performance tune SQL Server. Consider using the **lightweight pooling** option so that SQL Server switches to a fiber-based scheduling model versus the default thread-based scheduling model. Think of fibers as lightweight threads. Use command **sp_configure 'lightweight pooling', 1** to enable fiber-based scheduling. Watch processor queuing and context switching to monitor the effect.

For more information about I/O, memory, and CPU use mapped to SPID, see the DBCC SQLPERF (THREADS) statement in SQL Server Books Online.

Disk I/O Counters

The **Disk Write Bytes/sec** and **Disk Read Bytes/sec** counters provide the data throughput in bytes per second per logical drive. Weigh these numbers carefully along with the values of the **Disk Reads/sec** and **Disk Writes/sec** counters. Do not allow few bytes per second to lead you to believe that the disk I/O subsystem is not busy. A single hard disk drive is capable of supporting a total of 75 nonsequential and 150 sequential disk reads and disk writes per second.

Monitor the **Disk Queue Length** counter for all drives associated with SQL Server files and determine which files are associated with excessive disk queuing.

If Performance Monitor indicates that some drives are not as busy as others, you can move SQL Server files from drives that are bottlenecking to drives that are not as busy. This spreads disk I/O activity more evenly across hard disk drives. If one large drive pool is used for SQL Server files, the resolution to disk queuing is to make the I/O capacity of the pool bigger by adding more physical drives to the pool.

Disk queuing may be a symptom that one SCSI channel is saturated with I/O requests. Performance Monitor cannot directly detect if this is true. Hardware vendors can provide tools to detect the amount of I/O serviced by a RAID controller and whether the controller is queuing I/O requests. This is more likely to occur if many disk drives (10 or more) are attached to the SCSI channel, and they all perform I/O at full speed. To resolve this issue, take half of the disk drives and connect them to another SCSI channel or RAID controller to balance the I/O. Rebalancing drives across SCSI channels requires a rebuild of the RAID arrays and full backup and restore of the SQL Server database files.

Performance Monitor Graph Output

The illustration shows typical counters that Performance Monitor uses to observe performance. The **Processor Queue Length** counter is being observed. Click **BackSpace** to highlight the current counter. This helps to distinguish the current counter from other counters being observed and can be particularly helpful when observing many counters at the same time with Performance Monitor.

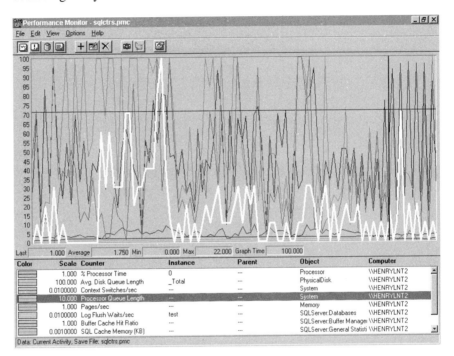

The Max value for **Processor Queue Length** is 22.000. The values of Max, Min, and Average for the Performance Monitor Graph cover only the current time window for the graph, as indicated by Graph Time. By default, graph time covers 100 seconds. To monitor longer periods and to ensure getting representative Max, Min, and Average values for those time periods, use the logging feature of Performance Monitor.

The shape of the Processor Queue Length graph line indicates that the Max of 22 occurred only for a short period. But there is a period preceding the 22 value when Processor Queue Length is greater than 5, 100 percent is 22. And there is a period prior to the 22 value when the graph has values above 25 percent, which is approximately 5. In this example, the database server **HENRYLNT2** has only one processor and should not sustain Processor Queue Length greater than 2. Therefore, Performance Monitor indicates that the processor on this computer is being overtaxed. Further investigation should be made to reduce the load on the processor or more processors should be added to **HENRYLNT2** to handle these periods of higher processor workloads.

Other Performance Topics

This section presents other factors that can influence the performance of Microsoft SQL Server.

Reduce Network Traffic and Resource Consumption

When you work with the relatively easy to use SQL Server interfaces such as Microsoft ActiveX Data Objects (ADO), Remote Data Objects (RDO), and Data Access Objects (DAO) database APIs, you must remain aware of the result sets they are building. ADO, RDO, and DAO provide database development interfaces that allow rich database rowset functionality without requiring a lot of database programming experience. You can encounter performance problems if you neither account for the data your application is returning to the client nor remain aware of where the SQL Server indexes are placed and how the SQL Server data is arranged. SQL Server Profiler, Index Tuning Wizard, and showplan are helpful tools for pinpointing and fixing problem queries.

Look for opportunities to reduce the size of the result set by eliminating columns in the select list that do not have to be returned, or by returning only the required rows. This reduces I/O and CPU consumption.

For more information, see SQL Server Books Online.

Deadlocking

You may avoid deadlocking if applications accessing SQL Server are built so that transactions access tables in the same chronological order across all user transactions. You should explain the concept of chronological table access to SQL Server application developers as early as possible during the application design process to avoid deadlocking problems, which are expensive to solve later.

By reducing SQL Server query I/O and shortening transaction time you can help prevent deadlocking. This can make queries faster, ensure lock resources are held for a shorter period, and reduce all locking contention (including deadlocking). Use the SQL Server Query Analyzer **Show stats I/O** option to determine the number of logical page fetches associated with large queries. Use the SQL Server Query Analyzer **Show query plan** option to review index use, and then consider a SQL Server query redesign that is more efficient and uses less I/O.

For more information, see SQL Server Books Online.

Language to Avoid in Queries

Use of inequality operators in SQL queries forces databases to use table scans to evaluate the inequalities. These queries generate high I/O if they run regularly against large tables.

For example, using any WHERE expression with NOT in it:

WHERE *column_name* != *some_value*

WHERE *column_name* <> *some_value*

If you must run these queries, restructure the queries to eliminate the NOT keyword or operator, for example:

```
SELECT * FROM tableA WHERE col1 < 'value' or col1 > 'value'
```

Instead of:

```
SELECT * FROM tableA WHERE col1 != 'value'
```

SQL Server can use the index (preferably clustered), if it is built on **col1**, rather than resorting to a table scan.

Smart Normalization

On frequently accessed tables, move columns that a database application does not need regularly to another table. By eliminating as many columns as possible, you can reduce I/O and increase performance. For more information, see SQL Server Books Online.

Partitioned Views

You can horizontally partition tables through views in SQL Server 7.0, which can provide I/O performance benefits when database users query subsections of large views. For example, if a large table documents sales for all sales departments for a year and if retrievals from this table are based on a single sales department, a partitioned view can be employed. A sales table is defined for each sales department, a constraint is defined on the sales department column on each table, and then a view is created on all of the tables to form a partitioned view. The query optimizer uses the constraint on the sales department column. When the view is queried, all of the sales department tables that do not match the sales department value provided in the query are ignored by the query optimizer and no I/O is performed against those base tables. This improves query performance by reducing I/O. For more information, see SQL Server Books Online.

Replication and Backup Performance

If you ensure that the disk I/O subsystem and CPUs are performing well, you ensure performance benefits to all SQL Server operations, including replication and backups. Transactional replication and transaction log backups read from transaction log files. Snapshot replication and backups perform serial scans of database files. The SQL Server 7.0 storage structures have made these operations fast and efficient, as long as there is no queuing occurring in the database server CPUs or disk subsystems. For more information, see SQL Server Books Online.

The EMC Disk I/O Tuning Scenario

For those implementing SQL Server database systems on the unique EMC Symmetrix Enterprise Storage Systems, some disk I/O balancing methods can help avoid disk I/O bottleneck problems and maximize performance.

Symmetrix storage systems contain up to 16 GB of RAM cache and contain internal processors within the disk array that help speed the I/O processing of data without using host server CPU resources. You must understand the four components in the Symmetrix storage system to balance disk I/O. One component is the 16-GB cache inside the Symmetrix. Up to 32 SA channels can be used to cable up to 32 SCSI cards from Windows NT–based host servers into the Symmetrix; all of these SA channels can be requesting data simultaneously from the 16-GB cache. Within the Symmetrix storage system, there are up to 32 connectors called DA controllers (internal SCSI controllers) that connect all of the internal disk drives within the Symmetrix into the 4-GB internal cache. And finally, there are the hard disk drives within the Symmetrix.

EMC hard disk drives are SCSI hard disk drives with the same I/O capability of the other SCSI drives referred to in this chapter. One feature commonly used with EMC technology is referred to as *hyper-volumes*. A hyper-volume is the logical division of an EMC hard disk drives, so the hyper-volume looks like another physical drive to the Windows NT Disk Administrator and can be manipulated with Windows NT Disk Administrator like any other disk drive. Multiple hyper-volumes can be defined on each physical drive. You should work closely with EMC field engineers to identify how hyper-volumes are defined when conducting database performance tuning on EMC storage. You can overload a physical drive with database I/O if you think two or more hyper-volumes are separate physical drives but actually are two or more hyper-volumes on the same physical drive.

SQL Server I/O activities should be divided evenly among distinct DA controllers because DA controllers are assigned to a defined set of hard disk drives. DA controllers are not likely to suffer an I/O bottleneck, but the set of hard disk drives associated with a DA controller may be more susceptible. SQL Server disk I/O balancing is accomplished the same way with DA controllers and their associated disk drives as with other vendors disk drives and controllers.

To monitor the I/O on a DA channel or on separate physical hard disk drives, get help from EMC technical support staff, because I/O activity occurs beneath the EMC internal cache and is not visible to Performance Monitor. EMC storage units have internal monitoring tools that allow an EMC technical support engineer to monitor I/O statistics within the Symmetrix. Performance Monitor can see I/O coming to and from an EMC storage unit only by the I/O coming from an SA channel. This is enough information to indicate that a SA channel is queuing disk I/O requests, but is not enough information to determine the disk or disks that are causing the disk queuing. If an SA channel is queuing, the bottleneck may be caused by the disk drives, not by the SA channel. One way to isolate the disk I/O bottleneck between the SA channels and the DA channels and drives is to add a SCSI card to the host server and connect it to another SA channel. If Performance Monitor indicates that I/O across both SA channels has not changed in volume and disk queuing is still occurring, then the SA channels are not causing the bottleneck. Another way to isolate the I/O bottleneck is to have an EMC engineer use EMC monitoring tools to monitor the EMC system and analyze the drives or DA channels that are bottlenecking.

Divide SQL Server activities evenly across as many disk drives as are available. When working with a smaller database that sustains a large amount of I/O and resides on EMC hardware using hypervolumes, you should continually monitor hyper-volumes definitions. Observing SQL Server activity will help you avoid overloading multiple hyper-volumes on one disk. For example, suppose the SQL Server consists of a 30-GB database. EMC hard disk drives can provide up to 23 GB in capacity, so you can fit the entire database onto 2 drives. For manageability and cost, this is appealing; but for I/O performance, it is not. An EMC storage unit can work with more than 100 internal drives. Involving only 2 drives for SQL Server can lead to I/O bottlenecks. Consider defining smaller hyper-volumes, perhaps of 2 GB each. Then approximately 12 hyper-volumes can be associated with a given 23-GB hard disk drive. Assuming 2-GB hyper-volumes, 15 hyper-volumes are required to store the database. Make sure that each hyper-volume is associated with a separate physical hard disk drive. Do not use 12 hyper-volumes from 1 physical drive and then 3 hyper-volumes associated on another physical drive, because this is the same as using 2 physical drives (150 nonsequential I/O / 300 sequential I/O across the two drives). But with 15 hyper-volumes, each of which is associated with a separate physical drive, SQL Server uses 15 physical drives for providing I/O (1125 nonsequential / 2250 sequential I/O activity per second across the 15 drives).

Also consider employing several SA channels from the host server to divide the I/O work across controllers for host servers that support more than a single PCI bus. Consider using one SA channel per host server PCI bus to divide I/O work across PCI buses as well as SA channels. On EMC storage systems, each SA channel is associated with a specific DA channel and a specific set of physical hard disk drives. Because SA channels read and write their data to and from the EMC internal cache, it is unlikely the SA channel is a point of I/O bottleneck. Because SCSI controller bottlenecks are not likely, it is probably best to concentrate on balancing SQL Server activities across physical drives rather than focus on how many SA channels to use.

C H A P T E R   7

Index Tuning Wizard

Enterprise-class databases require database administrators (DBAs) to select a physical database design appropriate for the system. An important component of physical database design is selecting indexes. In data intensive applications such as decision support and data warehousing, choosing the right set of indexes is crucial for performance. This chapter describes the Index Tuning Wizard: a Microsoft SQL Server 7.0 wizard that automates the challenge of index selection, while achieving performance competitive with that of indexes handpicked by DBAs.

Why Is Index Selection Difficult?

Despite a long history of development in the area of index selection, no widely deployed commercial products are available that select indexes automatically. Several factors make automating physical database design extremely difficult.

First, when viewed as a search problem, the variety of alternatives for indexes is large. A database may have many tables and each table may have many columns that need to be considered for indexing. An index may be clustered or nonclustered. Furthermore, in recommending a set of indexes, we cannot restrict ourselves to single-column indexes only. Considering multicolumn indexes increases the search space dramatically because for a given set of k columns, k! multicolumn indexes are possible.

Second, the textbook solution of using semantic information such as uniqueness, reference constraints, and rudimentary statistics ("small" versus "big" tables) to produce a physical database design leads to poor performance because it ignores valuable information on usage statistics. For example, the indexing requirement for a decision-support application is very different from the requirements of online transaction processing (OLTP) applications.

Third, even when index selection tools have taken the usage statistics into account, they suffer from being disconnected from the query processor. Modern query optimizers use complex strategies such as index intersection and index-only access. For example, if a table has 100 columns but a query references only 4 of the 100 columns, an index on those 4 columns may benefit the query significantly even if the query has no selection condition on any of the 4 columns. This is because the index acts as a vertical partition and saves the cost of scanning the remaining 96 columns of the table. Similarly, if a query has two selection conditions on columns **A** and **B** of a table, the query optimizer may choose to use indexes on both **A** and **B** to answer the query by taking their intersection. An index selection tool that does not take into account these strategies of the query processor can result in gross inefficiencies and poor quality of design. Therefore, even tools that adopt an expert system-like approach are unsatisfactory because they often rely on an inaccurate model of index usage by the query processor.

Finally, even if we are successful in identifying an ideal set of indexes for each Transact-SQL statement in the workload, it is challenging to obtain a set of indexes that acts as the best compromise, particularly when the workload contains queries as well as INSERT, DELETE, and UPDATE statements.

The Index Tuning Wizard in SQL Server 7.0 can help you avoid these problems. It is guided by usage statistics, synchronized with the query processor in evaluating promise of indexes, and it uses a unique search strategy to navigate the search space of indexes.

Using the Index Tuning Wizard

To use the Index Tuning Wizard, the server name and the database name must be specified. In addition, the wizard requires a workload file as its input. The workload file is used to capture the nature of the usage statistics against the database system. Any SQL Server Profiler trace can be used as a workload file. SQL Server Profiler is a graphical SQL Server client tool that makes it possible to monitor and record engine events in a workload file. A typical entry in such a workload file may consist of a variety of fields: event-class, text of the event (for example, text of the Transact-SQL query), start-time, and duration of the event. The Index Tuning Wizard can extract engine relevant events (such as Transact-SQL statements) and fields from a SQL Server Profiler trace automatically. Alternatively, any file that contains a set of Transact-SQL statements (separated by the delimiter GO) also can be used as a workload file. Such files may contain customer benchmarks for which the index selection must be tuned.

Customizing the Index Tuning Wizard

The Index Tuning Wizard provides a rich set of options to customize index selection:

- **Keep all existing indexes**

    This option can be exercised on the server and database choice screen. By selecting this option, the user instructs the wizard not to drop any of the existing indexes. Thus, this option allows conservative use of the tool and incremental changes in the design of the indexes. Unless the user is experienced, it is recommended that this mode of operation be used.

- **Exhaustive enumeration**

    For large workload files and large databases, index tuning may require a significant amount of time and resources. However, to lessen the elapsed time and the workload on the server, SQL Server allows the user to request the Index Tuning Wizard to be less extensive in its search for an appropriate set of indexes. Users can choose this mode by deselecting the exhaustive enumeration operation. This option is also presented on the server and database choice screen. Although this mode of operation searches fewer possibilities, in many cases it is able to provide a respectable set of recommendations. The Index Tuning Wizard deselects exhaustive enumeration by default.

Additional customization options are presented in the Advanced Options screen:

- **Maximum queries to tune**

    If this number is set to k, the Index Tuning Wizard ignores the workload that follows the first k queries (for example, Transact-SQL statements). By default, this number is set to 32,767. By reducing the value of this parameter, the size of the effective workload file can be controlled and the execution of the Index Tuning Wizard may be accelerated. However, it should be remembered that the Index Tuning Wizard considers the first k queries, not events. Specifically, events that are not considered by the Index Tuning Wizard to be queries are not counted towards this limit.

- **Maximum space for the recommended indexes**

    This parameter sets the limit on the sum total of all storage for all indexes. By default, this parameter is set to twice the size of the current data set. This limit includes the storage devoted to indexes that must be included due to integrity constraints (for example, uniqueness constraint). In case the **Keep all indexes** option is selected, this limit also includes the storage required for existing indexes. Because databases grow over time, the administrator should adjust the parameter so that the assigned storage is appropriate for the current data size.

- **Maximum columns per index**

    This parameter can be tuned to set the maximum width of indexes. An index with few columns potentially can be used in many queries in a workload. An index with many columns may enable index-only access and eliminate data scans for some of the queries even though it requires more storage space than an index with fewer columns. Given the complexity of the trade-off, it is recommended that only experienced administrators tune this parameter.

- **Select Tables to tune**

    Another significant way in which the Index Tuning Wizard can be customized is by restricting index tuning to only a subset of all tables by selecting the **Select Tables to Tune** option. This allows the user to focus the design on selected tables in the database without altering the indexes for the remaining tables.

Analyzing Index Tuning Wizard Output

The most important output from the Index Tuning Wizard is a set of recommended indexes. The **Index Recommendations** dialog box displays the list of these indexes, indicating the assigned index name, the order of columns in the index, whether the index is clustered, and whether the index exists. The wizard also produces an estimate of expected improvement in the execution of the workload compared to the existing configuration. The Index Tuning Wizard uses the optimizer component of the query processor to project the above estimate. Because the optimizer's projection is based on statistical information, the actual change in performance may be different from the projected estimate.

The Index Tuning Wizard recommendations are supplemented by a variety of reports that provide further analysis of the recommendations and their quantitative impact. These reports affect the decision about whether to accept or reject the recommendations. All the reports can be saved as text files for further analysis. In the **Index Recommendations** dialog box, click **Analyze** to view these report options:

- The **Index Usage Report** option (recommended configuration) presents information about the expected relative usage of the recommended indexes and their estimated sizes.

- The **Query Cost Report** option indicates to the user the estimated reduction or increase in the cost for execution of the most expensive, 100 Transact-SQL statements in the workload file if the recommended configuration is accepted.

- The **Table Analysis Report** option provides information about the relative hits of the queries in the workload by tables in the database.

- The **Workload Analysis Report** option provides information about the relative frequencies of SELECT, INSERT, UPDATE, and DELETE queries and their relative impact on total cost of the workload.

- The **Tuning Summary Report** option provides important summary information about the execution of the Index Tuning Wizard. In particular, this report indicates if the recommendations suggest dropping indexes. The report also indicates the total number of queries in the workload that were considered by the Index Tuning Wizard.

Finally, the Index Tuning Wizard allows the scheduling of a task to update the existing index configuration. The index creation/alteration step can be initiated immediately or can be scheduled to occur at a specific date and time. In addition, a script to perform the index update can be created. This is particularly useful because the index recommendations can be ported from the test computer to production computers by using the script. Furthermore, the script makes it easy to identify the indexes that will be dropped if the recommendations of the Index Tuning Wizard are accepted. Examining the script identifies two essential components of index tuning: a set of indexes and a set of statistics. Executing the recommendations to create a set of statistics is vital to harnessing the full benefits of indexing. This is because the query processor exploits statistical information during query optimization to determine whether to use an index.

Starting the Wizard

The Index Tuning Wizard can be started from SQL Server Enterprise Manager by selecting a database, and then clicking Index Tuning Wizard from the list of available wizards in the Management subgroup. Alternatively, it can be started from SQL Server Profiler on the **Tools** tab of the **Profiler** menu. After the wizard obtains all the necessary user input on required parameters, it carefully begins searching the space of possible configurations. If the search for the index configurations is terminated during this time, the wizard returns the best available configuration that has been considered thus far.

SQL Server Query Analyzer provides another mode in which the Index Tuning Wizard can be started for a workload consisting of a single Transact-SQL statement only. This is accomplished by selecting one Transact-SQL statement in the query buffer and then selecting **Perform index analysis** from the options available on the **Query** tab. In this mode, for all the customization options, the default settings are used and the workload file is assumed to contain only the single query. (The only exception is the **Perform Thorough Analysis** option, which is selected while starting Index Tuning Wizard from SQL Server Query Analyzer.) Because the **Keep all indexes** option is the default, all indexes suggested in this mode assume that existing indexes must be retained. Because single query workloads typically are not representative, the Index Tuning Wizard imposes an additional constraint that no changes in the clustering of data will be recommended, whether or not there is a clustered index. Such a restriction discourages clustering data based on index recommendations for a single query. The index recommendations are presented as a Transact-SQL script. You have the option of either accepting or rejecting the recommendations. The Index Tuning Wizard should be used on a representative workload and not on single queries. However, the ability to start the index tuning capability from SQL Server Query Analyzer is useful for tuning an under-performing query in an otherwise well-tuned system.

Understanding the Architecture of the Index Tuning Wizard

The Index Tuning Wizard takes as input a workload on a specified database. The tool iterates through several alternative sets of indexes called configurations, and chooses the configuration that results in the lowest cost for the given workload. Evaluating a configuration by materializing it physically is not practical because this approach requires adding and dropping indexes, which can be resource-intensive and affect operational queries on the system. Therefore, the Index Tuning Wizard must simulate a configuration without materializing it. SQL Server 7.0 has been extended to support the ability to simulate a configuration and estimate the cost of evaluating a query for a simulated configuration. The illustration shows the architectural overview of the Index Tuning Wizard and its interaction with SQL Server.

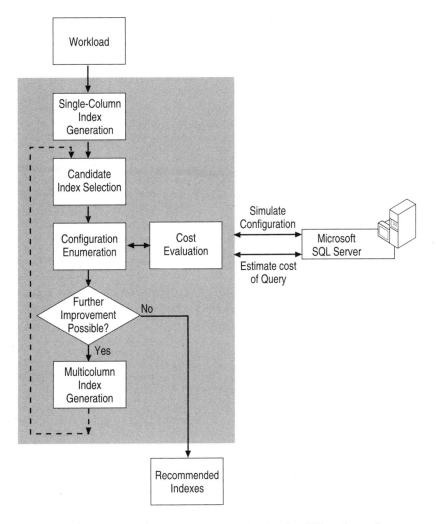

During the course of its execution, the Index Tuning Wizard may have to evaluate the cost of many alternative configurations.

- The Cost Evaluation module exploits the commonality among configurations to reduce the server work needed to estimate expected cost. The basic search module that picks the set of indexes has an iterative structure. The iterative structure arises from the consideration of multicolumn indexes of increasing width until wider indexes exceed the width threshold or fail to provide any additional reduction in the cost of the workload.

- The Candidate Index Selection module examines each query in the workload and helps eliminate from further consideration a large number of indexes from the current set that provide no tangible benefit for any query in the workload. The resulting candidate indexes provide significant improvement potentially to one or more queries in the workload.

- The Configuration Enumeration module uses a search algorithm to intelligently search the space of candidate indexes and pick a configuration with low total cost.

- The Multicolumn Index Generation module determines the initial set of multicolumn indexes to consider in the next iteration, based on indexes chosen by the configuration enumeration module in the current iteration.

In summary, the Index Tuning Wizard works with the query processor to determine the viability of a configuration. The wizard uses workload information and is therefore able to tune the selection of indexes to the expected usage of the system. By taking into account the space of multicolumn indexes, the wizard finds indexes appropriate for index-only access. Finally, the wizard has been designed to be scalable and can handle large schemas as well as large workloads by staging its execution steps appropriately.

Working with the Index Tuning Wizard

Because the index recommendations are made with respect to a workload file, the single most important prerequisite is to pick a workload that is representative of the database system's usage. Although tools such as SQL Server Profiler can help the user record a workload by logging activity on the server over a specified period of time, it is important to ensure that the logged events are representative. Furthermore, the choice of the indexes must be reevaluated periodically. In particular, if the data volume, the data distribution, or the queries against the system change, the Index Tuning Wizard must be executed to ensure that the choice of indexes remains sound.

Another important aspect to consider is that the projected reduction in the cost of the workload estimated by the index selection tool is based on statistical summary of data. Therefore, the actual decrease or increase in cost can diverge from the estimation. It is advisable to reexecute the workload with the new index configuration to verify the projected improvement before the index configuration update is applied to production servers.

Additional Tips

The following questions and answers provide additional tips for working with the Index Tuning Wizard.

Q: Why does the Index Tuning Wizard take so long to complete index recommendations?

A: You can reduce the execution time of the Index Tuning Wizard in several ways. First, make sure that **Perform Thorough Analysis** in the **Select Server and Database** dialog box is not selected. Next, consider tuning only a subset of the tables in the database. Finally, reduce the size of the workload file that you are using to significantly speed up the execution of the Index Tuning Wizard.

Q: I ran SQL Server Query Analyzer and want to accept the recommendations. How can I schedule the actual creation of indexes to occur at a later time?

A: You can save the script generated by SQL Server Query Analyzer and schedule that task at a convenient time.

Q: How can I determine the indexes that will be dropped if I accept the recommendations?

A: Select Save script file in the **Schedule Index Update Job** dialog box instead of applying the proposed changes immediately. By examining the script file, you can determine the indexes that will be dropped if you decide to accept the recommendations. You can edit the script to customize the recommendations if you want.

Q: An error occurred when I invoked **Perform Index Analysis** from SQL Server Query Analyzer on a query buffer consisting of multiple valid Transact-SQL statements. How do I avoid this?

A: Make sure that the query buffer consists purely of a consecutive set of Transact-SQL statements separated by blank lines. In particular, there should be no GO commands separating the Transact-SQL statements.

Q: Why do SQL Server Query Analyzer and the Index Tuning Wizard give different recommendations for the same query?

A: SQL Server Query Analyzer does not consider the option of building a clustered index. The Index Tuning Wizard may consider building a clustered index if none already exists. Therefore, the recommendations from the two tools may differ even for the same query.

P A R T   5

Integration

Part 5 addresses the integration of Microsoft Proxy Server with SQL Server for
the purpose of replication.

C H A P T E R   8

Configuring Proxy Server for Replication Across the Internet

Replication is an important and powerful technology for distributing data and stored procedures across an enterprise. The replication technology in Microsoft SQL Server allows you to make copies of data, move those copies to different locations, and synchronize the data automatically so that all copies have the same data values. Replication can be implemented between databases on the same server or between different servers connected by LANs, WANs, or the Internet.

By combining Microsoft SQL Server with Microsoft Proxy Server, you can replicate data over the Internet without compromising the security of your database. The steps involved in implementing replication over the Internet are configuring the network topology, understanding the security methodology, configuring Microsoft Proxy Server, and configuring SQL Server 7.0 for replication.

Configuring Network Topology

Configuring the network topology is the first step in defining how SQL Server and Microsoft Proxy Server will work together. As shown in the following illustration, Microsoft Proxy Server provides a gateway between the Internet and the internal network, which includes the server running SQL Server 7.0. The server running SQL Server is configured to be both a Publisher and a Distributor. A second server running SQL Server 7.0 and accessible on the Internet is configured as a pull Subscriber.

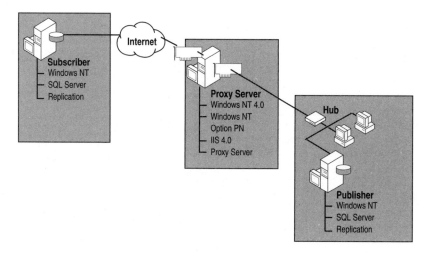

The software requirements for the proxy server are:

- Microsoft Windows NT 4.0 with Service Pack 4
- Microsoft Windows NT 4.0 Option Pack
- Microsoft Internet Information Services 4.0 (IIS)
- Microsoft Proxy Server 2.0 (MSP)

The software requirements for the server running SQL Server are:

- Microsoft Windows NT Server 4.0 with Service Pack 4
- Microsoft Internet Explorer 4.01 Service Pack 1
- Microsoft SQL Server 7.0

The proxy server is configured as a multihomed server to prevent unauthorized users on the Internet from accessing the internal server running SQL Server.

A multihomed server is created by using two network interface cards (NICs). The first NIC, called the external proxy interface, isolates the Internet traffic from the internal network. The internal network is accessed through the second NIC, called the internal proxy interface.

This special Internet configuration does not affect the basic security properties of SQL Server. Users with appropriate permissions on the internal network can access data on SQL Server. Users on the Internet with appropriate permissions to SQL Server must have a valid account on the Proxy Server and be authenticated prior to gaining access to any data on SQL Server.

Using Subnets

Do not specify a default gateway for the internal subnets of either the server running SQL Server or the proxy server. The default gateway of the external interface must point to its respective router's IP address.

Security Overview

Security considerations are an important part of the design and implementation of your distributed application. Because replication applies data changes from one server to many others across the network, understanding the layers of network security is essential.

The decentralized availability of replicated data increases the complexity of managing or restricting access to that data. Microsoft SQL Server replication uses a combination of security mechanisms to protect the data and business logic in your application.

One way to consider security requirements is to view the requirements as different layers of access. Each lower layer must work properly before any successive layer is added. Each successive layer is dependent on the proper operation of any preceding layer. These are the four layers of security to configure:

- Windows NT user accounts
- Proxy Server security
- SQL Server Agent account access
- SQL Server replication account security

Windows NT User Accounts

The first step in replicating data over the Internet is to establish a connection between the Subscriber and the proxy server. This process requires that Windows NT user accounts be configured on each computer. These accounts should differ from those used to log on to the Windows NT Server or to start SQL Server; otherwise, users might gain administrative access to the Windows NT Server or to SQL Server.

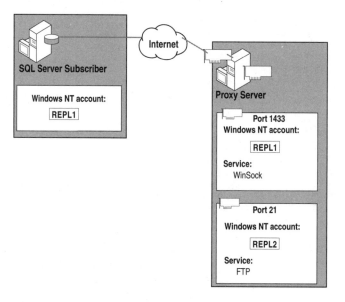

Windows NT Subscriber Account

You must set up a Windows NT user account to start SQL Server Agent. If your organization uses SQL Server Agent services, such as alerts and SQL Mail, and has not established a separate account for SQL Server Agent, the new account must be configured with the minimum access rights required by these services.

Windows NT Proxy Server Accounts

The SQL Server Agent account on the Subscriber must be configured as a user account on the proxy server. This account is entered in the WinSock service on the proxy server to authenticate the Subscriber's request for a connection. You either can use the same account or create a new account for FTP service authentication of the Subscriber. If you are creating separate accounts, the WinSock Proxy user account does not need any special access rights to the proxy server. The FTP user account must have read permission granted so the Subscriber can retrieve data from the snapshot folder.

Proxy Server Security

After the user accounts have been configured, they must be entered into the appropriate services on the proxy server. Microsoft Proxy Server provides a line of defense against unauthorized connections to the internal network. The Distribution Agent or Merge Agent on the Subscriber uses the user account information in the SQL Server Agent account profile to gain access to the FTP and WinSock proxy services on the proxy server. If you have configured a separate user account for the FTP service on the proxy server, the Distribution Agent or Merge Agent accesses the **MSsubscription_properties** table in the Subscription database to retrieve the FTP user account name and password.

When authentication is completed, the Subscriber gains access to SQL Server on port 1433 configured in the WinSock Proxy service. A logon to SQL Server is not established at this point. When the initial connection is made, only port 1433 is active. No access is granted to the FTP port 21. The Distributor server must validate the Subscriber and the subscription as well as identify the type of replication requested. Only then is a connection made to the FTP port.

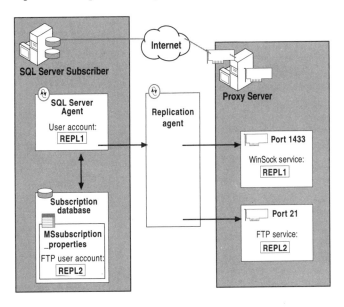

Configuring SQL Server Agent Account Access

After proxy server security has been established, access to all the servers required for replication has been gained. Permission has been granted to port 1433, which allows the Subscriber to initiate a direct connection to SQL Server. Using WinSock port 1433, the Subscriber establishes a connection to the Distributor server for transaction replication and to both the Distributor and Publisher servers for merge replication. You must ensure that a user account has been configured to allow the Subscriber to log in to the Publication database. This user account should not be granted any permissions, but is required for the replication process to work properly. If you are running separate Publisher and Distributor servers, you must configure a logon account on each server.

SQL Server Replication Login Account

For pull subscriptions, replication requires that the Publisher server be registered on the Subscriber. The registration process requires a username and password to gain access to the SQL Server database on the Publisher server. The ability to register the Publisher server on the Subscriber means that you have established a communications link at the Windows NT level and at the SQL Server level. If you are not able to register the Publisher on the Subscriber, you must check each user account to ensure they have been granted permission to access Windows NT and SQL Server. For more information about registering SQL Server, see SQL Server Books Online.

An existing Windows NT or SQL Server login account must be used to register the Publisher server on the Subscriber. This account does not need to be granted special access rights on SQL Server except to enter the Publication database. Access rights can be as a guest or by explicitly adding this user to the database. This account must also be included in the Publication Access List (PAL) of each publication you want to grant subscription permission to the Subscriber.

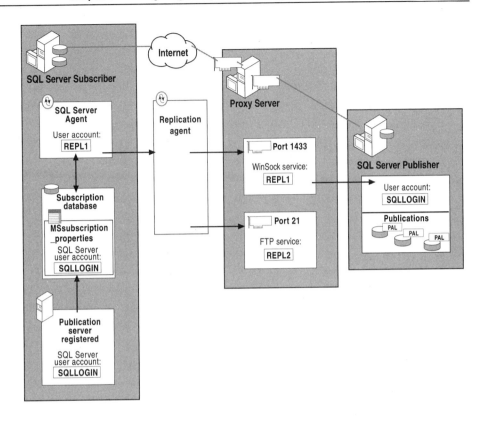

Publication Access

This is the final security check prior to exposing data. The login used by the Replication Agent is validated against the PAL of each publication it tries to access. If the Subscriber's login is not found in the PAL, access is denied. Using separate logins for different Subscribers in the PAL can help limit access to data in the publication.

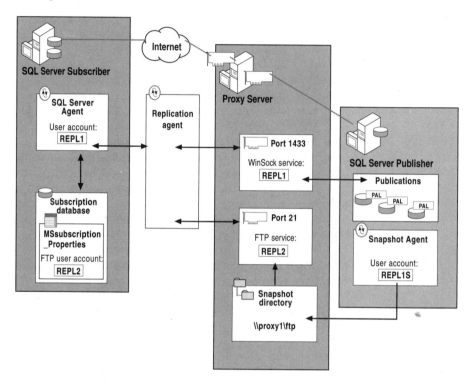

Configuring Proxy Server

Microsoft SQL Server uses two methods of access for replicated data: FTP and ODBC. Both services are required for replication over the Internet. Microsoft Proxy Server must be configured correctly to establish a link through ODBC and then to transfer data. Before configuring SQL Server replication, you must test the proxy server by connecting to it and then transferring data to and from it. There are four key steps to configuring Microsoft Proxy Server:

1. Disable IP forwarding.

2. Configure the FTP service.

3. Configure the WinSock Proxy service.

4. Validate the Microsoft Proxy Server configuration.

Disabling IP Forwarding

The Internet provides a cost-effective way to publish and collect (pull/subscribe) data over long distances, but it also can make the internal network and data vulnerable. To protect the network, disable listening on inbound service ports and disable IP forwarding. When IP forwarding is disabled, only your Network Operations–assigned IP address is visible to users on the Internet, reducing the potential for unauthorized intrusion.

The proxy server can block external ranges of IP addresses. When IP forwarding is disabled, Internet users cannot initiate connections unless an application service port is specifically enabled.

▶ **To disable IP forwarding**

1. In Control Panel, double-click Network.

2. Click the **Protocols** tab.

3. Select **TCP/IP**, and then click **Properties**.

4. In the **Microsoft TCP/IP Properties** dialog box, click **Routing**.

5. Verify that the **Enable IP Forwarding** check box is cleared.

In large Windows NT environments, you can provide maximum security by establishing a separate domain for your proxy server with a single one-way trust relationship to another domain where SQL Server will be located on your private network. For configuration information, see your Windows NT documentation.

Configuring the FTP Service

SQL Server replication uses FTP to transfer initial data and schema from one location to another over the Internet. The Snapshot Agent places in the snapshot folder data that is retrieved by the Merge Agent or Distribution Agent on the Subscriber.

When SQL Server replication transmits data over the Internet, it uses the FTP directory on the proxy server as the snapshot folder. An ODBC connection to the Distributor is first established to obtain the location of the snapshot folder. The Merge Agent on the Subscriber then initiates an FTP connection to the proxy server and retrieves any information stored in the snapshot folder.

To configure the FTP service on the proxy server, set the FTP home directory to the drop location in which SQL Server data is placed for replication. Stop and restart the FTP service for the changes to take effect.

▶ **To configure the FTP Service**

1. On the **Start** menu, point to **Programs/Microsoft Proxy Server**, and then click **Microsoft Management Console**.

2. Expand **Internet Information Service** and expand the computer name.

3. Right-click **Default FTP Site**.

4. Point to **New**, and then click **site** to start the New FTP Site Wizard.

5. Enter the following information when requested:

FTP Site Description	FTP Replication Site
Select the IP Address to use for this FTP Site	Enter the IP address for this site.
TCP Port this FTP Site should use	21
Enter the Path for your home directory	For example, C:\repldata\ftp
What access permissions do you want to set for the home directory	Allow Read Access

To complete the configuration of the FTP site, alter the default security settings. To increase security, turn off Anonymous Access or guest account access. A user account with appropriate permission should be defined for SQL Server Agent to gain access to all Windows NT servers. This same account is used to gain access to FTP and WinSock Services. For more information about SQL Server Agent account access, see "Configuring SQL Server Agent Account Access" earlier in this chapter.

▶ **To control FTP access through Proxy Server**

1. On the **Start** menu, point to **Programs/Microsoft Proxy Server**, and then click **Microsoft Management Console**.

2. Expand **Internet Information Service** and expand the computer name.

3. Right-click the FTP site defined for replication, and then select **Properties**.

4. In the *site name* **Properties** dialog box, click the **Security Accounts** tab, and then clear the **Allow Anonymous Access** check box.

5. Under **FTP Site Operators**, grant operator privileges only to the User Accounts that require access to this FTP site. In this case it will be the same account used for SQL Server Agent on the Subscriber.

6. In the **Internet Service Manager** dialog box, click **Yes** to continue.

7. Click the **FTP Site** tab.

8. Under **Connections**, select **Limited To**, and then enter a maximum number of replication connections.

9. Under the **Directory Security** tab, in the **By default, all computers will be:** dialog box, click **Denied Access**.

> **Note** This excludes any FTP Site Operator account entered in step 5 unless the IP address entered here is a static IP address for that account.

10. Click **Add**, and then enter the IP addresses for all replication servers that will be communicating to this server.

Configuring the WinSock Proxy Service

Before data can be transferred, the Subscriber must initialize an ODBC connection by using the WinSock Proxy service.

The WinSock Proxy service requires a protocol definition to identify valid network protocols when access control is enabled. The WinSock Proxy service uses the defined protocols to determine which Windows Sockets applications can be used to access the Internet.

If access control is enabled, the Replication Agent on the Subscriber uses the user account configured for the SQL Server Agent to gain access to system resources. The FTP user account can also be used by the WinSock Proxy for server connections.

▶ **To configure a protocol definition for WinSock Proxy to SQL Server**

1. On the **Start** menu, point to **Programs/Microsoft Proxy Server**, and then click **Microsoft Management Console**.

2. Expand **Internet Information Service** and expand the server running Proxy Server.

3. Right-click WinSock Proxy service and select **Properties**.

4. In the **WinSock Proxy Service Properties For** *computername* dialog box, click **Protocols**, and then click **Add**.

5. In the **Protocol name** text box, enter a name to identify the server on which the replication Distributor is running.

> **Note** The protocol name has no significance. It is a mnemonic used to identify the socket and the accounts or servers that will be granted access.

6. At **Initial Connection**, enter 1433 in the **Port** text box.

7. Under **Type** select **TCP**, and under **Direction** select **Inbound**.

▶ **To configure the WinSock Proxy service permissions**

1. On the **Start** menu, point to **Programs/Microsoft Proxy Server**, and then click **Microsoft Management Console**.

2. Expand **Internet Information Service** and expand the computer name.

3. Right-click WinSock Proxy service and select **Properties**.

4. In the **WinSock Proxy Service Properties For** *computername* dialog box, click the **Permissions** tab.

5. In the **Protocol** list, select the *Protocol* name defined when you configured a protocol definition.

6. Click **Edit**, and then in the *protocol name* **Permissions** dialog box, click **Add**.

7. In the **Add Users Groups** dialog box, select the user account that will provide access to the replication server. This account is the same User Account used for the FTP Service and must configured for the SQL Server Agent account on the Subscriber with appropriate permissions to gain access.

Validating the Proxy Server Configuration

After all servers have been configured, it is recommended that you establish a connection and attempt to transfer data. Using SQL Server Agent user account, test the connection thoroughly. If the servers cannot connect, replication will not function properly.

Configuring SQL Server

To configure Internet replication, key parameters must be set on both the Publisher and Subscriber. SQL Server must be configured to interoperate with the FTP and WinSock Proxy services on the proxy server. There are four key steps to configuring SQL Server replication:

1. Configure SQL Server to work with Microsoft Proxy Server.

2. Configure SQL Server to work with the FTP service on the proxy server.

3. Configure a SQL Server Subscriber for the Internet.

4. Verify SQL Server is working with Microsoft Proxy Server.

Configuring SQL Server to Work with Proxy Server

After Microsoft Proxy Server has been installed on the proxy server, you must configure the server running SQL Server to be a proxy client. This requires binding SQL Server to a WinSock port to allow communication over the Internet.

Binding a WinSock Port for Data Communications

Configuring SQL Server to work with Microsoft Proxy Server requires changes to the file \Mssql7\Binn\Wspcfg.ini on the server running SQL Server. If the file does not exist, create it by using Notepad. The file must contain these entries:

```
[sqlservr]
ServerBindTcpPorts=1433
Persistent=1
KillOldSession=1
```

SQL Server listens on service port 1433. When a user or anonymous subscriber is authenticated by SQL Server, a session is established between the user or anonymous subscriber and SQL Server using service port 1433.

Configuring SQL Server as a Proxy Client

When the server running Microsoft Proxy Server is set up, it creates a share called **mspclnt** that points to the directory C:\Msp\Clients. You must connect to this share and run the proxy client configuration utility (**mpclnt**) to establish SQL Server as a proxy client. After setup is complete, SQL Server is an internal client to the proxy server.

▶   **To run the Proxy Client configuration utility**

1. From the server running SQL Server, click **Start**, and then click **Run**.

2. Under **Open** type: ***servername*\mspclnt**, and run the Proxy Server client setup program.

3. When setup is complete, restart the SQL Server server for the changes to take effect.

Configuring SQL Server to Work with the FTP Service

Before you can publish articles over the Internet, the Publisher and Distributor must be enabled to listen on either the TCP/IP or the Multiprotocol network protocol. Microsoft SQL Server uses TCP/IP Sockets or Multiprotocol Net-Libraries over TCP/IP to establish the initial ODBC connection between the Distributor on one side of the Internet and the Subscriber on the other. TCP/IP Sockets Net-Library is enabled during the default SQL Server setup, but may not be enabled if you did a custom installation.

▶ **To enable access control for SQL Server**

1. On the **Start** menu, click **Programs/MS SQL Server 7.0**, and then click **Client Network Utility**.

2. In the **SQL Server Client Network Utility** dialog box, on the **General** tab, click **TCP/IP** in the list.

3. Click **Add**.

4. At **Server alias**, enter the *protocol name* defined for the WinSock Proxy Service above.

Note There is no requirement to use the same name for the Server Alias and the Protocol Name created in WinSock Proxy.

---

5. At **Network libraries**, ensure that the **TCP/IP** option is selected.

6. At **Connection parameters**, ensure that port 1433 appears.

SQL Server must be informed of the FTP home directory location on the proxy server. The snapshot folder (by default \Mssql7\Repldata\Ftp) is redirected to the FTP home directory on the proxy server, enabling data to be transferred to the Subscriber. A new snapshot folder is set up during the FTP service configuration.

▶ **To set the FTP home directory**

1. On the **Start** menu, point to **Programs/Microsoft SQL Server 7.0**, and then click **Enterprise Manager**.

2. Expand **SQL Server Group**, and then click the Publication Server.

3. On the **Tools** menu, choose **Wizards**.

4. In the **Select Wizard** dialog box, expand **Replication**.

5. Click **Configure Publishing and Distribution Wizard**.

6. Click the **Publishers** tab.

7. Double click the Publishing server that will be placing files into the snapshot folder.

8. Enter the UNC path name ***ProxyServerName*\\Repldata\\ftp**, and then click **By impersonating the SQL Server Agent Account on *PublishingServername* (Trusted connection)**.

Configuring a SQL Server Subscriber for the Internet

To ensure the Subscriber can access information on the Publisher by using Microsoft Proxy Server, a pull subscription must be configured with information that helps it resolve the address of the Publisher.

Note For a Subscriber to subscribe to a Publication over the Internet, the Publication on the Publisher must have the **Allow Snapshots to be downloaded using FTP** option enabled.

▶ **To configure a pull subscription**

1. In SQL Server Enterprise Manager, click the subscribing server.

2. On the **Tools** menu, point to **Replication**, and then click **Pull Subscriptions to *SubscriptionServerName*.**

3. Click **Pull New Subscription**.

   The Pull Subscription Wizard starts.

4. When the Choose Publication screen appears, click the publishing server. If the publishing server does not appear in the list, click the **Register Server** button and register the Publisher.

5. At **Specify Synchronization Agent Login**, enter an account with appropriate security settings.

6. At **Choose Destination Database**, select an existing database in the list or click **New Database** to configure a new Subscription database.

7. At **Initialize Subscription**, select **Yes, initialize schema and data at the Subscriber**.

8. If the **Snapshot Delivery** option appears, select **Yes, use FTP to copy the Snapshot files**.

9. At **Set Distribution Agent Schedule**, select an appropriate scheduling scheme.

10. At **Allow Anonymous Subscriptions**, select **Yes, make the Subscriptions anonymous**.

11. Continue through the remaining sections of the wizard, and then click **Finish**.

12. When the **Pull Subscriptions to** *SubscriptionServerName* dialog box appears, click **Properties**.

13. When the **Pull Subscription Properties -** *PublisherName:databasename:replicationtype* dialog box appears, click **Snapshot Delivery**.

14. Ensure the **Use File Transfer Protocol (FTP)** check box is selected.

15. At **FTP parameters** for **Server address of the Distributor**, enter the IP address of the NIC card that connects to the Internet on the Proxy Server used to interface with the Publisher.

16. At **Port** enter the FTP port number of the Publisher's Proxy Server connection (usually port 21).

17. At **Login**, enter an account that has been configured with appropriate security clearance.

18. At **Password** enter the password configured for this account.

19. Click **OK**, and then click **Close**.

Verifying SQL Server is Working with Proxy Server

To verify that a connection to Proxy Server has been established through port 1433, check the WinSock Proxy service on the proxy server. You should see a session in Proxy Server for the user account that SQL Server is running under.

The user account may not appear immediately. Allow SQL Server a few moments and click the **Refresh** button periodically. If the account for SQL Server Agent does not appear in the list, stop and restart SQL Server. SQL Server is a client to the proxy server and the service account in which SQL Server was configured to run should appear in the list.

Note You must use a fully qualified name; computer accounts will not work.

▶ **To verify a connection**

1. On the **Start** menu, point to **Programs/Microsoft Proxy Server**, and then click **Microsoft Management Console**.

2. Expand **Internet Information Service** and expand the server running Proxy Server.

3. Click **WinSock Proxy Service**, and then select **Properties**.

4. On the **Services** tab, click **Current Sessions**.

5. Click **WinSock Proxy service**.

Alternatively, you can verify your IP connection and port information on any of the computers by using the **netstat** command. The following is output from the SQL Server server using **netstat –a** command. This lists both client- and server-side connections as well as their status and port numbers. Use **netstat** without any options to client sessions only. If you want to display only ports 1433 and 21, use **netstat –an** to display TCP connections only.

You may notice that several ports other than 1433 are listed. Keep in mind that 1433 is configured as the incoming port. The outgoing port is dynamic and Proxy Server assigns it when a connection is established. The dynamic port ranges between 1025 and 5000.

```
Active Connections

  Proto  Local Address          Foreign Address      State
  TCP    SQLReplServer:1026      0.0.0.0:0            LISTENING
  TCP    SQLReplServer:1031      0.0.0.0:0            LISTENING
  TCP    SQLReplServer:1033      0.0.0.0:0            LISTENING
  TCP    SQLReplServer:ftp       0.0.0.0:0            LISTENING
  TCP    SQLReplServer:1058      0.0.0.0:0            LISTENING
  TCP    SQLReplServer:1059      0.0.0.0:0            LISTENING
  TCP    SQLReplServer:135       0.0.0.0:0            LISTENING
  TCP    SQLReplServer:135       0.0.0.0:0            LISTENING
  TCP    SQLReplServer:1433      0.0.0.0:0            LISTENING
  TCP    SQLReplServer:1025      0.0.0.0:0            LISTENING
  TCP    SQLReplServer:1025      localhost:1026       ESTABLISHED
  TCP    SQLReplServer:1026      localhost:1025       ESTABLISHED
  TCP    SQLReplServer:1029      0.0.0.0:0            LISTENING
  TCP    SQLReplServer:1030      0.0.0.0:0            LISTENING
  TCP    SQLReplServer:1032      0.0.0.0:0            LISTENING
  TCP    SQLReplServer:1056      0.0.0.0:0            LISTENING
  TCP    SQLReplServer:1057      0.0.0.0:0            LISTENING
  TCP    SQLReplServer:137       0.0.0.0:0            LISTENING
  TCP    SQLReplServer:138       0.0.0.0:0            LISTENING
  TCP    SQLReplServer:nbsession 0.0.0.0:0            LISTENING
  UDP    SQLReplServer:1059      *:*
  UDP    SQLReplServer:1088      *:*
  UDP    SQLReplServer:135       *:*
  UDP    SQLReplServer:nbname    *:*
  UDP    SQLReplServer:nbdatagram *:*
```

P A R T   6

Tools and Utilities

Part 6 provides an overview of the tools available on the *Microsoft BackOffice 4.5 Resource Kit* CD-ROM. Most tools are available for Intel platforms only and are available only in English.

Many of these tools were developed internally at Microsoft. These tools are provided "as is," without warranty of any kind. Although every effort has been made to test the utilities provided with the *Microsoft BackOffice 4.5 Resource Kit*, these programs are to be used at your own risk. Microsoft disclaims any implied warranty of merchantability and/or fitness for a particular purpose. Use of these tools is governed by the terms specified in the End-User License Agreement that accompanies such tools.

These tools have not been localized. Using these tools with a version of Microsoft SQL Server in a language other than U.S. English may produce unpredictable results.

C H A P T E R   9

Tools and Utilities

The tools and utilities described in this chapter can help you manage and troubleshoot your databases and integrate SQL Server with other Microsoft products.

Detailed information about the tools can be found on the CD-ROM that accompanies *Microsoft BackOffice Server 4.5 Resource Kit.*

You can install the entire set of tools by running the Setup program for the BackOffice resource kit. You can install individual tools by running Setup.exe from the *platform*\sql*tool_name* subdirectory on the CD-ROM:

- *platform* = **i386** (for *x*86-based computers) or **alpha** (for alpha-based computers)
- *tool_name* = the name of the tool

The following is a list of the tools and utilities, with *tool_name* in parentheses.

Data Simulator (**DataSim**)
Generates simulated data based on random sampling of an existing database.

Data Sizer (**DataSizer**)
Approximates the sizes of database tables, with and without clustered indexes.

Database Generator (**Dbgen**)
An ODBC-based tool that helps users fill tables in a database. The generated data conforms to the distribution types chosen by the user for each column.

Database Library Gateway (**DBLib Gateway**)
Allows SQL Server 7.0 to connect to any SQL Server 6.*x* or SQL Server 4.*x* gateway.

Deadlock Demonstration (**DeadlockDemo**)
Demonstrates a deadlock and how to resolve it in Transact-SQL.

Log Shipping (**Log Shipping**)
Provides a foundation for building customized "warm-backup" solutions.

Quick Reference to Transact-SQL (**Quick Reference to TSQL**)
Documents which Transact-SQL statements are ANSI standard.

Service Tools (**Service Tools**)
Two command-prompt tools. One checks service status from within batch files; the other stops and starts SQL Server services like MSSQLServer and SQLServerAgent from a remote computer.

SQL Execution Timer XP (**SQL Execution Timer**)
An extended stored procedure that is an execution timer.

SQL Hard Disk Test Utility (**Sqlhdtst**)
Tests a hard drive for functionality and errors.

SQL Load Simulator (**SqlLS**)
Provides the ability to simulate a large number of connections to SQL Server from a single workstation.

SQL Namespace Browser (**SQL Namespace Browser**)
Is a graphical browser for SQL Namespace objects.

SQL Synchronization Tools (**SQL Synchronization Tools**)
Is a command-prompt utility that synchronizes batch files using named events.

Trace Analyzer Application (**TraceAnalyzerApp**)
Is an OLAP trace analyzer.

Trace Reader (**TraceReader**)
Is a trace reader for COM objects.

Trace Scripts (**TraceScripts**)
Creates traces using the SQL Server trace extended stored procedures.

VB to Transact-SQL Converter (**Vbtosql**)
Changes the formatting of a query so that it fits conveniently in a Visual Basic application.

P A R T   7

Troubleshooting

Part 7 provides solutions and preventative strategies for common problems encountered in the SQL Server environment.

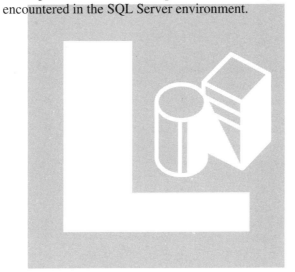

C H A P T E R   1 0

Troubleshooting

This chapter provides information about troubleshooting and resolving the most common errors you may encounter while using Microsoft SQL Server. If you encounter a problem while using SQL Server, check the SQL Server error log for entries that might help identify the cause. For more information, see SQL Server Books Online.

Isolating Connection Problems

When a DB-Library application has problems connecting to Microsoft SQL Server, there might be a problem with SQL Server, the network, or both. Regardless of which network you are running on, there are several items that you can check to isolate the problem. Check that:

- For servers running Microsoft Windows NT, the local connection to SQL Server over Named Pipes is available. You can test a local Named Pipes connection by using **osql** with no *servername* argument. If you cannot make a local connection using Named Pipes, either you are using an invalid login or there is a problem with SQL Server.

  For servers running Microsoft Windows 95 or Windows 98 operating systems, the local connection to SQL Server uses the Shared Memory Net-Library.

- The network components match the requirements specified in SQL Server Books Online.

- The default client Net-Library is appropriate for your network. You can determine and, if necessary, change the default client Net-Library by using SQL Server Client Network Utility in the Microsoft SQL Server program group.

- The network connection information on the server is appropriate for your network (if you are running SQL Server and listening on other interprocess communication (IPC) mechanisms in addition to Named Pipes). You can determine and, if necessary, change which networks SQL Server is listening on using SQL Server Network Utility in the Microsoft SQL Server program group.

- The network connection between the client workstation and the server is established. (The procedures for testing network connections for all supported networks are provided in the following sections.) If you test the network connection and determine that it is not open, check that:

  - The hardware connection is not disabled due to loose connectors or plugs.

  - The network software is installed and running on both the client workstation and the server.

Orphaned Sessions

A client may have its connection abruptly severed from the server, and as a result, the client process may be unable to tell the network to close the connection properly. This may occur for many reasons, including power failures on the client. Microsoft SQL Server does not proactively probe the status of a client connection. Instead, it relies on Microsoft Windows NT to notify it when a connection needs to be terminated or closed. Windows NT monitors connections and continues to report them as active to SQL Server for the duration of the KeepAliveTime for TCP/IP or SessionKeepAlive for NetBios, which affects Named Pipes clients. SQL Server continues to keep locks owned by the client active until they are killed, or until the connection is terminated or closed by Windows NT.

The following questions and answers provide frequently requested information on orphaned sessions.

Q: What is an orphaned session?

A: An orphaned session is a session that remains open on the server side after the client has disconnected.

Do not confuse orphaned sessions with orphaned users. Orphaned users are created when a database is backed up and restored to another system that does not have a corresponding user account configured. For more information about orphaned users, see SQL Server Books Online.

Q: When do orphaned sessions occur?

A: Orphaned sessions occur when the client is unable to free network connections it is holding when it terminates.

If the client terminates cleanly, Windows NT closes the connection and notifies SQL Server. If SQL Server is processing a client command, it will detect the closed connection when it ends the session. Client applications that crash or have their processes killed (for example, from Task Manager), are cleaned up immediately by Windows NT, rarely resulting in an orphaned session.

Orphaned sessions often are caused by a client computer losing power unexpectedly or being shut down improperly. Orphaned sessions can also occur due to a "hung" application that never completely terminates, resulting in a dead connection. Windows NT will not know that the connection is dead and will continue to report the action as active to SQL Server. SQL Server, in turn, keeps the session open and continues to wait for a command from the client.

Q: What problems can orphaned sessions cause?

A: Open sessions take up one of the SQL Server network connections. The maximum number of connections is limited by the number of server CALs; therefore, orphaned sessions may prevent other clients from connecting.

Typically, a more important issue is that open sessions use server resources, and may have open cursors, temporary tables, or locks. These locks can block other connections from performing useful work, and can sometimes be the result of a major backlog of locks. In severe cases, it can appear that SQL Server has stopped working.

Q: How can I tell if an orphaned session exists and what problems it might be causing?

A: **sysprocesses** (or stored procedures, such as **sp_who**) reports information on existing server sessions. Possible orphaned sessions can be identified if the status of a process is AWAITING COMMAND and the interval of time, found by subtracting **last_batch** from GETDATE(), is longer than usual for the process. If the session hostname is known to be down, it is orphaned.

Q: How do I resolve orphaned sessions?

Windows NT checks inactive sessions periodically to ensure they are active. If a session does not respond, it is closed and SQL Server is notified. The frequency of the checking depends on the network protocol and registry settings. However, by default, Windows NT performs a check only every one or two hours, depending on the protocol used. These configuration settings can be changed in the registry.

To close an orphaned SQL Server session, use the KILL command. All resources held by the session are then released.

If orphaned sessions become a problem, registry settings can be changed on Windows NT to increase the frequency at which clients are checked to verify they are active.

Warning Do not change these settings on computers running Microsoft Windows 95 or Windows 98 operating systems.

Consider the effect changing these settings may have on other applications on your system, in particular, applications with Internet connectivity, such as Microsoft Internet Information Services (IIS) or Microsoft Internet Explorer. In addition, consider the effects of using connections that are charged on a per-packet basis.

Caution Editing the registry is not recommended; inappropriate or incorrect changes can cause serious configuration problems for your system. Only experienced users should use the Registry Editor. For more information, see your Windows NT documentation.

The registry entries can be altered from HKEY_LOCAL_MACHINE by double-clicking SYSTEM, expanding CurrentControlSet, and then clicking Services.

KeepAliveTime for TCP/IP

    Key: Tcpip\Parameters

    Value Type: REG_DWORD - Time in milliseconds

    Valid Range: 1 - 0xFFFFFFFF

    Default: 7,200,000 (two hours)

    Description: The parameter controls how often TCP attempts to verify that an idle connection is still intact by sending a keep alive packet. If the remote system is still reachable and functioning, it will acknowledge the keep alive transmission. Keep alive packets are not sent by default; this feature may be enabled on a connection by an application.

SessionKeepAlive for Named Pipes
Key: Netbt\Parameters

Value Type: REG_DWORD - Time in milliseconds

Valid Range: 60,000 - 0xFFFFFFFF

Default: 3,600,000 (1 hour)

Description: This value determines the time interval between keep alive transmissions on a session. Setting the value to 0xFFFFFFFF disables keep alives.

Note Do not increase the ping frequency to less than 1 minute, as network I/O and CPU usage for pings may become excessive.

Named Pipes Client Connections

The following procedure describes how to test a network connection when using Named Pipes as the IPC mechanism.

▶ **To test a Named Pipes connection**

- At the operating system command prompt on the client workstation, type:

  net view *servername*

When using **net view**, *servername* is the name of the server to which you want to connect.

For example, to check the connection between a Named Pipes client and a server named \\SEATTLE1, type the following on the client:

```
net view \\SEATTLE1
```

If the connection is open, the output looks something like this:

```
Shared resources at \\SEATTLE1
SQL Server

Sharename       Type            Used as  Comment
---------------------------------------------------------
PUBLIC          Disk                     Public Files

The command completed successfully.
```

▶   **To verify connection to a server's named pipe**

- From a command prompt, type:

  net use *servername***\IPC$**

When using **net use**, *servername* is the server to which you want to connect.

For example:

```
net use \\SEATTLE1\IPC$

The command completed successfully
```

If the connection between the client workstation and the server is open but you still cannot connect to Microsoft SQL Server, test the network and local Named Pipes using the **makepipe** and **readpipe** utilities.

Two utilities included with SQL Server are designed to help test the integrity of network Named Pipes. The **makepipe** and **readpipe** utilities are installed during installation of both the client and server components. There are different versions of these utilities for the different operating systems on which they run: **makepipe** runs on Microsoft Windows NT; **readpipe** runs on Windows NT, Microsoft Windows, and MS-DOS. Be sure to use the correct version for the operating system that you are testing. (The version that runs on Windows is named **readpipe**. If the SQL Server tools are installed, **readpipe** is located in the \Msqql7\Binn directory; no icon is created for it.)

▶   **To test the integrity of the network Named Pipe services**

1. At the operating system command prompt on the server, type:

   makepipe

   The **makepipe** utility returns the following information:

   ```
   Making PIPE:\pipe\abc
   read to write delay (seconds):0
   Waiting for Client to Connect...
   ```

   SQL Server is waiting for a client to connect.

2. At the operating system command prompt on the client workstation, type:

   readpipe /S*server_name* **/D***string*

   When using **readpipe**, *server_name* is the network server name of the SQL Server on which **makepipe** was started and *string* is a test character string. If the string contains spaces, it must be enclosed in double quotation marks. There are no spaces between **/S** and the server name, and no spaces between **/D** and the string.

For example, to connect to a SQL Server installation named MYSERVER, type one of the following:

```
readpipe /Smyserver /Dhello
readpipe /Smyserver /D"hello there"
readpipe /Smyserver /D'hello there'
```

The strings specified in the first two **readpipe** statements are treated identically.

If a network Named Pipes connection can be established, the client workstation returns the following information to each of the commands above, respectively:

```
SvrName:\\myserver
PIPE    :\\myserver\pipe\abc
DATA    :hello
Data Sent: 1 : hello
Data Read: 1 : hello

SvrName:\\myserver
PIPE    :\\myserver\pipe\abc
DATA    :hello there
Data Sent: 1 :hello there
Data Read: 1 :hello there

SvrName:\\myserver
PIPE    :\\myserver\pipe\abc
DATA    :hello
Data Sent: 1 : 'hello
Data Read: 1 : 'hello
```

If a network named pipe connection can be established, the **makepipe** utility returns information similar to this:

```
Waiting for Client to Connect...
Waiting for client to send... 1

Data Read:
hello

Waiting for client to send... 2

Pipe closed

Waiting for Client to Connect...
Waiting for client to send... 1
```

```
Data Read:
hello there

Waiting for client to send...  2

Pipe closed

Waiting for Client to Connect...
Waiting for client to send...  1

Data Read:
'hello

Waiting for client to send...  2
Pipe closed

Waiting for Client to Connect...
```

At this point, SQL Server is waiting for a client to connect. The **readpipe** utility can be run from other workstations.

3. When testing is complete, go to the server where the **makepipe** utility is running and press either CTRL+BREAK or CTRL+C.

If the results are different from those in Step 2, network named pipe services are not available. If you are using Named Pipes as the IPC mechanism, clients cannot connect to SQL Server until a Named Pipe is available. These utilities attempt to open and use a named pipe; they do not stress the named pipe connection.

TCP/IP Sockets Client Connections

The following procedure describes how to test a network connection when using TCP/IP Sockets as the IPC mechanism.

▶   **To test a TCP/IP Sockets connection**

●   At the operating system command prompt on the client workstation, type:

    ping {*ip_address* | *server_name*}

When using **ping**, *ip_address* is the TCP/IP address of the server to which you want to connect and *server_name* is the name of the server to which you want to connect.

For example, to check the connection between a TCP/IP Sockets client workstation and a server at the TCP/IP address 11.1.4.70, type the following on the client workstation:

```
ping 11.1.4.70
```

If the connection is open, the output looks something like this:

```
[1] echo received from 11.1.4.70 with roundtrip < 50 sec
```

This example checks the connection between a TCP/IP Sockets client and a server named SEATTLE1:

```
ping SEATTLE1
```

If the connection is open, the output looks something like this:

```
[1] echo received from SEATTLE1 with roundtrip < 50 sec
```

Troubleshooting SQL Server Setup

SQL Server Setup is designed to be as problem free as possible; however, there may be situations that will interfere with the installation of Microsoft SQL Server. The most common errors are simple to diagnose and resolve. The resolution may involve freeing up disk space, shutting down other applications, or restarting the computer to unlock shared files.

For more information, see SQL Server Books Online.

If the installation fails, the Setup program might remove all installed components.

Before running the Setup program or installing additional SQL Server components, be sure to:

- Shut down all services.

  Use Services in Control Panel to shut down the MSSQLServer and SQLServerAgent services. Shut down the MSSearch service if you installed Full-text Search. Shut down the MSDTC service if you installed MS DTC.

- Check that the **SQL Server Service Manager** icon in the taskbar is closed.

  Any attempt to run the Setup program with the **SQL Server Service Manager** icon present (or any services still running) may cause the setup process to fail.

- Remove the read-only attribute for all ODBC* files. On computers running Microsoft Windows NT these files are located in the \System32 directory. On computers running Microsoft Windows 95 or Windows 98 operating systems, these files are located in the system directory.

  If you cannot remove the read-only attribute on the ODBC* files, SQL Server produces a dialog box that allows you to retry the updating of the ODBC* files.

- Understand that servers running Windows NT require Named Pipes. Cleaning named pipes during SQL Server installation does not prevent installation of named pipes. Because servers running Windows NT require named pipes, there is no way to uninstall Named Pipes on a server running Windows NT.

Setup Troubleshooting: Checklist

1. Read the error message. SQL Server Setup translates most error codes received from the operating system.

2. With the error dialog box showing, open Sqlstp.log in the \Windows or \WinNT directory. Check the last few events in the log to see if any problems occurred before the error message was generated.

3. If this is a custom installation and the component that failed to install properly is the Full-text Search (MSSearch) service, check the Mssearch.log in the \Temp directory to see if any problems occurred.

4. Continue past the error message dialog box. Some error messages are just warnings. The Setup program may still finish successfully.

5. If the Setup program fails, and you cannot diagnose and fix the problem yourself, make a copy of Sqlstp.log and Setup.iss from the \Windows or \WinNT directory and, if you installed Full-text Search, make a copy of the Mssearch.log from the \Temp directory.

Note The Setup program may encounter problems installing MS DTC on computers with multiple network cards or SPX installed. If the Setup program stops responding, check the Sqlstp.log in the \Windows or \WinNT directory to see if MS DTC is being installed. If this is the problem, uninstall one of the network cards or SPX, and then retry the Setup program.

Testing an Installation of SQL Server 7.0

Before a server installation is complete, SQL Server Setup starts and connects to the server multiple times. When the installation is complete, you can test the installation yourself and connect to it locally by running the **osql** utility from the server.

SQL Server Setup Frequently Asked Questions

Here are some of the frequently asked questions regarding SQL Server Setup.

Q: What do I need to do if I have an unsuccessful installation or I find an error in the Setup program?

A: If your installation fails and you are unable to determine the cause, or you find an error in the Setup program, find and save:

- The Sqlstp.log file, located in your \Windows or \WinNT directory.
- The Setup.log files, located in your \Windows or \WinNT directory.
- Any other files left in the target program directory (by default, \Mssql7).
- The Cnfgsvr.out file located in the \Install directory of the target program directory (by default, \Mssql7\Install).
- Any error logs located in the \Mssql7\Log directory.

If the Setup program fails, changes to the operating system are rolled back, including removal of any copied files and removal of changes to the registry.

Q: Why aren't some directories deleted on uninstall? Why does the final uninstall report always report that it cannot remove folders?

A: The UnInstallshield installer removes only what it installs.

Files created after installation is complete, such as **tempdb,** are not part of the installation record and will be unknown to UnInstallshield. Therefore, UnInstallshield is not able to remove these files or their associated directories. Sqlsun.dll, which runs after UnInstallshield is complete, removes files such as **tempdb** and their associated folders. Sqlsun.dll will not remove error logs, trace files, user data, or their associated folders if they are generated in the original directory structure.

Informational Files Created by SQL Server Setup

These informational files are generated to locate any problems during setup:

- The Sqlstp.log file, located in your \Windows or \WinNT directory. For example, C:\WinNT\Sqlstp.log.
- The most recent error log, located in the \Log directory of the target installation directory (by default, \Mssql7). For example, C:\Mssql7\Log\Errorlog.
- The Cnfgsvr.out file, located in the Install directory of the target installation directory (by default, Mssql7). For example, C:\Mssql7\Install\Cnfgsvr.out.

Troubleshooting the SQL Server Upgrade Wizard

The SQL Server Upgrade Wizard is designed to be as problem free as possible; however, there are situations that may interfere with upgrading Microsoft SQL Server version 6.*x* databases to SQL Server 7.0. The most common upgrade error is the failure to create an object in SQL Server 7.0. In many cases, the problem is simple, such as running out of disk space. In any case, the SQL Server Upgrade Wizard creates detailed logs specifying the problem.

Completing the SQL Server Upgrade Wizard

The SQL Server Upgrade Wizard performs a version upgrade using the options you specified. The Microsoft SQL Server version 6.*x* server and data are left intact throughout the version upgrade process.

During the SQL Server Upgrade Wizard process:

- User stored procedures are verified against the contents of **syscomments** for inconsistencies.
- All logins, users, and permissions are validated.

If the SQL Server Upgrade Wizard detects any problems, a dialog box is displayed with this text:

```
One or more warnings have been logged. Please read the next screen
carefully before you begin your upgrade.
```

The **Summary of Warnings** dialog box displays inconsistencies found in the user objects of accounts. Users should not continue until these are resolved. This output file is located in the \Mssql\Upgrade\<SQLServer_date_time> directory. The file name is associated with the database name and ID, "check65-<dbid><dbname>_err.out" (for example, "check65-007mypubs_err.out"). If the user continues without fixing the listed errors, check the relevant files for objects, logins, and invalid permissions.

If stored procedures have been renamed using **sp_rename**, the source stored in **syscomments** must be changed. Drop and re-create the procedure using the new name in the CREATE PROCEDURE syntax.

Upgrade Log Files

Each time you run the SQL Server Upgrade Wizard, a subdirectory is created in the C:\Mssql7\Upgrade directory. The subdirectory name consists of the server name and the current date and time to distinguish multiple runs of the SQL Server Upgrade Wizard (for example, SQLCONV1_092198_151900).

Inside this subdirectory are a number of descriptively named log files describing each of the upgrade steps. Also inside is another subdirectory for each upgraded database, including the **master** database. Inside each database folder are log files indicating the success of the creation of different types of objects in that database. Files that end in .ok indicate that all instances of that type of object were created successfully. Files that end in .err indicate that at least one instance of that type of object was not created successfully. The error files list each failed object creation statement and the reason the object was not created successfully.

Any log files that indicate a problem are listed at the end of the SQL Server Upgrade Wizard for easy access.

Programming Troubleshooting

Problems reported by the Microsoft SQL Server ODBC driver are not all related to ODBC errors. The driver is the interface between an ODBC application and all of the SQL Server components. All SQL Server errors are returned through the SQL Server ODBC driver. Diagnosing errors reported by the driver includes:

- Diagnosing ODBC connection errors.
- Diagnosing general ODBC errors.

Troubleshooting the SQL Server ODBC Driver

Troubleshooting the Microsoft SQL Server ODBC driver should include a review of the following issues:

- If applications prepare a lot of SQL, it is recommended that these clients release the SQL as soon as possible to free memory. For more information, see SQL Server Books Online.
- Few or no servers appear in the Register Server Wizard in SQL Server Enterprise Manager after either clicking **Next** in the **Welcome** dialog box or executing **osql-L**.

  Microsoft Windows NT enumerates servers, but Microsoft Windows 95 and Windows 98 do not. On Windows 95 or Windows 98 operating systems, the only servers enumerated either by using the **Register Server Wizard** or by executing **osql-L** are those servers configured explicitly using the Client Network Utility.

  Windows NT enumerates servers by network broadcast, listening for a fixed time period. Only those servers added explicitly or those receiving the broadcast and replying within the specified time limit are enumerated.

Therefore, on a Windows NT server, it is possible to see a large list of enumerated servers at one point in time, and then see a smaller list of enumerated servers just a few seconds later. This absence of enumerated servers can be caused by one or more temporarily busy or unavailable network computers.

- On the Windows 95 or Windows 98 operating systems, a connection cannot be established to any ODBC application if the Shared Memory Net-Library file named dbmsshrn.dll was either renamed or deleted. This Shared Memory Net-Library file is required for local connections.

- All driver-specific connection attributes are reset when an application uses connection pooling. After a connection is complete, an application using connection pooling must set all driver-specific connection attributes.

- To eliminate the row count messages from DML statements inside a procedure, use SET NOCOUNT ON as the first statement in the procedure.

- Character and binary parameters are padded to the size specified in **SQLBindParameter**. To disable, clear the **AnsiNPW** check box.

- The code page of the server must be installed on the client workstation unless automatic translation is disabled.

- Parameters must be specified as SQL_PARAM_INPUT unless the parameters are used with a stored procedure and declared as OUTPUT parameters.

- When a 2.65 or earlier version of the SQL Server ODBC driver is used and connected to a server running SQL Server 7.0, the server classifies the application as a pre-SQL Server 7.0 client and does not support certain features introduced in SQL Server 7.0. For more information, see SQL Server Books Online.

For more information about the changes from the version 2.0 ODBC driver to the version 3.0 ODBC driver, see the *Microsoft ODBC 3.0 Programmer's Reference and SDK Guide*.

Diagnosing ODBC Connection Errors

This topic discusses how to diagnose issues that may arise when connecting to Microsoft SQL Server using the SQL Server ODBC driver.

- A connection attempt using an ODBC data source fails and a call to SLQDiagRec () returns:

```
szSqlState = "IM002", *pfNativeError = 0,
szErrorMsg="[Microsoft][ODBC Driver Manager] Data source name not
found and no default driver specified"
```

The ODBC driver manager could not find the ODBC data source. Make sure the data source name was given correctly. Also make sure the data source name was defined using the same Microsoft Windows account the application is running under, or is a system data source. If the application is running as a Microsoft Windows NT service, the data source must be a system data source.

For more information, see SQL Server Books Online.

- A connection attempt fails and a call to SQL Error () returns:

```
szSqlState = "IM003", *pfNativeError = 0,
szErrorMsg="[Microsoft][ODBC Driver Manager] specified driver could
not be loaded"
```

The driver manager could not load the driver DLL, Sqlsrv32.dll, successfully. Make sure a valid version of Sqlsrv32.dll is in the client's path.

- A connection attempt fails and a call to SQLError () returns:

```
szSqlState = "S1000", *pfNativeError = 126,
szErrorMsg="[Microsoft][ODBC Driver Manager] Unable to load
communication module. Driver has not been correctly installed."
```

The SQL Server driver could not load the SQL Server client Net-Library. Verify that the ODBC data source specifies a valid Net-Library name. Verify that a valid version of the Net-Library .dll is in the client's path. This may also occur if the .dlls and files making up the underlying network protocol stack, such as Novell's SPX/IPX, or a TCP/IP protocol stack, are not installed properly. Verify the components with the network administrator, or reinstall the client network components.

- For other network connectivity errors, SQLDiagRec() will return errors in which the szErrorMsg string has this format:

```
[Microsoft][ODBC SQL Server Driver][Net-Libraryname]
```

Net-Libraryname is the display name of a SQL Server client Net-Library (for example, Named Pipes, Shared Memory, Multiprotocol, TCP/IP Sockets, NwLink IPX/SPX, or Banyan VINES). The remainder of the error messages contains the Net-Library function called and the function called in the underlying network API by the TDS function. The *pfNative* error code returned with these errors is the error code from the underlying network protocol stack. Work with the network administrator or your SQL Server support vendor to determine a likely cause for the network error.

Diagnosing General ODBC Errors

This topic discusses how to diagnose issues that may arise when using the
Microsoft SQL Server ODBC Driver.

- The szErrorMsg string returned by SQLDiagRec() starts with:

  ```
  "[Microsoft][ODBC SQL Server driver][DBMSxxxx]"
  ```

  If DBMSxxxx is the name of a SQL Server client Net-Library, the problem is a
  connectivity or network problem. For more information, see SQL Server
  Books Online.

- The szErrorMsg string returned by SQLDiagRec() starts with:

  ```
  "[Microsoft][ODBC SQL Server driver][SQL Server]"
  ```

  The error is coming from SQL Server. The pfNative variable returned by
  SQLError() is the SQL Server error code. Follow the directions for this error
  number in ODBC Error Message Format. Also, you should review the problem
  with the database administrator.

- If you are experiencing difficulties with stored procedures that reference
  temporary tables on SQL Server 6.0 or later, make sure that the CREATE
  TABLE statements for the temporary tables specify NULL or NOT NULL for
  each column. For more information, see SQL Server Books Online.

- If you are experiencing differences in behavior between DB-Library and
  ODBC clients, or in ODBC clients upgraded from earlier versions of
  SQL Server, these could be due to different options set by the SQL Server
  ODBC driver. For more information, see SQL Server Books Online.

- If you are experiencing Microsoft Access conformance errors, or if calls to the
  ODBC catalog API functions are failing, check that the right version of
  Instcat.sql was run in the target server. For more information, see SQL Server
  Books Online.

- If you are experiencing syntax errors from either SQL Server:

  ```
  szSqlState = "37000", *pfNativeError = 170,
  szErrorMsg="[Microsoft][ODBC SQL Server Driver][SQL Server]
              Line 1: Incorrect syntax near '*'."
  ```

  or the ODBC SQL Server Driver, you need to determine if the problem is with
  the SQL statements given to the SQL Server ODBC driver by the application,
  or with the Transact-SQL statements generated by the driver.

  Use the ODBC trace to see the SQL statements passed from the application to
  the SQL Server ODBC driver. The ODBC trace is activated from the **ODBC**
  icon in Control Panel.

If the trace shows that the SQL statements coming from the application are not using valid Transact-SQL or ODBC SQL syntax, diagnose the application.

If the trace shows that the application is passing valid Transact-SQL or ODBC SQL statements to the driver, use SQL Server Profiler to trace the Transact-SQL statements sent from the SQL Server ODBC driver to SQL Server. For more information, see SQL Server Books Online.

Troubleshooting SQL-DMO

After a successful installation of the Microsoft SQL Server version 7.0 client utilities, SQL-DMO files can be found in these locations with these names:

- In the \Mssql7\Binn directory:
    - Sqldmo.dll
    - Sqldmo.Hlp
    - Sqlrsld.dll
    - Sqlsvc.dll
    - Sqlwid.dll
    - W95scm.dll

- In the \Mssql7\Binn\Resources\<*language*> directory (where <*language*> is the installed language number.) For the installed language of U.S. English, for example, the language number is 1033. Therefore, these files would be in the \Mssql7\Binn\Resources\1033 directory:
    - Sqldmo.rll
    - Sqlsvc.rll

- In the %SystemRoot%\system32 directory, Sqlwoa.dll.

In addition to the above files, a successful installation of SQL-DMO includes:

- ODBC version 3.5
- SQL Server ODBC driver version 3.70
- Odbcbcp.dll

If the installation of client utilities fails, it is possible that not all SQL-DMO files will be present or some may not be registered properly.

▶   **To register the SQL-DMO components**

- From \Mssql7\Binn\Resources\<*language*> directory, execute:

```
\MSSQL7\BINN\REGSVR32 SQLDMO.RLL
```

- From any directory, execute:

```
\MSSQL7\BINN\REGSVR32.EXE \MSSQL7\BINN\resources\1033\SQLDMO.RLL
```

SQL Namespace

To use SQL Namespace (SQL-NS), you must have these files in these locations with these names and the SQL-DMO files mentioned above:

- In the \Mssql7\Binn directory:
  - Semcomn.dll
  - Sfc.dll
  - Sqlgui.dll
  - Sqlns.dll
  - Sqlresld.dll
  - Sqlsvc.dll
  - Sqlwid.dll

- In the \Mssql7\Binn\Resources\<*language*> directory (where <*language*> is the installed language number.) For the installed language of U.S. English, for example, the language number is 1033. Therefore, these files would be in the \Mssql7\Binn\Resources\1033 directory:
  - Semcomn.rll
  - Sfc.rll
  - Sqlgui.rll
  - Sqlns.rll
  - Sqlsvc.rll

- In the %SystemRoot%\system32 directory, Sqlwoa.dll.

If the installation of client utilities fails, it is possible that not all SQL-NS files will be present or some may not be registered properly.

▶ **To register the SQL-NS components**

- From \Mssql7\Binn\Resources\<*language*> directory, execute:

```
\MSSQL7\BINN\REGSVR32 SQLNS.RLL
```

- From any directory, execute:

```
\MSSQL7\BINN\REGSVR32.EXE \MSSQL7\BINN\resources\1033\SQLNS.RLL
```

Server and Database Troubleshooting

Servers running Microsoft SQL Server databases can have errors specific to the following areas:

- Databases marked as suspect
- Alerts
- Locks
- Jobs
- Microsoft Windows NT services related to SQL Server
- Interaction with the operating system
- SQL Server Agent

Resetting the Suspect Status

Microsoft SQL Server returns error 1105 and sets the **status** column of **sysdatabases** to suspect if SQL Server is unable to complete recovery on a database because the disk drive no longer has any free space. Follow these steps to resolve the problem:

1. Execute **sp_resetstatus**.
2. Use ALTER DATABASE to add a data file or log file to the database.
3. Stop and restart SQL Server.

   With the extra space provided by the new data file or log file, SQL Server should be able to complete recovery of the database.
4. Free disk space and rerun recovery.

sp_resetstatus, shown below, turns off the suspect flag on a database but leaves all other database options intact.

Caution   Use **sp_resetstatus** only when directed by your primary support provider. Otherwise, you might damage your database. For more information, see SQL Server Books Online.

Because this procedure modifies the system tables, the system administrator must enable updates to the system tables before creating this procedure. To enable updates, use this procedure:

```
USE master
GO
sp_configure 'allow updates', 1
GO
RECONFIGURE WITH OVERRIDE
GO
```

After the procedure is created, immediately disable updates to the system tables:

```
sp_configure 'allow updates', 0
GO
RECONFIGURE WITH OVERRIDE
GO
```

sp_resetstatus can be executed only by the system administrator. Always shut down SQL Server immediately after executing this procedure. The syntax is:

sp_resetstatus *database_name*

This example turns off the suspect flag on the **PRODUCTION** database.

```
sp_resetstatus PRODUCTION
```

Here is the result set:

```
Database 'PRODUCTION' status reset!
WARNING: You must reboot SQL Server prior to accessing this database!
```

sp_resetstatus Stored Procedure Code

Here is the code of the **sp_resetstatus** stored procedure:

```
CREATE PROC sp_resetstatus @dbname varchar(30) AS
DECLARE @msg varchar(80)
IF @@trancount > 0
        BEGIN
            PRINT "Can't run sp_resetstatus from within a transaction."
            RETURN (1)
        END
IF suser_id() != 1
        BEGIN
            SELECT @msg =  "You must be the System Administrator (SA)"
            SELECT @msg = @msg + " to execute this procedure."
            RETURN (1)
        END
IF (SELECT COUNT(*) FROM master..sysdatabases
            WHERE name = @dbname) != 1
        BEGIN
            SELECT @msg = "Database '" + @dbname + "' does not exist!"
            PRINT @msg
            RETURN (1)
        END
IF (SELECT COUNT(*) FROM master..sysdatabases
            WHERE name = @dbname AND status & 256 = 256) != 1
        BEGIN
            PRINT "sp_resetstatus can only be run on suspect databases."
            RETURN (1)
        END
BEGIN TRAN
        UPDATE master..sysdatabases SET status = status ^ 256
            WHERE name = @dbname
        IF @@error != 0 OR @@rowcount != 1
            ROLLBACK TRAN
        ELSE
            BEGIN
                COMMIT TRAN
                SELECT @msg = "Database '" + @dbname + "' status reset!"
                PRINT @msg
                PRINT " "
                PRINT "WARNING: You must reboot SQL Server prior to  "
                PRINT "        accessing this database!"
                PRINT " "
            END
GO
```

Troubleshooting Alerts

If you are experiencing problems with alerts, read the solutions detailed here.

An alert is not firing.

- Verify that the SQLServerAgent and EventLog services are running.
- Verify that the event appears in the Microsoft Windows NT application log.

  Launch the Windows NT Event Viewer. If the event is not in the log, check the log settings. On the **Log** menu, click **Log Settings**, and then in the **Change Settings for Log** box, select **Application**. If needed, set these options to the specified values.

Setting	Value
Maximum Log Size	Minimum of 2,048 KB (2 MB)
Event Log Wrapping	Overwrite Events as Needed

Note   Also check the Microsoft SQL Server error log; events written to the Windows NT application log are also written to the SQL Server error log. To focus the search on the cause of the problem, compare the dates and times for events between the SQL Server error log, the SQL Server Agent error log, and the Windows NT application log.

- Verify that the alert is enabled.
- Verify that the history values of the alert (for example, the occurrence count and last occurred values) are changing.
- Verify that the counter value is at, above, or below the defined threshold value for a minimum of 20 seconds.

  SQL Server Agent polls the performance counters at 20-second intervals.

Important   Using a frequency higher than 20 seconds increases the processing overhead for SQL Server.

If a counter spikes for only a few seconds, which satisfies the performance condition, there is a high likelihood that SQL Server Agent will fail to see the spike; the alert will not fire.

An alert is firing, but the responsible operator is not receiving notification.

- Check the operator and notification information to verify you have entered the correct e-mail, pager, and **net send** addresses.
- Test the e-mail, pager, and **net send** addresses.
- Check the operator's on-duty schedule.
- Check the SQL Server Agent error log for any e-mail problems.

An alert is firing, but the notification is not timely.

The probable causes for this include:

- The **Delay between responses** setting for the alert is too high.
- The alert response is complex, requiring many operator notifications.

Note   Send notifications to as few operators as possible. For example, send notifications to one group e-mail address rather than notifying several individual operators.

This error appears in the SQLServerAgent error log on Windows 95 or Windows 98 servers: "The common event system is being restarted after function ProduceEventsFromSS returned error 44, 'Unable To Connect'"

This may indicate incorrect registered server information. Verify that the registered server information for the local server is correct and that the registered login name is a member of the **sysadmin** fixed database role.

The Windows NT application log fills rapidly with the same error.

The CPU usage is high.

The number of alert responses is high.

Because SQL Server Agent both depends on and monitors SQL Server, SQL Server Agent can become caught in an endless loop of firing the same alert. This generally occurs when SQL Server runs out of an essential global resource and an alert has been defined on this event.

When the number of alerts raised exceeds the SQL Server Agent alert processing rate, a backlog is created.

▶   **To eliminate an alert processing backlog**

1. Increase the amount of time in the **Delay between responses** setting.
2. Correct the global resource problem to prevent recurring alerts from using all your resources.
3. Configure an error to be nonalert-generating.

Important   Configuring an error to not generate an alert can be performed only within the registry. This solution should be used only as a last resort.

---

4. Clear the Windows NT application log if: the backlog is not clearing, you do not want to wait for SQL Server Agent to clear the backlog, or you want an empty, unpopulated Windows NT application log.

> **Caution** Clearing the Windows NT application log using the **Clear All Events** option on the **Log** menu deletes all events from the error log, including those unrelated to SQL Server.

▶ **To configure an error to not generate an alert**

1. Start the Registry Editor.

2. Locate the following registry key:

```
HKEY_LOCAL_MACHINE
\SOFTWARE
\Microsoft
\MSSQLServer
\SQLServerAgent
\NonAlertableErrors
```

3. Type the error number.

   The list of nonalertable errors can be a maximum of 1,024 characters, should not contain spaces, and items must be separated by commas (,). Any error number in the list that appears after the number 0 will generate an alert. In this way, the entire list can be suspended temporarily if a 0 is the first list item. For example, assume that the list consists of

```
1204,0,100
```

   In this example, only error number 1204 does not generate an alert. Because error number 100 follows error number 0 in the list, it will generate an alert.

> **Important** Never remove the default nonalert-generating error, error 1204. Error 1204 defines those conditions known to lead to recursive alert generation. Removing this error will hamper attempts to resolve recursive alert generation.

Troubleshooting Data Transformation Services

Following is information about errors that might be generated while using DTS Designer:

- When using DTS on Alpha platforms, the Microsoft OLE DB Provider for Jet, supplied by default with Microsoft SQL Server, works when configuring connections to Microsoft Access. However, the ISAM components needed to make connections between that provider and data sources such as Microsoft Excel, Paradox, and dBase files are not installed. If you try to configure any of these data sources on an Alpha computer, you will receive an error message.

- If a connection is created for a database user who does not have permission to access the **model** database, when opening the transformation properties, the user will receive the message "Unspecified error. Server user '<user name>' is not a valid user in database 'model'". This message occurs because the user cannot see the provider type information. However, the error is informational and does not prevent the user from creating the transformations.

If you receive the message "Cannot find the specified file" when attempting to access a DTS package saved to a COM-structured storage file, verify that:

- The directory path is specified correctly.

- Permissions are set correctly.

Note   It is possible that the file is corrupt and that the stream cannot be detected.

Troubleshooting Locking

Two locking problems that an application may encounter are deadlocking and blocking.

Deadlocking

Deadlocking is a condition that can occur on any system with multiple users, not only on a relational database management system (RDBMS). A deadlock occurs when two users (or sessions) have locks on separate objects and each user wants a lock on the other's object. Each user waits for the other to release their lock. Microsoft SQL Server detects when two connections have gotten into a deadlock. One of the connections is chosen as a deadlock victim. The connection's transaction is rolled back and the application receives an error.

If deadlocks become a common occurrence to the point that their rollbacks are causing excessive performance degradation, you may need to perform more in-depth investigation. Use trace flag 1204. For example, this command starts SQL Server from the command prompt and enables trace flag 1204.

```
c:\mssql7\binn\sqlservr -T1204 /dc:\mssql7\data\master.mdf
```

All messages will now appear in the console screen where SQL Server was started and in the error log.

Deadlocking can also occur when using distributed transactions. For information about resolving deadlocks with distributed transactions, see SQL Server Books Online.

Blocking

An unavoidable characteristic of any lock-based concurrent system is that blocking may occur under some conditions. Blocking happens when one connection holds a lock and a second connection wants a conflicting lock type. This forces the second connection to either wait or block on the first.

In this discussion, the term "connection" refers to a single logged-on session of the database. Each connection appears as a system process ID (SPID). Each of these SPIDs is often referred to as a process, although it is not a separate process context in the usual sense. Rather, each SPID consists of the server resources and data structures necessary to service the requests of a single connection from a given client. A single client application may have one or more connections. From the perspective of SQL Server, there is no difference between multiple connections from a single client application on a single client computer and multiple connections from multiple client applications or multiple client computers. One connection can block another connection, regardless of whether they emanate from the same application or separate applications on two different client computers.

To eliminate deadlocking or blocking problems, contact your system administrator. The system administrator should check the **waittype**, **waittime**, **lastwaittype**, and the **waitresource** columns of **sysprocesses** to see what activities each SPID is performing.

Troubleshooting SQL Server Services Accounts

If you have difficulty starting either the MSSQLServer or SQLServerAgent service under a particular user account, you can:

- Use Windows NT User Manager to verify that the account has **Log on as a service** rights on the computer. (Both of these must be assigned within the security context of the local computer, not the domain.)

If services are started by someone who is not a member of the Windows NT local administrators group, the service account must have these permissions:

- Full control of the main Microsoft SQL Server directory (by default, \Mssql7).
- Full control of the SQL Server database files, regardless of storage location.
- The **Log on as a service** right. Ensure that all logon hours are allowed in the **Logon Hours** dialog box.
- Full control of registry keys at and below HKEY_LOCAL_MACHINE\SOFTWARE\Microsoft\MSSQLServer.

- Selection of the **Password Never Expires** box.
- Full control of registry keys at and below HKEY_LOCAL_MACHINE\SYSTEM\CurrentControlSet\Services\MSSQLServer.
- Full control of registry keys at and below HKEY_LOCAL_MACHINE\SOFTWARE\Microsoft\Windows NT\CurrentVersion\Perflib.

If the service does not have the appropriate permissions, certain functionality cannot be accomplished. For example, to write to a mail slot, the service must have a Windows NT domain user account, not just local system, with network write privileges. The service must be a Windows NT account with local administrator privileges to:

- Create SQL Server Agent CmdExec and ActiveX Script jobs not belonging to members of the **sysadmin** role.
- Use the automatic server restart feature of SQL Server Agent.
- Create SQL Server Agent jobs to be run when the server is idle.

- For the MSSQLServer service, right-click the server, click **Properties**, and then click the **Security** tab. Under **Startup service account**, enter the appropriate account and password. If the password is incorrect or has changed, the service cannot be started until the correct password is entered.

Caution For the MSDTC service only, use Services in Control Panel to reenter the user account password. If the password is incorrect or has changed, the service cannot be started until the correct password is entered. If necessary, change the account's password using User Manager, and then enter that password for the service using Services in Control Panel.

- For the SQLServerAgent service, expand the server, and then expand Management. Right-click SQLServerAgent and click **Properties**. On the **General** tab (the default) in the **Service startup account** section, enter the account and password.
- Assign the account experiencing the problem to another service. If you still have difficulty starting the MSSQLServer or SQLServerAgent service under a particular user account, assign that account to another service (for example, the Spooler service) and verify that the service can be started successfully. If not, the account is either not configured properly or cannot be validated by the domain controller (for example, if no domain controller is available).

Troubleshooting Full-Text Search

If you installed the Full-Text Search feature, it runs as the Microsoft Search service (MSSearch) in Control Panel. If Full-Text Search is not working properly, make sure that the Full-Text Search feature was installed and is running. In SQL Server Service Manager, in the **Services** box, make sure the **Microsoft Search** option is selected. For more information, see SQL Server Books Online.

MSSearch runs in the context of the local system account. During SQL Server Setup, SQL Server adds itself to MSSearch service as an administrator. All subsequent changes to the MSSQLServer service account must be made through SQL Server Enterprise Manager. While MSSearch service is running, right-click the server, click **Properties**, and then click the **Security** tab. Under **Startup Service Account**, enter the appropriate account and password. If the password is incorrect or has changed, the service cannot be started until the correct password is entered. This approach ensures that any service account change gets updated in the Microsoft Search service.

Caution Do not use Services in Control Panel to change user account information. Changing user account information through Control Panel results in a mismatch of account information between the MSSQLServer and MSSearch services, and causes full-text catalog population and querying to fail.

If a mismatch of user account information between the MSSQLServer and MSSearch services occurs, verify that both the MSSQLServer and MSSearch services are running. Then, launch SQL Server Enterprise Manager. Using the **Properties** option and the **Security** tab as described earlier, change the password for the MSSQLServer service. Changing the password for the MSSQLServer service implicitly updates the account information for the MSSearch service.

Before Uninstalling Site Server 3.0

If the computer running Microsoft SQL Server and Full-Text Search also has Microsoft Site Server version 3.0 installed, verify that Site Server 3.0 Service Pack 1 (SP1) is installed before uninstalling Site Server. If this service pack is not applied, Full-Text Search will not work properly after Site Server 3.0 has been uninstalled.

Presence of UNC path in PATH Environment Variable

If your computer running Microsoft Windows NT does have a UNC path specification present in the system PATH variable or in the user PATH variable, you may experience problems with full-text indexing and Full-Text Search. First, double-check whether you have a UNC path specification in your PATH variable. To do this, issue **echo %path%** from the command prompt. If you have a UNC path specification, you will see one or more paths of the form *computer_name**share_name*.

The symptoms of these problems may include one or more of the following:

- When attempting to issue a full-text query, you receive an error message stating "Full-text query failed because full-text catalog '<*your_fulltext_catalog_name*>' is not yet ready for queries."

- The **Item count**, **Catalog size**, and **Unique word count** options (located in the **Properties** dialog box in SQL Server Enterprise Manager) are all set to 0, even though you populated this full-text catalog.

- The Windows NT application log has "stop event" items logged, where **Source** is Microsoft Search and **Category** is Indexer. In addition, one of these error event items contains the following error message:

  "Unable to load DLL <X:\Program Files\Common Files\system\ContentIndex\ontciutl.dll>. Error 5 - Access is denied."

Note X refers to the drive letter where your Program Files\Common Files directory resides on your computer.

Two possible solutions to this problem are:

- If possible, remove the UNC path specification(s) in the SYSTEM and USER PATH variables. Replace these UNC path(s) with remapped drive(s).

- Add the location \%SYSTEMDRIVE%\Program Files\Common Files\SYSTEM\ContentIndex in front of any UNC path specification in the SYSTEM path.

Note After making any of these changes, restart your computer. SYSTEM path changes do not take effect until the computer is restarted.

If you have not attempted to repopulate your full-text catalog(s) after the addition of the UNC path specification(s) in your user or system PATH variables, you can use Full-Text Search. If you have attempted repopulation, you must rebuild your full-text catalog(s) and then repopulate them before you can issue full-text queries.

Troubleshooting Multiserver Jobs

When using multiserver jobs, you may experience one or more of these problems.

The job will not download.

Check the download list at the master server (MSX) either through the user interface or by executing **sp_help_downloadlist**.

Check the SQL Server Agent error log at the target server (TSX).

After resolving the problem, clear the blocking error at the MSX with the user interface.

There are problems with enlisting or defecting.

- Verify that an operator named **MSXOperator** exists at the MSX.
- Verify that the MSX is running Mixed Mode Security (SQL Server Authentication and Windows NT Authentication).
- Verify that the MSX is running Microsoft Windows NT, not Microsoft Windows 95 or Windows 98 operating systems.
- Check named pipes connectivity using **makepipe** at the MSX and **readpipe** at the TSX.

What if a TSX is reinstalled while it is still enlisted?

The uninstall portion of SQL Server Setup issues a warning that the server should be defected before uninstalling the TSX. If the warning is ignored, or the warning is noted but the MSX is unavailable when the defection occurs, it becomes necessary to resolve the dangling enlistment at the MSX.

▶ **To resolve the dangling enlistment**

- At the MSX, execute:

```
EXECUTE sp_delete_targetserver @server_name = '<TSX server name>',
    @post_defection = 0
```

What if I need to reinstall msdb on a TSX server?

Either a backup of **msdb** exists and the **msdb** database is successfully restored or the **msdb** database is damaged and no backup is available.

If a backup of **msdb** is available and **msdb** is successfully restored, MSX jobs that have been deleted after the **msdb** backup may also have been restored. To ensure that the deleted jobs are removed, delete all jobs that originated from the MSX and repost the jobs.

▶ **To delete and repost jobs**

- At the MSX, execute:

```
EXECUTE sp_resync_targetserver '<server name>'
```

Or

- In SQL Server Enterprise Manager, in the **Multi Server Job Execution Status** dialog box, click **Synchronize Jobs**.

If the **msdb** database is damaged and no backup is available, the TSX must be reenlisted.

▶ **To reenlist the TSX**

1. At the MSX:

   All jobs that were targeted at the reenlisted TSX must be retargeted using **sp_add_jobserver**. To generate the Transact-SQL statements to retarget jobs using **sp_add_jobserver**, execute **sp_generate_target_server_job_assignment_sql** and save the result set:

```
EXECUTE sp_generate_target_server_job_assignment_sql
    '<TSX server name>'
```

2. At the TSX, execute:

```
EXECUTE sp_msx_enlist '<MSX server name>'
```

3. At the MSX, execute the previously saved result set of **sp_generate_target_server_job_assignment_sql**.

What if I need to restore a backup of msdb on the MSX?

If possible, for all TSX servers that have enlisted after the last backup:

1. At the MSX, execute **sp_generate_target_server_job_assignment_sql** and save the result set:

```
EXECUTE sp_generate_target_server_job_assignment_sql
    '<TSX server name>'
```

2. At the MSX, restore the **msdb** database from a backup. Any TSX that has defected after the last **msdb** backup must be defected manually.

▶ **To defect a TSX server manually**

- At the MSX, execute:

```
EXECUTE sp_delete_targetserver @server_name = '<TSX server name>,
    @post_defection = 0
```

Any TSX that has enlisted after the last **msdb** backup must then be reenlisted.

▶ **To reenlist a TSX that was enlisted after the last msdb backup**

1. At the TSX, execute:

```
EXECUTE sp_msx_defect
EXECUTE sp_msx_enlist '<MSX server name>'
```

2. At the MSX, execute the previously saved result set of **sp_generate_target_server_job_assignment_sql**.

Note If a defected server is not reenlisted, it will generate many "Incomplete enlistment" errors in the SQL Server Agent error log of the TSX.

If jobs or job assignments have been added, deleted, or changed after the last **msdb** backup, all remaining TSX servers must be resynchronized.

▶ **To resynchronize TSX servers after the last msdb backup**

• Execute:

```
EXECUTE sp_resync_targetserver 'ALL'
```

This EXECUTE statement causes each TSX to delete all its MSX jobs and then download them again. This is a very expensive command. An alternative to executing **sp_resync_targetserver** with the **ALL** option is to resynchronize the TSX servers manually by selectively posting instructions for all the changes. This approach may work if only a very few changes occurred. However, it is recommended that **sp_resync_targetserver** with the **ALL** option be used to resynchronize TSX servers.

What if a TSX computer is renamed while enlisted?

The TSX server can be defected from the TSX side, but must be defected manually from the MSX side. Jobs that were targeted at the TSX must be retargeted by executing **sp_add_jobserver**. To generate the Transact-SQL statements to retarget jobs using **sp_add_jobserver**, execute **sp_generate_target_server_job_assignment_sql**.

1. At the MSX, execute **sp_generate_target_server_job_assignment_sql** and save the result set:

```
EXECUTE sp_generate_target_server_job_assignment_sql
    '<Old TSX server name>', '<New TSX server name>'
```

2. At the TSX, execute:

```
EXECUTE sp_msx_defect
```

3. At the MSX, execute:

```
EXECUTE sp_delete_targetserver
    @server_name = '<Old TSX server name>',
    @post_defection = 0
```

4. At the TSX, back up the **msdb** database. Then, uninstall and reinstall SQL Server.

Important   Uninstalling and reinstalling SQL Server is necessary because SQL Server does not support renaming of the computer.

---

5. Restore the backup of the **msdb** database.

6. At the TSX, execute:

```
EXECUTE sp_msx_enlist '<MSX server name>'
```

7. At the MSX, execute the previously saved result set of **sp_generate_target_server_job_assignment_sql**.

Troubleshooting the Operating System

When installing Microsoft SQL Server on a Microsoft Windows NTFS partition, make sure that the NTFS file permissions allow read/write access. Otherwise, this error message may appear in the Microsoft Windows NT application log (for each installation attempt):

```
Msg 17050: initerrlog: Could not open error log file
'C:\MSSQL7\log\ERRORLOG'. Operating system error =5(Access is denied.).
```

Verify that all system requirements are met, including installation of Microsoft Windows NT Service Pack 4 (SP4). For more information about system requirements, see SQL Server Books Online.

Internet Connection Dialog Box at Startup

If remote connections are enabled in Microsoft Windows 95 or Windows 98 operating systems, the system may initiate an Internet connection at Windows startup or at the start of many applications. This behavior is sometimes called autodial or autoconnect. This behavior can be disabled by setting the registry key EnableRemoteConnect to N.

To do this, create a text file named DisbleAutoConnect.reg with the following three lines:

```
REGEDIT4
[HKEY_LOCAL_MACHINE\SOFTWARE\Microsoft\OLE]
"EnableRemoteConnect"="N"
```

Changing this setting to disable remote connections should not prevent any of your usual Internet activities. This setting is the default for most systems. However, enabling remote connections is necessary for some features of DCOM. For more information, see http://support.microsoft.com/support/.

If there are instances when you need to have remote connections enabled, create a second REG file, named EnableRemoteConnect.reg, with the following three lines:

```
REGEDIT4
[HKEY_LOCAL_MACHINE\SOFTWARE\Microsoft\OLE]
"EnableRemoteConnect"="Y"
```

Run EnableAutoConnect.reg to make the setting, then run DisbleAutoConnect.reg to disable it when autoconnect is no longer needed.

Thread Pooling

The Microsoft SQL Server error log may display the message:

```
The working thread limit of 255 has been reached
```

This message is an informational message and does not indicate any problem with the system.

SQL Server maintains a pool of operating system threads for executing batches of SQL statements as they arrive from clients. On Microsoft Windows NT, if the server **lightweight pooling** configuration option is set to 1, SQL Server maintains a pool of fibers instead of threads; fibers use fewer resources than threads. Using a pool of threads or fibers allows SQL Server to optimize the allocation of processing time when executing multiple SQL statements at the same time. The threads or fibers in this pool are known collectively as the worker threads. For more information, see SQL Server Books Online.

The number of worker threads is controlled by the **max worker threads** server configuration option. The default is 255 and rarely needs to be changed.

When a batch of Transact-SQL statements is received from a client, if an existing worker thread is free, it is allocated to execute the batch. If no existing worker threads are free and the number of worker threads is less than **max worker threads**, a new worker thread is allocated. If no worker threads are free and **max worker threads** is reached, the new batch waits until an existing worker thread completes its current batch and becomes free. When the number of worker threads reaches **max worker threads**, SQL Server displays this message:

```
The working thread limit of 255 has been reached
```

Having all worker threads allocated does not mean that the performance of SQL Server will degrade. Typically, a new batch has only a short wait for a free thread. Allocating more threads may degrade performance because of the increased work required to coordinate resources among the threads. Many SQL Server systems running in production reach this state and run with very high performance levels.

Insufficient Virtual Memory on the Server

When the applications running on a server request more memory than is available on the server, Microsoft Windows opens the **Server Process - Out of Virtual Memory** dialog box with the following text:

```
Your system is running low on virtual memory. Please close some
applications. You can then start the System option in the Control Panel
and choose the Virtual Memory button to create an additional paging file
or increase the size of your current paging file.
```

Use Virtual Memory in Control Panel to make sure that the amount of virtual memory at least 1.5 times the amount of physical memory available on the server. Microsoft SQL Server dynamically requests or frees memory as needed on Microsoft Windows NT systems. SQL Server should not cause this error on Windows NT when running with the default configuration options. For more information, see SQL Server Books Online.

If the virtual memory setting seems appropriate, consider the following actions:

- Check that the SQL Server **max server memory** and **min server memory** configuration options are not set high enough to use most of the virtual memory. For more information, see SQL Server Books Online.
- Check that other applications on the server are not using the available virtual memory.
- Use the **max server memory** and **min server memory** configuration options to control the amount of memory requested by SQL Server.

Insufficient Resource Space

If a Microsoft SQL Server configuration option is set too high for the amount of available resources, SQL Server fails to start. For example, if the **max server memory** setting is too high, other applications may take some time to start.

Reset configuration options to their default values as described in SQL Server Books Online, or start SQL Server with minimal configuration by using the **-f** startup option of the **sqlservr** application.

Determining When SQL Server Causes a Windows NT Blue Screen

Infrequently, Microsoft Windows NT may either halt with a STOP screen or the console may become completely frozen and unresponsive. This is commonly called a blue screen. This may sometimes happen on a computer where Microsoft SQL Server is running, or may coincide with a particular SQL Server operation such as the **bcp** utility, a long-running query, and so on.

The vast majority of time, this indicates an operating system, device driver, or hardware problem and should be pursued as such. The Windows NT user or kernel mode process isolation ensures that a user mode application problem does not cause the operating system to stop responding. This section discusses exceptions to this and ways to determine whether to troubleshoot the problem at the system or application layer.

Sometimes the cause of a computer failing to respond or blue screen may be a nonmaskable interrupt (NMI) error. This is sometimes visible as an error code stating NMI, parity check, or I/O parity check. NMI errors are almost always hardware. Usually they are caused by a memory failure; however, they can originate in other hardware subsystems such as video boards. Even if the NMI error happens only during certain SQL Server operations, and if the system passes initial hardware diagnostics, it should still be considered a hardware problem and pursued as such. It may be necessary to use a dedicated memory SIMM testing device, which can often find a transient memory error that eludes software-based diagnostics.

Processes exist on Windows NT in either user mode or kernel mode (sometimes called supervisor or privileged mode). In the Intel x86 architecture, user mode maps to ring 3 and kernel mode to ring 0 of the 4-ring protection system. The x86 architecture has been carried forward with little change in all Intel and compatible processors to date, including the Pentium Pro and Pentium II. Processors such as the Alpha AXP typically have unprivileged and privileged modes as well.

Kernel mode is a privileged processor mode in which a thread has access to system-wide memory (including that of all user-mode processes) and to hardware. By contrast, user mode is a nonprivileged processor mode in which a thread can only access system resources by calling system services.

A user mode process cannot access kernel mode memory, or access memory of another user mode process. This is enforced by processor hardware, in conjunction with kernel mode data structures such as Page Tables. For more information, see the *80386 Programmer's Reference Manual*, the *80386 System Software Writer's Guide*, or equivalent Alpha AXP documentation.

As a result of this protection system, a user mode application generally cannot stop responding, cause a blue screen, or otherwise cause a failure in the Windows NT operating system. Such problems should be pursued primarily at the system layer as an operating system, device driver, or hardware issue.

Although an application error cannot cause a failure in the operating system, an operating system error can cause an application to stop responding. This is because of the general rule: applications must call inward (to kernel mode), but the operating system can reference outward to user mode freely at any time. A microkernel-influenced architecture such as Windows NT may in turn dispatch certain work to a user-mode system process rather than perform the work in kernel mode. However, the overall principal remains the same: processor hardware enforces process-context isolation, which prevents one process from causing a failure in another, whether one or both are in user mode.

If a user mode application passes an invalid parameter in a Win32 API call, it is the operating system's responsibility to validate this parameter. In very rare cases, passing an invalid parameter may cause a Windows NT blue screen error. However, this is an operating system issue, and should be debugged and pursued as such.

There are a few narrow exceptions to the above guidelines. These exceptions can be easily and quickly eliminated.

Winlogon Problem Caused by SQL Extensible Performance Counters

Current Microsoft Windows NT architecture stipulates that any extensible performance counters added by a service will run in the process context of the Windows NT Winlogon process. Because Winlogon is a vital component of the operating system, a bug or resource leak in any performance counter DLL may disrupt Winlogon, and hence the operating system. The Microsoft SQL Server extensible performance counter DLL is called Sqlctr70.dll, and it exports several SQL Server-specific objects from SQL Server to the operating system. You can use Windows NT Performance Monitor to monitor these objects.

Although it is very rare for Sqlctr70.dll to cause a Winlogon problem, you can find problems more quickly when pursuing a Windows NT failure or blue screen problem on a computer running SQL Server by renaming this DLL. This eliminates the use of SQL Server performance counters; however, you can still use Windows NT Performance Monitor to monitor SQL Server by using regular Windows NT performance counters (such as threads, process, memory, and so on).

If renaming Sqlctr70.dll fixes the problem, and if this is confirmed by reinstating and removing the DLL several times, the problem should be pursued as a SQL Server issue. Otherwise, it should be pursued as a system layer issue.

Resource Leak

If a resource leak continues for a long period of time, the operating system should return the appropriate return code to the application, which should log this. For example, if you receive operating system error 8, "Not enough storage," the operating system should handle the situation by not granting further resource requests. However, a continued application resource leak may not be handled by the operating system under all conditions, resulting in a blue screen or operating system or application failure.

Almost all resource leaks will manifest themselves as a gradual increase in consumption of some resource, such as handles, virtual memory, private bytes, and so on. Therefore, the easiest way to rule in or out a resource leak is to run Windows NT Performance Monitor and log all objects to a file. When the problem occurs, examine the logged performance data for signs of a leak. Some good counters to examine are: handle count, page file bytes, pool paged bytes, pool nonpaged bytes, private bytes, thread count, virtual bytes, and working set for each process running on the computer.

It is not necessary to classify certain values as normal or abnormal. Focus on identifying leaks by the continuous nature of the increase, not by the absolute value at a given time. Remember it is normal for the Windows NT Performance Monitor **private bytes** counter for Microsoft SQL Server to start well below the configured **min server memory** setting value, and then increase with activity until it roughly approaches, but does not significantly exceed, that value.

If one of the logged Windows NT Performance Monitor counters continuously increases for the Sqlservr.exe process, and if reaching a certain value repeatedly coincides with a Microsoft Windows NT blue screen or operating system failure, it should be pursued temporarily as a Microsoft Windows operating system issue until the cause of the continuous SQL Server resource leak is understood. Otherwise, it should be pursued as a system layer problem.

CPU Monopolization

If a process spawns high priority threads that are continuously in a runnable state, this process can dominate the computer and prevent the operating system from running. A properly configured Microsoft SQL Server computer will not cause this problem. However, under some conditions, the operating system may appear to stop responding. For example, boosting the **priority boost** too high may drain resources from essential operating system and network functions, resulting in problems shutting down SQL Server or using other Microsoft Windows NT tasks on the server. In general, you should leave **priority boost** setting at the default.

When pursuing an operating system failure, verify that the SQL Server configuration settings mentioned above are at their default values. Then, if the operating system or application failure recurs, it should be pursued as a system layer problem.

Troubleshooting Replication

Replication is a complex process, and although Microsoft SQL Server is designed to detect and correct problems automatically, you may encounter problems when implementing your application. Most replication problems can be resolved by following a general troubleshooting approach. Other problems require a specific set of instructions.

General Approach to Replication Troubleshooting

You can begin troubleshooting replication problems by viewing the task history to determine which task failed and the reason for failure. Message details cannot always identify the problem, but can often provide an indicator of the issues, for example, connectivity problems, permissions restrictions, log full errors, and so on.

You can also begin troubleshooting using Replication Monitor to view the status of replication agents:

1. In Replication Monitor, right-click the distribution agent serving the subscriber, then click **Agent Properties.** This allows you to view the job properties.

2. Click the **Steps** tab, then double-click **Run Replication Agent.**

3. Cut the string from the command window.

4. Paste the string into a console window, with Distrib.exe at the beginning, and with an extra parameter **-Output**.

5. Review the output for indications of the problem.

You can increase the amount of history logged by a replication agent and use the additional information to get a more detailed understanding of actions and failures at each point in the replication process. Set the **HistoryVerboseLevel** to its highest value in the replication agent profile.

If you suspect there is a problem with data consistency in your application, use **sp_table_validation** to test for row count or checksum differences.

If you encounter one of the following problems, follow the procedures described. For current information about SQL Server replication and suggested solutions to problems, see www.microsoft.com/sql/ and www.microsoft.com/support/.

Cannot Start a Replication Agent

A replication agent may not start because SQLServerAgent always calls the **xp_logininfo** stored procedure to validate that you still belong to your Microsoft Windows NT user groups and to verify your login permissions to the server. The called stored procedure always makes a round trip to the domain controller to do this work. If the agent will not start, an error is returned. This error shows only in the Jobs folder. It never gets propagated to the monitoring node because the agents never actually run, so no notification can be returned. The workaround for the agent not starting is to use standard security or a local computer login as the owner for your jobs.

Cannot Start Another Replication Job

Some replication agents allow only one instance of a particular job to run at a time, for example, one log reader per publication database, one Distributor or Merge Agent per publication/Subscriber pair, one snapshot per publication, and so on. If these jobs fail due to connection failure, it is possible you will not be able to start another job until the network connection time-out is reached or you kill the system process ID (SPID) of the failed job.

Cannot Find Conflicts

If you receive a message that conflicts occurred during the merge process, you can use Replication Conflict Viewer to review the outcomes of the conflicts and to make changes to these outcomes. Make sure you connect to the correct server to view the conflicts. The location of the conflict table varies depending upon whether replication has been configured for centralized or decentralized logging of conflicts. Conflict reporting is usually centralized (the default). If centralized, the conflict table is stored at the Publisher and you must connect to the Publisher to view the conflicts. If decentralized, the conflict table is stored at either the Publisher or the Subscriber, depending upon who lost the conflicts.

Access Denied Reading or Writing Snapshot Files

If you cannot start Snapshot Agent, and receive an "Access Denied" message, run Dcomcnfg.exe. Click the **Default Security** tab, then make sure the Windows NT account that SQL Server Agent runs under is enabled to have default access and launch permissions.

If the replication agents cannot access the snapshot folder on the Distributor, make sure that the folder is shared correctly. On a Distributor server running Windows NT, the snapshot folder defaults to using the <drive>$ share and a path of \\<computer>\<drive>$\Mssql7\Repldata.

On a Distributor server running the Microsoft Windows 95 or Windows 98 operating systems, the snapshot folder defaults to using the <drive> without a share and a path of <drive>:\Mssql7\Repldata. If your application requires the ability to create pull subscriptions on a server running the Windows 95 or Windows 98 operating systems, you must change the snapshot folder to a network path accessible by replication agents running at the Publisher and Subscribers. You can change the local path to a network path by sharing the folder manually.

Replicating from SQL Server 7.0 to SQL Server 6.5

If you are attempting to replicate from SQL Server 7.0 to SQL Server 6.5 and receive an error message that **MSreplication_ subscripions** is an invalid object error, try the following procedures:

1. Run Replp70.sql at the SQL Server 6.5 Subscriber.

2. Run **sp_addpublisher** at the Subscriber. Make sure you have the syntax correct:

    ```
    sp_addpublisher 70 <publisher server name>, <NT account used by
    Dist. agent>
    ```

3. Register the SQL Server 6.5 Subscriber at the SQL Server 7.0 Enterprise Manager.

4. Create a publication at the SQL Server 7.0 Publisher and perform a push subscription to the SQL Server 6.5 Publisher.

For more information about replicating between different versions of SQL Server, see SQL Server Books Online.

Merge Agent or Distribution Agent Fails on Time-out

If the Merge Agent or Distribution Agent fails because of a time-out, increase the **QueryTimeout** value in the Merge Agent or Distribution Agent profile.

Merge Agent Fails While Enumerating Deletions at the Subscriber

If the Merge Agent fails while enumerating deletions at the Subscriber, examine the error details. This condition is often the result of a large number of deletes to process and a small **QueryTimeout** value. Increase the **QueryTimeout** value in the Merge Agent profile.

Errors Occur Applying Constraints During the Initialization of a Partitioned, Merge Publication at a Subscriber.

If errors occur when the snapshot of a partitioned merge publication is applied at a Subscriber, the publication filter may not be defining all of the data needed at the Subscriber to support the constraints referenced at the Subscriber. For example, if you have an **EMPLOYEES** table that contains a self-referencing constraint on the **EMPLOYEES.SUPERVISOR_ID** column, make sure your partitioned data set includes all of the supervisors for the employees in the partition as well.

Conflicts Occur When Merging Newly Inserted Rows That Contain Identity Columns

If conflicts occur when merging newly inserted rows that contain identity columns, use the Replication Conflict Viewer to determine the cause of the conflict. An insert conflict is usually caused by inconsistent enforcement of constraints between Publishers and Subscribers. Also, identity columns must be used with caution. You must assign each Subscriber that will insert new rows containing an identity a unique range of identity values.

Data Validation Appears to Fail

Data validation uses rowcounts and checksums to determine if data at the Subscriber has diverged from data at the Publisher. However, there are several conditions other than actual data divergence that could cause data validation to fail.

- Checksum computes a 32-bit cyclic redundancy check (CRC) on the entire row image on the page. It does not check columns selectively and cannot operate on a view or vertical partition of the table. Also, the checksum skips the contents of **text** and **image** columns (by design).

- When doing a checksum, the structure of the table must be identical between the two servers; that is, the tables must have the same columns created and existing in the same order, same data types and lengths, and same NULL/NOT NULL conditions. For example, if the Publisher did a CREATE TABLE, then an ALTER TABLE to add columns, but the script applied at the Publisher is a simple CREATE table, the structure is NOT the same. If you are not certain that the structure of the two tables is identical, look at **syscolumns** and confirm that the offset in each table is the same.

- Floating point values are likely to generate checksum differences if character-mode **bcp** was used, which is the case if the publication has heterogeneous subscribers. These are due to minor and unavoidable differences in precision when doing conversion to and from character mode.

- The custom resolver may not ensure data convergence because it does not handle all conflicts. For example, the custom resolver may only resolve downloads to the Subscriber and not uploads to the Publisher.

If you suspect something is wrong, first check conflict tables and error tables for possible explanations. For example, if the Subscriber database or log is full, SQL Server may be unable to download all of the changes. SQL Server would log an error in the conflict table at the Publisher indicating that not all updates were processed at the Subscriber.

Note   You cannot use OPENROWSET on a server running Windows NT Authentication only.

For example, the following FULL OPEN JOIN query uses OPENROWSET to identify differences between two tables.

```
SELECT authors.au_id AS Local_PK, remote.au_id AS Remote_PK,
(getchecksum(authors.au_id,1),0) AS Local_chksum,remchksum
FROM authors
FULL OUTER JOIN
OPENROWSET('SQLOLEDB','RONSOU4';'sa';'',"SELECT
au_id,(getchecksum(NULL,1),0) AS remchksum FROM pubs.dbo.authors" ) AS
remote
ON (authors.au_id=remote.au_id)
WHERE
-- Find rows with same primary key but different checksums
(getchecksum(authors.au_id,1),0) <> remchksum
OR
-- Find rows which do not exist on one side or the other
authors.au_id IS NULL OR remote.au_id IS NULL
```

If the query returns rowcount differences, comment out the checksums. The checksums are unnecessary at that point and are more resource intensive than rowcounts to execute.

For more information on data validation, see SQL Server Books Online.

Troubleshooting Statistics

Here are some problems you may encounter when using statistics:

- When a table has a large number of indexes, and statistics are being either created or updated, you may receive this error:

  ```
  Cannot create more than 250 indexes on a table.
  ```

- Columns larger than 900 bytes cannot have statistics created on them.

- Verify that the query is using indexes by viewing the showplan output.

- Indexes are ignored. Verify the statistics information by executing DBCC SHOW_STATISTICS.

- Verify that there are no distribution page references in **sysindexes**.

SQL Server Tools Troubleshooting

This section contains information about troubleshooting problems you may encounter when using other tools with Microsoft SQL Server.

Troubleshooting SQL Mail with Exchange Server

Typically, errors in starting a SQL Mail session or sending mail from SQL Mail with Microsoft Exchange Server fall into two categories: permissions problems and Exchange client setup problems. For more information about SQL Mail, see SQL Server Books Online.

Examine this list of items, in this order:

1. Log on to Microsoft Windows NT with the user account that will be used for the MSSQLServer service. This user account must be an administrator of the local computer and a domain account.

2. Confirm that the Exchange Server client, Exchnge32.exe, or the Microsoft Outlook client, Outlook.exe, can connect to Exchange Server and that e-mail can be sent.

3. Confirm that the Exchange Server profile used does not have a Personal Message Store (.pst).

4. On the **Services** tab, confirm that the only services available are Microsoft Exchange Server and Personal Address Book, and then click the **Delivery** tab. Confirm that the selection in the **Deliver To** box is the mailbox on Exchange Server, which should have a name similar to "Mailbox - <Friendly User Name>" (where <Friendly User Name> is the name of the user who logged on to Windows NT in Step 1).

5. To run SQL Mail with Exchange Server, the MSSQLServer service must be run under the same user account that logged on in Step 1. In Control Panel, double-click Services, select the MSSQLServer service, and then click **Startup**.

6. Confirm that the SQL Mail profile is correct. In SQL Server Enterprise Manager, expand the server, expand the Support Services folder, select SQL Mail, and then right-click. Click **Properties**, and then on the **General** tab, verify that the profile name specified in the **Profile name** box is correct. If needed, click **Test**. The profile name must match the profile name used in Step 3.

7. Test Microsoft SQL Server access permissions to Exchange Server by executing **xp_cmdshell**, which executes with the same permissions as SQL Mail. Use this command to test connectivity to the server, assuming Exchange Server is located on a computer named "NTServer".

```
xp_cmdshell "NET USE \\NTServer\IPC$"
```

If this command fails, Step 3 was not completed correctly.

It should now be possible to start SQL Mail either automatically or manually using **xp_startmail**. When using **xp_startmail**, the profile can be replaced by replacing <Profile name> below with the profile name used in Step 3:

```
xp_startmail '<Profile name>',''
```

Troubleshooting SQL Server Profiler

Here are some problems you may encounter when using SQL Server Profiler:

- If you do not see all SQL Server Profiler event classes on the **Events** tab of the trace definition property sheet, on the **Tools** menu, click **Options**. On the **General** tab, under **Events**, select **All event classes**.

- If you do not see all SQL Server Profiler data columns on the **Data Columns** tab of the trace definition property sheet, on the **Tools** menu, click **Options**. On the **General** tab, under **Events**, select **All data columns**.

- SQL Server Profiler can display the object name (instead of the object ID) if the **Server Name** and **Database ID** data columns also appear in your trace.

- When setting filters, a blank include filter includes all items in the SQL Server Profiler output. A filter on a data column is not applied to event classes that do not populate that data column.

- Because the SQL Server Profiler Extended Stored Procedures save trace queue definitions on the server rather than on the client, SQL Server Profiler is unable to edit or start a trace created originally with the extended stored procedures.

- For security reasons, batches containing stored procedures with password arguments are not traced. Instead, an event is produced, which replaces the batch text with a comment.

- In Microsoft Windows 95 or Windows 98 operating systems, SQL Server Profiler does not accept client configuration changes until the SQL Server Profiler is closed and restarted.

- Due to file locking incompatibilities, Microsoft Windows NT cannot open trace or script files in a Windows 95 or Windows 98 shared directory.

- SQL Server Profiler can incur problems accessing files on a remote computer if those files become unavailable.

Here are some common problems you may encounter when replaying a SQL Server Profiler trace:

- Replay errors may occur when logins and users captured in the trace do not exist in the target database. If the logins and users exist in the database, they must have the same permissions as they did in the source (traced) database, and they must have the same password as the SQL Server Profiler user replaying the trace. For security reasons, Microsoft Windows NT authenticated logins cannot be impersonated.

- Replay errors may occur when the database ID (DBID) of the target database is different from the DBID captured in the trace. To correct this problem, restore a backup of the **master** database of the source (traced) server onto the target server. Then, restore the user database or databases. As an alternative, the DBID data column can be removed from the trace and the default database set to the target database for each user captured in the trace.

- Replay errors may occur when attempting to replay a trace against a database if it is in a different state than the source (traced) database. Updates may fail if data is missing or changed.

- Unexpected results may be returned, or replay errors may occur, if replaying a trace containing Session events (Connect, Disconnect, and Existing Connection, for example) and the **Binary Data** column has not been captured. For Session event classes, the **Binary Data** column contains information required to set ANSI and quoted identifiers.

- System performance may degrade if replaying a trace that contains more concurrent connections than the replay computer can manage. In this case, the trace may be filtered by **Application Name**, **SQL User Name**, or another filter if one or more of these data columns were captured in the trace.

- Replaying captured events containing the KILL statement may cause unexpected replay results; the SPID that is terminated may not exist or, if it does exist, the SPID may be assigned to a different user or connection than the one traced originally.

- When replaying a trace file as fast as possible, SPIDs may become blocked, halting the progress of the replay. To free the blocked SPID and allow the trace to continue, kill the blocking SPID.

Troubleshooting SQL Server Query Analyzer

Here is a problem that you may encounter when using SQL Server Query Analyzer to execute a script:

- Showplan does not return a plan for Transact-SQL statements referencing temporary objects. You can trace the **SQL:BatchStarting** and **Execution Plan** events in SQL Server Profiler while executing the Transact-SQL statements to see the plan.

Here are some problems that you may encounter when using SQL Server Query Analyzer to tune a database for a query:

- Unable to recommend indexes because the query did not reference only tunable tables. This problem was caused by one or both of the following reasons:
  - The query did not reference any tunable tables.
  - The query or batch contained the USE statement.

- No indexes suggested. This problem can be caused by any of these reasons:
  - The tables are very small.
  - Supporting indexes may already exist.
  - Only a clustered index would have improved performance.

Note SQL Server Query Analyzer will not recommend clustered indexes when tuning a single query.

- Unable to parse query. This problem can be caused by any of these reasons:
  - The GO command after the query was selected for tuning. The GO command should be excluded from the selected query text for analysis.
  - The wrong database was selected for the query.
  - The text of the query selected for analysis is not parseable.

Troubleshooting the Web Assistant Wizard

This section describes how the Web Assistant Wizard handles HTML page generation using the **When the SQL Server data changes** scheduling option.

With the Web Assistant Wizard, you can generate an HTML file whenever the data changes for one or more tables, by using the **Schedule the Web Assistant Job** dialog box and selecting **When the SQL Server data changes**. This is accomplished by building an INSERT, UPDATE, and DELETE trigger for each of the tables selected by the user. Any existing triggers are detected automatically by the Web Assistant Wizard and retained. Additional Transact-SQL statements are appended to the existing trigger code.

The trigger object built by the Web Assistant Wizard will have a name generated according to the following:

```
Web_tableObjectId_1 -> INSERT trigger
Web_tableObjectId_2 -> UPDATE trigger
Web_tableObjectId_4 -> DELETE trigger
```

For example, if the **authors** table from the **pubs** database is selected as one of the tables to be considered when the data changes, the three triggers generated by the Web Assistant Wizard will be: Web_16003088_1, Web_16003088_2, and Web_16003088_4 for the INSERT, UPDATE, and DELETE respectively (where 16003088 is the object ID corresponding to the **authors** table in the **pubs** database).

sp_depends does not enlist any of the Web Assistant Wizard generated triggers for a given table. You can use **sp_helptrigger** to return trigger information for the specified table for the current database.

Use the following steps to drop any of the triggers generated by the Web Assistant Wizard:

1. Identify the object ID for the table in question:

```
SELECT OBJECT_ID('tabName') tabObjId
```

2. List all the triggers for this table object:

```
USE master
GO
SELECT *
FROM sysobjects
WHERE name LIKE 'Web_tabObjId%'
GO
```

3. Run the DROP TRIGGER command for each of the triggers you want to drop:

```
DROP TRIGGER <Webtriggername>
```

PART 8

Disaster Recovery

Part 8 provides guidelines for and tips about backup and recovery procedures for SQL Server databases running in production environments.

CHAPTER 11

Backup and Recovery

You should back up your databases and transaction logs on a regular basis. In case of system problems, you can restore the backed up files and return to work more quickly than if you had neglected to back up your database. Additionally, every time Microsoft SQL Server starts, recovery is performed on all system and user databases.

The following sections address frequently asked questions about SQL Server 7.0 backup and restore functionality, as well as problems you may encounter when backing up and restoring databases and transaction logs. Additionally, information about resolving performance and insufficient disk space problems related to recovery is included.

Frequently Asked Questions

Here are some frequently asked questions regarding backup and restore functionality, as well as problems you may encounter when backing up and restoring databases and transaction logs.

Q: What are the conditions under which deferred updates occur in SQL Server 7.0?

A: In SQL Server 7.0, all updates are in-place (direct), provided that the column or columns participating in the clustered index key are not changed. If a change is made to a UNIQUE clustered key, the update plan runs in a hybrid mode where the query processor combines direct and deferred updates. If the clustered key is not UNIQUE, all of the updates are run as deferred.

You can use SHOWPLAN to see examples of this behavior. Look for the SPLIT and COLLAPSE operators in the plan. If you find a SPLIT below the clustered index update, one of the clustering keys has been changed. If a COLLAPSE operator is found, the update is running in a hybrid mode. SQL Server collapses delete and insert to the same key values into an in-place update.

Note that this behavior holds true for any index.

Q: Does enabling the **torn page detection** database option add any measurable performance overhead to a server?

A: The **torn page detection** option does not add much CPU cost, but it can increase contention on hot pages. With **torn page detection** off, a page can be accessed while it is being written to disk. This is not true if **torn page detection** is on.

Q: When does SQL Server check for torn pages?

A: **torn page detection** is performed whenever a page is read from disk. In practice, this is likely to happen during recovery, because any page on which the write did not complete during normal operations is very likely to be read by recovery (except for nonlogged operations, such as index creation, bulk copy, and so on).

Q: What happens when SQL Server detects a torn page?

A: When a torn page is detected, a severe I/O error is raised. This error closes the connection. The database is marked suspect only if the torn page is detected during recovery.

Q: How can I recover from torn pages?

A: Restoring the database from a backup and rolling the transaction log forward should correct the problem with no data loss.

Q: What situations are most likely to cause torn pages?

A: Lab tests have shown that torn pages are quite likely to happen when disk writes are occurring and power is lost. If you do not have a battery backup or Uninterruptible Power Supply (UPS), you should consider enabling this option.

Q: Will my query result sets be returned in order if I am running in SQL Server 6.5 compatibility mode?

A: If you do not provide a GROUP BY clause explicitly while in SQL Server 6.5 compatibility mode, the query processor adds one. In SQL Server 7.0 compatibility mode, not having an ORDER BY clause means that any ordering is acceptable to the user or application.

GROUP BY is always sorted in SQL Server 6.5 because the only way that SQL Server 6.5 can form groups is by first sorting the data. However, SQL Server 7.0 has other algorithms for grouping data (most involving hashing of some sort) that can work many times faster than sorting the data to form the groups. This prevents SQL Server from paying the penalty for a slower sort if one is not needed.

Adding an index hint does not force order; it only forces a scan of that particular index. If there is no ORDER BY clause in the query, the query processor is free to decide the cheapest execution strategy. This can be either a logical order scan of the index or a physical order scan of the index. The latter scan may return rows out of order for the index. If ordering is required, use the ORDER BY clause.

Q: Why is my reported log space never 0 (zero), even after truncating the log?

A: In SQL Server 7.0, the log truncation granularity is the virtual log file; in SQL Server 6.x it is a page. Consider an example in which a log configuration consists of four virtual log files. Even if there are no outstanding or unreplicated transactions that prevent truncation of the log after backup, at least 25 percent of the log is always in use, thereby causing at least one virtual log file to be marked as busy.

Efficiency is one of the primary reasons for implementing this schema in SQL Server 7.0. In SQL Server 6.x, truncating the log (even to throw it away) requires scanning through the page chain and deallocating pages. In SQL Server 7.0, truncating the log is as simple as changing the status on a virtual log file from a "used but doesn't contain active log" state to "usable."

It is still possible to have a process back up the log when it reaches some level of being full. However, SQL Server 7.0 differs from SQL Server 6.x in that the smallest fullness level that can be achieved through a transaction log backup and truncation is $(1/n * 100)$ percent, where n is the number of virtual log files in the database configuration.

Q: Why does using SET QUOTED_IDENTIFIER ON within my stored procedures not affect the stored procedure's behavior?

A: Stored procedures maintain the QUOTED_IDENTIFIER setting that was active at the time the stored procedures were compiled. Stored procedures go through distinct compile and execute phases, and the entire stored procedure is compiled as a unit. This means that by the time the SET QUOTED_IDENTIFIER statement is executed, the entire stored procedure has already been compiled. Therefore, changes to the setting cannot affect the stored procedure.

Furthermore, because the QUOTED_IDENTIFIER setting actually affects parsing, a change to the setting cannot be caught midway through compilation and enforce a mode switch.

Pushing the unit of compilation down to individual statements can potentially resolve this situation. In this case, doing so would require that all subsequent statements be recompiled when a SET QUOTED_IDENTIFIER statement is encountered, thereby negating the performance benefits of a stored procedure.

Q: How does SQL Server decide whether to use indexes?

A: SQL Server is a cost-based query optimizer, not a rule-based system. Being cost-based, SQL Server is syntax independent and literally analyzes the cost of each execution strategy based on the projected number and size of the result sets. If you want to force table scans or index strategies, you can guarantee their use only by using index hints. This is generally not recommended, although at times it may become necessary.

It is difficult to generalize and specify a basic set of rules under which the query processor will always pick a table scan or index seek. In general, the use of an index access strategy is favored over table scans unless the choice is very clear, for example, if all rows are wanted. Table scans acquire shared locks and thereby can reduce concurrency (that is, multiuser access) greatly. As a result, table scans are avoided whenever possible.

Scan decisions are based on anticipated execution costs, so there is no size limit below which indexes are ignored. However, if the entire table fits on a single page, there are very few cases, if any, in which indexes will be of value.

Q: DBCC SHRINKDB is not shrinking my log. Why?

A: DBCC SHRINKDB shrinks data files on a per-file basis, but shrinks log files as if all the log files existed in one contiguous log pool. The shrinking of log files is not immediate and does not occur until the active portion of the log moves. As updates are performed on the database, the shrink operation occurs at checkpoints or during transaction log backups. Each log file is marked with the *target_percent* for the shrink operation. Each subsequent log backup or log truncation attempts to shrink the file as close as possible to the *target_percent* size. Because a log file can be shrunk only to a virtual log file boundary, it may not be possible to shrink a log file to a size smaller than the size of a virtual log file, even if it is not being used.

Q: Why does the creation of a UNIQUE index stop on multiple null values in a column?

A: SQL Server does not support the occurrence of multiple null values in a UNIQUE index. For the purposes of the index key, a NULL is considered a value and can occur only once in a given UNIQUE index.

Q: What is the bulk copy TABLOCK hint or property?

A: The TABLOCK hint or property increases the performance of bulk copy operations by reducing the locking contention of the operation. SQL Server 7.0 introduces a new bulk update (BU) lock type. BU locks have reduced contention with other types of locks acquired by non-bulk copy operations. Bulk copy operations use bulk update locks by specifying the TABLOCK hint or property on either the **bcp** command prompt utility, the BULK INSERT Transact-SQL statement, the bulk copy API supported by the SQL Server ODBC driver, or the **IRowsetFastLoad** interface supported by the OLE DB Provider for SQL Server. If TABLOCK is not specified in a bulk copy operation, it acquires row locks on the bulk copied rows. These row locks have more overhead than a BU lock taken at the table level.

Tips for Using Backup and Restore

Several differences between the backup and restore functionality of Microsoft SQL Server 7.0 and earlier versions warrant a brief explanation and tips about how to exploit their benefits fully.

In SQL Server 7.0, database creation and backup operations use parallelism

The ALTER DATABASE statement uses parallelism to extend each file on a distinct logical drive. Likewise, the BACKUP DATABASE statement uses a separate thread per logical drive. Although this is a useful performance feature in certain circumstances, it does not mean that creating many logical drives is generally preferred over combining those drives in a RAID array. SQL Server uses asynchronous I/O and can usually leverage all available I/O capacity in a multidisk RAID array. Combining most available drive spindles to a large RAID array (of the appropriate type) often provides the best performance for the broadest circumstances.

SQL Server 7.0 documents in the error log backups with INIT or FORMAT

It may appear that SQL Server backup no longer documents whether a backup device has been initialized in the error log. Actually, this is documented, but not in the same format as in SQL Server 6.5.

The FILE= attribute in the error log provides the necessary information. For example, if the error log says FILE = 1, either an INIT or a FORMAT command was issued.

- FILE = 1 means the backup device was initialized.

- FILE = >1 means the backup device was not initialized.

The following examples show SQL Server 7.0 messages in the error log:

```
1998-11-17 18:17:47.98 backup    Database backed up with following
information: Database: bck_db, creation date and time:
11/17/98(18:09:42), pages dumped: 107, first LSN: 4:32:1, last LSN:
4:34:1, sort order: 52, striped: 0, number of dump devices: 1, device
information: (FILE=1, TYPE=DISK: {'c:\temp\fb1.bck'}).

1998-11-17 18:33:54.28 backup    Database backed up with following
information: Database: bck_db, creation date and time:
11/17/98(18:09:42), pages dumped: 106, first LSN: 4:42:1, last LSN:
4:44:1, sort order: 52, striped: 0, number of dump devices: 1, device
information: (FILE=2, TYPE=DISK: {'c:\temp\doit.bck'}).
```

The following examples show SQL Server 6.5 messages in the error log:

```
98/12/07 10:54:00.30 backup    DATABASE dumped with following info:
Database Name:pubs, Creation Date and Time:Dec 7, 98(10:53), Pages
dumped:161, Current Sequence:36075 11572328, Sort Order:52, Striped:NO,
Number of Dump Devices:1, device info:(VOLID=SQL0001
NAME=D:\temp\65pubs.dat TYPE=DISK FILE=1)

98/12/07 10:54:13.34 backup    DATABASE dumped with following info:
Database Name:pubs, Creation Date and Time:Dec 7, 98(10:54), Pages
dumped:161, Current Sequence:36075 11572328, Sort Order:52, Striped:NO,
Number of Dump Devices:1, device info:(VOLID=SQL0001
NAME=D:\temp\65pubs.dat TYPE=DISK FILE=2)
```

Differential backup time considerations

A differential backup records only changes made to the database since the last full backup. Although typically much faster than a full database backup, elapsed time for SQL Server 7.0 differential backup is roughly proportional to the allocated space in the database. Consequently, a differential backup on a very large database may take longer than expected, even if few changes have occurred since the last full database backup.

If the amount of time required for a differential backup is too large, you should consider doing log backups instead.

Common Backup and Restore Problems

Here are the solutions to some problems you may encounter when backing up and restoring databases and transaction logs:

- A syntax error occurred when using the BACKUP or RESTORE statements, which indicates that the database is in Microsoft SQL Server version 6.5 compatibility mode. The BACKUP and RESTORE keywords are valid only with SQL Server 7.0 databases.

  Set the SQL Server compatibility level to 70 before using BACKUP or RESTORE statements. For more information, see SQL Server Books Online.

- The BACKUP statement cannot be performed at the same time as these operations:

  - DBCC CHECKALLOC
  - DBCC SHRINKDATABASE
  - **bcp** Utility
  - SELECT INTO
  - File manipulation

  Reissue the backup operation after the conflicting operation has finished. For more information, see "Error 3023" in SQL Server Books Online.

- A standby database cannot be backed up if it has not yet been recovered.

  Use backups from your primary server until operations have switched to the standby. For more information, see SQL Server Books Online.

- A database cannot be restored unless its sort order, collation sequence, Unicode locale ID, and Unicode comparison style match those of the server.

  For more information, see "Error 3120" or "Error 3149" in SQL Server Books Online.

- The backup being restored is a valid Microsoft Tape Format, but it is not a SQL Server backup.

  To determine the backup contents, use RESTORE HEADERONLY. For more information, see "Error 3143" in SQL Server Books Online.

- The backup set is a backup of a database with the same name as the database to which you are restoring. However, the database being restored to was created by a different CREATE DATABASE statement than the database in the backup set.

  Either overwrite the existing database or restore the backup set to a different database name. For more information, see "Error 3154" in SQL Server Books Online.

- A restore operation failed because ALTER DATABASE was used to add or remove one or more database or transaction log files.

  Restore a full database backup created after the files were added or removed. For more information, see "Error 3155" in SQL Server Books Online.

- An attempt was made to use a logical device that is not a defined backup device.

  Either create the device or use the TAPE = or DISK = syntax of the BACKUP statement. For more information, see "Error 3206" or "Error 3209" in SQL Server Books Online.

- The media family spans multiple volumes. The restore operation has already processed the data on the specified volume.

  Replace the current volume with a volume not yet processed. For more information, see "Error 3227" in SQL Server Books Online.

- The backup device does not contain data in Microsoft Tape Format. For more information, see "Error 3242" in SQL Server Books Online.

- The media family spans multiple volumes. The restore operation expected to process the volume number specified in the error message but found a different volume number instead.

  To continue the restore operation, replace the current volume with the volume number specified in the error message. For more information, see "Error 3247" in SQL Server Books Online.

- The media family spans multiple volumes. The backup set to be processed by the restore operation starts on an earlier volume than the one inserted into the named device.

  Replace the current volume with a volume containing the start of the target backup set. For more information, see "Error 3249" in SQL Server Books Online.

- The restore operation has completely processed the media family on the named device and is now ready to reuse the device to restore one of the remaining media families.

  Replace the current volume with the first volume of a media family that has not yet been processed. For more information, see "Error 3251" in SQL Server Books Online.

- The BACKUP operation that created the backup set did not finish successfully.

  Either restore a different database backup, if restoring a database backup, and apply transaction logs; or apply the next transaction log backup, if restoring a transaction log backup. For more information, see "Error 3256" in SQL Server Books Online.

- The volume on the named device does not belong to the same RAID media set as the other volumes being processed.

  Either remove the offending volume and insert the next volume of the media family, for tape media sets; or, for disks, reissue the command, naming only those backup devices part of the same RAID media set. For more information, see "Error 3258" in SQL Server Books Online.

- The server will not initialize the volume inserted into the named device as a continuation volume for the designated media family because the RAID media set spans multiple volumes.

  Replace the current volume with a fresh tape that can be overwritten. For more information, see "Error 3263" in SQL Server Books Online.

- The server is too busy to perform the backup or restore operation.

  Retry the operation after reducing the server load. For more information, see "Error 3267" or "Error 3627" in SQL Server Books Online.

- If the **trunc. log on chkpt.** database option is enabled, the log is truncated when periodic checkpoints occur. Only full database and differential database backups are allowed because the log has been truncated and any log backups made would be unusable.

  Either perform full and differential backups, leaving **trunc. log on chkpt.** enabled, or maintain a full set of transaction log backups, disabling **trunc. log on chkpt.** For more information, see "Error 4208" in SQL Server Books Online.

- To restore the database after failure you must begin with either a full database backup or a complete set of file backups.

  Perform a full database backup before backing up the transaction log. For more information, see "Error 4214" in SQL Server Books Online.

- The restore operation found a gap between the last restore and the transaction log that you attempted to apply.

  Apply the transaction log backups in the order they were created originally. For more information, see "Error 4305" in SQL Server Books Online.

- No further restore operations can be performed after a database has been recovered.

  Restart the restore sequence and use the NORECOVERY option on all but the final RESTORE statement. For more information, see "Error 4306" in SQL Server Books Online.

- You cannot recover the database to the state that it was in at the time the current log backup occurred. At least one file was modified; therefore, recovery is not possible because the database will be left in an inconsistent state.

  Recover the database to either its most recent state or a specific point in time. For more information, see "Error 4318" in SQL Server Books Online.

Troubleshooting Orphaned Users

When restoring a database backup to another server, you may experience a problem with orphaned users. This scenario displays and resolves the problem:

1. Alias the login **janetl** to **dbo** by executing **sp_addlogin**.

   ```
   sp_addlogin 'janetl', 'dbo'
   ```

2. Back up a database. In this example, back up **Northwind**.

   ```
   BACKUP DATABASE Northwind
   TO DISK = 'c:\mssql7\backup\northwnd'
   ```

3. Drop the database that was just backed up.

   ```
   DROP DATABASE Northwind
   ```

4. Drop the login.

   ```
   sp_droplogin 'janetl'
   ```

5. Restore the backed up database.

   ```
   RESTORE DATABASE Northwind
   FROM DISK = 'c:\mssql7\backup\northwnd'
   ```

   The **janetl** login is not allowed into the **Northwind** database unless the **guest** login is allowed. Even though the **janetl** login has been deleted, it still shows up (as an orphaned row) in the **sysusers** table:

   ```
   USE Northwind
   SELECT *
   FROM sysusers
   WHERE name = 'janetl'
   ```

▶ **To resolve orphaned users**

1. Add a temporary login using **sp_addlogin**. Specify the security identifier (SID) (from **sysusers**) for the orphaned user.

   ```
   sp_addlogin @loginame = 'nancyd',
       @sid = 0x32C864A70427D211B4DD00104B9E8A00
   ```

2. Drop the temporary alias that belongs to the aliased SID using **sp_dropalias**.

   ```
   sp_dropalias 'nancyd'
   ```

3. Drop the original user (now orphaned) using **sp_dropuser**.

   ```
   sp_dropuser 'janetl'
   ```

4. Drop the original login using **sp_droplogin**.

   ```
   sp_droplogin 'nancyd'
   ```

Recovery Performance

Recovery time is determined by how much work has been done since the last checkpoint, and by how much work has been done by all active transactions at the time of the server crash. Microsoft SQL Server uses the **recovery interval** configuration option to set the maximum number of minutes per database that SQL Server needs to recover databases. This **recovery interval** option controls checkpoint frequency. For an online transaction processing (OLTP) system (using short transactions), **recovery interval** is the primary factor determining recovery time.

After installation, SQL Server sets **recovery interval** to a default value of 0. As long as **recovery interval** is at the default setting and long-running transactions are not present, recovery for each database should take approximately one minute or less. If long-running transactions were active at the time of the server crash, recovery time is controlled by the time it takes to roll back the effects of these transactions.

If recovery routinely takes significantly longer than one minute for a database, **recovery interval** has a value of 0, and there are no long-running transactions to roll back, consider contacting your primary support provider to resolve the recovery performance problem.

Recovery reports progress (based on the virtual log files for a database). At the beginning of recovery, recovery analyzes and scans the log since the last checkpoint. Based on the analysis phase, recovery estimates how much log will be read during recovery. The amount of log read is used to report recovery progress.

If **recovery interval** is changed from the default value, database recovery takes that many times longer to complete. For example, if **recovery interval** is changed to 10, recovery would take approximately 10 times longer to complete than if **recovery interval** remained at the default setting of 0.

When growing the log, use larger chunks to ensure a shorter startup time for SQL Server. The greater the number of small chunks, the longer SQL Server takes to initialize them.

If a long-running transaction is terminated, let the server finish the rollback process. If you are concerned about the length of the rollback process, ask your system administrator to confirm that activity is taking place on the server. Terminating the server process during the rollback of a long-running transaction results in long recovery time.

If you have a long-running transaction and a crash occurs during this transaction, SQL Server begins the recovery process. This may take some time. If you are concerned that this recovery process is taking too long and you believe it is halted, contact your system administrator.

Insufficient Disk Space

During recovery, it is a rare but possible occurrence for the server to require additional log or data space. If additional space is unavailable and either the log or data files cannot grow, the server:

- Reports error message 9002 or 1105 in the Microsoft SQL Server error log.
- Marks the database as suspect.
- Takes the database offline.

▶ **To resolve the 9002 error message and bring the database online**

1. Free disk space on any disk drive containing the log file for the related database. Freeing disk space allows the recovery system to grow the log file automatically.
2. Reset the suspect status by executing **sp_resetstatus**.
3. Run recovery by executing DBCC DBRECOVER (*database*).

   Or

1. Free disk space on a different disk drive.
2. Move the transaction log files with an insufficient amount of free disk space to the disk drive in Step 1.
3. Detach the database by executing **sp_detach_db**.
4. Attach the database by executing **sp_attach_db**, pointing to the moved files.

   Or

- Add a log file to the suspect database and run recovery on the database by executing **sp_add_log_file_recover_suspect_db**.

▶ **To resolve the 1105 error message and bring the database online**

1. Free disk space on any disk containing a file in the filegroup mentioned in the 1105 error message. Freeing disk space allows the files in the filegroup to grow.
2. Reset the suspect status by executing **sp_resetstatus**.
3. Run recovery by executing DBCC DBRECOVER (*database*).

Or

1. Free disk space on a different disk drive.
2. Move the data files in the filegroup with an insufficient amount of free disk space to the disk drive in Step 1.
3. Detach the database by executing **sp_detach_db**.
4. Attach the database by executing **sp_attach_db**, pointing to the moved files.

Or

- Add a data file to the suspect database and run recovery on the database by executing **sp_add_file_recover_suspect_db**.

PART 9

Architecture

The chapters in Part 9 explain the basic structure and behavior of SQL Server:

- Data Warehousing Framework
- OLAP Services
- Query Processor
- Storage Engine

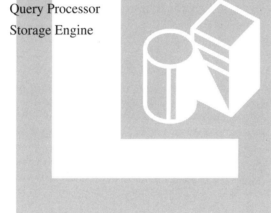

CHAPTER 12

Data Warehousing Framework

Making better business decisions quickly is the key to succeeding in today's competitive marketplace. Organizations seeking to improve their decision-making ability can be overwhelmed by the sheer volume and complexity of data available from their varied operational and production systems. In response to this challenge, many organizations choose to build a data warehouse to unlock the information in their operational systems.

What is Data Warehousing?

A data warehouse is an integrated store of information collected from other systems that becomes the foundation for decision support and data analysis. Although there are many types of data warehouses, based on different design methodologies and philosophical approaches, they all have these common traits:

- Information is organized around the major subjects of the enterprise (for example, customers, products, sales, or vendors), reflecting a data-driven design.

- Raw data is gathered from nonintegrated operational and legacy applications, cleansed, and then summarized and presented in a way that makes sense to end users.

- Based on feedback from end users and discoveries in the data warehouse, the data warehouse architecture will change over time, reflecting the iterative nature of the process.

The data warehousing process is inherently complex and, as a result, is costly and time-consuming. Over the past several years, Microsoft has been working within the software industry to create a data warehousing platform that consists of both component technology and leading products that can be used to lower the costs and improve the effectiveness of data warehouse creation, administration, and usage. Microsoft also has been developing a number of products and facilities, such as Microsoft SQL Server version 7.0, that are well suited to the data warehousing process. Coupled with third-party products that can be integrated using the Microsoft Data Warehousing Framework, customers have a large selection of interoperable, best-of-breed products from which to choose for their data warehousing needs.

SQL Server 7.0 offers broad functionality in support of the data warehousing process. In conjunction with the Data Warehousing Framework, Microsoft plans to deliver a platform for data warehousing that helps reduce costs and complexity, and improves effectiveness of data warehousing efforts.

Data Warehousing Process

From the information technology perspective, data warehousing is aimed at the timely delivery of the right information to the right individuals in an organization. This is an ongoing process, not a one-time solution, and requires an approach different from that required in the development of transaction-oriented systems.

A data warehouse is a collection of data in support of management's decision-making process that is subject-oriented, integrated, time-variant, and nonvolatile. The data warehouse is focused on the concept (for example, sales) rather than the process (for example, issuing invoices). It contains all the relevant information on a concept gathered from multiple processing systems. This information is collected and stored at regular intervals and is relatively stable.

A data warehouse integrates operational data by using consistent naming conventions, measurements, physical attributes, and semantics. The first steps in the physical design of the data warehouse are determining which subject areas should be included and developing a set of agreed-upon definitions. This requires interviewing end users, analysts, and executives to understand and document the scope of the information requirements. The issues must be thoroughly understood before the logical process can be translated into a physical data warehouse.

Following the physical design, operational systems are put in place to populate the data warehouse. Because the operational systems and the data warehouse contain different representations of the data, populating the data warehouse requires transformations of the data: summarizing, translating, decoding, eliminating invalid data, and so on. These processes need to be automated so that they can be performed on an ongoing basis: extracting, transforming, and moving the source data as often as needed to meet the business requirements of the data warehouse.

In the operational system, data is current-valued and accurate as of the moment of access. For example, an order entry application always shows the current value of inventory on hand for each product. This value could differ between two queries issued only moments apart. In the data warehouse, data represents information gathered over a long period, and is accurate as of a particular point in time. In effect, the data warehouse contains a long series of snapshots about the key subject areas of the business.

Finally, information is made available for browsing, analyzing, and reporting. Many tools assist in analysis, from simple report writers to advanced data miners. Ultimately, analysis drives the final iterations of the data warehousing process, causing revisions in the design of the data warehouse to accommodate new information, improve system performance, or allow new types of analysis. With these changes, the process restarts and continues throughout the life of the data warehouse.

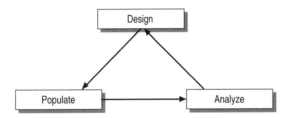

Data Warehousing Architecture

Many methodologies have been proposed to simplify the information technology efforts required to support the data warehousing process on an ongoing basis. This has led to debates about the best architecture for delivering data warehouses in organizations.

Two basic types of data warehouse architecture exist: *enterprise* data warehouses and *data marts*.

The enterprise data warehouse contains enterprise-wide information integrated from multiple operational data sources for consolidated data analysis. Typically, it is composed of several subject areas, such as customers, products, and sales, and is used for both tactical and strategic decision making. The enterprise data warehouse contains both detailed point-in-time data and summarized information, and can range in size from 50 gigabytes (GB) to more than 1 terabyte. Enterprise data warehouses can be very expensive and time-consuming to build and manage. They are usually created from the top down by centralized information services organizations.

The data mart contains a subset of enterprise-wide data that is built for use by an individual department or division in an organization. Unlike the enterprise data warehouse, the data mart is usually built from the bottom up by departmental resources for a specific decision-support application or group of users. Data marts contain summarized and often detailed data about a subject area. The information in the data mart can be a subset of an enterprise data warehouse (dependent data mart) or can come directly from the operational data sources (independent data mart).

Enterprise data warehouses and data marts are constructed and maintained through the same iterative process described earlier. Furthermore, both approaches share a similar set of technological components.

Data Warehousing Components

A data warehouse always consists of a number of components, including:

- Operational data sources.
- Design/development tools.
- Data extraction and transformation tools.
- Database management system (DBMS).
- Data access and analysis tools.
- System management tools.

Several years ago, Microsoft recognized the need for a set of technologies that would integrate these components. This led to the creation of the Microsoft Data Warehousing Framework, a roadmap not only for the development of Microsoft products such as SQL Server 7.0, but also for the technologies necessary to integrate products from other vendors.

Microsoft Data Warehousing Framework

The goal of the Microsoft Data Warehousing Framework is to simplify the design, implementation, and management of data warehousing solutions. This framework has been designed to provide:

- Open architecture that is easily integrated with and extended by third-party vendors.
- Heterogeneous data import, export, validation, and cleansing services with optional data lineage.

- Integrated metadata for data warehouse design, data extraction/transformation, server management, and end-user analysis tools.
- Core management services for scheduling, storage management, performance monitoring, alerts/events, and notification.

The Data Warehousing Framework has been designed from the ground up to provide an open architecture that can be extended easily by Microsoft customers and third-party businesses using industry-standard technology. This allows organizations to choose best-of-breed components and still be assured of integration.

Ease of use is a compelling reason for customers and independent software vendors (ISVs) to choose the Data Warehousing Framework. Microsoft provides an object-oriented set of components designed to manage information in the distributed environment. Microsoft also provides both entry-level and best-of-breed products to address the many steps in the data warehousing process.

Data Warehousing Framework Components

Building the data warehouse requires a set of components for describing the logical and physical design of the data sources and their destinations in the enterprise data warehouse or data mart.

To conform to definitions laid out during the design stage, operational data must pass through a cleansing and transformation stage before being placed in the enterprise data warehouse or data mart. This data staging process can be many levels deep, especially with enterprise data warehousing architectures, but is necessarily simplified in this illustration.

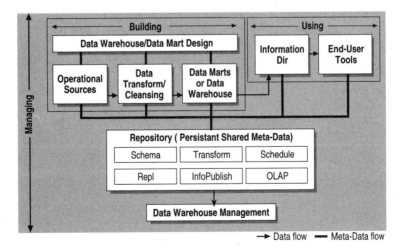

End-user tools, including desktop productivity products, specialized analysis products, and custom programs, are used to gain access to information in the data warehouse. Ideally, user access is through a directory facility that enables end-user searches for appropriate and relevant data to resolve questions and that provides a layer of security between the end users and the data warehouse systems.

Finally, a variety of components can come into play for the management of the data warehousing environment, such as for scheduling repeated tasks and managing multiserver networks.

The Data Warehousing Framework describes the relationships between the various components used in the process of building, using, and managing a data warehouse. Two enabling technologies comprise the core Data Warehousing Framework: the integrated metadata repository and the data transport layer (OLE DB). These technologies make possible the interoperability of many products and components involved in data warehousing.

OLE DB provides for standardized, high-performance access to a wide variety of data, and allows for integration of multiple data types.

Microsoft Repository provides an integrated metadata repository that is shared by the various components used in the data warehousing process. Shared metadata allows for the transparent integration of multiple products from a variety of vendors, without the need for specialized interfaces between each of the products:

- Mainframe indexed sequential access method/virtual storage access method (ISAM/VSAM) and hierarchical databases
- E-mail and file system stores
- Text, graphical, and geographical data
- Custom business objects

OLE DB defines a collection of COM interfaces that encapsulates various database management system services. These interfaces enable the creation of software components that implement such services. OLE DB components consist of data providers (which contain and expose data), data consumers (which use data), and service components (which process and transport data).

OLE DB interfaces are designed to integrate components smoothly so that vendors can bring high-quality OLE DB components to the market quickly. In addition, OLE DB includes a bridge to ODBC that enables continued support for the broad range of ODBC relational database drivers available today.

Defining ActiveX Data Objects

Microsoft ActiveX Data Objects (ADO) is a strategic application-level programming interface to data and information. ADO provides consistent, high-performance access to data and supports a variety of development needs, including creating front-end database clients and middle-tier business objects, and using applications, tools, languages, or Internet browsers. ADO is designed to be a data interface for one-to-multitier, client/server, and Web-based solution development.

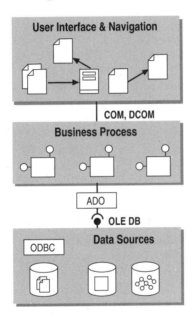

ADO provides an easy-to-use application-level interface to OLE DB, which in turn provides underlying access to data. ADO is implemented with a small footprint, minimal network traffic in key scenarios, and minimal layers between the front end and data source. The result is a lightweight, high-performance interface. ADO is called using the COM automation interface, a familiar metaphor available from all leading rapid application development (RAD) environments, database tools, and languages on the market today. And because ADO was designed to combine the best features of Remote Data Object (RDO) and Data Access Object (DAO), and eventually to replace them, ADO uses similar conventions with simplified semantics, making it a natural next step for today's developers.

Microsoft Repository: The Glue that Binds the Data Warehouse

One of the greatest implementation challenges is integrating all of the tools required to design, transform, store, and manage a data warehouse. The ability to share and reuse metadata reduces the cost and complexity of building, using, and managing data warehouses. Many data warehousing products include a proprietary metadata repository that cannot be used by any other components in the data warehouse. Each tool must be able to access, create, or enhance the metadata created by any other tool easily, while also extending the metadata model to meet the specific needs of the tool.

Consider the example of a data warehouse built with shared metadata. Metadata from operational systems is stored in the repository by design and data transformation tools. This physical and logical model is used by transformation products to extract, validate, and cleanse the data prior to loading it into the database. The database management system may be relational, multidimensional, or a combination of both. The data-access and data-analysis tools provide access to the information in the data warehouse. The information directory integrates the technical and business metadata, making it easy to find and launch existing queries, reports, and applications for the data warehouse.

The Microsoft Data Warehousing Framework is centered upon shared metadata in Microsoft Repository, which is a component of Microsoft SQL Server 7.0. Microsoft Repository is a database that stores descriptive information about software components and their relationships. It consists of an open information model (OIM) and a set of published COM interfaces.

OIMs are object models for specific types of information and are flexible enough to support new information types as well as extensible enough to fit the needs of specific users or vendors. Microsoft has developed OIMs in collaboration with the software industry for database schema, data transformations, and online analytical processing (OLAP). Future models may include replication, task scheduling, semantic models, and an information directory that combines business and technical metadata.

The Meta Data Coalition, an industry consortium of 53 vendors dedicated to fostering a standard means for vendors to exchange metadata, has announced support for Microsoft Repository, and Microsoft Repository OIMs have received broad third-party support.

Designing the Data Warehouse

The development phase of the data warehousing process often begins with the creation of a dimensional model that describes the important metrics and dimensions of the selected subject area based on user requirements. Unlike online transaction processing (OLTP) systems that organize data in a highly normalized manner, the data in the data warehouse is organized in a highly denormalized manner to improve query performance when stored in a relational database management system.

Relational databases often use star or snowflake schemas to provide the fastest possible response times to complex queries. Star schemas contain a denormalized central fact table for the subject area and multiple dimension tables for descriptive information about the subject's dimensions. The fact table can contain many millions of rows. Commonly accessed information is often preaggregated and summarized to further improve performance.

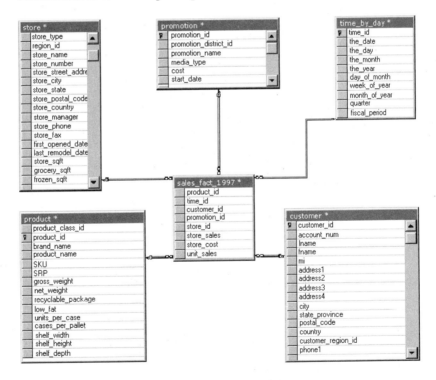

Although the star schema is primarily considered a tool for the database administrator to increase performance and simplify data warehouse design, it also represents data warehouse information in a way that makes better sense to end users.

The Data Warehouse Database

At the heart of the data warehouse is the database. It is crucial to build the data warehouse on a high-performance database engine that will meet both current and future needs of the organization. Relational database management systems (RDBMS) are the most common reservoirs for the large volumes of information stored in data warehouses. Increasingly, relational systems are being augmented with multidimensional OLAP (MOLAP) servers that provide enhanced navigational capabilities and increased performance for complex queries. Also important are facilities for replicating databases reliably from central data warehouses to dependent data marts, and ensuring consistency between mirrored data marts distributed geographically.

Scalable and Robust RDBMS

Microsoft SQL Server 7.0 contains a number of features that makes it an excellent RDBMS for enterprise data warehouses and data marts, including:

- Support for terabyte-sized databases to manage the largest data warehouses.

- Scalability for large databases, but also for departmental servers and laptop computers with the 100 percent code-compatible Desktop Edition, providing the ultimate flexibility and access to central data sources.

- Advanced query processing to support the optimization and execution of complex queries typical in data warehouse applications, including star schemas.

- Intraquery parallelism to provide faster performance by breaking a complex single query into component parts and distributing the workload to multiple processors, including remotely linked servers.

- High-performance utilities to provide performance tuning, data loading, and index construction.

- Heterogeneous join capabilities to enable retrieval and consolidation of information from any OLE DB source.

SQL Server 7.0 is appropriate for nearly every data warehouse size and complexity. However, data warehouse implementations usually require more than one central database. In practice, organizations will implement decision support systems with additional analytical tools and with distributed information architectures. SQL Server 7.0 includes essential facilities for managing these additional tasks.

Integrated OLAP Analytical Capabilities

OLAP is an increasingly popular technology that can dramatically improve business analysis. Historically, OLAP has been characterized by expensive tools, difficult implementation, and inflexible deployment. Microsoft SQL Server OLAP Services is a new, fully featured OLAP capability provided as a component of SQL Server 7.0. OLAP Services includes a middle-tier server that allows users to perform sophisticated analysis on large volumes of data with exceptional results. OLAP Services also includes a client-side cache and calculation engine called Microsoft PivotTable Service, which helps improve performance and reduce network traffic. PivotTable Service allows end users to conduct analyses while disconnected from the network.

OLAP Services is a middle-tier OLAP server that simplifies user navigation and helps improve performance for queries against information in the data warehouse.

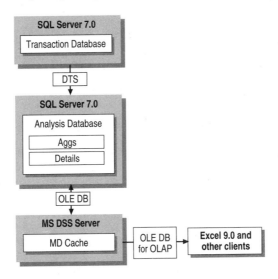

OLAP is a key component of data warehousing, and OLAP Services provides essential functionality for a wide array of applications ranging from reporting to advanced decision support. OLAP functionality within SQL Server 7.0 helps make multidimensional analysis much more affordable and bring the benefits of OLAP to a wider audience, from smaller organizations to groups and individuals within larger corporations. Coupled with the wide variety of tools and applications supporting OLAP applications through Microsoft OLE DB for OLAP, OLAP Services helps increase the number of organizations that have access to sophisticated analytical tools and can help reduce the costs of data warehousing.

For more information about Microsoft SQL Server OLAP Services, see SQL Server Books Online.

Replication

Creating distributed, dependent data marts from a central data warehouse, or even duplicating the contents of an independent data mart, requires the ability to replicate information reliably. SQL Server 7.0 includes facilities for reliably distributing information from a central publishing data warehouse to multiple subscribing data marts. Information can be partitioned by time, geography, and so on as part of the replication process.

SQL Server 7.0 provides a variety of replication technologies that can be tailored to your application's specific requirements. Each replication technology produces different benefits and restrictions across these dimensions:

- Transactional consistency
- Site autonomy
- Data partitioning

Requirements along and across these three dimensions vary from one distributed application to the next.

In most decision-support applications, data is not updated at individual sites. Instead, information is prepared at a central staging area and pushed to distributed database servers for remote access. For this reason, snapshot replication is often used to distribute data.

As its name implies, snapshot replication takes a picture, or snapshot, of the published data in the database at one moment in time. Instead of copying INSERT, UPDATE, and DELETE statements (characteristic of transactional replication) or data modifications (characteristic of merge replication), Subscribers are updated by a total refresh of the data set. Hence, snapshot replication sends all the data to the Subscriber instead of sending the changes only. If the information being sent is extremely large, it can require substantial network resources to transmit. In deciding if snapshot replication is appropriate, you must balance the size of the entire data set against the volatility of the data.

Snapshot replication is the simplest type of replication, and it guarantees latent consistency between the Publisher and Subscriber. It also provides high autonomy if Subscribers do not update the data. Snapshot replication is a good solution for read-only Subscribers that do not require the most recent data and can be totally disconnected from the network when updates are not occurring. However, SQL Server provides a full range of choices for replication depending on application requirements.

For more information about replication in SQL Server 7.0, see SQL Server Books Online.

Importing, Exporting, and Transforming Data

Before the data can be loaded into the data warehouse, it must first be transformed into an integrated and consistent format. A transformation is a sequence of procedural operations that is applied to the information in a data source before it can be stored in the specified destination. Data Transformation Services (DTS) is a new facility in Microsoft SQL Server 7.0 that supports many types of transformations, such as simple column mappings, calculation of new values from one or more source fields, decomposition of a single field into multiple destination columns, and so on.

DTS Goals

DTS was created to:

- Provide better importing, exporting, and transformation of heterogeneous data using OLE DB.
- Provide an extensible architecture accessible to ISVs, customers, and consultants.
- Share rich metadata about the sources, destinations, transformations, and lineage through integration with Microsoft Repository OIMs.

DTS allows the user to import, export, and transform data to and from multiple data sources using 100 percent OLE DB–based architecture. OLE DB data sources include not only database systems, but also desktop applications such as Microsoft Excel. Microsoft provides native OLE DB interfaces for SQL Server and for Oracle. In addition, Microsoft has developed an OLE DB wrapper that works in conjunction with existing ODBC drivers to provide access to other relational sources. Delimited and fixed-field text files are also supported natively.

DTS Architecture

DTS transformation definitions are stored in Microsoft Repository, SQL Server, or COM-structured storage files. Relational and nonrelational data sources are accessed using OLE DB. The data pump opens a rowset from the data source and pulls each row from the data source into the data pump. The data pump executes Microsoft ActiveX scripting functions (Microsoft Visual Basic, Scripting Edition; JScript development software; and PerlScript) to copy, validate, or transform data from the data source to the destination. Custom transform objects can be created for advanced data scrubbing. The new values for the destination are returned to the pump and sent to the destination by means of high-speed data transfers. Destinations can be OLE DB, ODBC, ASCII fixed field, ASCII delimited files, and HTML.

In DTS architecture, data is pulled from the data source with an OLE DB data pump, and optionally transformed before being sent to OLE DB destinations.

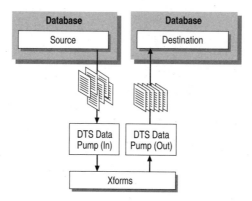

Complex transformation and data validation logic can be implemented using ActiveX scripting. These scripts can invoke methods from any OLE object to modify or validate the value of a column. Advanced developers can create reusable COM transformation objects that provide advanced scrubbing capabilities. Custom tasks can be created that transfer files by means of FTP or launch external processes.

ISVs and consultants can create new data sources and destinations by providing OLE DB interfaces. The data pump will query the OLE DB interface for any provider to determine whether high-speed data loading is supported; if not, then standard loading mechanisms will be used.

Although standards like SQL-92 have improved interoperability between relational database engines, vendors still differentiate themselves in the marketplace by adding useful but proprietary extensions to SQL-92. SQL Server offers a simple programming language known as Transact-SQL that provides basic conditional processing and simple repetition control. Oracle Corporation, Informix Software, Inc., and other vendors offer similar SQL extensions.

The DTS Transformation Engine pass-through SQL architecture helps guarantee that most of the functionality of the source and destination are available to customers using the DTS Transformation Engine. This allows customers to leverage scripts and stored procedures that they have already developed and tested by simply invoking them from the DTS Transformation Engine. The pass-through architecture dramatically simplifies development and testing, since DTS does not modify or interpret the SQL statement being executed. Any statement that works through the native interface of the DBMS will work exactly the same way during a transformation.

DTS records and documents the lineage of each transformation in the repository so customers can know where their data came from. Data lineage can be tracked at both the table and row levels. This provides a complete audit trail for the information in the data warehouse. Data lineage is shared across vendor products. DTS packages and data lineage can be stored centrally in Microsoft Repository. This includes transformation definitions, Visual Basic scripting, Java scripting, and package execution history. Integration with Microsoft Repository allows third parties to build on the infrastructure provided by the DTS Transformation Engine. DTS packages can be scheduled for execution through an integrated calendar, and then executed interactively or in response to system events.

DTS Package

The DTS package is a complete description of all the work to be performed as part of the transformation process. Each package defines one or more tasks to be executed in a coordinated sequence. A DTS package can be created interactively using the graphical user interface or any language that supports OLE Automation. The DTS package can be stored in Microsoft Repository, in SQL Server, or as a COM-structured storage file. After being retrieved from the repository or structured storage file, the package can be executed in the same way as a DTS package that was created interactively.

A DTS package can contain multiple tasks, and each task can be as uninvolved as table-to-table mapping or as complex as invoking an external data cleansing process.

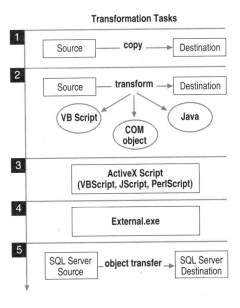

A task defines a piece of work to be performed as part of the transformation process. A task can move and transform heterogeneous data from an OLE DB source to an OLE DB destination using the DTS Data Pump, and can execute ActiveX scripting or launch an external program. Tasks are executed by step objects.

Step objects coordinate the flow of control and execution of tasks in the DTS package. Some tasks must be executed in a certain sequence. For example, a database must be created successfully (Task A) before a table can be created (Task B). This is an example of a finish-start relationship between Task A and Task B; Task B, therefore, has a precedence constraint on Task A.

Each task is executed when all preceding constraints have been satisfied. Tasks can be executed conditionally based on run-time conditions. Multiple tasks can be executed in parallel to improve performance. For example, a package can load data simultaneously from Oracle and DB2 into separate tables. The step object also controls the priority of a task. The priority of a step determines the priority of the Win32 API thread running the task.

The DTS Data Pump is an OLE DB service provider that provides the infrastructure to import, export, and transform data between heterogeneous data stores. The OLE DB strategic data access interface provides access to the broadest possible range of relational and nonrelational data stores. The DTS Data Pump is a high-speed, in-process COM server that moves and transforms OLE DB rowsets.

A transformation is a set of procedural operations that must be applied to the source rowset before it can be stored in the desired destination. The DTS Data Pump provides an extensible, COM-based architecture that allows complex data validations and transformations as the data moves from the source to the destination. The DTS Data Pump makes the full power of ActiveX scripting available to the DTS package, allowing complex procedural logic to be expressed as simple, reusable ActiveX scripts. These scripts can validate, convert, or transform the column values using the scripting language of their choice as they move from the source, through DTS Data Pump, to the destination. New values can be calculated easily from one or more columns in the source rowset. Source columns also decompose a single field into multiple destination columns. ActiveX scripts can invoke and use the services of any COM object that supports automation.

DTS Packages

DTS packages can be created using import/export wizards, the DTS Package Designer, or a COM interface. The import/export wizards provide the simplest mechanism for moving data into or out of a data warehouse, but the transformation complexity is limited by the wizards' scope. For example, only single sources and single destinations are allowed in the wizard.

The DTS Package Designer exposes all the capabilities of DTS through an easy-to-use, visual interface. Within the DTS Package Designer, users can define precedence relationships, complex queries, flow of control, and access to multiple, heterogeneous sources.

The DTS Package Designer provides a graphical environment for describing data flow and package execution.

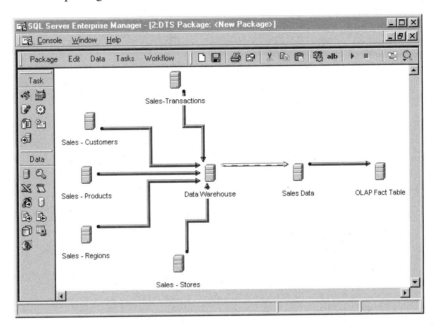

Finally, applications can define and execute DTS package programming through a COM interface. This approach is primarily used by ISVs who want to use the features of DTS without requiring a user to define the packages separately.

Analyzing and Presenting the Data

In the Microsoft Office suite of productivity tools, both Microsoft Access and Microsoft Excel offer facilities for query and analysis of information in a data warehouse. Microsoft SQL Server 7.0 includes a component called English Query, which allows users to query the database using natural, English-language sentences. In addition, through the Data Warehousing Framework, many compatible products are available for sophisticated viewing and analysis of data.

Microsoft Office

Two of the most common tools used to access and manipulate data for decision support are Microsoft Access and Microsoft Excel. With the introduction of Microsoft Office 2000, users will have access to more facilities for analyzing and presenting the information in their data warehouses.

Excel 2000 will allow tabular and graphical representation of OLAP data sources through the OLE DB for OLAP interfaces. At the same time, the existing PivotTable dynamic views capability will be replaced with a more advanced OLAP facility based on the PivotTable Service component of Microsoft SQL Server OLAP Services.

Access 2000 will provide transparent support for SQL Server databases in addition to the existing Access database facilities. These new capabilities will allow customers to use their familiar desktop tools to perform increasingly sophisticated data analyses.

Microsoft Office 2000 will include components for simplifying the construction of Web-based applications by using prebuilt controls. These controls will provide access to relational databases and OLAP databases, allowing widespread viewing of information in the data warehouse.

English Query

English Query is a component of SQL Server 7.0 that allows an application builder to create an application to the data warehouse that allows users to retrieve information from a SQL Server database using natural language rather than a formal query language like SQL. For example, you can ask, "How many widgets were sold in Washington last year?" instead of using these SQL statements:

```
SELECT sum(Orders.Quantity) from Orders, Parts
WHERE Orders.State='WA'
and Datepart(Orders.Purchase_Date,'Year')='1996'
and Parts.PartName='widget'
and Orders.Part_ID=Parts.Part_ID
```

English Query accepts natural, English-language commands, statements, and questions as input and determines their meaning. It then writes and executes a database query in SQL and formats the answer. English Query also can request additional information from a user if it cannot interpret a question.

English Query contains a deep knowledge of language syntax and usage, but the application developer must create a domain of information about the data being made available to the user. In English Query, a domain is the collection of all information that is known about the objects in the English Query application. This information includes the specified database objects (such as tables, fields, and joins), semantic objects (such as entities, the relationships between them, and additional dictionary entries), and global domain default options.

The first step to building an English Query application is to model the semantics of the data warehouse. The developer maps the English-language entities (nouns) and relationships (verbs, adjectives, traits, and subsets) to tables, fields, and joins in the database. This is accomplished by using an authoring tool that allows for domain testing outside the application.

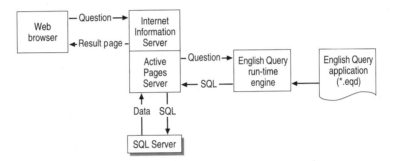

After the domain is modeled sufficiently for user testing and access, the developer makes the English Query application accessible through a Visual Basic-based application or a Web-based implementation using Active Server Pages (ASPs). With the increase of intranet-based information delivery to data warehouses, English Query is an excellent tool for providing access without costly query tools and training.

At run time, an end user of an English Query application connects to a Web page through Microsoft Internet Explorer software (or another Web browser) and enters a question. Microsoft Internet Explorer then passes the question to the Windows NT Server's built-in Web server, Internet Information Services (IIS), along with the URL of the ASP that executes the Visual Basic scripting.

The script passes the question to English Query for translation into an SQL statement. English Query uses domain knowledge about the target database (in the form of an English Query application) to parse the question and translate it into an SQL statement. The script then retrieves this SQL statement, executes it (using an ASP database control), formats the result as HTML, and returns the result page to the user.

English Query includes sample ASPs that can be used as delivered for rapid prototyping, or customized to fit the appearance and behavior of an existing Web application.

Third-Party Products

A fundamental philosophy of the Data Warehousing Framework is the openness of the solution to third-party components. Through the ODBC and OLE DB database interface standards, dozens of products can access and manipulate the information stored in SQL Server or another relational database. Likewise, the OLE DB for OLAP multidimensional database interface makes available the information in OLAP Services and other OLAP data stores. Because of these two access standards, organizations can select the most appropriate analytical tools for their needs. The reduced expenses for ISVs due to standardization also means that the costs of acquiring best-in-class products may diminish over time.

System Administration

One of the most significant hidden costs of implementing a data warehouse is the ongoing system maintenance and administration. With conventional technology, specialized skills typically are required to manage the relational database, the OLAP server, and the design and transformation technology. This means that multiple individuals with specific training often are needed to perform integral, related tasks. The Microsoft Data Warehousing Framework provides an integrated management and administration layer that can be shared across components in the data warehousing process.

Microsoft provides a console for the Microsoft product lines that simplifies the transition from task to task, even between separate products. Microsoft Management Console (MMC) is extensible by customers, consultants, and ISVs, providing a highly customized interface for specific environments. Applications are delivered as snap-ins to the console, and can be either a packaged user interface developed by an ISV or a customized interface developed separately, but accessing the capabilities of an underlying product such as SQL Server. Like much of the Microsoft BackOffice family of products, SQL Server 7.0 is delivered as a snap-in to MMC.

Microsoft Management Console

MMC provides a consistent, familiar interface for accessing the capabilities of Microsoft server products. The MMC user interface is similar to the Windows Explorer environment, with a vertically split work area containing a *console tree* of categories and objects relevant to a particular server on the left side, and a *details pane* about a selected item on the right. Detailed information in the details pane can be displayed in a variety of ways, including as an HTML document.

MMC allows for more sophisticated tools to assist the novice or infrequent database administrator. One significant addition is taskpads, which group multifaceted activities such as building a database, establishing user security, and monitoring the SQL Server database. Taskpads combine tutorial information, guided activities, and wizards.

Wizards

SQL Server 7.0 contains more than 25 wizards designed to simplify frequent tasks, including:

- Creating databases, views, indexes, and stored procedures.
- Backing up or restoring a database.
- Configuring a publishing and distribution server for replication, and creating a publication for replication.
- Managing SQL Server database security.
- Creating a maintenance file that can be run regularly.
- Defining full-text indexing on SQL Server character-based columns.
- Creating a Web task that creates an HTML page, imports data from an HTML page, or runs an existing Web task.

Wizards can help reduce the learning curve required for a database administrator to become productive with SQL Server. In the data warehousing environment, where database administrators are often supporting many steps of the process with multiple products, this can translate into saving time and money.

Visual Database Diagrams

Because data warehousing applications are more iterative than OLTP systems, the database structures and schemas can change more often. Visual database diagrams provide physical data modeling tools for SQL Server database administrators, which can simplify the definition and change cycles.

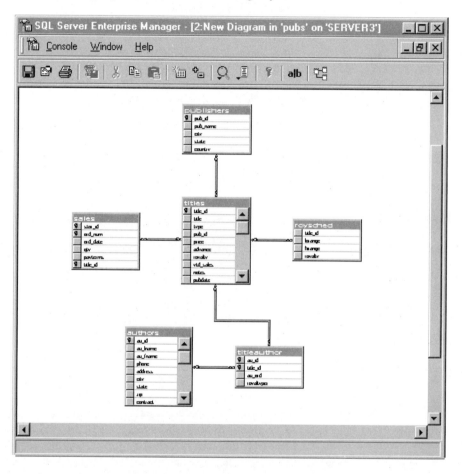

The visual database diagrams are stored on the database server using SQL Server Enterprise Manager. Changes to either the database or the diagrams are reflected in the other.

A wizard is available that automates the selection and layout of tables in an existing database. However, database entities (tables and their relationships) can be defined entirely within the diagram tool. The visual database diagram shows tables and their relationships, and allows changes to the structure of individual tables and to the constraints linking the tables.

SQL Server Profiler

Proper tuning of a relational database requires knowing how the database is used on a regular basis. SQL Server Profiler is a graphical tool that allows system administrators to monitor engine events in SQL Server by capturing a continuous record of server activity in real time. SQL Server Profiler monitors events that occur in SQL Server, filters events based on user-specified criteria, and directs the trace output to the screen, a file, or a table. SQL Server Profiler then allows the database administrator to replay previously captured traces to test changes to database structures, to identify slow-performing queries, to troubleshoot problems, or to re-create past conditions.

Examples of engine events that can be monitored include:

- Login connects, fails, and disconnects.
- SELECT, INSERT, UPDATE, and DELETE statements.
- Errors written to the SQL Server error log.
- Locks acquired or released on a database object.

Data from each event can be captured and saved to a file or SQL Server table for later analysis. Data from the engine events is collected by creating traces, which can contain information about the SQL statements and their results, the user and computer executing the statements, and the time the event started and ended.

Database administrators can filter event data to collect only the event data of interest to them. For example, they can collect only the events that affect a specific database or user and ignore all other events; or they can collect only data from queries that take longer than a specified time to execute.

SQL Server Profiler provides a graphical user interface to a set of extended stored procedures, which you can use directly. Therefore, it is possible to create your own application to monitor SQL Server that uses the SQL Server Profiler extended stored procedures.

SQL Server Query Analyzer

SQL Server Query Analyzer is an excellent tool for the ad hoc, interactive execution of Transact-SQL statements and scripts. Because users must understand Transact-SQL in order to use SQL Server Query Analyzer, this tool is primarily meant for database administrators and power users. Users can enter Transact-SQL statements in a full-text window, execute the statements, and view the results in a text window or tabular output. Users also can open a text file containing Transact-SQL statements, execute the statements, and view the results in the results window.

SQL Server Query Analyzer provides excellent tools for determining how SQL Server is interpreting and working with a Transact-SQL statement. A user can:

- Display a graphical representation of the execution plan generated for the statement.

- Start the Index Tuning Wizard to determine what indexes can be defined for the underlying tables to optimize the performance of the statement.

- Display statistics about the performance of the statement.

SQL Server Query Analyzer shows how complex queries are resolved. In this illustration, portions of a query are parallelized for performance improvement.

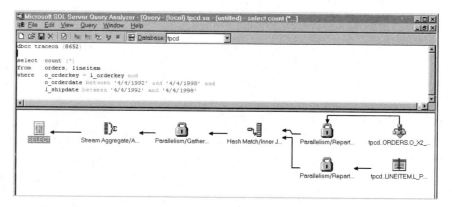

Index Tuning Wizard

One of the most time-consuming and inexact processes in managing a relational database is the creation of indexes to optimize the performance of user queries. The Index Tuning Wizard is a new tool that allows a database administrator to create and implement indexes without an expert understanding of the structure of the database, hardware platforms, and components, or of how end-user applications interact with the relational engine. The Index Tuning Wizard analyzes database workload and recommends an optimal index configuration for the SQL Server database.

The Index Tuning Wizard can:

- Compare, contrast, and select the best mix of indexes using the Graphical Showplan cost formula.

- Recommend the best mix of indexes for a workload (trace file or SQL script) against a database.

- Provide index, workload, table use, and query cost analysis.

- Allow the database administrator to tune the database for a small set of problem queries without changing the index configuration.

- Allow the database administrator to prototype index configuration recommendations for different disk-space constraints.

The Index Tuning Wizard can analyze an SQL script or the output from a SQL Server Profiler trace and make recommendations regarding the effectiveness of the current indexes referenced in the trace file or SQL script. The recommendations consist of SQL statements that can be executed to drop existing indexes and create new, more effective indexes. The recommendations suggested by the wizard can then be saved to an SQL script to be executed manually by the user at a later time, immediately implemented, or automatically scheduled for later implementation by creating a SQL Server job that executes the SQL script.

If an existing SQL script or trace is not available for the Index Tuning Wizard to analyze, the wizard can create one immediately or schedule one using SQL Server Profiler. When the database administrator has determined that the trace file has captured a representative sample of the normal workload of the database being monitored, the wizard can analyze the captured data and recommend an index configuration to improve database performance.

SQLServerAgent Service

Data warehouse administrators can benefit significantly from automation of routine tasks such as database backups. By using SQLServerAgent service, they can automate administrative tasks by establishing which tasks occur regularly, and can be administered programmatically by defining a set of jobs and alerts. Automated administration can include single server or multiserver environments.

The key components of automated administration are jobs, operators, and alerts. Jobs define an administrative task once so it can be executed one or more times and monitored for success or failure each time it executes. Jobs can be executed on one local server or on multiple remote servers; executed according to one or more schedules; executed by one or more alerts; and made up of one or more job steps. Job steps can be executable programs, Windows NT commands, Transact-SQL statements, ActiveX scripting, or replication agents.

Operators are individuals responsible for the maintenance of one or more servers running SQL Server. In some enterprises, operator responsibilities are assigned to one individual. In larger enterprises with multiple servers, many individuals share operator responsibilities. Operators are notified though e-mail, pager, or network messaging.

Alerts are definitions that match one or more SQL Server events and a response, should those events occur. In general, database administrators cannot control the occurrence of events, but they can control the response to those events with alerts. Alerts can be defined to respond to SQL Server events by notifying one or more operators, by forwarding the event to another server, or by raising an error condition that is visible to other software tools.

Through a combination of notifications and actions that can be automated through the SQLServerAgent service, administrators can construct a robust, self-managing environment for much of their day-to-day operational tasks. This frees administrators to tend to more complex tasks that cannot be automated.

CHAPTER 13

OLAP Services

Online analytical processing (OLAP) is an increasingly popular technology that can improve business analysis dramatically, but one that has been characterized historically by expensive tools, difficult implementation, and inflexible deployment. Microsoft has addressed the OLAP problem and created a solution that makes multidimensional analysis accessible to a broader audience and potentially at a significantly lower cost of ownership.

What is OLAP Services?

Microsoft SQL Server OLAP Services is a fully featured OLAP capability that is a component of Microsoft SQL Server version 7.0. OLAP Services includes a middle-tier server that allows users to perform sophisticated analyses on large volumes of data, with exceptional performance. A second feature of OLAP Services is a client cache and calculation engine called PivotTable Service, which helps improve performance and reduce network traffic. PivotTable Service allows users to conduct analyses while disconnected from the corporate network.

OLAP is a key component in the data warehousing process, and OLAP Services provides essential functionality for a wide array of applications ranging from corporate reporting to advanced decision support. The inclusion of OLAP functionality within SQL Server can help make multidimensional analysis more affordable and bring the benefits of OLAP to a wider audience. This includes not only smaller organizations, but also groups and individuals within larger corporations that have been excluded from the OLAP industry by the cost and complexity of today's products.

Coupled with a wide variety of tools and applications that support OLAP applications through the Microsoft OLE DB for OLAP interface, OLAP Services can increase access to sophisticated analytical tools and can reduce the costs of data warehousing.

Rationale for OLAP Systems

Historically, the bulk of investment in corporate computing has been in systems that generate or capture data, such as accounting, order processing, manufacturing, and customer information. Increasingly, organizations are investing in applications and technologies that deliver additional value from this collected data. Data warehousing is the process of collecting, cleansing, and sifting data from a variety of operational systems and making the resultant information available to a wide audience of end users for analysis and reporting. *Data warehouse* and *data mart* are terms used to describe these nonvolatile stores of cleansed and summarized information that are available for browsing by users.

Microsoft Data Warehousing Strategy

Several years ago, Microsoft undertook a pair of initiatives with the overall goal of expanding the availability of data warehousing and decision support capabilities in the business world. The two initiatives are the Microsoft Data Warehousing Framework, which is a roadmap for Microsoft product development, and the Microsoft Alliance for Data Warehousing, which is a coalition of industry businesses committed to the Microsoft platform and the Data Warehousing Framework for development and marketing purposes. The initiatives were based on a central strategy of Microsoft Corporation contributing to the data warehousing process by:

- Lowering the costs of acquisition, implementation, and maintenance.
- Redefining scalability to serve not only the large systems, but also to serve the individual user.
- Increasing the integration tools provided by third-party vendors.

Microsoft Data Warehousing Framework

The Data Warehousing Framework is an open architecture that describes mechanisms for sharing data and metadata in the construction and management of data warehouses and data marts. The essential technologies underlying the Data Warehousing Framework are the OLE DB data interfaces and the instance of Microsoft Repository running on SQL Server.

Repository is a database that stores descriptive information about software components and their relationships (metadata). Metadata models have been defined in Repository for database schemas, data transformations, and OLAP database schemas.

The Data Warehousing Framework components represent integral steps in the data warehousing process, some of which are being delivered by Microsoft but that can be extended easily by Microsoft customers and third-party businesses using alternative technology.

SQL Server 7.0 provides many of the basic components required for building and maintaining a data warehouse: database design with a graphical schema designer; high-capacity data storage; data transformation capabilities through Data Transformation Services (DTS); OLAP capabilities through OLAP Services; and so on.

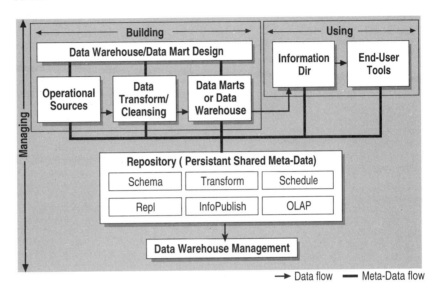

For more information about the Data Warehousing Framework, see "Data Warehousing Framework" earlier in this volume.

Data Complexity

Although the data warehousing process prepares data for end user consumption, most information in a relational data warehouse is not easily browsed.

Data structures are often difficult for the end user to comprehend and questions such as "Who are the top sales people in each region for the last year by month?" are complex when expressed in SQL. Some of these challenges can be addressed with advanced query tools, which hide the database complexity from the end user, but for the larger class of applications in which the end user is viewing multidimensional data, Microsoft believes the optimal solution is OLAP technology.

All organizations, regardless of size, must manage complex multidimensional data. Even the smallest organization may need to track sales by product, salesperson, geography, customer, and time. Organizations have sought tools to access, navigate, and analyze multidimensional data in an easy, natural way.

OLAP is not a new concept, but the OLAP name has been given to this technology only recently. In 1993, Dr. E. F. Codd, the database researcher and inventor of the relational database model, coined the term in his paper, "Providing OLAP to User Analysis: An IT Mandate," wherein he laid out 12 rules that defined the characteristics of OLAP applications. Nigel Pendse and Richard Creeth of the OLAP Report (www.olapreport.com/fasmi.htm) later refined his definition with what is called the FASMI test. This test states that OLAP applications should deliver fast analysis of shared multidimensional information following these guidelines:

Fast
  Delivers information to the user at a fairly constant rate. Most queries should be delivered to the user in five seconds or less.

Analysis
  Performs basic numeric and statistical analysis of the data, predefined by an application developer or defined ad hoc by the user.

Shared
  Implements the security requirements necessary for sharing potentially confidential data across a large user population.

Multidimensional
  Is the essential characteristic of OLAP.

Information
  Accesses all the data and information necessary and relevant for the application, wherever it may reside and not limited by volume.

Value to Organizations

OLAP provides organizations with a means of accessing, viewing, and analyzing data with high flexibility and performance. First and foremost, OLAP presents data to end users through a natural and intuitive data model. Using this navigational style, end users can view and understand the information in their data warehouses more effectively, thereby allowing organizations to better recognize the value of their data.

Second, OLAP accelerates the delivery of information to end users viewing these multidimensional structures by preparing some computed values in the data in advance, rather than at execution time. The combination of easy navigation and fast performance allows end users to view and analyze data more quickly and efficiently than is possible with relational database technology only. The end result is more time spent analyzing data and less time analyzing databases.

OLAP Data Model

In an OLAP data model, information is viewed conceptually as cubes that consist of descriptive categories (dimensions) and quantitative values (measures). The multidimensional data model makes it easy for users to formulate complex queries, arrange data on a report, switch from summary to detail data, and filter or slice data into meaningful subsets. For example, typical dimensions in a cube containing sales information include time, geography, product, channel, organization, and scenario (budget or actual). Typical measures include dollar sales, unit sales, inventory, headcount, income, and expense.

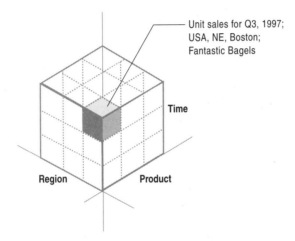

Within each dimension of an OLAP data model, data can be organized into a hierarchy that represents levels of detail on the data. For example, within the time dimension, you may have the levels years, months, and days; similarly, within the geography dimension, you may have the levels country, region, state/province, and city. A particular instance of the OLAP data model would have the specific values for each level in the hierarchy. A user viewing OLAP data can move up or down between levels to view information that is either more or less detailed.

Aggregation and Storage Models

Cubes, dimensions, hierarchies, and measures are the essence of the multidimensional navigation of OLAP.

By describing and presenting data in this fashion, users can navigate a complex set of data intuitively. However, describing the data model intuitively does little to speed delivery of the information to the user.

A key tenet of OLAP is that users should see consistent response times for each view, or slice, of the data they request. Because data is usually collected at the detail level only, the information summary usually is computed in advance. These precomputed values, or aggregations, are the basis of the OLAP performance gains.

In the early days of OLAP technology, most vendors assumed that the only possible solution for OLAP applications was a specialized, nonrelational storage model. Later, other vendors discovered that through the use of database structures (star and snowflake schemas), indexing, and storage of aggregates, relational database management systems (RDBMS) could be used for OLAP. These vendors called their technology Relational OLAP (ROLAP). The earlier OLAP vendors then adopted the term multidimensional OLAP (MOLAP).

MOLAP implementations usually outperform ROLAP technology, but have problems with scalability. On the other hand, ROLAP implementations are more scalable and are often attractive to customers because they leverage investments in existing relational database technology.

A recent development has been a hybrid OLAP (HOLAP) solution, which combines the ROLAP and MOLAP architectures to yield a solution with the best features of both: superior performance and extensive scalability. One approach to HOLAP maintains detail records (the largest volumes) in the relational database, while maintaining aggregations in a separate, MOLAP store.

OLAP Services Architecture

Microsoft SQL Server OLAP Services has been designed from the ground up to help minimize the most significant ownership costs of building and maintaining OLAP applications. OLAP Services consists of both server and client (middle-tier) software components.

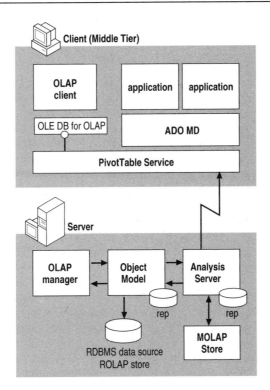

On the server side, OLAP Services OLAP server operates as a Microsoft Windows NT service and provides the core computational functionality. Programmatic access to administrative functions in the OLAP server is through an object model called Decision Support Objects (DSO), which is documented by Microsoft.

OLAP Manager, the built-in administrative user interface for OLAP Services, also is developed on DSO and provides a rich user experience without the need for programming. OLAP Manager, which can execute on a computer separate from the OLAP server, allows the database administrator to design OLAP data models, access information in RDBMS stores, design aggregations, and populate OLAP data stores, among other functions. The OLAP metadata definitions are stored in a private repository, but can be exported to Repository with the OLAP Open Information Model (OIM) by using a simple utility.

OLAP Services can access source data in any supported OLE DB data provider, which includes not only SQL Server but also a large number of desktop and server databases, including Microsoft Access, Microsoft FoxPro, Oracle, Sybase, and Informix. Any database source that provides an Open Database Connectivity (ODBC) interface is also accessible through a facility in OLE DB that wraps ODBC drivers and exposes them as if they were native OLE DB interfaces. These data sources can also reside on platforms other than the Windows NT operating system, for example, UNIX or mainframe systems and databases like IBM DB2 or Teradata. Through the multiplatform capabilities of OLE DB, data can be accessed from a wide variety of systems as if they were local to the OLAP Services server.

On the client side, OLAP Services includes a component called PivotTable Service. PivotTable Service is the facility that connects OLAP client applications to the OLAP Services server. All access to data managed by OLAP Services, by custom programs or client tools, is through the OLE DB for OLAP interface provided by PivotTable Service.

Both the client and server components of OLAP Services are extensible in functionality. Customer sites, independent software vendors (ISVs), and consultants all can extend the calculation, data management, or application functionality using the well-documented features in DSO. With this built-in extensibility, customers can be assured that OLAP Services will have the functionality necessary to address their application needs.

Challenges of OLAP Implementation

There are several challenges that must be overcome in the implementation of OLAP:

- Building the OLAP data model
- Performance and scalability

Building the OLAP Data Model

A fundamental challenge in OLAP implementation is mapping the initial database schema to the multidimensional model. This requires a significant programming effort with many of the products on the market today. In the evolution of OLAP products, OLAP database design has become a specialized and arcane process, intricately linked to the specific OLAP technology being deployed. Consequently, OLAP database developers are specialized, which has led to high costs in developing applications, concentrated at the data design stage.

In most OLAP implementations, it is assumed that the data has been prepared for analysis through data warehousing, whereby information has been extracted from operational systems, cleansed, validated, and summarized prior to incorporation into an OLAP application. This is a vital step in the process, which ensures that the data being viewed by the OLAP user is correct, consistent, and matches organizational definitions for the data.

Increasingly, information in a data warehouse is organized in star (or snowflake) schemas, which simplify user understanding of the data, maximize performance for decision support applications, and require less storage for large databases.

The following illustration is an example of a star schema. In this database schema, a central fact table is linked to related dimension tables.

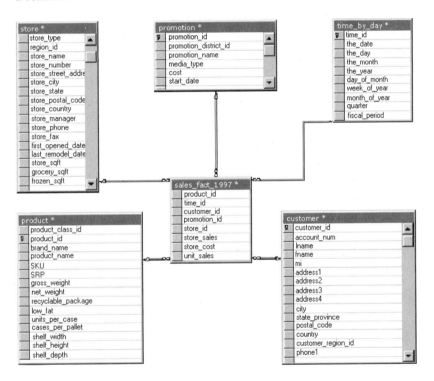

A star (snowflake) schema is a relational approximation of the OLAP data model and can be an excellent starting point for building OLAP cube definitions. Few OLAP products, however, have taken advantage of this trend. Generally, they have not provided easy tools to map a star schema to an OLAP model, and as a result keep the cost of building OLAP models extremely high and the development time unnecessarily long.

Intuitive User Interfaces

One of the key differences in Microsoft SQL Server OLAP Services version 7.0 is the OLAP Manager user interface, which has been created with the infrequent OLAP database administrator in mind. The OLAP Manager is delivered as a snap-in to the Microsoft Management Console (MMC), and it shares the same administrative user interface as the entire Microsoft BackOffice family of products. The obvious benefit is that the OLAP database administrator is better able to translate skills from SQL Server and other Microsoft products.

More value becomes apparent when the power and flexibility of MMC are understood. OLAP Services includes a full range of taskpads that guide the novice or infrequent user through common tasks. OLAP Services also includes a full tutorial on OLAP concepts and a step-by-step guide to building an OLAP cube. A full complement of wizards is available for automating the most common activities, such as creating a dimension definition.

Furthermore, OLAP Services is optimized for developing data warehouses in which star or snowflake schemas have been designed. The Cube Wizard is especially suited to these prebuilt schemas, and translation to the multidimensional model is extremely rapid. OLAP Services can easily accommodate other source schemas should they be encountered.

To ensure successful interpretation of the OLAP Services user interface concepts, Microsoft conducted usability tests. Finally, large-scale beta testing has provided broad exposure and customer input to OLAP Services. As a result of the energy spent on the database administrator requirements, most users are able to build their first cube in less than 30 minutes.

Managing Data Explosion with Aggregation

As noted earlier, precomputing aggregations is a key performance strategy for most OLAP products. However, preaggregation comes at a significant cost: The number of aggregations can easily outstrip the number of initial detail points, and the volume of data stored expands dramatically. The number of aggregations in an OLAP model is a function of the number of dimensions, the number of levels in the hierarchies, and the parent-child ratios. For more information, see the OLAP Report at www.olapreport.com.

Real-world examples of the effects of this data explosion abound. A recently published standard benchmark test of another OLAP product resulted in a data explosion factor of 240, requiring 2.4 gigabytes (GB) of storage to manage 10 megabytes (MB) of input data. Providing adequate disk storage to handle the huge expansion in data is a significant cost of large-scale OLAP implementations, and it creates distinct limits on the ability of an organization to analyze all the desired source-level data.

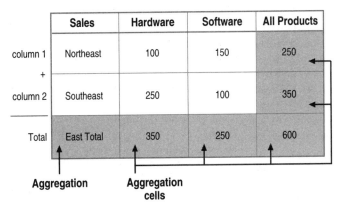

Sales	Hardware	Software	All Products
Northeast	100	150	250
Southeast	250	100	350
East Total	350	250	600

column 1 + column 2 (Northeast and Southeast rows)

Total — East Total

Aggregation   **Aggregation cells**

Sales	Hardware	Software	All Products
Northeast		150	150
Southeast	250		250
East Total	250	150	400

Missing / Invalid data

Because of data explosion, OLAP applications can suffer even more when the source or detail data is distributed sparsely throughout the multidimensional cube. Missing or invalid data values create sparsity in the OLAP data model. In the worst case, an OLAP product would nonetheless save an empty value. For example, a company may not sell all products in all regions, so no values would appear at the intersection where products are not sold in a particular region.

Reducing data sparsity is a challenge that has been met with varying degrees of success by different OLAP vendors. The worst implementation results in databases that stored empty values, thus having low density and wasting space and resources. OLAP Services does not store empty values, and as a result, even sparsely populated cubes do not balloon in size. While this issue is frequently highlighted by some OLAP vendors as a deciding factor in OLAP architectures, the differences between vendor implementations of sparsity management is minor compared to the more significant data explosion caused by precalculating too many aggregates.

Flexible Storage Choices

Microsoft believes OLAP Services leads the market in offering a flexible solution that allows the OLAP database administrator to decide which storage model is most appropriate. OLAP Services supports a full MOLAP implementation, full ROLAP implementation, or a HOLAP solution. For example, a database administrator may opt to put frequently accessed data in MOLAP and historical data, which has more scalability problems, in ROLAP. However, the underlying data model is completely invisible to the client application, and its user perceives only cubes.

Whether one chooses to implement a MOLAP, ROLAP, or HOLAP data model, the integration of OLAP Services with relational databases is superior. OLAP Services maintains strong links between the source data, the OLAP multidimensional metadata, and the aggregations themselves by tying the graphical user interface design tools and wizards directly to OLE DB.

When implementing ROLAP data models, OLAP Services defines, populates, and maintains all of the relational database structures. This frees the developer from having to perform these tasks, or worse, from having to manage complex queries across multiple tables and servers.

Intelligent Preaggregation

Also, OLAP Services has minimized a fundamental problem of OLAP technology: data explosion caused by excessive preaggregation. As described earlier, OLAP data explosion is the result of multidimensional preaggregation. In traditional OLAP systems, data that has not been preaggregated is not available for reporting and analysis purposes unless calculated at run time. By precalculating and storing all possible combinations of aggregates (for example, the sum of all products and product levels across all time periods, across all organizations, across all distribution channels, and so on), traditional OLAP products create a massive data explosion.

In contrast to the approach of calculating all possible aggregations, OLAP Services determines which aggregations provide the greatest performance improvements, but also allows the OLAP database administrator to make a trade-off between system speed and the disk space required to manage aggregations through the Storage Design Wizard. (See the following illustration.) If the developer were to precalculate all aggregations, disk space requirements would be maximized (hence the data explosion syndrome). On the other hand, if the developer were to precalculate nothing, disk requirements would be zero, but performance would not be improved.

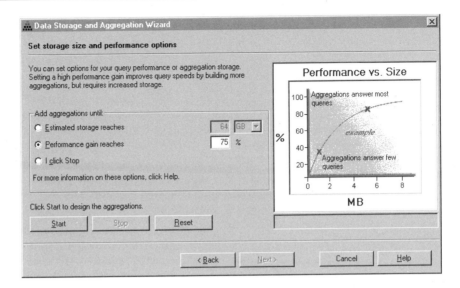

In most cases, OLAP Services can gain about 80 percent improvement in query performance without excessive precomputation of aggregations (the exponential explosion of data typically occurs during the last 20 percent of aggregations). OLAP Services analyzes the OLAP metadata model and heuristically determines the optimum set of aggregations from which all other aggregations can be derived. The result is that OLAP Services derives nonaggregated data from a few existing aggregate values rather than having to scan the entire data warehouse. This strategy of partial preaggregation, however, is only the starting point.

Although the OLAP Services heuristics are excellent, they are based on mathematical models that may or may not correspond to actual usage patterns. To optimize performance according to actual usage patterns, OLAP Services optionally logs queries sent to the server. These logs then can be used to fine-tune the set of aggregations that OLAP Services maintains. For example, the Usage-Based Optimization Wizard allows the database administrator to tell OLAP Services to create a new set of aggregations for all queries that take longer than n seconds to answer (where n might be 10 seconds or more).

Disk space can be purchased whereas time cannot. If the extraction time of critical information outweighs the cost of purchasing more disk space, the solution is apparent.

The OLAP Services solution for data explosion reduces the time required to process initial loads and incremental updates, as well as minimizes the amount of disk space necessary. If an application begins with a 10-GB data warehouse and generates 10 GB of aggregations, then the processing time required is a fraction of that required to process the fully exploded set of aggregations.

OLAP Services also has taken an innovative approach to data sparsity. Although the details of the internal implementation are proprietary, the net result is that both MOLAP and ROLAP implementations manage storage requirements extremely well, often resulting in databases with smaller OLAP storage needs than the original detail data.

Virtual cubes can be used whenever the user wants to view joined information from two dissimilar cubes that share as few as one common dimension. Similar in concept to a relational view, virtual cubes are two or more cubes linked at query time along one or more common dimensions. One benefit of virtual cubes applies to situations in which data sparsity is a significant problem. For example, a cube that contains measures for sales by unit and selling price could also have a measure for list price to compute discounts, but the list price value would be repeated many times. By building a list price cube that is joined in a virtual cube with the sales by unit and selling price information, the database administrator can eliminate much of the data redundancy. The ability to create virtual cubes means that many unnecessary values can be eliminated from the OLAP data storage altogether.

Performance and Scalability

The specific performance metrics of an OLAP application are a function of several factors, including database size, hardware computing power, and disk space allocated to preaggregated data. However, in real-world implementations, OLAP Services–based applications respond to most queries in less than 5 seconds and to nearly all queries within 10 seconds.

The OLAP Services implementation of partitioned cubes makes the technology highly scalable. A partitioned cube allows one logical cube of data to be spread over multiple physical cubes and even separate physical servers. In response to a user query, OLAP Services distributes the query among the partitioned servers, allowing the data to be retrieved in parallel.

For example, consider the case of an application tracking telephone calls for 10 geographic regions, where one would expect several million calls per day. For the purpose of analysis, one could partition the data among 10 servers, each containing the data for a particular region. From the user perspective, however, there is simply one logical cube of data. In response to user requests for this information, OLAP Services seamlessly transforms the queries as appropriate for each of the 10 servers and returns a single result set to the user. Each of the 10 databases is also available for separate access by analysts seeking information for that particular region.

Delivering OLAP Information to the User

Historically, because OLAP server technology has been tightly linked to proprietary client technology, customers have had little choice in their selection of mixed, best-of-breed products. This has led to high implementation costs and often inadequate choices for applications that require both client/server and Web-based OLAP information delivery. As was recognized years ago in the relational database industry, a common interface is necessary to promote openness in the selection of applications and databases. The industry standard became ODBC.

Industry Standards

The issue of openness in OLAP tools was first taken up in 1996, when a vendor consortium called the OLAP Council announced an interoperability standard, multidimensional application programming interface (MDAPI), which was meant to open the marketplace to greater vendor participation. In spite of much customer anticipation, the vendor community, including the members of the OLAP Council, generally shunned MDAPI.

Recognizing the need for a unifying standard that leveraged existing customer investments, Microsoft extended the definition of the existing OLE DB data access API to include multidimensional capabilities. In one year, Microsoft published two drafts of the API, sought feedback from vendors and the public, and ultimately delivered a final version in February 1998 that was endorsed by 18 vendors at beta release.

Today, the OLE DB for OLAP API has the support of more than 30 vendors, many of which are listed on the Microsoft Web site at www.microsoft.com/data/oledb/olap. This list includes almost every member of the OLAP Council. Many of these vendors already are delivering beta products based on the specification to OLAP Services users. For an index of the vendors with products currently supporting SQL Server OLAP Services, see www.microsoft.com/industry/bi/solutions/olap/olap.stm.

Disconnected and Web-based Delivery

Individuals often need to analyze data multidimensionally while they are disconnected from the corporate network, such as when traveling with a laptop computer. Disconnected users typically want to view and analyze small slices of their entire cube; for example, a sales manager may want to view a revenue summary for a particular region while visiting a regional office. The need is so common that desktop OLAP (DOLAP), which does not require a shared server for multidimensional data access, was created.

Most OLAP server technologies do not provide transparent creation of DOLAP cubes. As a result, this step has been left as yet another development-intensive effort or relegated to OLAP client tools that have added functionality to support desktop usage. Overall, this has increased the cost and complexity of delivering applications that require both connected and disconnected clients.

A popular viewing tool for any type of information, especially multidimensional information, is a Web browser. A key means of reducing the cost per user in large-scale OLAP applications, Web browsers open the world of multidimensional access to a wider audience. At present, there are some good products and tools for delivering OLAP data over an intranet, but there is no easy mechanism for an application developer to create custom OLAP viewing tools.

PivotTable Service

The OLAP Services server caches user queries and metadata as well as data. Cached query definitions and metadata make it possible for OLAP Services to answer new queries by calculating previously cached data rather than accessing the disk. For example, one user asks for sales data for January, February, and March. Another user asks for sales data for the first quarter. OLAP Services can summarize January through March from random access memory (RAM) faster than it can fetch the first-quarter data from disk.

OLAP Services is unique in that it provides much of the same functionality on the client. Every client connects to OLAP Services servers by using PivotTable Service. PivotTable Service acts as a driver to manage the connection between the client and server. PivotTable Service shares much of the same code as the OLAP Services server, bringing the server's multidimensional calculation engine, caching features, and query management directly to the client. The result is an innovative client/server, data-management model that optimizes performance and minimizes network traffic. This comes at a very small computing cost: The disk space required for PivotTable Service is approximately 2 MB, and the memory requirements are only 500 KB in addition to the cached data.

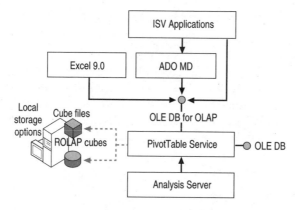

The OLAP Services intelligent client/server architecture is capable of determining how to answer a user request as quickly as possible, while eliminating redundant network traffic. The key to this architecture is shared metadata between client and server. When a user requests information from the server, both data and metadata (definitions of the cube structure) are downloaded to the client. Having the cube metadata present on the client allows PivotTable Service to resolve which requests need to be returned to the server for resolution.

For example, recall the three-month sales data scenario. Assume that both the OLAP Services server and the client application have just been started. When the user asks for sales data for January, February, and March, the data will be cached on both the server and the client. If the user then asks for data for the first quarter, PivotTable Service will derive the results locally (at the client) without sending the query to the server. If the user subsequently asks to see data from the first quarter of this year compared to that of last year, PivotTable Service has the intelligence to access the server for last year's data only.

PivotTable Service also provides the mechanism for disconnected usage. Portions of cubes defined and accessed from a server can be saved on the client for later access when disconnected from the network. In this way, business users can take portions of their database while travelling and still have complete analysis capabilities. In addition, PivotTable Service allows users to create simple OLAP models locally, accessing information in OLE DB compatible data sources, from flat files to desktop databases.

Finally, PivotTable Service provides the connectivity for Web-based applications. While OLE DB for OLAP is a low-level programming interface, a new extension to ActiveX Data Objects (ADO) provides multidimensional data access. This extension, called ADO/MD, can be used to create ActiveX controls in the Microsoft Visual Basic development system to browse, chart, or report on data in OLAP Services from a Web page. ADO/MD is the corporate application programmer's tool for gaining access to the full functionality of OLAP Services.

Affording OLAP Tools

Typically, OLAP products can cost $50,000 to $100,000 for less than 50 users. Microsoft recognizes that OLAP is a natural extension of database technology and has included OLAP Services as a feature of SQL Server 7.0.

SQL Server 7.0 includes other complementary data warehousing features:

- Visual Database Tools, for creating database schemas
- Data Transformation Services (DTS), for extracting and transforming operational data into the data warehouse
- Microsoft Repository, for providing a unified metadata store built on SQL Server

CHAPTER 14

Query Processor

This chapter describes the new features of the Microsoft SQL Server query processor. The query processor is that portion of SQL Server that accepts, parses, and executes SQL syntax. This chapter includes these topics:

- Query processor goals
- Query execution
- Query optimization
- Distributed queries
- Working with queries

The query processor is closely related to the storage engine, another part of SQL Server. For more information, see "Storage Engine" later in this volume.

What Is a Query Processor?

A relational database consists of many parts, but at its heart are two major components: the *storage engine* and the *query processor*. The storage engine writes data to and reads data from the disk. It manages records, controls concurrency, and maintains log files.

The query processor accepts SQL syntax, selects a plan for executing the syntax, and then executes the chosen plan. The user or program interacts with the query processor, and the query processor in turn interacts with the storage engine. The query processor isolates the user from the details of execution: The user specifies the result, and the query processor determines how this result is obtained.

Query Processing Phases

There are two major phases in query processing: *query optimization* and *query execution.*

Query optimization is the process of choosing the fastest execution plan. In the optimization phase, the query processor chooses:

- Which, if any, indexes to use.
- The order in which joins are executed.
- The order in which constraints such as WHERE clauses are applied.
- Which algorithms are likely to lead to the best performance, based on cost information derived from statistics.

Query execution is the process of executing the plan chosen during query optimization. The query execution component also determines the techniques available to the query optimizer. For example, SQL Server implements a hash join algorithm and a merge join algorithm, both of which are available to the query optimizer.

The query optimizer is the brain of a relational database system, enabling it to work intelligently and efficiently.

A relational database with a sophisticated query optimizer is more likely to complete a query, especially a complex query, faster than a relational database with a simple query optimizer.

Types of Query Optimizers

There are two major types of query optimizers in relational databases: *syntax-based* and *cost-based.*

Syntax-based Query Optimizers

A syntax-based query optimizer creates a procedural plan for obtaining the answer to an SQL query, but the particular plan it chooses is dependent on the exact syntax of the query and the order of the clauses within the query. A syntax-based query optimizer executes the same plan every time, regardless of whether the number or composition of records in the database changes over time. Unlike a cost-based query optimizer, it neither maintains nor considers statistics about the database.

Cost-based Query Optimizers

A cost-based query optimizer chooses among alternative plans to answer an SQL query. Selection is based on cost estimates for different plans. The factors in making cost estimates include the number of I/O operations, the amount of CPU time, and so on. A cost-based query optimizer estimates these costs by keeping statistics about the number and composition of records in a table or index and is not dependent on the exact syntax of the query or the order of clauses within the query (unlike a syntax-based query optimizer).

Query Processor Goals

One of the goals for SQL Server 7.0 is to provide improved query processor support for a range of database activities, including large queries, complex queries, data warehousing, and online analytical processing (OLAP). These are some of the specific ways in which this goal is addressed by SQL Server:

- More Choices for the Query Optimizer

  Earlier versions of SQL Server provided limited ways of optimizing queries. For example, SQL Server 6.5 supports only one method for performing a join: nested loops iteration. SQL Server 7.0 adds hash join and merge join, which give the optimizer more options to choose from and are the algorithms of choice for many large queries.

- Improved Query Execution

  SQL Server 7.0 improves execution of a plan after it is chosen. Faster scans, sort improvements, and large memory support all offer potential performance advantages.

- Parallel Execution of Queries

  Symmetric multiprocessing (SMP) computers and striped disk sets are increasingly common. SQL Server 6.5 implemented parallel I/O and inter-query parallelism (assigning different queries to different processors), but it could not execute different parts of a single query in parallel. SQL Server 7.0 breaks a single query into multiple subtasks and distributes them across multiple processors for parallel execution.

- Optimized Data Warehouse Queries

  Star schemas and star queries are common in data warehousing applications. A star query joins a large central table, called a *fact table*, to one or more smaller tables, called *dimension tables*. SQL Server 7.0 recognizes these queries automatically and makes a cost-based choice among multiple types of star join plans.

Query Execution

Query execution is the process of executing the plan chosen during query optimization. The objective is to execute the plan quickly by returning the answer to the user (or more often, the program run by the user) in the least amount of time. This is not the same as executing the plan with the fewest resources (CPU, I/O, and memory). For example, a parallel query almost always uses more resources than a nonparallel query, but it is often desirable because it returns the result more quickly.

Query execution is presented before query optimization because the set of available execution techniques determines the set of choices available to the optimizer. The techniques include disk I/O, sorting, join and hash operations, index intersections, index joins, and parallelism.

Disk I/O

The foundation for efficient query processing is efficient data transfer between disks and memory. SQL Server 7.0 incorporates many improvements in disk I/O.

Sequential I/O vs. Random I/O

Disk I/O is one of the more expensive computer operations. There are two types of disk I/O: sequential I/O, which reads data in the same order as it is stored on the disk, and random I/O, which reads data in random order, jumping from one location to another on the disk. Random I/O can be more expensive than sequential I/O, particularly when large amounts of data are involved.

Microsoft SQL Server 7.0 maintains an on-disk structure that minimizes random I/O and allows rapid scans of large *heap tables*. These are tables without a clustered index, meaning that the data rows are not stored in any particular order. This is an important feature for decision support queries. Such disk-order scans can also be employed for clustered and nonclustered indexes if the index's sort order is not required in subsequent processing steps.

Earlier versions of SQL Server use a page chain, in which each page has a pointer to the next page holding data for the table. This results in random I/O and prevents read-ahead because, until the server reads a page, it does not have the location of the next page.

SQL Server 7.0 takes a different approach. An Index Allocation Map (IAM) maps the pages used by a table or index. The IAM is a bitmap, in disk order, of the data pages for a particular table. To read all the pages, the server scans the bitmap, determining which pages need to be read in what order. It then can use sequential I/O to retrieve the pages and issue read-aheads.

If the server can scan an index rather than reading the table, it will attempt to do so. This is useful if the index is a covering index (one that has all the fields necessary to satisfy the query). The server may satisfy a query by reading the B-tree index in disk order rather than in sort order. This results in sequential I/O and faster performance.

Large I/O

In SQL Server 7.0, all database pages are 8 KB and data is read in 64-KB extents (in earlier releases these figures were 2 KB and 16 KB, respectively). Both of these changes increase performance by allowing the server to read larger amounts of data in a single I/O request. This is particularly important for very large databases and decision support queries, in which a single request can process large numbers of rows.

Scanning Read-Ahead

SQL Server 7.0 takes increased advantage of striped disk sets by reading multiple extents ahead of the actual query processor request. This results in faster scans of heap tables and B-tree indexes.

Prefetch Hints

Disk-order scans speed up scans of large amounts of data. SQL Server 7.0 also speeds up fetching data using a nonclustered index.

When searching for data using a nonclustered index, the index is searched for a particular value. When that value is found, the index points to the disk address. The traditional approach is to issue immediately an I/O for that row, given the disk address. The result is one synchronous I/O per row and, at most, one disk at a time working to evaluate the query. This does not take advantage of striped disk sets.

SQL Server 7.0 takes a different approach. It continues looking for more record pointers in the nonclustered index. When it has collected a number of them, it provides the storage engine with prefetch hints. These hints tell the storage engine that the query processor needs these particular records soon. The storage engine then can issue several I/O requests simultaneously, taking advantage of striped disk sets.

Sort Improvements

Many different areas of the query processor rely on the sort algorithms: merge joins, index creations, stream aggregations, and so on. Sort performance is dramatically improved in SQL Server 7.0.

Many internal improvements make each sort operation faster: simpler comparisons, larger I/O operations, asynchronous I/O, and large memory. In addition, SQL Server 7.0 pipelines data between a sort operation and the query operations on its input and output sides, thus avoiding query plan phases, which were traditionally used in SQL Server and require writing and scanning intermediate work tables.

Merge Joins, Hash Joins, and Hash Teams

SQL Server 6.5 uses nested loops iteration, which is excellent for row-to-row navigation such as moving from an order record to three or four order-line items. However, it is not efficient for joins of many records, such as typical data warehouse queries.

SQL Server 7.0 introduces three new techniques: merge joins, hash joins, and hash teams, the last of which is a significant innovation not available in any other relational database.

Merge Joins

A merge join simultaneously passes over two sorted inputs to perform inner joins, outer joins, semi-joins, intersections, and unions. A merge join exploits sorted scans of B-tree indexes and is generally the method of choice if the join fields are indexed and if the columns represented in the index cover the query.

Hash Joins

A hash join hashes input values, based on a repeatable randomizing function, and compares values in the hash table for matches. For inputs smaller than the available memory, the hash table remains in memory; for larger inputs, overflow files on disk are employed. Hashing is the method of choice for large, nonindexed tables, particularly for intermediate results.

The hashing operation can be used to process GROUP BY clauses, distincts, intersections, unions, differences, inner joins, outer joins, and semi-joins. SQL Server 7.0 implements all the well-known hashing techniques including cache-optimized in-memory hashing, large memory, recursive partitioning, hybrid hashing, bit-vector filtering, and role reversal.

Hash Teams

The hash team is an innovation in SQL Server 7.0. Many queries consist of multiple execution phases; where possible, the query optimizer should take advantage of similar operations across multiple phases. For example, suppose you want to know how many order-line items have been entered for each part number and each supplier, as shown in this SQL code:

```
SELECT  1_partkey, count (*)
FROM    lineitem, part, partsupp
WHERE   1_partkey = p_partkey and p_partkey = ps_partkey
GROUP BY 1_partkey
```

In response to this code, the query processor generates this execution plan.

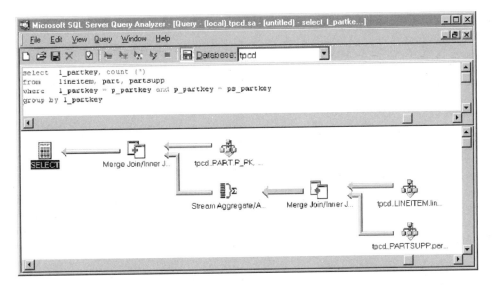

This query plan performs a merge inner join between the **lineitem** table and the **partsupp** table. It calculates the count (stream aggregate), and then joins the result with the **part** table. This query never requires a sort operation. It begins by retrieving records in sorted order from the **lineitem** and **partsupp** tables using sorted scans over an index. This provides a sorted input into the merge join, which provides sorted input into the aggregation, which in turn provides sorted input into the final merge join.

Interesting Ordering

Interesting ordering refers to avoiding sort operations by keeping track of the ordering of intermediate results that move from operator to operator. SQL Server 7.0 applies this concept to hash joins. Consider the same query, but assume that the crucial index on **lineitems** has been dropped, so that the previous plan would have to be augmented with an expensive sort operation on the large **lineitems** table.

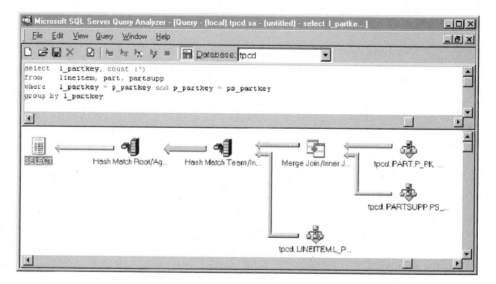

This query plan employs a hash join instead of a merge join; one of the merge joins is not affected by the dropped index and is therefore still very fast. The two hash operations are marked specially as the root and a member of a team. As data moves from the hash join to the grouping operation, work to partition rows in the hash join is exploited in the grouping operation. This eliminates overflow files for one of the inputs of the grouping operation, and thus reduces I/O costs for the query. The benefit is faster processing for complex queries.

Index Intersections

Microsoft SQL Server 6.5 selects the one best index for each table, even when a query has multiple predicates. SQL Server 7.0 takes advantage of multiple indexes, selecting small subsets of data based on each index, and then performing an intersection of the two subsets (that is, returning only those rows that meet all the criteria). For example, suppose you want to count orders for certain ranges of customers and order dates:

```
SELECT   count (*)
FROM     orders
WHERE        o_orderdate between '9/15/1992' and '10/15/1992' and
                 o_custkey between 100 and 200
```

SQL Server 7.0 can exploit indexes on both **o_custkey** and **o_orderdate**, and then employ a join algorithm to obtain the index intersection between the two subsets. This execution plan exploits two indexes, both on the **orders** table.

Index Joins

Index joins are a variation on index intersections. When using any index, if all the columns required for a given query are available in the index itself, it is not necessary to fetch the full row. This is called a *covering index* because the index covers or contains all the columns needed for the query.

The covering index is a common and well-understood technique. SQL Server 7.0 takes it a step further by applying it to the index intersection. If no single index can cover a query, but multiple indexes together can cover the query, SQL Server considers joining these indexes. The alternative chosen is based on the cost prediction of the query optimizer.

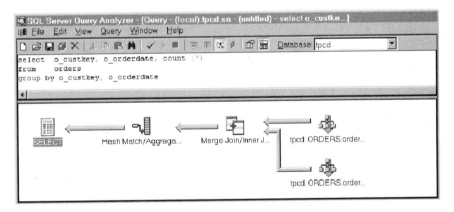

Parallel Queries

Microsoft SQL Server 7.0 introduces *intra-query parallelism,* which is the ability to break a single query into multiple subtasks and execute them on multiple processors in an SMP computer.

SQL Server accomplishes this by automatically detecting that it is running on an SMP computer and determining the best degree of parallelism for each instance of a parallel query execution. By examining the current system workload and configuration, SQL Server determines the optimal number of threads and spreads the parallel query execution across those threads. When a query starts executing, it uses the same number of threads until completion. SQL Server chooses the optimal number of threads each time a parallel query execution plan is retrieved from the procedure cache. As a result, one execution of a query can use a single thread, and another execution of the same query (at a different time) can use two or more threads.

In addition to parallel queries, Microsoft SQL Server 7.0 supports parallel backup, parallel restore, and parallel load using multiple clients. For more information, see SQL Server Books Online.

Query Optimization

This section includes information about some of the new query optimization features in SQL Server 7.0. These include:

- Multi-phase optimization
- Automatic parameters
- Transitive predicates
- Nested queries
- Moving GROUP BY clauses
- Partitioned views
- Star queries
- Optimized updates

Multiphase Optimization

The SQL Server 7.0 query optimizer proceeds in multiple phases. First, it looks for a simple but reasonable plan of execution that satisfies the query. If that plan takes less time than a cost threshold value (for example, a fraction of a second), the query optimizer does not bother looking for more efficient plans. This prevents over-optimization, in which the query optimizer uses more resources to determine the best plan than are required to execute the plan.

If the first plan chosen takes more time than the cost threshold value, then the optimizer continues to look at other plans, always choosing the least-cost plan. The use of multiple phases provides a good trade-off between the time it takes to choose the most efficient plan and the time it takes to optimize for that plan.

Automatic Parameters

Most query processors allow you to precompile and store an execution plan—for example, a stored procedure. Precompiling is efficient because it supports reuse of the execution plan and allows users to submit variables as parameters to the plan. A new Open Database Connectivity (ODBC) interface for preparing requests for repeated execution also exploits this efficiency.

Many commercial applications and all ad hoc queries, however, do not use stored procedures. Instead, they use dynamic SQL. SQL Server 7.0 implements a new feature called *automatic parameters* that caches a plan created for dynamic SQL, turning constants into parameters. The result is less compilation effort, providing many of the efficiencies of stored procedures, even for those applications that do not employ stored procedures.

SQL Server 7.0 also introduces full support for parameterized queries, in which the application identifies the parameters. This is typical with ODBC, OLE DB, and PREPARE/EXECUTE.

Transitive Predicates

The transitive property of numbers states that if A = B and B = C, then A = C. This property can be applied to queries:

```
SELECT   *
FROM     part, partsupp, lineitem
WHERE       ps_partkey = l_partkey and l_partkey = p_partkey and
               ps_availqty > l_quantity and ps_supplycost >
p_retailprice
```

Because both **ps_partkey** and **p_partkey** are equal to **l_partkey**, **ps_partkey** must be equal to **p_partkey**. The query processor takes advantage of this by deriving the third join predicate (**ps_partkey** equal to **p_partkey**). For example, in this query, the query processor begins by joining the partkey in the **parts** table to the partkey in the **partsupp** table, even though this particular join predicate is never specified in the query. It can do so because of transitive predicates.

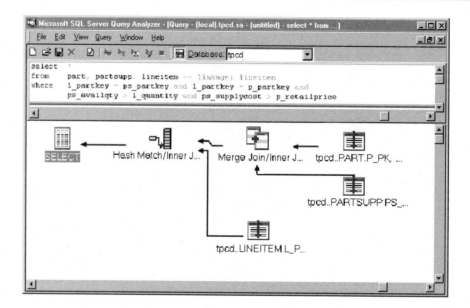

Nested Queries

Correlated subqueries present special challenges for any SQL query processor. SQL Server applies some specific techniques to correlated subqueries, and it flattens them to semi-joins if possible. The advantage of flattening is that all the join algorithms can be applied. For large queries, this means that the query optimizer can consider hash joins or merge joins, rather than using the less efficient nested iteration join.

Moving GROUP BY Clauses

The SQL standards require processing a query in the following order:

1. Execute FROM and WHERE clauses.
2. Reduce data using the GROUP BY clause.
3. Apply any conditions in the HAVING clause.

However, any plan that produces the same result is also correct. Therefore, in some queries, you can evaluate the GROUP BY clause earlier, before one or more join operations required for the WHERE clause, thus reducing the join input and the join cost, for example:

```
SELECT   c_name, c_custkey, count (*), sum (l_tax)
FROM     customer, orders, lineitem
WHERE        c_custkey = o_custkey and o_orderkey = l_orderkey and
                 o_orderdate between '9/1/1994' and '12/31/1994'
GROUP BY c_name, c_custkey
```

The query processor looks at the GROUP BY clause and determines that the primary key **c_custkey** determines **c_name**, so there is no need to group on **c_name** in addition to **c_custkey**. The query optimizer then determines that grouping on **c_custkey** and **o_custkey** produces the same result. Because the **orders** table has a customer key (**o_custkey**), the query processor can group by customer key as soon as it has the records for the **orders** table and before it joins to the **customer** table. This becomes evident in this execution plan.

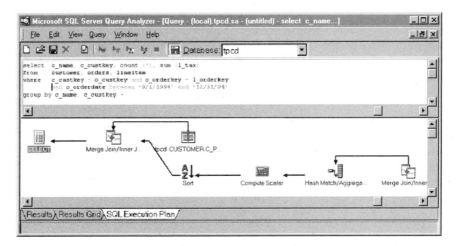

The query processor first uses a merge join of the **orders** table (within the specified date range) and the **lineitem** table to get all order-line items. The second step is a hash aggregation, that is, the grouping operation. In this step, SQL Server aggregates the order-line items at the customer key level, counting them and calculating a sum of **l_tax**. SQL Server then sorts the output of the hash join and joins it to the **customer** table to produce the requested result. The advantage of this query plan is that the input into the final join is substantially reduced due to the earlier grouping operation.

Partitioned Views

The SQL Server query processor supports queries that rely on partitioned views. Partitioned views allow you to create multiple tables with constraints (essentially one table for each partition) and have the tables logically reunited in response to queries. Here is an example:

```
CREATE table Sales96Q1  constraint "Month between 1 and 3"
CREATE table Sales96Q2  constraint "Month between 4 and 6"

CREATE view Sales96 as
    SELECT * from Sales96Q1 union all
    SELECT * from Sales96Q2 union all
```

This data definition language (DDL) creates four tables, one for each quarter of sales, each with an appropriate constraint. The DDL then creates a view that reunites all four tables. Programmers must be aware of the partitioning for updates, but for decision support queries the partitioning is transparent. When the query processor receives a query against the view **Sales96**, it automatically identifies and removes tables that do not fall within the constraints of the query.

```
SELECT *
FROM Sales96   -- remember, this view has four tables
WHERE   s_date between '6/21/1996' and '9/21/1996'
```

If you issue this query, the query processor generates a plan that touches only two of the tables in the view (**Sales96Q2** and **Sales96Q3**), because the WHERE clause makes the other two tables irrelevant to the query. Different access paths can be used for the individual quarters. For example, you can use an index scan for the few days in Q2 (6/21-6/30) and a table scan for Q3. This is a useful method of improving the performance of queries that tend to select subsets of large tables on a well-known column. Time and location are typical examples.

The query processor detects all empty results when a constraint contradicts the selection criteria, even if you have not declared a view.

Star Queries

Databases designed for decision support, particularly data warehouses and data marts, often have very different table structures than OLTP databases. A common approach is to implement a star schema, a type of database schema designed to allow a user to intuitively navigate information in the database, as well as to provide better performance for large, ad hoc queries.

A star schema begins with the observation that information can be classified into facts, the numeric data that is the core of what is being analyzed, and dimensions, the attributes of facts. Examples of facts include sales, units, budgets, and forecasts. Examples of dimensions include geography, time, product, and sales channel. Users often express their queries by saying "I want to look at these facts by these dimensions," or "I want to look at sales and units sold by quarter."

A star schema takes advantage of this observation by organizing data into a central fact table and surrounding dimension tables.

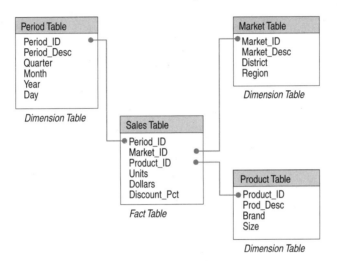

Microsoft SQL Server 7.0 has several techniques for optimizing queries against star schemas. The query processor automatically recognizes these queries and applies any and all of the techniques presented here, as well as combinations of these techniques. It is important to understand that the choice of which technique to apply is entirely cost-based; no hints are required to force these optimizations.

The tables in a star schema do not contain equal numbers of records. Typically, the fact table has many more records. This difference becomes important in many of the query optimization techniques.

A straightforward execution strategy is to read the entire fact table and join it in turn to each of the dimension tables. If no filter conditions are specified in the query, this can be a reasonable strategy. However, when filter conditions are present, the star query optimizations avoid having to read the entire fact table by taking full advantage of indexes.

Cartesian Products and Composite Indexes

Because dimension tables typically have fewer records than the fact table, it can make sense to compute the Cartesian product and use the result to view fact table rows in a multicolumn index.

For example, assume that the **sales** (fact) table has 10 million rows, the **period** table has 20 rows, the **market** table has 5 rows, and the **product** table has 200 rows. Also assume that a user generates this query using a front-end tool:

```
SELECT      sales.market_id, period.period_id, sum(units), sum(dollars)
FROM    sales, period, market
WHERE       period.period_id = sales.period_id and
            sales.market_id = market.market_id and
            period.period_Desc in
('Period2','Period3','Period4','Period5')
            and market.market_Desc in ('Market1','Market2')
GROUP BY sales.market_id, period.period_id
```

A simple approach is to join the **period** table to the **sales** table. Assuming an even distribution of data, the input is 10 million rows, the output is 4/20 (4 periods out of a possible 20), or 2 million rows. This can be done using a hash join or merge join and involves reading the entire 10 million rows in the fact table or retrieving 2 million rows through index lookups, whichever costs less. This partial result is then joined to the reduced **market** table to produce 800K rows of output, which are finally aggregated.

If there is a multicolumn index on the fact table (for example, on **period_id** or **market_id**) the Cartesian product strategy can be used. Because there are 4 rows selected from the **period** table and 2 rows from the **market** table, the Cartesian product is 8 rows. These eight combinations of values are used to look up the resulting 800K rows of output. Multicolumn indexes used this way are sometimes called star indexes.

Semi-Join Reductions and Index Intersection

If the joins to the fact table occur on fields other than those contained in a composite index, the query optimizer can use other indexes and reduce the number of rows read from the fact table by performing an intersection of the qualifying rows from joins to each dimension table.

For example, if **period_id** or **product_id** is selected, the query optimizer cannot use the composite index because the two fields of interest are not a leading subset of the index. However, if there are separate single-column indexes on **period_id** and **product_id**, the query optimizer may choose a join between the **period** table and the **sales** table (retrieving 2 million index entries) and, separately, a join between the **product** table and the **sales** table (retrieving 4 million index entries). In both cases, the optimizer will do the join using an index; thus, the two preliminary joins compute sets of record IDs for the **sales** table but not full rows of the **sales** table. Before retrieving the actual rows in the **sales** table (the most expensive process), an intersection of the two sets is computed to determine the qualifying rows. Only rows that satisfy both joins are included in this intermediate result of 800K rows and only these rows are actually read from the **sales** table.

Combined Techniques

Occasionally, semi-join reduction can be combined with Cartesian products and composite indexes. For example, if you select from three dimension tables, where two of the three tables are the initial fields of a composite index but the third dimension has a separate index, the query optimizer can use Cartesian products to satisfy the first two joins, use semi-joins to satisfy the third join, and then combine the results.

Several factors influence the effectiveness of these techniques. These factors include the size of the indexes to be used compared to the base table, and whether the set of indexes used covers all the columns required by the query, obviating the need to look up rows in the base table. These factors are taken into account by the query optimizer, which will choose the least expensive plan.

If that plan is more expensive than the cost threshold for parallelism, all required operations, including scans, joins, intersection, and row fetching, can be executed by multiple threads in parallel.

Optimized Updates

If a row in a table is updated, indexes on the table also must be updated. For small updates, such as OLTP operations, it is appropriate to update the indexes row-by-row as you update each row of the base table.

For large updates, such as a data warehouse refresh, row-by-row updates can be inefficient, resulting in a high volume of random I/O to the index records. A better approach is to delay updating the indexes until all the base tables are updated, then presort the changes per index and simultaneously merge all the changes into the index. This assures that each index leaf page is touched once at most and that SQL Server traverses each B-tree index sequentially.

The query optimizer takes this approach if it is the least expensive approach. The benefit is that large data warehouse refreshes can be accomplished more efficiently.

The query optimizer also plans the join operations required to enforce referential integrity constraints, making a cost-based choice among (index) nested loops join, merge join, and hash join.

Distributed Queries

In addition to storing and searching data locally, Microsoft SQL Server 7.0 also can be used as a gateway to many other data stores, both relational and nonrelational data sources.

SQL Server 7.0 performs distributed queries, that is, queries that involve data from two or more servers. It supports retrievals, updates, and cursors across servers, and ensures transaction semantics across nodes using the Microsoft Distributed Transaction Coordinator (MS DTC). It also maintains security across servers.

If any remote servers support indexes or SQL queries, the SQL Server query optimizer determines the largest possible query that can be sent to each remote server. In other words, the query optimizer assigns the maximum possible data reduction to each remote server. For example, if a remote query is issued against a 1-million row table, with a WHERE clause or an aggregation that returns only 10 records, the 1 million rows are processed at the remote server, and only 10 records are sent across the network. This reduces network traffic and overall query time. Typical operations that are pushed toward the data source are selections, joins, and sorts.

Heterogeneous Queries

Distributed queries may be heterogeneous, supporting any OLE DB or ODBC data source. The SQL Server 7.0 compact disc includes OLE DB drivers for Oracle 7.*x*, Oracle 8.*x*, Microsoft Excel, Microsoft Access, dBASE, Paradox, and Microsoft Visual FoxPro database development system, as well as an OBDC gateway for other relational databases. OLE DB providers for other server databases (IBM DB2, SYBASE, and Informix) are available from third parties.

Pass-through Queries

If a remote server supports syntax that is not standard SQL, or if the remote data source supports a query language other than SQL, the OPENQUERY operator is provided to pass through the query syntax unchanged.

Working with Queries

In addition to improved query processing capabilities in the server, Microsoft SQL Server 7.0 also offers these improved tools and features to work with database queries:

- SQL Server Query Analyzer
- Query Governor
- SQL Server Profiler

SQL Server Query Analyzer

SQL Server 7.0 provides SQL Server Query Analyzer, an interactive, graphical tool that allows a database administrator or developer to write queries, execute multiple queries simultaneously, view results, analyze the plan of a query, and receive assistance to improve the performance of a query. The **Showplan** option graphically displays the data retrieval methods chosen by the SQL Server query optimizer. This is useful for understanding the performance characteristics of a query. In addition, SQL Server Query Analyzer suggests additional indexes and statistics on nonindexed columns that will improve the query optimizer's ability to process a query efficiently. In particular, SQL Server Query Analyzer shows what statistics are missing, thus forcing the query optimizer to guess about predicate selectivity, and permits the creation of those statistics.

Query Governor

Query cost refers to the estimated elapsed time, in seconds, required to execute a query on a specific hardware configuration. On other hardware configurations, there is a correlation between cost units and elapsed time, but cost units do not equal seconds. The query governor lets you specify an upper cost limit for a query; a query that exceeds this limit is not run.

Because it is based on estimated query cost rather than actual elapsed time, the query governor does not have any run-time overhead. It also stops long-running queries before they start, rather than running them until they reach a predefined limit.

SQL Server Profiler

SQL Server Profiler is a graphical tool that allows system administrators to monitor engine events, such as:

- Login connects, fails, and disconnects
- Transact-SQL SELECT, INSERT, UPDATE, and DELETE statements
- Remote procedure call (RPC) batch status
- Start or end of a stored procedure
- Start or end of statements within stored procedures
- Start or end of an SQL batch
- Lock acquired or released on a database object
- An opened cursor
- Missing statistics that force the query optimizer to guess a predicate's selectivity

Data about each event can be captured and saved to a file or a SQL Server table for later analysis. Event data can be filtered so that only a relevant subset is collected. For example, only the events that affect a specific database, or those for a particular user, are collected; all others are ignored. Alternatively, data could be collected about only those queries that take longer than 30 seconds to execute.

SQL Server Profiler allows captured event data to be replayed against SQL Server, thereby effectively reexecuting the saved events as they originally occurred. You can troubleshoot problems in SQL Server by capturing all the events that lead up to a problem, and then, by replaying the events on a test system, replicate and isolate the problem.

Index Tuning Wizard

The Index Tuning Wizard is a new and powerful tool that analyzes your workload and recommends an optimal index configuration for your database.

Features of the Index Tuning Wizard include:

- Comparing, contrasting, and selecting the best mix of indexes using the query optimizer's cost calculations.
- Recommending the best mix of indexes for a workload (trace file or SQL Script) against a database.
- Providing index, workload, table-use, and query-cost analysis.
- Tuning for an entire workload, which may include dropping existing indexes to reduce maintenance costs.
- Tuning the database for a set of problem queries without dropping existing indexes.
- Prototyping index configuration recommendations for different disk space constraints.

The Index Tuning Wizard creates SQL statements that can be used to drop ineffective indexes or to create new, more effective indexes and statistics on nonindexed columns. The SQL statements can be saved for manual execution as necessary.

For more information, see "Index Tuning Wizard" earlier in this volume.

Automatic Statistics Creation and Refresh

When you create an index, SQL Server 7.0 automatically stores statistical information regarding the distribution of values in the indexed columns. It also supports statistics on nonindexed columns. The query optimizer uses these statistics to estimate the size of intermediate query results as well as the cost of using the index for a query.

If the query optimizer determines that the statistics needed to optimize a query are missing, it automatically creates them and saves them in the database. Moreover, it automatically updates the statistics as the data in a table changes, and it eventually discards the statistics if they are not reused.

Statistics are created and refreshed very efficiently by sampling. The sampling is random across data pages and taken from a table or nonclustered index for the smallest index containing the columns needed by the statistics. The volume of data in the table and the amount of changing data determine the frequency with which the statistical information is updated. For example, the statistics for a table containing 10,000 rows may need updating when 1,000 rows have changed because 1,000 is a significant percentage of the table. However, for a table containing 10 million rows, 1,000 changes are less significant.

CHAPTER 15

Storage Engine

Ten years ago, it was common for database application development to take months or years. When databases were built, everything was worked out in advance: the database size, schema, number of users, and so on. Now database applications are developed over weeks or months, evolve during the process, and are put into production before all issues are fully understood.

This rapid deployment of mission-critical applications places rigorous demands on the storage engine, which needs to be highly available and have a fast recovery system and automatic management utilities.

Storage Engine Goals

There are several important goals for the Microsoft SQL Server 7.0 storage engine. The defining strategy is to further improve ease of use so that applications using database technology can be deployed widely. Ideally, the database becomes completely transparent to end users and nearly transparent to database administrators.

Ease of Use

Customers are looking for solutions to business problems. Most database solutions bring multiple layers of cost and complexity. SQL Server versions 6.0 and 6.5 defined ease of use as a relational database management system (RDBMS) feature. SQL Server 7.0 takes this concept to the next level, firmly establishing the product as one of the least complex databases for building, managing, and deploying business applications.

For the SQL Server 7.0 storage engine, ease of use includes many innovative features, including:

- No database administrator for standard operations. This allows branch-office automation, and desktop and mobile database applications.
- Transparent server configuration, database consistency checker (DBCC), index statistics, and database backups.
- Streamlined and simplified configuration options, which automatically adapt to the specific needs of the environment.

Scalability

Customers must protect their investments in business applications, and as organizations grow, the database must grow to handle more data, transactions, and users. SQL Server 7.0 delivers a single database engine that scales from a laptop computer running the Microsoft Windows 95 or Windows 98 operating system to terabyte-size symmetric multiprocessing (SMP) clusters running the Microsoft Windows NT Server, Enterprise Edition, operating system. All of these systems must maintain the security and reliability demanded by mission-critical business systems.

These storage engine features are the foundation for scalability:

- New disk format and storage subsystem to provide storage that is scalable from small to large databases
- Redesigned utilities to support terabyte-size databases efficiently
- Large memory support to reduce the need for frequent disk access
- Dynamic row-level locking to allow increased concurrency, especially for online transaction processing (OLTP) applications
- Unicode support to allow for multinational applications

Reliability

SQL Server 7.0 eliminates many concurrency, scalability, and reliability problems by replacing complex data structures and algorithms with simple structures. The new structures scale better and do not have concurrency problems. They are also less complex, and therefore more reliable.

SQL Server 7.0 eliminates the need to run DBCC checks prior to every backup. Run-time checks of critical data structures result in a more robust database. SQL Server 7.0 drops the recommendation to run DBCC prior to every backup, resulting in a significantly faster DBCC.

Storage Engine Features

The table summarizes the storage engine features of SQL Server 7.0.

Feature	Description and benefits
Data type sizes	Size limitations of data types increased dramatically.
Databases and files	Database creation simplified. Databases now reside on operating-system files instead of logical devices.
Dynamic memory	Performance improved by optimizing memory allocation and usage. Simplified design minimizes contention with other resource managers.
Dynamic row-level locking	Full row-level locking implemented for both data rows and index entries. Dynamic locking chooses the optimal level of lock (row, page, multiple page, table) for all database operations automatically. Improved concurrency provided with no tuning. Database supports hints to force a particular level of locking.
Dynamic space management	Automatic grow and shrink allowed within configurable limits, minimizing the need for database administrator intervention. It is not necessary to preallocate space and manage data structures.
Evolution	New architecture designed for extensibility, with a foundation for object-relational features.
Large memory support	Memory addressing supported for greater than 4 gigabytes (GB) in conjunction with Windows NT Server 5.0, Alpha-processor based systems, and other techniques.
Log manager	Design simplified to improve performance for truncation, online backup, and recovery operations.
Read ahead	Smart read-ahead logic implemented to improve performance and eliminate manual tuning.
Text and image	Text and image data stored separately in an optimized format.
Unicode	Native Unicode implemented, with Open Database Connectivity (ODBC) and OLE DB Unicode application programming interfaces (APIs), to improve multilingual support.

Storage Engine Architecture

Microsoft SQL Server 7.0 scales to both large enterprise applications and laptop applications. This scalability is based on a completely new set of on-disk structures designed to handle applications for years to come. The new formats allow the server to scale from low-end to high-end systems to improve performance and manageability.

The benefits to the SQL Server 7.0 on-disk structures include:

- Improved scalability and integration with Windows NT Server.
- Better performance with larger I/O operations.
- Stable record locators to allow more indexes.
- More indexes to speed decision support queries.
- Simpler data structures to provide better quality.
- Greater extensibility, so that subsequent releases will have a cleaner development process and new features will be faster to implement.

Storage Engine Subsystems

Most relational database products have two primary components, a relational engine and a storage engine. Storage engine subsystems include:

- Mechanisms that store data in files and find pages, files, and extents
- Record management for accessing records on pages
- Access methods by using B-trees, which help find records quickly by using record identifiers
- Concurrency control for locking, which helps implement the physical lock manager and locking protocols for page-level or record-level locking
- I/O buffer management
- Logging and recovery
- Utilities for backup and restore, consistency checking, and bulk data loading

Physical Database Organization

Microsoft SQL Server 7.0 databases are now stored in operating-system files, not on SQL Server logical devices. The UNIX legacy of database devices and segments has been replaced with a simple system that maps each database to its own set of files.

Pages and Extents

The fundamental unit of data storage in SQL Server is the page. In SQL Server 7.0, the page size is 8 KB, increased from 2 KB. At the start of each page is a 96-byte header used to store system information such as the type of page, the amount of free space on the page, and the ID of the object owning the page.

There are seven page types in the data files of a SQL Server 7.0 database.

Page type	Contains
Data	Data rows with all data types except **text**, **ntext**, and **image**
Index	Index entries
Log	Log records recording data changes for use in recovery
Text/Image	**text**, **ntext**, and **image** data types
Global Allocation Map	Information about allocated extents
Page Free Space	Information about free space available on pages
Index Allocation Map	Information about extents used by a table or index

Data pages contain all the data types in data rows except **text**, **ntext**, and **image**, which are stored in separate pages. Data rows are placed serially on the page starting immediately after the header. A row-offset table starts at the end of the page.

The row-offset table contains one entry for each row on the page. Each entry records how far from the start of the page the first byte of the row is. The entries in the row-offset table are in reverse sequence from the sequence of the rows on the page. In SQL Server 7.0, rows cannot span pages, and the maximum amount of data contained in a single row is 8,060 bytes, not including the **text**, **ntext**, and **image** data types.

Extents are the basic unit in which space is allocated to tables and indexes. An extent is eight contiguous pages, or 64 KB. To make its space allocation efficient, SQL Server 7.0 does not allocate entire extents to tables with small amounts of data.

SQL Server 7.0 has two types of extents: *uniform* and *mixed*. Uniform extents are owned by a single object; all pages in the extent can be used only by the owning object.

Mixed extents, introduced in SQL Server 7.0, work well for small applications. In SQL Server, space is added to tables one extent at a time. In SQL Server 7.0, this can lead to a large overhead for tiny tables because pages are 8 KB. A mixed extent allows allocation of a single page to a small table or index. Only when the table or index has allocated more than eight pages will it begin to allocate uniform extents. Mixed extents are shared by up to eight objects. A new table or index is allocated pages from mixed extents. When a table or index grows to eight pages, it is switched to uniform extents.

Torn Page Detection

Torn page detection ensures database consistency. In SQL Server 7.0, pages are 8 KB, and Windows NT Server performs I/O in 512-byte segments. This discrepancy makes it possible for a page to be written partially, which could happen if there is a power failure or another problem between the time when the first 512-byte segment is written and the 8 KB of I/O is complete.

If the first 512-byte segment is written, it may appear that the page has been updated when it was not. (The timestamp for the page is in the header, the first 96 bytes of the page.) There are several ways to deal with this problem. You can use battery-backed cached I/O devices that guarantee all-or-nothing I/O. If you have one of these systems, torn page detection is unnecessary.

SQL Server can detect incomplete I/O by creating a mask of bits, one bit from each segment in the page. Every time a page is written, the bit is flipped from its previous state (as it was on disk), and the actual state is saved in the page header. If a page is read and a bit is in the wrong state, it indicates that an I/O did not complete and there is a torn page. This mechanism is less expensive than computing a checksum.

You can set torn page detection on and off because the page header is marked when the bit is flipped. If torn page detection is set on and off, then the state in the pages that have been flipped is observed and corrected the next time they are read.

Files and Filegroups

SQL Server 7.0 creates a database using a set of operating-system files, with a separate file for each database. Multiple databases no longer can exist in the same file. There are several important benefits to this simplification: Files can grow and shrink, and space management is simplified.

All data and objects in the database, such as tables, stored procedures, triggers, and views, are stored within the following operating-system files only.

File	Description
Primary data file	This file is the starting point of the database. Every database has only one primary data file. The recommended file extension is .mdf.
Secondary data files	These files are optional and can hold all data and objects that are not on the primary data file. Some databases may not have any secondary data files, while others may have multiple secondary data files. The recommended file extension is .ndf.
Log files	These files hold all the transaction log information used to recover the database. Every database has at least one log file. The recommended file extension is .ldf.

When a database is created, all the files that comprise the database are zeroed out (filled with zeros) to overwrite any data left on the disk by previously deleted files. Although this means that the files take longer to create, it prevents Windows NT from clearing out the files when data is written to the files for the first time (because they are already zeroed out) during normal database operations. This improves the performance of day-to-day operations.

A database consists of one or more data files and one or more log files. The data files can be grouped into user-defined filegroups. Tables and indexes then can be mapped to different filegroups to control data placement on physical disks.

Filegroups are a convenient unit of administration that improve flexibility. With a terabyte-size database, regardless of backup speed, it is impossible to back up the entire database within a reasonable window. SQL Server 7.0 allows you to back up a different portion of the database each night on a rotating schedule.

Filegroups work well for sophisticated users who know where they want to place indexes and tables. SQL Server 7.0 can work effectively without filegroups; therefore, many systems will not need to specify user-defined filegroups. In this case, all files are included in the default filegroup, and SQL Server 7.0 can allocate data effectively within the database.

Log files are never a part of a filegroup; log space is managed separately from data space.

Using Files and Filegroups

Files and filegroups improve database performance by allowing a database to be created across multiple disks, multiple disk controllers, or redundant array of inexpensive disks (RAID) systems. For example, if your computer has four disks, you can create a database that comprises three data files and one log file, with one file on each disk. As data is accessed, four read/write heads can access the data simultaneously, which speeds up database operations.

Additionally, files and filegroups permit better data placement because a table can be created in a specific filegroup. Performance is improved because all I/O for a specific table can be directed at a specific disk. For example, a heavily used table in a database can be placed on one file in one filegroup located on one disk, and another less heavily accessed table can be placed on another file in another filegroup located on a second disk.

Here are some recommendations for files and filegroups:

- Most databases work well with a single data file and a single log file.

- If you plan to use multiple files, use the primary data file for system tables and objects only. Create at least one secondary data file to store user data and objects.

- To maximize performance, create files or filegroups on as many different local physical disks as are available, and place objects that compete heavily for space in different filegroups.

- Use filegroups to allow placement of objects on specific physical disks.

- Place different tables used in the same join queries in different filegroups. This improves performance due to parallel disk I/O searching for joined data.

- Place heavily accessed tables and nonclustered indexes belonging to those tables in different filegroups. This will improve performance due to parallel I/O if the files are located on different physical disks.

- Do not place log files on the same physical disk as other files and filegroups.

Space Management

SQL Server 7.0 features many improvements in space allocation and space management within files. For example, the data structures that track page-to-object relationships have been redesigned. Instead of linked lists of pages, bitmaps are used because they are cleaner, simpler, and facilitate parallel scans. Now each file is more autonomous; it has more data about itself, within itself. This works well for copying or mailing database files.

SQL Server 7.0 also has a more efficient system for tracking table space. The changes allow:

- File shrink and file grow.
- Better support for large I/O.
- Row-space management within a table.
- Less expensive extent allocations.

In earlier versions of SQL Server, space allocations can cause blocking when large amounts of data were added. The SQL Server 7.0 space allocation algorithms and data structures are simple and efficient and will not cause blocking because SQL Server 7.0 tracks free space on a page. As rows are deleted from a table that does not have a clustered index, that space can be reused for new inserts. This is a more efficient use of disk space and speeds table scans by packing data more densely.

SQL Server 7.0 allocates pages to objects quickly and reuses space freed by deleted rows. These operations are internal to the system and use data structures not visible to users, yet the processes and structures are referenced occasionally in SQL Server messages. This information about space-allocation algorithms and data structures will help users and administrators understand the messages generated by SQL Server.

SQL Server 7.0 introduces some significant changes in the internal data structures that manage the allocation and reuse of pages. These data structures are not visible to end users, so the changes do not affect users other than by improving speed.

File Shrink

Laptop and desktop systems may have restricted disk space, so you can shrink database files automatically if the option is enabled. The server checks the space usage in each database periodically. If a database is found with a lot of empty space, the size of the files in the database is reduced. Both data and log files can be shrunk. This activity occurs in the background and does not affect any user activity within the database. You also can use SQL Server Enterprise Manager or DBCC to shrink files individually or as a group.

File shrink works by moving rows from pages at the end of a file to pages allocated earlier in the file. In an index, nodes are moved from the end of a file to pages at the beginning of a file. In both cases, pages are freed at the end of files and returned to the file system. Databases can shrink only to the point that no free space is remaining; there is no data compression.

File Grow

Automated file growth reduces the need for database management and eliminates many problems that occur when logs or databases run out of space. When creating a database, an initial size for the file must be given. SQL Server creates the data files based on the size provided by the database creator, and data is added to the database that these files fill. By default, data files are allowed to grow as much as necessary until disk space is exhausted. Alternatively, data files can be configured to grow automatically when they fill with data, but only to a predefined limit. This prevents disk drives from running out of space.

This feature is useful when SQL Server is used as a database embedded in an application, in which the user does not have ready access to a system administrator. The user can let the files grow automatically as needed to lessen the administrative burden of monitoring the amount of free space in the database and allocating additional space manually.

When creating a database, data files should be as large as possible, based on the maximum amount of data expected in the database. You can permit the data files to grow automatically, but place a limit on the growth. If the initial data file size is exceeded and the file starts to grow automatically, reevaluate the expected maximum database size and plan accordingly by adding more disk space or by creating and adding more files or filegroups to the database.

Databases can be prevented from growing beyond their initial size. If the files fill, no more data can be added unless more data files are added. Allowing files to grow automatically can cause fragmentation if many files share the same disk. Therefore, it is recommended that files or filegroups be created on as many different local physical disks as are available. Objects that compete for space should be placed in different filegroups.

Lock Enhancements

Microsoft SQL Server 7.0 offers these types of lock enhancements:

- Row-level locking
- Dynamic locking
- Locking modes

Row-Level Locking

SQL Server 6.5 introduced row-level locking on inserts. SQL Server 7.0 supports full row-level locking for both data rows and index entries. Transactions can update individual records without blocking the pages. Many OLTP applications experience increased concurrency, especially when applications append rows to tables and indexes. The lock manager dynamically adjusts the resources it uses for larger databases, eliminating the need to adjust the locks' server configuration option manually. The lock manager automatically chooses between page locking (preferable for table scans) and row-level locking (preferable for inserting, updating, and deleting data).

Dynamic Locking

SQL Server 7.0 has a superior locking mechanism that is unusual in the database industry: dynamic locking. At run time, the storage engine dynamically cooperates with the query processor to choose the lowest-cost locking strategy based on the characteristics of the schema and query.

Dynamic locking has these advantages:

- Simplified database administration, because database administrators no longer need to be concerned with adjusting lock-escalation thresholds

- Increased performance, because SQL Server minimizes system overhead by using locks appropriate to the task

- Concentrated development by application developers, because SQL Server adjusts locking automatically

Dynamic locking allows different types of resources to be locked by a transaction. To minimize the cost of locking, SQL Server locks resources automatically at a level appropriate to the task. Locking at a smaller granularity, such as rows, increases concurrency but has a higher overhead because more locks must be held if many rows are locked. Locking at a larger granularity, such as tables, is expensive in terms of concurrency because locking an entire table restricts access to any part of the table by other transactions. However, it has a lower overhead because fewer locks are being maintained.

SQL Server can dynamically lock the following resources (thereby increasing granularity).

Resource	Description
RID	A row identifier. Used to lock a single row within a table.
Key	A row lock within an index. Used to protect key ranges in serializable transactions.
Page	An 8-KB data page or index page.
Extent	A contiguous group of eight data pages or index pages.
Table	An entire table, including all data and indexes.
DB	A database.

Locking Modes

SQL Server locks resources by using different locking modes that determine how the resources can be accessed by concurrent transactions. SQL Server uses several resource locking modes:

- Shared
- Update
- Exclusive
- Intent
- Schema

Shared Locks

Shared locks allow concurrent transactions to read a resource. No other transactions can modify the data while shared locks exist on the resource. Shared locks are released as soon as the data on a resource has been read, unless the transaction isolation level is set to repeatable read or higher, or a locking hint is used to retain the shared locks for the duration of the transaction.

Update Locks

Update locks are used on resources that can be updated. Update locks prevent a common form of deadlock. If two transactions acquire shared locks on a resource and then attempt to update data concurrently, an attempted conversion to exclusive locks occurs. Both transactions are waiting for the other to release its shared lock, and a deadlock occurs. Update locks eliminate this problem, because only one transaction at a time can obtain an update lock to a resource.

Exclusive Locks

Exclusive locks are used for data-modification operations, such as updates, inserts, or deletes. Exclusive locks ensure that multiple updates cannot be made to the same resource at the same time (concurrent transactions). No other transactions can read or modify data locked with an exclusive lock.

Intent Locks

Intent locks indicate that SQL Server is attempting to acquire a shared or exclusive lock on some of the resources lower in the hierarchy. Intent locks improve performance because SQL Server must examine intent locks only at the table level to determine if a transaction can safely acquire a lock on that table. This removes the need to examine every row or page lock on the table to determine if a transaction can lock the entire table.

Schema Locks

There are two types of schema locks: Sch-M and Sch-S. Sch-M locks are taken when a table data definition language (DDL) operation is being performed (such as adding a column or dropping a table). Sch-S locks are taken while compiling queries. Sch-S locks do not block out any transactional locks, including exclusive locks. Therefore, other transactions can run while a query is being compiled, even transactions with exclusive locks on a table. However, DDL operations cannot be performed on the table.

Base Table and Index Architecture

Fundamental changes were made in Microsoft SQL Server 7.0 base-table organization that allow the query processor to make use of more secondary indexes, which greatly improves performance for decision support applications. The query optimizer has a wide set of execution strategies, and many of the optimization limitations of earlier versions of SQL Server have been removed. In particular, SQL Server 7.0 is less sensitive to index-selection issues, resulting in less need for tuning.

Table Organization

The data for each table now is stored in a collection of 8-KB data pages. Each data page has a 96-byte header containing system information, such as the ID of the table that owns the page and pointers to the next and previous pages for pages linked in a list. A row-offset table is at the end of the page; data rows fill the rest of the page.

SQL Server 7.0 tables use one of two methods to organize data pages:

- Clustered tables, which are tables that have a clustered index. The data rows are stored in order based on the clustered index key. The data pages are linked in a doubly linked list, and the index is implemented as a B-tree index structure that supports fast retrieval of the rows based on their clustered index key values.

- Heaps, which are tables that have nonclustered indexes. The data rows are not stored in any particular order, and there is no particular order to the sequence of the data pages. The data pages are not linked in a linked list.

Index Organization

An index (clustered or nonclustered) speeds retrieval of the rows in a table. An index contains key values built from one or more columns in a table. These keys are stored in a structure that allows SQL Server to find rows associated with the key values quickly and efficiently. If a table has no indexes, the data rows are not stored in any particular order, which is called a heap.

Clustered Indexes

In a clustered index, the order of the values in the index is the same as the order of the data in the table. (To some degree, the storage of the data is the index.) A clustered index is analogous to the alphabetic listings contained in a telephone directory.

Because a clustered index dictates the storage of the table's data, a table can contain only one clustered index; however, an index can be created on multiple columns. For example, a telephone directory is organized by last name, and then by first name.

A clustered index contains a hierarchical tree, with the range of values stored in a given area of the index. When searching for data based on a clustered-index value, SQL Server quickly isolates the page with the specified value, and then searches the page for the records with the specified value. The lowest level, or leaf node, of the index tree is the page that contains the data.

Nonclustered Indexes

A nonclustered index is analogous to an index in a textbook, in which the data is stored in one place and the index is stored in another. Pointers indicate the storage location of the index items in the data. The leaf node of a nonclustered index is the storage location (its page number and offset in the page) of the index entry. Therefore, a nonclustered index has an extra level between the index structure and the data itself.

When SQL Server searches for data based on a nonclustered index, it searches the index for the specified value to obtain the location of the rows of data, and then retrieves the data directly from its storage locations. This makes nonclustered indexes the optimal choice for exact-match queries.

Some nonclustered indexes contain multiple indexes. You can define a nonclustered index for each of the columns commonly used to find data in the table.

Because nonclustered indexes store clustered index keys as pointers to data rows, it is important to keep clustered index keys as small as possible. Avoid choosing large columns as the keys to clustered indexes if a table also has nonclustered indexes.

SQL Server 7.0 supports up to 249 nonclustered indexes on each table. Nonclustered indexes and clustered indexes share a similar B-tree structure. The difference is that nonclustered indexes have no effect on the order of the data rows. The collection of data pages for a heap is not affected if nonclustered indexes are defined for the table.

Index Distribution Statistics

All indexes have distribution statistics that describe the selectivity and distribution of the key values in the index. Selectivity is a property that relates to how many rows are typically identified by a key value. A unique key value has high selectivity; a nonunique key value (one found in 1,000 rows, for example) has poor selectivity.

The selectivity and distribution statistics are used by SQL Server to optimize its navigation through tables when processing Transact-SQL statements. The statistics for each index are not limited to a single page, but are stored as a long string of bits across multiple pages in the same way image data is stored.

Data Type Enhancements

Microsoft SQL Server 7.0 introduces enhancements to data storage and to text and image handling.

Unicode Data Types

SQL Server 7.0 supports Unicode data types, which makes it easier to store data in multiple languages within one database by eliminating conversion of characters and installation of multiple code pages. Unicode stores character data using 2 bytes for each character (rather than 1 byte). There are 65,536 different bit patterns in 2 bytes; therefore, Unicode can use one standard set of bit patterns to encode each character in all languages, including languages such as Chinese that have many characters. Programming languages also support Unicode data types.

The fact that Unicode data needs twice as much storage space is offset by the elimination of the need to convert extended characters between code pages. The new data types that support Unicode are **ntext**, **nchar**, and **nvarchar**. They are the same as **text**, **char**, and **varchar** except for the wider range of characters supported and the increased storage space used.

Traditional non-Unicode data types in SQL Server allow the use of characters that are defined by a particular character set. A character set is chosen during SQL Server setup and is immutable throughout the life of the installation. By using Unicode data types, a column can store any character that is defined by the Unicode Standard, which includes all characters defined in the various character sets.

Storage of Data Types

Data storage flexibility is improved in SQL Server 7.0 with the expansion of maximum limits for **char**, **varchar**, **binary**, and **varbinary** data types from 255 bytes to 8,000 bytes. It is no longer necessary to use **text** and **image** data types for anything but extremely large data values. The Transact-SQL string functions also support the large **char** and **varchar** data types, and the SUBSTRING function can be used to process **text** and **image** columns.

Additionally, the handling of nulls and empty strings has been improved. And a new **uniqueidentifier** data type is provided for storing a globally unique identifier (GUID).

text, ntext, and image Data Types

SQL Server provides a solid foundation for building object-relational features. One SQL Server 7.0 enhancement is for text and image storage, which uses a new, efficient data structure.

The SQL Server 7.0 **ntext**, **text**, and **image** data types are capable of storing extremely large amounts of data (up to 2 GB) in a single value. A single data value is typically larger than can be retrieved in one step by an application; some values may be larger than the virtual memory available on the client. This means that special steps may be necessary to retrieve these values. If the value for these data types is no longer than a Unicode, character, or binary string (4,000 characters, 8,000 characters, or 8,000 bytes), the value can be referenced in SELECT, UPDATE, and INSERT statements much the same as smaller data types.

text, **ntext**, and **image** data type values are not stored as part of the data row but in a separate collection of pages. For each value, only a 16-byte pointer is stored. For each row, the pointer points to the location of data. A row containing multiple **text**, **ntext**, or **image** columns has one pointer for each column.

The data is stored in a collection of 8-KB pages that are not necessarily located next to each other. In SQL Server 7.0, the pages are organized logically in a B-tree structure. In earlier versions, they are linked in a page chain. The advantage of the B-tree structure is that operations starting in the middle of the string are more efficient, making the B-tree quicker to navigate. This is in contrast to page chains, which often take a somewhat random path through the files of a database. The structure of the B-tree differs slightly depending on whether there is more or less than 32 KB of data.

Log Manager Architecture

A Microsoft SQL Server 7.0 log file consists of one or more physical files that contain log entries only. Previously, the log file was a system table that used ordinary database pages. These log pages were allocated and deallocated in the same way as pages of other tables, and they competed with data pages for space in the memory cache.

Each log file is divided logically into smaller segments called virtual log files, which are the unit of truncation for the transaction log. When a virtual log file no longer contains log records for active transactions, it can be truncated and the space becomes available for logging new transactions.

SQL Server 7.0 avoids having lots of small virtual log files. The number of virtual log files grows more slowly than their size. If a log file grows in small increments, it usually will have many small virtual log files. If the log file grows in larger increments, SQL Server will create a smaller number of larger virtual log files.

As records are written to the log file, the end of the log file grows from one virtual log file to the next. If there is more than one physical log file for a database, the end of the log file grows through each virtual log file in each physical log file before circling back to the first virtual log file in the first physical log file.

The smallest size for a virtual log file is 256 KB. The minimum size for a transaction log is 512 KB, or two virtual log files of 256 KB each. Both the number and size of the virtual log files in a transaction log increase as the size of the log file increases. A small log file might have a very few small virtual log files. A very large log file will have larger virtual log files.

Log files can grow and shrink automatically. If there is no reusable space available, the log file will be extended by adding another logical log file chunk. If more space is needed, another logical log file is added. Internally, the log manager divides physical log files into logical log files. The logical log files are either active or reusable. A logical log file can be backed up if it does not contain any portion of the active log. A log file can be reused if it has been backed up.

Transaction Log Management

Transaction logs assist in recovering database integrity in the event of system failure. Log records for a single database are maintained on one or more operating-system files called log files, which are serial recordings of all modifications that have occurred in the database and of which transaction performed each modification.

A log file grows continuously as logged operations occur in the database. For some large operations, the file records only the fact that the operation took place. The log file records the commit or rollback of each transaction. This allows SQL Server to roll a transaction either back or forward.

Rolling a transaction back occurs when SQL Server is backing out of an incomplete transaction. SQL Server restores the database to the state it was in before the transaction began by reversing the sequence of alterations.

Rolling a transaction forward occurs when SQL Server is restoring a transaction log. Modifications to the database are applied in the same sequence in which they originally occurred. At the end of this process, the database is in the same state it was in at the time the log was backed up.

The SQL Server 7.0 transaction log manager features these improvements:

- Does not compete with data for buffer cache pages
- Can be spread over one or more physical files
- Grows and shrinks automatically
- Allows for quick and nonintrusive truncation
- Enables larger I/O operations

Memory Management

Microsoft SQL Server 7.0 dynamically acquires and frees memory as needed. It is no longer necessary for an administrator to specify how much memory should be allocated to SQL Server, although the option still exists.

There are several competing subsystems in SQL Server that must share available memory. The log and recovery systems need memory to read and undo pages, and the query processor needs memory to perform hashing and sorting. Other subsystems that use memory are the procedure cache, buffer pool, lock manager, and data structures. In SQL Server 7.0, these systems allocate the memory they need dynamically and can return memory when it is no longer needed.

Microsoft Windows NT, Microsoft Windows 95, and Microsoft Windows 98 operating systems support virtual memory, a method of extending the available physical memory on a computer. In a virtual memory system, the operating system creates a pagefile, or swapfile, and divides memory into units called pages. Recently referenced pages are located in physical memory, or RAM. If a page of memory is not referenced for a while, it is written, or swapped out, to the pagefile. If the page is later referenced by an application, it is read, or swapped into physical memory, from the pagefile. The total memory available to applications is the amount of RAM plus the size of the pagefile.

One of the primary design goals of database software is minimizing disk I/O, because disk reads and writes are among the most resource-intensive operations on a computer. SQL Server builds a buffer cache in memory to hold pages read from the database. Much of the code in SQL Server is dedicated to minimizing the number of physical reads and writes between the disk and the buffer cache. The larger the buffer cache, the less I/O SQL Server has to do. However, if the buffer cache causes the SQL Server memory requirements to exceed the available physical memory on the server, then the operating system starts swapping memory to and from the pagefile. All that has happened is that the physical I/O to the database files has been traded for physical I/O to the swap file.

Having a lot of physical I/O to the database files is an inherent factor of database software. By default, SQL Server attempts to balance between two goals:

- Minimizing or eliminating pagefile I/O to concentrate I/O resources for reads and writes of the database files
- Minimizing physical I/O to the database files by maximizing the size of the buffer cache

SQL Server starts with a default memory value. As more applications are started, the system is queried periodically to determine the amount of free physical memory available. SQL Server grows or shrinks the buffer cache to keep free physical memory at around 5 MB, which also prevents Windows NT from paging. If there is less than 5 MB of free memory, then SQL Server releases memory to Windows NT that usually goes on the free list. If there is more than 5 MB of free memory, SQL Server recommits memory to the buffer cache. SQL Server adds memory to the buffer cache when its work load requires more memory; a server at rest does not grow its buffer cache.

Buffer Management and I/O

SQL Server 7.0 uses a clocking mechanism to manage buffer I/O instead of a least recently used list. The clocking mechanism improves performance because there is less synchronization required. This improves scaling on large SMP systems, but does not have much effect on small systems. Query performance is improved because it makes use of both parallel I/O and large I/O on the files that comprise the database object.

The **SQL Server: Buffer Manager** object provides counters to monitor how SQL Server uses memory to store data pages, internal data structures, the procedure cache, and physical I/O as SQL Server reads database pages from and writes database pages to disk.

Monitoring the memory used by SQL Server can help determine, for example, whether bottlenecks exist due to a lack of available physical memory for storing frequently accessed data in cache, in which case SQL Server must retrieve the data from disk. By monitoring memory, you can determine if query performance can be improved by adding more memory or by making more memory available to the data cache or SQL Server internal structures. Monitoring the physical I/O is especially important to determine how often SQL Server needs to read data from the disk.

Compared to other operations, such as memory access, physical I/O consumes a lot of time. Minimizing physical I/O can improve query performance.

Read Ahead

The read requests generated by the system are controlled by the relational engine and are optimized further by the storage engine. The access method used to read pages from a table determines the general pattern of reads performed. The relational engine determines the most effective access method, such as a table scan, an index scan, or a keyed read. This request is then given to the storage engine, which optimizes the reads required to implement the access method. The reads are requested by the thread executing the batch.

The SQL Server 7.0 read-ahead mechanism is improved and significantly simplified. By putting hints and directions in both the query processor and the storage engine, more than 1,000 lines of code were eliminated, as well as configuration parameters.

Table scans benefit from the new data structures introduced in SQL Server 7.0. In a SQL Server 7.0 database, the storage engine can build a serial list of the disk addresses that must be read. This allows SQL Server to optimize its I/O operations as large sequential reads in disk order. SQL Server issues multiple serial read-ahead reads immediately for each file in the scan. This takes advantage of striped disk sets.

The parallel read-ahead mechanism allows the disk subsystem to work at maximum speed. The inputs and outputs are decoupled, and the mechanism pulls in data pages and then passes them to the next available CPU. I/O operations are simultaneously issued against multiple files.

SQL Server 7.0 eliminates separate read-ahead threads and minimizes context switches. The new allocation data structures allow read ahead without following a page chain. The query processor helps with read ahead by using the middle tier of an index to predict the next page of an index scan (including clustered table scans).

SQL Server 7.0 also reads index pages serially in disk order, thereby improving the performance of index scans. Index processing is further improved by the use of prefetch hints to allow serial read-ahead processing of a nonclustered index.

P A R T   1 0

Security

Part 10 explains the security parameters of SQL Server.

C H A P T E R   1 6

Product Security

This chapter introduces some of the security features of the Microsoft Windows NT operating system and explains how to use them with Microsoft SQL Server 7.0 and other applications in the BackOffice family of products. The chapter focuses on how these components use Windows NT security features. It also provides information about the enabling technologies that make it easy for applications to use the security features and the basic security principles on which the features rest.

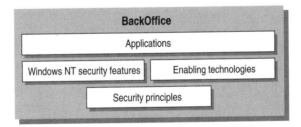

Security in the Enterprise Environment

The Microsoft approach to security is based on six fundamental principles:

authentication
 Identifies the user, and the all-important single-logon automatically promulgates this identity to all local and remote services.

access control
 Restricts access to data based on that identity.

cryptography
 Protects the privacy and integrity of data, especially when in transit across a network.

firewalls
> Restrict traffic between your LAN and an external network, such as the Internet.

system integrity
> Ensures the underlying security software cannot be tampered with.

auditing
> Records security events.

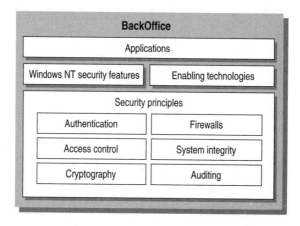

Authentication and Access Control

The root of enterprise security lies in controlling access to data—that is, in controlling each user's ability to see, modify, and delete data. Data can be extremely diverse, including:

- E-mail, address books, or collaborative documents (such as those in Microsoft Exchange)
- Heterogeneous data stored in centrally managed relational databases (such as Microsoft SQL Server)
- Communications with host mainframes (perhaps managed by SNA Server)
- Information on a Web site (perhaps accessed by Internet Information Services)
- Documents that you download using Windows NT Remote Access Service
- Simple memos on your desktop computer

Although there is no single security mechanism for handling all of these cases, the principles for handling them are relatively simple and stem from a basic, well-understood set of threats.

Security starts with legitimate users: employees, system administrators, business partners, and customers. You do not trust them all with the same information. The process of identifying these users is called authentication (or simply logging on). As with most commercial operating systems, passwords dominate authentication in the Windows NT arena, though smart card authentication may soon be available as a common, cost-effective alternative. Although the public key certificates (see "Certificates" later in this chapter) are often a critical component in network-wide authentication, a password or smart card always unlocks the first door.

Single-logon is perhaps the most important property of Microsoft authentication. Under single-logon, you first log on to the workstation running Windows NT. For the duration of your logon session, your identity is automatically and securely passed to all the local and network services you request. With single-logon you do not have to remember alternative usernames or passwords, or use them in interactions that can compromise them. Single-logon also makes it easier to incorporate advanced authentication techniques, such as smart cards. Although single-logon may sound simple, it requires a great deal of infrastructure and is a key goal of the enabling technologies, which are described later in this chapter.

Establishing the user's identity is only half the challenge. The other half is attaching information to various data objects denoting who can and cannot access that object and in what manner (read, write, delete, change access control permissions, and so forth). Access Control Lists (ACLs) appear throughout the Windows NT enterprise environment, and those on the Windows NT native file system (NTFS) are the very basis of its security. Briefly, an ACL is a list of Windows NT users or user groups with access permissions for an object. The permissions are usually targeted to the object the ACL protects. For example, shared printers typically have Print and Manage permissions, and files and directories have Read and Write permissions. In some cases users who create an object manage its ACL, but in other cases management is restricted to administrators.

Cryptography and Firewalls

Although authentication and access control provide adequate protection with regard to legitimate users, security is also concerned with unidentified, illegitimate, and usually unseen attempts to penetrate a system. These attempts pose two major threats. The first threat involves attacking data that is in transit across a network (or perhaps stored in an intermediary location, such as a mail server). The attack may involve eavesdropping on your data, modifying it, or attempting to impersonate you on the network. The only solution to this type of threat is cryptography.

The second threat seeks to introduce a malicious program (for example, a Trojan horse or virus) into your system, and is particularly virulent in the Internet environment. Microsoft Internet Explorer contains special cryptographic technology (Authenticode) and security zones that screen certain kinds of downloaded programs and scripts against common networking threats, and the system integrity of Windows NT make it inherently less prone to viruses than its predecessors.

Assuring Your Privacy

Encryption ensures that network elements cannot eavesdrop on your communications by "scrambling" the data. Microsoft currently uses the RC4 algorithm from RSA, Inc., and the U.S. Government standard DES algorithm for most of its encryption (the cryptographic infrastructure is open so that alternative algorithms are easily added). RC4 is a "symmetric" algorithm that requires both sender and receiver to have the same shared secret, or encryption "key." The standard key lengths, which determine the degree of protection, are 40- and 128-bits (the latter is subject to U.S. export control). Although 40-bit keys can be compromised by known, determined attacks, compromising 128-bit keys by means other than flaws in the RC4 algorithm would be extremely difficult. RC4 and DES are long-standing algorithms and have no publicly known flaws.

Key management is the process of distributing keys between sender and receiver, and there are many common key management protocols. Sometimes both parties already know a secret user password that can be used as the seed for an encryption key. Other protocols use previously established keys to transmit the encryption key. Public key algorithms are particularly well suited for this purpose. Like referees at a sporting event, the best key management is unseen by its users.

Assuring the Integrity of Your Data

Integrity is protection against malicious modification of data. Integrity techniques attach a cryptographic signature to the message that both identifies the sender and ensures that the message has not been modified in transit. Microsoft technology currently uses the RSA public key and MD5 hash algorithms, a technique that dominates the Internet community. In a public key cryptosystem, each user has a matched pair of keys: a private key they keep secret, and a public key they publish freely. The public key is presented in a certificate signed by a Certification Authority (CA) that attests to the key's authenticity.

The unique property of public key ciphers is deceptively simple: Data encrypted by the private key can be decrypted only by the public key, and data encrypted by the public key can be decrypted only by the private key. For example, if you encrypt a message for a colleague with her public key, only she can decrypt it.

A hashing algorithm produces a small value (usually 16 bytes) from an arbitrarily long stream of data. We call this value a "hash" or, more formally, a "message digest." Its unique property is that it is computationally infeasible for someone to construct a data stream that reproduces a specific hash value. For example, if you compute a hash from a document you send to a colleague and then transmit the hash value securely, your colleague could determine if the document had been tampered with by recomputing its hash and comparing it with your original. Although a nefarious intermediary (traditionally named "Mallet") might modify the document in transit, the intermediary simply cannot produce a fake document that has the same hash value.

The only question left is how to securely transmit the hash, but that is easy: You encrypt it with your private key and send the result as a signature that accompanies the document. Your colleague uses your public key to decipher the transmitted hash and checks the document as before. Although it may not be obvious, there is no way Mallet can modify the document or its signature that your colleague's software will not detect.

Microsoft uses this common, basic integrity algorithm in many situations. Perhaps the most visible is the Authenticode technology that ensures that Microsoft ActiveX, Java, and other active components downloaded from the Web come from identifiable sources and have not been tampered with. Public keys and hash algorithms are also used for symmetric key management and to ensure that a communicant is genuine and not a masquerader.

Secure Sockets Layer (SSL) is a popular protocol that incorporates both encryption and integrity. While SSL is predominantly used for Web traffic, Microsoft's cryptographic enabling technologies, called Secure Channel and Security Support Provider Interface (S-Channel and SSPI), make it available to all applications. Microsoft also supports Private Communication Technology (PCT), an improved version of SSL and Transport Layer Security (TLS), an upcoming Internet standard that merges SSL and the ideas in PCT. Throughout the rest of this chapter, this entire collection of protocols is referred to as SSL.

Certificates

The distribution and management of certificates are central to the successful deployment of public key technology. In the example, how does your colleague reliably obtain your public key? If you send it unprotected, Mallet can change it and compromise your communication without your knowledge (or your colleague's). A certificate holds your name, your public key, and other information, all of which are signed by a Certification Authority (CA) using a private key and the integrity algorithm. If your colleague reliably knows the public key of that CA, she can verify that the certificate you send her has not been tampered with. For example, most mail systems simply package the sender's certificate with the mail message. The recipient software first verifies the certificate, and then uses its public key to check the integrity of the message.

It may seem that the issue has been deferred: How do you reliably obtain from the CA the certificate that holds the public key? The answer is that you have to use a previously established, secure communication path. There are many techniques for doing this, for example, Microsoft delivers many commercial CA certificates preinstalled in Internet Explorer. You only have to obtain a small number of CA certificates. Your software automatically uses these to verify the user certificates signed by those CAs. You can even have CAs that verify and sign the certificates of other CAs.

You also need confidence that the CA uses a degree of diligence when signing a user's key. It is poor practice for a CA to sign a certificate with an intentionally supplied false name. However, there are limits to what CAs can ensure, and certificates often contain a value that denotes the degree of diligence. It is also important for the CA to be able to revoke certificates. The usual technique is for the CA to regularly publish Certificate Revocation Lists that are downloaded by various CA validation agents.

Firewalls

You can think of a firewall as a filter that restricts the direction and type of requests that can pass between your LAN and an external network such as the Internet. The more effective firewalls serve as a "proxy" for specific services; that is, a program on the firewall serves as intermediary between the LAN and entities on the external network for a specific service like Web browsing. Proxy programs understand the details of the communication and can apply sophisticated restrictions on the data. Firewalls also can hide your internal network addresses from the external network and reject packets from specified external network addresses.

Cryptography Support in Windows NT

The Windows NT security environment provides pervasive cryptographic support for these ideas. For example, Personal Store securely groups a user's keys and certificates together for storage, Certificate Server lets you issue and manage your company's own certificates, and CryptoAPI fully supports Certificate Management.

System Integrity and Auditing

System integrity ensures that the software and hardware responsible for enforcing the system's security cannot themselves be compromised by regular users or their programs. Unlike many desktop operating systems, Windows NT is built around a security kernel that ultimately protects the system itself. The security kernel also enforces the access controls that protect all sensitive files and data outside the kernel, making the protection complete. System integrity is the foundation upon which all other security protections rely.

The importance of an audit trail, a tamper-proof record of security-related events, speaks for itself. Windows NT has a rich auditing system, and many applications produce security logs particular to their services.

The Windows NT Security Environment

The basis of Microsoft's security environment lies in Windows NT security features and the technologies that enable them. The BackOffice family of products and other applications take advantage of both. An enabling technology is a set of software libraries that encapsulates certain algorithms or procedures that the operating system makes available to other applications and system services. These enabling technologies can be used by other parts of the operating system and also by applications developed either by Microsoft or independent, third-party developers. Although enabling technologies do not by themselves make your system more secure, they are crucial to assuring a strong, consistent, ongoing stream of security applications for the Windows NT environment.

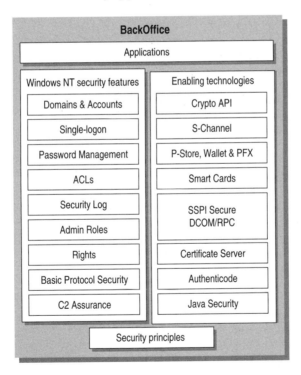

Windows NT Security Features

This section provides information about the security features of Windows NT.

Domains and Accounts

The most fundamental security issue in a computer network is posed by the question: Which computers can a given user access? For both local and remote users, the answer to this question is governed primarily by the domain structure of Windows NT.

Administrators assign each Windows NT–based computer, whether a server or desktop computer, to a single Windows NT domain. (This is usually permanent, but it can change.) Each domain has a Windows NT Domain Controller that serves as a repository for security information, most notably a set of domain-wide user accounts and group definitions. A user's account holds a logon name, password, capabilities, and other information, such as the user's real name. Each account in a domain can locally log on to and remotely access each computer in the domain, although there are other controls that can restrict access on an account-by-account basis.

If the administrators agree, one domain can trust another. When this happens, accounts in the second domain have the same access to computers as accounts in the first domain. In setting up the trust, the first administrator is in effect saying, "Your users may access the computers in my domain" (although there are many limitations on that access). Usernames across a multidomain network must be unique only within a domain and are implicitly prefixed by their domain name, such as SALES\JJones, where SALES is the domain and JJones the user. Trust is one-way. In the current example, accounts from the first domain cannot access the computers in the second domain. However, two domains can trust each other, and a domain can trust, and be trusted by, more than one other domain.

There are many popular practices for structuring domain trust relationships (domain models) and some are based on criteria other than security, for example, network browsers group computers and their shared resources by domain. In all cases, however, the fundamental security of domains is based on the same question: Which computers can a given user access?

There are two features that further allow administrators to control access to computers. User rights are special capabilities that administrators assign to accounts that can use a given computer. Most rights are used internally by Windows NT, and the default assignments seldom change. However, two rights are noteworthy: the right to log on locally and the right to log on remotely. These allow each computer to tightly limit each kind of logon. Further, each account has an optional list of workstations to which its user can locally log on.

Remote Sessions and Single-Logon

When you locally log on to a Windows NT–based computer, your logon session runs under the name you present along with your password at logon. When you attempt to access a remote computer (for example, connecting to one of its shared directories or printers, or performing remote administration), the remote computer transparently authenticates you and establishes a remote session for your activities there. If the domain structure allows, the remote account is the same as your local one. Otherwise, you sometimes can specify a name and password of an account that is allowed on the remote computer. But under no circumstances can you establish a remote session without being authenticated—that is, without demonstrating you know the name and password of an account that is legal on the remote computer. And without a remote session your programs can obtain no significant services.

After you have been logged on to the remote computer, remote server applications can assume the identity of your user account through a simple process called impersonation. When they do so, they are running under your permissions and capabilities, and their actions are appropriately constrained by controls in the remote environment, for example, ACLs on the remote file systems. This is our first and perhaps best example of how the Windows NT environment implements single-logon and propagates it to server applications. A server in this scenario need know nothing about authentication or accounts. It simply impersonates its client user (whose name it may not even choose to discover), and the Windows NT environment restricts the program's actions accordingly. The BackOffice family of products and other Microsoft applications universally use this fundamental security model, and Microsoft strongly encourages all BackOffice-compatible applications to do so as well.

Logon and Password Management

Under single-logon, you log on only once, so that logon should be quite strong. For this purpose, Windows NT uses a technique called trusted path, which is typically found only in highly secure operating systems. The trusted path prevents what is commonly called the spoofing scheme, in which a malicious program already running on a computer presents what appears to be a legitimate logon window in order to capture a user's password. Under the trusted path approach, users of Windows NT are trained always to call up the logon window by pressing the CTRL+ALT+DEL keys simultaneously. When they do, Windows NT reliably displays its Security Window, which allows them to safely enter the password. (You also use the trusted path approach to change your password and log off, which prevents similar spoofs.) Windows NT also includes a variety of password controls, including the ability to lock an account when its password appears to be under attack.

There are two important enabling technologies that can strengthen Windows NT logon and password management: PASSFILT and GINA. PASSFILT lets an administrator install a trusted program that is called every time a user changes a password. The program receives the new password and can ensure that it meets certain strength criteria such as length and the use of randomly chosen characters. Microsoft includes an optional PASSFILT module in Windows NT that enforces an example password policy. This addresses the time-honored but still troublesome problem posed by users who choose nonsecure passwords. GINA is a replaceable program that is part of the Windows NT local logon system. Although not for the novice, vendors can supply alternative GINA modules that strengthen the logon process. Prime examples include support for smart card authentication (see "Enabling Technologies" later in this chapter) and biometric authentication (devices such as fingerprint or retinal scanners).

Access Control Lists

All objects in the Windows NT environment can have an Access Control List (ACL). An ACL defines a set of users and groups, and the kind of access each has on the object. The most visible and important ACLs are those that protect all elements in the Windows NT native file system format (NTFS) and the Windows NT registry. These house all software that enforces Windows NT security, and ACLs are therefore important in protecting the system's integrity. (Windows NT sometimes uses encryption for additional protection, for example, its user accounts and other key security data.)

Users have full control of ACLs on the files, directories, and other objects they create, and use simple window interfaces to manage them. They also can specify the ACL to be given by default to all newly created objects in the directories they manage.

ACLs protect other objects, such as file shares and printers, and most of the BackOffice applications extend the ACL model to data they manage. It is often necessary for an application to have a customized ACL format for the objects it manages. In both cases the purpose and intent are the same.

Central Administration and Roles

Windows NT uses a simple administrative hierarchy. Full administrators, members of the local Administrators group on each computer, have complete power over that computer. Windows NT Server includes several operator roles each of limited power, for example, account operators who manage user accounts and server operators who look after day-to-day server operations. Windows NT administration is based simply on membership in certain groups so you can devise network-wide administrative roles flexibly. For example, you can include domain administrators from the local domain (or remote domains) to the administrators who control your LAN workstations. You also can create a group for accounts that administer only user workstations and not the more critical network servers.

Security Audit Trail

Windows NT and its applications can record an extensive set of system events in the security log. You can define an audit policy that designates which of six categories the system records (logons and logoffs, user and group management, and so on). You also can attach auditing information (which looks much like an ACL) to any Windows NT object (this is typically done for NTFS files, NTFS directories, and Registry keys). An object's category determines when the system audits access to the object-based on the user and group, and the success or failure of the operation. You can even stipulate that the system shut down if the audit trail exceeds the allowed storage.

Microsoft provides extensive software libraries that allow trustable programs to insert their own custom audit records into the audit trail. The libraries also give audit tools easy, high-level access to the security log.

Remote Access Service and Point-to-Point Tunneling Protocol

Remote Access Service (RAS) allows remote users to dial in to a Windows NT RAS server and use the resources of its network as if directly connected. In its simplest mode, users logging on to Windows NT remotely simply check a small box on their logon window that automatically establishes the RAS connection and authenticates the session. RAS uses the Windows NT standard single-logon technique, and users can log on under their office account. Overall, working from the road is identical to working from one's office, and it is secure.

Administrators designate which accounts can use RAS. They also can set up RAS to automatically "call back" a specific number for each account. This ensures that a user's remote access comes only from a specific phone number. RAS uses the Windows NT standard "challenge/response" logon, which prevents passwords from passing over the communication link. RAS clients and servers can require that all communication be encrypted, currently by the 40-bit or 128-bit RC4 cipher. You also can limit remote access to the resources of the RAS server itself (as opposed to its networks).

Microsoft's Virtual Private Networking technology uses the industry-supported Point-to-Point Tunneling Protocol (PPTP) to extend the use of RAS to the Internet. Instead of dialing directly into the RAS server using a telephone line, the remote RAS client dials a local Internet service provider and establishes an Internet link to the provider's PPTP RAS server. This virtual private network allows a remote user to securely access a central network over the nonsecure Internet.

Basic Protocol Security

Not all networks are prone to attack, and Windows NT does not impose performance penalties by applying cryptographic techniques to all network traffic. Instead, its philosophy is to support specific applications that must cryptographically protect data in transit across a network. However, it does use some common-sense and basic cryptographic techniques in its standard, underlying protocols.

Local logon requests are encrypted when they pass between the workstation and its domain controller. This helps ensure that passwords are not exposed and that interlopers cannot interfere with the primary authentication process. The remote (or secondary) authentication we discussed uses the NTLM challenge/response protocol to ensure that passwords never appear on the network unencrypted.

Windows NT uses the Microsoft SMB protocol for file and printer sharing and many for other remote services. SMB also applies integrity protection to this protocol. The protection does not encrypt data, but it does prevent a broad range of attacks that seek to modify the data while in transit or to impersonate the client's identity.

C2 and Its Companions

Windows NT is one of the few commercial operating systems that has successfully completed the U.S. Government C2 evaluation process, as well as the FC2/E3 evaluation under its companion European criteria, Information Technology Security Evaluation Criteria (ITSEC). This is important for two reasons. First, it ensures that the base operating system has certain important security features. Second, and more importantly, it provides an opinion about the system's security from an independent, trained, experienced, and unbiased team of government security analysts. This team has had the full cooperation of Microsoft developers and core software architects, as well as access to source code and internal design documents. The team, which meets regularly with the developers and architects to gauge Microsoft expertise, commitment, and thoroughness with regard to security, concentrates on fundamental security architecture and is guided by what is commonly called the "Orange Book" (Trusted Computer Systems Evaluation Criteria).

The C2 evaluation process is therefore not a detailed search for security bugs, but rather an opinion that the overall security architecture is sound. For more information, see www.microsoft.com/ntserver/info/default.asp.

Planned Additions to Windows NT

Future releases of the Windows operating system may bring many new security features, for example:

- Expanded Domain Trust Relationships

  To ease domain administration in larger sites, a future version of Windows may allow administrators to group domains so that each domain implicitly trusts every other domain in the group, and that accounts in a domain can be used in all other domains in the same group.

- Kerberos and Public Key Authentication

  Invisible to most users, Kerberos offers a variety of expanded authentication capabilities. For example, it allows servers to pass client user identities for use by other servers in a multitier client/server arrangement and allows mutual client/server authentication. It also allows users of the Windows operating system to securely access remote services other than Windows NT services that use this popular technology. Future versions of the Windows operating system may also authenticate users using public keys and certificate technology, including SSL. This facilitates authentication from sources other than Windows operating systems sources and eliminates some of the disadvantages of traditional passwords.

- Active Directories

  The Active Directory is logically a single, network-based storage hierarchy based on X.500 standards (and, of course, protected by ACLs, which have some interesting new properties of their own). When upgrading from Windows NT 4.0 to Windows 2000 or later, many security parameters may migrate to the Active Directory from their current location in the Windows NT Registry, including all user accounts. This significantly enhances central security administration. Administrators also can delegate detailed operations to lesser administrative users who must perform specific functions; for example, letting a help desk attendant assign a new password to a user without otherwise changing the user's privileges. Because these privileges are based on the ACLs that protect the Active Directory elements, managers can devise custom administrative hierarchies that fit their own particular needs.

- Encrypted File System

  Future versions of the Windows operating system may allow users automatically to encrypt information stored in the native NTFS file system format in much the same way they can automatically compress files today. It has provisions for data recovery that allow trusted administrators to recover data if users forget their own encryption keys or leave the company. This is a welcome and essential feature for people who use laptops or removable hard drives.

Enabling Technologies

In many ways, enabling technologies are the most exciting part of this security story because they portend a rich, ongoing stream of trusted applications that are more economical, more secure, and easier to administrator because they take advantage of the Windows NT security infrastructure. This section about enabling technologies begins with the Microsoft cryptographic application programming interface, CryptoAPI, and a public key security protocol called Secure Channel (S-Channel).

CryptoAPI and Secure Channel

Cryptography is the essential component of networking security. Unfortunately, it is a difficult technology to learn and implement. Microsoft created the CryptoAPI to address this problem. The CryptoAPI is a set of software libraries with high-level cryptographic interfaces (APIs) that manage the many details of key management, formatting, and cipher algorithms, presenting applications with a single interface that serves different underlying ciphers. CryptoAPI uses Cryptographic Service Providers (CSP), plug-in cipher modules that cryptographers create and market. In short, CryptoAPI joins application developers, who know little of cryptography but need to use it, with cryptographers who develop the base technology.

Each CSP implements a specific set of cryptographic algorithms. Microsoft provides a base CSP that includes a full complement of cryptographic ciphers and hash functions licensed from RSA Data Security, Inc. Under CryptoAPI, you can replace one CSP with another of the same type without affecting any of the applications that use that type. For example, Microsoft provides an enhanced version of the RSA-based CSP that supports stronger encryption. This also allows you to upgrade your security to hardware devices such as smart cards, by simply replacing the CSP.

A second advantage of the CryptoAPI is that it fully encapsulates the storage and protection of crypto keys and the ciphers themselves. A CSP can implement its schemes either in software or on smart cards. Smart cards present significant security advantages over software because they are portable and can better physically protect a user's secret keys.

Microsoft delivers a basic set of CSPs with Windows NT (you may need special third-party licenses if you develop and sell products using these CSPs). All BackOffice applications are moving quickly to fully utilize CryptoAPI. The recently released CryptoAPI 2.0 includes a complete set of certificate management APIs that implement the latest X.509 certificate formats.

Secure Channel (S-Channel) is a security service provider module that implements the popular public key security protocols between Web clients and servers. These include SSL, PCT, and TLS (an upcoming standard that merges SSL and PCT). S-Channel is layered on top of CryptoAPI for key and certificate management services. Independent software vendors and developers can use S-Channel to add these cryptographic protocols to any client/server application.

P-Store, Microsoft Wallet, and PFX

Traditionally, on a single-logon system such as the Windows NT operating system, users were required to remember only their logons and passwords. However, increased security in heterogeneous environments imposes additional burdens. These include private keys and certificates, trusted CA certificates, credit card and bank account numbers, other personal identification information (such as driver's license numbers), and data that helps their applications use this information automatically and transparently. There needs to be a single place to store and protect this information that applications can share. On the Windows NT operating system, the Protected Store (P-Store) is the technology that meets this need.

P-Store is a set of software libraries that allow applications to fetch and retrieve security and other information from a personal storage location, hiding the implementation and details of the storage itself. For example, the storage location could be the user's Windows NT profile, a preferences file, a diskette, or a smart card.

Microsoft Wallet is a generic name for a window application that serves as the user interface to the P-Store. Microsoft Site Server already uses the Wallet with Microsoft Internet Explorer.

Personal Information Exchange (PFX) is a protocol that securely transfers the contents of a P-Store from one location to another, for example, from an office computer to a home computer.

SSPI, Secure RPC, and DCOM

As intranets become more secure, client applications (such as Web browsers and e-mail programs) and servers (such as Web servers and e-mail hosts) become more complicated because different situations require different types of authentication and cryptography. Microsoft's Security Support Provider Interface (SSPI) makes common network authentication and cryptographic data protection schemes available to both client and server applications through simplified software libraries. Programs that use SSPI do not need to encode the details of specific authentication or cryptographic schemes. Instead, the SSPI libraries do all the complicated work.

A Security Support Provider (SSP) is a library that manages a particular scheme. Applications interact with all SSPs through a common SSP interface (hence, the name SSPI), which further hides the details of the specific scheme. SSPs rely heavily on other enabling technologies like CryptoAPI and S-Channel whenever possible. SSPI currently includes four SSPs:

Kerberos
   Kerberos is the cryptographic, industry-standard mutual authentication protocol.

NT LAN Manager (NTLM)
   NTLM is the traditional password-based authentication protocol for Windows-based networks. Although this time-honored standard continues to be supported, Kerberos will gradually replace its use for newer, Windows NT environments.

SSL (Including PCT and TLS)
   SSL is a cryptographic protocol for mutual authentication and data protection popular today only in the Web community, but nonetheless a strong, general-purpose security protocol.

Distributed Password Protocol (DPA)
   DPA is a password-based authentication protocol used by many commercial online services such as The Microsoft Network. Its advantage is that users can use the same credentials (name and password) to log on to more than one online service.

Distributed and client/server applications use SSPI in several ways, from calling its SSPs directly to selecting security options when using Distributed COM (DCOM), Remote Procedure Call (RPC), and other popular Internet APIs. DCOM and RPC are enabling technologies that make it easier for users to create distributed applications. (Distributed applications use cooperating components that run on different computers, and perhaps even different operating systems, such as Windows NT, UNIX, or Macintosh). For example, Windows NT remote administration uses RPC extensively. DCOM and RPC manage and hide the details of how the different parts communicate with each other. Both DCOM and RPC have simple options that automatically use SSPI authentication and message encryption. These options are sometimes called "Secure DCOM" or "Secure RPC." These are among the easiest ways to use SSPI.

For example, most authentication protocols begin by exchanging a series of packets between the client and server.

1. The SSPI client begins by calling a particular SSP requesting an initial client request packet. The SSP formulates the packet and instructs the client to deliver it to the server. The client and server never look inside these packets. Each simply delivers a packet to the other for processing by the other's SSP module. The server sends the packet to its corresponding SSP as an initial client request.

2. The server SSP returns a packet to the server with instructions to send the packet back to the client SSP. This packet might, for example, contain the challenge used in a challenge/response protocol.

3. Finally, the client SSP formulates the last packet and instructs the client to send it to the server. In our example, this includes the response to the challenge. The server passes this final packet to its SSP, which then informs the server that the authentication succeeded. (In our example, the client's SSP produced a response to the challenge that only the user's password could produce.)

SSPI also supports server impersonation, so at this point the server might impersonate the client user—that is, it might begin working under the client user's identity. If the client and server are cryptographically protecting their data, each one passes each of its outgoing packets to the SSP for encryption or signing, and each incoming packet for decryption or signature checking. In this case the initial exchange usually negotiates the encryption keys for the session.

Certificate Server

Certificate Management refers to the process whereby public and private encryption keys are securely and reliably managed by a Certification Authority (CA). A key component of this process is that the CA creates a user's certificate (essentially, signs the user's public key) after verifying that the user has presented a legitimate name (often a full name or e-mail address). Although there are several companies that provide this service, large Windows NT–based networks want and need their own certificate authorization services. This need is met by Microsoft's Certificate Server (CS).

You can think of CS as a toolkit for CAs. It accepts certificate requests from users in a variety of popular, standard formats (such as e-mail), subjects the requests to any number of "approval modules" that the CA easily can add to the server, and then constructs and returns a certificate to the user. Each site adds its own approval modules. A module might engage in an e-mail exchange with the user's listed e-mail address or send a request to an assistant who researches the requester. CS can also manage Certificate Revision Lists. The value of CS is that it decreases costs by creating certificates in-house and also allows you to establish the certification policies important to your organization. You can even use it to establish your own public certification service.

Authenticode and Java Security

In the early days of the Web, when you clicked a hyperlink, your browser printed the link's contents on your screen. But today your browser may invisibly download and locally run a number of small programs that manage the presentation of the page on your screen. These active Web page elements, including ActiveX controls, Java applets, and .exe files, pervade the Web and are the wave of the future. Their presence as local programs is automatic and transparent.

Unfortunately, you have no way of knowing whether these active elements attempt to act maliciously on your system. They run under your identity with your capabilities and can do everything you can do. This can include deleting files, e-mailing files to third parties, and installing malicious programs on your computer.

Microsoft's Authenticode technology uses the simple cryptographic integrity features presented earlier to help ensure that your browser accepts only active elements you think are safe. Reputable software vendors join a software vendor organization and receive a certificate signed by the CA of the organization. People who browse the Web install that CA certificate on their workstation. (It usually comes preinstalled in the browser.) Vendors sign their active elements using the integrity algorithm described earlier.

Your browser can now determine two important things: first, that an active element comes from a genuine member of that organization and, second, that it has not been tampered with since the vendor signed it. You can easily instruct your browser to ignore elements that fail these tests or allow only elements from a list of vendors you specify. Microsoft Internet Explorer can check Authenticode on any active element (ActiveX, Java, and so forth).

Is this sufficient assurance? Suppose you visit your favorite computer store and buy a shrink-wrapped program from a software vendor that produces a wide selection of PC programs. You probably have no reservations about the safety of the software because you have no reason to think it is malicious. No legitimate software house risks its business by selling what it knows or suspects to be a tainted program. It is always possible, of course, that someone tampered with the package or substituted a fake CD-ROM, but that is unlikely.

Authenticode assurance is analogous but even stronger. It is more difficult to tamper with cryptographic signatures than with shrink-wrapped software, and the software vendor organization attests that the software vendor is genuine and willingly joined the organization. If shrink-wrap tampering is unlikely, then Authenticode tampering is as unlikely.

Java offers some additional security possibilities. Java applets do not necessarily gain full access to your system. Your browser (more properly, the local software that runs the Java applets) can limit these applets, for example, preventing them from writing onto your file systems. The scope of a Java applet is often called its sandbox. With the proper Java security model this can be an effective security restraint, but it involves an inevitable trade-off against the capabilities of the applet. For example, when you prevent an applet from writing to your hard drive you may be removing its ability to give you the services it is designed to provide. Internet Explorer 3.0 fully enforces the standard Java "sandbox," and Microsoft is working with industry groups to make the sandbox walls more flexible.

There is no question that for some applets, the sandbox is an effective protection. But there is also no question that in general, it is not enough. Authenticode does not have this trade-off and need not make these concessions to usability.

SQL Server Security

As this illustration shows, all four components of the BackOffice family of products leverage the security infrastructure and enabling technologies of Windows NT, but these remarks are restricted to SQL Server.

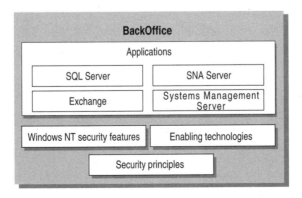

SQL Server 7.0 is a distributed, client/server, relational database server that supports the popular SQL query language. It often serves an enterprise back-end server for a variety of network client applications, such as Exchange Server. SQL Server is an interesting security story and perhaps best illustrates the convergence of BackOffice products around Windows NT. The popularity of SQL Server predates Windows NT, and therefore SQL Server implemented most of its own security. With the emergence of SQL Server version 7.0, SQL Server is now firmly integrated into the Windows NT security environment.

SQL Server fully supports Windows NT single-logon and user groups and will later leverage Kerberos authentication. It also implements its own internal roles, which are similar to Windows NT groups. SQL Server uses these roles for internal administration, and the advantage is that you do not need to clutter the Windows NT group list with groups internal to the server.

SQL Server applies access control to the database elements it manages (tables, views, stored procedures, and column-level permissions). Relational databases have a traditional format they use to present this access control, and therefore the format is different from other Windows NT ACLs, but the intent and degree of control are the same. You can assign a variety of database-specific permissions to Windows NT users, groups, or SQL Server roles. As in the Windows NT file system ACLs, you can also allow a group to control access to database element.

SQL Server creates a full transaction log, supports many internal administrative roles, and includes many other database-specific security features. Future plans may include using Secure RPC to encrypt network traffic.

Windows NT and Enabling Technologies

Microsoft's security architecture is based on fundamental security principles manifested in the security features of the Windows NT operating system; these principles are supported by various enabling technologies that bring powerful security technology within easy grasp of application programs. The BackOffice suite and its companion applications leverage this technology to create and support a powerful set of consistently secure applications that are illustrated here.

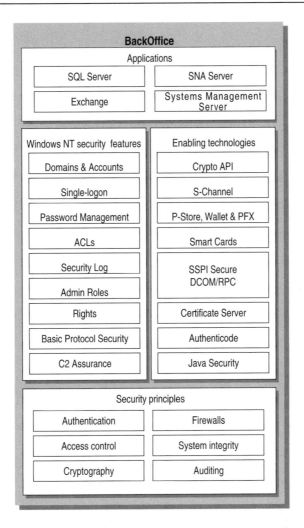

For more information about security, see www.microsoft.com/security/.

PART 11

Upgrading and Migrating

The chapters in Part 11 provide a reference for planning, customizing, and deploying your system upgrade or migration:

- Upgrading to Microsoft SQL Server 7.0
- Migrating Oracle Databases to Microsoft SQL Server 7.0
- Migrating Your Access Database to Microsoft SQL Server 7.0
- Migrating Sybase Applications to Microsoft SQL Server 7.0
- Migrating Btrieve Applications to Microsoft SQL Server 7.0

CHAPTER 17

Upgrading to SQL Server 7.0

Microsoft SQL Server version 7.0 offers many new features and product improvements, and it contains significant internal architectural developments. These developments provide an architectural foundation for now and years to come. One key aspect of the new architecture is an on-disk format for all data. The new format supports improvements such as 8-kilobyte (KB) pages, bitmaps to keep track of tables (instead of doubly-linked lists), and index enhancements that result in a faster, more reliable, and more scalable product.

This chapter contains the information you need to prepare for the upgrade process, and includes these topics:

- Preparing for an upgrade.
- Using the SQL Server Upgrade Wizard.
- Understanding backward compatibility after you have upgraded.
- Learning about Microsoft's upgrade experiences with SQL Server 7.0.

Overview for Upgrading SQL Server

Because SQL Server 7.0 introduces a new on-disk format, the upgrade is different from earlier upgrades (for example, from SQL Server version 6.0 to SQL Server version 6.5). However, the SQL Server Upgrade Wizard makes upgrading from SQL Server 6.0 or SQL Server 6.5 to SQL Server 7.0 a simple operation.

The SQL Server Upgrade Wizard is designed with a typical user in mind. Usually, most users can go through the SQL Server Upgrade Wizard, accept the default values and options, and complete a successful upgrade to SQL Server 7.0. Even so, you should prepare for and understand the upgrade process and what the SQL Server Upgrade Wizard can do for you.

The SQL Server Upgrade is built on some fundamental assumptions. The wizard is designed to upgrade all the databases in a single pass. The purpose of the SQL Server Upgrade Wizard is to upgrade a single instance of SQL Server 6.x to a single instance of SQL Server 7.0 in a single pass. You can run multiple upgrades (for example, one database at a time) as long as they use the same SQL Server 6.x installation; however, this is not recommended because cross-database dependencies cannot be resolved if you upgrade only one database at a time. You cannot run SQL Server 6.x and SQL Server 7.0 on one computer simultaneously.

After you upgrade to SQL Server 7.0, there is no correlation, data mapping, or data sharing with an earlier installation of SQL Server 6.x. If you choose not to delete the SQL Server 6.x data files, you have two full copies of the data on disk: one for the SQL Server 6.x installation and one for the SQL Server 7.0 installation. When you are satisfied with the upgrade, use the custom uninstaller for SQL Server 6.x on the **Microsoft SQL Server–Switch** menu to delete the SQL Server 6.x data files. You may also want to plan a test-run of an upgrade to determine if there is any reason to prepare a fallback plan.

Prerequisites for Upgrading

You should make some key decisions before you begin upgrading to SQL Server 7.0. A little planning can go a long way to prevent redoing difficult and time-consuming work. You must consider issues such as:

- Is the present version of SQL Server supported for upgrade to SQL Server 7.0?
- Where will SQL Server 7.0 be installed?
- Does the SQL Server 6.x installation have the required software?
- Is there enough disk space available for the upgrade?

Examining each area in detail can help you understand the upgrade requirements and plan a successful upgrade.

SQL Server 7.0 is the first release of SQL Server to run on the Windows 95 and Windows 98 platforms. However, the Windows 95 and Windows 98 operating-system installations of SQL Server do not have the SQL Server Upgrade Wizard, because upgrades to the Windows 95 and Windows 98 operating systems are not supported. Only Microsoft Windows NT to Windows NT upgrades are supported.

Versions Supported for Upgrade

The SQL Server Upgrade Wizard supports upgrading from SQL Server 6.0 and SQL Server 6.5. Before upgrading from SQL Server 6.0, Service Pack 3 for SQL Server 6.0 must be installed. Before upgrading from SQL Server 6.5, Service Pack 3 for SQL Server 6.5 (or a later service pack) must be installed. If you are currently running SQL Server version 4.21a (or earlier), you must upgrade to SQL Server 6.0 or 6.5 first, and then upgrade to SQL Server 7.0. It is recommended that you upgrade to SQL Server 6.5 directly and then upgrade to SQL Server 7.0.

SQL Server 6.0 requires Microsoft Windows NT version 3.5 or later. SQL Server 6.5 requires Windows NT 3.51 or later. SQL Server 7.0 requires Windows NT version 4.0 with Service Pack 4 or later. If you are planning to use the same computer for SQL Server 7.0, you must first upgrade the computer to Windows NT 4.0, apply Service Pack 4 for Windows NT, install SQL Server 7.0, and then begin the upgrade process.

Microsoft supports SQL Server 6.0 on Windows NT 4.0 only during the process of a one-computer upgrade to SQL Server 7.0. If you are running SQL Server 6.0 on Windows NT 3.5, you must first upgrade to Windows NT 3.51 (Service Pack 5 is recommended) for a two-computer upgrade, or to Windows NT 4.0 for a one-computer upgrade before you begin the upgrade process.

Where to Install SQL Server 7.0

SQL Server 7.0 requires at minimum a Pentium 166 with 32 MB of random access memory (RAM). If your SQL Server 6.0 or SQL Server 6.5 installation is on a computer that meets these minimum hardware requirements, you might consider a one-computer upgrade. You must also consider the disk space requirements for an upgrade; otherwise, you should consider a two-computer upgrade.

One-computer Upgrades

If you want to perform a one-computer upgrade, you must install SQL Server 7.0 on the same computer that is currently running SQL Server 6.x. The computer may require some operating-system upgrades. SQL Server 7.0 requires:

- Windows NT 4.0
- Windows NT 4.0 with Service Pack 4 (or later)
- Microsoft Internet Explorer version 4.01 with Service Pack 1 (or later)

You must complete these upgrades before you begin installing SQL Server 7.0. Because you will likely have to reboot your computer after installing each of these products, you should schedule time to prevent production users from accessing the SQL Server 6.x installation.

When the minimum operating-system requirements have been met, you can set up SQL Server 7.0. The SQL Server 6.*x* installation is not available during the installation of SQL Server 7.0. SQL Server 7.0 requires varying amounts of disk space, depending upon the components you choose to install; however, a typical installation requires about 170 megabytes (MB) of hard disk space. You should have free space equal to at least 1.5 times the amount of space that is used by the SQL Server 6.*x* data files. By default, the SQL Server 6.*x* data files are located in the \Sql60\Data or \Mssql\Data directories (for SQL Server 6.0 and 6.5, respectively). This free space is in addition to the space needed for the installation of SQL Server 7.0. Furthermore, you should have 1 MB of free space for files and logs on the hard drive on which SQL Server is installed for each gigabyte (GB) of SQL Server 6.*x* devices you plan to upgrade.

For example, if you intend to upgrade a 10-GB SQL Server 6.5 installation installed on C:\mssql, you need approximately 10 MB of free space on drive C for temporary files and logs, and 15 GB of free disk space available on the computer for use during the upgrade. Some of the 15 GB of disk space is used by the upgrade process for temporary storage, and the rest is used to store the SQL Server 7.0 data files. Most Microsoft databases shrink in size when they are upgraded; therefore, the data files may take less than 10 GB of space after they have been upgraded to SQL Server 7.0.

If the required space is not available on the hard disks, but you want to perform a one-computer upgrade, you must use the **Tape** option in the SQL Server Upgrade Wizard. The **Tape** option requires that the tape drive be installed on the local computer. During the upgrade process, you can specify that the SQL Server 6.*x* devices be deleted. You must delete the SQL Server 6.*x* device files to create the disk space for the SQL Server 7.0 data files. The speed of an upgrade using the **Tape** option is limited by the tape media and may be substantially slower.

Two-computer Upgrades

If you choose a two-computer upgrade to SQL Server 7.0, you must meet the same requirements for a one-computer upgrade (Windows NT 4.0 with Service Pack 4 or later, and Internet Explorer 4.01 with Service Pack 1 or later). In a two-computer upgrade, the SQL Server 7.0 server requires at least 1.5 times the free space used by the SQL Server 6.*x* data files. The same temporary work space (1 MB for each 1 GB of data upgraded) is required on the hard drive on which SQL Server 7.0 is installed.

The SQL Server 7.0 server, or the import server, must be in the same administrative domain (or at least in the same domain structure) as the SQL Server 6.x server, or the export server. Therefore, both servers must have a common trusted domain. The system administrator performing the upgrade must be a Windows NT local administrator on both computers. The MSSQLServer service account on the import server must be running with a domain user account from a common trusted domain, and the user account must be a local administrator on both computers. The MSSQLServer service account must not be running using the Windows NT **LocalSystem** account on the import server.

This illustration shows a multiple domain upgrade scenario.

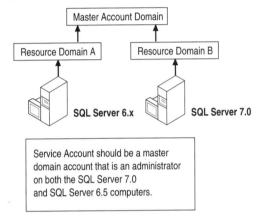

If the export server is in Resource Domain A but the import server is in Resource Domain B, the MSSQLServer service on the import server must use a service account that is in a common trusted domain (such as the Master Account Domain in the illustration) and must be a member of the Windows NT **Administrators** local group on both the export and import servers. (The service account used on the export server does not affect the upgrade.)

This is most easily accomplished if both the export and import computers are installed as member computers in the same domain and use the same service account for the MSSQLServer service.

Preparing to Upgrade

Whether you decide to perform a one-computer upgrade (installing SQL Server 7.0 on existing hardware), or a two-computer upgrade (installing SQL Server 7.0 on a new computer), the information in the rest of this chapter relates to these upgrades similarly. A one-computer upgrade is simply a special case of a two-computer upgrade for which the import and export computers are the same physical computer.

The first step is to obtain the system administrator user password for both the export and import servers. Your Windows NT logon must also be a member of the Windows NT **Administrators** local group on both the export and import servers. You must leave the SQL Server 7.0 installation in SQL Server and Windows NT Authentication Mode for the duration of the upgrade. If you want to run in Windows NT–only mode (Integrated Security mode in SQL Server 6.*x*), switch to this mode after the upgrade is complete.

If you use SQL Server 6.*x* Integrated Security logins that are mapped to any Windows NT local groups, those groups must exist on the import server with the same group and user membership that exists on the export server.

Prepare the SQL Server 6.*x* Installation

It is essential that you verify the SQL Server 6.*x* installation before you begin the upgrade. The SQL Server 6.*x* (export) installation must meet the following requirements or the SQL Server Upgrade Wizard will not allow you to continue:

- The **tempdb** database must be at least 10 MB.

  The **tempdb** database must be at least 10 MB to support queries that SQL Server Upgrade Wizard runs against the SQL Server 6.*x* installation. If the **tempdb** database is not at least 10 MB, the upgrade will not continue. By default, the **tempdb** database in SQL Server 6.0 and SQL Server 6.5 is 2 MB; therefore, you may need to change the size of the database. Use **exec sp_helpdb tempdb** or SQL Server Enterprise Manager to verify the size of the **tempdb** database.

- The @@SERVERNAME must not be NULL.

  The SQL Server Upgrade Wizard uses the @@SERVERNAME function during the upgrade process. It is recommended that @@SERVERNAME be set to the same name as the computer name during the upgrade. If you run SELECT @@SERVERNAME and receive NULL, run **exec sp_addserver 'computername', 'local'** to reset the @@SERVERNAME function. For example, if the computer name is SQLPROD1, run **exec sp_addserver 'SQLPROD1', 'local'**.

- The **master** database must have 3 MB of free space.

When you run the SQL Server Upgrade Wizard, a Transact-SQL script is run against the export server to upgrade the system tables and stored procedures in the **master** database for SQL Distributed Management Objects (SQL-DMO) and other connectivity components. These changes are fully backward compatible, but allow later versions of Open Database Connectivity (ODBC) and SQL-DMO to use the SQL Server 6.*x* installation. To verify that you have 3 MB of free space, run the following script or use SQL Server Enterprise Manager:

```
Use master
Go
exec sp_spaceused @updateusage = 'TRUE'
```

Verify that unallocated space is at least 3 MB (or 3072 KB).

- The text for objects must be intact in the **syscomments** system table.

If you create a nontable object such as a trigger, view, or stored procedure, the text of the CREATE statement is stored in the **syscomments** system table. If a system administrator has deleted the text for an object, that object is not upgraded.

The **sp_rename** system stored procedure does not change an object's name in **syscomments**.

If you use the **sp_rename** system stored procedure to rename an object, such as a view or stored procedure, the text of the original CREATE statement for that object is not modified. Therefore, when the object is migrated to SQL Server 7.0, it retains the name that it had before the rename.

- Logins must exist for every database user.

If you have moved a database or restored a database to the SQL Server 6.*x* installation, you must verify that a login exists and is mapped properly for each user. You can do this manually in SQL Server 6.0 or use the **sp_change_users_login** stored procedure in SQL Server 6.5. If you run the stored procedure with no parameters in either database, it reports the users who do not have a correct login. You must correct login-to-user mappings before you begin an upgrade.

Note Stored procedures that modify system tables are not upgraded. Permissions that had no effect, such as EXECUTE on a table, are not upgraded.

Back Up the SQL Server 6.x Installation

Before upgrading the databases, you should check them for errors that can prevent a successful migration. It is recommended that you run database integrity checks against all of the databases with the DBCC CHECKDB, DBCC CHECKCATALOG, DBCC NEWALLOC, and DBCC TEXTALL commands. In the event that database inconsistencies are found, you must repair the database or restore to a clean one before you begin the upgrade process. You should then back up the SQL Server 6.x installation, including the **master**, **model**, and **msdb** databases, as well as all of the user-defined databases. Also, you may want to back up the actual data and log files. Perform any repair or restoration work after all production activity has been stopped for the upgrade, and the DBCC consistency checks have completed successfully.

Replication Considerations

SQL Server 7.0 can perform transactional replication to SQL Server 6.5 installations. You cannot take advantage of new replication features until all servers involved in the replication (such as Publisher, Distributor, and Subscriber) have been upgraded to SQL Server 7.0. If you have enabled replication, you do not have to disable it to perform an upgrade to SQL Server 7.0.

Replication can be upgraded only if you are upgrading from SQL Server 6.5 and then only with a one-computer upgrade. Otherwise, you must upgrade the databases, and then manually reestablish replication with SQL Server 7.0.

You upgrade the Distributor server first. Before you begin the upgrade from SQL Server 6.5, ensure:

- No new Subscribers have been added that have not completed initial synchronization.
- No updates occur to the Publisher server(s) that correspond to the Distributor server you are about to upgrade.
- All transactions have been copied from the transaction log of the Publisher to the distribution database by running the log reader task for the production server.
- All transactions have been distributed to the Subscribers before you begin the upgrade of the SQL Server containing the distribution database, by running the distribution task.

To verify there are no undistributed transactions, run **exec sp_repltrans** against the Publisher database. If activity has stopped, no rows are returned. Then, run **exec sp_MSDistribution_counter @publisher = 'publisher_servername'** on the distribution database for each supported Publisher. The no rows returned message should have 0 in the **undelivered_jobs** column.

Install SQL Server 7.0

When you install SQL Server 7.0, use the same sort order and character set that is used in SQL Server 6.*x*. (SQL Server Setup chooses this by default if it can connect to the SQL Server 6.*x* server at the beginning of setup for a one-computer upgrade). If you do not know the character set and sort order used for the SQL Server 6.*x* installation, run the **sp_helpsort** system stored procedure against the SQL Server 6.*x* server.

If you choose a one-computer upgrade, you can start the SQL Server Upgrade Wizard automatically at the end of the installation. Otherwise, you can start the SQL Server Upgrade Wizard manually anytime after the Setup program is complete. If you plan to perform a two-computer upgrade, you cannot use the Windows NT **LocalSystem** account for the SQL Server services.

Starting the SQL Server Upgrade Wizard

The SQL Server Upgrade Wizard is a fast, reliable way to upgrade the databases. The wizard is easy to use and understand, but still allows flexibility. Microsoft's extensive testing has shown that simply taking the default path through the wizard results in a successful upgrade for a majority of installations.

You can estimate how long the upgrade will take based on the approximate size of the SQL Server 6.*x* data devices:

- 1 GB: 1 hour
- 10 GB: less than 4 hours
- 50 GB: less than 12 hours
- 100 GB: less than 24 hours

These numbers can vary depending upon the hardware and the database schema (the number of tables, for example, to be upgraded). Double these times if you want to perform an upgrade using the tape data transfer option.

After you complete the preparatory work, start the SQL Server Upgrade Wizard. You can start the wizard from SQL Server Setup, or on the **Start** menu, point to **Programs** and **Microsoft SQL Server – Switch**. (Upgrading is supported only on Windows NT–based installations of SQL Server.)

When the wizard begins, the welcome screen warns that both the SQL Server 6.*x* and SQL Server 7.0 installations (the MSSQLServer service(s)) will be stopped and restarted several times during the upgrade process. Therefore, users cannot use any instance of SQL Server while the upgrade process is running.

Click **Next** to view the **Data and Object Transfer** dialog box.

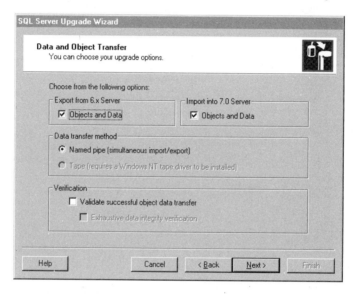

The **Data and Object Transfer** dialog box contains key choices that affect what you see as you continue with the upgrade wizard. As for most dialog boxes in the wizard, it is recommended that you accept the defaults. However, you should be aware of the options:

- The **Export from 6.*x* Server** option allows you to export the objects and data from the SQL Server 6.*x* installation. If you upgrade using the tape data transfer method, you may choose to upgrade in two steps: an export only to tape, followed by an import only to the SQL Server 7.0 installation after you increase the free disk space. For a named pipe data transfer, this option is always selected. It is recommended that you select this option and, whenever possible, upgrade with a single pass through the wizard that uses the **Named Pipe** data transfer option.

- The **Import into 7.0 Server** option can be cleared only for a tape data transfer method. If you use the upgrade scenario of multiple passes through the SQL Server Upgrade Wizard, check or clear this option as appropriate. It is recommended that you select this option and, whenever possible, upgrade with a single pass through the wizard that uses the **Named Pipe** data transfer option.

- The **Data transfer method** option allows you to select either a **Named Pipe** transfer or a **Tape** transfer of the data. If you perform a two-computer upgrade to SQL Server 7.0, you must use a named pipe transfer. If you perform a one-computer upgrade and are short of disk space, you can use a locally installed tape drive and the tape data transfer method. However, in all cases, **Named Pipe** transfer is the fastest and recommended option.

   If the tape option is unavailable (as shown in the preceding illustration) but you have a tape drive installed and you want to perform a tape data transfer method upgrade, you probably have some other tape program running, such as the Microsoft Windows NT Backup program. Cancel the wizard, close the open applications that might be using the tape drive, and then restart the SQL Server Upgrade Wizard.

- The **Verification** option allows you to verify the successful transfer of the objects and data. The **Validate successful object data transfer** option verifies that the tables, views, triggers, stored procedures, indexes, rules, defaults, and constraints were created correctly in SQL Server 7.0. If you select this option, you can select **Exhaustive data integrity verification**. This option performs a byte-by-byte comparison between SQL Server 6.x and SQL Server 7.0.

   Neither of these options is selected by default. When you choose these options, you receive a warning that the time it takes to perform an upgrade may increase significantly. Select these options if you want 100 percent verification of your upgrade. Selecting the **Validate successful object data transfer** option can add a significant amount of time to the upgrade, depending on how many objects you have to upgrade. Performing the exhaustive data integrity verification can add approximately one hour for each GB of data you want to upgrade, and is CPU-intensive.

After you specify the options you want to use, click **Next** to view the **Logon** dialog box.

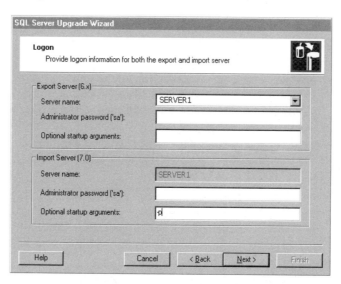

In this dialog box, you can select the export server and the import server. You must supply the system administrator password for both installations of SQL Server.

The optional startup arguments allow you to specify any flags that you want to use during the upgrade process. Unless you are instructed to do so by Microsoft SQL Server Product Support or your Independent Software Vendor (ISV), you should not specify any options here. The **-p** option is the most common option to specify. The **-p** option raises the precision of **decimal** and **numeric** data types to 38 digits, instead of the SQL Server default of 28 digits. You can specify this option for SQL Server 7.0 if you have used it for SQL Server 6.x and you want numeric values with digits of precision greater than 28 to transfer correctly.

You can verify startup parameters by selecting the **Configure** option for the server in SQL Server Enterprise Manager, and then clicking **Parameters** for SQL Server 6.5 as shown in this illustration.

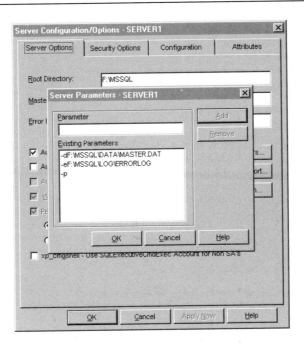

The optional startup parameters you use for the SQL Server 7.0 server are not added to the SQL Server 7.0 configuration. You do not need to specify the **–d** or **–e** options on either SQL Server 6.x or SQL Server 7.0. The only options necessary are those that are not part of the existing SQL Server 6.x and SQL Server 7.0 startup parameters.

After you click **Next** in the **Logon** dialog box, a message warns that the SQL Server 6.x and SQL Server 7.0 installations will stop and restart.

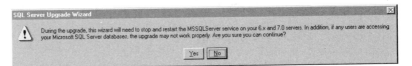

Click **Yes** to continue. At that point, several background checks occur. You must correct any problems before you can continue with the SQL Server Upgrade Wizard. For a list of the checks that occur at this stage, see "Prepare the SQL Server 6.x Installation" earlier in this chapter.

The **Code Page Selection** dialog box appears.

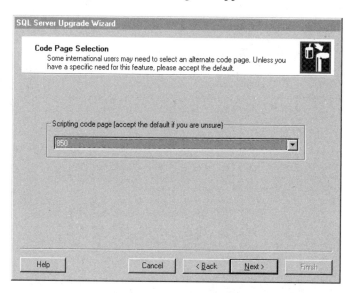

The SQL Server Upgrade Wizard determines the code page in use by the SQL Server 6.*x* installation and recommends the code page to use during the upgrade. Do not change this selection unless you have been instructed to change it by Microsoft SQL Server Product Support or your ISV, or you have advanced experience with code page issues.

If you have selected a tape data transfer method, after you click **Next**, the **Data Transfer** dialog box appears.

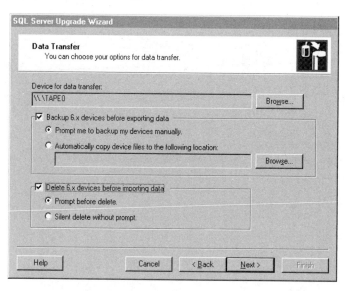

In the **Data Transfer** dialog box, you can select which tape drive to use if you have multiple tape drives installed, whether to back up the SQL Server 6.*x* devices, and whether to delete the SQL Server 6.*x* devices:

- Select the **Backup 6.*x* devices before exporting data** option if you want the SQL Server Upgrade Wizard to back up the data files (rather than backing them up before you begin the upgrade process, as was recommended). If you choose to be prompted, the SQL Server Upgrade Wizard prompts you when it is time to back up the SQL Server 6.*x* device files. If you select **Automatically copy device files to the following location**, click **Browse**, and then select a network location on which to save your data files. At the appropriate point in the wizard, all of the SQL Server 6.*x* devices are copied to this network share.

- If you select **Delete 6.*x* devices before importing data**, you must select how those devices will be deleted. Use this option if you do not have enough disk space to keep the SQL Server 6.*x* devices on the computer and to upgrade successfully to SQL Server 7.0. If you select **Prompt before delete**, you can choose to delete the SQL Server 6.*x* files. If you select **Silent delete without prompt**, the files are deleted.

  Both of these options delete all of the SQL Server 6.*x* device files, including Master.dat. Use this option only if you are performing a complete upgrade of all databases to SQL Server 7.0. Make sure that you have backed up all of the SQL Server 6.*x* databases and the SQL Server 6.*x* device files before selecting this option.

If you click the **Browse** button next to **Device for data transfer**, the **Detected Tape Drives** dialog box lists the names of tape devices. Select the one you want to use to hold the data that will be exported from the SQL Server 6.*x* databases.

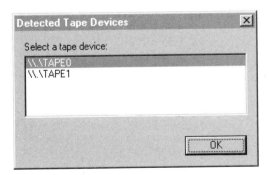

Click **Next** to view the **Upgrade Databases to SQL Server 7.0** dialog box, in which you can select the databases you want to upgrade to SQL Server 7.0.

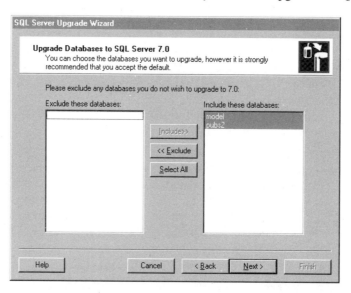

You should upgrade all of the databases in a single pass, which is the default configuration. If you run the SQL Server Upgrade Wizard multiple times, the databases that have been upgraded previously appear in the **Exclude these databases** list by default.

The **model** database is selected for upgrade so that custom users or objects in the SQL Server 6.*x* **model** database will transfer to in the SQL Server 7.0 **model** database. Upgrade the SQL Server 6.*x* **model** database even if you have not modified it.

A database marked offline cannot be upgraded until the database is placed back online. Additionally, raw partitions are not supported during upgrade; therefore, databases that use raw partitions do not appear in this dialog box.

Click **Next** to view the **Database Creation** dialog box.

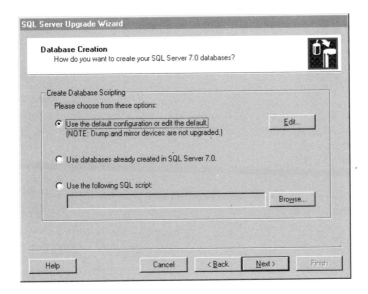

By default, the SQL Server Upgrade Wizard creates databases and files for you in SQL Server 7.0 for each database you have selected to upgrade. The number and layout of the files in SQL Server 7.0 is similar to the number and location of files that are used in SQL Server 6.*x*. In most cases, this option is recommended for the upgrade.

However, you may want to review or edit the default. Click **Edit** to configure the names, sizes, and locations of the files.

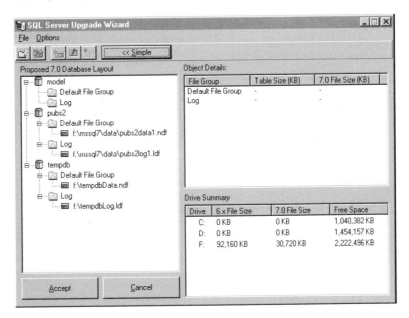

If you want to see the entire dialog box, click **Advanced**. You can modify the name, location, and size of the file, as well as the autogrowth increment. Right-click each file you want to modify, and change the attributes as needed. Also, you can remove or add files or filegroups as appropriate for your server configuration. When you complete your changes, click **Accept**.

If you have created the databases in SQL Server 7.0, in the **Database Creation** dialog box, select **Use databases already created in SQL Server 7.0**. Using this option is not recommended. The databases are matched by name. If you select this option, make sure that the databases are large enough to hold the data when it is imported into SQL Server 7.0, and configure the database compatibility mode. In addition, you must have a sufficiently large **tempdb**, assign database ownership, and set the compatibility level of the databases to the version of the export server by using **sp_dbcmptlevel dbname, 65** (use 60 if the export server is SQL Server 6.0).

Also, you can specify a Transact-SQL create database script. This option is useful, however, only if you are familiar with SQL Server 7.0 CREATE DATABASE syntax. This is an advanced option and is recommended only for advanced users or ISVs who have tested their scripts carefully (unless you are performing an import-only upgrade from tape).

After you select any changes or accept the default configuration, click **Next**.

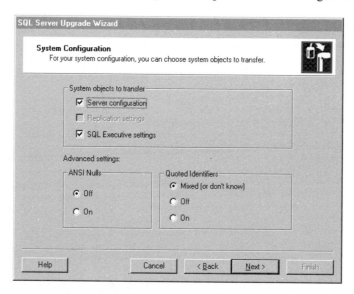

In the **System Configuration** dialog box, you can specify the system options you want to transfer. These include relevant server configuration options, replication settings, and SQL Server Agent settings (scheduled tasks, alerts, and operators). It is recommended that you transfer the server configuration options and SQL Server Agent settings, which includes tasks such as scheduled backup. If you do not use replication, the **Replication settings** check box is unavailable. If replication was enabled in the SQL Server 6.5 configuration, this option is selected the first time you run the SQL Server Upgrade Wizard.

You also can determine advanced settings, such as whether to use the **ANSI Nulls** option during transfer, and whether to use the **Quoted Identifiers** options. Unless a prior upgrade has failed, accept the defaults.

When you click **Next**, the **syscomments** system table in each SQL Server 6.*x* database you want to upgrade is examined. If a problem is encountered, those objects may not be upgraded.

After **syscomments** has been selected for integrity in each database you are upgrading, the **Completing the SQL Server Upgrade Wizard** dialog box appears.

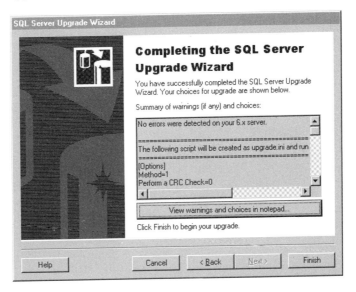

If the message indicating no errors were detected does not appear, click **View warnings and choices in notepad** to view any problem reports. If problems are reported, repair them before continuing.

After all errors are repaired (the initial state for most configurations), click **Finish** to start the SQL Server Upgrade Script Interpreter.

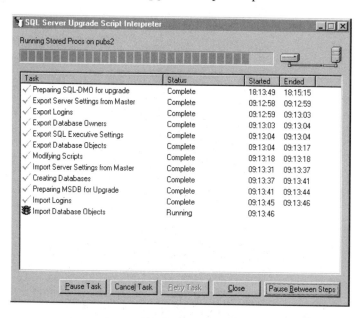

The SQL Server Upgrade Script Interpreter is the program that performs most of the work during the upgrade process. The tasks that run depend on the choices you made in the SQL Server Upgrade Wizard. If you selected a default upgrade path, the first step is to run a script against the SQL Server 6.x database to upgrade the SQL-DMO capabilities. Then, the SQL Server Upgrade Script Interpreter exports the schema for all databases that are to be upgraded and includes the row counts and byte comparison values if you requested those options. System settings, including replication settings, are exported. Next, the process begins on the import server, including creating the database(s), importing the schema for those databases, and then loading the data from the SQL Server 6.x data files. Finally, the schema is verified, and row counts and byte comparison values are verified if you requested this step.

Files Created by the Upgrade Process

After the upgrade process is complete, you can view the files that are created. Each time you run the SQL Server Upgrade Wizard, a new directory is created in the \Mssql7\Upgrade directory. This directory name is in the format EXPORTSERVER_DATE_TIME. For example, on the server used for this chapter, the directory SERVER1_102898_134353 indicates the server name is SERVER1, the date is 28 October 1998, and the time is 1:43:53 PM. Within that directory, each database has its own directory.

In each database directory, you can find the results of running the create scripts for each type of object (such as .tab for tables). The root directory contains reports for various parts of the upgrade that are not related necessarily to the scripts run in each database. You do not have to examine any of these files unless there is a problem with the upgrade. A separate copy of the data is not kept; only scripts of objects, logins, users, scheduled tasks, and any other options you requested are kept.

Do not delete this directory until you are comfortable that you have upgraded fully to SQL Server 7.0.

Database Compatibility in SQL Server 7.0

SQL Server 7.0 has built-in backward compatibility. When you upgrade the databases to SQL Server 7.0, they are left in a backward compatible state. If you upgrade from SQL Server 6.0, the databases are in 6.0 mode. If you upgrade from SQL Server 6.5, the databases are in 6.5 mode. Databases in native SQL Server 7.0 mode are said to be in 7.0 mode.

Backward compatibility modes allow your application to function as it did in SQL Server 6.*x*. For example, the TOP keyword in SQL Server 7.0 is not valid in a SQL Server 6.*x* backward compatibility mode, because this word may have been used as a column name, a column alias, or in another context that is not valid in SQL Server 7.0.

In addition to syntax changes, some functional behaviors are affected also. In SQL Server 6.*x*, a SELECT statement with a GROUP BY clause always implies an ORDER BY on the same columns. In SQL Server 7.0, this is not the case; however, in SQL Server 6.*x* backward compatibility modes, an ORDER BY is implicitly added to GROUP BY queries so that the data is returned in the same sequence that it would have been in SQL Server 6.*x*. For more information about backward compatibility, see SQL Server Books Online.

You can run the **sp_dbcmptlevel** system stored procedure to switch between backward compatibility modes. For example, if you upgrade a database named **upgrade_test**, you run **exec sp_dbcmptlevel 'upgrade_test', 70** to change the database compatibility level to SQL Server 7.0 mode. No other database on the server is affected by this change. To switch back to SQL Server 6.5 mode instantly, simply run **exec sp_dbcmptlevel 'upgrade_test', 65**. This switching mechanism allows you to switch compatibility modes easily and test your application. If no problems are encountered, you can leave the database in 7.0 mode. If you do encounter issues that require coding changes, you can switch back to the compatibility mode of the earlier version until you have time to complete the code changes. You still get most of the performance enhancements and the other benefits of SQL Server 7.0 while running your applications in backward compatibility mode.

> **Note** The **master** database must always be in 7.0 compatibility mode; therefore, applications that use the **master** database must change immediately when upgrading.

Testing the Upgrade Process

The SQL Server Upgrade Wizard has been tested extensively. Microsoft upgraded literally thousands of production databases to determine problems that might be encountered and ways to handle them appropriately. Microsoft worked with ISVs and businesses to upgrade SQL Server 6.*x* databases to SQL Server 7.0 to ascertain requirements for backward compatibility. Microsoft assisted its internal information technology department with the upgrade to SQL Server 7.0.

Because of this testing, the SQL Server Upgrade Wizard and the backward compatibility modes changed during development to meet the needs of customers.

In addition to backward compatibility support in SQL Server 7.0, Microsoft implemented several other projects to help ensure the integrity and simplicity of the upgrade process.

The 1K Challenge Project

The 1K Challenge was a Microsoft project to upgrade 1,000 real customer databases before shipping SQL Server 7.0. Customers (under nondisclosure) sent Microsoft their SQL Server 6.0 and SQL Server 6.5 production databases to be upgraded to SQL Server 7.0.

More than 92 percent of all customer databases converted during the 1K Challenge project were 100 percent successful. These databases were received from 27 countries and varying in complexity and size ranging from 25 MB to 200 GB. Because these databases represent a random sampling of databases from Microsoft's worldwide customer base, these numbers should accurately predict the customer's upgrade experience. An additional 6.4 percent of the converted databases required only minor changes to migrate to SQL Server 7.0. Based on these results, the majority of customers can upgrade their databases successfully on their first attempt.

The ISV Migration Lab Project

The ISV Migration Lab invited certain companies that sell SQL Server as part of their solutions to upgrade to SQL Server 7.0 at the SQL Server development site. ISVs participating in the lab upgraded their databases by using the SQL Server Upgrade Wizard, and then tested their applications by using the configurations that their customers use in production. The ISVs tested SQL Server versions 6.5 and 7.0 client libraries (for example, DB-Library, ODBC, OLE DB) with their converted databases in both 6.5 and 7.0 compatibility modes.

More than 96 percent of all applications tested during the ISV Migration Lab project run unchanged with SQL Server 7.0 in 6.5 backward compatibility mode. That is, the client computers using the ISV application run unchanged against a database that has been upgraded to SQL Server 7.0 with the SQL Server Upgrade Wizard.

Internal Database Migrations at Microsoft

Microsoft has migrated most of its internal SQL Server databases to SQL Server 7.0, including all mission-critical systems. Each of these upgrades occurred with beta versions of SQL Server 7.0.

The SAP R/3 enterprise resource planning (ERP) environment at Microsoft manages the company's worldwide financials, human resources, OEM contracts and all procurement transactions. Moving SAP R/3 to SQL Server 7.0 has drastically reduced the update performance time from an average of more than 5 seconds to 0.7 seconds. In addition, the total database size has been reduced from 140 GB to 80 GB, system availability has increased substantially, and backup throughput has increased 450 percent.

Microsoft Sales, Microsoft's revenue-reporting data warehouse, contains 150 GB of sales data that supports business intelligence throughout the corporation, and is used concurrently by more than 1,600 employees worldwide, primarily accountants and sales and marketing people. Since the move to SQL Server 7.0, query performance has increased 57 percent, and backup speed has increased 25 percent. The Microsoft Sales database upgraded quickly and easily in about 24 hours.

With SQL Server 7.0, Microsoft's product support systems used for call tracking, credit card billing, and customer contract information can be used concurrently by up to 3,600 support specialists worldwide. SQL Server 7.0 provides Microsoft with the enhanced reliability and scalability imperative to keep the system up and running continuously, an advantage that translates into better customer service and lower support costs.

Microsoft has also converted its corporate Web site, www.microsoft.com/, to SQL Server 7.0. This site, one of the 10 busiest Web sites on the Internet, receiving between 140 million and 200 million hits a day, is run by multiple SQL Server databases, each of which has been upgraded to SQL Server 7.0. Additionally, MSNBC and MSN have upgraded to SQL Server 7.0.

C H A P T E R   1 8

Migrating Oracle Databases to Microsoft SQL Server 7.0

This chapter is for developers of Oracle applications who want to convert their applications to Microsoft SQL Server applications. The tools, processes, and techniques required for a successful conversion are described. Also highlighted are the essential design points that allow you to create high-performance, high-concurrency SQL Server applications.

Target Audience

The target audience can be new to Microsoft SQL Server and its operation but should have a solid foundation in the Oracle RDBMS and database concepts. The target audience should possess:

- A strong background in Oracle RDBMS fundamentals.
- General database management knowledge.
- Familiarity with the Oracle SQL and PL/SQL languages.
- A working knowledge of the C/C++ programming language.
- Membership in the **sysadmin** fixed server role.

This chapter assumes that you are familiar with the terms, concepts, and tools associated with the Oracle RDBMS. For more information about the Oracle RDBMS and its architecture, see the *Oracle 7 Server Concepts Manual*. For using the Oracle scripts and examples, it is also assumed that you are familiar with the Oracle Server Manager and Oracle SQL*Plus tools. For more information about these tools, see your Oracle documentation.

Development and Application Platforms

For clarity and ease of presentation, the reference development and application platform is assumed to be Microsoft Visual Studio version 6.0, Microsoft Windows NT version 4 (Service Pack 4), SQL Server 7.0, and Oracle 7.3. The Visigenic Software ODBC driver (version 2.00.0300) is used with Oracle 7.3, and the Microsoft Corporation ODBC driver (version 3.70) is used with SQL Server 7.0. Microsoft SQL Server 7.0 includes an OLE DB driver for Oracle, but that driver is not discussed extensively in this chapter.

Overview

The application migration process can appear complicated. There are many architectural differences between each RDBMS. The words and terminology used to describe Oracle architecture often have completely different meanings in Microsoft SQL Server. Additionally, both Oracle and SQL Server have made many proprietary extensions to the SQL-92 standard.

From an application developer's perspective, Oracle and SQL Server manage data in similar ways. The internal differences between Oracle and SQL Server are significant, but if managed properly, have minimal impact on a migrated application.

SQL Language Extensions

The most significant migration issue that confronts the developer is the implementation of the SQL-92 SQL language standard and the extensions that each RDBMS has to offer. Some developers use only standard SQL language statements, preferring to keep their program code as generic as possible. Generally, this means restricting program code to the entry-level SQL-92 standard, which is implemented consistently across many database products, including Oracle and SQL Server.

This approach can produce unneeded complexity in the program code and can substantially affect program performance. For example, Oracle's DECODE function is a nonstandard SQL extension specific to Oracle. Microsoft SQL Server's CASE expression is a SQL-92 extension beyond entry level and is not implemented in all database products.

Both the Oracle DECODE and the SQL Server CASE expressions can perform sophisticated conditional evaluation from within a query. The alternative to not using these functions is to perform the function programmatically, which might require that substantially more data be retrieved from the RDBMS.

Also, procedural extensions to the SQL language can cause difficulties. The Oracle PL/SQL and SQL Server Transact-SQL languages are similar in function, but different in syntax. There is no exact symmetry between each RDBMS and its procedural extensions. Consequently, you might decide not to use stored programs such as procedures and triggers. This is unfortunate because they can offer substantial performance and security benefits that cannot be duplicated in any other way.

The use of proprietary development interfaces introduces additional issues. The conversion of a program using the Oracle OCI (Oracle Call Interface) often requires a significant investment in resources. When developing an application that may use multiple RDBMSs, consider using the Open Database Connectivity (ODBC) interface.

ODBC

ODBC is designed to work with numerous database management systems. ODBC provides a consistent application programming interface (API) that works with different databases through the services of a database-specific driver.   .

A consistent API means that the functions a program calls to make a connection, execute a command, and retrieve results are identical whether the program is talking to Oracle or SQL Server.

ODBC also defines a standardized call-level interface and uses standard escape sequences to specify SQL functions that perform common tasks but have different syntax in different databases. The ODBC drivers can automatically convert this ODBC syntax to either Oracle native or Microsoft SQL Server native SQL syntax without requiring the revision of any program code. In some situations, the best approach is to write one program and allow ODBC to perform the conversion process at run time.

ODBC is not a magical solution for achieving complete database independence, full functionality, and high performance from all databases. Different databases and third-party vendors offer varying levels of ODBC support. Some drivers just implement core API functions mapped on top of other interface libraries. Other drivers, such as the Microsoft SQL Server driver, offer full Level 2 support in a native, high-performance driver.

If a program uses only the core ODBC API, it will likely forego features and performance capabilities with some databases. Furthermore, not all native SQL extensions can be represented in ODBC escape sequences (such as Oracle DECODE and SQL Server CASE expressions).

Additionally, it is common practice to write SQL statements to take advantage of the database's optimizer. The techniques and methods that enhance performance within Oracle are not necessarily optimal within Microsoft SQL Server 7.0. The ODBC interface can not translate techniques from one RDBMS to another.

ODBC does not prevent an application from using database-specific features and tuning for performance, but the application needs some database-specific sections of code. ODBC makes it easy to keep the program structure and the majority of the program code consistent across multiple databases.

OLE DB

OLE DB is the next generation of data access technology. Microsoft SQL Server 7.0 takes advantage of OLE DB within the components of SQL Server itself. Additionally, application developers should consider OLE DB for new development with SQL Server 7.0. Microsoft includes an OLE DB provider for Oracle 7.3 with SQL Server 7.0.

OLE DB is Microsoft's strategic system-level programming interface to manage data across the organization. OLE DB is an open specification designed to build on the features of ODBC. ODBC was created to access relational databases, and OLE DB is designed to access relational and nonrelational information sources, such as mainframe ISAM/VSAM and hierarchical databases, e-mail and file system stores, text, graphical and geographical data, and custom business objects.

OLE DB defines a collection of COM interfaces that encapsulate various database management system services and allows the creation of software components that implement such services. OLE DB components consist of data providers (that contain and expose data), data consumers (that use data), and service components (that process and transport data, for example, query processors and cursor engines).

OLE DB interfaces are designed to help components integrate smoothly so that OLE DB component vendors can bring high quality OLE DB components to the market quickly. In addition, OLE DB includes a bridge to ODBC to allow continued support for the broad range of ODBC relational database drivers available today.

Organization of this Chapter

To assist you in implementing a step-by-step migration from Oracle to SQL Server, each section includes an overview of the relevant differences between Oracle 7.3 and Microsoft SQL Server 7.0. It also includes conversion considerations, SQL Server 7.0 advantages, and multiple examples.

Architecture and Terminology

To start a successful migration, you should understand the basic architecture and terminology associated with Microsoft SQL Server 7.0. Many of the examples in this section have been drawn from the sample Oracle and SQL Server applications included as part of this chapter.

Definition of Database

In Oracle, a *database* refers to the entire Oracle RDBMS environment and includes these components.

- Oracle database processes and buffers (instance).
- SYSTEM tablespace containing one centralized system catalog.
- Other tablespaces as defined by the DBA (optional).
- Two or more online Redo Logs.
- Archived Redo Logs (optional).
- Miscellaneous other files (control file, Init.ora, and so on).

A Microsoft SQL Server database provides a logical separation of data, applications, and security mechanisms, much like a tablespace. Where Oracle supports multiple tablespaces, SQL Server supports multiple databases. Tablespaces also can be used to support the physical placement of data; SQL Server provides this same functionality with filegroups.

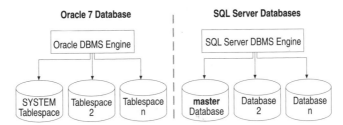

Microsoft SQL Server also installs the following databases by default:

- The **model** database is a template for all newly created user databases.
- The **tempdb** database is similar to an Oracle temporary tablespace in that it is used for temporary working storage and sort operations. Unlike the Oracle temporary tablespace, users can create temporary tables that are automatically dropped when the user logs off.

- The **msdb** database supports the SQL Server Agent and its scheduled jobs, alerts, and replication information.

- The **pubs** and **Northwind** databases are provided as sample databases for training.

For more information about the default databases, see SQL Server Books Online.

Database System Catalogs

Each Oracle database runs on one centralized system catalog, or data dictionary, which resides in the SYSTEM tablespace. Each Microsoft SQL Server 7.0 database maintains its own system catalog, which contains information about:

- Database objects (tables, indexes, stored procedures, views, triggers, and so on).

- Constraints.

- Users and permissions.

- User-defined data types.

- Replication definitions.

- Files used by the database.

SQL Server also contains a centralized system catalog in the **master** database, which contains system catalogs as well as some information about the individual databases:

- Database names and the primary file location for each database.

- SQL Server login accounts.

- System messages.

- Database configuration values.

- Remote and/or linked servers.

- Current activity information.

- System stored procedures.

Like the SYSTEM tablespace in Oracle, the SQL Server **master** database must be available to access any other database. As such, it is important to protect against failures by backing up the **master** database after any significant changes are made in the database. Database administrators can also mirror the files that make up the **master** database.

Physical and Logical Storage Structures

The Oracle RDBMS is comprised of tablespaces, which in turn are comprised of data files. Tablespace data files are formatted into internal units termed *blocks*. The block size, set by the DBA when the Oracle database is first created, can range from 512 to 8192 bytes. When an object is created in an Oracle tablespace, the user specifies its space in units called *extents* (initial extent, next extent, min extents, and max extents). An Oracle extent varies in size and must contain a chain of at least five contiguous blocks.

Microsoft SQL Server uses filegroups at the database level to control the physical placement of tables and indexes. Filegroups are logical containers of one or more files, and data contained within a filegroup is proportionally filled across all files belonging to the filegroup.

If filegroups are not defined and used, database objects are placed in a default filegroup that is implicitly defined during the creation of a database. Filegroups allow you to:

- Distribute large tables across multiple files to improve I/O throughput.
- Store indexes on different files than their respective tables, again to improve I/O throughput and disk concurrency.
- Store **text**, **ntext**, and **image** columns (large objects) on separate files from the table.
- Place database objects on specific disk spindles.
- Back up and restore individual tables or sets of tables within a filegroup.

SQL Server formats files into internal units called pages. The page size is fixed at 8192 bytes (8 KB). Pages are organized into extents that are fixed in size at 8 contiguous pages. When a table or index is created in a SQL Server database, it is automatically allocated one page. This allows for more efficient storage of smaller tables and indexes when compared to allocating an entire extent.

Striping Data

Oracle-type segments are not needed for most Microsoft SQL Server installations. Instead, SQL Server can distribute, or stripe, data better with hardware-based RAID or Windows NT software–based RAID. Windows NT software–based RAID or hardware-based RAID can set up stripe sets consisting of multiple disk drives that appear as one logical drive. If database files are created on this stripe set, the disk subsystem assumes responsibility for distributing I/O load across multiple disks. It is recommended that administrators spread out the data over multiple physical disks using RAID.

The recommended RAID configuration for SQL Server is RAID 1 (mirroring) or RAID 5 (stripe sets with an extra parity drive, for redundancy). RAID 10 (mirroring of striped sets with parity) is also recommended, but is much more expensive than the first two options. Stripe sets work very well to spread out the usually random I/O done on database files.

If RAID is not an option, filegroups are an attractive alternative and provide some of the same benefits available with RAID. Additionally, for very large databases that might span multiple physical RAID arrays, filegroups may be an attractive way to further distribute your I/O across multiple RAID arrays in a controlled fashion.

Transaction log files must be optimized for sequential I/O and must be secured against a single point of failure. Accordingly, RAID 1 (mirroring) is recommended for transaction logs. The size of this drive should be at least as large as the sum of the size of the online redo logs and the rollback segment tablespace(s). Create one or more log files that take up all the space defined on the logical drive. Unlike data stored in filegroups, transaction log entries are always written sequentially and are not proportionally filled.

For more information about RAID, see SQL Server Books Online, your Windows NT Server documentation, and the Microsoft Windows NT Resource Kit.

Transaction Logs and Automatic Recovery

The Oracle RDBMS performs automatic recovery each time it is started. It verifies that the contents of the tablespace files are coordinated with the contents of the online redo log files. If they are not, Oracle applies the contents of the online redo log files to the tablespace files (roll forward), and then removes any uncommitted transactions that are found in the rollback segments (roll back). If Oracle cannot obtain the information it requires from the online redo log files, it consults the archived redo log files.

Microsoft SQL Server 7.0 also performs automatic data recovery by checking each database in the system each time it is started. It first checks the **master** database and then launches threads to recover all of the other databases in the system. For each SQL Server database, the automatic recovery mechanism checks the transaction log. If the transaction log contains any uncommitted transactions, the transactions are rolled back. The recovery mechanism then checks the transaction log for committed transactions that have not yet been written out to the database. If it finds any, it performs those transactions again, rolling forward.

Each SQL Server transaction log has the combined functionality of an Oracle rollback segment and an Oracle online redo log. Each database has its own transaction log that records all changes to the database and is shared by all users of that database. When a transaction begins and a data modification occurs, a BEGIN TRANSACTION event (as well as the modification event) is recorded in the log. This event is used during automatic recovery to determine the starting point of a transaction. As each data modification statement is received, the changes are written to the transaction log prior to being written to the database itself. For more information, see the "Transactions, Locking, and Concurrency" section later in this chapter.

SQL Server has an automatic checkpoint mechanism that ensures completed transactions are regularly written from the SQL Server disk cache to the transaction log file. A checkpoint writes any cached page that has been modified since the last checkpoint to the database. Checkpointing these cached pages, known as dirty pages, onto the database, ensures that all completed transactions are written out to disk. This process shortens the time that it takes to recover from a system failure, such as a power outage. This setting can be changed by modifying the recovery interval setting by using SQL Server Enterprise Manager or with Transact-SQL (**sp_configure** system stored procedure).

Backing Up and Restoring Data

Microsoft SQL Server offers several options for backing up data:

Full database backup
> To make a full database backup, use the BACKUP DATABASE statement or the Backup Wizard.

Differential backup
> After a full database backup, regularly back up just the changed data and index pages using the BACKUP DATABASE WITH DIFFERENTIAL statement or the Backup Wizard.

Transaction log backup
> Transaction logs in Microsoft SQL Server are associated with individual databases. The transaction log fills until it is backed up or truncated. The default configuration of SQL Server 7.0 is that the transaction log grows automatically until it uses all available disk space or it meets its maximum configured size. When a transaction log gets too full, it can create an error and prevent further data modifications until it is backed up or truncated. Other databases are not affected. Transaction logs can be backed up using the BACKUP LOG statement or the Backup Wizard.

File or filegroup backup
> SQL Server can back up files and filegroups. For more information, see SQL Server Books Online.

Backups can be performed while the database is in use, allowing backups to be made of systems that must run continually. The backup processing and internal data structures of SQL Server 7.0 have been improved so that backups maximize their rate of data transfer with minimal effect on transaction throughput.

Both Oracle and SQL Server require a specific format for log files. In SQL Server, these files, called backup devices, are created using SQL Server Enterprise Manager, the Transact-SQL **sp_addumpdevice** stored procedure, or the equivalent SQL-DMO command.

Although backups can be performed manually, it is recommended that you use SQL Server Enterprise Manager and/or the Database Maintenance Plan Wizard to schedule periodic backups, or backups based on database activity.

A database can be restored to a certain point in time by applying transaction log backups and/or differential backups to a full database backup (device). A database restore overwrites the data with the information contained in the backups. Restores can be performed using SQL Server Enterprise Manager, Transact-SQL (RESTORE DATABASE), or SQL-DMO.

Just as you can turn off the Oracle archiver to override automatic backups, in Microsoft SQL Server, members of the **db_owner** fixed database role can force the transaction log to erase its contents every time a checkpoint occurs. This can be accomplished by using SQL Server Enterprise Manager (truncate log on checkpoint), Transact-SQL (**sp_dboption** stored procedure), or SQL-DMO.

Networks

Oracle SQL*Net supports networked connections between Oracle database servers and their clients. It communicates with the Transparent Network Substrate (TNS) data stream protocol, and allows users to run many different network protocols without writing specialized code. SQL*Net is not included with the core Oracle database software product.

With Microsoft SQL Server, *Net-Libraries* (network libraries) support the networked connections between the clients and the server by using the Tabular Data Stream (TDS) protocol. They enable simultaneous connections from clients running Named Pipes, TCP/IP Sockets, or other Inter-Process Communication (IPC) mechanisms. The SQL Server CD-ROM includes all client Net-Libraries so that there is no need to purchase them.

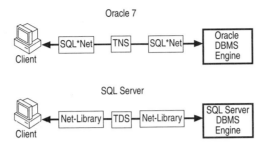

SQL Server Net-Library options can be changed after installation. The Client Network utility configures the default Net-Library and server connection information for a client running the Windows NT, Windows 95, or Windows 98 operating systems. All ODBC client applications use the same default Net-Library and server connection information, unless it is changed during ODBC data source setup or explicitly coded in the ODBC connection string. For more information about Net-Libraries, see SQL Server Books Online.

Database Security and Roles

To adequately migrate your Oracle applications to Microsoft SQL Server 7.0, you must understand SQL Server's implementation of database security and roles.

Login Accounts

A login account allows a user to access SQL Server data or administrative options. The login account allows users only to log in to SQL Server and view databases that allow guest access. (The **guest** account is not set up by default and must be created.)

SQL Server offers two types of login security: Windows NT Authentication Mode (also known as integrated) and SQL Server Authentication Mode (also known as standard). SQL Server 7.0 also supports a combination of standard and integrated security, known as mixed.

The Windows NT Authentication Mode uses the security mechanisms within Windows NT when validating login connections, and relies on a user's Windows NT security credentials. Users do not need to enter login IDs or passwords for SQL Server—their login information is taken directly from the network connection. When this occurs, an entry is written to the **syslogins** table and is verified between Windows NT and SQL Server. This is known as a trusted connection and works like a trust relationship between two Windows NT servers. This functions like the IDENTIFIED EXTERNALLY option associated with Oracle user accounts.

The SQL Server Authentication Mode requires that a user enter a login ID and password when requesting access to SQL Server. This is known as a nontrusted connection. This functions like the IDENTIFIED BY PASSWORD option associated with Oracle user accounts. With the use of the standard security model, the login provides access to the SQL Server database engine only; it does not provide access to the user databases.

For more information about these security mechanisms, see SQL Server Books Online.

Groups, Roles, and Permissions

Microsoft SQL Server and Oracle use permissions to enforce database security. SQL Server statement-level permissions are used to restrict the ability to create new database objects (similar to the Oracle system-level permissions).

SQL Server also offers object-level permissions. As in Oracle, object-level ownership is assigned to the creator of the object and cannot be transferred. Object-level permissions must be granted to other database users before they can access the object. Members of the **sysadmin** fixed server role, **db_owner** fixed database role, or **db_securityadmin** fixed database role can also grant permissions on one user's objects to other users.

SQL Server statement- and object-level permissions can be granted directly to database user accounts. However, it is often simpler to administer permissions to database roles. SQL Server roles are used for granting and revoking privileges to groups of database users (much like Oracle roles). Roles are database objects associated with a specific database. There are a few specific fixed server roles associated with each installation, which work across databases. An example of a fixed server role is **sysadmin**. Windows NT groups can also be added as SQL Server logins, as well as database users. Permissions can be granted to a Windows NT group or a Windows NT user.

A database can have any number of roles or Windows NT groups. The default role **public** is always found in every database and cannot be removed. The **public** role functions much like the PUBLIC account in Oracle. Each database user is always a member of the **public** role. A database user can be a member of any number of roles in addition to the **public** role. A Windows NT user or group can also be a member of any number of roles, and is also always in the **public** role.

Database Users and the guest Account

In Microsoft SQL Server, a user login account must be authorized to use a database and its objects. One of the following methods can be used by a login account to access a database:

- The login account can be specified as a database user.

- The login account can use a guest account in the database.
- A Windows NT group login can be mapped to a database role. Individual Windows NT accounts that are members of that group can then connect to the database.

Members of the **db_owner** or **db_accessadmin** roles, or the **sysadmin** fixed server role, create the database user account roles. An account can include several parameters: the SQL Server login ID, database username (optional), and up to one role name (optional). The database username does not have to be the same as the user's login ID. If a database username is not provided, the user's login ID and database username are identical. If a role name is not provided, the database user is only a member of the **public** role. After creating the database user, the user can be assigned to as many roles as necessary.

Members of the **db_owner** or **db_accessadmin** roles can also create a **guest** account. The **guest** account allows any valid SQL Server login account to access a database even without a database user account. By default, the **guest** account inherits any privileges that have been assigned to the **public** role; however, these privileges can be changed to be greater or less than that of the **public** role.

A Windows NT user account or group account can be granted access to a database, just as a SQL Server login can. When a Windows NT user who is a member in a group connects to the database, the user receives the permissions assigned to the Windows NT group. If a member of more than one Windows NT group that has been granted access to the database, the user receives the combined rights of all of the groups to which he belongs.

The sysadmin Role

Members of the Microsoft SQL Server **sysadmin** fixed server role have similar permissions to that of an Oracle DBA. In SQL Server 7.0, the **sa** SQL Server Authentication Mode login account is a member of this role by default, as are members of the local **Administrators** group if SQL Server is installed on a Windows NT computer. A member of the **sysadmin** role can add or remove Windows NT users and groups, as well as SQL Server logins. Members of this role typically have the following responsibilities:

- Installing SQL Server.
- Configuring servers and clients.
- Creating databases.*
- Establishing login rights and user permissions.*
- Transferring data in and out of SQL Server databases.*
- Backing up and restoring databases.*
- Implementing and maintaining replication.

- Scheduling unattended operations.*
- Monitoring and tuning SQL Server performance.*
- Diagnosing system problems.

*These items can be delegated to other security roles or users.

There are no restrictions on what a member of the **sysadmin** fixed server role can do in SQL Server 7.0. Therefore, a member of this role can access any database and all of the objects (including data) on a particular instance of SQL Server. Like an Oracle DBA, there are several commands and system procedures that only members of the **sysadmin** role can issue.

The db_owner Role

Although a Microsoft SQL Server database is similar to an Oracle tablespace in use, it is administered differently. Each SQL Server database is a self-contained administrative domain. Each database is assigned a database owner (**dbo**). This user is always a member of the **db_owner** fixed database role. Other users can also be members of the **db_owner** role. Any user who is a member of this role has the ability to manage the administrative tasks related to her database (unlike Oracle, in which one DBA manages the administrative tasks for all tablespaces). These tasks include:

- Managing database access.
- Changing database options (read-only, single user, and so on).
- Backing up and restoring the database contents.
- Granting and revoking database permissions.
- Creating and dropping database objects.

Members of the **db_owner** role have permissions to do anything within their database. Most rights assigned to this role are separated into several fixed database roles, or can be granted to database users. It is not necessary to have **sysadmin** server-wide privileges to have **db_owner** privileges in a database.

Installing and Configuring Microsoft SQL Server

With an understanding of the basic structural differences between Oracle and SQL Server, you are ready to perform the first step in the migration process. SQL Server Query Analyzer should be used to run these scripts:

1. Use Windows NT software–based RAID or hardware-based RAID level 5 to create a logical drive large enough to hold all of your data. An estimate of space can be calculated by adding the total file space used by the Oracle system, temporary, and application tablespaces.

2. Create a second logical drive for holding transaction logs by using Windows NT software–based RAID or hardware-based RAID level 1. The size of this drive should be at least as large as the sum of the size of the online redo and rollback segment tablespace(s).

3. Use SQL Server Enterprise Manager to create a database with the same name as the Oracle application's tablespace. (The sample application uses the database name **USER_DB**.) Specify the file locations to coincide with the disks you created in steps 1 and 2 for the data and transaction logs, respectively. If you are using multiple Oracle tablespaces, it is not necessary or even recommended that you create multiple SQL Server databases. RAID will distribute the data for you.

4. Create the SQL Server login accounts:

```
USE MASTER
EXEC SP_ADDLOGIN STUDENT_ADMIN, STUDENT_ADMIN
EXEC SP_ADDLOGIN DEPT_ADMIN, DEPT_ADMIN
EXEC SP_ADDLOGIN ENDUSER1, ENDUSER1
GO
```

5. Add the roles to the database:

```
USE USER_DB
EXEC SP_ADDROLE DATA_ADMIN
EXEC SP_ADDROLE USER_LOGON
GO
```

6. Grant permissions to the roles:

```
GRANT CREATE TABLE, CREATE TRIGGER, CREATE VIEW,
CREATE PROCEDURE TO DATA_ADMIN
GO
```

7. Add the login accounts as database user accounts:

```
EXEC SP_ADDUSER ENDUSER1, ENDUSER1, USER_LOGON
EXEC SP_ADDUSER DEPT_ADMIN, DEPT_ADMIN, DATA_ADMIN
EXEC SP_ADDUSER STUDENT_ADMIN, STUDENT_ADMIN, DATA_ADMIN
GO
```

The illustration shows the SQL Server and Oracle environments after this process is completed.

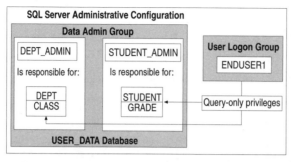

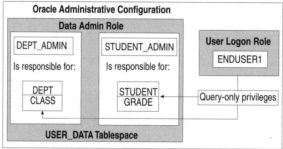

Defining Database Objects

Oracle database objects (tables, views, and indexes) can be migrated to Microsoft SQL Server easily because each RDBMS closely follows the SQL-92 standard that regards object definitions. Converting Oracle SQL table, index, and view definitions to SQL Server table, index, and view definitions requires relatively simple syntax changes. The table highlights some differences in database objects between Oracle and Microsoft SQL Server.

Category	Microsoft SQL Server	Oracle
Number of columns	1024	254
Row size	8060 bytes, plus 16 bytes to point to each **text** or **image** column	Unlimited (only one long or long raw allowed per row)
Maximum number of rows	Unlimited	Unlimited
BLOB type storage	16-byte pointer stored with row. Data stored on other data pages.	One long or long raw per table. Must be at end of row. Data stored on same block(s) with row.
Clustered table indexes	One per table	One per table (index-organized tables)

(continued)

Category	Microsoft SQL Server	Oracle
Nonclustered table indexes	249 per table	Unlimited
Maximum number of indexed columns in single index	16	16
Maximum length of column values within of an index	900 bytes	½ block
Table naming convention	[[[server.]database.]owner.] table_name	[schema.]table_name
View naming convention	[[[server.]database.]owner.] table_name	[schema.]table_name
Index naming convention	[[[server.]database.]owner.] table_name	[schema.]table_name

It is assumed that you are starting with an Oracle SQL script or program that is used to create your database objects. Simply copy this script or program and make the following modifications. Each change is discussed throughout the rest of this section. The examples have been taken from the sample application scripts Oratable.sql and Sstable.sql:

1. Ensure database object identifiers comply to Microsoft SQL Server naming conventions. You may need to change only the names of indexes.

2. Modify the data storage parameters to work with SQL Server. If you are using RAID, no storage parameters are required.

3. Modify Oracle constraint definitions to work in SQL Server. Create triggers to support the foreign key DELETE CASCADE statement if necessary. If tables cross databases, use triggers to enforce foreign key relationships.

4. Modify the CREATE INDEX statements to take advantage of clustered indexes.

5. Use Data Transformation Services to create new CREATE TABLE statements. Review the statements, taking note of how Oracle data types are mapped to SQL Server data types.

6. Remove any CREATE SEQUENCE statements. Replace the use of sequences with identity columns in CREATE TABLE or ALTER TABLE statements.

7. Modify CREATE VIEW statements if necessary.

8. Remove any reference to synonyms.

9. Evaluate the use of Microsoft SQL Server temporary tables and their usefulness in your application.

10. Change any Oracle CREATE TABLE...AS SELECT commands to SQL Server SELECT...INTO statements.

11. Evaluate the potential use of user-defined rules, data types, and defaults.

Database Object Identifiers

The following chart compares how Oracle and Microsoft SQL Server handle object identifiers. In most cases, you do not need to change the names of objects when migrating to SQL Server.

Oracle	Microsoft SQL Server
1-30 characters in length. Database names: up to 8 characters long. Database link names: up to 128 characters long.	1-128 Unicode characters in length. Temporary table names: up to 116 characters.
Identifier names must begin with an alphabetic character and contain alphanumeric characters, or the characters _, $, and #.	Identifier names can begin with an alphanumeric character, or an _, and they can contain virtually any character. If the identifier begins with a space, or contains characters other than _, @, #, or $, you must use [ ] (delimiters) around the identifier name. If an object begins with: @ it is a local variable. # it is a local temporary object. ## it is a global temporary object.
Tablespace names must be unique.	Database names must be unique.
Identifier names must be unique within user accounts (schemas).	Identifier names must be unique within database user accounts.
Column names must be unique within tables and views.	Column names must be unique within tables and views.
Index names must be unique within a users schema.	Index names must be unique within database table names.

Qualifying Table Names

When accessing tables that exist in your Oracle user account, the table can be selected simply by its unqualified name. Accessing tables in other Oracle schemas requires that the schema name be prefixed to the table name with a single period (.). Oracle synonyms can provide additional location transparency.

Microsoft SQL Server uses a different convention when it references tables. Because one SQL Server login account can create a table by the same name in multiple databases, the following convention is used to access tables and views: [[*database_name.*]*owner_name.*]*table_name*

Accessing a table in...	Oracle	Microsoft SQL Server
Your user account	SELECT * FROM **STUDENT**	SELECT * FROM **USER_DB.STUDENT_ ADMIN.STUDENT**

Accessing a table in...	Oracle	Microsoft SQL Server
Other schema	SELECT * FROM STUDENT_ADMIN.STUDENT	SELECT * FROM OTHER_DB.STUDENT_ADMIN.STUDENT

Here are guidelines for naming Microsoft SQL Server tables and views:

- Using the database name and username is optional. When a table is referenced only by name (for example, **STUDENT**), SQL Server searches for that table in the current user's account in the current database. If it does not find one, it looks for an object of the same name owned by the reserved username of **dbo** in the database. Table names must be unique within a user's account within a database.

- The same SQL Server login account can own tables with the same name in multiple databases. For example, the **ENDUSER1** account owns the following database objects: **USER_DB.ENDUSER1.STUDENT** and **OTHER_DB.ENDUSER1.STUDENT**. The qualifier is the database username, not the SQL Server login name, because they do not have to be the same.

At the same time, other users in these databases might own objects by the same name:

- **USER_DB.DBO.STUDENT**

- **USER_DB.DEPT_ADMIN.STUDENT**

- **USER_DB.STUDENT_ADMIN.STUDENT**

- **OTHER_DB.DBO.STUDENT**

Therefore, it is recommended that you include the owner name as part of the reference to a database object. If the application has multiple databases, it is recommended that the database name also is included as part of the reference. If the query spans multiple servers, include the server name.

- Every connection to SQL Server has a current database context, set at login time with the USE statement. For example, assume the following scenario:

  A user, using the **ENDUSER1** account, is logged in to the **USER_DB** database. The user requests the **STUDENT** table. SQL Server searches for the table **ENDUSER1.STUDENT**. If the table is found, SQL Server performs the requested database operation on **USER_DB.ENDUSER1.STUDENT**. If the table is not found in the **ENDUSER1** database account, SQL Server searches for **USER_DB.DBO.STUDENT** in the **dbo** account for that database. If the table is still not found, SQL Server returns an error message indicating the table does not exist.

- If another user, for example **DEPT_ADMIN**, owns the table, the table name must be prefixed with the database user's name (**DEPT_ADMIN.STUDENT**). Otherwise, the database name defaults to the database that is currently in context.

- If the referenced table exists in another database, the database name must be used as part of the reference. For example, to access the **STUDENT** table owned by **ENDUSER1** in the **OTHERDB** database, use **OTHER_DB.ENDUSER1.STUDENT**.

The object's owner can be omitted by separating the database and table name by two periods. For example, if an application references **STUDENT_DB..STUDENT**, SQL Server searches as follows:

1. **STUDENT_DB.***current_user***.STUDENT**

2. **STUDENT_DB.DBO.STUDENT**

If the application uses only a single database at a time, omitting the database name from an object reference makes it easy to use the application with another database. All object references implicitly access the database that is currently being used. This is useful when you want to maintain a test database and a production database on the same server.

Creating Tables

Because Oracle and SQL Server support SQL-92 entry-level conventions for identifying RDBMS objects, the CREATE TABLE syntax is similar.

Oracle	Microsoft SQL Server
CREATE TABLE [*schema.*]*table_name* ({*col_name column_properties* [*default_expression*] [*constraint* [*constraint* [*...constraint*]]]∣ [[,] *constraint*]} [[,] {*next_col_name* ∣ *next_constraint*}...]) [Oracle Specific Data Storage Parameters]	CREATE TABLE [*server.*][*database.*][*owner.*] *table_name* ({*col_name column_properties*[*constraint* [*constraint* [*...constraint*]]]∣ [[,] *constraint*]} [[,] {*next_col_name* ∣ *next_constraint*}...]) [ON *filegroup_name*]

Oracle database object names are not case-sensitive. In Microsoft SQL Server, database object names can be case-sensitive, depending on the installation options selected.

When SQL Server is first set up, the default sort order is dictionary order, case-insensitive. (This can be configured differently using SQL Server Setup.) Because Oracle object names are always unique, you should not have any problems migrating the database objects to SQL Server. It is recommended that all table and column names in both Oracle and SQL Server be uppercase to avoid problems if a user installs on a case-sensitive SQL Server.

Table and Index Storage Parameters

With Microsoft SQL Server, using RAID usually simplifies the placement of database objects. A SQL Server clustered index is integrated into the structure of the table, like an Oracle index-organized table.

Oracle	Microsoft SQL Server

CREATE TABLE DEPT_ADMIN.DEPT (
DEPT   **VARCHAR2**(4) NOT NULL,
DNAME   **VARCHAR2**(30) NOT NULL,
CONSTRAINT DEPT_DEPT_PK
              PRIMARY KEY (DEPT)
USING INDEX TABLESPACE USER_DATA
PCTFREE 0 STORAGE (INITIAL 10K NEXT
10K
MINEXTENTS 1 MAXEXTENTS
UNLIMITED),
CONSTRAINT DEPT_DNAME_UNIQUE
              UNIQUE (DNAME)
USING INDEX TABLESPACE USER_DATA
PCTFREE 0 STORAGE (INITIAL 10K NEXT
10K
MINEXTENTS 1 MAXEXTENTS
UNLIMITED)
)
PCTFREE 10   PCTUSED 40
TABLESPACE USER_DATA
STORAGE (INITIAL 10K NEXT 10K
MINEXTENTS 1 MAXEXTENTS UNLIMITED
FREELISTS 1)
	CREATE TABLE
	USER_DB.DEPT_ADMIN.DEPT (
	DEPT **VARCHAR**(4) NOT NULL,
	DNAME **VARCHAR**(30) NOT NULL,
	CONSTRAINT DEPT_DEPT_PK
	              PRIMARY KEY **CLUSTERED** (DEPT),
	CONSTRAINT DEPT_DNAME_UNIQUE
	              UNIQUE **NONCLUSTERED** (DNAME)
	)

Creating Tables with SELECT Statements

Using Oracle, a table can be created with any valid SELECT command. Microsoft SQL Server provides the same functionality with different syntax.

Oracle	Microsoft SQL Server
CREATE TABLE **STUDENTBACKUP** AS SELECT * FROM **STUDENT**	SELECT * INTO **STUDENTBACKUP** FROM **STUDENT**

SELECT...INTO does not work unless the database to which this is applied has the database configuration option **select into/bulkcopy** set to **true**. (The database owner can set this option using SQL Server Enterprise Manager or the Transact-SQL **sp_dboption** system stored procedure.) Use the **sp_helpdb** system stored procedure to check the status of the database. If **select into/bulkcopy** is not set to **true**, you can still use a SELECT statement to copy into a temporary table:

```
SELECT * INTO #student_backup FROM user_db.student_admin.student
```

When new tables are created using SELECT.. INTO statements, referential integrity definitions are not transferred to the new table.

The need to have the **select into/bulkcopy** option set to **true** may complicate the migration process. If you must copy data into tables by using a SELECT statement, create the table first, and then use the INSERT INTO...SELECT statement to load the table. The syntax is the same for Oracle and SQL Server, and does not require that any database option be set.

Views

The syntax used to create views in Microsoft SQL Server is similar to that of Oracle.

Oracle	Microsoft SQL Server
CREATE [OR REPLACE] [FORCE | NOFORCE] VIEW [*schema.*]*view_name* [(*column_name* [, *column_name*]...)] AS *select_statement* [WITH CHECK OPTION [CONSTRAINT *name*]] [WITH READ ONLY]	CREATE VIEW [*owner.*]*view_name* [(*column_name* [, *column_name*]...)] [WITH ENCRYPTION] AS *select_statement* [WITH CHECK OPTION]

SQL Server views require that the tables exist and that the view owner has privileges to access the requested tables(s) specified in the SELECT statement (similar to the Oracle FORCE option).

By default, data modification statements on views are not checked to determine whether the rows affected are within the scope of the view. To check all modifications, use the WITH CHECK OPTION. The primary difference between the WITH CHECK OPTION is that Oracle defines it as a constraint, while SQL Server does not. Otherwise, it functions the same in both.

Oracle provides a WITH READ ONLY option when defining views. SQL Server applications can achieve the same result by granting only SELECT permission to the users of the view.

Both SQL Server and Oracle views support derived columns, using arithmetic expressions, functions, and constant expressions. Some of the specific SQL Server differences are:

- Data modification statements (INSERT or UPDATE) are allowed on multitable views if the data modification statement affects only one base table. Data modification statements cannot be used on more than one table in a single statement.

- READTEXT or WRITETEXT cannot be used on **text** or **image** columns in views.

- ORDER BY, COMPUTE, FOR BROWSE, or COMPUTE BY clauses cannot be used.

- The INTO keyword cannot be used in a view.

When a view is defined with an outer join and is queried with a qualification on a column from the inner table of the outer join, the results from SQL Server and Oracle can differ. In most cases, Oracle views are easily translated into SQL Server views.

Oracle	Microsoft SQL Server
CREATE VIEW STUDENT_ADMIN.STUDENT_GPA (SSN, GPA) AS SELECT SSN, ROUND(AVG(**DECODE(grade** ,**'A'**, **4** ,**'A+'**, **4.3** ,**'A-'**, **3.7** ,**'B'**, **3** ,**'B+'**, **3.3** ,**'B-'**, **2.7** ,**'C'**, **2** ,**'C+'**, **2.3** ,**'C-'**, **1.7** ,**'D'**, **1** ,**'D+'**, **1.3** ,**'D-'**, **0.7** ,**0**))**,2**) FROM STUDENT_ADMIN.GRADE GROUP BY SSN	CREATE VIEW STUDENT_ADMIN.STUDENT_GPA (SSN, GPA) AS SELECT SSN, ROUND(AVG(**CASE grade** **WHEN 'A' THEN 4** **WHEN 'A+' THEN 4.3** **WHEN 'A-' THEN 3.7** **WHEN 'B' THEN 3** **WHEN 'B+' THEN 3.3** **WHEN 'B-' THEN 2.7** **WHEN 'C' THEN 2** **WHEN 'C+' THEN 2.3** **WHEN 'C-' THEN 1.7** **WHEN 'D' THEN 1** **WHEN 'D+' THEN 1.3** **WHEN 'D-' THEN 0.7** **ELSE 0** **END**)**,2**) FROM STUDENT_ADMIN.GRADE GROUP BY SSN

Indexes

Microsoft SQL Server offers clustered and nonclustered index structures. These indexes are made up of pages that form a branching structure known as a B-tree (similar to the Oracle B-tree index structure). The starting page (root level) specifies ranges of values within the table. Each range on the root-level page points to another page (decision node), which contains a more limited range of values for the table. In turn, these decision nodes can point to other decision nodes, further narrowing the search range. The final level in the branching structure is called the leaf level.

B-Tree Architecture

Clustered Indexes

Clustered indexes are implemented in Oracle as index-organized tables. A clustered index is an index that has been physically merged with a table. The table and index share the same storage area. The clustered index physically rearranges the rows of data in indexed order, forming the intermediate decision nodes. The leaf pages of the index contain the actual table data. This architecture permits only one clustered index per table. Microsoft SQL Server automatically creates a clustered index for the table whenever a PRIMARY KEY or UNIQUE constraint is placed on the table. Clustered indexes are useful for:

- Primary keys.

- Columns that are not updated.

- Queries that return a range of values, using operators such as BETWEEN, >, >=, <, and <=, for example:

```
SELECT * FROM STUDENT WHERE GRAD_DATE
BETWEEN '1/1/97' AND '12/31/97'
```

- Queries that return large result sets:

```
SELECT * FROM STUDENT WHERE LNAME = 'SMITH'
```

- Columns that are used in sort operations (ORDER BY, GROUP BY).

  For example, on the **STUDENT** table, it might be helpful to include a nonclustered index on the primary key of **ssn**, and a clustered index could be created on **lname, fname**, (last name, first name), because this is the way students are often grouped.

- Distributing update activity in a table to avoid *hot spots*. Hot spots are often caused by multiple users inserting into a table with an ascending key. This application scenario is usually addressed by row-level locking.

Dropping and re-creating a clustered index is a common technique for reorganizing a table in SQL Server. It is an easy way to ensure that data pages are contiguous on disk and to reestablish some free space in the table. This is similar to exporting, dropping, and importing a table in Oracle.

A SQL Server clustered index is not at all like an Oracle cluster. An Oracle cluster is a physical grouping of two or more tables that share the same data blocks and use common columns as a cluster key. SQL Server does not have a structure similar to an Oracle cluster.

As a general rule, defining a clustered index on a table improves SQL Server performance and space management. If you do not know the query or update patterns for a given table, you can create the clustered index on the primary key.

The table shows an excerpt from the sample application source code. Note the use of the SQL Server clustered index.

Oracle	Microsoft SQL Server

CREATE TABLE STUDENT_ADMIN.GRADE (
 SSN   CHAR(9) NOT NULL,
 CCODE VARCHAR2(4) NOT NULL,
 GRADE VARCHAR2(2) NULL,
 CONSTRAINT   GRADE_SSN_CCODE_PK
    PRIMARY KEY (SSN, CCODE)
 CONSTRAINT GRADE_SSN_FK
     FOREIGN KEY (SSN) REFERENCES
     STUDENT_ADMIN.STUDENT (SSN),
 CONSTRAINT GRADE_CCODE_FK
     FOREIGN KEY (CCODE) REFERENCES
     DEPT_ADMIN.CLASS (CCODE)
)
	CREATE TABLE STUDENT_ADMIN.GRADE (
	 SSN CHAR(9) NOT NULL,
	 CCODE VARCHAR(4) NOT NULL,
	 GRADE VARCHAR(2) NULL,
	 CONSTRAINT
	   GRADE_SSN_CCODE_PK
	   PRIMARY KEY **CLUSTERED** (SSN,
	 CCODE),
	 CONSTRAINT GRADE_SSN_FK
	    FOREIGN KEY (SSN) REFERENCES
	    STUDENT_ADMIN.STUDENT (SSN),
	 CONSTRAINT GRADE_CCODE_FK
	    FOREIGN KEY (CCODE) REFERENCES
	    DEPT_ADMIN.CLASS (CCODE)
	)

Nonclustered Indexes

In nonclustered indexes, the index data and the table data are physically separate, and the rows in the table are not stored in the order of the index. You can move Oracle index definitions to Microsoft SQL Server nonclustered index definitions (as shown in the following example). For performance reasons, however, you might want to choose one of the indexes of a given table and create it as a clustered index.

Oracle	Microsoft SQL Server

CREATE INDEX
STUDENT_ADMIN.STUDENT_
    MAJOR_IDX
ON STUDENT_ADMIN.STUDENT   (MAJOR)
TABLESPACE USER_DATA
PCTFREE 0
STORAGE (INITIAL 10K NEXT 10K
    MINEXTENTS 1 MAXEXTENTS
    UNLIMITED)
	CREATE **NONCLUSTERED** INDEX
	STUDENT_MAJOR_IDX
	ON **USER_DB.**STUDENT_
	    ADMIN.STUDENT (MAJOR)

Index Syntax and Naming

In Oracle, an index name is unique within a user account. In Microsoft SQL Server, an index name must be unique within a table name, but it does not have to be unique within a user account or database. Therefore, when creating or dropping an index in SQL Server, you must specify both the table name and the index name. Additionally, the SQL Server DROP INDEX statement can drop multiple indexes at one time.

Oracle	Microsoft SQL Server

CREATE [UNIQUE] INDEX [*schema*].*index_name*
    ON [*schema*.]*table_name* (*column_name*
    [, *column_name*]...)
[INITRANS *n*]
[MAXTRANS *n*]
[TABLESPACE *tablespace_name*]
[STORAGE *storage_parameters*]
[PCTFREE *n*]
[NOSORT]
 	
DROP INDEX ABC;
	CREATE [UNIQUE] [CLUSTERED |
	NONCLUSTERED]
	    INDEX index_name ON table (column [,...*n*])
	[WITH
	    [PAD_INDEX]
	    [[,] FILLFACTOR = *fillfactor*]
	    [[,] IGNORE_DUP_KEY]
	    [[,] DROP_EXISTING]
	    [[,] STATISTICS_NORECOMPUTE]
	]
	[ON *filegroup*]
	
	  DROP INDEX
	  USER_DB.STUDENT.DEMO_IDX,
	  USER_DB.GRADE.DEMO_IDX

Index Data Storage Parameters

The FILLFACTOR option in Microsoft SQL Server functions in much the same way as the PCTFREE variable does in Oracle. As tables grow in size, index pages split to accommodate new data. The index must reorganize itself to accommodate new data values. The fill factor percentage is used only when the index is created, and it is not maintained afterwards.

The FILLFACTOR option (values are 0 through 100) controls how much space is left on an index page when the index is initially created. The default fill factor of 0 is used if none is specified—this will completely fill index leaf pages and leave space on each decision node page for at least one entry (two for nonunique clustered indexes).

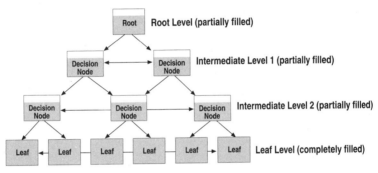

Fill Factor of 0

A lower fill factor value initially reduces the splitting of index pages and increases the number of levels in the B-tree index structure. A higher fill factor value uses index page space more efficiently, requires fewer disk I/Os to access index data, and reduces the number of levels in the B-tree index structure.

The PAD_INDEX option specifies that the fill factor setting be applied to the decision node pages as well as to the data pages in the index.

While it may be necessary to adjust the PCTFREE parameter for optimal performance in Oracle, it is seldom necessary to include the FILLFACTOR option in a CREATE INDEX statement. The fill factor is provided for fine-tuning performance. It is useful only when creating a new index on a table with existing data, and then it is useful only when you can accurately predict future changes in that data.

If you have set PCTFREE to 0 for your Oracle indexes, consider using a fill factor of 100. This is used when there will be no inserts or updates occurring in the table (a read-only table). When fill factor is set to 100, SQL Server creates indexes with each page 100 percent full.

Ignoring Duplicate Keys

With both Oracle and Microsoft SQL Server, users cannot insert duplicate values for a uniquely indexed column or columns. An attempt to do so generates an error message. Nevertheless, SQL Server lets the developer choose how the INSERT or UPDATE statement will respond to the error.

If IGNORE_DUP_KEY was specified in the CREATE INDEX statement, and an INSERT or UPDATE statement that creates a duplicate key is executed, SQL Server issues a warning message and ignores (does not insert) the duplicate row. If IGNORE_DUP_KEY was not specified for the index, SQL Server issues an error message and rolls back the entire INSERT statement. For more information about these options, see SQL Server Books Online.

Using Temporary Tables

An Oracle application might have to create tables that exist for short periods. The application must ensure that all tables created for this purpose are dropped at some point. If the application fails to do this, tablespaces can quickly become cluttered and unmanageable.

Microsoft SQL Server provides temporary table database objects, which are created for just such a purpose. These tables are always created in the **tempdb** database. The table name determines how long they reside within the **tempdb** database.

Table name	Description
#table_name	This local temporary table only exists for the duration of a user session or the procedure that created it. It is automatically dropped when the user logs off or the procedure that created the table completes. These tables cannot be shared between multiple users. No other database users can access this table. Permissions cannot be granted or revoked on this table.
##table_name	This global temporary table also typically exists for the duration of a user session or procedure that created it. This table can be shared among multiple users. It is automatically dropped when the last user session referencing it disconnects. All other database users can access this table. Permissions cannot be granted or revoked on this table.

Indexes can be defined for temporary tables. Views can be defined only on tables explicitly created in **tempdb** without the # or ## prefix. The following example shows the creation of a temporary table and its associated index. When the user exits, the table and index are automatically dropped.

```
SELECT SUM(ISNULL(TUITION_PAID,0)) SUM_PAID, MAJOR INTO #SUM_STUDENT
FROM USER_DB.STUDENT_ADMIN.STUDENT GROUP BY MAJOR

CREATE UNIQUE INDEX SUM STUDENT IDX ON #SUM STUDENT (MAJOR)
```

You may find that the benefits associated with using temporary tables justify a revision in your program code.

Data Types

Microsoft SQL Server has a more robust selection of data types than Oracle. There are many possible conversions between the Oracle and SQL Server data types. It is recommended that you use the DTS Wizard to automate the creation of the new CREATE TABLE statements. You can then modify these statements as necessary.

Oracle	Microsoft SQL Server
CHAR	**char** is recommended. **char** type columns are accessed somewhat faster than **varchar** columns because they use a fixed storage length.
VARCHAR2 and LONG	**varchar** or **text**. (If the length of the data values in your Oracle column is 8000 bytes of less, use **varchar**; otherwise, you must use **text**.)
RAW and LONG RAW	**varbinary** or **image**. (If the length of the data values in your Oracle column is 8000 bytes of less, use **varbinary**; otherwise, you must use **image**.)
NUMBER	If integer between 1 and 255, use **tinyint**. If integer between -32768 and 32767, use **smallint**. If integer between -2,147,483,648 and 2,147,483,647 use **int**. If you require a float type number, use **numeric** (has precision and scale). **Note**: Do not use **float** or **real**, because rounding may occur (Oracle NUMBER and SQL Server **numeric** do not round). If you are not sure, use **numeric**; it most closely resembles Oracle NUMBER data type.
DATE	**datetime**.
ROWID	Use the **identity** column type.
CURRVAL, NEXTVAL	Use the **identity** column type, and @@IDENTITY, IDENT_SEED(), and IDENT_INCR() functions.
SYSDATE	GETDATE().
USER	USER.

Using Unicode Data

The Unicode specification defines a single encoding scheme for practically all characters widely used in businesses around the world. All computers consistently translate the bit patterns in Unicode data into characters using the single Unicode specification. This ensures that the same bit pattern is always converted to the same character on all computers. Data can be freely transferred from one database or computer to another without concern that the receiving system will correctly translate the bit patterns into characters.

One problem with data types that use 1 byte to encode each character is that the data type can represent only 256 different characters. This forces multiple encoding specifications (or code pages) for different alphabets. It is also impossible to handle systems such as the Japanese Kanji or Korean Hangul alphabets that have thousands of characters.

Microsoft SQL Server translates the bit patterns in **char**, **varchar**, and **text** columns to characters using the definitions in the code page installed with SQL Server. Client computers use the code page installed with the operating system to interpret character bit patterns. There are many different code pages. Some characters appear on some code pages, but not on others. Some characters are defined with one bit pattern on some code pages, and with a different bit pattern on other code pages. When you build international systems that must handle different languages, it becomes difficult to pick code pages for all the computers that meet the language requirements of multiple countries. It is also difficult to ensure that every computer performs the correct translations when interfacing with a system that uses a different code page.

The Unicode specification addresses this problem by using 2 bytes to encode each character. There are enough different patterns (65,536) in 2 bytes for a single specification covering the most common business languages. Because all Unicode systems consistently use the same bit patterns to represent all characters, there is no problem with characters being converted incorrectly when moving from one system to another.

In SQL Server, **nchar**, **nvarchar**, and **ntext** data types support Unicode data. For more information about SQL Server data types, see SQL Server Books Online.

User-defined Data Types

User-defined data types can be created for the **model** database or for a single user database. If the user-defined data type is defined for **model**, that data type is available to all new user databases created from that point forward. The user-defined data type is defined with the **sp_addtype** system stored procedure. For more information, see SQL Server Books Online.

You can use a user-defined data type in the CREATE TABLE and ALTER TABLE statements, and bind defaults and rules to it. If nullability is explicitly defined when the user-defined data type is used during table creation, it takes precedence over the nullability defined when the data type was created.

This example shows how to create a user-defined data type. The arguments are the user-type name, data type, and nullability:

```
sp_addtype gender_type, 'varchar(1)', 'not null'
go
```

This capability might initially appear to solve the problem of migrating Oracle table creation scripts to SQL Server. For example, it is quite easy to add the Oracle DATE data type:

```
sp_addtype date, datetime
```

This does not work with data types that require variable sizes, such as the Oracle data type NUMBER. An error message is returned indicating that a length must also be specified:

```
sp_addtype varchar2, varchar
Go
Msg 15091, Level 16, State 1
You must specify a length with this physical type.
```

Microsoft timestamp Columns

The **timestamp** columns enable BROWSE-mode updates and make cursor update operations more efficient. The **timestamp** is a data type that is automatically updated every time a row containing a **timestamp** column is inserted or updated.

Values in **timestamp** columns are not stored as an actual date or time, but are stored as **binary(8)** or **varbinary(8)**, which indicates the sequence of events on rows in the table. A table can have only one **timestamp** column.

For more information, see SQL Server Books Online.

Object-level Permissions

Microsoft SQL Server object privileges can be granted to, denied from, and revoked from other database users, database groups, and the **public** role. SQL Server does not allow an object owner to grant ALTER TABLE and CREATE INDEX privileges for the object as Oracle does. Those privileges must remain with the object owner.

The GRANT statement creates an entry in the security system that allows a user in the current database to work with data in the current database or to execute specific Transact-SQL statements. The syntax of the GRANT statement is identical in Oracle and SQL Server.

The DENY statement creates an entry in the security system that denies a permission from a security account in the current database and prevents the security account from inheriting the permission through its group or role memberships. Oracle does not have a DENY statement. The REVOKE statement removes a previously granted or denied permission from a user in the current database.

Oracle	Microsoft SQL Server
GRANT {ALL [PRIVILEGES][*column_list*] | *permission_list* [*column_list*]} ON {*table_name* [(*column_list*)]] | *view_name* [(*column_list*)]] | *stored_procedure_name*} TO {PUBLIC | *name_list* } [WITH GRANT OPTION]	GRANT {ALL [PRIVILEGES] | *permission*[,...*n*]} { [(*column*[,...*n*])] ON {*table* | *view*} | ON {*table* | *view*}[(*column*[,...*n*])] | ON {*stored_procedure* | *extended_procedure*} } TO *security_account*[,...*n*] [WITH GRANT OPTION] [AS {*group* | *role*}] REVOKE [GRANT OPTION FOR] {ALL [PRIVILEGES] | *permission*[,...*n*]} { [(*column*[,...*n*])] ON {*table* | *view*} | ON {*table* | *view*}[(*column*[,...*n*])] | {*stored_procedure* | *extended_procedure*} } {TO | FROM} *security_account*[,...*n*] [CASCADE] [AS {*group* | *role*}] DENY {ALL [PRIVILEGES] | permission[,...*n*]} { [(*column*[,...*n*])] ON {*table* | *view*} | ON {table | view}[(*column*[,...*n*])] | ON {*stored_procedure* | *extended_procedure*} } TO *security_account*[,...*n*] [CASCADE]

For more information about object-level permissions, see SQL Server Books Online.

In Oracle, the REFERENCES privilege can be granted only to a user. SQL Server allows the REFERENCES privilege to be granted to both database users and database groups. The INSERT, UPDATE, DELETE, and SELECT privileges are granted in the same way in both Oracle and SQL Server.

Enforcing Data Integrity and Business Rules

Enforcing data integrity ensures the quality of the data in the database. Two important steps when planning tables are identifying valid values for a column and deciding how to enforce the integrity of the data in the column. Data integrity falls into four categories, and is enforced in various ways.

Integrity type	How enforced
Entity integrity	PRIMARY KEY constraint UNIQUE constraint IDENTITY property
Domain integrity	Domain DEFAULT definition FOREIGN KEY constraint CHECK constraint Nullability
Referential integrity	Domain DEFAULT definition FOREIGN KEY constraint CHECK constraint Nullability
User-defined integrity	All column- and table-level constraints in CREATE TABLE Stored procedures Triggers

Entity Integrity

Entity integrity defines a row as a unique entity for a particular table. Entity integrity enforces the integrity of the identifier column(s) or the primary key of a table through indexes, UNIQUE constraints, PRIMARY KEY constraints, or IDENTITY properties.

Naming Constraints

You should always name your constraints explicitly. If you do not, Oracle and Microsoft SQL Server will use different naming conventions to name the constraint implicitly. These differences in naming can complicate your migration process unnecessarily. The discrepancy appears when dropping or disabling constraints, because constraints must be dropped by name. The syntax for explicitly naming constraints is the same for Oracle and SQL Server:

```
CONSTRAINT constraint_name
```

Primary Keys and Unique Columns

The SQL-92 standard requires that all values in a primary key be unique and that the column not allow null values. Both Oracle and Microsoft SQL Server enforce uniqueness by automatically creating unique indexes whenever a PRIMARY KEY or UNIQUE constraint is defined. Additionally, primary key columns are automatically defined as NOT NULL. Only one primary key is allowed per table.

A SQL Server clustered index is created by default for a primary key, though a nonclustered index can be requested. The Oracle index on primary keys can be removed by either dropping or disabling the constraint, whereas the SQL Server index can be removed only by dropping the constraint.

In either RDBMS, alternate keys can be defined with a UNIQUE constraint. Multiple UNIQUE constraints can be defined on any table. UNIQUE constraint columns are nullable. In SQL Server, a nonclustered index is created by default, unless otherwise specified.

When migrating your application, it is important to note that SQL Server allows only one row to contain the value NULL for the complete unique key (single or multiple column index), and Oracle allows any number of rows to contain the value NULL for the complete unique key.

Oracle	Microsoft SQL Server

CREATE TABLE DEPT_ADMIN.DEPT (DEPT **VARCHAR2**(4) NOT NULL, DNAME **VARCHAR2**(30) NOT NULL, CONSTRAINT DEPT_DEPT_PK
    PRIMARY KEY (DEPT)
    USING INDEX TABLESPACE
    USER_DATA
    PCTFREE 0 STORAGE (
    INITIAL 10K NEXT 10K
    MINEXTENTS 1 MAXEXTENTS
    UNLIMITED),
CONSTRAINT DEPT_DNAME_UNIQUE
    UNIQUE (DNAME)
    USING INDEX TABLESPACE USER_DATA
    PCTFREE 0 STORAGE (
    INITIAL 10K NEXT 10K
    MINEXTENTS 1 MAXEXTENTS
    UNLIMITED)
)
	CREATE TABLE **USER_DB**.DEPT_ADMIN.DEPT (DEPT **VARCHAR**(4) NOT NULL, DNAME **VARCHAR**(30) NOT NULL, CONSTRAINT DEPT_DEPT_PK
	    PRIMARY KEY CLUSTERED (DEPT),
	CONSTRAINT DEPT_DNAME_UNIQUE
	    UNIQUE NONCLUSTERED (DNAME)
	)

Adding and Removing Constraints

Disabling constraints can improve database performance and streamline the data replication process. For example, when you rebuild or replicate table data at a remote site, you do not have to repeat constraint checks, because the integrity of the data was checked when it was originally entered into the table. You can program an Oracle application to disable and enable constraints (except for PRIMARY KEY and UNIQUE). You can accomplish this in Microsoft SQL Server using the CHECK and WITH NOCHECK options with the ALTER TABLE statement.

This illustration shows a comparison of this process.

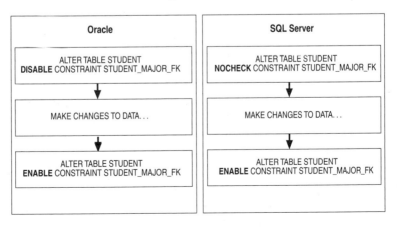

With SQL Server, you can defer all of the table constraints by using the ALL keyword with the NOCHECK clause.

If your Oracle application uses the CASCADE option to disable or drop PRIMARY KEY or UNIQUE constraints, you may need to rewrite some code because the CASCADE option disables or drops both the parent and any related child integrity constraints.

This is an example of the syntax:

```
DROP CONSTRAINT DEPT_DEPT_PK CASCADE
```

The SQL Server application must be modified to first drop the child constraints and then the parent constraints. For example, in order to drop the PRIMARY KEY constraint on the **DEPT** table, the foreign keys for the columns **STUDENT.MAJOR** and **CLASS.DEPT** must be dropped. This is an example of the syntax:

```
ALTER TABLE STUDENT
DROP CONSTRAINT STUDENT_MAJOR_FK
ALTER TABLE CLASS
DROP CONSTRAINT CLASS_DEPT_FK
ALTER TABLE DEPT
DROP CONSTRAINT DEPT_DEPT_PK
```

The ALTER TABLE syntax that adds and drops constraints is almost identical for Oracle and SQL Server.

Generating Sequential Numeric Values

If your Oracle application uses SEQUENCEs, it can be altered easily to take advantage of the Microsoft SQL Server IDENTITY property.

Category	Microsoft SQL Server IDENTITY
Syntax	CREATE TABLE new_employees (Empid int IDENTITY (1,1), Employee_Name varchar(60), CONSTRAINT Emp_PK PRIMARY KEY (Empid)) If increment interval is 5: CREATE TABLE new_employees (Empid int IDENTITY (1,5), Employee_Name varchar(60), CONSTRAINT Emp_PK PRIMARY KEY (Empid))
Identity columns per table	One
Null values allowed	No
Use of default constraints, values	Cannot be used.

(continued)

Category	Microsoft SQL Server IDENTITY
Enforcing uniqueness	Yes
Querying for maximum current identity number after an INSERT, SELECT INTO, or bulk copy statement completes	@@IDENTITY (function)
Returns the seed value specified during the creation of an identity column	IDENT_SEED('*table_name*')
Returns the increment value specified during the creation of an identity column	IDENT_INCR('*table_name*')
SELECT syntax	The keyword IDENTITYCOL can be used in place of a column name when you reference a column that has the IDENTITY property, in SELECT, INSERT, UPDATE, and DELETE statements.

Although the IDENTITY property automates row numbering within one table, separate tables, each with its own identifier column, can generate the same values. This is because the IDENTITY property is guaranteed to be unique only for the table on which it is used. If an application must generate an identifier column that is unique across the entire database, or every database on every networked computer in the world, use the ROWGUIDCOL property, the **uniqueidentifier** data type, and the NEWID function. SQL Server uses globally unique identifier columns for merge replication to ensure that rows are uniquely identified across multiple copies of the table.

For more information about creating and modifying identifier columns, see SQL Server Books Online.

Domain Integrity

Domain integrity enforces valid entries for a given column. Domain integrity is enforced by restricting the type (through data types), the format (through CHECK constraints), or the range of possible values (through REFERENCE and CHECK constraints).

DEFAULT and CHECK Constraints

Oracle treats a default as a column property, and Microsoft SQL Server treats a default as a constraint. The SQL Server DEFAULT constraint can contain constant values, built-in functions that do not take arguments (niladic functions), or NULL.

To easily migrate the Oracle DEFAULT column property, you should define DEFAULT constraints at the column level in SQL Server without applying constraint names. SQL Server generates a unique name for each DEFAULT constraint.

The syntax used to define CHECK constraints is the same in Oracle and SQL Server. The search condition must evaluate to a Boolean expression and cannot contain subqueries. A column-level CHECK constraint can reference only the constrained column, and a table-level check constraint can reference only columns of the constrained table. Multiple CHECK constraints can be defined for a table. SQL Server syntax allows only one column-level CHECK constraint to be created on a column in a CREATE TABLE statement, and the constraint can have multiple conditions.

The best way to test your modified CREATE TABLE statements is to use the SQL Server Query Analyzer in SQL Server, and parse only the syntax. The results pane indicate any errors. For more information about constraint syntax, see SQL Server Books Online.

Oracle	Microsoft SQL Server
CREATE TABLE STUDENT_ADMIN.STUDENT (SSN CHAR(9) NOT NULL, FNAME **VARCHAR2**(12) NULL, LNAME **VARCHAR2**(20) NOT NULL, GENDER CHAR(1) NOT NULL **CONSTRAINT** **STUDENT_GENDER_CK** **CHECK (GENDER IN ('M','F')),** MAJOR **VARCHAR2**(4) **DEFAULT 'Undc' NOT NULL,** BIRTH_DATE **DATE** NULL, TUITION_PAID **NUMBER**(12,2) NULL, TUITION_TOTAL **NUMBER**(12,2) NULL, START_DATE **DATE** NULL, GRAD_DATE **DATE** NULL, LOAN_AMOUNT **NUMBER**(12,2) NULL, DEGREE_PROGRAM CHAR(1) **DEFAULT 'U' NOT NULL** **CONSTRAINT** **STUDENT_DEGREE_CK CHECK** **(DEGREE_PROGRAM IN ('U', 'M', 'P',** **'D')),** ...	CREATE TABLE **USER_DB**.STUDENT _ADMIN.STUDENT (SSN CHAR(9) NOT NULL, FNAME **VARCHAR**(12) NULL, LNAME **VARCHAR**(20) NOT NULL, GENDER CHAR(1) NOT NULL **CONSTRAINT STUDENT_GENDER_CK** **CHECK (GENDER IN ('M','F')),** MAJOR **VARCHAR**(4) **DEFAULT 'Undc' NOT NULL,** BIRTH_DATE **DATETIME** NULL, TUITION_PAID **NUMERIC**(12,2) NULL, TUITION_TOTAL **NUMERIC**(12,2) NULL, START_DATE **DATETIME** NULL, GRAD_DATE **DATETIME** NULL, LOAN_AMOUNT **NUMERIC**(12,2) NULL, DEGREE_PROGRAM CHAR(1) **DEFAULT 'U' NOT NULL** **CONSTRAINT STUDENT_DEGREE_CK** **CHECK** **(DEGREE_PROGRAM IN ('U', 'M',** **'P','D')),** ...

A note about user-defined rules and defaults: The syntax for Microsoft SQL Server rules and defaults remains for backward compatibility purposes, but CHECK constraints and DEFAULT constraints are recommended for new application development. For more information, see SQL Server Books Online.

Nullability

Microsoft SQL Server and Oracle create column constraints to enforce nullability. An Oracle column defaults to NULL, unless NOT NULL is specified in the CREATE TABLE or ALTER TABLE statements. In Microsoft SQL Server, database and session settings can override the nullability of the data type used in a column definition.

All of your SQL scripts (whether Oracle or SQL Server) should explicitly define both NULL and NOT NULL for each column. To see how this strategy is implemented, see Oratable.sql and Sstable.sql, the sample table creation scripts. When not explicitly specified, column nullability follows these rules.

Null settings	Description
Column is defined with a user-defined data type	SQL Server uses the nullability specified when the data type was created. Use the **sp_help** system stored procedure to get the data type's default nullability.
Column is defined with a system-supplied data type	If the system-supplied data type has only one option, it takes precedence. Currently, the **bit** data type can be defined only as NOT NULL. If any session settings are ON (turned on with the SET), then: 　If ANSI_NULL_DFLT_ON is ON, NULL is assigned. 　If ANSI_NULL_DFLT_OFF is ON, NOT NULL is assigned. If any database settings are configured (changed with the **sp_dboption** system stored procedure), then: 　If **ANSI null default** is **true**, NULL is assigned. 　If **ANSI null default** is **false**, NOT NULL is assigned.
NULL/NOT NULL Not defined	When not explicitly defined (neither of the ANSI_NULL_DFLT options are set), the session has not been changed and the database is sct to the default (**ANSI null default** is **false**), then SQL Server assigns it NOT NULL.

Referential Integrity

The table provides a comparison of the syntax used to define referential integrity constraints.

Constraint	Oracle	Microsoft SQL Server
PRIMARY KEY	[CONSTRAINT *constraint_name*] PRIMARY KEY (*col_name* [, *col_name2* [..., *col_name16*]]) [USING INDEX *storage_parameters*]	[CONSTRAINT *constraint_name*] PRIMARY KEY [CLUSTERED | NONCLUSTERED] (*col_name* [, *col_name2* [..., *col_name16*]]) [ON *segment_name*] [NOT FOR REPLICATION]
UNIQUE	[CONSTRAINT *constraint_name*] UNIQUE (*col_name* [, *col_name2* [..., *col_name16*]]) [USING INDEX *storage_parameters*]	[CONSTRAINT *constraint_name*] UNIQUE [CLUSTERED | NONCLUSTERED](*col_name* [, *col_name2* [..., *col_name16*]]) [ON *segment_name*] [NOT FOR REPLICATION]
FOREIGN KEY	[CONSTRAINT *constraint_name*] [FOREIGN KEY (*col_name* [, *col_name2* [..., *col_name16*]])] REFERENCES [*owner.*]*ref_table* [(*ref_col* [, *ref_col2* [..., *ref_col16*]])] [ON DELETE CASCADE]	[CONSTRAINT *constraint_name*] [FOREIGN KEY (*col_name* [, *col_name2* [..., *col_name16*]])] REFERENCES [*owner.*]*ref_table* [(*ref_col* [, *ref_col2* [..., *ref_col16*]])] [NOT FOR REPLICATION]
DEFAULT	Column property, not a constraint DEFAULT (*constant_expression*)	[CONSTRAINT *constraint_name*] DEFAULT {*constant_expression* | *niladic-function* | NULL} [FOR *col_name*] [NOT FOR REPLICATION]
CHECK	[CONSTRAINT *constraint_name*] CHECK (*expression*)	[CONSTRAINT *constraint_name*] CHECK [NOT FOR REPLICATION] (*expression*)

The NOT FOR REPLICATION clause is used to suspend column-level, FOREIGN KEY, and CHECK constraints during replication.

Foreign Keys

The rules for defining foreign keys are similar in each RDBMS. The number of columns and data type of each column specified in the foreign key clause must match the REFERENCES clause. A nonnull value entered in this column(s) must exist in the table and column(s) defined in the REFERENCES clause, and the referenced table's columns must have a PRIMARY KEY or UNIQUE constraint.

Microsoft SQL Server constraints provide the ability to reference tables within the same database. To implement referential integrity across databases, use table-based triggers.

Both Oracle and SQL Server support self-referenced tables, tables in which a reference (foreign key) can be placed against one or more columns on the same table. For example, the column **prereq** in the **CLASS** table can reference the column **ccode** in the **CLASS** table to ensure that a valid course code is entered as a course prerequisite.

Whereas cascading deletes and updates are implemented in Oracle with the CASCADE DELETE clause, SQL Server provides the same functionality with table triggers. For more information, see "SQL Language Support" later in this chapter.

User-defined Integrity

User-defined integrity allows you to define specific business rules that do not fall into one of the other integrity categories.

Stored Procedures

Microsoft SQL Server stored procedures use the CREATE PROCEDURE statement to accept and return user-supplied parameters. With the exception of temporary stored procedures, stored procedures are created in the current database. The table shows the syntax for Oracle and SQL Server.

Oracle	Microsoft SQL Server

CREATE OR REPLACE PROCEDURE [*user.*]*procedure*
    [(*argument* [IN I OUT] *datatype*
    [, *argument* [IN I OUT] *datatype*]
{IS I AS} block
	CREATE PROC[EDURE] *procedure_name*
	    [;*number*]
	    [
	    { @*parameter data_type*} [VARYING] [= *default*] [OUTPUT]
	    ]
	    [,...*n*]
	[WITH
	    { RECOMPILE I ENCRYPTION I
	      RECOMPILE, ENCRYPTION}]
	[FOR REPLICATION]
	AS
	    sql_statement [...*n*]

In SQL Server, temporary procedures are created in the **tempdb** database by prefacing *procedure_name* with a single number sign (*#procedure_name*) for local temporary procedures and a double number sign (*##procedure_name*) for global temporary procedures.

A local temporary procedure can be used only by the user who created it. Permission to execute a local temporary procedure cannot be granted to other users. Local temporary procedures are automatically dropped at the end of the user session.

A global temporary procedure is available to all SQL Server users. If a global temporary procedure is created, all users can access it, and permissions cannot be explicitly revoked. Global temporary procedures are dropped at the end of the last user session using the procedure.

SQL Server stored procedures can be nested up to 32 levels. The nesting level is incremented when the called procedure starts execution, and it is decremented when the called procedure finishes execution.

The following example demonstrates how a Transact-SQL stored procedure can be used to replace an Oracle PL/SQL packaged function. The Transact-SQL version is much simpler because of SQL Server's ability to return result sets directly from SELECT statements in a stored procedure, without using a cursor.

Oracle	Microsoft SQL Server
CREATE OR REPLACE PACKAGE STUDENT_ADMIN.P1 AS ROWCOUNT NUMBER :=0; CURSOR C1 RETURN STUDENT%ROWTYPE; FUNCTION SHOW_RELUCTANT_STUDENTS (WORKVAR OUT VARCHAR2) RETURN NUMBER; END P1; /	CREATE PROCEDURE STUDENT_ADMIN.SHOW_ RELUCTANT_STUDENTS AS SELECT FNAME+" +LNAME+', social security number'+ SSN+' is not enrolled in any classes!' FROM STUDENT_ADMIN.STUDENT S WHERE NOT EXISTS (SELECT 'X' FROM STUDENT_ADMIN.GRADE G WHERE G.SSN=S.SSN) ORDER BY SSN RETURN@ @ROWCOUNT GO

```
CREATE OR REPLACE PACKAGE BODY
  STUDENT_ADMIN.P1 AS CURSOR C1
  RETURN STUDENT%ROWTYPE IS
    SELECT * FROM
    STUDENT_ADMIN.STUDENT
      WHERE NOT EXISTS
    (SELECT 'X' FROM
    STUDENT_ADMIN.GRADE
    WHERE
    GRADE.SSN=STUDENT.SSN) ORDER
    BY SSN;

FUNCTION SHOW_RELUCTANT_STUDENTS
  (WORKVAR OUT VARCHAR2) RETURN
  NUMBER IS
  WORKREC STUDENT%ROWTYPE;
  BEGIN
    IF NOT C1%ISOPEN THEN OPEN C1;
    ROWCOUNT :=0;
    ENDIF;
    FETCH C1 INTO WORKREC;
    IF (C1%NOTFOUND) THEN
      CLOSE C1;
      ROWCOUNT :=0;
    ELSE
      WORKVAR := WORKREC.FNAME||'
      '||WORKREC.LNAME||
      ', social security number
      '||WORKREC.SSN||' is not enrolled
        in any classes!';
      ROWCOUNT := ROWCOUNT + 1;
    ENDIF;
RETURN(ROWCOUNT);
```

(continued)

Oracle	Microsoft SQL Server

```
    EXCEPTION
    WHEN OTHERS THEN
        IF C1%ISOPEN THEN CLOSE C1;
            ROWCOUNT :=0;
        ENDIF;
        RAISE_APPLICATION_ERROR(-
20001,SQLERRM);
END SHOW_RELUCTANT_STUDENTS;
END P1;
/
```

SQL Server does not support constructs similar to Oracle packages or functions, and does not support the CREATE OR REPLACE option for creating stored procedures.

Delaying the Execution of a Stored Procedure

Microsoft SQL Server provides WAITFOR, which allows developers to specify a time, time interval, or event that triggers the execution of a statement block, stored procedure, or transaction. This is the Transact-SQL equivalent to the Oracle dbms_lock.sleep.

WAITFOR {DELAY '*time*' | TIME '*time*'}

where

DELAY

Instructs Microsoft SQL Server to wait until the specified amount of time has passed, up to a maximum of 24 hours.

'*time*'

The amount of time to wait. *time* can be specified in one of the acceptable formats for **datetime** data, or it can be specified as a local variable. Dates cannot be specified; therefore, the data portion of the **datetime** value is not allowed.

TIME

Instructs SQL Server to wait until the specified time.

For example:

```
BEGIN
    WAITFOR TIME '22:20'
    EXECUTE update_all_stats
END
```

Specifying Parameters in a Stored Procedure

To specify a parameter within a stored procedure, use this syntax.

Oracle	Microsoft SQL Server
Varname datatype DEFAULT <value>;	{@*parameter data_type*} [VARYING] [= *default*] [OUTPUT]

Triggers

Both Oracle and Microsoft SQL Server have triggers, which have some differences in their implementations.

Description	Oracle	Microsoft SQL Server
Number of triggers per table	Unlimited	Unlimited
Triggers executed before INSERT, UPDATE, DELETE	Yes	No
Triggers executed after INSERT, UPDATE, DELETE	Yes	Yes
Statement-level triggers	Yes	Yes
Row-level triggers	Yes	No
Constraints checked prior to execution	Yes, unless trigger is disabled.	Yes. In addition, this is an option in Data Transformation Services.
Referring to old or previous values in an UPDATE or DELETE trigger	:old	DELETED.*column*
Referring to new values in an INSERT trigger	:new	INSERTED.*column*
Disabling triggers	ALTER TRIGGER	Option in Data Transformation Services

DELETED and **INSERTED** are logical (conceptual) tables created by SQL Server for trigger statements. They are structurally similar to the table on which the trigger is defined and hold the old values or new values of the rows that might be changed by the user action. The tables track row-level changes in Transact-SQL. These tables provide the same functionality as Oracle row-level triggers. When an INSERT, UPDATE, or DELETE statement is executed in SQL Server, rows are added to the trigger table and to the INSERTED and DELETED table(s) simultaneously.

The **INSERTED** and **DELETED** tables are identical to the trigger table. They have the same column names and the same data types. For example, if a trigger is placed on the **GRADE** table, the **INSERTED** and **DELETED** tables have this structure.

GRADE	INSERTED	DELETED
SSN CHAR(9)	SSN CHAR(9)	SSN CHAR(9)
CCODE VARCHAR(4)	CCODE VARCHAR(4)	CCODE VARCHAR(4)
GRADE VARCHAR(2)	GRADE VARCHAR(2)	GRADE VARCHAR(2)

The **INSERTED** and **DELETED** tables can be examined by the trigger to determine what types of trigger actions should be carried out. The **INSERTED** table is used with the INSERT and UPDATE statements. The **DELETED** table is used with DELETE and UPDATE statements.

The UPDATE statement uses both the **INSERTED** and **DELETED** tables because SQL Server always deletes the old row and inserts a new row whenever an UPDATE operation is performed. Consequently, when an UPDATE is performed, the rows in the **INSERTED** table are always duplicates of the rows in the **DELETED** table.

The following example uses the **INSERTED** and **DELETED** tables to replace a PL/SQL row-level trigger. A full outer join is used to query all rows from either table.

Oracle	Microsoft SQL Server
CREATE TRIGGER	CREATE TRIGGER
STUDENT_ADMIN.TRACK_GRADES	STUDENT_ADMIN.TRACK_GRADES
AFTER	ON STUDENT_ADMIN.GRADE
INSERT OR UPDATE OR DELETE	FOR INSERT, UPDATE, DELETE
ON STUDENT_ADMIN.GRADE	AS
FOR EACH ROW	INSERT INTO GRADE_HISTORY(
BEGIN	TABLE_USER, ACTION_DATE,
INSERT INTO GRADE_HISTORY(	OLD_SSN, OLD_CCODE, OLD_GRADE
TABLE_USER, ACTION_DATE,	NEW_SSN, NEW_CCODE, NEW_GRADE)
OLD_SSN, OLD_CCODE,	SELECT USER, GETDATE(),
OLD_GRADE, NEW_SSN,	OLD.SSN, OLD.CCODE, OLD.GRADE,
NEW_CCODE, NEW_GRADE)	NEW.SSN, NEW.CCODE, NEW.GRADE
VALUES (USER, SYSDATE,	FROM INSERTED NEW FULL OUTER JOIN
:OLD.SSN, :OLD.CCODE, :OLD.GRADE,	DELETED OLD ON NEW.SSN = OLD.SSN
:NEW.SSN, :NEW.CCODE,	
:NEW.GRADE),	
END;	

You can create a trigger only in the current database, though you can reference objects outside the current database. If you use an owner name to qualify a trigger, qualify the table name the same way.

Triggers can be nested 32 levels deep. If a trigger changes a table on which there is another trigger, the second trigger is activated and can then call a third trigger, and so on. If any trigger in the chain sets off an infinite loop, the nesting level is exceeded and the trigger is canceled. Additionally, if an update trigger on one column of a table results in an update to another column, the update trigger is activated only once.

Microsoft SQL Server declarative referential integrity (DRI) does not provide cross-database referential integrity. If cross-database referential integrity is required, use triggers.

The following statements are not allowed in a Transact-SQL trigger:

- CREATE statements (DATABASE, TABLE, INDEX, PROCEDURE, DEFAULT, RULE, TRIGGER, SCHEMA, and VIEW)
- DROP statements (TRIGGER, INDEX, TABLE, PROCEDURE, DATABASE, VIEW, DEFAULT, RULE)
- ALTER statements (DATABASE, TABLE, VIEW, PROCEDURE, TRIGGER)
- TRUNCATE TABLE
- GRANT, REVOKE, DENY
- UPDATE STATISTICS
- RECONFIGURE
- UPDATE STATISTICS
- RESTORE DATABASE, RESTORE LOG
- LOAD LOG, DATABASE
- DISK statements
- SELECT INTO (because it creates a table)

For more information about triggers, see SQL Server Books Online.

Transactions, Locking, and Concurrency

This section explains how transactions are executed in both Oracle and Microsoft SQL Server and presents the differences between the locking processes and concurrency issues in both database types.

Transactions

In Oracle, a transaction is started automatically when an insert, update, or delete operation is performed. An application must issue a COMMIT command to save all changes to the database. If a COMMIT is not performed, all changes are rolled back or undone automatically.

By default, Microsoft SQL Server automatically performs a COMMIT statement after every insert, update, or delete operation. Because the data is automatically saved, you are unable to roll back any changes. You can use implicit or explicit transaction modes to change this default behavior.

The implicit transaction mode, allowing SQL Server to behave like Oracle, is activated with the SET IMPLICIT_TRANSACTIONS ON statement. If this option is ON and there are no outstanding transactions, every SQL statement automatically starts a transaction. If there is an open transaction, no new transaction is started. The open transaction must be committed by the user explicitly with the COMMIT TRANSACTION statement for the changes to take effect and for all locks to be released.

An explicit transaction is a grouping of SQL statements surrounded by the following transaction delimiters:

- BEGIN TRANSACTION [*transaction_name*]
- COMMIT TRANSACTION [*transaction_name*]
- ROLLBACK TRANSACTION [*transaction_name* | *savepoint_name*]

In the following example, the English department is changed to the Literature department. Note the use of the BEGIN TRANSACTION and COMMIT TRANSACTION statements.

Oracle	Microsoft SQL Server
INSERT INTO DEPT_ADMIN.DEPT (DEPT, DNAME)	BEGIN TRANSACTION
VALUES ('LIT', 'Literature')	
/	INSERT INTO DEPT_ADMIN.DEPT (DEPT, DNAME)
UPDATE DEPT_ADMIN.CLASS	VALUES ('LIT', 'Literature')
SET MAJOR = 'LIT'	
WHERE MAJOR = 'ENG'	UPDATE DEPT_ADMIN.CLASS
/	SET DEPT = 'LIT'
UPDATE STUDENT_ADMIN.STUDENT	WHERE DEPT = 'ENG'
SET MAJOR = 'LIT'	
WHERE MAJOR = 'ENG'	UPDATE STUDENT_ADMIN.STUDENT
/	SET MAJOR = 'LIT'
DELETE FROM DEPT_ADMIN.DEPT	WHERE MAJOR = 'ENG'
WHERE DEPT = 'ENG'	
/	DELETE FROM DEPT_ADMIN.DEPT
COMMIT	WHERE DEPT = 'ENG'
/	
	COMMIT TRANSACTION
	GO

All explicit transactions must be enclosed within BEGIN TRANSACTION...COMMIT TRANSACTION statements. The SAVE TRANSACTION statement functions in the same way as the Oracle SAVEPOINT command, setting a savepoint in the transaction that allows partial rollbacks.

Transactions can be nested one within another. If this occurs, the outermost pair creates and commits the transaction, and the inner pairs track the nesting level. When a nested transaction is encountered, the @@TRANCOUNT function is incremented. Usually, this apparent transaction nesting occurs as stored procedures or triggers with BEGIN...COMMIT pairs calling each other. Although transactions can be nested, they have little effect on the behavior of ROLLBACK TRANSACTION statements.

In stored procedures and triggers, the number of BEGIN TRANSACTION statements must match the number of COMMIT TRANSACTION statements. A stored procedure or trigger that contains unpaired BEGIN TRANSACTION and COMMIT TRANSACTION statements produces an error message when executed. The syntax allows stored procedures and triggers to be called from within transactions if they contain BEGIN TRANSACTION and COMMIT TRANSACTION statements.

Wherever possible, break large transactions into smaller transactions. Make sure each transaction is well-defined within a single batch. To minimize possible concurrency conflicts, transactions should not span multiple batches nor wait for user input. Grouping many Transact-SQL statements into one long-running transaction can negatively affect recovery time and cause concurrency problems.

When programming with ODBC, you can select either the implicit or explicit transaction mode by using the **SQLSetConnectOption** function. An ODBC program's selection of one or the other depends on the AUTOCOMMIT connect option. If AUTOCOMMIT is ON (the default), you are in explicit mode. If AUTOCOMMIT is OFF, you are in implicit mode.

If you are issuing a script through SQL Server Query Analyzer or other query tools, you can either include the explicit BEGIN TRANSACTION statement shown previously, or start the script with the SET IMPLICIT_TRANSACTIONS ON statement. The BEGIN TRANSACTION approach is more flexible, and the implicit approach is more compatible with Oracle.

Locking and Transaction Isolation

Oracle and Microsoft SQL Server have very different locking and isolation strategies. You must consider these differences to ensure application scalability when you convert an application from Oracle to SQL Server.

Oracle uses a multiversion consistency model for all SQL statements that read data, either explicitly or implicitly. In this model, data readers by default neither acquire locks nor wait for other locks to be released before reading rows of data. When a reader requests data that has been changed but not yet committed by other writers, Oracle re-creates the old data by using its rollback segments to reconstruct a snapshot of rows.

Data writers in Oracle request locks on data that is updated, deleted, or inserted. These locks are held until the end of a transaction, and they prevent other users from overwriting uncommitted changes.

Microsoft SQL Server has multigranular locking that allows different types of resources to be locked by a transaction. To minimize the cost of locking, SQL Server automatically locks resources at a level appropriate to the task. Locking at a smaller granularity, such as rows, increases concurrency but has a higher overhead because more locks must be held if many rows are locked. Locking at a larger granularity, such as tables, is expensive in terms of concurrency because locking an entire table restricts access to any part of the table by other transactions, but has a lower overhead because fewer locks are being maintained. SQL Server can lock these resources (listed in order of increasing granularity).

Resource	Description
RID	Row identifier. Used to individually lock a single row table.
Key	Key; a row lock within an index. Used to protect key ranges in serializable transactions.
Page	8-KB data page or index page.
Extent	Contiguous group of eight data pages or index pages.
Table	Entire table, including all data and indexes.
DB	Database.

SQL Server locks resources with different lock modes that determine how the resources can be accessed by concurrent transactions.

Lock mode	Description
Shared (S)	Used for operations that do not change or update data (read only operations), such as a SELECT statement.
Update (U)	Used on resources that can be updated. Prevents a common form of deadlock that occurs when multiple sessions are read, locking and then potentially updating resources later.
Exclusive (X)	Used for data-modification operations, such as UPDATE, INSERT, or DELETE. Ensures that multiple updates cannot be made to the same resource at the same time.
Intent	Used to establish a lock hierarchy.
Schema	Used when an operation dependent on the schema of a table is executing. There are two types of schema locks: schema stability (Sch-S) and schema modification (Sch-M).

It is important in any RDBMS that locks be released quickly to provide the maximum concurrency. You can ensure you are releasing locks quickly by keeping transactions as short as possible. If possible, a transaction should not span multiple round-trips to the server, nor include user "think" time. If you use cursors, you also need to code your application to fetch data quickly, because unfetched data scans can hold share locks at the server and thus block updaters. For more information, see "Using ODBC" later in this chapter.

Changing Default Locking Behavior

Both Microsoft SQL Server and Oracle allow the developer to request nondefault locking and isolation behavior. In Oracle, the most common mechanisms for this are the FOR UPDATE clause on a SELECT command, the SET TRANSACTION READ ONLY command, and the explicit LOCK TABLE command.

Because their locking and isolation strategies are so different, it is difficult to map these locking options directly between Oracle and SQL Server. To obtain a better understanding of this process, it is important to understand the options that SQL Server provides for changing its default locking behavior.

In SQL Server, the most common mechanisms for changing default locking behavior are the SET TRANSACTION ISOLATION LEVEL statement and the locking hints that are supported in the SELECT and UPDATE statements. The SET TRANSACTION ISOLATION LEVEL statement sets transaction isolation levels for the duration of a user's session. This becomes the default behavior for the session unless a locking hint is specified at the table level in the FROM clause of an SQL statement. The transaction isolation is set like this:

```
SET TRANSACTION ISOLATION LEVEL
    {
        READ COMMITTED
        | READ UNCOMMITTED
        | REPEATABLE READ
        | SERIALIZABLE
    }
```

READ COMMITTED

Is the default isolation level for SQL Server. When you use this option, your application cannot read data that has not yet been committed by other transactions. In this mode, however, shared locks are released as soon as the data has been read from a page. If the application rereads the same data range within the same transaction, it sees other users' changes.

SERIALIZABLE

With this option set, transactions are isolated from one another. If you do not want to see other user's changes during a query, set the transaction isolation level to SERIALIZABLE. SQL Server holds all shared locks until the end of a transaction. You can achieve the same effect on a more granular level by using the HOLDLOCK hint after the table name in the SELECT statement. Either of these options represents a trade-off of concurrency for strict consistency, and should be used only when necessary.

READ UNCOMMITTED

With this option set, SQL Server readers are nonblocking, as in Oracle. This option implements dirty read or isolation level 0 locking, which means that no shared locks are issued and no exclusive locks are honored. When this option is set, it is possible to read uncommitted or *dirty* data; values in the data can be changed and rows can appear or disappear in the data set before the end of the transaction. This option has the same effect as setting NOLOCK on all tables in all SELECT statements in a transaction. This is the least restrictive of the four isolation levels. Use this isolation level only after you thoroughly analyze how it affects the accuracy of the results in your application.

SQL Server supports Oracle READ ONLY functionality in two ways:

- If some transactions in an application require repeatable read behavior, you may need to use the SERIALIZABLE isolation level offered by SQL Server.

- If all of the database access is read-only, you can improve performance by setting the SQL Server database option to READ ONLY.

SELECT...FOR UPDATE

The SELECT...FOR UPDATE statement in Oracle is used primarily when an application needs to issue a positioned update or delete on a cursor by using the WHERE CURRENT OF syntax. In this case, optionally remove the FOR UPDATE clause, because Microsoft SQL Server cursors are updatable by default.

By default, SQL Server cursors do not hold locks under the fetched row. SQL Server uses an optimistic concurrency strategy to prevent updates from overwriting each other. If one user attempts to update or delete a row that has been changed since it was read into the cursor, SQL Server issues an error message. The application can trap this error message and retry the update or delete as appropriate. To override this behavior, developers can use SCROLL_LOCKS in a cursor declaration.

The optimistic concurrency strategy supports higher concurrency in the usual case in which collisions between updaters are rare. If your application really needs to ensure that a row cannot be changed after it is fetched, use the UPDLOCK hint in your SELECT statement. This hint does not block other readers, but it prevents other potential writers from also obtaining an update lock on the data. When using ODBC, you can achieve this effect by using SQLSETSTMTOPTION (...,SQL_CONCURRENCY)= SQL_CONCUR_LOCK. Either of these options reduces concurrency, however.

Table-level Locks

Microsoft SQL Server can lock an entire table by using the SELECT...*table_name* (TABLOCK) statement. This performs the same operation as the Oracle LOCK TABLE...IN SHARE MODE statement. The lock allows others to read a table, but prevents them from updating it. By default, the lock is held until the end of the statement. If you also add the keyword HOLDLOCK (SELECT...*table_name* (TABLOCK HOLDLOCK)), the table lock is held until the end of the transaction.

An exclusive lock can be placed on a SQL Server table with the SELECT...*table_name* (TABLOCKX) statement. This statement requests an exclusive lock on a table. It is used to prevent others from reading or updating the table and is held until the end of the command or transaction. It is similar in function to the Oracle LOCK TABLE...IN EXCLUSIVE MODE statement.

SQL Server does not provide a NOWAIT option for its explicit lock requests.

Lock Escalation

When a query requests rows from a table, Microsoft SQL Server automatically generates page-level locks. However, if the query requests a large percentage of the table's rows, SQL Server escalates the locking from page level to table level. This process is called *lock escalation*.

Lock escalation makes table scans and operations against a large result set more efficient because it reduces locking overhead. SQL statements that lack WHERE clauses typically cause lock escalation.

A shared table lock (TABLOCK) is applied when a shared page lock is escalated to a table lock during a read operation. Shared table locks are applied when:

- A HOLDLOCK or SET TRANSACTION ISOLATION LEVEL SERIALIZABLE statement is used.
- A table scan is chosen by the optimizers.
- The number of share locks accumulated in a table exceeds the lock escalation threshold.

The lock escalation threshold defaults to 200 pages in a table, but this can be customized to be based on a percentage of table size with minimum and maximum bounds. A shared table lock is also used when building a nonclustered index. For more information about the lock escalation threshold, see the SQL Server Books Online.

An exclusive table lock (TABLOCKX) is applied when an UPDATE lock has been escalated to a table lock during a write operation. Exclusive table locks are applied when:

- No index can be used for an update or delete operation.
- The number of pages in a table that has an exclusive lock exceeds the lock escalation threshold.
- A clustered index is created.

Oracle's inability to escalate row-level locks can cause problems in some queries that include the FOR UPDATE clause. For example, assume that the **STUDENT** table has 100,000 rows of data, and the following statement is issued by an Oracle user:

```
SELECT * FROM STUDENT FOR UPDATE
```

This statement forces the Oracle RDBMS to lock the **STUDENT** table one row at a time; this can take quite a while. It never escalates the request to lock the entire table.

The same query in SQL Server is:

```
SELECT * FROM STUDENT (UPDLOCK)
```

When this query is run, page-level locking escalates to table-level locking, which is much more efficient and significantly faster.

Deadlocks

A deadlock occurs when one process locks a page or table needed by another process, and the second process locks a page that the first process needs. A deadlock is also known as a *deadly embrace*. SQL Server automatically detects and resolves deadlocks. If a deadlock is found, the server terminates the user process that has completed the deadly embrace.

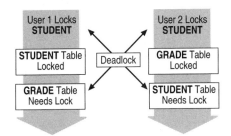

After every data modification, your program code should check for message number 1205, which indicates a deadlock. If this message number is returned, a deadlock has occurred and the transaction was rolled back. In this situation, your application must restart the transaction.

Deadlocks can usually be avoided by using a few simple techniques:

- Access tables in the same order in all parts of your application.
- Use a clustered index on every table to force an explicit row ordering.
- Keep transactions short.

For more information, see the Microsoft Knowledge Base article, "Detecting and Avoiding Deadlocks in Microsoft SQL Server."

Remote Transactions

To perform remote transactions in Oracle, you must have access to a remote database node with a database link. In SQL Server, you must have access to a *remote server*. A remote server is a server running SQL Server on the network that users can access by using their local server. When a server is set up as a remote server, users can use the system procedures and the stored procedures on it without explicitly logging in to it.

Remote servers are set up in pairs. You must configure both servers to recognize each other as remote servers. The name of each server must be added to its partner with the **sp_addlinkedserver** system stored procedure or SQL Server Enterprise Manager.

After you set up a remote server, use the **sp_addremotelogin** system stored procedure or SQL Server Enterprise Manager to set up remote login IDs for the users who must access that remote server. After this step is completed, you must grant permissions to execute the stored procedures.

The EXECUTE statement is then used to run procedures on the remote server. This example executes the **validate_student** stored procedure on the remote server **STUDSVR1** and stores the return status indicating success or failure in **@retvalue1**:

```
DECLARE @retvalue1 int
EXECUTE @retvalue = STUDSVR1.student_db.student_admin.validate_student
    '111111111'
```

For more information, see SQL Server Books Online.

Distributed Transactions

Oracle automatically initiates a distributed transaction if changes are made to tables in two or more networked database nodes. SQL Server distributed transactions use the two-phase commit services of the Microsoft Distributed Transaction Coordinator (MS DTC) included with SQL Server.

By default, SQL Server must be instructed to participate in a distributed transaction. SQL Server's participation in an MS DTC transaction can be started by either of the following:

- The BEGIN DISTRIBUTED TRANSACTION statement. This statement begins a new MS DTC transaction.

- A client application calling DTC transaction interfaces directly.

In the example, notice the distributed update to both the local table **GRADE** and the remote table **CLASS** (using a **class_name** procedure):

```
BEGIN DISTRIBUTED TRANSACTION
UPDATE STUDENT_ADMIN.GRADE
    SET GRADE = 'B+' WHERE SSN = '111111111' AND CCODE = '1234'
DECLARE @retvalue1 int
EXECUTE @retvalue1 = CLASS_SVR1.dept_db.dept_admin.class_name '1234',
    'Basketweaving'
COMMIT TRANSACTION
GO
```

If the application cannot complete the transaction, the application program cancels it by using the ROLLBACK TRANSACTION statement. If the application fails or a participating resource manager fails, MS DTC cancels the transaction. MS DTC does not support distributed savepoints or the SAVE TRANSACTION statement. If an MS DTC transaction is aborted or rolled back, the entire transaction is rolled back to the beginning of the distributed transaction, regardless of any savepoints.

Two-phase Commit Processing

The Oracle and MS DTC two-phase commit mechanisms are similar in operation. In the first phase of a SQL Server two-phase commit, the transaction manager requests each enlisted resource manager to prepare to commit. If any resource manager cannot prepare, the transaction manager broadcasts an abort decision to everyone involved in the transaction.

If all resource managers can successfully prepare, the transaction manager broadcasts the commit decision. This is the second phase of the commit process. While a resource manager is prepared, it is in doubt about whether the transaction is committed or aborted. MS DTC keeps a sequential log so that its commit or abort decisions are durable. If a resource manager or transaction manager fails, they reconcile in-doubt transactions when they reconnect.

SQL Language Support

This section outlines the similarities and differences between Transact-SQL and PL/SQL language syntax and presents conversion strategies.

SELECT and Data Manipulation Statements

Use the following when migrating your Oracle DML statements and PL/SQL programs to SQL Server.

1. Verify that the syntax of all SELECT, INSERT, UPDATE, and DELETE statements is valid. Make any required modifications.

2. Change all outer joins to SQL-92 standard outer join syntax.

3. Replace Oracle functions with the appropriate SQL Server functions.

4. Check all comparison operators.

5. Replace the "||" string concatenation operator with the "+" string concatenation operator.

6. Replace PL/SQL programs with Transact-SQL programs.

7. Change all PL/SQL cursors to either noncursor SELECT statements or Transact-SQL cursors.

8. Replace PL/SQL procedures, functions, and packages with Transact-SQL procedures.

9. Convert PL/SQL triggers to Transact-SQL triggers.

10. Use the SET SHOWPLAN statement to tune your queries for performance.

SELECT Statements

The SELECT statement syntax used by Oracle and Microsoft SQL Server is similar.

Oracle	Microsoft SQL Server
SELECT [/*+ optimizer_hints*/]	SELECT select_list
[ALL I DISTINCT] select_list	[INTO new_table_]
[FROM	FROM table_source
{table_name I view_name I select_statement}]	[WHERE search_condition]
[WHERE clause]	[GROUP BY [ALL] group_by_expression [,...n]
[GROUP BY group_by_expression]	[WITH { CUBE I ROLLUP }]
[HAVING search_condition]	[HAVING search_condition]
[START WITH ... CONNECT BY]	[ORDER BY order_expression [ASC I DESC]]
[{UNION I UNION ALL I INTERSECT I MINUS} SELECT ...]	In addition:
[ORDER BY clause]	UNION Operator
[FOR UPDATE]	COMPUTE Clause
	FOR BROWSE Clause
	OPTION Clause

Oracle-specific cost-based optimizer hints are not supported by SQL Server, and must be removed. The recommended technique is to use SQL Server cost-based optimization. For more information, see "Tuning SQL Statements" later in this chapter.

SQL Server does not support the Oracle START WITH...CONNECT BY clause. You can replace this in SQL Server by creating a stored procedure that performs the same task.

The Oracle INTERSECT and MINUS set operators are not supported by SQL Server. The SQL Server EXISTS and NOT EXISTS clauses can be used to accomplish the same result.

The following example uses the INTERSECT operator to find the course code and course name for all classes that have students. Notice how the EXISTS operator replaces the use of the INTERSECT operator. The data that is returned is identical.

Oracle	Microsoft SQL Server
SELECT CCODE, CNAME FROM DEPT_ADMIN.CLASS **INTERSECT** **SELECT C.CCODE, C.CNAME** **FROM STUDENT_ADMIN.GRADE G,** **DEPT_ADMIN.CLASS C** **WHERE C.CCODE = G.CCODE**	SELECT CCODE, CNAME FROM DEPT_ADMIN.CLASS C **WHERE EXISTS** **(SELECT 'X' FROM** **STUDENT_ADMIN.GRADE G** **WHERE C.CCODE = G.CCODE)**

This example uses the MINUS operator to find those classes that do not have any students.

Oracle	Microsoft SQL Server
SELECT CCODE, CNAME FROM DEPT_ADMIN.CLASS **MINUS** **SELECT C.CCODE, C.CNAME** **FROM STUDENT_ADMIN.GRADE G,** **DEPT_ADMIN.CLASS C** **WHERE C.CCODE = G.CCODE**	SELECT CCODE, CNAME FROM DEPT_ADMIN.CLASSC **WHERE NOT EXISTS** **(SELECT 'X' FROM** **STUDENT_ADMIN.GRADE G** **WHERE C.CCODE = G.CCODE)**

INSERT Statements

The INSERT statement syntax used by Oracle and Microsoft SQL Server is similar.

Oracle	Microsoft SQL Server

INSERT INTO
{*table_name* | *view_name* | **select_statement**}
[(*column_list*)]
{**values_list** | *select_statement*}
	INSERT [INTO]
	  {
	  table_name [[AS] *table_alias*] WITH (
	  <table_hint_limited> [...*n*])
	   | *view_name* [[AS] *table_alias*]
	   | *rowset_function_limited*
	  }
	
	  { [(*column_list*)]
	    { VALUES ({ DEFAULT
	            | NULL
	            | *expression*
	          }[,...*n*]
	      )
	   | *derived_table*
	   | *execute_statement*
	   }
	  }
	 | DEFAULT VALUES

The Transact-SQL language supports inserts into tables and views, but does not support INSERT operations into SELECT statements. If your Oracle application code performs inserts into SELECT statements, this must be changed.

Oracle	Microsoft SQL Server

INSERT INTO (**SELECT SSN, CCODE,**
  GRADE FROM GRADE)
VALUES ('111111111', '1111',NULL)
	INSERT INTO **GRADE (SSN, CCODE,**
	  GRADE)
	VALUES ('111111111', '1111',NULL)

The Transact-SQL *values_list* parameter offers the SQL-92 standard keyword DEFAULT, which is not supported by Oracle. This keyword specifies that the default value for the column be used when an insert is performed. If a default value does not exist for the specified column, a NULL is inserted. If the column does not allow NULLs, an error message is returned. If the column is defined as a **timestamp** data type, the next sequential value is inserted.

The DEFAULT keyword cannot be used with an identity column. To generate the next sequential number, columns with the IDENTITY property must not be listed in the *column_list* or *values_clause*. You do not have to use the DEFAULT keyword to obtain the default value for a column. As in Oracle, if the column is not referenced in the *column_list* and it has a default value, the default value is placed in the column. This is the most compatible approach to use when performing the migration.

One useful Transact-SQL option (EXECute *procedure_name*) is to execute a procedure and pipe its output into a target table or view. Oracle does not allow you to do this.

UPDATE Statements

Because Transact-SQL supports most of the syntax used by the Oracle UPDATE command, minimal revision is required.

Oracle	Microsoft SQL Server

UPDATE
{*table_name* I *view_name* I   **select_statement**}
SET [*column_name(s)* = {*constant_value* I
  expression I *select_statement* I *column_list* I
  variable_list]
{*where_statement*}
	UPDATE
	{
	table_name [[AS] *table_alias*] WITH (
	<table_hint_limited> [...*n*])
	view_name [[AS] *table_alias*]
	I *rowset_function_limited*
	}
	SET
	{*column_name* = {*expression* I DEFAULT I NULL}
	I @*variable* = *expression*
	I @*variable* = *column* = *expression* } [,...*n*]
	
	{{[FROM {<table_source>} [,..*n*]]
	
	[WHERE
	<search_condition>] }
	I
	[WHERE CURRENT OF
	{ { [GLOBAL] *cursor_name* } I
	cursor_variable_name}
	] }
	[OPTION (<query_hint> [,...*n*])]

The Transact-SQL UPDATE statement does not support update operations against SELECT statements. If your Oracle application code performs updates against SELECT statements, you can turn the SELECT statement into a view, and then use the view name in the SQL Server UPDATE statement. See the example shown previously in "INSERT Statements."

The Oracle UPDATE command can use only program variables from within a PL/SQL block. The Transact-SQL language does not require the use of blocks to use variables.

Oracle	Microsoft SQL Server

DECLARE
VAR1 NUMBER(10,2);
BEGIN
  VAR1 := 2500;
  UPDATE   STUDENT_ADMIN.STUDENT
  SET TUITION_TOTAL = VAR1;
END;
	DECLARE
	@VAR1 NUMERIC(10,2)
	SELECT @VAR1 = 2500
	UPDATE STUDENT_ADMIN.STUDENT
	SET TUITION_TOTAL=@VAR1

The keyword DEFAULT can be used to set a column to its default value in SQL Server. You cannot set a column to a default value with the Oracle UPDATE command.

Transact-SQL and Oracle SQL support the use of subqueries in an UPDATE statement. However, the Transact-SQL FROM clause can be used to create an UPDATE based on a join. This capability makes your UPDATE syntax more readable and in some cases can improve performance.

Oracle	Microsoft SQL Server

UPDATE
  STUDENT_ADMIN.STUDENT S
SET TUITION_TOTAL = 1500
WHERE SSN IN (SELECT SSN
      FROM GRADE G
         WHERE G.SSN = S.SSN
         AND G.CCODE = '1234')
	Subquery:
	
	UPDATE
	  STUDENT_ADMIN.STUDENT S
	SET TUITION_TOTAL = 1500
	WHERE SSN IN (SELECT SSN
	      FROM GRADE G
	         WHERE G.SSN = S.SSN
	         AND G.CCODE = '1234')
	
	FROM clause:
	
	UPDATE
	  STUDENT_ADMIN.STUDENT S
	SET TUITION_TOTAL = 1500
	  FROM GRADE G
	    WHERE S.SSN = G.SSN
	    AND G.CCODE = '1234'

DELETE Statements

In most cases, you do not need to modify DELETE statements. If you perform deletes against SELECT statements in Oracle, you must modify the syntax for SQL Server because this functionality is not supported by Transact-SQL.

Transact-SQL supports the use of subqueries in the WHERE clause, as well as joins in the FROM clause. The latter can produce more efficient statements. See the example shown previously in "UPDATE Statements."

Oracle	Microsoft SQL Server

DELETE [FROM]
 {*table_name*
	view_name	***select_statement***}
		 [WHERE clause]
			DELETE
			 [FROM]
			 {
			 table_name [[AS] *table_alias*] WITH (
			 <table_hint_limited> [...*n*])
			
				view_name [[AS] *table_alias*]
				
					rowset_function_limited
					 }
					
					 [FROM {<table_source>} [,...*n*]]
					
					 [WHERE
					 { <search_condition>
					
						{ [CURRENT OF
						 {
						 { [GLOBAL] *cursor_name* }
						 cursor_variable_name
						 }
						]
						 }
						]
						 [OPTION (<query_hint> [,...*n*])]

TRUNCATE TABLE Statement

The TRUNCATE TABLE syntax used by Oracle and Microsoft SQL Server is similar. TRUNCATE TABLE is used to remove all of the rows from a table and cannot be rolled back. The table structure and all of its indexes continue to exist. DELETE triggers are not executed. If a table is referenced by a FOREIGN KEY constraint, it cannot be truncated.

Oracle	Microsoft SQL Server
TRUNCATE TABLE *table_name* [{DROP	REUSE} STORAGE]	TRUNCATE TABLE *table_name*

In SQL Server, this statement can be issued only by the table owner. In Oracle, this command can be issued if you are the table owner or have the DELETE TABLE system privilege.

The Oracle TRUNCATE TABLE command can optionally release the storage space occupied by the rows in the table. The SQL Server TRUNCATE TABLE statement always reclaims space occupied by the table data and its associated indexes.

Manipulating Data in identity and timestamp Columns

Oracle sequences are database objects that are not directly related to any given table or column. The relationship between a column and a sequence is implemented in the application, by assigning the sequence value to a column programmatically. Therefore, Oracle does not enforce any rules when it works with sequences. However, in Microsoft SQL Server identity columns, values cannot be updated and the DEFAULT keyword cannot be used.

By default, data cannot be inserted directly into an identity column. The identity column automatically generates a unique, sequential number for each new row inserted in the table. This default can be overridden using the following SET statement:

```
SET IDENTITY_INSERT table_name ON
```

With IDENTITY_INSERT set to ON, the user can insert any value into the identity column of a new row. To prevent the entry of duplicate numbers, a unique index must be created against the column. The purpose of this statement is to allow a user to re-create a value for a row that has been deleted accidentally. The @@IDENTITY function can be used to obtain the last identity value.

The TRUNCATE TABLE statement resets an identity column to its original SEED value. If you do not want to reset the identity value for a column, use the DELETE statement without a WHERE clause instead of the TRUNCATE TABLE statement. You will have to evaluate how this affects your Oracle migration, because ORACLE SEQUENCES are not reset following the TRUNCATE TABLE command.

You can perform only inserts or deletes when working with **timestamp** columns. If you attempt to update a **timestamp** column, you receive this error message:

```
Msg 272, Level 16, State 1 Can't update a TIMESTAMP column.
```

Locking Requested Rows

Oracle uses the FOR UPDATE clause to lock rows specified in the SELECT command. You do not need to use the equivalent clause in Microsoft SQL Server because this is the default behavior.

Row Aggregates and the Compute Clause

The SQL Server COMPUTE clause is used to generate row aggregate functions (SUM, AVG, MIN, MAX, and COUNT), which appear as additional rows in the query results. It allows you to see detail and summary rows in one set of results. You can calculate summary values for subgroups, and you can calculate more than one aggregate function for the same group.

The Oracle SELECT command syntax does not support the COMPUTE clause. Nevertheless, the SQL Server COMPUTE clause works just like the COMPUTE command found in the Oracle SQL*Plus query tool.

Join Clauses

Microsoft SQL Server 7.0 allows up to 256 tables to be joined in a join clause, including both temporary and permanent tables. There is no join limit in Oracle.

When using outer joins in Oracle, the outer join operator (+) is placed typically next to the child (foreign key) column in the join. The (+) identifies the column with fewer unique values. This always occurs unless the foreign key allows null values, in which case (+) can be placed on the parent (PRIMARY KEY or UNIQUE constraint) column. You cannot place the (+) on both sides of the equal sign (=).

With SQL Server, you can use the *= and =* outer join operators. The * is used to identify the column that has more unique values. If the child (foreign key) column does not allow null values, the * is placed on the parent (PRIMARY KEY or UNIQUE constraint) column side of the equal sign. The placement of the * is essentially reversed in Oracle. You cannot place the * on both sides of the equal sign (=).

The *= and =* are considered legacy join operators. SQL Server also supports the SQL-92 standard join operators listed below. It is recommended that you use this syntax. The SQL-92 standard syntax is more powerful and has fewer restrictions than the * operators.

Join operation	Description
CROSS JOIN	This is the cross product of two tables. It returns the same rows as if no WHERE clause was specified in an old-style join. This type of join is called a Cartesian-join in Oracle.
INNER	This join specifies that all inner rows be returned. Any unmatched rows are discarded. This is identical to a standard Oracle table join.
LEFT[OUTER]	This type of join specifies that all of the left table outer rows be returned, even if no column matches are found. This operates just like an Oracle outer join (+).
RIGHT[OUTER]	This type of join specifies that all of the right table outer rows be returned, even if no column matches are found. This operates just like an Oracle outer join (+).
FULL [OUTER]	If a row from either table does not match the selection criteria, specifies the row be included in the result set and its output columns that correspond to the other table be set to NULL. This would be the same as placing the Oracle outer join operator on both sides of the "=" sign (col1(+) = col2(+)), which is not allowed.

The following code examples return lists of classes taken by all students. Outer joins are defined between the student and grade tables that allow all students to appear, even those who are not enrolled in any classes. Outer joins are also added to the class table in order to return the class names. If outer joins are not added to the class tables, those students who are not enrolled in any classes are not returned because they have null course codes (**CCODE**).

Oracle	Microsoft SQL Server
SELECT S.SSN AS SSN, FNAME, LNAME **FROM STUDENT_ADMIN.STUDENT S,** **DEPT_ADMIN.CLASS C,** **STUDENT_ADMIN.GRADE G** **WHERE S.SSN = G.SSN(+)** **AND G.CCODE = C.CCODE(+)**	SELECT S.SSN AS SSN, FNAME, LNAME **FROM STUDENT_ADMIN.GRADE G** **RIGHT OUTER JOIN** **STUDENT_ADMIN.STUDENT S** **ON G.SSN = S.SSN** **LEFT OUTER JOIN** **DEPT_ADMIN.CLASS C** **ON G.CCODE = C.CCODE**

Using SELECT Statements as Table Names

Microsoft SQL Server and Oracle support the use of SELECT statements as the source of tables when performing queries. SQL Server requires an alias; the use of an alias is optional with Oracle.

Oracle	Microsoft SQL Server
SELECT SSN, LNAME, FNAME, TUITION_PAID, SUM_PAID FROM STUDENT_ADMIN.STUDENT, **(SELECT SUM(TUITION_PAID) SUM_PAID** **FROM STUDENT_ADMIN.STUDENT)**	SELECT SSN, LNAME, FNAME, TUITION_PAID, SUM_PAID FROM STUDENT_ADMIN.STUDENT, **(SELECT SUM(TUITION_PAID) SUM_PAID** **FROM STUDENT_ADMIN.STUDENT)** **SUM_STUDENT**

Reading and Modifying BLOBs

Microsoft SQL Server implements binary large objects (BLOBs) with **text** and **image** columns. Oracle implements BLOBs with LONG and LONG RAW columns. In Oracle, a SELECT command can query the values in LONG and LONG RAW columns.

In SQL Server, you can use a standard Transact-SQL statement or the specialized READTEXT statement to read data in **text** and **image** columns. The READTEXT statement allows you to read partial sections of a **text** or **image** column. Oracle does not provide an equivalent statement for working with LONG and LONG RAW columns.

The READTEXT statement makes use of a *text_pointer*, which can be obtained using the TEXTPTR function. The TEXTPTR function returns a pointer to the **text** or **image** column in the specified row or to the **text** or **image** column in the last row returned by the query if more than one row is returned. Because the TEXTPTR function returns a 16-byte binary string, it is best to declare a local variable to hold the text pointer, and then use the variable with READTEXT.

The READTEXT statement specifies how many bytes to return. The value in the @@TEXTSIZE function, which is the limit on the number of characters or bytes to be returned, supersedes the size specified by the READTEXT statement if it is less than the specified size for READTEXT.

The SET statement can be used with the TEXTSIZE parameter to specify the size, in bytes, of text data to be returned with a SELECT statement. If you specify a TEXTSIZE of 0, the size is reset to the default (4 KB). Setting the TEXTSIZE parameter affects the @@TEXTSIZE function. The SQL Server ODBC driver automatically sets the TEXTSIZE parameter when the SQL_MAX_LENGTH statement option is changed.

In Oracle, UPDATE and INSERT commands are used to change values in LONG and LONG RAW columns. In SQL Server, you can use standard UPDATE and INSERT statements, or you can use the UPDATETEXT and WRITETEXT statements. Both UPDATETEXT and WRITETEXT allow a nonlogged option, and UPDATETEXT allows for partial updating of a **text** or **image** column.

The UPDATETEXT statement can be used to replace existing data, delete existing data, or insert new data. Newly inserted data can be a constant value, table name, column name, or text pointer.

The WRITETEXT statement completely overwrites any existing data in the column it affects. Use WRITETEXT to replace text data and UPDATETEXT to modify text data. The UPDATETEXT statement is more flexible because it changes only a portion of a text of image value rather than the entire value.

For more information, see SQL Server Books Online.

Functions

The tables in this section show the relationship between Oracle and SQL Server scalar-valued and aggregate functions. Although the names appear to be the same, it is important to note that functions vary in numbers and types of arguments. Also, functions that are supplied only by Microsoft SQL Server are not mentioned in this list as this chapter is limited to easing migration from existing Oracle applications. Examples of functions not supported by Oracle are: degrees (DEGREES), PI (PI), and random number (RAND).

Number/Mathematical Functions

The following are number/mathematical functions supported by Oracle and their Microsoft SQL Server equivalents.

Function	Oracle	Microsoft SQL Server
Absolute value	ABS	ABS
Arc cosine	ACOS	ACOS
Arc sine	ASIN	ASIN
Arc tangent of n	ATAN	ATAN
Arc tangent of n and m	ATAN2	ATN2
Smallest integer >= value	CEIL	CEILING
Cosine	COS	COS
Hyperbolic cosine	COSH	COT
Exponential value	EXP	EXP
Largest integer <= value	FLOOR	FLOOR
Natural logarithm	LN	LOG
Logarithm, any base	LOG(N)	N/A
Logarithm, base 10	LOG(10)	LOG10
Modulus (remainder)	MOD	USE MODULO (%) OPERATOR
Power	POWER	POWER
Random number	N/A	RAND
Round	ROUND	ROUND
Sign of number	SIGN	SIGN
Sine	SIN	SIN
Hyperbolic sine	SINH	N/A
Square root	SQRT	SQRT
Tangent	TAN	TAN
Hyperbolic tangent	TANH	N/A
Truncate	TRUNC	N/A
Largest number in list	GREATEST	N/A
Smallest number in list	LEAST	N/A
Convert number if NULL	NVL	ISNULL

Character Functions

The following are character functions supported by Oracle and their Microsoft SQL Server equivalents.

Function	Oracle	Microsoft SQL Server
Convert character to ASCII	ASCII	ASCII
String concatenate	CONCAT	(*expression + expression*)
Convert ASCII to character	CHR	CHAR
Returns starting point of character in character string (from left)	INSTR	CHARINDEX
Convert characters to lowercase	LOWER	LOWER
Convert characters to uppercase	UPPER	UPPER
Pad left side of character string	LPAD	N/A
Remove leading blanks	LTRIM	LTRIM
Remove trailing blanks	RTRIM	RTRIM
Starting point of pattern in character string	INSTR	PATINDEX
Repeat character string multiple times	RPAD	REPLICATE
Phonetic representation of character string	SOUNDEX	SOUNDEX
String of repeated spaces	RPAD	SPACE
Character data converted from numeric data	TO_CHAR	STR
Substring	SUBSTR	SUBSTRING
Replace characters	REPLACE	STUFF
Capitalize first letter of each word in string	INITCAP	N/A
Translate character string	TRANSLATE	N/A
Length of character string	LENGTH	DATELENGTH or LEN
Greatest character string in list	GREATEST	N/A
Least character string in list	LEAST	N/A
Convert string if NULL	NVL	ISNULL

Date Functions

The following are date functions supported by Oracle and their Microsoft
SQL Server equivalents.

Function	Oracle	Microsoft SQL Server
Date addition	(date column +/- value) or ADD_MONTHS	DATEADD
Difference between dates	(date column +/- value) or MONTHS_BETWEEN	DATEDIFF
Current date and time	SYSDATE	GETDATE()
Last day of month	LAST_DAY	N/A
Time zone conversion	NEW_TIME	N/A
First weekday after date	NEXT_DAY	N/A
Character string representation of date	TO_CHAR	DATENAME
Integer representation of date	TO_NUMBER (TO_CHAR))	DATEPART
Date round	ROUND	CONVERT
Date truncate	TRUNC	CONVERT
Character string to date	TO_DATE	CONVERT
Convert date if NULL	NVL	ISNULL

Conversion Functions

The following are conversion functions supported by Oracle and their Microsoft
SQL Server equivalents.

Function	Oracle	Microsoft SQL Server
Number to character	TO_CHAR	CONVERT
Character to number	TO_NUMBER	CONVERT
Date to character	TO_CHAR	CONVERT
Character to date	TO_DATE	CONVERT
Hex to binary	HEX_TO_RAW	CONVERT
Binary to hex	RAW_TO_HEX	CONVERT

Other Row-level Functions

The following are other row-level functions supported by Oracle and their Microsoft SQL Server equivalents.

Function	Oracle	Microsoft SQL Server
Return first nonnull expression	DECODE	COALESCE
Current sequence value	CURRVAL	N/A
Next sequence value	NEXTVAL	N/A
If exp1 = exp2, return null	DECODE	NULLIF
User's login ID number	UID	SUSER_ID
User's login name	USER	SUSER_NAME
User's database ID number	UID	USER_ID
User's database name	USER	USER_NAME
Current user	CURRENT_USER	CURRENT_USER
User environment (audit trail)	USERENV	N/A
Level in CONNECT BY clause	LEVEL	N/A

Aggregate Functions

The following are aggregate functions supported by Oracle and their SQL Server equivalents.

Function	Oracle	Microsoft SQL Server
Average	AVG	AVG
Count	COUNT	COUNT
Maximum	MAX	MAX
Minimum	MIN	MIN
Standard deviation	STDDEV	STDEV or STDEVP
Summation	SUM	SUM
Variance	VARIANCE	VAR or VARP

Conditional Tests

Both the Oracle DECODE statement and the Microsoft SQL Server CASE expression perform conditional tests. When the value in *test_value* matches any following expression, the related value is returned. If no match is found, the *default_value* is returned. If no *default_value* is specified, both DECODE and CASE return NULL if there is no match. The table shows the syntax as well as an example of a converted DECODE command.

Oracle	Microsoft SQL Server
DECODE (*test_value*, *expression1*, *value1* [[,*expression2*, *value2*] [...]] [,*default_value*])	**CASE** *input_expression* **WHEN** *when_expression* **THEN** *result_expression* [[**WHEN** *when_expression* **THEN** *result_expression*] [...]] [**ELSE** *else_result_expression*] **END**

CREATE VIEW
 STUDENT_ADMIN.STUDENT_GPA
 (SSN, GPA)
 AS SELECT SSN,
 ROUND(AVG(**DECODE(grade**
          ,'A', 4
          ,'A+', 4.3
          ,'A-', 3.7
          ,'B', 3
          ,'B+', 3.3
          ,'B-', 2.7
          ,'C', 2
          ,'C+', 2.3
          ,'C-', 1.7
          ,'D', 1
          ,'D+', 1.3
          ,'D-', 0.7
          ,0)),2)
 FROM STUDENT_ADMIN.GRADE
 GROUP BY SSN
	CREATE VIEW
	 STUDENT_ADMIN.STUDENT_GPA
	 (SSN, GPA)
	 AS SELECT SSN, ROUND(AVG(**CASE grade**
	        WHEN 'A' THEN 4
	        WHEN 'A+' THEN 4.3
	        WHEN 'A-' THEN 3.7
	        WHEN 'B' THEN 3
	        WHEN 'B+' THEN 3.3
	        WHEN 'B-' THEN 2.7
	        WHEN 'C' THEN 2
	        WHEN 'C+' THEN 2.3
	        WHEN 'C-' THEN 1.7
	        WHEN 'D' THEN 1
	        WHEN 'D+' THEN 1.3
	        WHEN 'D-' THEN 0.7
	        ELSE 0
	        END),2)
	 FROM STUDENT_ADMIN.GRADE
	 GROUP BY SSN

The CASE expression can support the use of SELECT statements for performing Boolean tests, something the DECODE command does not allow. For more information about the CASE expression, see SQL Server Books Online.

Converting Values to Different Data Types

The Microsoft SQL Server CONVERT and CAST functions are multiple purpose conversion functions. They provide similar functionality, converting an expression of one data type to another data type, and supporting a variety of special date formats:

CAST(expression AS data_type)

CONVERT (data type[(length)], expression [, style])

CAST is a SQL-92 standard function. These functions perform the same operations as the Oracle TO_CHAR, TO_NUMBER, TO_DATE, HEXTORAW, and RAWTOHEX functions.

The data type is any system data type into which the expression is to be converted. User-defined data types cannot be used. The *length* parameter is optional and is used with **char**, **varchar**, **binary**, and **varbinary** data types. The maximum allowable length is 8000.

Conversion	Oracle	Microsoft SQL Server
Character to number	TO_NUMBER('10')	CONVERT(**numeric**, '10')
Number to character	TO_CHAR(10)	CONVERT(**char**, 10)
Character to date	TO_DATE('04-JUL-97') TO_DATE('04-JUL-1997', 'dd-mon-yyyy') TO_DATE('July 4, 1997', 'Month dd, yyyy')	CONVERT(**datetime**, '04-JUL-97') CONVERT(**datetime**, '04-JUL-1997') CONVERT(**datetime**, 'July 4, 1997')
Date to character	TO_CHAR(sysdate) TO_CHAR(sysdate, 'dd mon yyyy') TO_CHAR(sysdate, 'mm/dd/yyyy')	CONVERT(**char**, GETDATE()) CONVERT(**char**, GETDATE(), 106) CONVERT(**char**, GETDATE(), 101)
Hex to binary	HEXTORAW('1F')	CONVERT(**binary**, '1F')
Binary to hex	RAWTOHEX (binary_column)	CONVERT(**char**, *binary_column*)

Notice how character strings are converted to dates. In Oracle, the default date format model is "DD-MON-YY." If you use any other format, you must provide an appropriate date format model. The CONVERT function automatically converts standard date formats without the need for a format model.

When converting from a date to a character string, the default output for the CONVERT function is "dd mon yyyy hh:mm:ss:mmm(24h)". A numeric style code is used to format the output to other types of date format models. For more information about the CONVERT function, see SQL Server Books Online.

The following table shows the default output for Microsoft SQL Server dates.

Without Century	With Century	Standard	Output
-	0 or 100 (*)	Default	mon dd yyyy hh:miAM (or PM)
1	101	USA	mm/dd/yy
2	102	ANSI	yy.mm.dd
3	103	British/French	dd/mm/yy
4	104	German	dd.mm.yy
5	105	Italian	dd-mm-yy
6	106	-	dd mon yy
7	107	-	mon dd, yy
8	108	-	hh:mm:ss
-	9 or 109 (*)	Default milliseconds	mon dd yyyy hh:mi:ss:mmm (AM or PM)
10	110	USA	mm-dd-yy
11	111	Japan	yy/mm/dd
12	112	ISO	yymmdd
-	13 or 113 (*)	Europe default	dd mon yyyy hh:mm:ss:mmm(24h)
14	114	-	hh:mi:ss:mmm(24h)

User-defined Functions

Oracle PL/SQL functions can be used in Oracle SQL statements. This functionality can often be achieved in other ways with Microsoft SQL Server.

In the following example, the Oracle user-defined function GET_SUM_MAJOR is used to obtain a sum of tuition paid by major. It can be replaced in SQL Server by using a query as a table.

Oracle	Microsoft SQL Server

SELECT SSN, FNAME, LNAME,)
  TUITION_PAID,
  TUITION_PAID/**GET_SUM_**
  MAJOR(MAJOR)
  AS PERCENT_MAJOR
FROM STUDENT_ADMIN.STUDENT
	SELECT SSN, FNAME, LNAME,
	TUITION_PAID,
	TUITION_PAID/**SUM_MAJOR** AS
	PERCENT_MAJOR
	FROM STUDENT_ADMIN.STUDENT,
	  **(SELECT MAJOR,
	    SUM(TUITION_PAID) SUM_MAJOR
	  FROM STUDENT_ADMIN.STUDENT
	  GROUP BY MAJOR) SUM_STUDENT
	  WHERE STUDENT.MAJOR =
	    SUM_STUDENT.MAJOR**

CREATE OR REPLACE FUNCTION **GET_SUM_MAJOR** **(INMAJOR VARCHAR2) RETURN NUMBER** **AS SUM_PAID NUMBER;** **BEGIN** **SELECT SUM(TUITION_PAID) INTO** **SUM_PAID** **FROM STUDENT_ADMIN.STUDENT** **WHERE MAJOR = INMAJOR;** **RETURN(SUM_PAID);** **END GET_SUM_MAJOR;**	**No CREATE FUNCTION syntax is required;** **use CREATE PROCEDURE syntax.**

Comparison Operators

Oracle and Microsoft SQL Server comparison operators are nearly identical.

Operator	Oracle	Microsoft SQL Server
Equal to	(=)	(=)
Greater than	(>)	(>)
Less than	(<)	(<)
Greater than or equal to	(>=)	(>=)
Less than or equal to	(<=)	(<=)
Not equal to	(!=, <>, ^=)	(!=, <>, ^=)
Not greater than, not less than	N/A	!> , !<
In any member in set	IN	IN

(continued)

Operator	Oracle	Microsoft SQL Server
Not in any member in set	NOT IN	NOT IN
Any value in set	ANY, SOME	ANY, SOME
Referring to all values in set	!= ALL, <> ALL, < ALL, > ALL, <= ALL, >= ALL, != SOME, <> SOME, < SOME, > SOME, <= SOME, >= SOME	!= ALL, <> ALL, < ALL, > ALL, <= ALL, >= ALL, != SOME, <> SOME, < SOME, > SOME, <= SOME, >= SOME
Like pattern	LIKE	LIKE
Not like pattern	NOT LIKE	NOT LIKE
Value between x and y	BETWEEN x AND y	BETWEEN x AND y
Value not between	NOT BETWEEN	NOT BETWEEN
Value exists	EXISTS	EXISTS
Value does not exist	NOT EXISTS	NOT EXISTS
Value {is | is not} NULL	IS NULL, IS NOT NULL	Same. Also = NULL, != NULL for backward compatibility (not recommended).

Pattern Matches

The SQL Server LIKE keyword offers useful wildcard search options that are not supported by Oracle. In addition to supporting the % and _ wildcard characters common to both RDBMSs, the [ ] and [^] characters are also supported by SQL Server.

The [ ] character set is used to search for any single character within a specified range. For example, if you search for the characters a through f in a single character position, you can specify this with LIKE '[a-f]' or LIKE '[abcdef]'. The usefulness of these additional wildcard characters is shown in this table.

Oracle	Microsoft SQL Server

SELECT * FROM STUDENT_ADMIN.STUDENT WHERE LNAME LIKE 'A%'
     OR LNAME LIKE 'B%'
     OR LNAME LIKE 'C%'
	SELECT * FROM STUDENT_ADMIN.STUDENT WHERE LNAME LIKE '[ABC]%'

The [^] wildcard character set is used to specify characters NOT in the specified range. For example, if any character except a through f is acceptable, you use LIKE '[^a - f]' or LIKE '[^abcdef]'.

For more information about the LIKE keyword, see SQL Server Books Online.

Using NULL in Comparisons

Although Microsoft SQL Server traditionally has supported the SQL-92–standard as well as some nonstandard NULL behaviors, it supports the use of NULL in Oracle.

SET ANSI_NULLS should be set to ON for executing distributed queries.

The SQL Server ODBC driver and OLE DB Provider for SQL Server automatically SET ANSI_NULLS to ON when connecting. This setting can be configured in ODBC data sources, in ODBC connection attributes, or in OLE DB connection properties that are set in the application before connecting to SQL Server. SET ANSI_NULLS defaults to OFF for connections from DB-Library applications.

When SET ANSI_DEFAULTS is ON, SET ANSI_NULLS is enabled.

For more information about the use of NULL, see SQL Server Books Online.

String Concatenation

Oracle uses two pipe symbols (||) as the string concatenation operator, and SQL Server uses the plus sign (+). This difference requires minor revision in your application program code.

Oracle	Microsoft SQL Server
SELECT FNAME|| ' '||LNAME AS NAME FROM STUDENT_ADMIN.STUDENT	SELECT FNAME + ' '+ LNAME AS NAME FROM STUDENT_ADMIN.STUDENT

Control-of-Flow Language

The control-of-flow language controls the flow of execution of SQL statements, statement blocks, and stored procedures. PL/SQL and Transact-SQL provide many of the same constructs, although there are some syntax differences.

Keywords

These are the keywords supported by each RDBMS.

Statement	Oracle PL/SQL	Microsoft SQL Server Transact-SQL
Declare variables	DECLARE	DECLARE
Statement block	BEGIN...END;	BEGIN...END

(continued)

Statement	Oracle PL/SQL	Microsoft SQL Server Transact-SQL
Conditional processing	IF...THEN, ELSIF...THEN, ELSE ENDIF;	IF...[BEGIN...END] ELSE <condition> [BEGIN...END] ELSE IF <condition> CASE expression
Unconditional exit	RETURN	RETURN
Unconditional exit to the statement following the end of the current program block	EXIT	BREAK
Restarts a WHILE loop	N/A	CONTINUE
Wait for a specified interval	N/A (dbms_lock.sleep)	WAITFOR
Loop control	WHILE LOOP...END LOOP;	WHILE <condition> BEGIN... END
	LABEL...GOTO LABEL; FOR...END LOOP; LOOP...END LOOP;	LABEL...GOTO LABEL
Program comments	/* ... */, --	/* ... */, --
Print output	RDBMS_OUTPUT.PUT_LINE	PRINT
Raise program error	RAISE_APPLICATION_ERROR	RAISERROR
Execute program	EXECUTE	EXECUTE
Statement terminator	Semicolon (;)	N/A

Declaring Variables

Transact-SQL and PL/SQL variables are created with the DECLARE keyword. Transact-SQL variables are identified with @) and, like PL/SQL variables, are initialized to a null value when they are first created.

Oracle	Microsoft SQL Server
DECLARE	DECLARE
VSSN CHAR(9);	@VSSN CHAR(9),
VFNAME VARCHAR2(12);	@VFNAME VARCHAR2(12),
VLNAME VARCHAR2(20);	@VLNAME VARCHAR2(20),
VBIRTH_DATE DATE;	@VBIRTH_DATE DATETIME,
VLOAN_AMOUNT NUMBER(12,2);	@VLOAN_AMOUNT NUMERIC(12,2)

Transact-SQL does not support the %TYPE and %ROWTYPE variable data type definitions. A Transact-SQL variable cannot be initialized in the DECLARE command. The Oracle NOT NULL and CONSTANT keywords cannot be used in Microsoft SQL Server data type definitions.

Like Oracle LONG and LONG RAW data types, **text** and **image** data types cannot be used for variable declarations. Additionally, the PL/SQL style record and table definitions are not supported.

Assigning Variables

Oracle and Microsoft SQL Server offer these ways to assign values to local variables.

Oracle	Microsoft SQL Server
Assignment operator (:=)	SET @*local_variable* = value
SELECT...INTO syntax for selecting column values from a single row	SELECT @*local_variable = expression* [FROM...] for assigning a literal value, an expression involving other local variables, or a column value from a single row
FETCH...INTO syntax	FETCH...INTO syntax

Here are some syntax examples.

Oracle	Microsoft SQL Server

DECLARE VSSN CHAR(9);
 VFNAME VARCHAR2(12);
 VLNAME VARCHAR2(20);
 BEGIN
 VSSN := '123448887';
 SELECT **FNAME, LNAME INTO VFNAME,**
 VLNAME FROM STUDENTS WHERE
 SSN=VSSN;
 END;
	DECLARE @VSSN CHAR(9),
	 @VFNAME VARCHAR(12),
	 @VLNAME VARCHAR(20)
	 SET **@VSSN = '12355887'**
	 SELECT **@VFNAME=FNAME,**
	 @VLNAME=LNAME FROM STUDENTS
	 WHERE SSN = @VSSN

Statement Blocks

Oracle PL/SQL and Microsoft SQL Server Transact-SQL support the use of BEGIN...END terminology to specify statement blocks. Transact-SQL does not require the use of a statement block following the DECLARE statement. The BEGIN...END statement blocks are required in Microsoft SQL Server for IF statements and WHILE loops if more than one statement is executed.

Oracle	Microsoft SQL Server
DECLARE	DECLARE
DECLARE VARIABLES ...	DECLARE VARIABLES ...
BEGIN -- THIS IS REQUIRED SYNTAX	**BEGIN -- THIS IS OPTIONAL SYNTAX**
PROGRAM_STATEMENTS ...	PROGRAM_STATEMENTS ...
IF ...THEN	IF ...
STATEMENT1;	**BEGIN**
STATEMENT2;	STATEMENT1
STATEMENTN;	STATEMENT2
END IF;	STATEMENTN
WHILE ... **LOOP**	**END**
STATEMENT1;	WHILE ...
STATEMENT2;	**BEGIN**
STATEMENTN;	STATEMENT1
END LOOP;	STATEMENT2
END; -- THIS IS REQUIRED SYNTAX	STATEMENTN
	END
	END -- THIS IS REQUIRED SYNTAX

Conditional Processing

The Microsoft SQL Server Transact-SQL conditional statement includes IF and
ELSE rather than the ELSIF statement in Oracle PL/SQL. Multiple IF statements
can be nested to achieve the same effect. For extensive conditional tests, the
CASE expression may be easier to read.

Oracle	Microsoft SQL Server
DECLARE	DECLARE
VDEGREE_PROGRAM CHAR(1);	@VDEGREE_PROGRAM CHAR(1),
VDEGREE_PROGRAM_NAME	@VDEGREE_PROGRAM_NAME
VARCHAR2(20);	VARCHAR(20)
BEGIN	SELECT @VDEGREE_PROGRAM = 'U'
VDEGREE_PROGRAM := 'U';	SELECT @VDEGREE_PROGRAM_
IF VDEGREE_PROGRAM = 'U' THEN	NAME = CASE @VDEGREE_PROGRAM
VDEGREE_PROGRAM_NAME :=	WHEN 'U' THEN 'Undergraduate'
'Undergraduate';	WHEN 'M' THEN 'Masters'
ELSIF VDEGREE_PROGRAM = 'M'	WHEN 'P' THEN 'PhD'.
THEN VDEGREE_PROGRAM_	ELSE 'Unknown'
NAME := 'Masters';	END
ELSIF VDEGREE_PROGRAM = 'P'	
THEN VDEGREE_PROGRAM_	
NAME := 'PhD';	
ELSE VDEGREE_PROGRAM_	
NAME := 'Unknown';	
END IF;	
END;	

Repeated Statement Execution (Looping)

Oracle PL/SQL provides the unconditional LOOP and FOR LOOP. Transact-SQL offers the WHILE loop and the GOTO statement for looping purposes.

```
WHILE Boolean_expression
    {sql_statement | statement_block}
    [BREAK] [CONTINUE]
```

The WHILE loop tests a Boolean expression for the repeated execution of one or more statements. The statement(s) are executed repeatedly as long as the specified expression evaluates to TRUE. If multiple statements are to be executed, they must be placed within a BEGIN...END block.

Oracle	Microsoft SQL Server
DECLARE	DECLARE
COUNTER NUMBER;	@COUNTER NUMERIC
BEGIN	SELECT@COUNTER = 1
COUNTER := 0	WHILE (@COUNTER <5)
WHILE (COUNTER <5) LOOP	BEGIN
COUNTER := COUNTER + 1;	SELECT @COUNTER =
END LOOP;	@COUNTER +1
END;	END

Statement execution can be controlled from inside the loop with the BREAK and CONTINUE keywords. The BREAK keyword causes an unconditional exit from the WHILE loop, and the CONTINUE keyword causes the WHILE loop to restart, skipping any statements that follow. The BREAK keyword is equivalent to the Oracle PL/SQL EXIT keyword. Oracle does not have an equivalent to CONTINUE.

GOTO Statement

Both Oracle and Microsoft SQL Server have GOTO statements, with different syntax. The GOTO statement causes the execution of a Transact-SQL batch to jump to a label. None of the statements between the GOTO statement and the label are executed.

Oracle	Microsoft SQL Server
GOTO label;	GOTO *label*
<<label name here>>	

PRINT Statement

The Transact-SQL PRINT statement performs the same operation as the PL/SQL RDBMS_OUTPUT.*put_line* procedure. It is used for printing user-specified messages.

The message limit for the PRINT statement is 8,000 characters. Variables that are defined using the **char** or **varchar** data type can be embedded in the printed statement. If any other data type is used, the CONVERT or CAST function must be used. Local variables, global variables, and text can be printed. Both single and double quotation marks can be used to enclose text.

Returning from Stored Procedures

Both Microsoft SQL Server and Oracle have RETURN statements. RETURN lets your program exit unconditionally from a query or procedure. RETURN is immediate and complete and can be used at any point to exit from a procedure, batch, or statement block. Statements following RETURN are not executed.

Oracle	Microsoft SQL Server
RETURN *expression*:	RETURN [*integer_expression*]

Raising Program Errors

The Transact-SQL RAISERROR statement returns a user-defined error message and sets a system flag to record that an error has occurred. It is similar in function to the PL/SQL *raise_application_error* exception handler.

The RAISERROR statement allows the client to retrieve an entry from the **sysmessages** table or build a message dynamically with user-specified severity and state information. When defined, this message is sent back to the client as a server error message.

```
RAISERROR ({msg_id | msg_str}, severity, state
    [, argument1 [, argument2]])
    [WITH options]
```

When converting your PL/SQL programs, it may not be necessary to use the RAISERROR statement. In the following code example, the PL/SQL program uses the *raise_application_error* exception handler, while the Transact-SQL program uses nothing. The *raise_application_error* exception handler has been included to prevent the PL/SQL program from possibly returning an ambiguous *unhandled exception* error message. Instead, it always returns the Oracle error message (SQLERRM) when an unanticipated problem occurs.

When a Transact-SQL program fails, it always returns a detailed error message to the client program. Therefore, unless some specialized error handling is required, the RAISERROR statement is not always needed.

Oracle	Microsoft SQL Server
CREATE OR REPLACE FUNCTION DEPT_ADMIN.DELETE_DEPT (VDEPT IN VARCHAR2) RETURN NUMBER AS BEGIN DELETE FROM DEPT_ADMIN.DEPT WHERE DEPT = VDEPT; RETURN(SQL%ROWCOUNT); EXCEPTION WHEN OTHER THEN RAISE_APPLICATION_ERROR (-20001,SQLERRM); END DELETE_DEPT; /	CREATE PROCEDURE DEPT_ADMIN.DELETE_DEPT @VDEPT VARCHAR(4) AS DELETE FROM DEPT_DB.DBO.DEPT WHERE DEPT = @VDEPT RETURN @@ROWCOUNT GO

Implementing Cursors

Oracle always requires that cursors be used with SELECT statements, regardless of the number of rows requested from the database. In Microsoft SQL Server, a SELECT statement that is not enclosed within a cursor returns rows to the client as a default result set. This is an efficient way to return data to a client application.

SQL Server provides two interfaces for cursor functions. When cursors are used in Transact-SQL batches or stored procedures, SQL statements can be used to declare, open, and fetch from cursors as well as positioned updates and deletes. When cursors from a DB-Library, ODBC, or OLEDB program are used, the SQL Server client libraries transparently call built-in server functions to handle cursors more efficiently.

When porting a PL/SQL procedure from Oracle, first determine whether cursors are needed to do the same function in Transact-SQL. If the cursor returns only a set of rows to the client application, use a noncursor SELECT statement in Transact-SQL to return a default result set. If the cursor is used to load data a row at a time into local procedure variables, you must use cursors in Transact-SQL.

Syntax

The table shows the syntax for using cursors.

Operation	Oracle	Microsoft SQL Server
Declaring a cursor	**CURSOR** *cursor_name* [(*cursor_parameter(s)*)] **IS** *select_statement*;	**DECLARE** *cursor_name* **CURSOR** [LOCAL | GLOBAL] [FORWARD_ONLY | SCROLL] [STATIC | KEYSET | DYNAMIC | FAST_FORWARD] [READ_ONLY | SCROLL_LOCKS | OPTIMISTIC] [TYPE_WARNING] **FOR** *select_statement* [FOR UPDATE [OF *column_name* [,...*n*]]]
Opening a cursor	OPEN *cursor_name* [(*cursor_parameter(s)*)];	OPEN *cursor_name*
Fetching from a cursor	**FETCH** *cursor_name* **INTO** *variable(s)*	**FETCH** [[NEXT | PRIOR | FIRST | LAST | ABSOLUTE {*n* | @nvar} | RELATIVE {*n* | @nvar}] FROM] *cursor_name* [INTO @variable(s)]
Update fetched row	UPDATE *table_name* SET *statement(s)...* WHERE CURRENT OF *cursor_name*;	UPDATE *table_name* SET *statement(s)...* WHERE CURRENT OF *cursor_name*
Delete fetched row	DELETE FROM *table_name* WHERE CURRENT OF *cursor_name*;	DELETE FROM *table_name* WHERE CURRENT OF *cursor_name*
Closing cursor	CLOSE *cursor_name*;	CLOSE *cursor_name*
Remove cursor data structures	**N/A**	**DEALLOCATE** *cursor_name*

Declaring a Cursor

Although the Transact-SQL DECLARE CURSOR statement does not support the use of cursor arguments, it does support local variables. The values of these local variables are used in the cursor when it is opened. Microsoft SQL Server offers many additional capabilities in its DECLARE CURSOR statement.

The INSENSITIVE option is used to define a cursor that makes a temporary copy of the data to be used by that cursor. All of the requests to the cursor are answered by this temporary table. Consequently, modifications made to base tables are not reflected in the data returned by fetches made to this cursor. Data accessed by this type of cursor cannot be modified.

Applications can request a cursor type and then execute a Transact-SQL statement that is not supported by server cursors of the type requested. SQL Server returns an error that indicates the cursor type has changed, or given a set of factors, implicitly converts a cursor. For a complete list of factors that trigger SQL Server 7.0 to implicitly convert a cursor from one type to another, see SQL Server Books Online.

The SCROLL option allows backward, absolute, and relative fetches in addition to forward fetches. A scroll cursor uses a keyset cursor model in which committed deletes and updates made to the underlying tables by any user are reflected in subsequent fetches. This is true only if the cursor is not declared with the INSENSITIVE option.

If the READ ONLY option is chosen, updates are prevented from occurring against any row within the cursor. This option overrides the default capability of a cursor to be updated.

The UPDATE [OF *column_list*] statement is used to define updatable columns within the cursor. If [OF *column_list*] is supplied, only the columns listed allow modifications. If no list is supplied, all of the columns can be updated unless the cursor has been defined as READ ONLY.

It is important to note that the name scope for a SQL Server cursor is the connection itself. This is different from the name scope of a local variable. A second cursor with the same name as an existing cursor on the same user connection cannot be declared until the first cursor is deallocated.

Opening a Cursor

Transact-SQL does not support the passing of arguments to a cursor when it is opened, unlike PL/SQL. When a Transact-SQL cursor is opened, the result set membership and ordering are fixed. Updates and deletes that have been committed against the base tables of the cursor by other users are reflected in fetches made against all cursors defined without the INSENSITIVE option. In the case of an INSENSITIVE cursor, a temporary table is generated.

Fetching Data

Oracle cursors can move in a forward direction only—there is no backward or relative scrolling capability. SQL Server cursors can scroll forward and backward with the fetch options shown in the following table. These fetch options can be used only when the cursor is declared with the SCROLL option.

Scroll Option	Description
NEXT	Returns the first row of the result set if this is the first fetch against the cursor; otherwise, it moves the cursor one row within the result set. NEXT is the primary method used to move through a result set. NEXT is the default cursor fetch.
PRIOR	Returns the previous row within the result set.
FIRST	Moves the cursor to the first row within the result set and returns the first row.
LAST	Moves the cursor to the last row within the result set and returns the last row.
ABSOLUTE n	Returns the nth row within the result set. If n is a negative value, the returned row is the nth row counting backward from the last row of the result set.
RELATIVE n	Returns the nth row after the currently fetched row. If n is a negative value, the returned row is the nth row counting backward from the relative position of the cursor.

The Transact-SQL FETCH statement does not require the INTO clause. If return variables are not specified, the row is automatically returned to the client as a single-row result set. However, if your procedure must get the rows to the client, a noncursor SELECT statement is much more efficient.

The @@FETCH_STATUS function is updated following each FETCH. It is similar in use to the CURSOR_NAME%FOUND and CURSOR_NAME%NOTFOUND variables used in PL/SQL. The @@FETCH_STATUS function is set to the value of 0 following a successful fetch. If the fetch tries to read beyond the end of the cursor, a value of –1 is returned. If the requested row has been deleted from the table after the cursor was opened, the @@FETCH_STATUS function returns –2. The value of –2 usually occurs only in a cursor declared with the SCROLL option. This variable must be checked following each fetch to ensure the validity of the data.

SQL Server does not support Oracle's cursor FOR loop syntax.

CURRENT OF Clause

The CURRENT OF clause syntax and function for updates and deletes is the same in both PL/SQL and Transact-SQL. A positioned UPDATE or DELETE is performed against the current row within the specified cursor.

Closing a Cursor

The Transact-SQL CLOSE CURSOR statement closes the cursor but leaves the data structures accessible for reopening. The PL/SQL CLOSE CURSOR statement closes and releases all data structures.

Transact-SQL requires the use of the DEALLOCATE CURSOR statement to remove the cursor data structures. The DEALLOCATE CURSOR statement is different from CLOSE CURSOR in that a closed cursor can be reopened. The DEALLOCATE CURSOR statement releases all data structures associated with the cursor and removes the definition of the cursor.

Cursor Example

The example below shows equivalent cursor statements in PL/SQL and Transact-SQL.

Oracle	Microsoft SQL Server
DECLARE	DECLARE
VSSN CHAR(9);	@VSSN CHAR(9),
VFNAME VARCHAR(12);	@VFNAME VARCHAR(12),
VLNAME VARCHAR(20);	@VLNAME VARCHAR(20)

(continued)

Oracle	Microsoft SQL Server
CURSOR CUR1 IS	DECLARE curl CURSOR FOR
SELECT SSN, FNAME, LNAME	SELECT SSN, FNAME, LNAME
FROM STUDENT ORDER BY LNAME;	FROM STUDENT ORDER BY SSN
BEGIN	OPEN CUR1
OPEN CUR1;	FETCH NEXT FROM CUR1
FETCH CUR1 INTO VSSN, VFNAME, VLNAME;	INTO @VSSN, @VFNAME, @VLNAME
WHILE (CUR1%FOUND) LOOP	WHILE (@@FETCH_STATUS <> -1)
FETCH CUR1 INTO VSSN, VFNAME, VLNAME;	BEGIN
END LOOP;	FETCH NEXT FROM CUR1 INTO @VSSN, @VFNAME, @VLNAME
CLOSE CUR1;	END
END;	CLOSE CUR1
	DEALLOCATE CUR1

Tuning SQL Statements

This section provides information about several SQL Server tools you can use to tune Transact-SQL statements. For more information about tuning your SQL Server database, see "Performance Tuning" earlier in this volume.

SQL Server Query Analyzer

You can use the graphical showplan feature of SQL Server Query Analyzer to learn more about how the optimizer will process your statement.

SQL Server Profiler

This graphical tool captures a continuous record of server activity in real-time. SQL Server Profiler monitors many different server events and event categories, filters these events with user-specified criteria, and outputs a trace to the screen, a file, or another SQL Server.

SQL Server Profiler can be used to:

- Monitor the performance of SQL Server.
- Debug Transact-SQL statements and stored procedures.
- Identify slow-executing queries.

- Troubleshoot problems in SQL Server by capturing all the events that lead up to a particular problem, and then replaying the events on a test system to replicate and isolate the problem.

- Test SQL statements and stored procedures in the development phase of a project by single-stepping through statements, one line at a time, to confirm that the code works as expected.

- Capture events on a production system and replay those captured events on a test system, thereby re-creating what happened in the production environment for testing or debugging purposes. Replaying captured events on a separate system allows the users to continue using the production system without interference.

SQL Server Profiler provides a graphical user interface to a set of extended stored procedures. You can also use these extended stored procedures directly. Therefore, it is possible to create your own application that uses the SQL Server Profiler extended stored procedures to monitor SQL Server.

SET Statement

The SET statement can set SQL Server query-processing options for the duration of your work session, or for the duration of a running trigger or a stored procedure.

The SET FORCEPLAN ON statement forces the optimizer to process joins in the same order as the tables appear in the FROM clause, similar to the ORDERED hint used with the Oracle optimizer.

The SET SHOWPLAN_ALL and SET SHOWPLAN_TEXT statements return only query or statement execution plan information and do not execute the query or statement. To execute the query or statement, set the appropriate showplan statement OFF. The query or statement will then execute. The SHOWPLAN option provides results similar to the Oracle EXPLAIN PLAN tool.

With SET STATISTICS PROFILE ON, each executed query returns its regular result set, followed by an additional result set that shows a profile of the query execution. Other options include SET STATISTICS IO and SET STATISTICS TIME.

Transact-SQL statement processing consists of two phases, compilation and execution. The NOEXEC option compiles each query but does not execute it. After NOEXEC is set ON, no subsequent statements are executed (including other SET statements) until NOEXEC is set OFF.

```
SET SHOWPLAN ON
SET NOEXEC ON
go
SELECT * FROM DEPT_ADMIN.DEPT,
    STUDENT_ADMIN.STUDENT
WHERE MAJOR = DEPT
go
STEP 1
The type of query is SETON
STEP 1
The type of query is SETON
STEP 1
The type of query is SELECT
FROM TABLE
DEPT_ADMIN.DEPT
Nested iteration
Table Scan
FROM TABLE
STUDENT_ADMIN.STUDENT
Nested iteration
Table Scan
```

Query Optimization

Oracle requires the use of hints to influence the operation and performance of its cost-based optimizer. The Microsoft SQL Server cost-based optimizer does not require the use of hints to assist in its query evaluation process. They are offered, however, as some situations do warrant their use.

The INDEX = {*index_name* | *index_id*} hint specifies the index name or ID to use for that table. An *index_id* of 0 forces a table scan, while an *index_id* of 1 forces the use of a clustered index, if it exists. This is similar to the index hints used in Oracle.

The SQL Server FASTFIRSTROW hint directs the optimizer to use a nonclustered index if its column order matches the ORDER BY clause. This hint operates in a similar fashion to the Oracle FIRST_ROWS hint.

Using ODBC

This section provides information about the ways Oracle and SQL Server use ODBC and information about developing or migrating applications with ODBC.

Recommended Conversion Strategy

Use the following process when you convert your application code from Oracle to SQL Server:

1. Consider converting your application to ODBC if it is written using Oracle Pro*C or the Oracle Call Interface (OCI).

2. Understand SQL Server default result sets and cursor options, and choose the fetching strategy that is most efficient for your application.

3. Remap Oracle ODBC SQL data types to SQL Server ODBC SQL data types where appropriate.

4. Use the ODBC Extended SQL extensions to create generic SQL statements.

5. Determine if manual commit mode is required for the SQL Server application.

6. Test the performance of your application(s) and modify the program(s) as necessary.

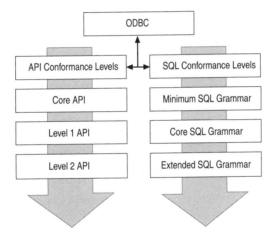

ODBC Architecture

Microsoft provides both 16-bit and 32-bit versions of its the ODBC SQL Server driver. The 32-bit ODBC SQL Server driver is thread-safe. The driver serializes shared access by multiple threads to shared statement handles (hstmt), connection handles (hdbc), and environment handles (henv). However, the ODBC program is still responsible for keeping operations within statements and connection spaces in the proper sequence, even when the program uses multiple threads.

Because the ODBC driver for Oracle can be supplied by one of many possible vendors, there are many possible scenarios regarding architecture and operation. You must contact the vendor to ensure that the ODBC driver meets your application's requirements.

In most cases, the ODBC driver for Oracle uses SQL*Net to connect to the Oracle RDBMS. SQL*Net may not be used, however, when connecting to Personal Oracle.

The illustration shows the application/driver architecture for 32-bit environments.

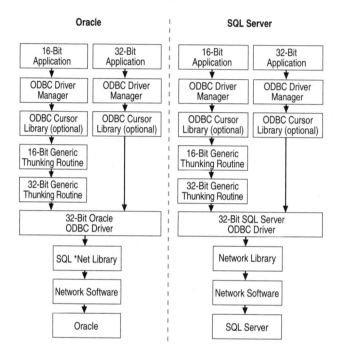

The term *thunking* means intercepting a function call, doing a special processing to translate between 16-bit and 32-bit code, and then transferring control to a target function. Note how the ODBC Cursor Library optionally resides between the driver manager and its driver. This library provides scrollable cursor services on top of drivers that support only forward-only cursors.

Forward-only Cursors

Oracle and SQL Server treat result sets and cursors differently. Understanding these differences is essential for successfully moving a client application from Oracle to SQL Server and having it perform optimally.

In Oracle, any result set from a SELECT command is treated as a forward-only cursor when fetched in the client application. This is true whether you are using ODBC, OCI, or Embedded SQL as your development tool.

By default, each Oracle FETCH command issued by the client program (for example, **SQLFetch** in ODBC) causes a round-trip across the network to the server to return one row. If a client application wants to fetch more than one row at a time across the network, it must set up an array in its program and perform an array fetch.

Between fetches, no locks are held at the server for a read-only cursor because of Oracle's multiversioning concurrency model. When the program specifies an updatable cursor with the FOR UPDATE clause, all of the requested rows in the SELECT command are locked when the statement is opened. These row-level locks remain in place until the program issues a COMMIT or ROLLBACK request.

In SQL Server, a SELECT statement is not always associated with a cursor at the server. By default, SQL Server simply streams all the result set rows from a SELECT statement back to the client. This streaming starts as soon as the SELECT is executed. Result set streams can also be returned by SELECT statements within stored procedures. Additionally, a single stored procedure or batch of commands can stream back multiple result sets in response to a single EXECUTE statement.

The SQL Server client is responsible for fetching these default result sets as soon as they are available. For default result sets, fetches at the client do not result in round-trips to the server. Instead, fetches from a default result set pull data from local network buffers into program variables. This default result set model creates an efficient mechanism to return multiple rows of data to the client in a single round-trip across this network. Minimizing network round-trips is usually the most important factor in client/server application performance.

Compared to Oracle's cursors, default result sets put some additional responsibilities on the SQL Server client application. The SQL Server client application must immediately fetch all the result set rows returned by an EXECUTE statement. If the application needs to present rows incrementally to other parts of the program, it must buffer the rows to an internal array. If it fails to fetch all result set rows, the connection to SQL Server remains busy.

If this occurs, no other work (such as UPDATE statements) can be executed on that connection until the entire result set rows are fetched or the client cancels the request. Moreover, the server continues to hold share locks on table data pages until the fetch has completed. The fact that these share locks are held until a fetch is complete make it mandatory that you fetch all rows as quickly as possible. This technique is in direct contrast to the incremental style of fetch that is commonly found in Oracle applications.

Server Cursors

Microsoft SQL Server offers *server cursors* to address the need for incremental fetching of result sets across the network. Server cursors can be requested in an application by simply calling **SQLSetStmtOption** to set the SQL_CURSOR_TYPE option.

When a SELECT statement is executed as a server cursor, only a cursor identifier is returned by the EXECUTE statement. Subsequent fetch requests pass the cursor identifier back to the server along with a parameter specifying the number of rows to fetch at once. The server returns the number of rows requested.

Between fetch requests, the connection remains free to issue other commands, including other cursor OPEN or FETCH requests. In ODBC terms, this means that server cursors allow the SQL Server driver to support multiple active statements on a single connection.

Furthermore, server cursors do not usually hold locks between fetch requests, so you are free to pause between fetches for user input without affecting other users. Server cursors can be updated in place using either optimistic conflict detection or pessimistic scroll locking concurrency options.

While these features make programming with server cursors more familiar to Oracle developers than using default result sets, they are not free. Compared to default result sets:

- Server cursors are more expensive in terms of server resources, because temporary storage space is used to maintain cursor state information at the server.

- Server cursors are more expensive to retrieve a given result set of data with, because the EXECUTE statement and each fetch request in a server cursor requires a separate round-trip to the server.

- Server cursors are less flexible in terms of the kind of batches and stored procedures they support. This is because a server cursor can execute only one SELECT statement at a time, whereas default result sets can be used for batches and stored procedures that return multiple result sets or include statements other than SELECT statements.

For these reasons, it is wise to limit the use of server cursors to those parts of your application that need their features. An example that illustrates the use of server cursors can be found in the LIST_STUDENTS function in the Ssdemo.cpp sample SQL Server ODBC program file.

Scrollable Cursors

The Oracle RDBMS supports only forward-scrolling cursors. Each row is fetched to the application in the order that it was specified in the query. Oracle does not accept requests to move backward to a previously fetched row. The only way to move backward is to close the cursor and reopen it. Unfortunately, you are repositioned back to the first row in the active query set.

Because SQL Server supports scrollable cursors, you can position a SQL Server cursor at any row location. You can scroll both forward and backward. For many applications involving a user interface, scrollability is a useful feature. With scrollable cursors, your application can fetch a screen full of rows at a time, and only fetch additional rows as the user asks for them.

Although Oracle does not directly support scrollable cursors, this limitation can be minimized by using one of several ODBC options. For example, some Oracle ODBC drivers, such as the one that ships with the Microsoft Developer Studio visual development system, offer client-based scrollable cursors in the driver itself.

Alternatively, the ODBC Cursor Library supports block scrollable cursors for any ODBC driver that complies with the Level One conformance level. Both of these client cursor options support scrolling by using the RDBMS for forward-only fetching, and by caching result set data in memory or on disk. When data is requested, the driver retrieves it from the RDBMS or its local cache as needed.

Client-based cursors also support positioned UPDATE and DELETE statements for the result sets generated by SELECT statements. The cursor library constructs an UPDATE or DELETE statement with a WHERE clause that specifies the cached value for each column in a row.

If you need scrollable cursors and are trying to maintain the same source code for both Oracle and SQL Server implementations, the ODBC Cursor Library is a useful option. For more information about the ODBC Cursor Library, see your ODBC documentation.

Strategies for Using SQL Server Default Result Sets and Server Cursors

With all of the options that SQL Server offers for fetching data, it is sometimes difficult to decide what to use and when. Here are some useful guidelines:

- Default result sets are always the fastest way to get an entire set of data from SQL Server to the client. Look for opportunities in your application where you can use this to your advantage. Batch report generation, for example, generally processes an entire result set to completion, with no user interaction and no updates in the middle of processing.

- If your program requires updatable cursors, use server cursors. Default result sets are never updatable when using positioned UPDATE or DELETE statements. Additionally, server cursors are better at updating than client-based cursors, which have to simulate a positioned UPDATE or DELETE by constructing an equivalent searched UPDATE or DELETE statement.

- If your program needs scrollable, read-only cursors, both the ODBC Cursor Library and server cursors are good choices. The ODBC Cursor Library gives you compatible behavior across SQL Server and Oracle, and server cursors give you more flexibility as to how much data to fetch across the network at one time.

- When you use default result sets or ODBC Cursor Library cursors built on top of default result sets, be sure to fetch to the end of a result set as quickly as possible to avoid holding share locks at the server.

- When you use server cursors, be sure to use **SQLExtendedFetch** to fetch in blocks of rows rather than a single row at a time. This is the same as array-type fetching in Oracle applications. Every fetch request on a server cursor requires a round-trip from the application to the RDBMS on the network.

  Grocery shopping provides an analogy. Assume you purchase 10 bags of groceries at the grocery store, load one bag into your car, drive home, drop it off, and return to the grocery store for the next bag. This is an unlikely scenario, but this is what you do to SQL Server and your program by making single-row fetches from a server cursor.

- If your program requires only forward-only, read-only cursors but depends on multiple open cursors on the same connection, use default result sets when you know you can fetch the entire result set immediately into program variables. Use server cursors when you do not know if you can fetch all of the rows immediately.

This strategy is not as difficult as it sounds. Most programmers know when they are issuing a singleton select that can return a maximum of one row. For singleton fetches, using a default result set is more efficient than using a server cursor.

For an example of this technique, see the LIST_STUDENTS function in the Ssdemo.cpp sample SQL Server ODBC program file. Note how a server cursor is requested only if the SELECT statement may return more than one row. Following the execute step, the rowset size is set to a reasonable batch size. This allows the same **SQLExtendedFetch** loop to work efficiently in either the default result set or the server cursor case.

For more information about cursor implementations, see SQL Server Books Online.

Multiple Active Statements (hstmt) per Connection

The ODBC driver uses a statement handle (hstmt) to track each active SQL statement within the program. The statement handle is always associated with a RDBMS connection handle (hdbc). The ODBC driver manager uses the connection handle to send the requested SQL statement to the specified RDBMS. Most ODBC drivers for Oracle allow multiple statement handles per connection. However, the SQL Server ODBC driver allows only one active statement handle per connection when using default result sets. The **SQLGetInfo** function of this SQL Server driver returns the value 1 when queried with the SQL_ACTIVE_STATEMENTS option. When statement options are set in a way that uses server cursors, multiple active statements per connection handle are supported.

For more information about setting statement options to request server cursors, see SQL Server Books Online.

Data Type Mappings

The SQL Server ODBC driver offers a richer set of data type mappings than any available Oracle ODBC driver.

SQL Server data type	ODBC SQL data type
binary	SQL_BINARY
bit	SQL_BIT
char, **character**	SQL_CHAR
datetime	SQL_TIMESTAMP
decimal, **dec**	SQL_DECIMAL
float, double precision, float(n) for n = 8-15	SQL_FLOAT
image	SQL_LONGVARBINARY
int, **integer**	SQL_INTEGER
money	SQL_DECIMAL
nchar	SQL_WCHAR
ntext	SQL_WLONGVARCHAR
numeric	SQL_NUMERIC
nvarchar	SQL_WVARCHAR
real, **float(n)** for n = 1-7	SQL_REAL

(continued)

SQL Server data type	ODBC SQL data type
smalldatetime	SQL_TIMESTAMP
smallint	SQL_SMALLINT
smallmoney	SQL_DECIMAL
sysname	SQL_VARCHAR
text	SQL_LONGVARCHAR
timestamp	SQL_BINARY
tinyint	SQL_TINYINT
uniqueidentifier	SQL_GUID
varbinary	SQL_VARBINARY
varchar	SQL_VARCHAR

The **timestamp** data type is converted to the SQL_BINARY data type. This is because the values in **timestamp** columns are not **datetime** data, but rather **binary(8)** data. They are used to indicate the sequence of SQL Server activity on the row.

The Oracle data type mappings for the Microsoft ODBC driver for Oracle are shown in this table.

Oracle data type	ODBC SQL data type
CHAR	SQL_CHAR
DATE	SQL_TIMESTAMP
LONG	SQL_LONGVARCHAR
LONG RAW	SQL_LONGVARBINARY
NUMBER	SQL_FLOAT
NUMBER(P)	SQL_DECIMAL
NUMBER(P,S)	SQL_DECIMAL
RAW	SQL_BINARY
VARCHAR2	SQL_VARCHAR

Oracle ODBC drivers from other vendors can have alternative data type mappings.

ODBC Extended SQL

The ODBC Extended SQL standard provides SQL extensions to ODBC that support the advanced nonstandard SQL feature set offered in both Oracle and SQL Server. This standard allows the ODBC driver to convert generic SQL statements to Oracle- and SQL Server–native SQL syntax.

This standard addresses outer joins, such as predicate escape characters, scalar functions, date/time/timestamp values, and stored programs. This syntax is used to identify these extensions:

```
--(*vendor(Microsoft), product(ODBC) extension *)--
OR
{extension}
```

The conversion takes place at run time and does not require the revision of any program code. In most application development scenarios, the best approach is to write one program and allow ODBC to perform the RDBMS conversion process when the program is run.

Outer Joins

Oracle and SQL Server do not have compatible outer join syntax. This can be solved by using the ODBC extended SQL outer join syntax. The Microsoft SQL Server syntax is the same as the ODBC Extended SQL/SQL-92 syntax. The only difference is the {oj   } container.

ODBC Extended SQL and SQL-92	Oracle	Microsoft SQL Server
SELECT STUDENT.SSN, FNAME, LNAME, CCODE, GRADE FROM {oj STUDENT LEFT OUTER JOIN GRADE ON STUDENT.SSN = GRADE.SSN}	SELECT **SUBSTR**(LNAME,1,5) FROM STUDENT	SELECT **SUBSTRING**(LNAME,1,5) FROM STUDENT

Date, Time, and Timestamp Values

ODBC provides three escape clauses for date, time, and timestamp values.

Category	Shorthand syntax	Format
Date	{d 'value'}	"yyyy-mm-dd"
Time	{t 'value'}	"hh:mm:ss"
Timestamp	{Ts 'value'}	"yyyy-mm-dd hh:mm:ss[.f...]"

The format of dates has more of an impact on Oracle applications than on SQL Server applications. Oracle expects the date format to be "DD-MON-YY". In any other case, the TO_CHAR or TO_DATE functions are used with a date format model to perform a format conversion.

Microsoft SQL Server automatically converts most common date formats, and also provides the CONVERT function when an automatic conversion cannot be performed.

As shown in the table, ODBC Extended SQL works with both databases. SQL Server does not require a conversion function. Nevertheless, the ODBC shorthand syntax can be generically applied to both Oracle and SQL Server.

ODBC Extended SQL	Oracle	Microsoft SQL Server
SELECT SSN, FNAME, LNAME, BIRTH_DATE FROM STUDENT WHERE BIRTH_DATE < {D '1970-07-04'}	SELECT SSN, FNAME, LNAME, BIRTH_DATE FROM STUDENT WHERE BIRTH_DATE < **TO_DATE**('1970-07-04', **'YYYY-MM-DD'**)	SELECT SSN, FNAME, LNAME, BIRTH_DATE FROM STUDENT WHERE BIRTH_DATE < '1970-07-04'

Calling Stored Procedures

The ODBC shorthand syntax for calling stored programs supports Microsoft SQL Server stored procedures, and Oracle stored procedures, functions, and packages. The optional "?=" captures the return value for an Oracle function or a SQL Server procedure. The parameter syntax is used to pass and return values to and from the called program. In most situations, the same syntax can be generically applied to Oracle and SQL Server applications.

In the following example, the SHOW_RELUCTANT_STUDENTS function is part of the Oracle package P1. This function must exist in a package because it returns multiple rows from a PL/SQL cursor. When you call a function or procedure that exists in a package, the package name must be placed in front of the program name.

The SHOW_RELUCTANT_STUDENTS function in the package P1 uses a package cursor to retrieve multiple rows of data. Each row must be requested with a call to this function. If there are no more rows to retrieve, the function returns the value of 0, indicating that there are no more rows to retrieve. The resulting performance of this sample Oracle package and its function might be less than satisfactory. SQL Server procedures are more efficient with this type of operation.

Generic ODBC Extended SQL	Oracle	Microsoft SQL Server
{?=} call *procedure_name*[(*parameter(s)*)]} SQLExecDirect(hstmt1,(SQLCHAR *)"{? = call *owner.procedure*(?)}", SQL_NTS);	SQLExecDirect(hstmt1, (SQLCHAR*)"{? = call **STUDENT_ADMIN.P1.** **SHOW_RELUCTANT** **_STUDENTS(?)}"**, SQL_NTS);	SQLExecDirect(hstmt1, (SQLCHAR*)"{? = call **STUDENT_ADMIN.** **SHOW_RELUCTANT** **_STUDENTS}"**, SQL_NTS);

Native SQL Translation

Because of the variety of ODBC drivers for both Oracle and SQL Server, you may not always get the same conversion string for the extended SQL functions. To assist with application debugging issues, you might want to consider using the **SQLNativeSql** function. This function returns the SQL string as translated by the driver.

The following are possible results for the following input SQL string that contains the scalar function CONVERT. The column **SSN** is defined as the type CHAR(9), and is converted to a numeric value.

Original statement	Converted Oracle statement	Converted SQL Server statement
SELECT **(fn CONVERT (SSN, SQL_INTEGER)}** FROM STUDENT	SELECT **TO_NUMBER(SSN)** FROM STUDENT	SELECT **CONVERT(INT, SSN)** FROM STUDENT

The Common.cpp Sample Program

The Common.cpp sample program does not take advantage of the ODBC Extended SQL syntax. Rather, it employs a series of views and procedures to hide statements and functions that are not common to both Oracle and SQL Server. This program, although written using ODBC, is intended to show how an application programmer can easily overcome any apparent hurdles when trying to write one common program.

These techniques and strategies are best employed in a non-ODBC development environment. If you are using ODBC, consider using the ODBC Extended SQL syntax to overcome any syntactical differences between Oracle and SQL Server.

Manual Commit Mode

Oracle automatically enters the transaction mode whenever a user modifies data. This must be followed by an explicit COMMIT to write the changes to the database. If a user wants to undo the changes, the user can issue the ROLLBACK statement.

By default, SQL Server automatically commits each change as it occurs. This is called autocommit mode in ODBC. If you do not want this to occur, you can use the BEGIN TRANSACTION statement to signal the start of a block of statements comprising a transaction. After this statement is issued, it is followed by an explicit COMMIT TRANSACTION or ROLLBACK TRANSACTION statement.

To ensure compatibility with your Oracle application, it is recommended that you use the **SQLConnectOption** function to place your SQL Server application in implicit transaction mode. The SQL_AUTOCOMMIT option must be set to SQL_AUTOCOMMIT_OFF in order to accomplish this. This code excerpt from the sample programs demonstrates this concept:

```
SQLSetConnectOption(hdbc1, SQL_AUTOCOMMIT,-sql_AUTOCOMMIT_OFF);
```

The SQL_AUTOCOMMIT_OFF option instructs the driver to use implicit transactions. The default option SQL_AUTOCOMMIT_ON instructs the driver to use autocommit mode, in which each statement is committed immediately after it is executed. Changing from manual commit mode to autocommit mode commits any open transactions on the connection.

If the SQL_AUTOCOMMIT_OFF option is set, the application must commit or roll back transactions explicitly with the **SQLTransact** function. This function requests a commit or rollback operation for all active operations on all statement handles associated with a connection handle. It can also request that a commit or rollback operation be performed for all connections associated with the environment handle.

```
SQLTransact(henv1, hdbc1, SQL_ROLLBACK);
(SQLTransact(henv1, hdbc1, SQL_COMMIT);
```

When autocommit mode is off, the driver issues SET IMPLICIT_TRANSACTIONS ON statement to the server. Starting with SQL Server 6.5, DDL statements are supported in this mode.

To commit or roll back a transaction in manual commit mode, the application must call **SQLTransact**. The SQL Server driver sends a COMMIT TRANSACTION statement to commit a transaction, and a ROLLBACK TRANSACTION statement to roll back a transaction.

Be aware that manual commit mode can adversely affect the performance of your SQL Server application. Every commit request requires a separate round-trip to the server to send the COMMIT TRANSACTION string.

If you have single atomic transactions (a single INSERT, UPDATE, or DELETE immediately followed by a COMMIT), use the autocommit mode.

In the sample programs, the manual commit mode has been turned on, even for atomic transactions, to demonstrate how easily a SQL Server application can be developed that closely mimics the operation of a similar application designed for the Oracle RDBMS.

Developing and Administering Database Replication

This section explains the differences between Oracle and Microsoft SQL Server replication support.

SQL Server implements snapshot replication in place of Oracle's read-only snapshot. As its name implies, snapshot replication takes a picture, or snapshot, of the published data in the database at a moment in time. Snapshot replication requires less constant processor overhead than transactional replication because it does not require continuous monitoring of data changes on source servers. Instead of copying INSERT, UPDATE, and DELETE statements (characteristic of transactional replication), or data modifications (characteristic of merge replication), Subscribers are updated by a total refresh of the data set. Hence, snapshot replication sends all the data to the Subscriber instead of sending only the changes.

SQL Server also offers transactional replication, a type of replication that marks selected transactions in the Publisher's database transaction log for replication and then distributes them asynchronously to Subscribers as incremental changes, while maintaining transactional consistency.

SQL Server implements merge replication in place of Oracle's updatable snapshots and Oracle's multimaster replication model. Merge replication is a type of replication that allows sites to make autonomous changes to replicated data, and at a later time, merge changes made at all sites. Merge replication does not guarantee transactional consistency.

SQL Server offers heterogeneous replication, which is the simplest way to publish data to a heterogeneous Subscriber by using ODBC and creating a push subscription from the Publisher to the ODBC Subscriber. As an alternative, however, you can create a publication and then create an application with an embedded distribution control. The embedded control implements the pull subscription from the Subscriber to the Publisher. For ODBC Subscribers, the subscribing database has no administrative capabilities regarding the replication being performed.

ODBC and Replication

A distribution server connects to all subscription servers as an ODBC client. Replication requires that the ODBC 32-bit driver be installed on all distribution servers. The SQL Server Setup program automatically installs the necessary driver on Windows NT–based computers.

You do not have to preconfigure ODBC Data Sources for SQL Server subscription servers because the distribution process simply uses the subscriber's network name to establish the connection.

SQL Server also includes an ODBC driver that supports Oracle subscriptions to SQL Server. The driver exists only for Intel-based computers. To replicate to Oracle ODBC subscribers, you must also obtain the appropriate Oracle SQL*Net driver from Oracle or from your software vendor.

If a password is provided in the Windows NT registry, the Oracle ODBC driver connects to Oracle without requesting a password. If a password is not provided in the Windows NT registry, you must enter a username and a password for the Oracle ODBC data source when specifying the DSN in the **New ODBC Subscriber** dialog box of SQL Server Enterprise Manager.

The following restrictions apply when replicating to an Oracle ODBC subscriber:

- The **datetime** data type is mapped to DATE. The range for the Oracle DATE data type is between 4712 B.C. and 4712 A.D. If you are replicating to Oracle, verify that SQL Server **datetime** entries in a replicated column are within this range.
- A replicated table can have only one **text** or **image** column.
- The **datetime** data type is mapped to the Oracle CHAR data type .
- The SQL Server ranges for **float** and **real** data types are different from the Oracle ranges.

Drivers for other ODBC subscriber types must conform to the SQL Server replication requirements for generic ODBC subscribers. The ODBC driver:

- Must be ODBC Level 1 compliant.
- Must be 32-bit and thread-safe for the processor architecture that the distribution process runs on.
- Must be transaction capable.
- Must support the data definition language (DDL).
- Cannot be read-only.

Migrating Your Data and Applications

This section presents various methods for migrating data from an Oracle database to a Microsoft SQL Server database.

Data Migration Using Data Transformation Services

The simplest method of migrating between Oracle and SQL Server is to use the Data Transformation Services (DTS) feature in Microsoft SQL Server 7.0. The DTS Wizard guides you through moving the data to SQL Server.

Oracle Call Interface (OCI)

If you have applications that were written by using the Oracle Call Interface (OCI), you may want to consider rewriting them by using ODBC. The OCI is specific to the Oracle RDBMS and cannot be used with Microsoft SQL Server or any other database.

In most cases, you can replace OCI functions with the appropriate ODBC functions, followed by relevant changes to the supporting program code. The remaining non-OCI program code should require minimal modification. The example shows a comparison of the OCI and ODBC statements required for establishing a connection to an Oracle database.

Oracle Call Interface	Oracle ODBC
rcl = olog(&logon_data_area, &host_data_area, user_name, -1, (text*) 0, -1, (text) 0, -1, OCI_LM_DEF);	rcl = SQLConnect(hdbc1, (SQLCHAR*) ODBC_dsn, (SQLSMALLINT) SQL_NTS, (SQLCHAR*) user_name, (SQLSMALLINT) SQL_NTS, (SQLCHAR*) user_password, (SQLSMALLINT) SQL_NTS);

The table suggests conversions between Oracle OCI function calls and ODBC functions. These suggested conversions are approximate. There may not be an exact match in the conversion process. Your program code might require additional revision to obtain similar functionality.

OCI function	ODBC function
Obindps	SQLBindParameter
Obndra	SQLBindParameter
Obndrn	SQLBindParameter
Obndrv	SQLBindParameter
Obreak	SQLCancel
Ocan	SQLCancel, SQLFreeStmt
Oclose	SQLFreeStmt
Ocof	SQLSetConnectOption
Ocom	SQLTransact
Ocon	SQLSetConnectOption
Odefin	SQLBindCol
Odefinps	SQLBindCol
Odescr	SQLDescribeCol
Oerhms	SQLError
Oexec	SQLExecute, SQLExecDirect
Oexfet	SQLExecute, SQLExecDirect, and SQLFetch
Oexn	SQLExecute, SQLExecDirect
Ofen	SQLExtendedFetch
Ofetch	SQLFetch
Oflng	SQLGetData
Ogetpi	SQLGetData
Olog	SQLConnect
Ologof	SQLDisconnect
Oopen	SQLExecute, SQLExecDirect
Oparse	SQLPrepare
Orol	SQLTransact

Embedded SQL

Many applications are written using the Oracle Programmatic Interfaces (Pro*C, Pro*Cobol, and so on). These interfaces support the use of SQL-92 standard embedded SQL. They also include nonstandard Oracle programmatic extensions.

Oracle embedded SQL applications can be migrated to SQL Server by using the Microsoft Embedded SQL (ESQL) for C development environment. This environment provides adequate but less than optimal control over the performance and the use of SQL Server features compared to an ODBC application.

Some of the Oracle Pro*C features are not supported in Microsoft's ESQL precompiler. If your Oracle application makes extensive use of these features, a rewrite to ODBC is probably a better migration choice. These features include:

- Host array variables.
- VAR and TYPE statements for data type equivalencing.
- Support for embedded SQL in C++ modules.
- Support for embedded PL/SQL or Transact-SQL blocks.
- Cursor variables.
- Multithreaded application support.
- Support for the Oracle Communication Area (ORACA).

If your Oracle application has been developed in Cobol, it can be moved to Embedded SQL for Cobol from Micro Focus. You may run into some of the same limitations in Cobol as with the Microsoft ESQL for C precompiler.

You can convert your Oracle embedded SQL application to the ODBC environment. This migration process is quite easy and offers many advantages. ODBC does not require the use of a precompiler, as does embedded SQL. Consequently, much of the overhead associated with program development is eliminated.

The table shows the approximate relationship between Embedded SQL statements and ODBC functions.

Embedded SQL statement	ODBC function
CONNECT	**SQLConnect**
PREPARE	**SQLPrepare**
EXECUTE	**SQLExecute**
DECLARE CURSOR and OPEN CURSOR	**SQLExecute**
EXECUTE IMMEDIATE	**SQLExecDirect**
DESCRIBE SELECT LIST	**SQLNumResultCols, SQLColAttributes, SQLDescribeCol**
FETCH	**SQLFetch**
SQLCA.SQLERRD[2]	**SQLRowCount**
CLOSE	**SQLFreeStmt**
COMMIT WORK, ROLLBACK WORK	**SQLTransact**

(continued)

Embedded SQL statement	ODBC function
COMMIT WORK RELEASE, ROLLBACK WORK RELEASE	**SQLDisconnect**
SQLCA, SQLSTATE	**SQLError**
ALTER, CREATE, DROP, GRANT, REVOKE	**SQLExecute, SQLExecDirect**

The most significant change when converting embedded SQL programs to ODBC involves the handling of SQL statement errors. The MODE = ORACLE option is often used when developing embedded SQL programs. When this option is used, the SQL Communications Area (SQLCA) is typically used for error handling operations.

The SQLCA structure provides:

- Oracle error codes.
- Oracle error messages.
- Warning flags.
- Information regarding program events.
- The number of rows processed by the most recent SQL statement.

In most cases, you should check the value in the **sqlca.sqlcode** variable following the execution of each SQL statement. If the value is less than zero, an error has occurred. If the value is greater than zero, the requested statement executed with warnings. The Oracle error message text can be retrieved from the **sqlca.sqlerrm.sqlerrmc** variable.

In ODBC, a function returns a numeric status code that indicates its success or failure following the requested operation. The status codes are defined as string literals, and include SQL_SUCCESS, SQL_SUCCESS_WITH_INFO, SQL_NEED_DATA, SQL_ERROR, and others. It is your responsibility to check these return values following each function call.

An associated SQLSTATE value can be obtained by calling the **SQLError** function. This function returns the SQLSTATE error code, the native error code (specific to the data source), and the error message text.

An application typically calls this function when a previous call to an ODBC function returns SQL_ERROR or SQL_SUCCESS_WITH_INFO. However, any ODBC function can post zero or more errors each time it is called, so an application may call **SQLError** after every ODBC function call.

Here are examples of error handling for each environment.

Oracle Pro*C and EMBEDDED SQL	Oracle ODBC

EXEC SQL DECLARE CURSOR C1
  CURSOR FOR SELECT SSN, FNAME,
  LNAME FROM STUDENT ORDER BY SSN;
EXEC SQL OPEN C1;
if (sqlca.sqlcode) != 0 {
/* handle error condition,
   look at sqlca.sqlerrm.sqlerrmc for error
   description...*/}
	if (SQLExecDirect(hstmtl,
	(SQLCHAR*)"SELECT SSN, FNAME,
	  LNAME FROM STUDENT ORDER BY
	  SSN", SQL_NTS) != SQL_SUCCESS) {
	/* handle error condition, use SQLError
	   for SQLSTATE details regarding error...*/}

Developer 2000 and Third-party Applications

If you have developed an application using Oracle Developer 2000 and want to use it with SQL Server, consider converting it to Microsoft Visual Basic. Visual Basic is a powerful development system that works well with both databases. You might also consider other development tools in Microsoft Visual Studio, or PowerBuilder, SQL Windows, and others.

If you are unable to immediately migrate from Developer 2000, consider the Oracle Gateway to SQL Server. It can be used as an intermediate step when migrating from Oracle to SQL Server. This gateway allows the Oracle RDBMS to connect to SQL Server. All requests for SQL Server data are automatically translated by the gateway. From the perspective of the Developer 2000 application, this connection is transparent. SQL Server data appears as Oracle data. Very few changes need to be made to the application program code.

Another intermediate step is to use the Developer 2000 application directly with SQL Server. Developer 2000 can directly access SQL Server using the Oracle Open Client Adapter (OCA). The OCA is ODBC Level 1 compliant and has limited support for ODBC Level 2 functions.

The OCA establishes a connection with the SQL Server ODBC driver. When connecting the Developer 2000 tools to SQL Server, you must specify an ODBC data source name as part of the database connection string. When you exit the Developer 2000 application, the OCA connection to the ODBC data source is disconnected.

The syntax for the logon connect string is demonstrated in the following example. In this example, the user logs on to the SQL Server **STUDENT_ADMIN** account. The name of the SQL Server ODBC data source is **STUDENT_DATA**:

```
STUDENT_ADMIN/STUDENT_ADMIN@ODBC:STUDENT_DATA
```

Using an ODBC driver does not ensure that a Developer 2000 application will work correctly with SQL Server. The application program code must be modified to work with a non-Oracle data source. For example, the column security property is Oracle-specific and does not work with SQL Server.

You must change the key mode that is used to identify each row of data. When using Oracle as the data source, a ROWID is used to identify each row. When using SQL Server, you must work with unique primary key values to ensure unique row values.

The locking mode also must be changed. When using Oracle, Developer 2000 attempts to lock a row of data immediately following any change to that row. When using SQL Server, the locking mode should be set to delayed so that the record is locked only when it is written to the database.

They are many other issues that must be resolved, including the potential for a deadlock situation if multiple inserts on a table access the same page of data in a PL/SQL program block. For more information, see "Transactions, Locking, and Concurrency" earlier in this chapter.

Internet Applications

Microsoft SQL Server includes the SQL Server Web Assistant, a wizard that generates standard HTML files from SQL Server data. The wizard can configure your Web page so that it is static, updated periodically, or updated when the data is updated. A wizard walks you through the process of creating the Web page.

Database Examples

A sample university RDBMS application has been created to support the sample program applications and code referenced throughout this chapter. This application was created specifically to illustrate many of the points, issues, and tricks involved in converting an Oracle 7 application to a SQL Server 7.0 application.

Sample University Application

This sample application uses four tables to track all university activity. The **DEPT** table is used to track department offerings within the university. The **CLASS** table is used to track class offerings within each department. The **STUDENT** table is used to track each student within the university. The **GRADE** table is used to track the enrollments of each student within each class.

Sample University Application

In this sample application, social security number (**ssn**) is used as the primary key for the **STUDENT** table. The **DEPT** table uses department code (**dept**) as the primary key, and course code (**ccode**) is used as the primary key for the **CLASS** table. The combination of social security number (**ssn**) and course code (**ccode**) makes up the primary key for the **GRADE** table.

The column major is defined as a foreign key in the **STUDENT** table. When selecting a major, the student must choose a valid department code (**dept**) from the **DEPT** table. The department (**dept**) column in the **CLASS** table is also defined as a foreign key. When a course is inserted into this table, it must be associated with a valid department (**dept**) from the **DEPT** table.

The **GRADE** table has two foreign keys. When enrolling a student in a class, the social security number (**ssn**) must exist in the **STUDENT** table, and the course code (**ccode**) must exist in the **CLASS** table. This ensures that students are not enrolled in nonexistent classes, and that classes are not filled with nonexistent students.

Sample Application and Code References

These sample applications are referenced throughout this chapter.

Orademo.cpp

Oracle ODBC application that accesses the sample university tables on an Oracle 7.3 database. This program is the starting point for the conversion process. It allows users to perform data entry and produce reports against the sample university application.

Ssdemo.cpp

SQL Server application written using ODBC. This program is the ending point for the conversion process. All of the Oracle SQL commands, procedures, packages, and functions have been converted to SQL Server Transact-SQL statements and procedures. Many of the advantages associated with SQL Server 7.0 are demonstrated in this program.

Common.cpp

ODBC application that works with both Oracle and SQL Server. To connect to Oracle or SQL Server, the user simply provides the ODBC Data Source Name (DSN). The program then logs on to the requested RDBMS. The program contains excellent examples of programming techniques that can be used when developing a multi-RDBMS program.

Orauser.sql

Creates the database user accounts and database roles required for the sample Oracle program.

Oratable.sql

Creates the tables and views required for the sample Oracle program.

Oraproc.sql

Creates the Oracle stored procedure, functions, and packages required for the sample Oracle program.

Oracommn.sql

Creates all of the additional Oracle database objects that are required to support the Common.cpp program.

Oradata.sql

Loads sample application data into the tables required for the sample Oracle program.

Ssuser.sql

Creates the SQL Server user accounts and database roles required for the sample SQL Server program.

Sstable.sql
> Creates the SQL Server tables and views required for the sample SQL Server program.

Ssproc.sql
> Creates the stored procedures required for the sample SQL Server program.

Sscommon.sql
> Creates all of the additional SQL Server database objects that are required to support the Common.cpp application.

Ssdata.sql
> Loads sample application data into the tables required for the sample SQL Server program.

Running the Supplied Scripts

The sample scripts must be run in the following sequence to create the sample applications on the target RDBMS platforms.

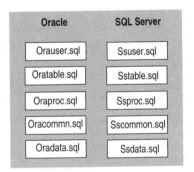

Prior to running these scripts for the SQL Server database, you must create an application database (named **USER_DB**) for these scripts and the sample SQL Server program to work. This database can be created using SQL Server Enterprise Manager or the Transact-SQL CREATE DATABASE statement. After the database has been created, log in to SQL Server 7.0 as a system administrator (the **sa** SQL Server user, or a member of the **sysadmin** fixed server role), use the SQL Server Query Analyzer, and run these scripts in the indicated order.

Prior to running these scripts for the Oracle 7.3 database, the sample scripts assume that the USER_DATA and TEMPORARY_DATA tablespaces exist. They are usually created during a default Oracle 7.3 database installation. If these tablespaces do not exist, you must either add them or modify the supplied sample scripts to use other tablespaces.

After verifying that these tablespaces exist, log on to SQL*Plus using the SYSTEM account. If the password is not the default value of MANAGER, change the password in the Oracle SQL scripts.

RDBMS User Accounts

Three user accounts are created for this application:

STUDENT_ADMIN
 This account is the administrative owner of the **STUDENT** and **GRADE** tables.

DEPT_ADMIN
 This account is the administrative owner of the **DEPT** and **CLASS** tables.

ENDUSER1
 This account is a query-only account that can access the **STUDENT**, **GRADE**, **DEPT**, and **CLASS** tables.

CHAPTER 19

Migrating Your Access Database to Microsoft SQL Server 7.0

As customer needs grow and demand for an enterprise-scale high-performance database increases, customers sometimes move from the file-server environment of the Microsoft Access Jet engine to the client/server environment of Microsoft SQL Server. The Access 2000 Upsizing Wizard, available with Microsoft Office 2000, moves Access tables and queries into SQL Server 7.0. If you are working with an earlier version of Access, you can migrate your applications to SQL Server by upgrading to Access 2000, and then using the Upsizing Wizard.

If you prefer not to use Access 2000 and the Upsizing Wizard to migrate, use this chapter as a guide for moving an Access application to SQL Server. Moving an Access application requires moving the data into SQL Server 7.0 and then migrating the Access queries into the database or into SQL files for execution at a later time. The final step involves migrating the applications.

SQL Server Tools Used in Migrations

Several tools in SQL Server can assist you with the migration of your Access data and applications.

SQL Server Enterprise Manager

SQL Server Enterprise Manager allows enterprise-wide configuration and management of SQL Server and SQL Server objects. SQL Server Enterprise Manager provides a powerful scheduling engine, administrative alert capabilities, and a built-in replication management interface. You can also use SQL Server Enterprise Manager to:

- Manage logins and user permissions.
- Create scripts.
- Manage backup of SQL Server objects.
- Back up databases and transaction logs.
- Manage tables, views, stored procedures, triggers, indexes, rules, defaults, and user-defined data types.
- Create full-text indexes, database diagrams, and database maintenance plans.
- Import and export data.
- Transform data.
- Perform various Web administration tasks.

By default, SQL Server Enterprise Manager is installed by SQL Server Setup as part of the server software on computers running the Microsoft Windows NT operating system, and as part of the client software on computers running Windows NT and the Microsoft Windows 95 operating system. You will likely launch Data Transformation Services (DTS) from the SQL Server Enterprise Manager graphical user interface.

Data Transformation Services (DTS)

Data Transformation Services (DTS) allows you to import and export data between multiple heterogeneous sources that use an OLE DB–based architecture such as Microsoft Excel spreadsheets, and to transfer databases and database objects (for example, indexes and stored procedures) between multiple computers running SQL Server 7.0. You can also use DTS to transform data so that it can be used more easily to build data warehouses and data marts from an online transaction processing (OLTP) system.

The DTS Wizard allows you to interactively create DTS packages that use OLE DB and ODBC to import, export, validate, and transform heterogeneous data. The wizard also allows you to copy schema and data between relational databases.

SQL Server Query Analyzer

SQL Server Query Analyzer is a graphical query tool that visually allows you to analyze the plan of a query, execute multiple queries simultaneously, view data, and obtain index recommendations. SQL Server Query Analyzer provides the **showplan** option, which is used to report data retrieval methods chosen by the SQL Server query optimizer.

SQL Server Profiler

SQL Server Profiler captures a continuous record of server activity in real time. SQL Server Profiler allows you to monitor events produced through SQL Server, filter events based on user-specified criteria, and direct the trace output to the screen, a file, or a table. Using SQL Server Profiler, you can replay previously captured traces. This tool helps application developers identify transactions that might be deteriorating the performance of an application. This can be useful when migrating an application from a file-based architecture to a client/server architecture, because the last step involves optimizing the application for its new client/server environment.

Moving Tables and Data

To use the DTS Wizard to transfer your Access data into SQL Server, you can use these steps:

1. In SQL Server Enterprise Manager, on the **Tools** menu, point to **Data Transformation Services**, and then click **Import Data**.
2. In the **Choose a Data Source** dialog box, select **Microsoft Access as the Source**, and then type the file name of your .mdb database (.mdb file extension) or browse for the file.
3. In the **Choose a Destination** dialog box, select **Microsoft OLE DB Provider for SQL Server**, select the database server, and then click the required authentication mode.
4. In the **Specify Table Copy or Query** dialog box, click **Copy tables**.
5. In the **Select Source Tables** dialog box, click **Select All**.

Migrating Microsoft Access Queries

You must move your existing Access queries into SQL Server in one of these formats:

- Transact-SQL scripts

  Transact-SQL statements are usually called from database programs, but you can use SQL Server Query Analyzer, included in SQL Server 7.0, to run them against the database directly. SQL Server Query Analyzer helps developers to test Transact-SQL statements against development databases, or to run Transact-SQL statements that perform queries, data manipulation (INSERT, UPDATE, DELETE), or data definition (CREATE TABLE).

- Stored procedures

  Developers can move most Transact-SQL statements that originate from Access queries (SELECT, INSERT, UPDATE, and DELETE) into stored procedures. Stored procedures written in Transact-SQL can be used to encapsulate and standardize your data access, and are actually stored within the database. Stored procedures can run with or without parameters and are called from database programs or manually from SQL Server Query Analyzer.

- Views

  Views are used as virtual tables that expose specific rows and columns from one or more tables. They allow users to create queries without directly implementing the complex joins that underlie the query. Views do not support the use of parameters. Views that join more than one table cannot be modified using INSERT, UPDATE, or DELETE statements. Views are called from Transact-SQL statements, and can also be used in *.scripts that are run in SQL Server Query Analyzer. SQL Server views and the SQL-92 standard do not support ORDER BY clauses in views.

For more information about Transact-SQL, stored procedures, or views, see SQL Server Books Online.

Access query type	SQL Server migration options and comments
SELECT	A SELECT statement can be stored in a Transact-SQL file, a stored procedure, or a view. Creating stored procedures is the best way to separate the database application development from the physical implementation of the database design. Stored procedures are created in one place, and are called from the application. Calls to stored procedures will not "break" if the underlying database changes and the stored procedure is carefully modified to reflect these changes.
CROSSTAB	Crosstabs are often used for summary reports. An Access CROSSTAB can be implemented as a Transact-SQL SELECT statement in a SQL script, a stored procedure, or a view. The data join is reexecuted each time a query is issued, ensuring that the latest data is always used. Depending on the application, it might be appropriate to store data from the crosstab as a temporary table (see MAKE TABLE in the next row). The temporary table requires fewer resources, but offers only a snapshot of the data at the time the temporary table is created.
MAKE TABLE	An Access MAKE TABLE can be implemented as a Transact-SQL CREATE TABLE statement in a Transact-SQL script or stored procedure. The syntax follows: ```SELECT [ALL	DISTINCT]` `[{TOP integer	TOP integer PERCENT} [` `WITH TIES]]` `<select_list>` `[INTO new_table]` `[FROM {<table_source>} [,…n]]` `[WHERE <search_condition>]` `[GROUP BY [ALL] group_by_expression` `[,…n]` `[WITH { CUBE	ROLLUP }]` ` CREATE TABLE mytable (low int, high` `int)```

(continued)

Access query type	SQL Server migration options and comments
UPDATE	An UPDATE statement can be stored in a Transact-SQL script; however, the recommended way to implement an UPDATE statement is to create a stored procedure.
APPEND	An APPEND statement can be stored in a Transact-SQL script; however, the recommended way to implement an APPEND statement is to create a stored procedure.
DELETE	A DELETE statement can be stored in a Transact-SQL script; however, the recommended way to implement a DELETE statement is to create a stored procedure.

Migrating Microsoft Access Queries into Stored Procedures and Views

Each Access query must be placed into this set of statements:

```
CREATE PROCEDURE <NAME_HERE> AS
< SELECT, UPDATE, DELETE, INSERT, CREATE TABLE statement from Microsoft
Access >
GO

CREATE VIEW  <NAME_HERE> AS
<Place (SELECT only, with no parameters) Microsoft Access Query>
GO
```

For each Access query:

1. Open Access, and then in SQL Server, open SQL Server Query Analyzer.

2. In Access, in the Database window, click the Queries tab, and then click **Design**.

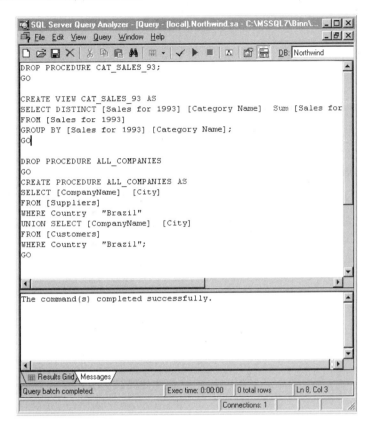

3. On the View menu, click **SQL**.

4. Paste the entire query into SQL Server Query Analyzer.

5. Either test the syntax and save the Transact-SQL statement for later use, or run the statement in the database. You can optionally save the Transact-SQL to a script.

Migrating Microsoft Access Queries into Transact-SQL Scripts

Most Access queries should be translated into stored procedures and views. Nevertheless, some statements run infrequently by an application developer can be stored as a Transact-SQL script, a text file that ends in the file extension .sql. These files can be run from within SQL Server Query Analyzer.

If you plan to transfer some of your Access queries into .sql files, consider separating the Transact-SQL statements into several scripts, depending on how they are used. For example, you can group together into a script those Transact-SQL statements that must be run with the same frequency. Another script might contain all Transact-SQL statements that are run only under certain conditions. Additionally, Transact-SQL statements that must be run in a specific order should be grouped together in a discrete script.

To move a statement from Access to a Transact-SQL file:

1. Copy the statement into SQL Server Query Analyzer.
2. Use the blue check mark icon to parse the statement.
3. Execute the statement if appropriate.

Developers with MAKE TABLE Access queries have several options in SQL Server. Developers can create either of these:

- A view.

  A view creates the effect of having a dynamic, virtual temporary table that provides the latest information. This is I/O intensive, because it requires the rejoining of the data tables each time a query is issued.

- A temporary table.

  A temporary table creates a snapshot of data for a connected user's session. You can create local and global temporary tables. Local temporary tables are visible only in the current session; global temporary tables are visible to all sessions. Prefix local temporary table names with single number sign (*#table_name*), and prefix global temporary table names with double number sign (*##table_name*). Queries run quickly against temporary tables because they generally use only one table rather than dynamically joining together several tables to obtain a result set.

For more information about temporary tables, see SQL Server Books Online.

Data Transformation Services (DTS) in SQL Server 7.0 allows you to standardize, automate, and schedule the creation of temporary tables by creating packages.

For example, when you migrate the Access 2.0 **Northwind** sample database, the crosstab that is created for reporting quarterly data becomes either a view or a data transformation that creates a temporary table on a regular basis. For more information about DTS, see SQL Server Books Online.

Additional Design Considerations

The following are some of the issues you must consider when migrating your Access application to SQL Server.

Using Parameters

SQL Server stored procedures that have parameters need a different syntax from Access queries, for example:

Access 2.0:

Query Name: Employee Sales By Country, in NWIND.mdb:

```
PARAMETERS [Beginning Date] DateTime, [Ending Date] DateTime;
SELECT Orders.[Order ID], [Last Name] & ", " & [First Name] AS
Salesperson, Employees.Country, Orders.[Shipped Date], [Order
Subtotals].Subtotal AS [Sale Amount]
FROM Employees INNER JOIN (Orders INNER JOIN [Order Subtotals] ON
Orders.[Order ID] = [Order Subtotals].[Order ID]) ON Employees.[Employee
ID] = Orders.[Employee ID]
WHERE (((Orders.[Shipped Date]) Between [Beginning Date] And [Ending
Date]))
ORDER BY [Last Name] & ", " & [First Name], Employees.Country,
Orders.[Shipped Date];
```

SQL Server 7.0:

```
CREATE PROCEDURE EMP_SALES_BY_COUNTRY
@BeginningDate datetime,
@EndingDate datetime
AS
SELECT Orders.[Order ID], [Last Name] + ", " + [First Name] AS
Salesperson, Employees.Country,
Orders.[Shipped Date], [Order Subtotals].Subtotal AS [Sale Amount]
FROM Employees INNER JOIN (Orders INNER JOIN [Order Subtotals] ON
Orders.[Order ID] = [Order Subtotals].[Order ID]) ON Employees.[Employee
ID] = Orders.[Employee ID]
WHERE (((Orders.[Shipped Date]) Between @BeginningDate And @EndingDate))
ORDER BY [Last Name] + ", " + [First Name], Employees.Country,
Orders.[Shipped Date]
GO
```

For more information, see SQL Server Books Online.

Nested Queries

Some Access queries are created on top of other queries in a nested fashion. Nested queries in Access become nested views in SQL Server. The ORDER BY clauses cannot be part of a view definition; instead they are appended to the SELECT statement that queries the VIEW. If you have nested Access queries, create several views, and then create stored procedures that both perform a SELECT operation on the view and append an ORDER BY clause to the SELECT statement.

For example, the following Access query:

```
SELECT *
FROM STUDENTS
WHERE COUNTRY = "USA"
ORDER BY LAST_NAME
```

Becomes a SQL Server view and a stored procedure:

```
CREATE VIEW US_STUDENTS AS
SELECT * FROM STUDENTS
WHERE COUNTRY = "USA"

CREATE PROCEDURE US_STUDENTS_ORDER AS
SELECT * FROM US_STUDENTS ORDER BY LAST NAME
```

Verifying SQL Server–compliant Syntax

You can use the **Parse** command on the **Query** menu in SQL Server Query Analyzer to verify whether a view or stored procedure functions in SQL Server. In the example below, the Access query uses DISTINCTROW. SQL Server uses the Transact-SQL command DISTINCT to perform the same operation. The **Parse** command allows developers to isolate and modify syntax problems in their Access queries.

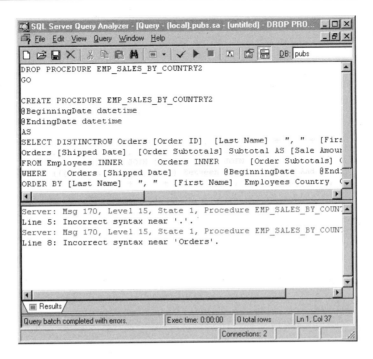

Connecting Your Applications

Many Access applications were written by using Microsoft Visual Basic for Applications or the Visual Basic for Applications Access user interface.

- Applications that use Visual Basic for Applications as the development environment can run against SQL Server, using the Jet ODBC driver.

- Applications that use the forms and reports found in the Access user interface can access SQL Server using linked tables. If your application will use linked tables, make sure that all Access tables get moved to SQL Server to increase performance. Creating queries against a mix of Access (Jet) and SQL Server using linked tables can be very resource-intensive.

The first step in migrating your file-server application to a client/server model is to ensure that the application works against the new database. The next step is to optimize the application for the client/server environment by:

- Monitoring Transact-SQL statements being sent to the server.

  SQL Server Profiler is a useful tool for monitoring how Transact-SQL statements are sent to the database. If you run an unmodified Access application on SQL Server, you might send suboptimal Transact-SQL to the database by using Data Access Objects (DAO) with the Jet/ODBC driver. For example, a DELETE statement that uses the Jet/ODBC driver to delete 1,000 rows makes 1,000 calls to the database, negatively impacting the performance of a production database. In this example, SQL Server Profiler displays 1,000 DELETE statements, allowing you to modify the application to use Microsoft ActiveX Data Objects (ADO) with the Microsoft OLE DB Provider for SQL Server, and thereby improve the application's efficiency.

- Implementing efficient indexes.

  After you determine that the Transact-SQL statements being sent to the database are efficient, you can fine-tune those statements by using indexes more effectively. The Index Tuning Wizard allows you to find bottlenecks, and it makes recommendations. Your Transact-SQL statements are not modified, but their performance improves with the correct use of indexes.

SQL Server and Access Query Syntax

The following table shows the corresponding differences between SQL Server and Access query syntax.

Access query syntax	SQL Server query syntax
ORDER BY in queries	ORDER BY in views not supported
DISTINCTROW	DISTINCT
String concatenation with "&"	String concatenation with "+"

(continued)

Access query syntax	SQL Server query syntax
Supported clauses/operators:	Supported clauses/operators:
SELECT	SELECT
SELECT TOP N	SELECT TOP N
INTO	INTO
FROM	FROM
WHERE	WHERE
GROUP BY	GROUP BY
HAVING	HAVING
UNION (ALL)	UNION (ALL)
ORDER BY	ORDER BY
WITH OWNERACCESS	COMPUTE
	FOR BROWSE
	OPTION
Not Supported: COMPUTE, FOR BROWSE, OPTION	Not Supported: WITH OWNERACCESS
Aggregate functions:	Aggregate functions:
AVG	AVG([ALL | DISTINCT] *expression*)
COUNT(column)	COUNT([ALL | DISTINCT] *expression*)
COUNT(*)	COUNT(*)
MIN	GROUPING (*column_name*)
MAX	MAX(*expression*)
FIRST	MIN(*expression*)
LAST	STDEV, STDEVP
STDEV, STDEVP	SUM([ALL | DISTINCT] *expression*)
SUM	VAR, VARP
VAR, VARP	Not supported: FIRST, LAST
TRANSFORM	WITH ROLLUP, WITH CUBE on SELECT statements
(SELECT statement)	
PIVOT	
MAKE TABLE, ALTER TABLE	CREATE TABLE, ALTER TABLE
Supported clauses:	Supported clauses:
CONSTRAINT	CONSTRAINT
ADD COLUMN	ADD COLUMN
DROP COLUMN	DROP COLUMN
DROP INDEX	
Also, stand-alone statement: DROP INDEX	Stand-alone statement: DROP INDEX

C H A P T E R   2 0

Migrating Sybase Applications to Microsoft SQL Server 7.0

Microsoft SQL Server and the Sybase database were developed together until their respective 4.2 versions. This similarity provides for a unique, low-cost opportunity for Sybase customers to migrate to Microsoft SQL Server and benefit from the new functionality of Microsoft SQL Server version 7.0.

This chapter outlines the steps to take in a migration and helps database application developers anticipate issues, based on the experiences of other customers. This chapter is intended for Sybase database administrators (DBAs) and managers who are planning a database application migration to Microsoft SQL Server 7.0. It assumes the reader knows Sybase databases (SQL Server or Adaptive Server Enterprise).

This chapter addresses the differences between Sybase T-SQL and Microsoft Transact-SQL statements, and differences in the applications and administrative procedures. Issues regarding conversion from CT-Library applications or the porting of ODBC applications from Sybase to Microsoft SQL Server databases are not addressed.

Understanding the Migration Process

Three areas must be considered during a migration from Sybase Adaptive Server Enterprise to Microsoft SQL Server: data and object definitions, Transact-SQL and system stored procedure language changes, and administrative changes.

The steps of the migration process are:

1. Review the architectural differences between Microsoft SQL Server and Sybase SQL Server that require changes to administrative procedures.

2. Migrate data and objects using Microsoft SQL Server Data Transformation Services (DTS).

3. Review Sybase stored procedures, triggers, SQL scripts, and applications for necessary language changes.

4. Make the necessary changes to client code. Sybase SQL statements issued by applications must reflect changes to object names forced by keyword conflicts. The Sybase application SQL must reflect any changes required to comply with Microsoft Transact-SQL syntax.

5. Test the client code.

6. Make required changes to the customer's administrative procedures.

7. Review the new features available in Microsoft SQL Server and make changes to take advantage of these features.

Reviewing Architectural Differences

The Data Definition Language (DDL) syntax of Sybase Adaptive Server Enterprise differs from that of Microsoft SQL Server when used to define most database objects. Conversely, Sybase and Microsoft dynamic link libraries (DLLs) share many system stored procedure similarities. You must address the major architectural differences between Sybase and Microsoft SQL Server as part of the migration.

Client Configuration and Net-Libraries

Although it is easier to use Microsoft DB-Library to migrate Sybase applications that use CT-Library, in order to take full advantage of Microsoft SQL Server version 7.0 functionality, it is recommended that Microsoft SQL Server–based clients use either an OLE DB provider or an ODBC driver to connect with the server. Microsoft supplies two components, Ntwdblib.dll (DB-Library) and Sqlsrv32.dll (ODBC driver), to replace the Sybase client components.

Microsoft SQL Server–based clients should use the appropriate Microsoft SQL Server Network Library components.

Net-Library	Win32 DLL
TCP/IP Windows Sockets	Dbmssocn.dll
Named Pipes	Dbnmpntw.dll
Multiprotocol	Dbmsrpcn.dll
Novell IPX/SPX	Dbmsspxn.dll
Banyan VINES	Dbmsvinn.dll
AppleTalk	Dbmsadsn.dll

One of the Microsoft SQL Server client-side components installed in the SQL Server program group, the SQL Server Client Network Utility, is used to manage the client-side Net-Libraries. The user can choose which Net-Library to use as the default. By using a Net-Library and the network name of the server, the user can make advanced entries to connect to servers that use other protocols. The **Advanced Entry** dialog box holds three components:

Server Alias
> The label by which the entry is referenced at connect time. For example, if an advanced entry is created with SERVER=XYZ, the server XYZ is used for the connection when osql is run with a /Sxyz switch.

Network Library
> The Microsoft SQL Server Net-Library used by the client to connect to the aliased server. Select the check box that corresponds with the appropriate Net-Library.

Connection Parameters
> The network address of the server. For example, if it is a Windows Sockets entry, specify the port and socket address of the server. If it is a Named Pipes or Multiprotocol entry, specify the network name of the server.

Sybase and Microsoft servers are compatible with each other's client software, provided the software is limited to SQL Server 4.2 features. Microsoft servers can host Sybase clients, and Sybase servers can host Microsoft clients. Since version 4.2, the servers diverge with their introduction of new data types, new Transact-SQL statements, new ANSI-based statements, and new administrative procedures. Sybase customers migrating to Microsoft SQL Server 7.0 should convert the client software to use OLE DB providers or ODBC drivers. This software is included with Microsoft SQL Server 7.0 or can be downloaded at no charge from www.microsoft.com/data/ (connect time charges may apply).

For more information about configuring the client Net-Libraries, see SQL Server Books Online.

System Databases

The table provides an overview of the implementation of Sybase and Microsoft system databases.

Database item	Sybase Adaptive Server Enterprise (SQL Server 10+)	Microsoft SQL Server 7.0	Comments
Stored Procedures	Stored in the **sybsystemprocs** database.	Stored in the **master** database.	Change references from **sybsystemprocs** to **master**.
Memory Management	Beginning with System 11, user-defined data caches allow each user to create an area of data cache that can be reserved for specific objects.	Dynamic memory management techniques eliminate the need for administrative configuration of memory.	
Information about the oldest open transaction	The **syslogshold** table records the oldest open transaction.	The DBCC OPENTRAN statement records the oldest open transaction.	Replace all references to **syslogshold** with DBCC OPENTRAN logic.

For an explanation of the Microsoft SQL Server system database structure, see "System Databases and Data" later in this chapter.

Keyword Conflicts

Migrate your Sybase databases to a test Microsoft database and fully test your applications and administrative procedures against the test Microsoft database, including stress testing, before you transfer the entire production system to Microsoft SQL Server.

Review your T-SQL statements and the names of SQL Server objects for keyword conflicts before transferring your objects and data to Microsoft SQL Server.

The following table lists Sybase System 11 keywords that will not function in Microsoft SQL Server and keywords that are reserved by Microsoft SQL Server. If your T-SQL statements use any of the listed keywords, replace them with other words before you migrate your Sybase database to Microsoft SQL Server.

Sybase System 11 keywords	Microsoft SQL Server reserved keywords
ARITH_OVERFLOW	CASE
AT	COALESCE
CHAR_CONVERT	COMMITTED
ENDTRAN	CROSS
ERRORDATA	CURRENT_DATE
MAX_ROWS_PER_PAGE	CURRENT_TIME
NATIONAL	CURRENT_TIMESTAMP
NOHOLDLOCK	CURRENT_USER
NUMERIC_TRANSACTION	DISTRIBUTED
ONLINE	DROP
PARTITION	FLOPPY
REPLACE	FULL
ROLE	IDENTITY
ROWS	IDENTITYCOL
SHARED	INNER
STRIPE	INSENSITIVE
SYB_IDENTITY	JOIN
SYB_RESTREE	LEFT
UNPARTITION	NOCHECK
USER_OPTION	NULLIF
USING	OUTER PIPE
	REPEATABLE
	REPLICATION
	RESTRICT
	RIGHT
	SCROLL
	SERIALIZABLE
	SESSION_USER
	SYSTEM_USER
	TAPE
	THEN
	UNCOMMITTED
	UPDATETEXT
	WHEN

Migrating Tables and Data

Using Data Transformation Services (DTS) allows you to import and export data between multiple heterogeneous sources that use an OLE DB–based architecture such as Microsoft Excel spreadsheets and flat text files, and to transfer databases and database objects (for example, indexes and stored procedures) between multiple computers running Microsoft SQL Server version 7.0. You can also use DTS to transform data so it can be used more easily to build data warehouses and data marts from an online transaction processing (OLTP) system.

The DTS Wizard allows you to interactively create DTS packages that use OLE DB and ODBC to import, export, validate, and transform heterogeneous data. The wizards also enable you to copy schema and data between relational databases.

Use the DTS Wizard to transfer your Sybase data into Microsoft SQL Server in a few steps.

1. Launch Enterprise Manager, click the **Tools** menu, and choose **Data Transformation Services, Import into SQL**.
2. In the **Choose a Data Source** dialog box, choose **Sybase System 11** as the Source. Choose the DSN that corresponds to your Sybase data source.
3. In the **Choose a Destination** dialog box, choose **Microsoft SQL Server 7.0 OLEDB Provider**, select the database server, and then choose the required authentication mode for the selected database server.
4. In the **Specify Table Copy or Query** dialog box, choose **Copy tables**.

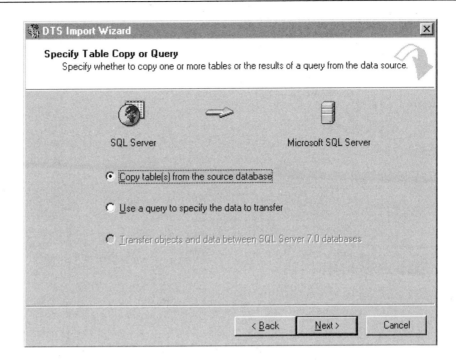

5. In the **Select Source Tables** dialog box, choose **Select All**. Click the gray box found within the Transform column of the **Select Source Tables** dialog box to change column names, data types, nullability, size, precision, and even write code to make unique transformations to your data before importing data into Microsoft SQL Server.

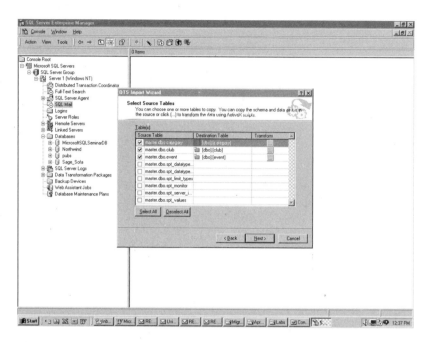

6. Run the data migration package immediately, or run it at a later time. The DTS Wizard shows you the progress and status of the data migration, step by step.

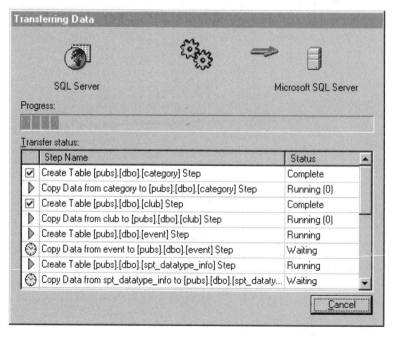

Reviewing Sybase T–SQL and Microsoft Transact–SQL Differences

Some differences between Sybase T-SQL and Microsoft Transact-SQL and system stored procedures must be addressed to ensure a successful migration. The following issues affect Transact-SQL in scripts, applications, triggers, and stored procedures.

Transaction Management

Both Sybase and Microsoft support explicit transactions managed with the statements BEGIN TRANSACTION, SAVE, COMMIT TRANSACTION, and ROLLBACK TRANSACTION.

Rollback Trigger

The Sybase ROLLBACK TRIGGER statement rolls back only the work performed by the statement that fired the trigger.

In Microsoft SQL Server version 7.0, you must replace the ROLLBACK TRIGGER statements with paired SAVE TRANSACTION (tr1)… ROLLBACK TRANSACTION (tr1) statements to roll back a single Transact-SQL statement without affecting the rest of the transaction. Sybase applications that currently use ROLLBACK TRIGGER should be changed to issue SAVE TRANSACTION (tr1), fire the trigger, and then issue the ROLLBACK TRANSACTION (tr1) statement if needed before executing any other Transact-SQL statements.

Chained Transactions

Sybase System 10 introduced chained transactions, which are transactions that have implicit starting points but must be explicitly committed. A connection can put itself into or out of a chained transaction state with the SET statement:

```
SET CHAINED [ON | OFF]
```

Microsoft SQL Server version 6.5 introduced a similar feature called implicit transactions that functions in the same way as Sybase chained transactions. Microsoft SQL Server implicit transactions are also controlled by the SET statement:

```
SET IMPLICIT_TRANSACTIONS [ON | OFF]
```

Change the SET CHAINED statements in Sybase applications to SET IMPLICIT_TRANSACTION statements for Microsoft SQL Server.

Sybase stored procedures are tagged with the transaction mode (chained or unchained) with which they were created, while Microsoft SQL Server procedures operate in the transaction mode that exists when they are executed. Therefore, Sybase procedures can have COMMIT TRANSACTIONS that are not matched with a BEGIN TRANSACTION statement; this is not allowed in Microsoft SQL Server procedures. Scan all Sybase procedures created in chained mode for COMMIT TRANSACTION statements that do not have matched BEGIN TRANSACTION statements. Either remove the COMMIT TRANSACTION from or add a BEGIN TRANSACTION to the procedure before it is migrated to Microsoft SQL Server.

The Sybase @@**tranchain** variable, indicating the current transaction mode (0=unchained, 1=chained), has no Microsoft SQL Server equivalent. The 2 bits in the Microsoft SQL Server @@OPTIONS function report the mode of implicit_transactions:

```
IF (@@OPTIONS & 2) > 0
    PRINT 'Implicit_transactions on'
ELSE
    PRINT 'Implicit_transactions off'
```

The Sybase @@**transtate** variable, indicating whether a transaction is in progress, successful, or canceled, has no Microsoft SQL Server equivalent. Replace @@**transtate** logic with either @@ERROR checking or SET XACT_ABORT ON to enable Microsoft SQL Server to roll back a transaction automatically when an error occurs.

The Sybase system stored procedure **sp_procxmode**, used to control the transaction modes of stored procedures, has no Microsoft SQL Server equivalent. Sybase procedures must have COMMIT statements matched with BEGIN TRANSACTION statements or be removed from the stored procedures before migrating to Microsoft SQL Server.

Transaction Isolation Levels

Sybase identifies its transaction isolation levels with numbers and Microsoft SQL Server identifies the levels with character tags. Scan for SET TRANSACTION ISOLATION LEVEL statements and change the Sybase level specifications to Microsoft specifications.

Note Microsoft SQL Server 7.0 implements REPEATABLE READ in the same way as SERIALIZABLE.

Sybase	Microsoft SQL Server
0	READ UNCOMMITTED
1	READ COMMITTED
2	REPEATABLE READ
3	SERIALIZABLE

Cursors

Microsoft SQL Server supports the Sybase cursor statements except for a minor difference in syntax for the DEALLOCATE CURSOR; the keyword CURSOR is not used by SQL Server with the DEALLOCATE cursor statement:

Sybase: DEALLOCATE CURSOR *cursor_name*
Microsoft: DEALLOCATE *cursor_name*

Error Checking

Error checking is implemented differently by Sybase and Microsoft SQL Server. Sybase cursors report errors through @@**sqlstatus**, and Microsoft reports errors through @@FETCH_STATUS. In addition, Microsoft and Sybase report different values.

Sybase @@sqlstatus	Microsoft @@FETCH_STATUS
	-2 = Row deleted from result set
	-1 = End of result set
0 = Success	0 = Success
1 = Type mismatch	
2 = End of result set	

Sybase allows different stored procedures to open cursors with identical names. Each cursor with the same name gets a separate result set. Microsoft SQL Server considers the scope of a cursor name to be the current session. The server does not allow different stored procedures that are executed by the same connection to open cursors with duplicate names.

Microsoft SQL Server cursors default to optimistic concurrency control, which does not place shared locks on tables. Sybase cursors generally default to pessimistic concurrency control, which places shared locks on the underlying tables. The pessimistic concurrency can reduce concurrency in high-use environments.

Index Optimizer Hints

Optimizer hints are important in Sybase implementations because Sybase does not update index statistics automatically. The Sybase query optimizer is not always reliable because it often optimizes based on outdated statistics.

Microsoft SQL Server 7.0 updates statistics automatically, so the Microsoft query optimizer is more likely than the Sybase query optimizer to make the best choice of index use. In addition, the graphical SQL Server Query Analyzer helps programmers and DBAs determine the system I/O bottlenecks. The automatically updated statistics, the accurate query optimizer, and the ability to troubleshoot using the graphical SQL Server Query Analyzer are all reasons to delete Sybase optimizer hints from the statements, not simply replace them. For more information about implementing optimizer hints, see SQL Server Books Online.

Optimizer Hints for Locking

A range of table-level locking hints can be specified by using the SELECT, INSERT, UPDATE, and DELETE statements to direct Microsoft SQL Server to the type of locks to be used. Table-level locking hints can be used when you need a finer control of the types of locks acquired on an object. These locking hints override the current transaction isolation level for the session.

The SQL Server query optimizer automatically makes the correct determination. It is recommended that table-level locking hints be used to change the default locking behavior only when absolutely necessary. Disallowing a locking level can adversely affect concurrency.

To implement optimizer hints for locking manually, you must remove the System 11 hints PREFETCH, LRU, or MRU because Microsoft SQL Server does not support them. Microsoft SQL Server automatically uses READ AHEAD (RA) processing when it is appropriate. This behavior can be tailored with new RA options on **sp_configure**, discussed in "System Stored Procedures" later in this chapter.

For more information about locking hints, see SQL Server Books Online.

Server Roles

The Sybase server roles of **sa_role**, **sso_role**, or **oper** are not supported by Microsoft SQL Server. GRANT and REVOKE statements referencing these roles must be removed.

In Microsoft SQL Server, the **sysadmin** role has functions equivalent to the Sybase **sa_role** and **sso_role**. By using the GRANT statement, you can give individual users permissions to perform the operator actions of dumping databases and transactions, but you cannot give them permissions to load databases and transactions.

The Sybase function **proc_name**, which validates a user's name, is not supported by Microsoft SQL Server and must be removed.

The table describes the fixed server roles in Microsoft SQL Server 7.0.

Fixed server role	Permission
sysadmin	Can perform any activity in SQL Server.
serveradmin	Can set serverwide configuration options and shut down the server.
setupadmin	Can manage linked servers and startup procedures.
securityadmin	Can manage logins and CREATE DATABASE permissions and read error logs.
processadmin	Can manage processes running in SQL Server.
dbcreator	Can create and alter databases.
diskadmin	Can manage disk files.

You can get a list of the fixed server roles from **sp_helpsrvrole**, and get the specific permissions for each role from **sp_srvrolepermission**.

Each database has a set of fixed database roles. While roles with the same names exist in each database, the scope of an individual role is only within a specific database. For example, if **Database1** and **Database2** both have user IDs named **UserX**, adding **UserX** in **Database1** to the **db_owner** fixed database role for **Database1** has no effect on whether **UserX** in **Database2** is a member of the **db_owner** role for **Database2**.

The table describes the fixed database roles in Microsoft SQL Server 7.0.

Fixed database role	Permission
db_owner	Has all permissions in the database.
db_accessadmin	Can add or remove user IDs.
db_securityadmin	Can manage all permissions, object ownerships, roles, and role memberships.
db_ddladmin	Can issue ALL DDL, but cannot issue GRANT, REVOKE, or DENY statements.
db_backupoperator	Can issue DBCC, CHECKPOINT, and BACKUP statements.
db_datareader	Can select all data from any user table in the database.
db_datawriter	Can modify any data in any user table in the database.
db_denydatareader	Can deny or revoke SELECT permissions on any object.
db_denydatawriter	Can deny or revoke INSERT, UPDATE, and DELETE permissions on any object.

Raising Errors

The Sybase version of RAISERROR allows argument substitution in any order, but the arguments must be of data type **varchar** or **char**.

The Microsoft SQL Server RAISERROR statement requires positional argument substitution, like the C language **printf**, but supports integer and string substitution: %d, %i, %s. This RAISERROR statement also supports the specification of a severity level (range 1 through 25).

The Microsoft RAISERROR statement includes a *WITH LOG* parameter so that the server enters the message in the error log. Messages raised with severities from 19 through 25 require the *WITH LOG* parameter.

PRINT

The Sybase version of PRINT allows argument substitution; the Microsoft version does not. The most straightforward solution is to change any Sybase PRINT that uses argument substitution to a RAISERROR with a severity of 10 or lower. Another solution is to print a string built of substrings in Microsoft SQL Server:

```
DECLARE @msg VARCHAR(255)
SELECT @msg = 'The object ' + @tablename + 'does not allow duplicate
keys.\n'
PRINT @msg
```

Partitioned Tables vs. Row Locking

In Sybase 11+, partitions are supported only on user tables that do not have clustered indexes. This System 11 feature helps to reduce the blocking caused by the lack of row-level locking.

Microsoft SQL Server supports row-level locking on all table types, and does not support the keyword **PARTITION** on the ALTER TABLE statement.

Setting SQL-92 NULL Behavior

Both Sybase 11+ and Microsoft SQL Server version 6.5 and later support SQL-92–compliant NULL behavior. However, the syntax in the two systems is different.

Sybase:

```
SET ANSINULL {ON|OFF}
```

Microsoft SQL Server:

```
SET ANSI_NULLS {ON|OFF}
SET ANSI_WARNINGS {ON|OFF}
```

Microsoft SQL Server supports setting options that define whether columns in CREATE TABLE statements take the ANSI NULL defaults:

```
SET ANSI_NULL_DFLT_ON {ON|OFF}
SET ANSI_NULL_DFLT_OFF {ON|OFF}
```

IDENTITY Columns

Microsoft and Sybase use the same syntax for defining identity columns. The Microsoft default name for an identity column is IDENTITYCOL; the Sybase default name is SYB_IDENTITY. All references to SYB_IDENTITY must be changed to IDENTITYCOL.

SET Statement

Since their respective 4.2 versions, the SET statement options implemented by both vendors have diverged. Although the new options may have the same or similar names, their defined characteristics can be slightly different. For example, the full effect of the Sybase ANSINULLS option combines behavior defined by the Microsoft options ANSI_NULLS and ANSI_WARNINGS.

The following table lists the Sybase-specific options that do not have exact Microsoft equivalents, and lists the Microsoft options that most closely match the desired Sybase behavior. Review the SQL Server documentation carefully to understand the differences between the Sybase statement and the alternative offered. The table does not list the options that the two vendors share.

Sybase option	Microsoft option
ANSINULLS	ANSI_NULLS, ANSI_WARNINGS
ANSI_PERMISSIONS	No equivalent.
ARITHABORT can take overflow or truncated options.	ARITHABORT does not support options.
ARITHIGNORE can take overflow option.	ARITHIGNORE does not support options.
CHAINED	IMPLICIT_TRANSACTION
CLOSE ON ENDTRAN	CURSOR_CLOSE_ON_COMMIT
CHAR_CONVERT	Set with either ODBC or DB-Library connect options.
CURSOR ROWS	No equivalent.
DUP_IN_SUBQUERY (System 10 only)	No equivalent.
FIPSFLAGGER takes ON/OFF.	FIPSFLAGGER takes a FIPS level identifier.
FLUSHMESSAGE	No equivalent.
PREFETCH	See READ AHEAD processing.
ROLE	No equivalent.

(continued)

Sybase option	Microsoft option
SELF_RECURSION	No equivalent.
STATISTICS SUBQUERYCACHE	No equivalent (STATS TIME and I/O supported).
STRING_RTRUNCATION	No equivalent.
TABLE COUNT	No equivalent.
TRANSACTION ISOLATION LEVEL {0|1|3}	Levels specified with strings (like READ COMMITTED).

Subquery Behavior

Sybase SQL Server 4.9.2 and Microsoft SQL Server 4.2x subqueries are not SQL-92 standard; subqueries can return duplicate rows.

Sybase System 10 defaults to SQL-92 standard behavior, but the old subquery behavior can be turned on to ease migration. Sybase 10 is backward compatible to the non-ANSI behavior if the SET DUP_IN_SUBQUERY option is turned ON. Sybase 11 and Microsoft SQL Server 7.0 support only SQL-92 subquery behavior. If you are migrating an application from Sybase 10 and the system uses SET DUP_IN_SUBQUERY ON, you must review the Sybase queries so that they do not cause errors. If you are migrating from a Sybase version previous to 10, you also must review queries that have subqueries.

System Stored Procedures

The Microsoft and Sybase implementations of the system stored procedures **sp_addmessage**, **sp_dboption**, and **sp_configure** are not the same.

sp_addmessage

In Sybase systems, the range for user-defined message numbers starts at 20,000. In SQL Server, the range starts at 50,000 and also requires a severity to be specified to support alerts (severity ranges from 1 through 25).

Microsoft SQL Server stores user messages in **master.dbo.sysmessages**, and Sybase stores them in **master.dbo.sysusermessages**.

sp_dboption

The table lists the parameters for **sp_dboption** that are different for Sybase and Microsoft implementations.

Sybase parameters	Microsoft parameters
ABORT TRAN ON LOG FULL	No equivalent.
ALLOW NULLS BY DEFAULT	ANSI NULL DEFAULT
AUTO IDENTITY	No equivalent.
DDL IN TRAN	SQL Server version 7.0 allows DDL in transactions.
IDENTITY IN NONUNIQUE INDEX	No equivalent.

Sybase requires a checkpoint in the affected database after **sp_dboption** completes, and Microsoft SQL Server automatically checkpoints the affected database. Also, Microsoft SQL Server allows DDL in transactions without requiring the system administrator to set any server or database options.

sp_configure

You can manage and optimize Microsoft SQL Server resources through configuration options by using SQL Server Enterprise Manager or the **sp_configure** system stored procedure. The most commonly used server configuration options are available through SQL Server Enterprise Manager; all configuration options are accessible through **sp_configure**.

Compared to earlier versions, SQL Server version 7.0 has more internal features for self-tuning and reconfiguring. These features reduce the need to set server configuration options manually. You should consider the effects on your system carefully before setting these options.

The options for the Sybase and Microsoft versions of **sp_configure** are quite different. Detailing all of the differences is beyond the scope of this chapter. Sybase DBAs should review the SQL Server documentation for **sp_configure** options.

sp_configure allows members of the **sysadmin** fixed server role to set defaults for user options, such as ANSI options, although individual connections can later change the settings. The current state of a connection's settings are made visible to it through the @@OPTIONS function. @@OPTIONS returns a numeric value that records the current option settings. For more information about a stored procedure that returns a character list of the options recorded by @@OPTIONS, see the Microsoft Knowledge Base article Q156498.

DUMP/LOAD

The DUMP statement is included in Microsoft SQL Server version 7.0 for backward compatibility. It is recommended that the BACKUP statement be used instead of the DUMP statement. In future versions of SQL Server, DUMP will not be supported. For more information about database back up and restore operations, see SQL Server Books Online.

Use DTS to perform imports and exports on a regular basis with Microsoft SQL Server.

DUMP/LOAD statements	Sybase Adaptive Server Enterprise	Microsoft SQL Server 7.0
dump devices	FILE	DISK
listing	LISTONLY	Not supported in the same way; closest statement is HEADERONLY.
	HEADERONLY only lists the first dump.	HEADERONLY lists information about all dumps in a device.
Striping	STRIPE=*n*	Remove the STRIPE=*n* parameter from the Sybase DUMP and LOAD statements and set the **sp_configure backup threads** parameter to *n*.

Replace all logic that uses the Sybase **syslogshold** table to determine the oldest outstanding transaction with logic that uses the Microsoft DBCC OPENTRAN statement.

Understanding Database Administration Differences

Microsoft SQL Server 7.0 offers several tools for database administration.

Graphical Administration

SQL Server Enterprise Manager allows easy enterprise-wide configuration and management of SQL Server and SQL Server objects. SQL Server Enterprise Manager provides a powerful scheduling engine, administrator alert capability, and a built-in replication management interface. You can also use SQL Server Enterprise Manager to:

- Manage logins, permissions, and users.
- Create scripts.
- Manage backup devices and databases.

- Back up databases and transaction logs.
- Manage tables, views, stored procedures, triggers, indexes, rules, defaults, and user-defined data types.
- Create full-text indexes, database diagrams, and database maintenance plans.
- Import and export data.
- Transform data.
- Perform various Web administration tasks.

By default, SQL Server Enterprise Manager is installed by SQL Server Setup as part of the server software on computers running Windows NT, and as part of the client software on computers running on the Windows NT and Windows 95/98 operating systems. Because SQL Server Enterprise Manager is a 32-bit application, it cannot be installed on computers running 16-bit operating systems.

Auditing

SQL Server Profiler is a graphical tool that allows system administrators to monitor engine events in Microsoft SQL Server 7.0. SQL Server Profiler captures a continuous record of server activity in real-time. SQL Server Profiler allows you to monitor events produced through SQL Server, filter events based on user-specified criteria, and direct the trace output to the screen, a file, or a table. Using SQL Server Profiler, you can replay previously captured traces. This tool helps application developers identify transactions that may be reducing the performance of an application. This can be useful when migrating an application from a file-based architecture to a client/server architecture, since the last step involves optimizing the application for its new client/server environment.

Examples of engine events include:

- Login connects, fails, and disconnects.
- Transact-SQL SELECT, INSERT, UPDATE, and DELETE statements.
- Remote procedure call (RPC) batch status.
- The start or end of a stored procedure.
- The start or end of statements within stored procedures.
- The start or end of a Transact-SQL batch.
- Errors written to the Microsoft SQL Server error log.
- Locks acquired or released on a database object.
- Open cursors.

Data about each event can be captured and saved to a file or a SQL Server table for later analysis.

Threshold Manager

Microsoft SQL Server uses two tools to manage transaction logs in a manner equivalent to the Sybase Threshold Manager:

- SQL Server Enterprise Manager allows you to set up a system of periodic, scheduled backups.

- SQL Server Agent monitors Windows NT Performance Monitor counters. You must set up an alert to execute a backup of the transaction log when the appropriate threshold is exceeded.

Rebuilding master

Sybase 4.*x* rebuilt its **master** databases using the **bldmstr** utility. In later versions of Sybase, the **sybinit** utility is used to rebuild the **master** database.

Microsoft SQL Server 7.0 has a Rebuild Master utility that provides the same functionality.

Graphical Query Analysis

SQL Server Query Analyzer is a graphical query tool that visually allows you to analyze the plan of a query, execute multiple queries simultaneously, view data, and obtain index recommendations. SQL Server Query Analyzer provides the Showplan option, which is used to report data retrieval methods chosen by the SQL Server query optimizer.

Migration Checklist

You must make the following changes to your Sybase database and applications before migrating to Microsoft SQL Server 7.0:

1. Change references to chained transaction mode to either unchained transactions or Microsoft implicit transactions. Change @@**trainchain** references to @@OPTIONS. Change @@**transtate** references to @@ERROR logic.

2. Convert ROLLBACK TRIGGER to savepoints.

3. Change transaction isolation levels from Sybase numeric-level identifiers to Microsoft string-based identifiers.

4. Move user-supplied stored procedures from **sybsystemprocs** to **master**.

5. Delete (preferably) or change index and locking optimizer hints to Microsoft format.

6. Change permanent temporary tables to global tables.

7. Change range and add severity to user-defined messages.

8. Remove:

   - Arguments from the PRINT statement.
   - Sybase server roles.
   - User-defined data cache references.
   - Thresholds.
   - Table partitioning.

9. Make required syntax changes:

   - Change DUMP and LOAD statements to BACKUP and RESTORE statements.
   - Change cursor processing (change @@**sqlstatus** to @@FETCH_STATUS).
   - Identity column default name changes to IDENTITYCOL.
   - SET TRANSACTION ISOLATION LEVEL.
   - SELECT statement optimizer hints.
   - **sp_addmessage** (message range and severity).
   - Reserved Microsoft keywords.
   - DBCC.
   - RAISERROR.

10. Change message ranges to >= 50,000.

11. Change argument substitution such as C **printf.**

Optionally, you can choose to make the following changes to your Sybase database and applications before migrating to Microsoft SQL Server 7.0:

- Change tuning options for read ahead.
- Change scrollable server cursors.
- Encrypt stored procedures in **syscomments**.
- Replace nested IF statements with the CASE statement.
- Use RPCs with result sets in INSERTS.
- Schedule automatic maintenance tasks, alerts, and replication.
- Use extended stored procedures for mail notification, paging, scheduling.
- Log user messages to the Windows NT application log and/or the SQL Server error log by using **xp_logevent**.
- Change trusted connections and *NT_username*.
- Start up stored procedures automatically.

- Change EXECUTE strings.
- Use the SQL Server Agent autostart functionality.
- Change the SELECT statement to use SQL-92–style joins (INNER JOIN, CROSS JOIN, LEFT OUTER JOIN, RIGHT OUTER JOIN, FULL OUTER JOIN).

System Databases and Data

Microsoft SQL Server systems have four system databases:

- **master**

  The **master** database records all of the system-level information for a SQL Server system. It records all login accounts and all system configuration settings. The **master** database records the existence of all other databases and the location of the primary files that contain the initialization information for the user databases. The **master** database records the initialization information for SQL Server; always have a recent backup of **master** available.

- **tempdb**

  The **tempdb** database holds all temporary tables and temporary stored procedures and fills any other temporary storage needs. The **tempdb** database is a global resource; the temporary tables and stored procedures for all users connected to the system are stored there. The **tempdb** database is re-created every time SQL Server is started so the system starts with a clean copy of the database. Because temporary tables and stored procedures are automatically dropped on disconnect, and no connections are active when the system is shut down, there is never anything in **tempdb** to be saved from one session of SQL Server to another.

  The **tempdb** database grows automatically as needed. Each time the system is started, **tempdb** is reset to its default size. You can avoid the overhead of having **tempdb** grow automatically by using ALTER TABLE to increase the size of **tempdb**.

- **model**

  The **model** database is used as the template for all databases created on a system. When a CREATE DATABASE statement is issued, the first part of the database is created by copying in the contents of the **model** database, then the remainder of the new database is filled with empty pages. Because **tempdb**, which uses the **model** database, is created every time SQL Server is started, the **model** database must always exist on a SQL Server system.

- **msdb**

  The **msdb** database is used by SQL Server Agent for scheduling alerts and jobs and for recording operators.

In SQL Server version 7.0, every database, including the system databases, has its own set of files and does not share those files with other databases. The default location for these files is the C:\Mssql7\Data directory.

Database file	Physical file name	Default size, typical setup
master primary data	Master.mdf	7.5 MB
master log	Mastlog.ldf	1.0 MB
tempdb primary data	Tempdb.mdf	8.0 MB
tempdb log	Templog.ldf	0.5 MB
model primary data	Model.mdf	0.75 MB
model log	Modellog.ldf	0.75 MB
msdb primary data	Msdbdata.mdf	3.5 MB
msdb log	Msdblog.ldf	0.75 MB

In SQL Server 7.0, each database has its own set of files that can grow independently of the others.

Each database in Microsoft SQL Server contains system tables that record the data needed by the SQL Server components. The successful operation of SQL Server depends on the integrity of information in the system tables; therefore, Microsoft does not support users who directly update information in the system tables.

Microsoft provides a complete set of administrative tools that allow users to fully administer their system and manage all users and objects in a database. Users can use the administration utilities, such as SQL Server Enterprise Manager, to directly manage the system. Programmers can use the SQL-DMO API to include complete functionality for administering SQL Server in their applications. Programmers building Transact-SQL scripts and stored procedures can use the system stored procedures and Transact-SQL DDL statements to support all administrative functions in their systems.

An important function of SQL-DMO, system stored procedures, and DDL statements is to shield applications from changes in the system tables. Microsoft sometimes needs to change the system tables in later versions of SQL Server to support new functionality being added in that version. Applications issuing SELECT statements that directly reference system tables are frequently dependent on the earlier format of the system tables. Customers may not be able to upgrade to a later version of SQL Server until they have rewritten applications that are selecting data from system tables. Microsoft considers the system stored procedures, DDL, and SQL-DMO published interfaces, and seeks to maintain the backward compatibility of these interfaces.

Microsoft does not support triggers defined on the system tables because they may alter the operation of the system.

Another important tool for querying the SQL Server catalog is the set of information schema views. These views comply with the information schema defined in the SQL-92 standard. These views provide applications with a standards-based component for querying the SQL Server catalog.

C H A P T E R   2 1

Migrating Btrieve Applications to Microsoft SQL Server 7.0

Many database application vendors are finding that their products are at a critical point in the product life cycle. They have released with a solid level of success several versions that use indexed sequential access method (ISAM)–based database management systems (DBMS) like Btrieve.

However, due to rapidly expanding customer needs and the powerful capabilities of relational database management systems (RDBMS) offerings, many Independent Software Vendors (ISVs) are now converting their applications to RDBMSs. Applications based on an RDBMS can offer better performance and scalability, and more replication features than ISAM-based solutions. Well-designed RDBMS solutions vary in size from a few megabytes to multiple terabytes.

Microsoft SQL Server 7.0 is a powerful and flexible RDBMS solution. The ease of use and scalability of SQL Server 7.0 has made it attractive for thousands of application developers. This chapter presents a strategy that will allow you to convert Btrieve applications to work with SQL Server. The strategy presents many of the features of SQL Server that make it a high-performance alternative to an ISAM platform. While the Btrieve platform is this chapter's focus, the chapter introduces many concepts that can be applied to any ISAM-based application.

Microsoft offers many programs and resources for developers. The benefits to developers include training, comarketing opportunities, and early bites of Microsoft products. Benefits vary based on the programs. For more information, see www.microsoft.com/developer/.

The Btrieve environment may seem simpler to use and administer than SQL Server. However, this simplicity comes at a price. Btrieve has several architectural shortcomings that add complexity to applications that access it. Btrieve does not:

- Enforce logging of all data changes.
- Provide a way to back up the data files while they are online and in use.

- Provide mechanisms to automate administrative tasks such as data file backups.

- Offer tools for monitoring performance.

The Microsoft strategy is to make SQL Server the easiest database for building, managing, and deploying business applications. This means providing a fast and efficient programming model for developers, eliminating database administration for standard operations, and providing sophisticated tools for more complex operations.

SQL Server 7.0 feature	Description
Administration Wizards	Many new wizards simplify advanced tasks such as creating databases, scheduling backups, importing and exporting data, and configuring replication.
DBA Profiling and Tuning Tools	New tools provide advanced profiling and tuning: ■ SQL Server Profiler improves debugging by allowing the capture and replay of server activity. ■ Index Tuning Wizard provides guidance through the index tuning process. ■ SQL Server Query Analyzer allows easy, in-depth query analysis.
Distributed Management Objects	Independent software vendors and corporate developers can easily develop custom management applications. The COM-based framework exposes all management interfaces for SQL Server. Automation components and custom applications can be written using the Microsoft Visual Studio development system, the Microsoft Visual Basic development system for Applications, and Java scripting.
Dynamic Self-Management	Reduces need for DBA intervention: memory and lock resources are adjusted dynamically; file sizes grow automatically; autotuning features guarantee consistent performance under variable-load conditions.

(continued)

SQL Server 7.0 feature	Description
Event/Alert Management	Enhances ability to monitor performance, availability, and security status through policy-based event management. Improved alert management provides automatic notification and recovery in response to thresholds and severity levels.
Job Scheduling and Execution	The job scheduling and execution environment is extended to allow stand-alone, multiserver, single-step, multistep jobs and job step with dependencies. Great flexibility is provided though a variety of scripting environments: Microsoft Visual Basic Scripting Edition, Java scripting, Microsoft Windows NT commands and custom ODBC and OLE DB programs.
Multisite Management	Improves power and flexibility for managing multiple servers. Drag-and-drop and single commands can be used to implement changes across groups of servers. Management is simplified through the use of a repository that maintains schema, profiles, and data transformation metadata for all servers in the enterprise.
Security	Security administration is improved and simplified through better integration with Windows NT security and SQL Server roles. Windows NT integration includes authentication, support for multiple groups, grant/revoke/deny permission management activities and dynamic use of groups.
Standards Compliance	Full compliance with the ANSI/ISO SQL-92 Entry-level standards. Views are included for the ANSI/ISO schema information tables as defined in SQL-92, providing a standard method for metadata examination.
Version Upgrade	Databases are easily transferred from version 6.x to 7.0, via a fully automated upgrade utility. Customers are able to get up and running quickly on the new version and take advantage of new features with minimal impact on operations.
Visual Data Modeler	New tools provide a graphical interface for building and managing schema and other database objects.

Introducing Microsoft SQL Server Version 7.0

Microsoft SQL Server version 7.0 is a defining release that builds on the solid foundation established by SQL Server version 6.5. As the most robust database for the family of Windows operating systems, SQL Server is the RDBMS of choice for a broad spectrum of corporate customers and ISVs who are building business applications. Customer needs and requirements have driven significant product innovations in ease of use, reliability, scalability, and data warehousing.

SQL Server Design Goals

SQL Server 7.0 was designed with several goals in mind:

- Leadership and innovation in the database industry
- Ease of use for customers
- Scalability and reliability
- Data warehousing

Leadership and Innovation

Innovations enable SQL Server 7.0 to lead several of the database industry's fastest growing application categories, including data warehousing, line-of-business applications, mobile computing, branch automation, and e-commerce.

Innovations with which SQL Server 7.0 leads the database industry include:

- Scalability from the laptop to branch offices using the same code base and offering 100 percent code compatibility.
- Support for autoconfiguration and self-tuning.
- Integrated online analytical processing (OLAP) server.
- Integrated Data Transformation Services (DTS).
- The Microsoft Data Warehousing Framework, the first comprehensive approach to solving the metadata problem.
- Multiserver management for large numbers of servers.
- A wide array of replication options, including replication to any database that supports OLE DB or ODBC.
- Integration with the Microsoft Windows NT Server operating system, Microsoft Office, and the Microsoft BackOffice family of products.
- Universal Data Access, the Microsoft strategy for enabling high-performance access to a variety of information sources.

Universal Data Access is a platform for developing multitier, enterprise applications that require access to diverse relational and nonrelational data. This collection of software components interacts using a common set of system-level interfaces called OLE DB, the Microsoft open specification for low-level interfacing with data. OLE DB is the next generation successor to the industry standard ODBC data access method.

OLE DB replaces DB-Library as the internal interface for all SQL Server database operations. OLE DB enables heterogeneous queries that use the SQL Server query processor to perform with the same high level of performance as queries to the SQL Server storage engine.

Ease of Use

Customers are looking for solutions to business problems. Most database solutions bring multiple layers of cost and complexity. The Microsoft strategy is to make SQL Server the easiest database for building, managing, and deploying business applications. This means providing a fast and simple programming model for developers, eliminating database administration for standard operations, and providing sophisticated tools for more complex operations.

SQL Server 7.0 lowers the total cost of ownership through features like multiserver, single-console management; event-based job execution and alerting; integrated security; and administrative scripting. This release also frees the database administrator for more sophisticated aspects of the job by automating routine tasks. Combining these powerful management facilities with new autoconfiguration features, SQL Server 7.0 is the ideal choice for branch automation and embedded database applications.

Scalability and Reliability

Customers make investments in database management systems in the form of the applications written to that database and the education that it takes for deployment and management. That investment must be protected: as the business grows, the database must grow to handle more data, transactions, and users. Customers also want to protect investments as they scale database applications down to laptops and up to branch offices.

To meet these needs, Microsoft delivers a single database engine that scales from a mobile laptop computer running the Microsoft Windows 95 and Windows 98 operating systems, to terabyte symmetric multiprocessor clusters running Windows NT Server, Enterprise Edition. All of these systems maintain the security and reliability demanded by mission-critical business systems.

New in SQL Server 7.0 is a low-memory footprint version with multisite replication capabilities. It is well suited to the growing needs of the mobile computing marketplace.

Other features such as dynamic row-level locking, intra-query parallelism, distributed query, and very large database (VLDB) enhancements make SQL Server 7.0 the ideal choice for high-end online transaction processing (OLTP) and data warehousing systems.

Data Warehousing

Transaction processing systems remain a key component of corporate database infrastructures. Companies are also investing heavily in improving understanding of their data. Microsoft's strategy is to reduce the cost and complexity of data warehousing while making the technology accessible to a wider audience.

Microsoft has established a comprehensive approach to the entire process of data warehousing. The goal is to make it easier to build and design cost-effective data warehousing solutions through a combination of technologies, services, and vendor alliances.

The Microsoft Alliance for Data Warehousing is a coalition that brings together the industry's leaders in data warehousing and applications. The Microsoft Data Warehousing Framework is a set of programming interfaces designed to simplify the integration and management of data warehousing solutions.

New product innovations in SQL Server 7.0 improve the data warehousing process with:

- Microsoft SQL Server OLAP Services, an essential component for enterprise solutions that require OLAP, from corporate reporting and analysis to data modeling and decision support.
- DTS, for importing, exporting, and transforming data.
- Handling of complex queries and very large databases.
- Microsoft Repository, a common infrastructure for sharing information.
- Visual Design Tools, for creating and maintaining database diagrams.
- Integrated replication, including multisite update, for maintaining dependent data marts.
- Integration with third-party solutions.

Getting Started with the Migration

For clarity and ease of presentation, the reference development and application platforms are assumed to be the Microsoft Visual C++ development system and Microsoft Windows NT 4.0 or later, or Microsoft Windows 95 or Windows 98 operating systems. The Btrieve function and dynamic-link library (DLL) references throughout this chapter reflect this assumption. However, these techniques can also be applied to other compilers that create Microsoft Windows-based applications.

Examples from the pubs Database

Several tables from the Microsoft SQL Server **pubs** sample database are used in both the sample applications and sample code referenced in this chapter. These tables were chosen because they are readily available to any SQL Server user and because their structure and entity relationships are presented in the SQL Server documentation.

Sample Application and Code References

The following sample applications and wrapper DLLs are referenced in this chapter and you can find the source files on the CD-ROM that accompanies this volume. See www.microsoft.com/sql/ for updates to these resources.

Resource	Description
Btrvapp.exe	Sample Btrieve application that references the Sales.btr and Titlepub.btr Btrieve data files. It is the starting point for the conversion strategy, and it is a simple data-entry and reporting application for a database that maintains information about publishing companies, the titles they manage, and current sales information for each title.
Mybtrv32.dll	Sample wrapper DLL that translates the Btrieve calls in Btrvapp.exe to ODBC and Transact-SQL calls. The wrapper provides a bare minimum conversion from a Btrieve ISAM implementation to a SQL Server client/server implementation. Using this wrapper DLL, Btrvapp.exe accesses nonnormalized tables from the SQL Server **pubs** database instead of the Btrieve data files.

(continued)

Resource	Description
Odbcapp.exe	Sample ODBC and SQL Server application that performs the same function as the Btrvapp.exe and Mybtrv32.dll combination by using ODBC and Transact-SQL only, and no Btrieve calls or references.
Morepubs.sql	Script file that creates the nonnormalized tables in the **pubs** database referenced by the wrapper DLL, as well as the stored procedures used by Odbcapp.exe for illustrative purposes.

Conversion Strategy

Converting an application from one database environment to another takes time, patience, and resources. Because of the differences between platforms, a multiple-step conversion process is recommended. This approach provides multiple analysis points and makes the overall project development process more flexible.

This strategy provides a framework you can use when converting an application from a Btrieve-based implementation to a full ODBC and structured query language (SQL) implementation that accesses Microsoft SQL Server. Converting the application in several steps creates separate checkpoints that allow you to evaluate the status and direction of the conversion process at each stage of the project life cycle. The conversion strategy addresses the following areas:

- Creating a wrapper DLL.
- Converting the application data using DTS.
- Converting the application to ODBC and SQL.
- Using server resources effectively.
- Ease-of-use features for administering a SQL Server 7.0 database.

The following illustration presents the application architecture implemented at each stage of the conversion process. The components of this illustration are analyzed in detail throughout the next two sections of this chapter.

Conversion Strategy: Application Architecture Stages

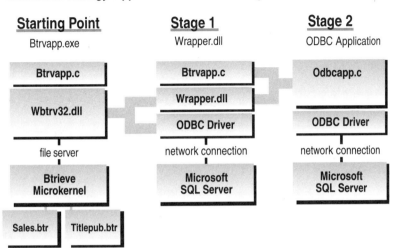

Starting Point: Btrieve Application

Btrvapp.exe is a simple data-entry and reporting application that maintains information about book titles, the publishers that own the titles, and sales information for each title. The Btrieve application accesses two Btrieve files, Sales.btr and Titlepub.btr, through the Btrieve microkernel engine. The Sales file contains sales information for each title, and the Titlepub file maintains the title and publisher information for each title. The Sales file and the Titlepub file each have two keys that correspond to a publisher and a title ID.

The Btrieve application uses these keys to position itself within these files when it performs all searches. The Btrieve application uses ISAM row-at-a-time searching techniques and result processing to perform its operations, and Btrieve concurrent transactions to manage the locks in the data file while information is updated, inserted, or deleted. The Btrieve application provides the following functionality:

- Searches for a particular title by its title ID key. The output of the search contains details about the title, its publisher, its recent sales, and a year-to-date sales total.

- Adds a title and its corresponding publisher information.
- Adds sales items for a title.
- Updates the year-to-date sales for all titles owned by a particular publisher. The output of the search contains details about each title affected and its new year-to-date sales total.

Stage 1: Wrapper DLL

The goal of this stage in the conversion process is to provide a layer of abstraction between the base application and Microsoft SQL Server. Using the concept of a wrapper DLL, the base application, Btrvapp.exe, can access SQL Server data without modification. Essentially, the wrapper disguises the SQL Server data and responses as Btrieve data and responses to Btrvapp.exe. The wrapper uses Btrieve-like result set processing techniques to access two nonnormalized tables, **bsales** and **titlepublisher**. These tables are structured to maintain the same details as the Sales and Titlepub files accessed by Btrvapp.exe. Although the ODBC and SQL Server implementation techniques presented in the wrapper DLL are not optimal, they present an initial access methodology that is similar to Btrieve.

Stage 2: ODBC and SQL Server Application

Odbcapp.exe is a full ODBC and SQL Server application that accesses SQL Server data directly and more efficiently than the techniques implemented by the wrapper DLL. The ODBC application accesses data in the three normalized tables (**titles**, **publishers**, and **sales**), taking advantage of the relational model provided by SQL Server. Odbcapp.exe also uses several of the performance-enhancing features of SQL Server such as indexes, default result sets and stored procedures to process result sets.

Migrating Btrieve Data to Microsoft SQL Server

The Data Transformation Services wizard (DTS Wizard) can help you move your data from Btrieve to SQL Server. First, you create a data source name (DSN) by using an ODBC driver or an OLE DB provider. Then the wizard leads you through the steps required for data migration.

Note Before you can begin migrating Btrieve data, you must have a Pervasive Btrieve ODBC driver. You can use the ODBC driver included with the Pervasive Btrieve product or a third-party driver.

First, you must create a Pervasive ODBC data source:

1. On the **Start** menu, click Control Panel, and then click ODBC.

2. In the **System DSN** dialog box, click **Add**, and then configure the Btrieve data source. Make sure that the data source points to your database.

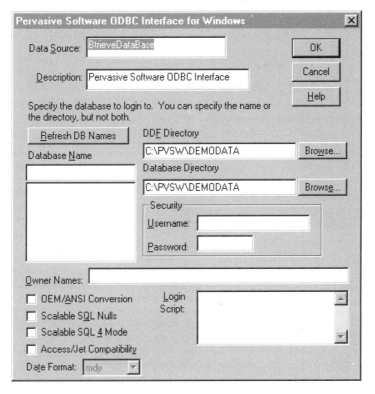

3. In the **ODBC Data Source Administrator** dialog box, verify that the driver is listed on the **File DSN** tab.

4. On the Start menu, point to **SQL Server 7.0**, and then click **Import and Export Data** to launch the Data Transformation Services Wizard.

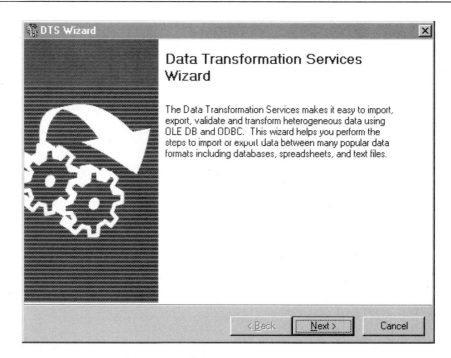

5. Select the Btrieve DSN when you are asked for a Source database.

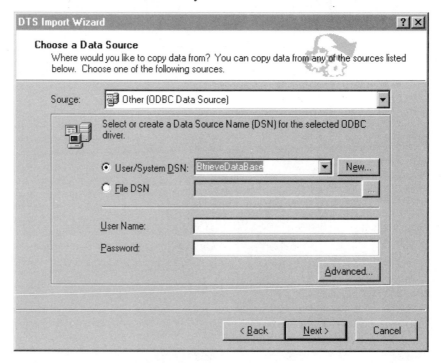

6. Select the name of the SQL Server database when you are asked for a destination database.

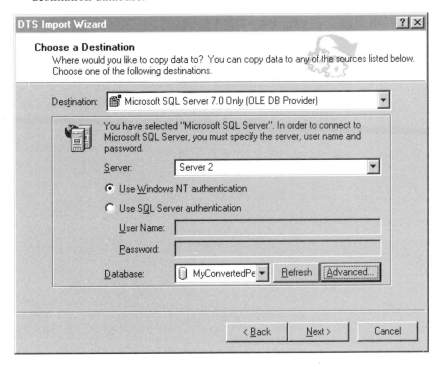

7. In the **Specify Table Copy or Query** dialog box, select **Copy Table(s)** from the source database.

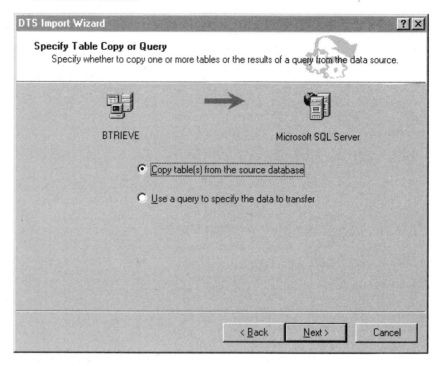

8. Select the tables to move.

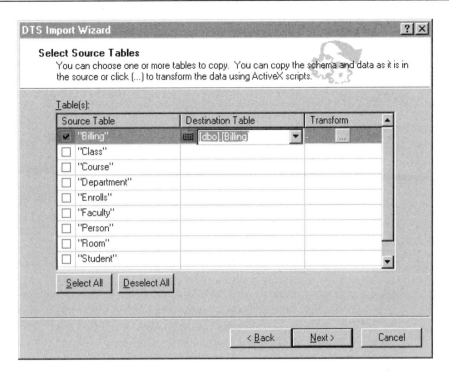

9. Select the data formats for the new Microsoft SQL Server database.

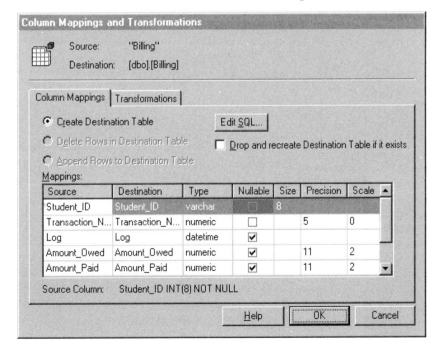

10. Optionally, modify the CREATE TABLE statement that was automatically generated.

11. Optionally, transform data as it is copied to its destination.

    You can use this functionality to help you check for potential year 2000 problems, and to change data to reflect standard coding such as country codes, state names, or phone number formatting.

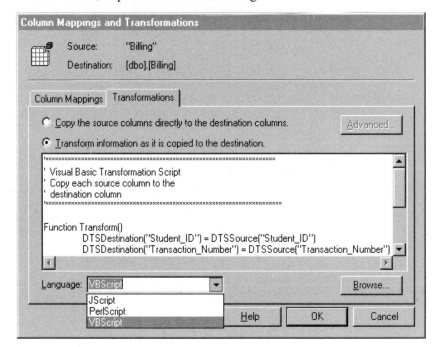

12. Select one or more source tables to copy to the destination database.

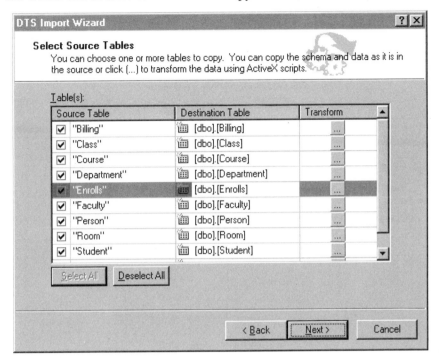

13. Do one of the following:

  - To run the data export/import now, click **Run Immediately**.
  - To save the DTS package later, click **Save Package on SQL Server**.

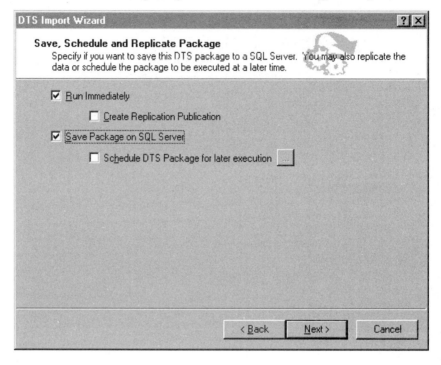

14. Optionally, schedule this export/import task to run on a recurring basis.

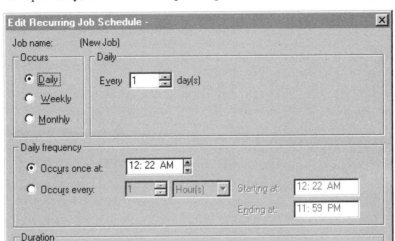

15. If you saved the DTS package, you can reexecute the routine from the Microsoft Management Console (MMC) at any time. The routine is located in the Data Transformation Services directory under Local Packages.

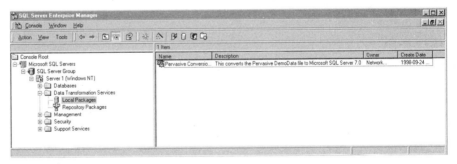

Using the Wrapper DLL

A wrapper DLL is a dynamic-link library that intercepts external library function calls made to an application. After a function call has been intercepted, the DLL controls the application or process that instantiated the DLL. The DLL can be designed to perform any task or set of tasks, or to do nothing at all. The developer can add to, change, or remove functionality or scope from the DLL without modifying the source code of the calling process or application.

For example, in the case of this conversion strategy, a wrapper DLL can intercept Btrieve calls made to an application and change them to use ODBC to access Microsoft SQL Server. This technique leaves the base application code intact while changing the scope and/or targets of the operation. The initial investment made in the application is preserved even though the application's capabilities have been extended to access SQL Server data.

Alternatively, the wrapper DLL could retrieve data from SQL Server into buffers maintained on the client or another computer. The application then fetches data from the buffers instead of from SQL Server directly by using ISAM-like processing techniques. Although this implementation enables the unmodified base application to access SQL Server, it is complex and can be difficult to implement. It is best suited for those instances when you do not want to use set operations or to develop a full ODBC- and SQL-based application. This methodology is not presented in this chapter.

Creating the Wrapper DLL

Four steps are involved in creating the wrapper DLL:

1. Determine which functions to wrap.
2. Map Btrieve import functions to export functions in the DLL.
3. Implement the Btrieve functions.
4. Link the application to the wrapper DLL.

Determining Which Functions to Wrap

The wrapper DLL must cover all the functions that the base application imports from the Btrieve library Wbtrv32.dll. Use a binary file dumping utility to list the functions imported from the various external link libraries and referenced by the application. In Microsoft Visual C++, the equivalent of the dumping utility is called Dumpbin.exe.

Use DUMPBIN /IMPORTS *application_file_name* to obtain the list of imported symbols for Wbtrv32.dll. In the following sample output, the function symbols in Btrvapp.exe imported from Wbtrv32.dll are ordinals 3, 2, and 1:

```
DUMPBIN /IMPORTS BTRVAPP.EXE
Microsoft (R) COFF Binary File Dumper Version 4.20.6164
Copyright (C) Microsoft Corp 1992-1997. All rights reserved.
Dump of file BTRVAPP.EXE
File Type: EXECUTABLE IMAGE
        Section contains the following Imports:
            wbtrv32.dll
                Ordinal     3
                Ordinal     2
                Ordinal     1
```

Use DUMPBIN /EXPORTS *DLL_file_name* to obtain the list of exported symbols for the DLL in question. The symbols appear in the **name** column of the table whose headings are "ordinal," "hint," and "name." In the example, these correspond to BTRCALL, BTRCALLID, and WBRQSHELLINIT.

```
DUMPBIN /EXPORTS WBTRV32.DLL
Microsoft (R) COFF Binary File Dumper Version 4.20.6164
Copyright (C) Microsoft Corp 1992-1997. All rights reserved.
Dump of file wbtrv32.dll
File Type: DLL
        Section contains the following Exports for wbtrv32.dll
                    0 characteristics
            31D30571 time date stamp Thu Jun 27 15:04:33 1996
                 0.00 version
                    1 ordinal base
                   10 number of functions
                   10 number of names
        ordinal hint    name
                1    0   BTRCALL  (000014EC)
                8    1   BTRCALLBACK  (00003799)fs
                2    2   BTRCALLID  (00001561)
                9    3   DBUGetInfo  (00008600)
               10    4   DBUSetInfo  (000089E8)
                3    5   WBRQSHELLINIT  (00002090)
                4    6   WBSHELLINIT  (00002A6A)
                7    7   WBTRVIDSTOP  (00001812)
                5    8   WBTRVINIT  (00002A4F)
                6    9   WBTRVSTOP  (000017D2)
```

The information presented in these output excerpts is used to create the definition file for the wrapper DLL. You need to implement only the exported functions from Wbtrv32.dll that are used by the base application in the wrapper DLL. This eliminates the need to implement exported functions that are never used by the base application.

Mapping Functions in a DEF File

After you have identified the Btrieve import functions and symbols in the base application as well as the exported symbols for the DLL, map these import functions to export functions in the wrapper DLL by using a definition file for the wrapper DLL.

Create a DEF file that contains an EXPORTS section with the names of the functions listed in the **name** column of the DUMPBIN output. The exact import/export combination varies depending on what Btrieve functionality is used in the application.

Implementing the Btrieve Functions Within the Wrapper

The next step is to develop the basic framework within the wrapper so that all of the Btrieve operations are implemented properly. Most of the Btrieve operations are performed by using the BTRCALL and BTRCALLID functions. Their equivalent functions within the wrapper must be designed to address the operations used by the base applications. Each of these functions has all of the data necessary to perform the operations by using the input parameters it receives.

The following code fragment shows how the B_GET_EQUAL operation is handled by the BTRCALL function within Mybtrv32.dll:

```
DllExport int __stdcall BTRCALL (BTI_WORD operation, BTI_VOID_PTR
posBlock,
    BTI_VOID_PTR dataBuffer, BTI_ULONG_PTR dataLen32,
        BTI_VOID_PTR keyBuffer, BTI_BYTE keyLength, BTI_CHAR ckeynum)
{
```

```
SQLRETURN rc;     // Btrieve operation return code
/*Perform tasks based on operation used in the calling application */
switch(operation){
case B_GET_EQUAL:
// Get the first Title-Publisher record that matches the search
// criteria
if (!strcmp(posBlock, "titlepub.btr")){//Are we accessing title-
publisher info
rc = GetTitlePublisher(henv1, hdbc1, hstmt, B_GET_EQUAL,
ckeynum,keyBuffer);
if (rc != B_NO_ERROR)
        return rc;
//Copy title-publisher data to titlepub record structure tpRec
memcpy(dataBuffer, &tpRec, sizeof(tpRec));
}
else {  // Accessing sales info
rc=GetSales(henv1, hdbc2, hstmt2, B_GET_EQUAL, keyBuffer);
    if (rc != B_NO_ERROR)
return rc;
//Copy sales data to sales record structure salesRec
memcpy(dataBuffer, &salesRec, sizeof(salesRec));
}
break;
```

The most important parameters are the posBlock, operation, dataBuffer, keyBuffer, and ckeynum parameters. The posBlock parameter is described in "Addressing the Btrieve posBlock Handle," later in this chapter. The operation parameter designates what operation is to be performed. The contents of the dataBuffer, keyBuffer, and ckeynum parameters depend on the operation being performed. You must use these parameters in the same way they would be used if the function was being processed by Btrieve.

The posBlock parameter in the preceding code fragment determines the target SQL Server table. After the target has been determined, a function is called to retrieve the first data record that matches the keyBuffer and ckeynum values from the appropriate SQL Server cursor.

The same methodology is used throughout the wrapper DLL. This illustration shows the wrapper DLL concept.

Wrapper.dll Concept

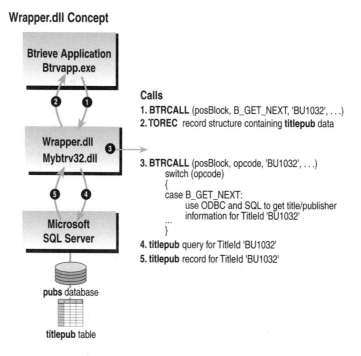

The base application, Btrvapp.exe, requests the title and publisher information for **TitleID** "BU1032." While the wrapper DLL processes this request, the Btrieve application calls the Btrieve function BTRCALL to get the next record from the Titlepub.btr file. The wrapper DLL mimics BTRCALL but accesses SQL Server data instead. It examines the opcode parameter and then performs the appropriate ODBC and Transact-SQL operations to satisfy the request. In this example, the wrapper DLL retrieves the record for **TitleID** "BU1032" from the **titlepub** table in the database. The wrapper DLL returns the retrieved data to the base Btrieve application by using the record data buffer passed as part of the original BTRCALL function call.

Accessing the Wrapper DLL in the Base Application

After the wrapper DLL has been created, the original application must reference the wrapper DLL instead of the Btrieve DLL. Link the application with the wrapper DLL and ODBC library files (LIB) rather than with the Btrieve library file. You do not have to recompile the base code. The base application will access SQL Server and not the Btrieve microkernel.

Translating Btrieve Calls to ODBC and Transact-SQL

Now, the base application, Btrvapp.exe, can use the wrapper DLL to access SQL Server data. Essentially, the wrapper makes SQL Server look like Btrieve to Btrvapp.exe. The next step is to consider how ODBC and Transact-SQL will access SQL Server data within the scope of the wrapper DLL. The wrapper is designed to use ISAM processing techniques to access SQL Server. Although this implementation successfully accesses SQL Server data without making changes to the base application code, the data is not accessed optimally.

Addressing the Btrieve posBlock Handle

In the Btrieve environment, posBlock is a unique area of memory that is associated with each open file and that contains logical positional information to access records. The Btrieve libraries initialize and use this memory area to perform data functions. The Btrieve application inserts into every Btrieve call a pointer to the posBlock.

The wrapper DLL does not need to maintain any Btrieve-specific data within the posBlock, so it is free to use this memory area for other operations. In the example DLL wrapper, the memory area is used to store the unique identifier for the SQL Server data affected by the requested operation. Regardless of the contents of the posBlock maintained by the wrapper DLL, each memory block must be unique to each corresponding SQL Server table set.

For example, Btrvapp.exe references two Btrieve files, Sales.btr and Titlepub.btr, where Sales.btr contains sales information for each title and Titlepub.btr maintains the title and publisher for each title. These files correspond to the **bsales** and **titlepublishers** tables that were created in the **pubs** database by the sample script, Morepubs.sql. In Btrvapp.exe, the B_OPEN operation opens the requested Btrieve file and creates its corresponding posBlock.

In the wrapper, the same posBlock now references a particular table by name. The wrapper DLL can be designed to store any form of a unique identifier that represents the SQL Server data that it accesses. Table names are used in the context of this migration strategy for ease of presentation. The keybuffer parameter contains the file name of the Btrieve file to be opened when B_OPEN is called. The wrapper DLL implementation of the B_OPEN function sets the posBlock equal to this file or table name.

The following code fragment, taken from the wrapper DLL B_OPEN implementation (For more information, see source file Mybtrv32.c on the CD-ROM that accompanies this volume), demonstrates this concept:

```
/*Step1:*/
if (strlen((BTI_CHAR *) keyBuffer) <= MAX_POSBLOCK_LEN)
memcpy((BTI_CHAR *) posBlock, (BTI_CHAR *) keyBuffer,  keyLength);
else
memcpy((BTI_CHAR *) posBlock, (BTI_CHAR* ) keyBuffer,
MAX_POSBLOCK_LEN -1);
```

In the example, the Sales.btr posBlock is set to Sales.btr and the Titlepub.btr posBlock is set to Titlepub.btr. Btrvapp.exe always knows what SQL Server table set is being referenced based on the file name referenced in the posBlock.

The same data record structure formats are used in both the base application and the wrapper DLL. This allows the wrapper DLL to transport record data between SQL Server and Btrvapp.exe in the same format as if the data were coming from Btrieve. The data record structures used in Btrvapp.exe and Mybtrv32.dll are presented in the following example. For more information, see source files Btrvapp.c and Mybtrv32.c.

```
/***********************************************************
    Data Record Structure Type Definitions
***********************************************************/
//titlepub record structure
struct{
    charTitleID[7]; //string
    charTitle[81];  //string
    charType[13];   //string
    charPubID[5];   //string
    float    Price;        //money
    float    Advance;//money
    int Royalty;//integer
    int YTD_Sales; //integer
    charPubName[41];//string
    charCity[21];   //string
    charState[3];   //string
    charCountry[31];//string
}tpRec;

//sales record structure
struct
{
```

```
charStorID[5];  //string
    charTitleID[7]; //string
    charOrdNum[21]; //string
    int Qty;     //integer
    charPayTerms[13];   //string
}salesRec;
```

Establishing the ODBC Connections and Initializing Data Access

Within the sample wrapper implementation, the B_OPEN operation establishes a connection to SQL Server for each table set referenced by the base application Btrvapp.exe. The operation also creates and opens the cursors used to reference the SQL Server tables. The cursors are opened on the entire table without a WHERE clause to restrict the number of rows returned. These connections and cursors are used throughout Mybtrv32.dll to reference the SQL Server tables. To avoid the time and processing overhead associated with making or breaking connections to the server, the connections are not terminated until the application is closed.

This connection and cursor implementation were chosen for two reasons. First, they simulate a Btrieve application accessing a Btrieve file: one posBlock for every open file referenced by the application. Second, they demonstrate the inefficient use of connection management when SQL Server is accessed. Only one connection is needed in the context of this wrapper implementation because multiple server cursors can be opened and fetched concurrently on a single connection. Thus, the second connection is only creating overhead within the application. A more efficient connection management methodology uses only a single connection with multiple cursors opened on that connection.

Understanding ODBC and SQL Implementation

There are many different ways to access SQL Server data with ODBC and SQL. The wrapper Mybtrv32.dll uses server-side cursors. Cursors were chosen for several reasons:

- Cursors and Btrieve files are accessed similarly, for example, through the use of FETCH, GET FIRST, and NEXT operations.

- Cursors demonstrate the use of ISAM-like row-at-a-time processing and positioned updating of SQL Server data.

- Cursors demonstrate the difference between the row-at-a-time processing model and the default result set processing model used in the Odbcapp.exe sample application.

Each Btrieve operation that is performed in the base application is ported to an ODBC and SQL equivalent within the wrapper DLL. Some of the operations, like the B_SET_DIR operation, are not applicable to the SQL Server environment and do nothing within the wrapper DLL. Optimal implementation strategies of ODBC and SQL for both the wrapper DLL and the final application port are presented in "Converting the Application to ODBC and SQL" later in this chapter.

Handling Errors

The wrapper DLL must use Btrieve return codes when exiting each function. Each wrapper function must return B_NO_ERROR or a Btrieve error code corresponding to the type of error that was encountered. By using a valid Btrieve return code, the base application code does not know that its library function is accessing SQL Server instead of Btrieve. You must return the Btrieve return codes that are expected by the base application in order for the wrapper DLL to work properly.

However, there is no direct mapping of SQL Server to Btrieve error codes. You must translate all SQL Server errors encountered in the ODBC code of the wrapper DLL to a Btrieve return code equivalent. The following example taken from the **MakeConn** function in the wrapper DLL source file Mybtrv32.c demonstrates this concept:

```
// Allocate a connection handle, set login timeout to 5 seconds, and
// connect to SQL Server
    rc = SQLAllocHandle(SQL_HANDLE_DBC, henv, hdbc);
// Set login timeout
    if (rc == SQL_SUCCESS || rc == SQL_SUCCESS_WITH_INFO)
        rc=SQLSetConnectAttr(*hdbc, SQL_LOGIN_TIMEOUT,(SQLPOINTER)5, 0);
    else{
    // An error has been encountered: notify the user and return
        ErrorDump("SQLAllocHandle HDBC", SQL_NULL_HENV, *hdbc,
SQL_NULL_HSTMT);
return B_UNRECOVERABLE_ERROR;
}
```

In case an error is encountered, the SQL Server error code must be mapped to an applicable Btrieve error code. For example, the preceding code fragment allocates a connection handle for use in the wrapper DLL. Because Btrieve does not have the concept of connection handles, it does not have a corresponding error code. The solution is to choose a Btrieve return code that closely matches the severity or context of the message. The connection handle error was severe enough to the application to warrant the Btrieve return code *B_UNRECOVERABLE_ERROR*. You can choose any Btrieve return code provided that the base application is designed to address it.

Converting the Application to ODBC and SQL

To produce a high-performance Microsoft SQL Server application, it is important to understand some of the basic differences between the SQL Server relational and the Btrieve ISAM models. The wrapper DLL described in the previous section successfully disguises SQL Server as Btrieve. However, this implementation is inefficient in the way that it accesses SQL Server data. In fact, the wrapper DLL implementation is likely to perform significantly worse than the original Btrieve application.

The wrapper DLL accesses two nonnormalized tables instead of taking advantage of the relational model capabilities that SQL Server provides. It also does not process result sets by using any of the powerful application performance enhancing features like effective Transact-SQL syntax, stored procedures, indexes, and triggers, to process result sets.

The next step in migrating Btrieve applications to SQL Server is to change the focus of processing techniques used by the base application to take full advantage of the relational model provided by SQL Server. This can be accomplished through the creation of a new application, Odbcapp.exe, that uses ODBC and SQL only to access SQL Server data.

The performance of your SQL Server database depends on the design of the database, index, and queries. These design issues should be addressed first because they can drastically improve performance with a relatively small effort. This section focuses on optimizing database, index, and query design using ODBC and SQL. Implementation comparisons between the Btrieve and SQL Server processing models will be made frequently to demonstrate the advantages that SQL Server provides.

Understanding Normalized Databases

Relational Database Management Systems (RDBMS) are designed to work best with normalized databases. One of the key differences between an indexed service access method database and a normalized database is that a normalized database has less data redundancy. For example, the file and table record formats used by Btrvapp.exe and Mybtrv32.dll for the Titlepub.btr file and the **titlepublisher** table have redundant data. Specifically, the publisher information is stored for every title. Therefore, if a publisher manages more than one title, its publisher information will be stored for every title entry it manages. An ISAM-based system such as Btrieve neither provides join functionality nor groups data from multiple files at the server. Therefore, ISAM-based systems such as Btrieve require that developers add the redundant publisher data to the **Titles** table to avoid manual join processing of two separate files at the client.

With a normalized database, the **titlepublisher** table is transformed into two tables: a **Title** table and a **Publisher** table. The **Title** table has a column that contains a unique identifier (consisting of numbers or letters) that corresponds to the correct publisher in the **Publisher** table. With relational databases, multiple tables can be referenced together in a query; this is called a join.

The Data Transformation Services (DTS) feature used in the data migration stage can help you automate the migration and transformation of your data from a source database to a destination database. A data transformation consists of one or more database update statements. Each software application requires specific data transformations. These migration and transformation routines should be designed and saved for reuse by the Independent Software Vendor (ISV) or application developer who understands the business logic of the database. DTS helps to ensure that the data transformations occur in the right order and can be repeated hundreds of times for different ISV customers.

Consider using DTS to automate the migration and normalization of your customers' databases. The ability of DTS to save routines helps you repeat the migration process easily for many customers. DTS can migrate any data that can be accessed through ODBC drivers or OLE DB providers and move the data directly into another ODBC/OLE DB data store.

Comparing Data Retrieval Models

Choose the implementation methodologies for data retrieval, modification, insertions, and deletions based on how the data is used in the application. Microsoft SQL Server is a powerful and flexible RDBMS. While many of the aspects of processing data in Btrieve can be applied to the SQL Server environment, you should avoid using Btrieve ISAM-like, client-side, result-set processing techniques and take full advantage of the server processing that SQL Server provides. The following discussion compares the result-set processing models of both Btrieve and SQL Server. The goal is to briefly expose the differences in these processing models and to show you how to design this functionality effectively and, in many cases, more efficiently in the SQL Server environment.

Btrieve Navigational Model

Btrieve processes result sets based on the navigational data processing model. The navigational model accesses a single data file at a time; any operation involving multiple files must be performed in the application itself. When the data file is searched, all of the record data is returned to the client regardless of the number of record attributes needed to satisfy the requests. The navigational model is characteristic of positional-based operations. The application and the Btrieve engine maintain a position within the data file, and all operations that are performed against this file are based upon this position. All updates in Btrieve are positional, requiring the application to search for and lock the record to be updated. Because the operations are position based, the application cannot change or delete database records based on search criteria.

In most cases, you use an index to perform the searches. You must know all of the fields that are indexed within each data file that the application references. (Non-index fields can be filtered using the extended get call). The Btrieve navigational model is capable of simple search arguments using the =, <>, >, <, >=, and <= comparison operators to filter the records retrieved from the data file. These search arguments are normally performed between a single indexed field and a constant. Btrieve offers an extended fetch call that can set up a search filter composed of multiple search arguments that are combined using the logical AND or OR operators, but the logical combinations of criteria in these filters are limited.

Transact-SQL

The structured query language of SQL Server is called Transact-SQL. Transact-SQL is rich and robust and, if used effectively, can make application development easy and efficient. Transact-SQL can reference both nonnormalized and normalized tables. Transact-SQL also allows you to query specific columns needed to satisfy a request, instead of returning all of the columns. Query capabilities are not limited to indexed fields; you can query any column in any table referenced in the FROM clause. To increase the speed of an operation, the query optimizer chooses among existing indexes to find the fastest access path. More details on indexes can be found later in this chapter.

Transact-SQL provides advanced searching capabilities in addition to the basic comparison operators also provided by Btrieve. Using Transact-SQL, you can perform complex joins, aggregate functions such as SUM, MAX, and MIN, and data grouping and ordering. One of the strengths of Microsoft SQL Server is its ability to rapidly access and process data at the server. Processing query results at the server reduces the client workload and the number of trips between the client and the server needed to process data.

Transact-SQL uses joins to combine information from multiple tables on the server concurrently. The following example taken from the **GetTitlePubRec** function Odbcapp.exe demonstrates this. The function calls a stored procedure to return all of the title and publisher information for a particular **TitleID**.

```
/***********************************************************************
Returns Title and Publisher information for @titleID.  The query in
this stored procedure performs a join between the Titles and the
Publishers table based on Publisher ID
***********************************************************************/
CREATE PROCEDURE GetTPByTitleId @titleid char(6) AS
SELECT T.TITLE_ID, T.TITLE, T.TYPE, T.PUB_ID, T.PRICE, T.ADVANCE,
    T.ROYALTY, T.YTD_SALES, P.PUB_NAME, P.CITY, P.STATE,
    P.COUNTRY
FROM TITLES T, PUBLISHERS P
WHERE T.TITLE_ID = @titleid AND T.PUB_ID = P.PUB_ID
```

After the client issues the call to the stored procedure **GetTPByTitleID**, the server executes the stored procedure, retrieves all of the requested columns for all of the records that match the criteria in the WHERE clause, and sends the result set back to the client.

To take advantage of these server-side resources and to reduce performance problems and overhead, application developers should use Transact-SQL fully, rather than create Transact-SQL statements underneath an ISAM-like interface. With direct access to the tables using Transact-SQL, you have complete control over the way data is processed throughout the application. You can fine-tune individual data requests to optimize performance and maximize throughput and data concurrency. You may find that optimizing the most frequently used queries improves performance drastically.

Comparing Default Result Sets and Cursors

SQL Server allows you to process data within your application by using both set-based operations (called default result sets) and row-at-a-time techniques with server cursors (processed similarly to Btrieve operations). Each of these processing models has its own distinct role in the application development process. In the following section, these processing options are compared and contrasted to help you choose the one that satisfies the data processing requirements within your application.

Default Result Sets

When an application uses Transact-SQL effectively to request only the rows it needs from the server, the most efficient way to retrieve these rows is a default result set. An application requests a default result set by leaving the ODBC statement options at their default values prior to executing **SQLExecute** or **SQLExecDirect**. For a default result set, the server returns the rows from a Transact-SQL statement as quickly as possible and maintains no position within this set of rows. The client application is responsible for immediately fetching these rows into application memory. Most data processing activity within an application can and should be accomplished using default result sets. Default result sets offer several distinct advantages:

- Reduce network traffic.

  One or multiple default result sets can be returned with only one round-trip between the client and the server.

- Conserve server resources.

  Between client calls, default result sets do not maintain position or other client state information at the server. This allows your application to support many users.

- Increase code efficiency.

  Stored procedures that return default result sets can also contain procedural logic, all at the server. This is more efficient than moving the data out of the server to apply procedural logic at the client. Stored procedures also allow data manipulation logic to be encapsulated and shared by all client applications.

SQL Server Cursors

Most data retrievals and modifications can be performed using SQL Server default result sets. However, in some cases, an application must use row-at-a-time capabilities to satisfy a certain application request. For example, the user may have to examine information one row at a time to make a decision or to use the information from the row to proceed with another task. SQL Server provides this functionality with server cursors. Like the Btrieve navigational model, server cursors maintain a position at the server. Server cursors act like an ISAM interface, except you cannot perform seek or find operations within the cursor result set. Cursors require that you perform this functionality within the client application.

Server Cursor Differences

Server cursors can be opened on the full table or any subset of a table just like default result sets. However, cursors differ from default result sets in the following distinct ways:

- Variety of fetching operations.

  Depending on the type of cursor chosen (static, keyset-driven, forward-only, dynamic, and so on), the application can perform a variety of different fetching operations (FETCH FIRST, NEXT, PREVIOUS, ABSOLUTE, RELATIVE, and so on) within the scope of the cursor result set at the server. With a default result set, an application can fetch only in a forward direction.

- Server cursors do not hold locks at the server on large unfetched result sets.

  When an application uses default result sets, shared locks may remain in effect until the client application processes the entire result set or cancels the operation. This can be a problem if the application waits for user input before it finishes fetching. If the application does not immediately fetch all data requested, the shared locks may be held for a long time, preventing others from updating or deleting. Because server cursors do not hold locks by default, they are unaffected by this application behavior.

- Server cursors allow you to perform positional updates.

  Default result sets, because of their set-based nature, do not provide this functionality. If a client application needs to update or delete a row retrieved from a default result set, it must use a SQL UPDATE or DELETE statement with a WHERE clause containing the row's primary key or call a stored procedure that takes the primary key and new values as parameters.

- Multiple active statements.

  By using ODBC, server cursors allow you to have multiple active statements on a single connection. An application that uses default result sets must fetch result rows entirely before a connection can be used for another statement execution.

Server Cursor Performance Costs and Limitations

Server cursors within SQL Server are powerful, flexible, and useful for ISAM-like, row-at-a-time processing and for positional updates. However, server cursors incur some cost and have some limitations:

- More resources are required.

    Opening a server cursor is more expensive than using default result sets within SQL Server in terms of parse, compile, and execute time and **tempdb** resources. The additional cost of a server cursor varies by query depending on the number of tables involved (for example, single table or join) and type chosen (static, keyset-driven, forward-only, dynamic, and so on).

- There are limits on their usage.

    Server cursors cannot be opened on Transact-SQL batches or stored procedures that return multiple result sets or involve conditional logic.

- There may be increased network traffic.

    Fetching from a server cursor requires one round-trip from client to server to open the cursor and retrieve the rowset number of rows specified within the application. In ODBC terms, this means one round-trip per call to **SQLFetchScroll** (or **SQLExtendedFetch** in ODBC 2.0).

Determining the Rowset Size of a SQL Server Cursor

The rowset size that is used to process a server cursor affects the processing throughput of your application. In ODBC, you can communicate the number of rows to fetch at a time by using the ROWSET SIZE statement option. The size you choose for the rowset depends on the operations performed by the application. Screen-based applications commonly follow one of two strategies: Setting the rowset size to the number of rows displayed on the screen or setting the rowset size to a larger number. If the user resizes the screen, the application changes the rowset size accordingly. Setting the rowset size low causes unnecessary fetching overhead. Setting the rowset size to a larger number, such as 100, reduces the number of fetches between the client and the server needed to scroll through the result set. Setting the rowset size high requires a larger buffer on the client, but minimizes the number of round-trips needed to return the result set between the client and server. An application that buffers many rows at the client enables the application to scroll within the client-side buffer instead of repeatedly requesting data from the server. In that case, the application only fetches additional rows when the user scrolls outside of the buffered portion of the result set.

Conclusions: Default Result Sets and SQL Server Cursors

You should carefully analyze the scope of each task within the application to decide whether default result sets or server cursors should be used. Default result sets should be used as much as possible. They require fewer resources, and their result sets are easier to process than those of server-side cursors. When a data request will retrieve a small number of rows or only one, and the application does not require positional updates, be sure to use a default result set.

Server cursors should be used sparingly and should be considered only for row-at-a-time processing within the application. If your application requires server cursors despite their performance disadvantages, make sure that the rowset size is set to a reasonably high value.

Understanding Data Access Interface Issues

Now that several different data processing implementation techniques have been compared, the next step is to use these methods to access SQL Server data effectively. The proper implementation of these concepts eliminates application overhead.

Accessing Tables Directly with Transact-SQL

Some third-party application development controls and objects provide properties and methods for accessing and retrieving data. These objects and controls expedite the development process by creating a simple interface that allows you to access tables while minimizing or eliminating the need to use Transact-SQL. This abstraction layer can put you at a disadvantage, however, because you will reduce your ability to tune the data-access operations.

By using Transact-SQL statements and stored procedures, you have direct access to the tables involved with your application. This allows you to determine how, and in what order, the data operations are performed. By accessing the tables directly, your application can issue Transact-SQL statements that are tuned for optimal performance.

In addition, stored procedures written in Transact-SQL can be used to encapsulate and standardize your data access.

Implementing Data Retrieval Effectively

You may be tempted to use server cursors to implement data seek operations at the client to emulate the ISAM-like processing techniques used in the Btrieve environment. However, using this methodology to implement data retrieval greatly diminishes the performance advantages of using SQL Server.

Introducing the Query Optimizer

SQL Server incorporates an intelligent, cost-based query optimizer that quickly determines the best access plan for executing a Transact-SQL statement. The query optimizer is invoked with every Transact-SQL statement that is sent to the database server. Its goal is to minimize execution time, which generally minimizes physical data accesses within the database. The query optimizer chooses from among the indexes you create on the tables. For more information about indexes, see "Using Effective Indexing Techniques," later in this chapter.

Joining Tables on the Server

Use table joins on the server rather than processing nested iterations of result set data on the client to reduce the amount of processing required at the client and the number of round-trips between the client and the server to process a result set.

Managing Concurrency and Locking Within the Application

Data concurrency and lock management are critical implementation issues in database application development. Effective lock management can have a substantial impact on data concurrency, scalability, and the overall performance of a database application system.

The row-level locking functionality of Microsoft SQL Server 7.0 resolves most application developers' database concurrency and locking issues. Nevertheless, a comparison of Btrieve (explicit) locking mechanisms and SQL Server (implicit) row-level locking capabilities ensures a smooth migration of the Btrieve application to SQL Server.

Locking and Concurrency Within the ISAM/Btrieve Model

In the Btrieve model, records can be locked by the application automatically. You can lock records automatically inside the scope of a transaction or manually on the statement level. Locks can be placed on a row, page, or the entire file; however, the decision of when and how to lock is left to you.

Because you are responsible for lock management, you must choose an optimistic or pessimistic locking concurrency approach in multiuser scenarios. Hard coding your locking scheme reduces the flexibility and scalability of the application. One locking scheme may not be optimal in all user environments due to varying database sizes and user-concurrency conditions. You must carefully examine each transaction and data modification made within the application to determine what locks are needed to satisfy its requirements.

Regardless of the locking scheme you choose in Btrieve, record reading, record writing, and the locks corresponding to each action are not implemented as an atomic unit. You must first read a record with a lock before it can be updated or deleted. This requires at least two round-trips between the client and the server for each data modification or deletion. For example, the following code retrieves a single record from Titlepub.btr by its **TitleID** with a single-row, wait-record lock (Btrieve lock bias 100) and then updates the record:

```
/* GET TITLE/PUBLISHERS RECORD WITH op and lock bias 100*/
memset( &tpRec, 0, sizeof(tpRec) );
dataLen = sizeof(tpRec);
tpStat = BTRV( op+100, tpPB, &tpRec, &dataLen, keyBuf, keyNum );
if (tpStat != B_NO_ERROR)
    return tpStat;
.
.
.

// Update with -1 key value because key for the record is not to be
// changed
tpStat = BTRV(B_UPDATE, tpPB, &tpRec, &dataLen, TitleID, -1 );
if (tpStat != B_NO_ERROR){
    printf( "\nBtrieve TitlePublishers UPDATE status = %d\n",     tpStat
);
    return B_UNRECOVERABLE_ERROR;
}
```

Because multiple round-trips are required to process these types of requests, their associated locks are maintained longer. This may reduce the concurrency and scalability of the application. SQL Server performs the locks and data modification or deletion in one step, reducing both the round-trips and the lock maintenance overhead. SQL Server can also automatically perform optimistic concurrency locking by using cursors.

Locking and Concurrency Within SQL Server

SQL Server 7.0 supports row-level locking, which virtually eliminates the locking problems that added complexity to ISAM and RDBMS programming in the past. This drastically reduces the development time and complexity of the client application.

SQL Server escalates lock granularity automatically based on the constraints of the query or data modification that is issued. SQL Server does not require you to perform a separate read and lock before the application can update or delete a record. SQL Server reads and performs the required lock in a single operation when an application issues an UPDATE or DELETE statement. The qualifications in the WHERE clause tell SQL Server exactly what data will be affected and ultimately locked. For example, the following stored procedure and ODBC code perform the same update of a record based on its **TitleID** as the preceding Btrieve example:

```
/****** Object:  Stored Procedure dbo.UpdtTitlesByPubID   ******/
CREATE PROCEDURE UpdtTitlesByPubID @PubID char(4) AS
    UPDATE TITLES SET YTD_SALES = YTD_SALES +
    (SELECT SUM(QTY) FROM SALES WHERE TITLES.TITLE_ID =
    SALES.TITLE_ID)
    WHERE PUB_ID = @PubID
GO
// Bind the PubID input parameter for the stored procedure
rc = SQLBindParameter(hstmtU, 1, SQL_PARAM_INPUT, SQL_C_CHAR, SQL_CHAR,
4, 0,
choice, 5, &cbInval);
if (rc!=SQL_SUCCESS && rc!=SQL_SUCCESS_WITH_INFO) {
    ErrorDump("SQLBIND SELECT TITLEPUB 1", SQL_NULL_HENV,
    SQL_NULL_HDBC, hstmtU);
    SQLFreeStmt(hstmtU, SQL_RESET_PARAMS);
    SQLFreeStmt(hstmtU, SQL_CLOSE);
    return FALSE;
}
// Execute the UPDATE
rc=SQLExecDirect(hstmtU, "{call UpdtTitlesByPubID(?)}", SQL_NTS);
if ((rc != SQL_SUCCESS && rc != SQL_SUCCESS_WITH_INFO)){
    ErrorDump("SQLEXECUTE UPDATE TITLEPUB", SQL_NULL_HENV,
    SQL_NULL_HDBC, hstmtU);
    return FALSE;
}
```

The numbers of operations needed to perform a task are reduced because SQL Server handles the row-level locking.

Emulating ISAM Processing and Locking Techniques with SQL Server

If you are accustomed to the nonrelational ISAM model, you may want to use ISAM data locking and concurrency management techniques within your SQL Server application code. These techniques, however, eliminate the performance-enhancing advantages that SQL Server provides. The following list presents two fundamental locking and concurrency implementation challenges that result from using ISAM processing and locking techniques, and a brief description of how each issue can be avoided.

- If you attempt to implement pessimistic SELECT FROM T (UPDLOCK) or locking cursors (using the SQL_CONCURRENCY statement option) to mimic the ISAM processing model, remember that Microsoft SQL Server performs the row-level locking automatically based on the query or data modification that has been issued; therefore, you do not have to lock the target record explicitly within your application.

- If SQL Server rereads the same record multiple times with lock to verify record existence before performing an update or delete, consider that in an ISAM environment such as Btrieve, you must verify a record's existence before it can be modified or deleted. This processing model incurs a great deal of overhead. It also reduces concurrency within the data due to the number of round-trips between the client and application that are needed to perform this verification and the number and durations of locks acquired by these checks.

SQL Server provides a mechanism for eliminating this overhead. The SQL Server @@ROWCOUNT function indicates the number of rows that were affected by the last operation. Use this function when you issue an UPDATE or DELETE statement within the application to verify how many records were affected. If no records exist that match the qualifications you specify in the WHERE clause, @@ROWCOUNT will be set to zero, and no records will be affected. The following example demonstrates the use of @@ROWCOUNT for this purpose:

```
UPDATE PUBLISHERS SET PUB_NAME = 'Microsoft Press', City = 'Redmond',
State= 'WA', Country = 'USA' WHERE = TITLE_ID = 'BU1032'
/* Verify that record was updated */
IF @@ROWCOUNT <1
    /* Record does not exist so create it with correct values */
    INSERT PUBLISHERS VALUES ('BU1032', 'Microsoft Press',
    'Redmond', 'WA', 'USA') WHERE TITLE_ID = 'BU1032'
```

In the preceding example, the UPDATE is performed, and @@ROWCOUNT is set to the number of records it affected. If no records were modified, then a new record is inserted.

Implementing Effective Database and Query Design

Database and query design have a dramatic impact on the performance of your SQL Server application. Successful planning and design at this stage can have positively influence your application's performance.

The first step in effective query design is to limit the amount of data transferred between the client and the server by limiting the columns specified in a Transact-SQL statement to the values required by the application (for example, through the efficient use of the SELECT and FROM clauses), and by limiting the number of rows fetched from the database (for example, through the efficient use of the WHERE clause).

After reviewing the Transact-SQL statements to ensure that they request only the required rows and columns, a database developer must consider the use of indexes, stored procedures, and efficient coding to improve application performance.

Selecting Specific Table Columns

In the Btrieve environment, most operations retrieve every column or attribute for each record involved in an operation. With SQL Server, this technique can be inefficient, especially in cases where only a small number of columns are actually required. For example, the **GetSales** function in Btrvapp.exe retrieves all of the sales record attributes from Sales.btr even though only the **TitleID** and **Qty** attributes are needed to complete the task. The following is the code fragment from the **GetSales** function in Mybtrv32.c that exhibits this behavior:

```
/* Get TITLE/PUBLISHER with OPERATION*/
// Copy the desired TitleID to the keyBuffer for use by Btrieve and
// initialize parameters
strcpy(TitleID, keyBuf);
memset( &salesRec, 0, sizeof(salesRec) );
dataLen = sizeof(salesRec);'
// Retrieve the sales record
salesStat = BTRV( op, salesPB, &salesRec, &dataLen, keyBuf, 1 );
    if (salesStat != B_NO_ERROR)
        return salesStat;
```

The same design inefficiency can be implemented in the SQL Server environment by selecting all of the columns from tables, views, or cursors involved in an operation. For example, the following code fragment from the **GetSales** function retrieves all of the sales record attributes from the BSALESCURSOR even though only **TitleID** and **Qty** are needed to complete the task.

```
// Bind result set columns to buffers
SQLBindCol(hstmt, 1, SQL_C_CHAR, salesRec.StorID, 5, &cbStorID);
```

```
SQLBindCol(hstmt, 2, SQL_C_CHAR, salesRec.TitleID, 7, &cbTitleID);
SQLBindCol(hstmt, 3, SQL_C_CHAR, salesRec.OrdNum, 21, &cbOrdNum);
SQLBindCol(hstmt, 4, SQL_C_SLONG, &salesRec.Qty, 0, &QtyInd);
SQLBindCol(hstmt, 5, SQL_C_CHAR, salesRec.PayTerms, 13, &cbPayTerms);
// Fetch records one-at-a-time from the server until the desired
// record is found
while(!found)
{
memset(&salesRec, 0, sizeof(salesRec)); // Initialize the record buffer
// Fetch the record from the server cursor
rc = SQLFetchScroll(hstmt, FetchOrientation, FetchOffset);
if ((rc != SQL_SUCCESS && rc != SQL_SUCCESS_WITH_INFO))
         .
         .
         .
```

You can avoid design inefficiency by accessing only the record attributes required to satisfy a particular task. Odbcapp.exe demonstrates a more efficient design concept in its **GetSales** function. The **GetSales** function in Odbcapp.exe calls the **GetSales** stored procedure from the SQL Server **pubs** database to retrieve only the **TitleID** and **Qty** columns for the desired title. The following code fragment presents the **GetSales** stored procedure. It demonstrates how the stored procedure is executed and its results processed in the Odbcapp.exe **GetSales** function.

```
/*Get Sales stored procedure */
CREATE PROCEDURE GetSales @titleid char(6) AS
SELECT TITLE_ID, QTY FROM SALES WHERE TITLE_ID = @titleid
GO
// Execute the stored procedure and bind client buffers for each
// column of the result
rc = SQLExecDirect(hstmtS, "{callGetSales(?)}", SQL_NTS);

         .

         .

         .
    SQLBindCol(hstmtS,1, SQL_C_CHAR, TitleID, 7, &cbTitleID);
    SQLBindCol(hstmtS, 2, SQL_C_SLONG, & Qty, 0, &QtyInd);
// Fetch result set from the server until SQL_NO_DATA_FOUND
    while( rc == SQL_SUCCESS || rc == SQL_SUCCESS_WITH_INFO)
    {
        rc = SQLFetch(hstmtS);
    .
    .
    .
```

Using WHERE Clauses to Reduce the Result Set Size

Use WHERE clauses to restrict the quantity of rows returned. Using WHERE clauses reduces the total amount of data affected by the operation, reduces unnecessary processing, and minimizes the number of locks needed to process the request. By using the WHERE clause to reduce the result set, you can avoid table contention, reduce the amount of data transferred between the client and the server, and increase the processing speed of the request.

For example, the following cursor code was taken from the **CreateCursor** function of Mybtrv32.c:

```
// Creates the BSALESCURSOR
if (!strcmp(curname, "BSALESCURSOR"))
    rc=SQLExecDirect(*hstmt2,
"SELECT STOR_ID, TITLE_ID, ORDNUM, QTY, PAYTERMS FROM
BSALES",SQL_NTS);
```

The BSALESCURSOR is created without using a WHERE clause. As a result, the server creates a cursor that retrieves all rows in the **bsales** table. This cursor results in more resources and processing at the client than it needs.

The application actually requires that the query obtain the sales information for a particular **TitleID** column. It would be more efficient to use a WHERE clause that defines the exact **TitleID** or even a range of **TitleID** columns. This would reduce the amount of data sent for client-side examination and the number of round-trips between the client and the server. This example is shown below. Notice that the cursor is more efficient because it only requests the **TitleID** and **Qty** columns from the **bsales** table; in this application, only those columns are used by the business logic.

```
if (!strcmp(curname, "BSALESCURSOR")){
    SQLBindParameter(hstmtU, 1, SQL_PARAM_INPUT, SQL_C_CHAR,
        SQL_CHAR, 6, 0, inval, 7, &cbInval);
    rc=SQLExecDirect(*hstmt2,
    "SELECT  TITLE_ID, QTY FROM BSALES WHERE TITLE_ID LIKE ?",
    SQL_NTS);
```

Using the Singleton SELECT

A singleton SELECT returns one row based on the criteria defined in the WHERE clause of the statement. Singleton SELECTs are often performed in applications and are worthy of special attention. Because only one row is returned, you should always use a default result set SELECT statement rather than a server-side cursor to retrieve the record. The default result set SELECT statement retrieves the record faster and requires far fewer resources on both the client and the server. The following code fragment is an example of a singleton SELECT that returns the **Pub_ID** and **Title** for a single **Title_ID**:

```
SELECT PUB_ID, TITLE FROM TITLES WHERE TITLE_ID = 'PC8888'
```

Because singleton SELECTs are performed frequently in applications, consider creating stored procedures to perform these SELECT statements. By using a stored procedure rather than issuing a SELECT statement directly, you can reduce the parse, compile, and execute time necessary to process the request. The following code, taken from the **GetTitlePubRec** function in Odbcapp.exe, executes a singleton SELECT through the **GetTPByTitleId** stored procedure. Notice the small amount of processing needed in Odbcapp.exe to execute this stored procedure.

```
switch(key)
    {
    case 1: // Title_ID search
        strcpy(StoredProc, "{call GetTPByTitleID(?)}");
        // Identify stored procedure to call
        // Bind the input parameter buffer
        SQLBindParameter(hstmtU, 1, SQL_PARAM_INPUT,
        SQL_C_CHAR,
        SQL_CHAR, 6, 0, inval, 7, &cbInval);
        break;

        .
        .
        .

// Execute the stored procedure and bind result set row columns to
variables
        memset( &tpRec, 0, sizeof(tpRec) );  // Initialize buffer record
                            // structure
        rc=SQLExecDirect(hstmtU, StoredProc, SQL_NTS );
        .
        .
        .

        SQLBindCol(hstmtU, 1, SQL_C_CHAR, tpRec.TitleID, 7,
        &cbTitleID);
        SQLBindCol(hstmtU, 2, SQL_C_CHAR, tpRec.Title, 81, &cbTitle);
        .
        .
        .
```

```
        SQLBindCol(hstmtU, 12, SQL_C_CHAR, tpRec.Country, 31,
        &cbCountry);
// Process the results until SQL_NO_DATA_FOUND
    while (rc==SQL_SUCCESS || rc==SQL_SUCCESS_WITH_INFO)
    {
        rc=SQLFetch(hstmtU);
        if (rc==SQL_SUCCESS || rc==SQL_SUCCESS_WITH_INFO) {
    .
    .
    .
```

Using Effective Indexing Techniques

Careful index design improves the performance of a SQL Server database. The query optimizer in SQL Server selects the most effective index for most cases; however, the following new features of SQL Server 7.0 allow you to create the best indexes for your application:

- The Index Tuning Wizard allows you to select and create an optimal set of indexes and statistics for a SQL Server database without requiring an expert understanding of the structure of the database, the workload, or the internals of SQL Server.

- The graphical SQL Server Query Analyzer provides easy and in-depth query analysis. You may want to create one index per table as a starting point, and then run the SQL Server Query Analyzer after a few days in a test environment to further optimize the database.

For guidelines about index creation before you implement the Index Tuning Wizard and SQL Server Query Analyzer, see "Recommendations for Creating Indexes" later in this chapter.

Implementing Stored Procedures

Stored procedures enhance the power, efficiency, and flexibility of Transact-SQL and can dramatically improve the performance of Transact-SQL statements and batches. Stored procedures differ from individual Transact-SQL statements because they are precompiled. The first time a stored procedure is run, the SQL Server query engine creates an execution plan and stores the procedure in memory for future use. Subsequent calls to the stored procedure run almost instantaneously since most of the preprocessing work has already been completed. The Odbcapp.exe application demonstrates how stored procedures are called using ODBC within an application.

For more information on stored procedures, see SQL Server Books Online and the Microsoft Knowledge Base.

Keeping Transactions Short and Efficient

Short and efficient transactions decrease the number of row-level locks managed by the system at any given point in time and are considered to be good programming practice. This is especially true in mixed decision support and online transaction processing (OLTP) environments.

Updating and Deleting Data as Set Operations

Use the WHERE clause to implement UPDATE and DELETE statements as set-based operations, restricting the data involved with the operation to that which matches a specific criteria. By implementing these operations using this methodology, you only update or delete the rows you intend to update or delete, reduce the total amount of data affected by processing the operations, and reduce the number of row-level locks needed to process them.

These operations should be performed only by using server cursors if the criteria for determining the rows for the UPDATE or DELETE operations cannot be specified in the Transact-SQL statement itself.

The following two examples demonstrate the difference between a set-based update and a positional update using a cursor. Both of these examples update the **YTD_Sales** for each title covered by a specific **PubID**. The first example is a stored procedure used by Odbcapp.exe. It demonstrates the use of a default result set update that uses a WHERE clause.

```
/****** Object:  Stored Procedure dbo.UpdtTitlesByPubID ******/
CREATE PROCEDURE UpdtTitlesByPubID @PubID char(4) AS
    UPDATE TITLES SET YTD_SALES = YTD_SALES + (SELECT SUM(QTY) FROM
    SALES WHERE TITLES.TITLE_ID = SALES.TITLE_ID)
WHERE PUB_ID = @PubID
GO
```

The preceding example is efficient and uses the server to perform the processing and row selection for the UPDATE.

The following example taken from Mybtrv32.exe demonstrates the inefficient use of a positional update through a cursor. This example must fetch through the cursor, updating each record that has the desired **PubID**. Notice the amount of fetching (round-trips between the client and the server) needed to process this request.

```
// The following code is taken from the GetTitlePublisher function in
// Mybtrv32.c
// Scroll through the cursor a row-at-a-time until the row needing
// updated is found.
while (!found)
{
```

```
                    memset( &tpRec, 0, sizeof(tpRec) );  // Initialize
// the client row buffer
// Fetch the record
    rc=SQLFetchScroll(hstmt8, FetchOrientation, FetchOffset);
        if ((rc != SQL_SUCCESS && rc != SQL_SUCCESS_WITH_INFO))
    {
            if (rc!=SQL_NO_DATA_FOUND){
// Error encountered before end of cursor notify the user and return
        ErrorDump("SQLFetchScroll TitlePub", SQL_NULL_HENV,
SQL_NULL_HDBC, hstmt8);
                return B_UNRECOVERABLE_ERROR;
            }
else {
                return B_END_OF_FILE;} // End of cursor
// found. Record does not exist
}
// Check to see if this is the record we want to update
        if (!strcmp(keyBuffer, tpRec.PubID))
            found=1;
}
// The record to be updated has been found. The next step is to
// update it.
// The following code is taken from the CursorUPD function in
// Mybtrv32.c
// Initialize the client record buffer
memset( &tpRec, 0, sizeof(tpRec) );
memcpy(&tpRec, dataBuffer, sizeof(tpRec));
    // Initialize the tpRec data structure
    memset( &tpRec, 0, sizeof(tpRec) );
    memcpy(&tpRec, dataBuffer, sizeof(tpRec));
/*  Update the current row within the cursor. We rebind the columns
/*  to update the length of the NULL terminated string columns. We
/*  are using 0 for the numRows parameter to affect all rows in
/*  the rowset. Since we have a rowset size of 1 only the positioned
/*  row will be affected. The key value of the current record is not
/*  changing so we issue the positioned update using SQLSet
/*  Pos(SQL_UPDATE, SQL_LOCK_NO_CHANGE)*/
    SQLBindCol(hstmtS, 1, SQL_C_CHAR, tpRec.TitleID, 7, &cbTitleID);
    .
    .
    .
    rc=SQLSetPos(hstmtS, numRows, SQL_UPDATE,  SQL_LOCK_NO_CHANGE);
    if ((rc != SQL_SUCCESS && rc != SQL_SUCCESS_WITH_INFO))
        {
            ErrorDump("SQLSetPos SQL_UPDATE for TITLEPUBLISHER FAILED",
SQL_NULL_HENV, SQL_NULL_HDBC, hstmtS);
            return B_UNRECOVERABLE_ERROR;
        }
    return B_NO_ERROR;
```

Using Server Resources Effectively

This section focuses on maximizing the benefits of Microsoft SQL Server server-side resources. There are several areas on the server side that relate closely to the overall performance of your application system. Although these topics fall out of the scope of mainstream application development, when used effectively they provide benefits important to the overall performance of the system.

Three of the most versatile and powerful server-side resources are triggers, declarative referential integrity (DRI), and views. Triggers, DRI, and views are often used to reduce the complexity of the client and application. Used effectively, these features can improve the performance of your application.

Business Rules and Referential Integrity

In a SQL Server database, triggers are special stored procedures that take effect when data is modified in a specific table. Business rule consistency is enforced across logically related data in different tables by using triggers. Triggers are executed automatically when data modification occurs, regardless of the application interface that is used.

Referential integrity refers to the way in which an RDBMS manages relationships between tables. Referential integrity is implemented in the database using the CREATE TABLE or ALTER TABLE statements, with a clause that starts with FOREIGN KEY. For example, in a scenario with **Orders** and **OrderLineItems**, records should not exist in the **OrderLineItems** table if there is no corresponding record in the **Orders** table. Because Btrieve does not offer this feature, the Btrieve application performs all referential integrity at the client. Enforcing referential integrity at the server eliminates this processing from the client and can provide slight performance improvements.

Triggers and foreign key constraints also eliminate the need to change the application in multiple places if table schemas or relationships change. These modifications can be made at the server.

Views

A view is an alternate way of looking at data resulting from a query of one or more tables. Views allow users to focus on data that fits their particular needs. Views simplify the way users can look at the data and manipulate it. Frequently used joins and selections can be defined as views so that users can avoid respecifying conditions and qualifications each time additional data operations are performed. Views also provide logical data independence because they help to shield users from changes in the structure of the base tables. In many cases, if a base table is restructured, only the view has to be modified, rather than each individual reference to the table.

For more information about views and triggers, see SQL Server Books Online and the Microsoft Knowledge Base.

Recommendations for Creating Indexes

Users of Microsoft SQL Server 7.0 can benefit from the new graphical SQL Server Query Analyzer and Index Tuning Wizard. These tools remove the guesswork from index creation. Nevertheless, understanding some basic index design recommendations can be useful to developers new to RDBMS.

- Index to enforce a primary key

  The system creates a unique index on a column or columns referenced as a primary key in a CREATE TABLE or ALTER TABLE statement. The index ensures that no duplicate values are entered in the column(s) that comprise the primary key. SQL Server does not require you to declare a primary key for every table, but it is considered good programming practice for RDBMS developers.

- Indexes to improve performance

  You can optionally create unique or nonunique indexes on tables. These indexes can improve the performance of queries against the table.

- Unique indexes

  Unique indexes improve performance and ensure that the values in the specified columns are unique.

- Clustered indexes

  Clustered indexes physically order the table data on the indexed column(s). Because the table can be physically ordered in only one way, only one clustered index can be created per table. If you have only one index on a table, it should be a clustered index. PRIMARY KEY constraints create clustered indexes automatically if no clustered index already exists on the table and a nonclustered index is not specified when you create the PRIMARY KEY constraint.

Database Index Guidelines

The following are a few database index guidelines:

- The columns in a WHERE clause of a Transact-SQL query are the primary focus of the query optimizer.

  The column(s) listed in the WHERE clause of a Transact-SQL statement is a possible candidate for an index. For each table, consider creating optional indexes based on the frequency with which the columns are used in WHERE clauses, and take into account the results of the graphical SQL Server Query Analyzer.

- Use single-column indexes.

  Single-column indexes are often more effective than multicolumn indexes. First, they require less space, allowing more index values to fit on one data page. Secondly, the query optimizer can effectively analyze thousands of index-join possibilities. Maintaining a large number of single (or very few)-column indexes provides the query optimizer with more options from which to choose.

- Use clustered indexes.

  The SQL Server Query Analyzer helps you determine which clustered indexes to create. Appropriate use of clustered indexes can significantly improve performance.

For more information on indexing and performance, see SQL Server Books Online and the Microsoft Knowledge Base.

PART 12

Programming

The chapters in Part 12 provide advanced programming information for leveraging SQL Server technology in demanding business environments:

- Textual Searches on Database Data
- Textual Searches on File Data
- Developing with English Query
- Distributed Queries: OLE DB Connectivity

C H A P T E R 2 2

Textual Searches on Database Data

Microsoft SQL Server version 7.0 introduces facilities that support textual queries on data residing in SQL Server as well as textual queries on data in the file system.

This chapter describes support for textual queries against data within SQL Server tables. The full-text search concepts are introduced, followed by the form that a full-text search takes and the information that can be retrieved by means of such queries. The internal design and architecture of the full-text search system is presented, and then how this system can be administered by means of stored procedures or graphical user interfaces (GUIs) through SQL Server Enterprise Manager is described.

This chapter provides an overview of the capability of SQL Server 7.0 full-text support and describes how the various subcomponents interact to provide this support.

A large portion of digitally stored information is in the form of unstructured data, primarily text. While the bulk of this data is stored in the file system, some organizations have begun to manage it by storing it in relational databases in character-based columns such as **varchar** and **text**. This means that relational database users need a mechanism to effectively retrieve textual data from the database. Traditional relational database management systems (RDBMSs), such as Microsoft SQL Server version 6.5, were not designed for efficient full-text retrieval. For example, while SQL Server 6.5 has some capabilities for retrieving text based on pattern matching, it cannot search for words and phrases in proximity to one another.

There are two major types of textual searches:

- Property

  This search technology first applies filters to documents in order to extract properties such as author, subject, type, word count, printed page count, and time last written, and then issues searches against those properties.

- Full-text

  This search technology first creates indexes of all non noise words in the documents, and then uses these indexes to support linguistic searches and proximity searches.

The lack of integrated textual-search facilities in relational databases has forced customers to use third-party products. These solutions usually involve pulling data out of the database through bridges or gateways and storing the data as files in the file system so that full-text indexing can be applied. This is not a seamless way for a user to combine a full-text search with a regular structured relational query.

Some relational database products offer customers relational and full-text search conditions seamlessly integrated into the same query. A demonstration of how such a query might be specified follows.

Suppose that the contents of a set of plain-text documents reside in the **DocText** column of the **doc_collection** table, and that the table also contains the **StorName**, **Size**, and **DocAuthor** columns. It should be possible to issue the following query:

```
SELECT Q.StorName, Q.Size, Q.DocAuthor, W.Citizenship
FROM doc_collection as Q,
    writers as W
WHERE CONTAINS(DocText, ' "SQL Server" NEAR text')
  AND Q.DocAuthor = W.writer_name
```

This query is issued to obtain the names, authors, and sizes of all documents, where the document contains the phrase "SQL Server" in proximity to the word "text". This information is joined with the **writers** table to obtain the author's citizenship.

Microsoft has been engaged in a project that makes it possible to issue such queries. The objective is to introduce the Microsoft text search technology as part of SQL Server 7.0 so that users can issue entry-level full-text searches against plain-text data in relational database tables. The syntax is a natural extension to the structured query language (SQL).

Existing technologies have been leveraged to provide full-text searches against SQL Server data. The Microsoft information retrieval technologies have been around for some time and are included with Microsoft Indexing Services version 2.0 and Microsoft Site Server version 3.0. Various components have been combined within these technologies, and these have been integrated into SQL Server 7.0 to provide relational database customers with full-text retrieval support.

Two additional technologies outside of SQL Server also have been integrated:

- The Microsoft Search service, a full-text indexing and search service that is called both index engine and search engine in the context of this chapter. Within the context of SQL Server, this is called full-text search.
- The parser component of the OLE DB Provider for Indexing Services 2.0 that accepts full-text SQL extensions and maps them into a form that can be processed by the search engine.

This chapter has three purposes:

- To introduce the SQL extensions in support of full-text searches on database data
- To show how the various technologies have been brought together to allow full-text searches on database data
- To introduce the new SQL Server administrative facilities in support of full-text searches on database data

Full-Text Search Concepts

There are four major aspects of supporting full-text retrieval of plain-text data on a database:

- Managing the definition of the tables and columns that are registered for full-text searches.
- Indexing the data in registered columns. The indexing process scans the character streams, determines the word boundaries (this is called word breaking), removes all noise words (this is called stop words), and then populates a full-text index with the remaining words.
- Issuing queries against registered columns for populated full-text indexes.
- Ensuring that subsequent changes to the data in registered columns gets propagated to the index engine to keep the full-text indexes synchronized.

The underlying design principle for the indexing, querying, and synchronizing processes is the presence of a full-text unique key column (or single-column primary key) on all tables registered for full-text searches. The full-text index contains an entry for the non noise words in each row together with the value of the key column for each row.

When processing a full-text search, the search engine returns to SQL Server the key values of the rows that match the search criteria. The following example illustrates what is happening.

Suppose you have a **SciFi** table with the following columns, where the **Book_No** column is the primary key column.

Book No	Writer	Title
A025	Asimov	Foundation's Edge
A027	Asimov	Foundation and Empire
C011	Clarke	Childhood's End
V109	Verne	Mysterious Island

Next, suppose you have a full-text retrieval query where you want to find the book titles having the word "Foundation" in them. When the SQL Server relational engine encounters a full-text retrieval predicate, it calls the full-text search component to retrieve the values of **Book_No** that satisfy the text retrieval filter condition. In this case, the values A025 and A027 are returned. The relational engine then uses this information, together with other information under its direct control, to respond to the query.

Unlike classic relational database indexes, traditional full-text indexes are not modified instantly when values in full-text registered columns are updated, when rows are added to full-text registered tables, or when rows are deleted from full-text registered tables. Rather, full-text indexes usually are repopulated asynchronously. There are two reasons for this:

- It typically takes significantly more time to update a full-text index than a classic index.

- Full-text searches usually are fuzzy by nature and so do not need to be as precise as classic searches.

During repopulation, the unique key column values are passed to the index engine to identify those items that need to be reindexed. For example, if the title associated with V109 gets changed to "Mystery Island," then the index should be modified to reflect this new value.

The full-text administration process starts by designating a table and its columns of interest for full-text search. Either GUIs and wizards or built-in stored procedures are used first to register tables and columns as eligible for full-text search. Then, a separate request (again by means of a GUI and wizards or stored procedures) is issued to populate the full-text indexes.

The result is that the underlying index engine gets invoked and asynchronous index population begins. Full-text indexing tracks which significant words are used and where they are located. For example, a full-text index might indicate that the word "Microsoft" is found at word number 423 and word number 982 in the **Abstract** column of the **DevTools** table for the row associated with a **ProductID** of 6. This index structure supports an efficient search for all items containing indexed words as well as advanced search operations, such as phrase searches and proximity searches. (An example of a phrase search is looking for "white elephant," where "white" is followed by "elephant." An example of a proximity search is looking for "big" and "house" where "big" occurs near "house.")

To prevent the full-text index from becoming bloated, noise words such as "a," "and," and "the" are ignored. Noise word lists for many languages are available in the directory \Mssql\Ftdata\Sqlserver\Config. And the set of supported languages is growing. The choice of a particular noise word list is based on the language setting of the database server. These noise word lists should be sufficient for most operations, but they can be modified by using a regular text editor. For example, a computer company can add the word "computer" to its noise word list.

Extensions to Microsoft SQL Server Transact-SQL were made to allow users to pose full-text queries. The syntax of the CONTAINS and FREETEXT predicates, already supported for full-text search in both the Microsoft OLE DB Provider for Indexing Services 2.0 and the Microsoft OLE DB Provider for Site Server 3.0 Search, were used.

The CONTAINS predicate is used to search for:

- A word or phrase.
- The prefix of a word or phrase.
- A word or phrase that is near another.
- A word that is an inflectional form of another (for example, "drive" is the inflectional stem of "drives," "drove," "driving," and "driven").
- A set of words or phrases, each of which is assigned a different weighting.

The FREETEXT predicate is a basic form of natural language query. Any text, including words, phrases, or sentences, can be specified in the query. The search engine matches values that reflect the meaning, rather than the exact wording, of the query.

The SQL Server relational engine recognizes the CONTAINS and FREETEXT predicates and performs some minimal syntax and semantic checking, such as ensuring that the column referenced in the predicate has been registered for full-text searches. During query execution, a full-text predicate and other relevant information are passed to the full-text search component. After further syntax and semantic validation, the search engine is invoked and returns the set of unique key values identifying those rows in the table that satisfy the full-text search condition.

There currently are two mechanisms available to an administrator for keeping a full-text index synchronized with changes to the data in its table:

- Scheduled repopulation
- On-demand repopulation

Both GUIs and stored procedures are provided for repopulation tasks. If a table has a column with a **timestamp** data type, it is possible to request an incremental repopulation where only changes to the table since the last population participate in the repopulation. If a table does not have a **timestamp** column, then only a complete repopulation is possible.

An alternative to automatic update of full-text indexes based on log activity is a candidate for a future release of SQL Server.

Transact-SQL Extensions for Full-Text Searches

A point worth repeating is that these extensions are consistent with SQL supported for full-text searches in Indexing Services 2.0. Furthermore, the SQL support for full-text searches follows the SQL-3 functional methodology for full-text syntax extensions.

The primary extension to Transact-SQL consists of the CONTAINS and FREETEXT predicates. These predicates are used to find column values that match special full-text search criteria.

In addition, the new CONTAINSTABLE() and FREETEXTTABLE() rowset-valued functions are supported. These functions can be specified (in the FROM clause) to return a two-column table, where one column uniquely identifies the rows that match the specified full-text search criteria and the other contains rank values showing the degree to which the rows match the criteria.

To be consistent with similar features in other products and to make the new predicates more extensible, functional notation has been chosen. The high-level syntax is:

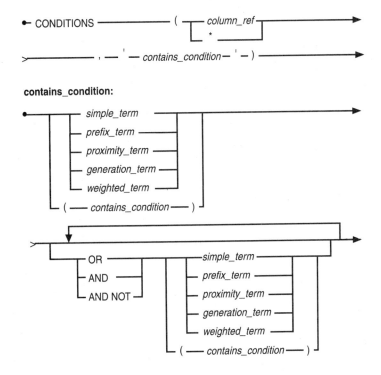

In Microsoft SQL Server 7.0, the language always is implied by the locale of the database holding the data. The flexibility of the functional style of these two predicates allows easy, upward-compatible future extension for a third parameter to designate the language to be used for the query.

These predicates can be used with the character family of data types: **char**, **varchar**, **text**, **nchar**, **nvarchar**, and **ntext**. Often, document formats stored in columns defined with the binary family of data types cannot be indexed or searched. Such support will be a candidate for a future release of SQL Server.

The CONTAINS Predicate

The CONTAINS predicate is used to determine whether values in full-text registered columns contain certain words and phrases. Currently, these predicates can reference base tables only.

The CONTAINS predicate syntax is as follows:

Here are the definitions of the syntax terminology.

column_ref **or** *
> The column or columns to be searched.

column_ref
> A specific column that is full-text registered.

*

> All columns in the table that are full-text registered.

AND, OR, **and** AND NOT
> The Boolean operators used to join, or combine, terms.

simple_term

This term is used to match the exact word or phrase being searched for.

The *simple_term* syntax is as follows, where word refers to one or more characters without spaces or punctuation, and phrase refers to multiple words with spaces in between. Asian languages can have phrases made up of multiple words without spaces in between.

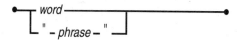

In keeping with the standard for full-text products, the search function is always case insensitive.

Here are some examples of simple terms used in the context of the CONTAINS predicate in a WHERE clause.

```
WHERE CONTAINS( context_col, 'hockey' )
WHERE CONTAINS( context_col, ' "ice hockey" ')
```

Suppose you have one row with a **context_col** value of "This is a dissertation on the use of ice cream sandwiches as hockey pucks," and another row with the value "Dissertation on new ways of splitting the atom." Since "this," "is," "a," and so on are noise words, they are not stored in the full-text index. Therefore, a query with the CONTAINS predicate:

```
CONTAINS (context_col, '"this is a dissertation"')
```

is the same as this query:

```
CONTAINS (context_col, 'dissertation')
```

Both rows are returned as hits because in the first query, the noise words are removed before processing the query.

Combining Terms

As with other SQL search conditions, more complex conditions can be specified by linking individual operands with Boolean operators. In this case, the operands are any of the types of terms being discussed. Except for the restrictions that the OR NOT combination is not supported and that NOT cannot be specified before the first term, the rules are exactly the same as those used to combine individual predicates to form search conditions. For instance, parentheses may be used to change the default priority order in which the operators are applied.

Here are some examples of simple terms being combined within a CONTAINS predicate in a WHERE clause.

```
WHERE CONTAINS( context_col, 'hockey OR curling' )
WHERE CONTAINS( context_col, 'hockey AND NOT field')
WHERE CONTAINS( context_col,
                ' ("ice hockey" OR curling) AND NOT
                Canada ' )
```

prefix_term

The *prefix_term* is used to match words or phrases that begin with the specified text.

The *prefix_term* syntax is as follows:

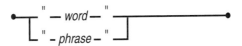

A prefix term consists of a simple term appended with an asterisk (*) to activate prefix matching on the word or phrase. All text that starts with the material before the * is matched. The wildcard symbol (*) in this case is similar to the % symbol in the LIKE predicate in that it matches zero, one or more characters of the root words in a word or phrase. In a phrase, each word within the phrase is considered to be a prefix; for example, the term "local bus *" matches "locality busy," "local bush," and "locale bust."

Here are some examples of prefix terms used in the context of the CONTAINS predicate in a WHERE clause.

```
WHERE CONTAINS( context_col, ' "atom*" ' )
```

This matches **context_col** values that contain the word "atom," "atomic," "atomism," "atomy," and so on.

```
WHERE CONTAINS( abstract, ' "wine*" OR "vine*" ')
```

This matches abstract values that contain the word "wine," or "vine," or, alternatively, words such as "winery," "wines," "vineyard," or "vinegar."

proximity_term

This is used when the words or phrases being searched for must be in proximity to one another.

The *proximity_term* syntax is as follows:

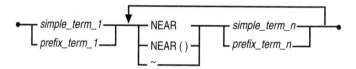

The proximity term is similar to the AND operator in that more than one word or phrase must exist in the column being searched. It differs from AND because the relevance of the match increases as the words appear closer together.

The syntax is designed to be extensible for possible future support for specification of units of proximity such as words, sentences, paragraphs, chapters, and so on.

NEAR(), NEAR, and ~ share the same meaning: the first word or the phrase is close to the second word or phrase. "Close" is a purposefully vague term that can mean "within 50 words," but the algorithm is complicated. While words within the same sentence are one word distance apart, larger distances are assigned between units such as sentences, paragraphs, and chapters. Even if words or phrases are very far apart, the query is still considered to be satisfied; the row just has a low (zero) rank value. However, if the *contains_condition* consists only of NEAR proximity terms, then SQL Server does not return rows with a rank value of zero.

It is possible to chain-code the proximity matching. For example, "a ~ b ~ c" means *a* should be near *b*, which should be near *c*. Because of the fuzzy nature of full-text searches, it is often desirable to see the rank values. The CONTAINSTABLE() rowset-valued function can be used to execute queries that return a rank value for each row.

Here are some examples of proximity terms used in the context of the CONTAINS predicate in a WHERE clause.

```
WHERE CONTAINS( context_col, ' hockey ~ player ' )
```

This matches **context_col** values that contain the word "hockey" in proximity to the word "player."

```
WHERE CONTAINS( context_col, ' hockey ~ "play*" ')
```

This matches **context_col** values that contain the word "hockey" in proximity to a word that starts with "play."

```
WHERE CONTAINS( context_col, '  "great*"
                        ~ "Mike Nash" ')
```

This matches **context_col** values that contain a word starting with "great" in proximity to the phrase "Mike Nash."

generation_term

The *generation_term* is used when the words being searched for need to be expanded to include the variants of the original word.

The *generation_term* syntax is as follows:

```
●── FORMSOF ─ ( ─ INFLECTIONAL ──┬──── , simple_term ──┴── ) ─●
```

The INFLECTIONAL keyword means that plural and singular forms of nouns or the various tenses of verbs are matched. A single term does not match both exclusive noun and exclusive verb forms. The syntax is designed to be extensible enough to handle other linguistically generated forms, such as derivational, soundex, and thesaurus.

Here is an example of a generation term used in the context of the CONTAINS predicate in a WHERE clause.

```
WHERE CONTAINS(curriculum_vite,
            ' FORMSOF (INFLECTIONAL, skate) ' )
```

This matches **curriculum_vite** values that contain words such as "skate," "skates," "skated," and "skating."

weighted_term

The *weighted_term* is used for queries that match a list of words and phrases, each optionally given its own weighting. Matching values must match only one element in the list.

The *weighted_term* syntax is as follows, where *n.nnn*: represents a decimal constant from zero through one:

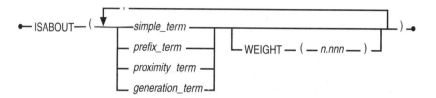

A row is returned if there is a match on any one of the ISABOUT elements.

Each component in the vector can be optionally weighted. The assigned weight forces a different measurement of the rank value that is assigned to each row that matches the query.

Here are some examples of weighted terms used in the context of the CONTAINS predicate in a WHERE clause.

```
WHERE CONTAINS( article,
                ' ISABOUT(hockey, puck, goalie) ' )
```

This matches article values that contain any of the words "hockey," "puck," or "goalie." The better matches will contain more than one of the words.

```
WHERE CONTAINS( article,
          'ISABOUT("Canadian ice hockey" WEIGHT(1.0),
                   "ice hockey" WEIGHT(.5),
                   hockey WEIGHT(.2) )
      ' )
```

This matches article values that may have information about Canadian ice hockey, with higher rank values assigned to articles that have more words from the phrase.

FREETEXT Predicate

The FREETEXT predicate is used to determine whether or not values in full-text registered columns reflect the meaning, rather than the exact words, specified in the predicate.

The FREETEXT predicate syntax is as follows:

```
●─ FREETEXT ── ( ─┬─ column_ref ─┬─ , ─ ' ─ freetext_string - ' ─ ) ──●
                  └─── * ─────────┘
```

This is a basic form of natural language query, where the index engine internally breaks the freetext string into a number of search terms, generates the stemmed form of the words, assigns heuristic weighting to each term, and then finds the matches.

Here is an example of a FREETEXT predicate used in a WHERE clause.

```
WHERE FREETEXT (articles, ' Who have been the most
        valuable players for the Montreal Canadien? ' )
```

Combining Predicates and Use of Predicates

Because CONTAINS and FREETEXT are SQL predicates, they can be used anywhere that SQL predicates are supported. In particular, they can be combined with each other and with other predicates, such as equality, LIKE, and BETWEEN, to specify extensive search conditions.

The WHERE clause in the following query uses both a CONTAINS predicate and a comparison predicate. It obtains the title and publication year of all the books in the **titles** table in the **pubs** database, where the book costs less than $20.00 and text in the **notes** column indicates that the book is about ice hockey.

```
SELECT title, DatePart(year, pubdate)
  FROM pubs
  WHERE price < 20.00
    AND CONTAINS (notes, ' "ice hockey" ')
```

The following query uses a CONTAINS predicate within a subquery. It obtains the titles of all the books in the **titles** table for the publisher who is located close to the flying saucer in Moonbeam, Ontario. This information about the publisher is known to exist in the **pr_info** column in the **pub_info** table, and it is also known that there is only one such publisher.

```
SELECT T.title, P.pub_name
  FROM publishers P,
       Titles T
  WHERE P.pub_id = T.pub_id
    AND P.pub_id = (SELECT pub_id
                      FROM pub_info
                      WHERE CONTAINS
                            (pr_info,
                             ' moonbeam AND
                               ontario AND
                               "flying saucer"
                             ') )
```

CONTAINSTABLE() Rowset-Valued Function

The CONTAINSTABLE() function is used to issue contains-type full-text queries that return relevance rankings for each row.

The CONTAINSTABLE syntax is as follows, where table_ref refers to a full-text registered table, column_ref: refers to a specific full-text registered column, or * refers to all columns in table_ref that are full-text registered.

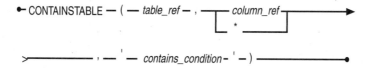

contains_condition:
    Is the same as described for the CONTAINS predicate.

Although both the CONTAINS predicate and CONTAINSTABLE() function are used for contains-type full-text queries, and the SQL used to specify the full-text search condition is the same in both, there are major differences in the way these are used:

- CONTAINS returns a true or false value, and so typically is specified in the WHERE clause of a SELECT statement.

    CONTAINTABLE() returns a table of zero, one, or more rows, and so always must be specified in the FROM clause.

- CONTAINS can be used only to specify selection criteria that SQL Server uses to determine the membership of the result set.

    CONTAINSTABLE() is also used to specify selection criteria. The table returned has a column named **key** that contains full-text key values. Each full-text registered table has a column that has values guaranteed to be unique, and the values returned in the **key** column are the full-text key values of the rows that match the selection criteria specified in the *contains_condition*. Furthermore, the table produced by the CONTAINSTABLE() function has a column named **rank** that contains values from zero to 1,000 that can be used to rank the returned rows according to how well they meet the selection criteria.

Queries that use the CONTAINSTABLE() function are more complex than those using the CONTAINS predicate because it is necessary to explicitly join qualifying rows returned by CONTAINSTABLE() with the rows in **table_ref**.

For example, the contents of some documents reside in the **DocText** column of the **doc_collection** table, and the table also contains the **StorName**, **Size**, and **DocAuthor** columns. The unique key column for the table is named **DocNo**. You want the rows in the result set to be ordered so that those with the highest **rank** value are returned first.

```
SELECT Q.StorName, Q.Size, Q.DocAuthor, W.Citizenship
FROM doc_collection as Q,
     writers as W,
     ContainsTable(doc_collection, DocText,
                   ' "SQL Server" NEAR() text'
                   ) AS K
WHERE Q.DocAuthor = W.writer_name
  AND K.[KEY] = Q.DocNo
ORDER BY K.RANK DESC
```

To simplify the use of CONTAINSTABLE() for queries that involve only one table and no grouping, use the following fixed template:

```
SELECT select_list ,KEY_TBL.RANK
FROM table_ref AS FT_TBL
CONTAINSTABLE (    table_ref
                 , { column_ref | * }
                 , ' contains_condition ' )
) AS KEY_TBL
WHERE FT_TBL.key_column = KEY_TBL.[KEY]
      AND predicate  ...
ORDER BY KEY_TBL.RANK DESC
```

The following example uses the previous template. In this example, the wording on the plaques in the Hockey Hall of Fame reside in the **PlaqueWording** column of **HockeyHall** table, and the table also contains the **PlayerName**, **StartYear**, and **LastYear** columns. The unique key column for the table is named **PlaqueNo**. You want to return the **PlayerName**, **PlaqueNo**, and **rank** values for players who might have played for the Kenora (also called Rat Portage) teams in the early 1900s. The higher ranking rows should be returned first.

```
SELECT PlayerName, PlaqueNo, KEY_TBL.RANK
FROM HockeyHall AS FT_TBL
     CONTAINSTABLE(HockeyHall, PlaqueWording,
                   ' CKenora OR "Rat Portage" '
                   ) AS KEY_TBL
WHERE FT_TBL.PlaqueNO = KEY_TBL.[KEY]
  AND StartYear < 1915 AND EndYear > 1899
ORDER BY KEY_TBL.RANK DESC
```

FREETEXTTABLE() Rowset-Valued Function

The FREETEXTTABLE() function is used to issue freetext-type full-text queries that return relevance ranking for each row.

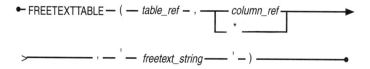

This function is used in the same manner as a CONTAINSTABLE() function, and the search condition is the same as specified by a FREETEXT predicate.

Textual Searches against File-System Data

It is worth noting that the ability to search against file-system data only already exists in Indexing Services 2.0. This capability is further enhanced by the SQL Server 7.0 Distributed Query Processor, which, in conjunction with the Microsoft OLE DB Provider for Indexing Services 2.0, can be used to issue both property and full-text searches against file-system data and to join the results with data in the database.

By recasting the first example in this chapter, we will introduce searches against the file system to obtain some of the data from the file system. The following query selects the names, sizes, and authors of all Microsoft Word files on drive D, where the document contains the phrase "SQL Server" in proximity to the word "text" and joins this result with the **writers** table to obtain the author's citizenship.

```
SELECT Q.FileName, Q.Size, Q.DocAuthor, W.Citizenship
FROM OpenQuery(MyLinkedServer,
              'SELECT FileName, Size, DocAuthor
               from SCOPE('' "D:\" '')
               WHERE CONTAINS(''"SQL Server"
                                    NEAR() text'')
               AND FileName LIKE ''%.doc%'' '
              ) as Q,
      writers as W
WHERE Q.DocAuthor = W.writer_name
```

The location of the data must be known to the person writing the queries. The SQL standards organization is developing a new **datalink** data type, which will allow seamless queries that access data both inside and outside the database. This emerging definition offers some interesting possibilities.

Component Architecture

There are two aspects to the component architecture: indexing components and query components.

Indexing Components

The indexing components manage the initial population and subsequent updating of the full-text indexes.

Before presenting the steps involved in the indexing process, various subcomponents are introduced, and then the flow among the subcomponents is described.

Enterprise Manager User Interface

SQL Server Enterprise Manager is the GUI for the full-text indexing administration utility. It takes the form of extensions to the current Microsoft SQL Server Enterprise Manager property sheets, and a new wizard. These have been designed to assist first-time and infrequent administrators of full-text indexed tables. The GUI also is appropriate for frequent users. It allows a user to select the desired tables for full-text indexing and walks the user through the various steps needed to set this up.

One option is to schedule regular refreshing of full-text indexes; this uses the scheduling facilities that already exist in SQL Server. The GUI also can be used to display properties of the full-text indexed tables. This GUI uses a set of new full-text administration system stored procedures, a set of full-text related properties available through the SQL Server property functions, as well as the existing SQL Server Agent job scheduler.

Full-Text Administration System Stored Procedures

This set of system stored procedures is used to:

- Set up full-text catalogs. A full-text catalog is an entity holding a collection of full-text indexes.
- Register a table and the selected columns within the table for full-text search.
- Request the population of the indexes within a full-text catalog.
- Undo any of the previous.

The setup and configuration capabilities of full-text indexing reside in the stored procedures, not in the GUI. It is possible to use these stored procedures directly rather than using SQL Server Enterprise Manager, and experienced administrators may choose to do this. Calls to the stored procedures also may be embedded in scripts and other stored procedures.

Scheduling Stored Procedures

The set of stored procedures (such as **sp_add_jobschedule**) that is used for scheduling regular jobs also can be used to schedule refreshes of full-text catalogs.

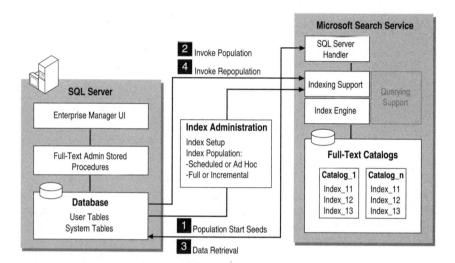

Full-Text Index Additions to System Tables

The **sysdatabases** system catalog has been extended to provide the new **IsFulltextEnabled** property, which is available through the DATABASEPROPERTY() function.

A new system table, **sysfulltextcatalogs**, is present for each database. This table holds metadata about the full-text catalogs that are linked to the database. A given full-text catalog is linked to only one database.

The **sysobjects**, **sysindexes**, and **syscolumns** tables that reside in each database are augmented with information about the tables and the associated columns in that database that have been full-text indexed. The information is:

- The **ftcatid** column of user table rows in **sysobjects**, which points to rows in **sysfulltextcatalogs**.

- The **TableHasActiveFulltextIndex** property, which is available through the OBJECTPROPERTY() function.

- The **TableFulltextKeyColumn** property, which is the column ID of the full-text unique key column and is available through the OBJECTPROPERTY() function.

- The **TableFulltextCatalogId** property, which is the full-text catalog ID associated with the table and is available through the OBJECTPROPERTY() function.

- The **IsFulltextKey** property, which is available through the INDEXPROPERTY() function.

- The **IsFulltextIndexed** property, which is available through the COLUMNPROPERTY() function.

Microsoft Search Service

This is a Windows NT service that has two roles:

- Indexing support accepts requests to populate the full-text index of a given table.

- Querying support processes full-text searches.

Microsoft Search Service operates under the context of the local system account. This service must be run on the same computer as SQL Server.

Indexing Support

The information about populating full-text indexes is submitted in the form of a population start seed value, which uniquely identifies both the database and the table that needs to be full-text indexed. When the service is ready to handle the population, it invokes the SQL Server Handler driver.

SQL Server Handler

This subcomponent is a driver that plugs into indexing support and is specially coded to handle SQL Server data stores.

SQL Server Handler always runs in the same process as Microsoft Search Service.

Index Engine

This subcomponent presents indexable units of text (in the form of character strings), each with an identifying key. It scans through character strings, determines the word boundaries, removes all noise words, and then populates a full-text index with the remaining words.

Full-Text Catalogs

This is where full-text indexes reside. This is a Windows NT file-system directory that is accessible only by Windows NT Administrator and Microsoft Search Service. The full-text indexes are organized into full-text catalogs, which are referenced by friendly names. Typically, the full-text index data for an entire database is placed into a single full-text catalog. However, administrators can partition the full-text index data for a database across more than one full-text catalog. This is useful if one or more of the tables being full-text indexed contains a large number of rows. A full-text catalog is limited to holding index data for 2^{31} to 64K rows.

In SQL Server 7.0, there are no facilities to coordinate backup and recovery relational database data in conjunction with the relevant indexes in the full-text catalogs (however there are facilities to resynchronize them). Coordinated backup and recovery is a candidate for a future release of SQL Server.

Full-Text Indexing Administration

The following steps are started by an administrator using GUIs or stored procedures (either on demand or as scheduled).

1. First, enable the database for full-text search and then identify the tables and columns that are to be registered for full-text search. This information is stored in the SQL Server system tables.

2. When a table is activated for full-text processing, a population start seed for that table is sent to indexing support.

3. Next, request the initial population of the full-text index for a table. Actually, the granularity of population is a full-text catalog, so if more than one table has been linked to a full-text catalog, the result is the full population of the full-text indexes for all tables linked to that catalog.

4. The knowledge of the tables and rows that require indexing resides in SQL Server, so when indexing support receives a population request for a full-text catalog, it calls back into SQL Server to obtain data from all the columns in the table that have been marked for indexing. When this data arrives, it is passed to the index engine where it is broken into words. Noise words are removed and the remaining words are stored in the index.

5. Full-text indexes are kept current by using a GUI that sets up a schedule for periodic refreshes of a full-text catalog. This GUI uses stored procedures from the SQL Server job scheduler. It also is possible to request a refresh at any time, either by means of a GUI or by direct use of a stored procedure.

   If a table has a row-versioning (**timestamp**) column, repopulation can be handled more efficiently. At the time the population start seed for a table is constructed, the largest row-versioning value in the database is remembered. When an incremental population is requested, the SQL Server handler connects to the database and requests only rows where the row-versioning value is greater than the remembered value.

   During an incremental population, if there is a full-text indexed table in a catalog that does not have a row-versioning column, then that table will be completely repopulated.

There are two cases where a complete repopulation is performed, even though there is a row-versioning column on the table. These are:

- In tables when the schema has changed.
- In tables activated since the last population.

After populating tables with a row-versioning column, the remembered row-versioning value is updated.

Since incremental repopulation on relatively static tables with **timestamp** columns can be completed faster than a complete repopulation, users can schedule repopulation on a more frequent basis. For a given database, users should take care not to mix index data from tables with **timestamp** columns with tables in the same full-text catalog, because these two groups of tables usually should be on separate repopulation schedules.

6. Additional tables and columns will be registered for full-text search, and full-text indexes will be generated for them. The full-text search capability may be removed from some tables and columns. Some full-text catalogs may be dropped. This step may be repeated several times.

Full-Text Query Component Architecture

The query components accept a full-text predicate or rowset-valued function from SQL Server, transform parts of the predicate into an internal format, and send it to Microsoft Search Service, which returns the matches in a rowset. The rowset is then sent back to SQL Server. SQL Server uses this information to create the result set that is then returned to the submitter of the query.

The SQL Server Relational Engine accepts the CONTAINS and FREETEXT predicates as well as the CONTAINSTABLE() and FREETEXTTABLE() rowset-valued functions. During parse time, this code checks for conditions such as attempting to query a column that has not been registered for full-text search. If valid, then at run time, the *ft_search_condition* and context information is sent to the full-text provider. Eventually, the full-text provider returns a rowset to SQL Server, which is used in any joins (specified or implied) in the original query.

The Full-Text Provider parses and validates *ft_search_condition*, constructs the appropriate internal representation of the full-text search condition, and then passes it to the search engine. The result is returned to the relational engine by means of a rowset of rows that satisfy *ft_search_condition*. The handling of this rowset is conceptually similar to the code used in support of the OPENROWSET() and OPENQUERY() rowset-valued functions.

Search Engine

This subcomponent processes full-text search queries. It determines which entries in the index meet the selection criteria. For each entry that meets the selection criteria, the value of the unique key column and a ranking value are returned.

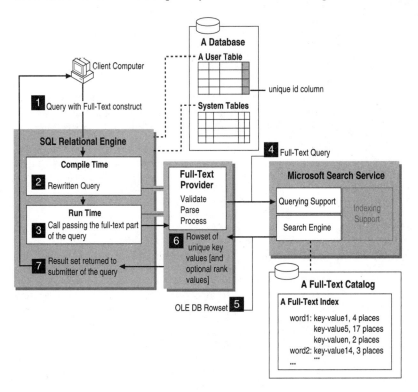

Full-Text Query Process

1. A query that uses one of the full-text constructs (that is CONTAINS, FREETEXT, CONTAINSTABLE(), or FREETEXTTABLE) is submitted to the SQL Relational Engine.

2. Queries containing either the CONTAINS or FREETEXT predicate are rewritten so that the rowset returned from the Full-Text Provider later will be automatically joined to the table that the predicate is acting upon. This rewrite is the mechanism used to ensure that these predicates are a seamless extension to SQL Server. By specifying CONTAINS and FREETEXT, you do not have to concern yourself with or even know about the details of the underlying invocation of the Microsoft Search Service.

3. The Full-Text Provider is invoked, passing the following information:

   - The *ft_search_condition*
   - The friendly name of the full-text catalog where the full-text index of a table resides
   - The locale ID to be used for language (for example, word breaking)
   - The identities of the database, table, and column

   If the query is comprised of more than one full-text construct, the full-text provider is invoked separately for each construct.

   The SQL Server Relational Engine does not look into the contents of the *ft_search_condition*. Instead, this is passed along to the full-text provider, which checks it for validity and then creates the appropriate internal representation of the full-text search condition.

4. The command is passed to Querying Support.

5. Querying Support returns a rowset that contains the unique key column values for the rows that match the full-text search criteria. A rank value also is returned for each row.

6. The rowset is passed to the SQL Server Relational Engine. If processing either a CONTAINSTABLE() or FREETEXTTABLE() function, RANK values are returned; otherwise, the rank value is filtered out.

7. The rowset values are plugged into the query with values obtained from the relational database, and the result set is returned to the user.

Administration

In the current implementation, full-text indexes are different from classic SQL Server indexes. These differences give rise to the need for the administrative tasks outlined here. Following is a summary of the main differences.

Classic SQL indexes	Full-text indexes
Stored in and under the control of the database.	Stored in the file system, but administered through the database.
Several indexes per table.	Only one full-text index definition per table.
Automatically updated when the data upon which they are based is inserted, updated, or deleted.	Population must be requested (either as scheduled or on demand).
Not grouped.	Grouped.
Created and dropped using SQL statements.	Created, managed, and dropped using stored procedures (either directly of by means of GUIs).

Full-Text Administration is carried out at several different levels:

- Certain server-wide properties can be set, such as those required for Microsoft Search Service to initialize and prepare for index population.

- A database must be enabled to use full-text search. Metadata for one or more full-text catalogs can be created and dropped in an enabled database.

- A full-text catalog must be populated using administrative facilities.

- A table must be registered as supporting full-text searches, at which time metadata is created for the full-text index of that table. A registered table must be activated before it can participate in the next full-text catalog population.

- Columns that support full-text searches can be added or dropped from an inactive registered table.

At all of these levels, there are facilities to retrieve information on property, status, and volume (for example, size of the full-text catalog). These facilities take the form of both GUIs and stored procedures, and almost all tasks can be accomplished either way. This chapter concentrates on the stored procedures and gives only a few examples of the use of GUIs. The term "stored procedures" has been used to illustrate the level at which an administrator is communicating with SQL Server. In fact, a combination of stored procedures and scalar-valued property functions is used.

Stored Procedures Scenario

Following is an outline of the steps that an administrator operating in the "stored procedure mode" could take to set up full-text search on selected tables and columns in the **pubs** database. This scenario does not demonstrate everything that is available, but only enough to provide insight as to how these procedures can be used.

1. Check that Microsoft Search Service is running by looking at the shape or color of the icon for full-text search in SQL Server Enterprise Manager.

   If necessary, the service can be started in one of several ways:

   - Through the context menu of the full-text search object in SQL Server Enterprise Manager

   - Outside SQL Server through the Service Control Manager (in the Service Control Manager, this service is called Microsoft Search Service)

   - From a MS-DOS prompt by typing **net start mssearch**

   - From SQL Server service manager

   The full-text service also can be stopped in all of these places.

   In this case, **pubs** has not been enabled.

2. Determine if the **pubs** database has been enabled for full-text processing. The SQL statement `SELECT DatabaseProperty('pubs', 'IsFulltextEnabled')` returns 1 if the service has been enabled, and 0 if it has not. In this case, the service has been enabled.

3. Connect to the **pubs** database by executing the Transact-SQL statement:

```
USE pubs
```

4. Enable **pubs** for full-text search by invoking the stored procedure:

```
sp_fulltext_database 'enable'
```

5. Create a full-text catalog named **PubsCatalog**, and choosing the default directory. This is done by invoking the stored procedure:

```
sp_fulltext_catalog 'PubsCatalog', 'create'
```

This procedure creates metadata about a full-text catalog in the system table of the database and builds an empty full-text catalog in the file system. The file is created in a default root directory that can be overridden, if desired, by using a third parameter.

6. Register the **authors**, **jobs**, **pub_info**, and **titles** tables for full-text processing. Tables so registered must have a column (called the **full-text unique key** column) that is guaranteed to have a unique value for each row. Because all of these tables have a primary key that consists of a single column, they all qualify.

To register such a table, you must specify the name of the index that enforces the unique value for the unique key column. For a given table, this information can be obtained using the **sp_helpindex** stored procedure. The indexes of interest in this scenario are:

authors	UPKCL_auidind
jobs	PK_jobs_22AA996
pub_info	UPKCL_pubinfo
titles	UPKCL_titleind

Knowing these names, it is now possible to register the tables by invoking the **sp_fulltext_table** stored procedure once for each table:

```
sp_fulltext_table 'authors', 'create', 'PubsCatalog', 'UPKCL_auidind'
sp_fulltext_table 'jobs', 'create', 'PubsCatalog', 'PK_jobs_22AA996'
sp_fulltext_table 'pub_info', 'create', 'PubsCatalog',
'UPKCL_pubinfo'
sp_fulltext_table 'titles', 'create', 'PubsCatalog', 'UPKCL_titleind'
```

The effect of these invocations is to update the metadata in the system tables both for this full-text catalog and for these tables.

7. For each of the newly registered tables, specify the names of the columns that are to be registered. This is done by invoking the **sp_fulltext_column** stored procedure once for each column:

```
sp_fulltext_column 'authors', 'address', 'add'
sp_fulltext_column 'jobs', 'job_desc', 'add'
sp_fulltext_column 'pub_info', 'pr_info', 'add'
sp_fulltext_column 'titles', 'type', 'add'
sp_fulltext_column 'titles', 'notes', 'add'
```

The effect of these invocations is to augment the metadata in the system tables.

Note A mistake was made for the sake of later illustration. For the **titles** table, the **type** column, rather than the **titles** column has been registered.

---

8. Before a full-text index can be created, it must be active. Activate the ability to create a full-text index for these tables by invoking the **sp_fulltext_table** stored procedure once for each table:

```
sp_fulltext_table 'authors', 'activate'
sp_fulltext_table 'jobs', 'activate'
sp_fulltext_table 'pub_info', 'activate'
sp_fulltext_table 'titles', 'activate'
```

This does not create the full-text indexes; it only registers the tables as active in the metadata of the full-text catalog so that data from these tables will be included in the next population. Additionally, this defines full-text population start seeds for each table to the full-text service.

9. Start a full population of the **PubsCatalog** full-text catalog by invoking the **sp_fulltext_catalog** stored procedure:

```
sp_fulltext_catalog 'PubsCatalog', 'start_full'
```

The population of a full-text catalog is an asynchronous operation. This means that immediately following the execution the procedure and the return to the procedure's caller, it is unlikely that the full-text indexes will have been created yet.

10. Inquire into the progress of the population of the **PubsCatalog** full-text catalog. This statement SELECT FulltextCatalogProperty ('PubsCatalog', 'PopulateStatus') returns 0 if the service is idle for the full-text catalog and therefore (supposedly) finished, and 1 or more to indicate various stages of population.

11. Issue some SQL queries to confirm that the administration was executed properly. For example, issue the following SQL statement:

```
SELECT P.pub_name, T.title, T.price
  FROM publishers P, titles.T
  WHERE P.pub_id = T.pub_id
    AND P.country = 'England'
    AND CONTAINS (T.notes,
                  '"case is altered" OR
                  "cat and custard pot" OR
                  "the monarch and the sphinx"
                  ' )
```

12. Issue the following SQL query:

```
SELECT title_id, title, pubdate
  FROM titles
  WHERE CONTAINS (T.title,
                  'classic ~ french ~ cooking')
```

This results in an error because the **title** column was not registered for full-text queries.

13. Check for mistakes by using this statement, which returns 1 if title is part of the full-text index for the books table, and 0 if it is not.

```
SELECT ColumnProperty ( ObjectId('titles'),
                        'titles',
                        'IsFulltextIndexed' )
```

In this case, the value returned is 0.

14. List the columns that participate in full-text processing for **titles** by invoking the stored procedure:

```
sp_help_fulltext_columns 'titles'
```

The results of this query will show that there was a mistake and that **type** instead of **title** was included in the full-text index definition.

15. Deactivate the **titles** table so that the **title** column can be added to the full-text index and the **type** column can be removed. This is done by invoking the stored procedure:

```
sp_fulltext_table 'titles', 'deactivate'
```

In addition to allowing columns to be added and deleted, the effect of deactivating the **titles** table means that the table no longer participates in the population of the **PubsCatalog** full-text catalog. However, the metadata remains and the table can be reactivated. The existing full-text index for the **titles** table remains in place until the next full population of **PubsCatalog**, but it is unused because SQL Server blocks queries on deactivated tables.

16. Add the **title** column and remove the **type** column from the metadata for the **title** table's full-text index. This is done by invoking the **sp_fulltext_column** stored procedure once for each column:

```
sp_fulltext_column 'titles', 'type', 'drop'
sp_fulltext_column 'titles', 'title', 'add'
```

17. Reactivate the books table by invoking the stored procedure:

```
sp_fulltext_table 'titles', 'activate'
```

If the table is reactivated and the index is not repopulated, the old index is still available for queries against all the full-text registered columns that remain (but not against any new full-text registered columns). Data from deleted columns will be matched on queries that specify a * search (that is, all full-text columns in a table).

18. Start an incremental population of the **PubsCatalog** full-text catalog by invoking the stored procedure:

```
sp_fulltext_catalog 'PubsCatalog',
                    'start_incremental'
```

An incremental population will refresh the full-text catalog by indexing data in the full-text enabled columns that meet any of the following criteria:

- Data from rows that have been updated or inserted since the last population in tables that have a **timestamp** column

- Data from all rows in tables that do not have a **timestamp** column, tables that were enabled for full-text processing since the last population, or tables whose schemas have been modified in any way since the last population

19. After the repopulation of **PubsCatalog** is complete, reissue the query from step 13. This time, no error is raised.

Graphical User Interfaces

GUIs are simple and straightforward to use. This chapter shows how they fit into the rest of GUI for the SQL Server Enterprise Manager.

A. Console Pane

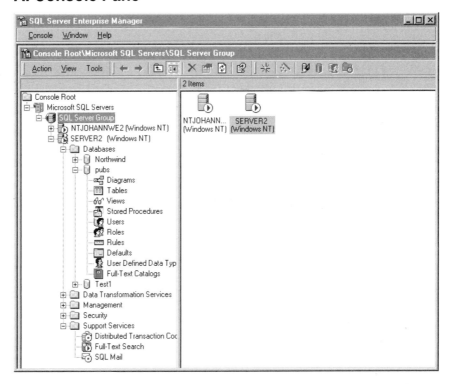

There are two full-text objects on the console (left) pane:

- **Full-Text Search**: A right-click brings up a menu that has options such as starting and stopping the full-text search service.

- **Full-Text Catalogs**: Selecting this causes a list of full-text catalogs for a database to be displayed in the details (right) pane. A right-click brings up a context menu that has options such as creating new full-text catalogs and rebuilding all the full-text catalogs for a database.

B. Tools Menu

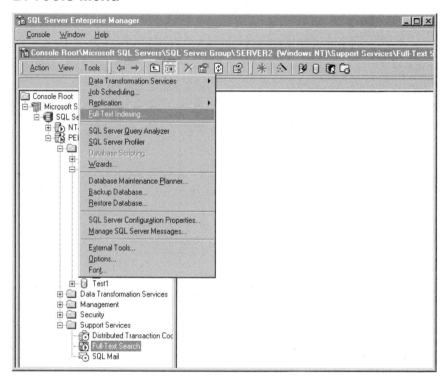

Selecting **Full-Text Indexing** launches the Full-Text Indexing Wizard.

C. Context Menu of a Typical Table

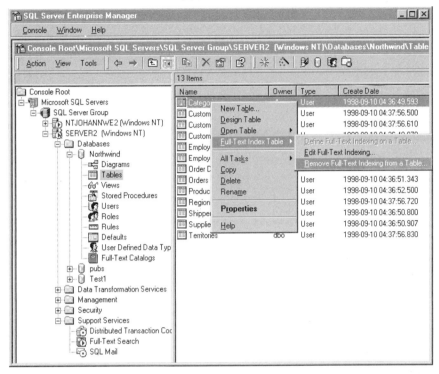

The **Full-Text Index Table** menu option has suboptions that can be used to launch the Full-Text Indexing Wizard to define or to modify the full-text index specifications for a table or to remove full-text indexing from the table.

D. Property Sheet Tabs of a Typical Table

Selecting the **Full-Text Indexing** tab selects a property page. The illustration shows a typical page.

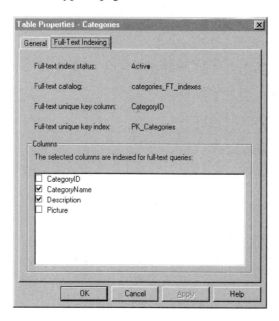

E. Catalog Pane and Context Menu

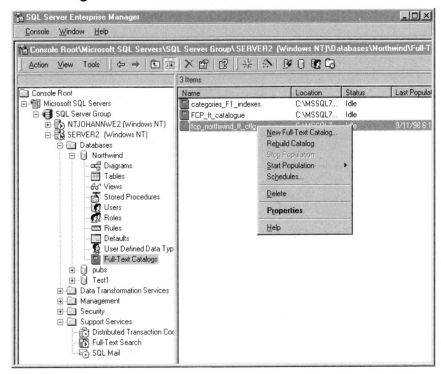

To view this menu follow these steps:

1. To view the list of full-text catalogs, select the **Full-Text Catalogs** object on the Console Pane A.

2. Right-click the **fcp.northwind.ft.ctlg** to view the context menu shown.

    Select **Properties** to view the **Full-Text Catalog Properties** dialog box.

F. Status Property Page

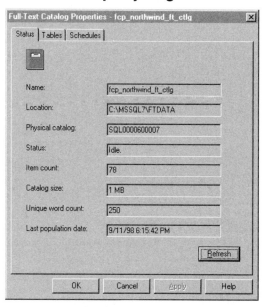

To view this property page, select **Properties** in the menu shown in E.

G. Schedules Property Page

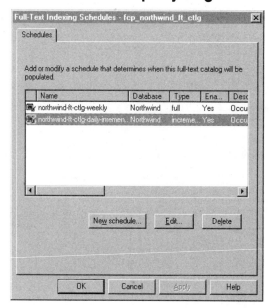

To view this property page, select **Schedules** in the menu shown in E.

H. Full-Text Indexing Wizard

This wizard can be invoked from many places: The two ways we have shown here are by selecting the **Full-Text Indexing...** option from the **Tools** Menu B or one of the **Full-Text Index Table** options from the Context Menu C. The wizard gathers all the information necessary to create and maintain a full-text index for a given table.

Registering and activating a table does not mean that the full-text queries can be issued against the table. A full-text index must be created first, and this is not a function of the wizard. After registering one or more tables, start a full population of the full-text catalogs for those tables by selecting **Start Population** on the **Pubs Catalog** context menu.

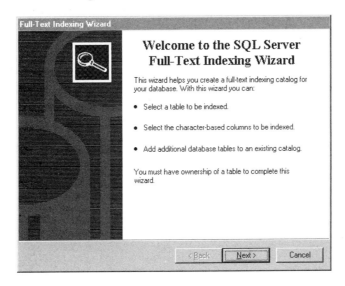

CHAPTER 23

Textual Searches on File Data

Microsoft SQL Server version 7.0 introduces facilities that support textual queries on data in SQL Server as well as on data in the file system. This chapter describes searches on data in the file system. Several products and features have been brought together to support this capability, including SQL Server distributed queries, Windows NT Server built-in Web server, Microsoft Internet Information Services (IIS) version 4.0, and Microsoft Index Services version 2.0. This chapter is for those who are familiar with SQL Server but not necessarily familiar with its textual search features and products.

This chapter introduces the types of textual searches supported by SQL Server and illustrates the roles performed by both the IIS and Index Services technologies. It also introduces SQL Server distributed queries and describes their use in the processing of textual searches. It then addresses the question of how SQL queries can be written against the file system when there are no tables in the file system. Finally, the SQL extensions to support full-text queries are described, and several examples, including examples that combine file data with database data, are provided.

This chapter provides an overview of how to incorporate file data into SQL queries and of how the various components of SQL Server and other software interact to provide support for such queries.

A large portion of digitally stored information is in the form of unstructured data, primarily text, which is stored in the file system. This data is often related to data within the database, and there are requirements to support searches that include both sources. However, it is often inappropriate to import this data into the file system. SQL Server 7.0 distributed queries, coupled with extensions to the SQL language, make it possible to write such queries without the data. This capability is called file content search.

There are two major types of textual searches:

Property
> This search technology first applies filters to documents to extract properties such as author, subject, type, word count, printed page count, and time last written, and then issues searches against those properties.

Full-text
> This search technology first creates indexes of all non-noise words in the documents, and then uses these indexes to support linguistic searches and proximity searches (searches for words or phrases that are "close" to each other).

File content search supports both these types of textual searches and couples them with the ability to incorporate such searches into a query that includes relational operations against database data. For example, the following search selects the names, sizes, and authors of all Microsoft Word files on drive D that contain the phrase "SQL Server" in proximity to the word "text." It then joins this result with the writers table to obtain the author's citizenship.

```
SELECT Q.FileName, Q.Size, Q.DocAuthor, W.Citizenship
FROM OpenQuery(MyLinkedServer,
               'SELECT FileName, Size, DocAuthor
               FROM SCOPE('' "D:\" '')
               WHERE CONTAINS('''"SQL Server"
                                     NEAR() text'')
               AND FileName LIKE ''%.doc%'' '
            ) AS Q,
     writers AS W
WHERE Q.DocAuthor = W.writer_name
```

File content search relies on the Microsoft OLE DB Provider for Index Services. It also relies on Index Services for support of underlying filters and full-text indexes.

Notice that the OLE DB Provider gives Index Services 2.0 the ability to support SQL queries against data in the file system independent of SQL Server. The core extensions SQL that support such queries are the same in Index Services and SQL Server.

This chapter has the following purposes:

- To illustrate the use of IIS 4.0, Index Services 2.0, and SQL Server 7.0 in support of file content search

- To introduce the SQL language extensions in support of textual searches on file data

- To present several sample queries to encourage you to start using textual searches

Only a small percentage of the facilities available in the supporting products are introduced in this chapter, and even when a facility is discussed, many of its options are not discussed. For more information, see SQL Server Books Online and your Windows NT documentation.

Internet Information Services and Index Services

Microsoft Internet Information Server (IIS) 4.0 and Index Services 2.0 (both part of the Microsoft Windows NT 4.0 Option Pack) combine to provide property filtering and searching as well as full-text indexing and searching of file data. Windows NT 4.01 Service Pack 4 must be installed for proper interaction between Index Services and SQL Server.

All of these capabilities are available completely independent of SQL Server. In particular, there are at least two ways to search that do not use SQL Server. One of these employs an Index Services specific query language; the other supports SQL-based queries within ActiveX Data Objects (ADO). Neither alternative is discussed in this chapter except to say that SQL used in ADO queries is consistent with the SQL extensions outlined here. This chapter discusses property filtering and full-text indexing.

Index Services provides filters for several file formats, including Microsoft Word, Microsoft PowerPoint, Microsoft Excel, and HTML. Filters are also available for plain–text documents. Filters can be written by customers and third-party vendors for other formats such as Adobe Acrobat. Filters provide support for non-plain–text documents and capture property values both from the file content and about the files. Assuming that every file is a document, examples of properties include the document's title, the number of its pages with notes (for PowerPoint documents), the number of paragraphs it contains, the date and time when it was last accessed, and its physical path. A full list of file properties is provided later in this chapter. For more information, see your Windows NT documentation.

Full-text indexes are created by scanning file content. The process consists of tracking which significant words are used and where they are located. For example, a full-text index might indicate that the word "Canada" is found at word number 227, word number 473, and word number 1,017 in a given file. This index structure supports an efficient search for all items containing indexed words, as well as advanced search operations such as phrase searches and proximity searches. An example of a phrase search is looking for "white elephant," where "white" is immediately followed by "elephant." An example of a proximity search is looking for "big," where "big" occurs near "house."

To prevent the full-text index from becoming bloated, noise words (words that are too common to expedite the search, such as "a," "and," "the," and "therefore") are ignored. SQL Server setup for version 7.0 installs noise-word lists for many languages in directory *\Mssql\Ftdata\Sqlserver\Config*. And the set of supported languages is growing. The choice of a particular noise-word list is based on the language of the material that is file-format dependent during the filtering process. Some files set the language per section or paragraph; some specify it for the entire document. These noise-word lists should be sufficient for most operations, but they can be modified.

Index Services stores indexes and property values in a text search catalog. By default, a text search catalog named **Web** is created when Index Services is installed. It is possible to specify more than one text search catalog, but this chapter confines itself to the use of **Web** and does not discuss the process used to create additional text search catalogs.

A given text search catalog references one or more IIS virtual directories. A virtual directory references one or more physical directories and, optionally, other virtual directories. When a real file is linked to the text search catalog by means of a virtual directory, Index Services is notified of any new files that need to be indexed and begins filtering and indexing the properties and content associated with those files. Index Services is also notified of any subsequent changes to the files and will refilter and reindex any updated files.

The following screen shot shows a directory for the default Web site on the computer Pellow-2. Notice that /Corpus is listed in both panes. /Corpus is the alias of a virtual directory that, in turn, points to the real directory, D:\Corpus. All of the files in D:\Corpus have their properties and full-text indexes maintained in the **Web** text search catalog.

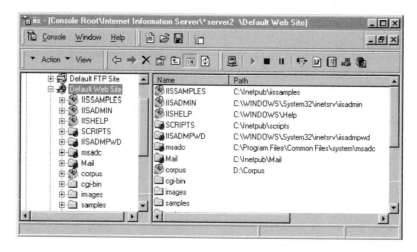

The following screen shot demonstrates how the Virtual Directory Wizard can be invoked to insert new virtual directories into the tree.

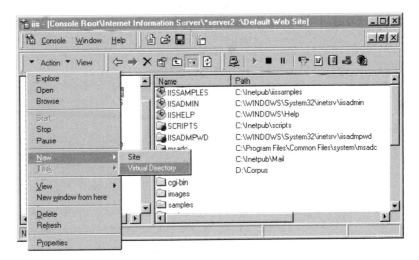

This final screen shot demonstrates the result of using the Virtual Directory Wizard to add the /SQL_standards virtual directory, which contains two virtual directories and one real directory.

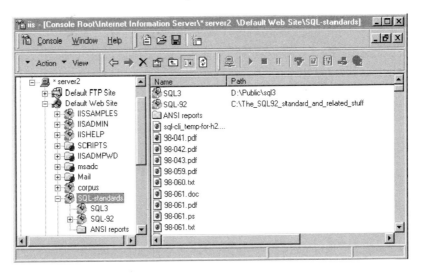

SQL Server Distributed Queries

SQL Server 7.0 supports access to data in multiple, heterogeneous data sources, which can be on either the same or different computers. The data can be stored in various relational and nonrelational data sources for which there is either an OLE DB provider or ODBC driver. The OLE DB provider exposes its data in tabular objects called rowsets. SQL Server 7.0 allows a rowset from an OLE DB provider to be referenced in the FROM clause of a SQL query as if it were a SQL Server table.

OLE DB Provider for Index Services

In the examples discussed in this chapter, OLE DB provider is supplied by Index Services.

The **sp_addlinkedserver** stored procedure may be used to register data sources that will be referenced in distributed queries. To register OLE DB Provider for Index Services for the **Web** text search catalog on the computer on which SQL Server is running, execute this statement:

```
EXECUTE sp_AddLinkedServer FileSystem,
                           'Index Services',
                           'MSIDXS',
                           'Web'
```

Here are the definitions of the syntax terminology:

FileSystem
   The *linked_server_name* assigned to this particular linked server.

Index Services
   The *product_name* of the data source.

MSIDXS
   The *provider_name* (PROGID) of OLE DB Provider for Index Services.

Web
   The name of the text search catalog that will be used for this linked server.

The OLE DB provider now can be referenced using the **FileSystem** *linked_server_name* in the new OPENQUERY() result-set–valued function. For example:

```
SELECT *
FROM OpenQuery(FileSystem,
              'SELECT Directory, FileName, DocAuthor, Size, Create
              FROM SCOPE()
              WHERE CONTAINS( Contents, ''Distributed'' ) ' )
```

Notice that there are two SELECT statements. The inner SELECT statement (within the OPENQUERY() function) returns a result set as a table that can then be used like any other table in the FROM clause. In this case, the outer SELECT statement is a simple SELECT *, which passes on all the rows from the inner SELECT statement. Also notice that because the inner SELECT statement is specified as a constant parameter value within single quotation marks, all single quotation characters within the inner SELECT statement must be doubled. That is why ' 'Distributed' ' appears as it does. Two adjacent single quote marks (') are not the same as one double quotation mark (").

In general, SQL Server distributed queries support both read and update access to the data source. In the case of Index Services, only read access is appropriate. Generally, distribution is supported to remote computers; however, the SQL Server file content search feature has been tested only with all components and all data residing in the same computer.

Notice that OPENQUERY() does not work when running with a compatibility mode earlier than SQL Server 7.0. The compatibility mode can be set using the **sp_dbcmptlevel** stored procedure.

Security

There are special security considerations with OLE DB Provider for Index Services on the Windows NT operating system. SQL Server supplies a username and password on the current SQL Server login and on the login mapping set up in SQL Server of the form (current login, linked server) -> (remote login, remote password). However, OLE DB Provider for Index Services ignores the username and password and instead uses the Windows NT security context of the client (as if the client asked for a Windows NT Authentication mode connection). This means that OLE DB Provider for Index Services uses the Windows NT account under which SQL Server is running. Because this account is likely to be powerful, it can expose information about files to which the original SQL Server login has no privileges.

This concern has been addressed by giving SQL Server administrators full control over who has access to OLE DB Provider for Index Services through SQL Server. The administrator can control the login mappings so that no one other than those who have explicit login mappings can gain access to the server (for example, an Index Services linked server). The administrator can also disable ad hoc access against a given provider so that no one can access Index Services through the ad hoc route without using a linked server.

For example, if SQL Server is running under the Windows NT account **sqlaccount**, consider a linked server called **mytextfiles** that has been configured to point to a particular Index Services text search catalog. On Windows NT 4.0, when a SQL Server user executes a distributed query against **mytextfiles**, this query is executed under the privileges of the Windows NT account under which SQL Server is running (**sqlaccount**). Given this, the SQL Server security administrator must decide which SQL Server logins should have access to **mytextfiles**. This can be done by performing the following steps.

When a linked server is created with the **sp_addlinkedserver** stored procedure, by default all SQL Server logins have access to that server through self-mapping. The default mapping needs to be removed so that no one other than the approved logins can gain access to **mytextfiles**. This is accomplished by executing the following procedure:

```
-- Remove login mappings for all logins (by specifying NULL value for
the @locallogin
parameter)
exec sp_droplinkedsrvlogin 'MyTextFiles', NULL
```

For each SQL Server login (either SQL Server Authentication or Windows NT Authentication) to be given access to the **mytextfiles** linked server, execute the following stored procedure:

```
-- Add a self mapping for local login to itself
exec sp_addlinkedsrvlogin 'MyTextFiles, true, 'local_login'
```

Remove the ability for ad hoc access to Index Services text search catalogs using the OPENROWSET() function. This task is accomplished through SQL Server Enterprise Manager by using the **Linked Server Properties** dialog box, which can be brought up by right-clicking on the corresponding linked server in SQL Server Enterprise Manager, and then clicking **Properties**.

Defined Tables

At least one defined table must be specified in every SQL query. A defined table is a table in which the number and types of columns are either known in advance or specified as part of the query. A relational database usually contains a number of defined tables, and metadata about the columns of these tables is stored in a schema.

The collection of files in a file system does not generally have a predefined structure. The closest thing to columns are the properties of a file, but there is no deterministic set of properties for files. The closest thing to a row is a file, but files are usually not grouped in a homogeneous collection akin to rows in a table. Thus, in this case, the table concept is unclear, SELECT * is meaningless, and both the rows and columns are unbounded. Another way of looking at this is that a file system effectively has a universal schema consisting of every possible file property, both known and unknown.

Index Services solves this problem by providing the SCOPE function as a means of defining the set of rows that makes up a virtual table and by providing file properties that substitute for columns.

SCOPE Function

The SCOPE function is specified in the FROM clause of the Index Services query. It specifies the set of files that make up a virtual table.

The syntax of the SCOPE function, simplified for this chapter, is as follows:

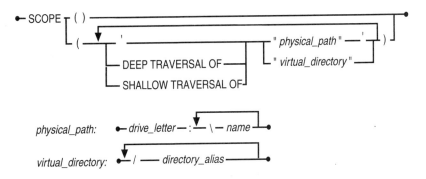

These are the definitions of the syntax terminology:

()

    The virtual table consists of all the files that have been registered in the text search catalog and data source for the linked server specified in the OPENQUERY() function.

DEEP TRAVERSAL OF

    The virtual table consists of all the files in the directory at the specified path or virtual directory as well as all the files in all the subdirectories (to any level) that are considered to be part of the virtual table. DEEP is the default.

SHALLOW TRAVERSAL OF

The virtual table consists only of the files in the top-level directory at the specified path or virtual directory that are considered to be part of the virtual table.

physical_path

A path to a real directory. If a real directory is specified, the filtering and indexing is done as part of the query processing, which can be time-consuming.

virtual_directory

The alias (or chain of aliases) assigned to a virtual directory that has been registered in the text search catalog and data source for the linked server specified in the OPENQUERY() function. In this case, the filtering and indexing will probably already have been done and, thus, the query will be much faster than when a physical path is specified.

File Properties

Index Services filters and maintains an excess of 50 file properties. All of these can be specified in text file search queries. From the perspective of writing a SELECT statement, there are three types of file properties:

- Those that can be specified only in a WHERE clause
- Those that can be specified in a WHERE clause and an ORDER BY clause.
- Those that can be specified in a WHERE clause and a select list.

This table outlines some of the file properties.

Property name	SQL Data Type	Description	Use in ORDER BY clause	Use in select list
Access	datetime	Most recent date and time that the file was accessed.	Yes	Yes
Characterization	nvarchar or ntext	Abstract of the contents of the file. In Index Services 2.0, this is usually the first paragraph or first section of a document. In future releases, it is planned to be a real summary.	–	Yes
Contents	nvarchar or ntext	Main contents of the file.	–	–
Create	datetime	Date and time that the file was created.	Yes	Yes
Directory	nvarchar	Physical path to the file, not including the file name.	Yes	Yes

(continued)

Property name	SQL Data Type	Description	Use in ORDER BY clause	Use in select list
DocAuthor	nvarchar	Document author.	Yes	Yes
DocComments	nvarchar	Comments about the document.	Yes	Yes
DocLastAuthor	nvarchar	Most recent user that edited the document.	Yes	Yes
DocLastPrinted	datetime	Date and time that the document was last printed.	Yes	–
DocPageCount	integer	Number of pages in the document.	Yes	–
DocPartTitles	array of varchar	Names of the document parts: ■ in Microsoft PowerPoint (slide titles). ■ in Microsoft Excel (spreadsheets). ■ in Microsoft Word (documents).	–	–
DocSubject	nvarchar	Subject of the document.	Yes	Yes
DocTitle	nvarchar	Title of the document.	Yes	Yes
DocWordCount	integer	Number of words in the document.	Yes	–
FileIndex	decimal (19,0)	Unique identifier of the file.	Yes	Yes
FileName	nvarchar	Name of the file.	Yes	Yes
HitCount	integer	Number of words matching the query.	Yes	Yes
Path	nvarchar	Full physical path to the file, including the file name.	Yes	Yes
Rank	integer	Value from 0 through 1,000, indicating how well this row matches the selection criteria.	Yes	Yes
Size	decimal (19, 0)	Size of the file (in bytes).	Yes	Yes
Write	datetime	Most recent date and time that the file was written.	Yes	Yes

Customers and third-party vendors can write filters to add to this set of file properties. They can also add properties, for example, by adding tags to an HTML document. In addition, to permit the query and retrieval of such user-defined file properties, the SQL extensions to Index Services include support for a SET statement that allows the specification of new file property names and their associated types.

Virtual Tables

It is possible to specify a query with the equivalent of a table in the file system, resulting in the select list and the FROM clause. For other parts of a SELECT statement, the properties can be used in place of columns in the WHERE and ORDER BY clauses. However, the GROUP BY and HAVING clauses are not supported by OLE DB Provider for Index Services. The following examples illustrate the use of all supported clauses.

The following query selects the full physical path and the file creation timestamp of all files in the /SQL-standards virtual directory and all its subdirectories, where the document contains the phrase "overloaded function."

```
SELECT *
FROM OpenQuery(FileSystem,
              'SELECT Path, Create
              FROM SCOPE('' "/SQL-standards" '')
              WHERE CONTAINS(Contents, '' "overloaded function" '')
              '
              )
```

The next query is similar to the previous one, except that only files directly in the /SQL-standards virtual directory are considered.

```
SELECT *
FROM OpenQuery(FileSystem,
              'SELECT Path, Create
              FROM SCOPE('' SHALLOW TRAVERSAL OF "/SQL-standards" '')
              WHERE CONTAINS(Contents, '' "overloaded function" '')
              '
              )
```

The next query is also similar, except that only files directly in the /SQL3 virtual subdirectory are considered.

```
SELECT *
FROM OpenQuery(FileSystem,
              'SELECT Path, Create
              FROM SCOPE('' "/SQL-standards/SQL3" '')
              WHERE CONTAINS(Contents, '' "overloaded function" '')
              '
              )
```

The final query selects author, title, subject, and file name of documents in all files that are either in the /Corpus virtual directory and its subdirectories or in the \Temp directory on drive C, where the document is at least 5,000 words, the author is either Wendy Vasse or Anas Abbar, and the rows representing those documents with the most pages are ordered highest.

```
SELECT *
FROM OpenQuery(FileSystem,
               'SELECT DocAuthor, DocTitle, DocSubject, FileName
                FROM SCOPE('' "/corpus" '',
                           '' "C:\temp" '' )
                WHERE DocWordCount >= 5000 AND
                      ( DocAuthor = ''Wendy Vasse'' OR
                        DocAuthor = ''Anas Abbar'' )
                ORDER BY DocPageCount DESC
                '
               )
```

Path Through the Components

The following figure contains the code for a typical query and a diagram that illustrates the part played by each component in processing the query.

```
SELECT Q.DocAuthor, Q.DocTitle, W. Citizenship
FROM OpenQuery (FileSystem,
               'SELECT DocAuthor, DocTitle
                FROM SCOPE ( ' ' "/corpus" ' ',
                    ' ' "C:\temp" ' ' )
                WHERE DocWordCount >= 5000
                ') AS Q
       writers AS W
WHERE Q.DocAuthor = w.writer_name
```

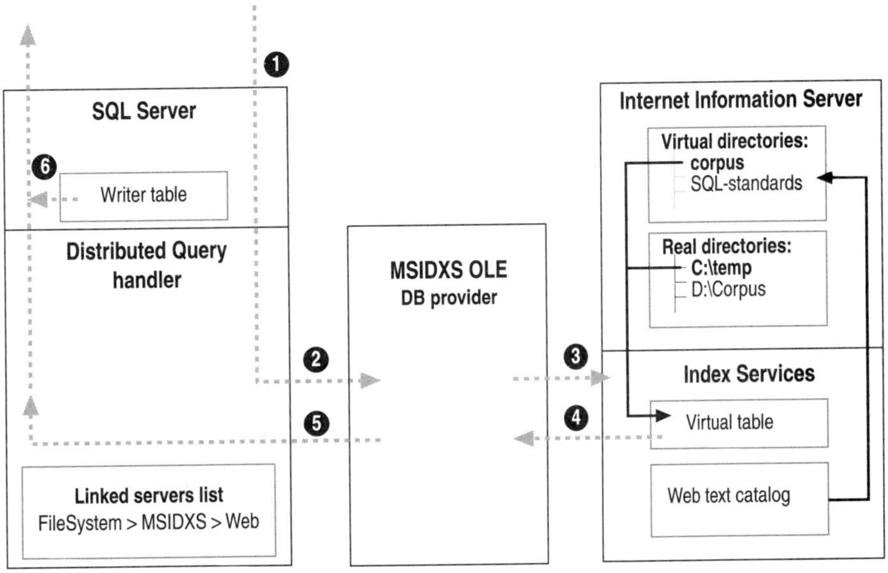

These items relate to the numbered items in the previous diagram.

1. The query is submitted to SQL Server, which separates the distributed portion of the query (the OPENQUERY() function) and forwards it to the SQL Server Distributed Query Handler.

2. The Distributed Query Handler passes the inner SELECT statement specified in the OPENQUERY() function to the to the OLE DB Provider for Index Services (MSIDXS) that has been linked to **FileSystem**.

3. MSIDXS parses the inner SELECT statement, then issues the appropriate commands to Index Services.

4. Index Services forms a virtual table by combining the files in the **Web** text search catalog's /Corpus virtual directory with the files in the C:\Temp path, selecting only files that contain 5,000 words or more. The results are returned as a rowset to MSIDXS.

5. MSIDXS returns the rowset to the Distributed Query Handler.

6. The Distributed Query Handler returns the rowset as a table to its calling component within SQL Server. This component, in turn, fulfills the rest of the query by joining this table with the **writers** table, and then returns the result set to the originator of the query.

SQL Extensions for Index Services Full-Text Queries

SQL extensions for Index Services are consistent with the SQL supported for full-text search against relational database data. Furthermore, SQL support for full-text searching follows the SQL-3 functional methodology for full-text syntax extensions.

The primary SQL extension consists of the CONTAINS and FREETEXT predicates. These predicates are used to find column values that match special full-text query criteria.

To be consistent with similar features in other products and to make these predicates more extensible, functional notation is used. The high-level syntax is as follows:

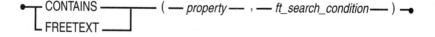

The flexibility of the functional style of these two predicates allows easy, upward-compatible future extensions for a third parameter to designate the language used for the query.

CONTAINS Predicate

The CONTAINS predicate determines whether the content of files contains certain words and phrases. The CONTAINS predicate syntax is as follows:

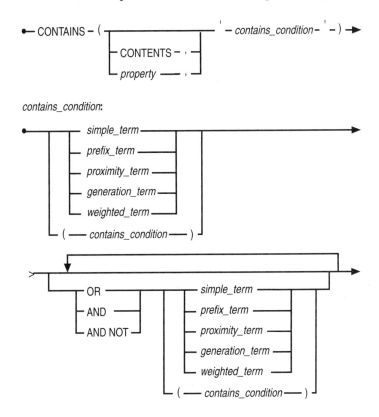

contains_condition:

property
> The property to be searched. Its data type must be character-based. If *property* is not specified, the CONTENTS property is assumed. The value of the CONTENTS clause is the contents of the file after conversion to plain text (if necessary) by a filter. It is good practice to explicitly code the CONTENTS clause, rather than to accept it as a default.

simple_term
> The term used to match the exact word or phrase being searched for. Its syntax is:

where word refers to one or more characters without spaces or punctuation and phrase refers to multiple words with spaces in between. Asian languages can have phrases made up of multiple words without any spaces in between.

Here are some examples of simple terms used in the context of the CONTAINS predicate in a WHERE clause:

```
WHERE CONTAINS( Contents, 'hockey' )
WHERE CONTAINS( Contents, ' "ice hockey" ')
```

In keeping with the standard for full-text products, the search for characters in a word or phrase is always case-insensitive, and noise words are not stored in the full-text index. For example, suppose there is one file with a value of "This is a dissertation on the use of ice-cream sandwiches as hockey pucks" and another file with the value "Dissertation on new ways of splitting the atom." Since "this," "is," "a," and so on are noise words, they are not stored in the full-text index, and the following two queries are effectively identical:

```
CONTAINS( Contents, ' "this is a dissertation" ' )
CONTAINS( Contents, 'dissertation' )
```

Both rows are returned as hits because in the first query, the noise words are removed before processing the query.

Combining Terms Using Boolean Operators

As with other SQL search conditions, more complex conditions can be specified by linking individual operands with the Boolean operators AND, OR, and AND NOT. In this case, the operands are any of the types of terms being discussed (simple_term, prefix_term, and so on). Except for the restriction that the OR NOT combination is not supported and that NOT cannot be specified before the first term, the rules are exactly the same as those used to combine individual predicates to form search conditions. For example, parentheses may be used to change the default priority order in which the operators are applied.

Here are some examples of simple terms being combined within a CONTAINS predicate in a WHERE clause.

```
WHERE CONTAINS( Contents, 'hockey OR curling' )
WHERE CONTAINS( Contents, 'hockey AND NOT field')
WHERE CONTAINS( Contents, ' ("ice hockey" OR curling) AND NOT Canada ')
```

prefix_term

prefix_term is used to match words or phrases that begin with specified text. Its syntax is:

A prefix term consists of a simple term appended with an asterisk (*) to activate prefix matching on a word or phrase. All text that starts with the material before the * is matched. The wildcard symbol (*) in this case is similar to the percent symbol (%) in the LIKE predicate in that it matches zero, one, or more characters of the root words in a word or phrase. In a phrase, each word within the phrase is considered to be a prefix; for example, the term "local bus*" matches "locality busy," "local bush," and "locale bust."

Here are two examples of prefix terms used in the context of the CONTAINS predicate in a WHERE clause. The first matches values that contain the word "atom," "atomic," "atomism," "atomy," and so on. The second matches values that contain the word "wine," "vine," or words such as "winery," "wines," "vineyard," or "vinegar."

```
WHERE CONTAINS( Contents, ' "atom*" ' )
WHERE CONTAINS( Contents, ' "wine*" OR "vine*" ')
```

proximity_term

proximity_term is used when the words or phrases being searched for must be close to one another. Its syntax is:

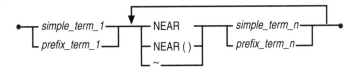

A proximity term is similar to an AND operator in that more than one word or phrase must exist in the value being searched. It differs from AND because the relevance of the match increases as the words appear closer together.

The syntax is designed to be extensible for possible future support for specification of units of proximity such as words, sentences, paragraphs, chapters, and so on.

NEAR, NEAR() and ~ share the same meaning: the first word or phrase is close to the second word or phrase. "Close" is a purposefully vague term that can mean "within 50 words," but the algorithm is complicated. While words within the same sentence are one word distance apart, larger distances are assigned between units such as sentences, paragraphs, and chapters. Even if words or phrases are very far apart, the query is still considered to be satisfied; the row just has a low (zero) rank value. This can be avoided by specifying RANK > 0 as one of the predicates in the WHERE clause.

It is possible to chain-code the proximity matching. For example," a ~ b ~ c " means that *a* should be near *b*, which should be near *c*. Because of the fuzzy nature of full-text searches, it is often desirable to see the rank values. This can be done by including the **RANK** property in the select list of the query.

Here are some examples of proximity terms used in the context of the CONTAINS predicate in a WHERE clause:

```
WHERE CONTAINS( Contents, ' hockey ~ player ' )
```

This matches values that contain the word "hockey" in proximity to the word "player."

```
WHERE CONTAINS( Contents, ' hockey ~ "play*" ')
```

This matches values that contain the word "hockey" in proximity to a word that starts with "play."

```
WHERE CONTAINS( Contents, '  "great*"  ~ "Mike Nash" ') AND Rank > 0
```

This matches values that contain words starting with "great" in proximity to the phrase "Mike Nash." Values that meet the criteria but have a ranking of 0 do not have rows returned.

generation_term

generation_term is used when the words being searched for need to be expanded to include the variants of the original word. Its syntax is:

```
●── FORMSOF ─ ( ─ INFLECTIONAL ────┬──── , simple_term ──┘ ) ─●
```

The INFLECTIONAL predicate means that plural and singular forms of nouns and the various tenses of verbs will be matched. A single term will not match both exclusive noun and exclusive verb forms. The syntax is designed to be extensible enough to handle other linguistically generated forms, such as derivational, soundex, and thesaurus.

Here is an example of a generation term used in the context of the CONTAINS predicate in a WHERE clause.

```
WHERE CONTAINS(' FORMSOF (INFLECTIONAL, skate) ' )
```

This matches values that contain words such as "skate," "skates," "skated," and "skating."

weighted_term

weighted_term is used for queries that match a list of words and phrases, each optionally given its own weighting. Matching values must match only one element in the list. Its syntax is as follows, where *n.nnn* represents a decimal constant from zero through one.

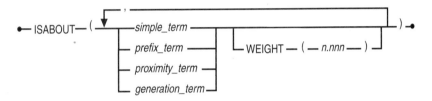

A row is returned if there is a match on any one of the ISABOUT elements.

Each component in the vector can be optionally weighted. The assigned weight forces a different measurement of the rank value that is assigned to each row that matches the query.

Here are some examples of weighted terms used in the context of the CONTAINS predicate in a WHERE clause.

```
WHERE CONTAINS( Contents, ' ISABOUT(hockey, puck, goalie) ' )
```

This matches article values that contain any of the words "hockey," "puck," or "goalie." The better matches will contain more than one of the words.

```
WHERE CONTAINS( Contents, 'ISABOUT("Canadian ice hockey" WEIGHT(1.0),
                          "ice hockey" WEIGHT(.5),
                          hockey WEIGHT(.2) )
                    ' )
```

This matches article values that may have information about Canadian ice hockey, with higher rank values assigned to articles that have more words from the phrase.

FREETEXT Predicate

The FREETEXT predicate determines whether or not a value reflects the meaning, rather than the exact words, specified in the predicate.

The FREETEXT predicate syntax is as follows:

This is a simple form of natural language query, where the index engine internally breaks the freetext string into a number of search terms, generates the stemmed form of the words, assigns heuristic weighting to each term, then finds the matches.

Here is an example of a FREETEXT predicate used in a WHERE clause.

```
WHERE FREETEXT( Contents, ' Who have been the most valuable ice hockey
                          players from 1975 through 1982? ' )
```

Search Condition Support in Index Services

The *search_condition* supported by Index Services is slightly different from the *search_condition* supported by SQL Server. Because these queries are distributed to the OLE DB provider for processing, the queries must follow the rules of the provider. The main difference is that OLE DB Provider for Index Services does not support the QUANTIFIED COMPARISON, BETWEEN, EXISTS, IN, or NULL predicates, but it does support two other predicates: MATCHES and ARRAY COMPARISON. These predicates are not yet directly supported by SQL Server.

Following is an introduction to the *search_condition* syntax as supported by Index Services. Some aspects have been omitted, and the syntax of other aspects is incomplete. For more information, see the Index Services documentation.

The *search_condition* syntax is as follows:

search_condition:

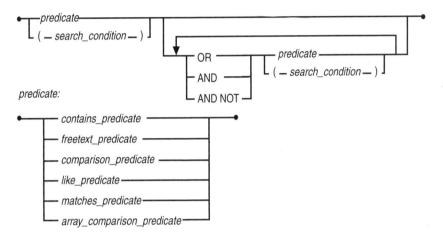

predicate:

contains_predicate and *freetext_predicate*: see above

comparison_predicate:

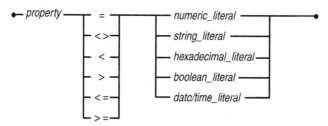

like_predicate:

● — *property* ——————— LIKE — *sql_server_wildcard_literal* ——————●
　　　　　　　└─ NOT ─┘

sql_server_wildcard_literal: The same as supported in SQL Server.

matches_predicate:

● — MATCHES — (—— *property* — , — ' — *matches_literal* — ' —) —●

matches_string: See Index Server documentation.

array_comparison_predicate:

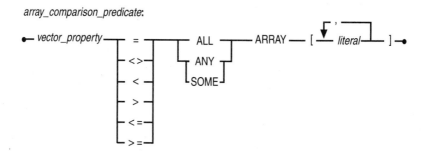

MATCHES and ARRAY COMPARISON Predicates

This section briefly introduces the MATCHES and ARRAY COMPARISON predicates. For more information, see your Windows NT documentation.

The MATCHES predicate provides more extensive pattern matching than the LIKE predicate. This added functionality bears the burden of a more complicated set of rules. The complete syntax and rules are not described here; rather, here are some examples to illustrate the use of this predicate.

Here is a grouped match against more than one pattern, where it is known that the author's first name is Peggy, but the spelling of her second name is uncertain.

```
WHERE MATCHES( DocAuthor, 'Peggy |(MacK|,McK|,MacC|,McC|)arson' )
Here, it is uncertain if Pellow is spelled with one "l" or two.
WHERE MATCHES( DocAuthor, '* Pel|{1,2|}ow' )
```

The ARRAY COMPARISON predicate is for use with the Index Services Vector properties. Some of the property values filtered by Index Services are multivalued. The data type of such values is a variable size array. SQL Server does not yet support such data types, but SQL-3 does. The SQL extension supported by OLE DB Provider for Index Services is consistent with that in SQL-3. For example, the virtual table contains a number of PowerPoint presentations, and you want to know the path to the presentations that contain any slide called "CONTAINS predicate," "FREETEXT predicate," or "Query Transformation."

```
SELECT *
FROM OpenQuery(FileSystem,
    'SELECT Path
     FROM SCOPE('' "/slide_presentations" '')
     WHERE DocPartTitles = SOME ARRAY[ ''CONTAINS predicate'',
                                       ''FREETEXT predicate'',
                                       ''Query Transformation'' ]
    ')
```

For more information, see your Windows NT documentation.

Sample Full-Text Queries

This section provides several examples that answer queries by combining database data and file data.

The following query returns the title and publication year of qualifying books that are represented by files in the virtual directory that has the /Pubs alias. In order to qualify, a book must cost less than $20.00, and text in the **Characterization** property must indicate that the book is about ice hockey. It is known that the **year** portion of the Create property is always the publication year of the book. The customer has defined the **BookCost** property (of type **money**), which filters out the cost of each book.

```
SELECT Q.DocTitle, DATEPART(year, Q.Create)
FROM OpenQuery(FileSystem,
              'SELECT DocTitle, Create
               FROM SCOPE('' "/pubs" '')
               WHERE BookCost <= 20.00
                 AND CONTAINS( Characterization, '' "ice hockey" '' )
              ') AS Q
```

Notice that the table alias value of Q has been assigned to the table returned by the OPENQUERY() function. This alias is then used to qualify the items in the outer select list. Previous examples specified the SELECT * statement and passed on all values returned by the inner SELECT statement. Here, the SQL Server DATEPART() function is used to pass on only the **year** portion of the **create datetime** value.

The following query returns the same information as the previous query. The difference is that the price of the book is obtained from the **document_cost** column in the BookCost table in the database, rather than from a property in the file system. The primary key of the BookCost table is the combination of the **document_author** and **document_title** columns.

```
SELECT Q.DocTitle, DATEPART(year, Q.Create)
FROM OpenQuery(FileSystem,
                'SELECT DocTitle, Create, DocAuthor, DocTitle
                 FROM SCOPE('' "/pubs" '')
                    AND CONTAINS( Characterization, '' "ice hockey" '' )
                ') AS Q,
    BookCost as B
WHERE Q.DocAuthor = B.document_author
  AND Q.DocTitle = B.document_title
  AND B.document_cost <= 20.00
```

The table returned by the OPENQUERY() function is joined to the real **BookCost** table in the database, then rows with a suitable cost are filtered for inclusion in the outer SELECT statement.

The next query also joins data from the file system and the database, and this time, data from both appears in the outer SELECT list. Furthermore, the **Rank** property, which indicates how well the selected rows met the selection criteria, appears in the select list and is used to ensure that higher-ranking rows appear before lower-ranking rows in the outer SELECT statement. In this example, the wording on the plaques in the Hockey Hall of Fame is recorded on files. There is a file for each plaque, and the plaque number can be obtained through the **DocSubject** property. The **HockeyHall** table contains **PlaqueNo**, **PlayerName**, **StartYear**, and **LastYear** columns, with the primary key in the **PlaqueNo** column. You want to return the **PlayerName** and **PlaqueNo** columns from the table and the **Rank** and **DocComments** properties from the file. Only players who might have played for Canadian or U.S. teams in the early 1900s are to be returned.

```
SELECT HH.PlayerName, HH.PlaqueNo, Q.Rank, Q.DocComments
FROM OpenQuery(FileSystem,
                'SELECT DocSubject, DocComments, Rank
                 FROM SCOPE('' "/hall_of_fame" '')
                 WHERE CONTAINS( Contents, '' Canada OR "United States"
                                                    '' )
                ') AS Q,
    HockeyHall as HH
WHERE Q.DocSubject = HH.PlaqueNo
  AND HH.StartYear < 1915
  AND HH.EndYear < 1899
ORDER BY Q.Rank DESC
```

In the next example, an international construction company stores a large number of onsite progress reports in a Microsoft Word document in a central site. All the documents have been registered within the /Site_report virtual directory. Each document can be identified by its unique **FileIndex** property. These documents are tracked in the database. The following tables in the database are of interest.

```
Projects:      project_number    char(8)          primary key,
               project_name      nvarchar(40),
               project_leader    smallint,        --employee number
               budgeted          money,
               spent             money,
               ...
Employees:     employee_number   smallint         primary key,
               employee_name     nvarchar(40),
               nationality       nvarchar(20),
               ...
Reports:       project_number    char(8),
               file_index        decimal(19,0),   --link to the file
               ...
               primary key is project_number and file_index
```

A rush order has been issued for 5,000 saunas in a heavily forested area with no electricity. The salesperson vaguely recalls a similar, successful project about 10 years ago. He issues a query that returns the project number, the paths to the onsite reports, and the ranking value of the projects managed by someone from a Scandinavian country that came in under budget between 8 and 12 years ago.

The highest ranking is given if the onsite report contains the phrase "wood burning" in proximity to "sauna." Points are also given if the document contains the phrase "Northern Ontario" or the word "island." Here is an example of what the query could look like:

```
SELECT P.project_number, Q.path, Q.Rank
FROM OpenQuery(FileSystem,
              'SELECT FileIndex, Path, Rank, Write
               FROM SCOPE('' "/site_reports" '')
               WHERE CONTAINS( Contents,
                       '' ISABOUT( Sauna ~ "wood burning" WEIGHT (.9),
                                   "Northern Ontario" WEIGHT (.4),
                                   Ontario            WEIGHT (.2),
                                   island             WEIGHT (.2) )
                       '' )
                 AND Rank > 5
               ') AS Q,
     Projects AS P,
     Employees AS E,
     Reports AS R
```

```
WHERE Q.FileIndex = R.file_index
  AND R.project_number = P.project_number
  AND P.project_leader = E.employee_number
  AND E.nationality IN ('FINNISH', 'DANISH', 'SWEDISH', 'NORWEGIAN')
  AND P.spent < P.budgeted
  AND YEAR(Q.Write) > 1986 AND YEAR(Q.Write) < 1992
```

SQL Extensions for Site Server Full-Text Queries

Microsoft Site Server version 3.0 also ships an OLE DB provider, the primary purpose of which is to allow users to write ADO application programs to query Web data. The OLE DB Provider for Site Server has not yet been tested with the SQL Server 7.0 query processor for distributed queries, and there is no official support for interoperability with SQL Server 7.0. However, users who want to experiment with this configuration will find the following information useful.

As with the OLE DB Provider for Index Services, the **sp_addlinkedserver** stored procedure is used to register OLE DB Provider for Site Server. For example, to register this provider for the WebTest text search catalog on the same computer that SQL Server is running on, the following statement must be executed:

```
EXECUTE sp_addlinkedserver  WebData,  'Site Server',  'MSSEARCHSQL',
'WebTest'
```

These are the definitions of the syntax terminology:

WebData
  The linked server name assigned to this particular linked sever.

Site Server
  The product name of the data source.

MSSEARCHSQL
  The provider name (PROGID) of OLE DB Provider for Site Server.

WebTest
  The name of the text search catalog that will be used for this linked server.

Notice that Site Server has additional syntax to support the union of results generated by a query across multiple catalogs. For more information, see your Site Server Search documentation.

C H A P T E R   2 4

Developing with English Query

Many database administrators have developed database-driven Web sites using Active Server Pages (ASP), Microsoft ActiveX Data Objects (ADO), and SQL Server or another database server only to find it difficult for their users to search the database and report on it.

It is easy enough to build a query form that allows users to search based on one or two fields, but it is much more difficult to build form-based Web pages that allow searches across multiple tables and multiple fields. A more flexible search is difficult to implement (there are many problems beyond the user-interface and Web-coding aspects, such as defining how the various tables and fields are related to each other) and even the best interface can be difficult for the casual Web visitor to use and understand.

Microsoft English Query, which was introduced in Microsoft SQL Server version 6.5, Enterprise Edition, and has been improved for SQL Server version 7.0, addresses this issue by providing users with the ability to use natural language when querying existing database-driven Web sites and applications.

Using English Query to develop an initial natural-language search is easy—it is only a small part of the effort of building your overall application—and the development process is more conceptual than traditional programming. In fact, the process can be mastered by nonprogrammers who have some database background, for example, database administrators and Web-content developers who work often with databases.

English Query ships with an engine, a component object model (COM) server, that is used at run time to convert a user's English language question to an SQL statement. English Query also provides sample ASPs that you can embed in a Web site to drive the engine, prompting a user for questions, executing the engine's returned SQL queries, and displaying query results to the user.

This chapter explains how to author an English Query domain and how to embed the domain and the English Query engine in your Web site.

Building with English Query

Microsoft English Query can be embedded into any application that supports COM. One common scenario is to embed it in a Web site built with ASP scripts.

A typical Web page can use the sample ASP scripts that come with English Query. For example, the user enters a question or clicks **Sample questions...** for predefined questions that show the kind of information available. The user clicks ENTER to submit the question to the English Query engine, which generates an SQL statement that is then submitted to SQL Server using ADO. The returned recordset is then displayed in the lower frame.

Authoring an English Query Domain

The first step to building a Microsoft English Query application is to model the semantics of your problem domain, that is, you must specify how English-language entities (nouns) and relationships (verbs, adjectives, traits, and subsets) map to tables, fields, and joins in your database. To do this, use the English Query authoring tool, which appears in the Microsoft English Query program group after installation.

▶   **To initialize your database structure**

- From the **File** menu on the Database tab, click **New**, and then select **Structure loaded from database**.

  This initializes the database structure from your SQL Server schema, filling the **Database** tab with tables and fields.

This illustration shows the database structure of the sample SQL Server **pubs** database.

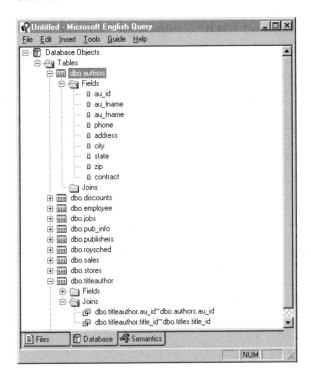

If any tables in the database are missing primary keys, edit them and supply one or more fields as the primary key. It is not necessary that the underlying database have a primary key, but all tables must have primary keys identified in the authoring tool for your application to build.

If tables will be related to each other in queries, then there should be joins indicated between those tables. The joins usually are retrieved from the foreign keys defined in your database. However, if the necessary foreign keys are not present (usually they are there to force referential integrity), then you should add the joins manually inside the authoring tool.

Creating Entities

Now you are ready to start adding semantic entities. This consists of defining the entities in your database and the tables or fields with which they are associated.

▶ **To create an entity**

1. On the **Semantics** tab, right-click Entities, and then click **Insert Entity…**.

2. In the **New Entity** dialog box, under **Semantic Properties**, in the **Words/phrases identifying entity** box, enter a description of the entity, for example, **author** or **writer**. In the **Entity type** box, enter a type.

3. Under **Database Properties**, in the **Table** or **Fields** boxes, identify which part of the database represents the entity.

   Major entities usually correspond to entire tables. If it is a major entity, then enter the fields that should be used to display the entity, such as **name** or **address**.

This illustration shows this process for the entity "author" in the **pubs** database.

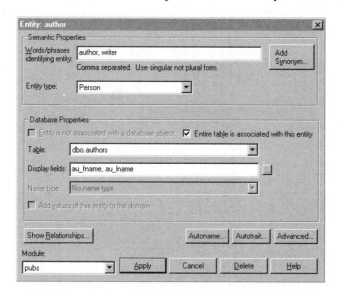

Major entities have two kinds of minor entities associated with them: names and traits. Names indicate how the entity is identified in questions and statements. By clicking **Autoname** for the author entity, you can create an entity that represents the name of the author entity, associated with the first and last name fields. You can create such name entities for major entities that are represented by entire tables so the user can identify the specific entity in question.

By clicking **Autotrait**, you can create traits for the entity: minor entities that the major entity *has*. Click **Accept All** to create minor entities for all of the semantically meaningful fields, as well as for trait relationships between the major entity and the newly created minor entities.

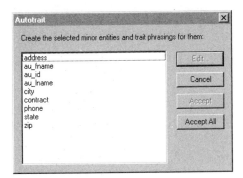

In general, you should create entities for all tables in the database. By using **Autotrait**, you can create entities for all fields in the database.

Creating Relationships

By establishing traits for the major entities, your model begins with several relationships. At this point, you can ask questions about things having traits, for example, "What authors have city Seattle?", "Show authors and their cities," "What book has the title The Busy Executive's Database Guide?", or "What publishers have country France?" But to ask the really interesting questions, you must create relationships between major entities, for example, "authors write books" and "publishers publish books."

▶ **To create a relationship between major entities**

1. On the **Semantics** tab, right-click **Relationships**, and then click **Insert Relationship…**.

2. In the **New Relationship** dialog box on the **Entities** tab, click **Add Entity…**.

3. In the **Select Entities** list, click all entities that participate in the relationship.

If the relationship occurs at a time or place, including the time or place entity helps English Query answer some questions. The entities associated with the relationship "authors write books" might appear as shown in this illustration.

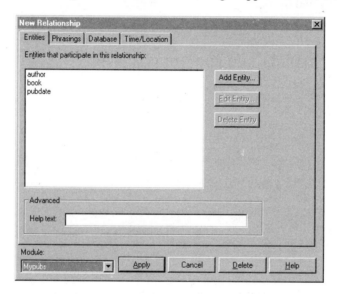

Phrasing

Next, you can create phrasings for the relationship. Phrasing types include verb phrasings ("authors write books"), preposition phrasings ("publishers are in cities"), adjective phrasings ("books are popular"), and subset phrasings ("some books are bestsellers"). Most trait phrasings ("books have royalties") and name phrasings ("author names are the names of authors") are created by **Autotrait** and **Autoname**.

This illustration shows the **Verb Phrasing** dialog box defined for "authors write books."

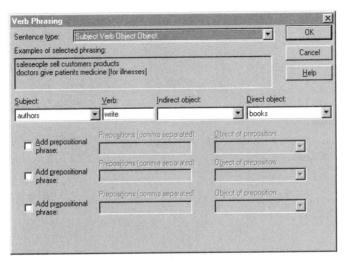

▶ **To create phrasings for a relationship**

1. On the **Semantics** tab, right-click **Relationships**, and then click **Insert Relationships…**.

2. In the **New Relationships** dialog box, on the **Phrasings** tab, click **Add…**.

3. In the **Select Phrasing** dialog box, select a phrasing type.

Time and Location

If a relationship occurs at a specific time or place, then it is helpful to anticipate some user questions and to supply the date or location entity on the **Time/Location** tab of the **New Relationship** dialog box.

You can create relationships for every kind of question you want the user to ask. For example, if you want the model to support questions about authors in cities, return to the "authors have cities" relationship and supply a new preposition phrasing that says "authors are in cities."

Testing Your Model

At any time during the development process, you can test what you have modeled by invoking **Test Application** from the **Tools** menu. For example, with only the "authors write books" relationship entered, English Query can answer questions such as "Who wrote the most books?", "Who wrote Net Etiquette?", and "What books did Anne Ringer write?"

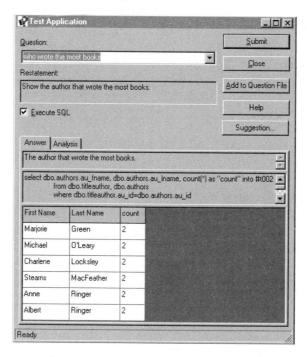

▶ **To test your application**

1. On the **Tools** menu, click **Test Application…**.

2. In the **Test Application** dialog box, in the **Question** box, enter your query as an English sentence, and then click **Submit**.

3. If you select **Execute SQL**, English Query submits the query to SQL Server and displays the answer.

4. If you think the question is useful as a sample, then click **Add to Question File**.

Another **Tools** menu item called **Regression Test** executes all queries in the question file and generates an output file. If you copy the output file to a reference file, then **Regression Test** allows you to compare the results of the most recent output against the reference file. This ensures that English Query can handle all questions as you continue to enhance your English Query domain. The question file questions also can be used as a set of sample questions that can be displayed on a Web page to give users an idea of the available information.

Building and Deploying

After you have developed and tested the model to your satisfaction inside the English Query authoring tool, you are ready to build the application. **Build Application** on the **Tools** menu creates the English Query domain (.eqd) file. The .eqd file and the English Query engine (the COM object called Mseq.Session) can be deployed inside any COM-supporting application.

Adding English Query to Your Web Site

An example framework for adding English Query to your Web site is provided in the Samples/Asp2 subdirectory of the Microsoft English Query directory. If you are running Microsoft Windows NT Server's built-in Web server, Microsoft Internet Information Services (IIS) version 4.0, and installing from your IIS computer, you can deploy a Web page that allows users to query your English Query domain by choosing the Setupasp.vbs file. This is a Windows Scripting Host (WSH) script that copies the ASP files and your created .eqd file to a directory on the Web server, creates an IIS virtual directory for the English Query pages, and sets options in a Params.inc file to point ASP scripts to your database.

If you are running IIS 3.0, perform the previous steps manually (the Readme.htm file also documents the steps).

Using English Query in ASP Applications

You can also use the sample application to begin integrating English Query into other ASP applications. For example, you might choose to have an English Query text box available on your search page or to supplement existing reporting mechanisms.

This code fragment (a simplified version of the ASP sample code) shows the essence of how to convert the questions supplied by users into SQL. You embed code such as this in the ASP that processed the user's query.

```
    ' create the English Query object
Set objEQSession = Server.CreateObject("Mseq.Session")
' load the domain
objEQSession.InitDomain ("c:\pubs\pubs.eqd")
' convert user's question to English Query response object
Set objEQResponse = objEQSession.ParseRequest(Request ("User Question"))
' determine what kind of response object it is
Select Case objEQResponse.Type
Case nlCommandResponse
    Set objCommands = objEQResponse.Commands
    For intCommand = 0 To objCommands.Count - 1
        Set objCommand = objCommands(intCommand)
        Select Case objCommand.CmdID
        Case nlQueryCmd
            ' execute the returned SQL and display to the user
            DoSQLCommand objCommand
        Case nlAnswerCmd
' just display the answer
    Response.Write objCommand.Answer
            End Select
Next
Case nlUserClarifyResponse
    DoClarification objEQResponse, strQuestion
Case nlErrorResponse
    Response.Write objEQResponse.Description & "<BR>"
End Select
```

Create an English Query object with **Server.CreateObject**(*"Mseq.Session"*). To load your domain, call the **InitDomain** method with the name of the .eqd file. Call **ParseRequest**() with the user's question and a **Response** object is returned. The **Response** object can be a **CommandResponse**, which is a collection of commands that are either SQL commands or direct answers. Each SQL command should be executed against your SQL Server database, and you can display the result as a table on the Web page. The process of executing the SQL command using ADO and displaying the result in a table is embedded in the **DoSQLCommand** function (available in Samples/Asp/Common.inc).

If the command is an answer, it is displayed directly to the user. The response might also be a request for clarification. For example, the question might be "What are all the compact cars in Washington?" and the clarification question might ask whether Washington is a city or a state. The **DoClarification** call (also available in Common.inc) encapsulates the code necessary to prompt the user to choose from possible values in the **UserInputs** collection on the **Response** object.

C H A P T E R   2 5

Distributed Queries: OLE DB Connectivity

This chapter describes how the Microsoft SQL Server version 7.0 query processor interacts with an OLE DB provider to enable distributed and heterogeneous queries. It is primarily intended for OLE DB provider developers, and assumes a good understanding of the OLE DB specification. The emphasis is on the OLE DB interface between the SQL Server query processor and the OLE DB provider, not on the distributed query functionality itself. For a full description of distributed querying functionality, see SQL Server Books Online.

Overview and Terminology

In Microsoft SQL Server version 7.0, distributed queries enable SQL Server users to access data outside a SQL Server-based server, either within other servers running SQL Server or other data sources that expose an OLE DB interface. OLE DB provides a way to uniformly access tabular data from heterogeneous data sources.

A distributed query for the purpose of this discussion is any SELECT, INSERT, UPDATE, or DELETE statement that references tables and rowsets from one or more external OLE DB data sources.

A remote table is a table that is stored in an OLE DB data source and is external to the server running SQL Server executing the query. A distributed query accesses one or more remote tables.

OLE DB Provider Categories

The following is a categorization of OLE DB providers based on their capabilities from a SQL Server distributed querying standpoint. As defined, these are not mutually exclusive; a given provider may belong to more than one of the following categories:

- SQL Command Providers
- Index Providers
- Simple Table Providers
- Non-SQL Command Providers

SQL Command Providers

Providers that support the **Command** object with a SQL standard dialect recognized by SQL Server belong to this category. The specific requirements for a given OLE DB provider to be treated as a SQL Command provider by SQL Server are:

- The provider must support the **Command** object and all of its mandatory OLE DB interfaces: **ICommand**, **ICommandText**, **IColumnsInfo**, **ICommandProperties**, and **IAccessor**.
- The SQL dialect supported by the provider must be at least ODBC Core level on the ODBC conformance scale or SQL 92 Entry level on the SQL-92 conformance scale. The dialect must be reported by the provider through the DBPROP_SQLSUPPORT property.

Examples of SQL Command providers are the Microsoft OLE DB Provider for SQL Server and the Microsoft OLE DB Provider for ODBC.

Index Providers

Index providers support and expose indexes according to OLE DB and allow index-based lookup of base tables. The specific requirements for a given OLE DB provider to be treated as an Index provider by SQL Server are:

- The provider must support the **IDBSchemaRowset** interface with the TABLES, COLUMNS and INDEXES schema rowsets.
- The provider must support opening a rowset on an index through **IOpenRowset** by specifying the index name and the corresponding base table name.
- The **Index** object must support all its mandatory interfaces: **IRowset**, **IRowsetIndex**, **IAccessor**, **IColumnsInfo**, **IRowsetInfo**, and **IConvertTypes**.

- Rowsets opened against the indexed base table (through **IOpenRowset**) must support the **IRowsetLocate** interface for positioning on a row based off a bookmark.

If the OLE DB provider meets the above requirements, users can set the **Index As Access Path** provider option to force SQL Server to use the provider's indexes to evaluate queries. By default, SQL Server does not attempt to use the provider's indexes unless this option is set.

Note SQL Server supports various options that influence how SQL Server accesses an OLE DB provider. The **Linked Server Properties** dialog box in SQL Server Enterprise Manager can be used to set these options.

Simple Table Providers

These are providers that expose the opening of a rowset against a base table through the **IOpenRowset** interface. Such providers are neither SQL Command providers nor Index providers; rather, they are the simplest class of providers that SQL Server distributed queries can work with.

Against such providers, SQL Server can perform only table scans during distributed query evaluation.

Non-SQL Command Providers

Providers that support the **Command** object and its mandatory interfaces but do not support a SQL standard dialect recognized by SQL Server fall into this category.

Two examples of Non-SQL Command providers are the Microsoft OLE DB Provider for Indexing Service and the Microsoft Windows NT® Active Directory Service Interfaces (ADSI) OLE DB provider.

Transact-SQL Subset

Each of the following classes of Transact-SQL statements is supported for distributed queries if the provider supports the required OLE DB interfaces.

- All SELECT statements are allowed except for SELECT INTO statements with a remote table as the destination table.
- INSERT statements are allowed against remote tables if the provider supports the required interfaces for insert. For more information about OLE DB requirements for INSERT, see "INSERT Statement" later in this chapter.

- UPDATE and DELETE statements are allowed against remote tables if the provider satisfies the OLE DB interface requirements on the specified table. For the OLE DB interface requirements and conditions under which a remote table can be updated or deleted, see "UPDATE and DELETE Statements" later in this chapter.

Cursor Support

Both snapshot and keyset cursors are supported against distributed queries if the provider supports the necessary OLE DB functionality. Dynamic cursors are not supported against distributed queries. A user request for a dynamic cursor against a distributed query is downgraded to a keyset cursor.

Snapshot cursors are populated at cursor open time and the result set remains unchanged; updates, inserts, and deletes to the underlying tables are not reflected in the cursor.

Keyset cursors are populated at cursor open time and the result set remains unchanged throughout the lifetime of the cursor. However, updates and deletes to underlying tables are visible in the cursor as the rows are visited. Inserts to underlying tables that may affect cursor membership are not visible.

A remote table can be updated or deleted through a cursor that is defined on a distributed query and references the remote table if the provider meets the conditions for updates and deletes on the remote table, for example, table UPDATE | DELETE <remote-table> WHERE CURRENT OF <cursor-name>. For more information, see "UPDATE and DELETE Statements" later in this chapter.

Keyset Cursor Support Requirements

A keyset cursor is supported on a distributed query if all the Transact-SQL syntax requirements are met and either of these exist:

- The OLE DB provider supports reusable bookmarks on all the remote tables in the query. Reusable bookmarks can be consumed from a rowset on a given table and used on a different rowset of the same table. The support for reusable bookmarks is indicated through the TABLES_INFO schema rowset of **IDBSchemaRowset** by setting the BOOKMARK_DURABILITY column to BMK_DURABILITY_INTRANSACTION or a higher durability.

- All the remote tables expose a unique key through the INDEXES rowset of **IDBSchemaRowset** interface. There should be an index entry with the UNIQUE column set to VARIANT_TRUE.

Updatable Keyset Cursor Requirements

A remote table can be updated or deleted through a keyset cursor that is defined on a distributed query, for example, UPDATE | DELETE <remote-table> WHERE CURRENT OF <cursor-name>. The following are the conditions under which updatable cursors against distributed queries are allowed:

- Updatable cursors are allowed if the provider also meets the conditions for updates and deletes on the remote table. For more information, see "UPDATE and DELETE Statements" later in this chapter.

- All the updatable keyset cursor operations must be in a user-defined transaction with read-repeatable isolation level or a higher isolation level. Furthermore, the provider must support distributed transactions with the **ITransactionJoin** interface.

OLE DB Provider Interaction Phases

These operations are common to all distributed query execution scenarios:

- Connection establishment and property retrieval operations indicate how SQL Server connects to an OLE DB provider and what provider properties are used.

- Table name resolution and metadata retrieval operations indicate how SQL Server resolves the remote table name (which is specified in one of two ways, either a linked server based name or an ad hoc name) into the appropriate data object in the provider. This also includes the table metadata that SQL Server retrieves from the provider in order to compile and optimize a distributed query.

- Transaction management operations specify all transaction-related interaction with the OLE DB provider.

- Data type handling operations indicate how OLE DB data types are handled by SQL Server when it consumes data from or exports data to an OLE DB provider while processing a distributed query.

- Error handling operations indicate how SQL Server uses extended error information from the provider.

- Security operations specify how SQL Server security interacts with the provider's security.

Connection Establishment and Property Retrieval

SQL Server supports two remote data object naming conventions: linked server-based four-part names and ad hoc names using the OPENROWSET function.

Linked server-based names

A linked server serves as an abstraction to an OLE DB data source. A linked server–based name is a four-part name of the form <linked-server>.<catalog>. <schema>.<object>, where <linked-server> is the name of the linked server. SQL Server interprets <linked-server> to derive the OLE DB provider and the connection attributes that identify the data source to the provider. The other three-name parts are interpreted by the OLE DB data source to identify the specific remote table.

Ad hoc names

An ad hoc name is a name based on the OPENROWSET function. It includes all the connection information (that is, the OLE DB provider to use, the attributes needed to identify the data source, the user ID and password) every time the remote table is referenced in a distributed query.

If a linked server name is used, SQL Server extracts from the linked server definition the OLE DB provider name and the initialization properties for the provider. If an ad hoc name is used, SQL Server extracts the same information from the arguments of the OPENROWSET function.

For detailed instructions about setting up a linked server using a four-part name and ad hoc name–based syntax, see SQL Server Books Online.

Connecting to an OLE DB Provider

These are the high-level steps that SQL Server performs when it connects to an OLE DB provider:

SQL Server creates a data source object.

SQL Server uses the provider's ProgID to instantiate its data source object (DSO). The ProgID is specified as the *provider_name* parameter of a linked server configuration or as the first argument of the OPENROWSET function in the case of an ad hoc name.

SQL Server instantiates the provider's DSO through the OLE DB service component interface **IDataInitialize**. This allows the Service Component Manager to aggregate its services, such as scrollability and update support, above the native functionality of the provider. Further, instantiating the provider through **IDataInitialize** allows the OLE DB service component to pool connections to the provider, thereby reducing some of the connection and initialization overhead.

A given provider can be configured to be instantiated either in the same process as SQL Server or in its own process. Instantiating in a separate process protects the SQL Server process from failures in the provider. At the same time, there is a performance overhead associated with marshalling OLE DB calls out-of-process from SQL Server. A provider can be configured to be instantiated in-process or out-of-process by setting the **Allow In Process** provider option. For information about setting provider options, see SQL Server Books Online.

To take advantage of the OLE DB service components and session pooling, see the OLE DB documentation for provider requirements.

The data source is initialized.

After the DSO has been created, the **IDBProperties** interface sets the DBPROP_INIT_TIMEOUT initialization property if the server configuration option **remote login timeout** is greater than 0; this is a required property.

These properties are set if they are specified or implied in either the linked server definition or in the second argument of the OPENROWSET function:

- DBPROP_INIT_PROVIDERSTRING
- DBPROP_INIT_DATASOURCE
- DBPROP_INIT_LOCATION
- DBPROP_INIT_CATALOG
- DBPROP_AUTH_USERID
- DBPROP_AUTH_PASSWORD

After these properties are set, **IDBInitialize::Initialize** is called to initialize the DSO with the specified properties.

SQL Server gathers provider-specific information.

SQL Server gathers several provider properties to be used in distributed query evaluation; these properties are retrieved by calling **IDBProperties::GetProperties**. All of these properties are optional; however, supporting all relevant properties allows SQL Server to take full advantage of the provider's capabilities. For instance, DBPROP_SQLSUPPORT is needed to determine whether SQL Server can send queries to the provider. If this property is not supported, SQL Server will not use the remote provider as a SQL command provider even if it is one. In the following table, the Default value column indicates what value SQL Server assumes if the provider does not support the property.

Property	Default value	Use
DBPROP_DBMSNAME	None	Used for error messages.
DBPROP_DBMSVER	None	Used for error messages.
DBPROP_PROVIDERNAME	None	Used for error messages.
DBPROP_PROVIDEROLEDBVER	1.5	Used to determine availability of 2.0 features.
DBPROP_CONCATNULLBEHAVIOR	None	Used to determine whether the NULL concatenation behavior of provider is the same as SQL Server.
DBPROP_NULLCOLLATION	None	Allows sorting/index-use only if NULLCOLLATION matches SQL Server's null collation behavior.
DBPROP_OLEOBJECTS	None	Determines whether provider supports structured storage interfaces for large data object columns.
DBPROP_STRUCTUREDSTORAGE	None	Determines which of the structured storage interfaces are supported for large object types (among **ILockBytes**, **Istream**, and **ISequentialStream**).
DBPROP_MULTIPLESTORAGEOBJECTS	False	Determines whether more than one large object column can be open at the same time.
DBPROP_SQLSUPPORT	None	Determines whether SQL queries can be sent to the provider.

(continued)

Property	Default value	Use
DBPROP_CATALOGLOCATION	DBDROPVAL CL_START	Used to construct multipart table names.
SQLPROP_DYNAMICSQL	False	SQL Server-specific property: if it returns VARIANT_TRUE, it indicates that '?' parameter markers are supported for parameterized query execution.
SQLPROP_NESTEDQUERIES	False	SQL Server specific property: if it returns VARIANT_TRUE, it indicates that the provider supports nested SELECT statements in the FROM clause.

The following three literals are retrieved from **IDBInfo::GetLiteralInfo**: DBLITERAL_CATALOG_SEPARATOR, DBLITERAL_SCHEMA_SEPARATOR (to construct a full object name given its catalog, schema, and object name parts), and DBLITERAL_QUOTE (to quote identifier names in a SQL query sent to the provider).

If the provider does not support the separator literals, SQL Server uses a period (.) as the default separator character. If the provider supports only the catalog separator character but not the schema separator character, SQL Server uses the catalog separator character as the schema separator character also. If the provider does not support DBLITERAL_QUOTE, SQL Server uses a single quotation mark (') as the quoting character.

Note If the provider's name separator literals do not match these default values, the provider must expose them through **IDBInfo** for SQL Server to access its tables through four-part names. If these literals are not exposed, only pass-through queries can be used against such a provider.

For information about exposing the SQLPROP_DYNAMICSQL and SQLPROP_NESTEDQUERIES properties, see "SQL Server-Specific Properties" later in this chapter.

Table Name Resolution and Metadata Retrieval

SQL Server resolves a given remote table name in a distributed query to a specific table or view in an OLE DB data source. Both the linked server–based and ad hoc naming schemes result in a three-part name to be interpreted by the provider. In the case of the linked server–based name, the last three parts of the four-part name form the catalog, schema, and object names. In the case of the ad hoc name, the third argument of the OPENROWSET function specifies a three-part name that describes the catalog, schema, and object names. One or both of the catalog and schema names can be empty. (A four-part name with an empty catalog name and schema name looks like <server-name>...<object-name>.) In such a case, SQL Server uses NULL as the corresponding value to look for in the schema rowset tables.

The name resolution rules and the metadata retrieval steps that SQL Server employs depend on whether the provider supports the **IDBSchemaRowset** interface on the **Session** object.

If **IDBSchemaRowset** is supported, TABLES, COLUMNS, INDEXES, and TABLES_INFO schema rowsets are used from the **IDBSchemaRowset** interface. (The TABLES_INFO schema rowset is defined in OLE DB 2.0.) SQL Server restricts the schema rowsets returned by the **IDBSchemaRowset** interface to look for schema rows that match the specified remote table name parts. The following are the rules related to the restrictions supported by the provider on the schema rowsets and how SQL Server uses them to retrieve a remote table's metadata:

- Restrictions on TABLE_NAME and COLUMN_NAME columns are always required.

- If the provider supports a restriction on TABLE_CATALOG (or TABLE_SCHEMA), SQL Server uses that restriction on TABLE_CATALOG (or TABLE_SCHEMA). If catalog (or schema) name is not specified in the remote table name, a null value is used as the corresponding restriction value. If a catalog (or schema) name is specified, the provider must support the corresponding restriction on TABLE_CATALOG (or TABLE_SCHEMA).

- The provider must either support restriction on the TABLE_SCHEMA column in both TABLES and COLUMNS or support them on neither. The provider must either support catalog name restriction on both TABLES and COLUMNS rowsets or support them on neither.

- If any restrictions are supported on INDEXES, the provider must support schema restriction on both TABLES and INDEXES or support them on neither. The provider must either support catalog name restriction on both TABLES and INDEXES rowsets or support them on neither.

From the TABLES schema rowset, SQL Server retrieves the
TABLE_CATALOG, TABLE_SCHEMA, TABLE_NAME, TABLE_TYPE,
TABLE_GUID columns by setting restrictions according to the above rules.

From the COLUMNS schema rowset, SQL Server retrieves the
TABLE_CATALOG, TABLE_SCHEMA, TABLE_NAME, COLUMN_NAME,
COLUMN_GUID, ORDINAL_POSITION, COLUMN_FLAGS,
IS_NULLABLE, DATA_TYPE, TYPE_GUID,
CHARACTER_MAXIMUM_LENGTH, NUMERIC_PRECISION, and
NUMERIC_SCALE columns. COLUMN_NAME, DATA_TYPE and
ORDINAL_POSITION must return valid nonnull values. If DATA_TYPE is
DBTYPE_NUMERIC or DBTYPE_DECIMAL, the corresponding
NUMERIC_PRECISION and NUMERIC_SCALE must be valid nonnull values.

From the optional INDEXES schema rowset, SQL Server looks for indexes on the
specified remote table by setting restrictions as per the previous rules. From the
matching index entries thus found, SQL Server retrieves the TABLE_CATALOG,
TABLE_SCHEMA, TABLE_NAME, INDEX_CATALOG, INDEX_SCHEMA,
INDEX_NAME, PRIMARY_KEY, UNIQUE, CLUSTERED, FILL_FACTOR,
ORDINAL_POSITION, COLUMN_NAME, COLLATION, CARDINALITY,
and PAGES columns.

From the optional TABLES_INFO rowset, SQL Server looks for additional
information on the specified remote table such as bookmark support, the type and
the length of the bookmark. All columns except the DESCRIPTION column of
the TABLES_INFO rowset are used. The information in TABLES_INFO rowset
is used as follows:

- The BOOKMARK_DURABILITY column is used to implement more
  efficient keyset cursors. If this column has a value of
  BMK_DURABILITY_INTRANSACTION or a higher durability value,
  SQL Server uses bookmark-based retrieval and updates of remote table rows
  for implementing a keyset cursor.

- The BOOKMARK_TYPE, BOOKMARK_DATA TYPE, and
  BOOKMARK_MAXIMUM_LENGTH columns are used to determine
  bookmark metadata at query compilation time. If these columns are not
  supported, SQL Server opens the base table rowset through **IOpenRowset**
  during compilation to get the bookmark information.

If **IDBSchemaRowset** is not supported and the remote table name includes a
catalog or schema name, SQL Server requires **IDBSchemaRowset** and returns an
error. However, if neither the catalog nor the schema names are supplied,
SQL Server opens the rowset that corresponds to the remote table and retrieves
the column metadata from the mandatory **IColumnsInfo** interface of the rowset
object.

SQL Server opens the rowset corresponding to the table by calling **IOpenRowset::OpenRowset**. The table name supplied to OPENROWSET is constructed from the catalog, schema, and object name parts.

- Each of the name parts (catalog, schema, object name) are quoted with the provider's quoting character (DBLITERAL_QUOTE) and then concatenated with the DBLITERAL_CATALOG_SEPARATOR character and the DBLITERAL_SCHEMA_SEPARATOR character embedded between them. The name construction follows the OLE DB rules in **IOpenRowset**.

- The column metadata for the table is retrieved through **IColumnsInfo::GetColumnInfo** after the rowset object is opened.

If **IDBSchemaRowset** is not supported with TABLES, COLUMNS, and TABLES_INFO rowsets, SQL Server opens the rowset against the base table twice: once during query compilation to retrieve metadata, and once during query execution. Providers that incur side effects from opening the rowset (for example, run code that alters the state of a real-time device, send e-mail, run arbitrary user-supplied code) must be aware of this behavior.

Transaction Management

SQL Server supports transaction-based access to distributed data by using the provider's **ITransactionLocal** (for local transaction) and **ITransactionJoin** (for distributed transactions) OLE DB interfaces. By starting a local transaction against the provider, SQL Server guarantees atomic write operations. By using distributed transactions, SQL Server ensures that a transaction that involves multiple nodes has the same result (either commit or abort) in all the nodes. If the provider does not support the requisite OLE DB transaction-related interfaces, update operations against that provider are not allowed depending on the local transaction context.

The following table describes what happens when the user executes a distributed query. A read operation against a provider involves either a SELECT statement or reading a remote table into the input side of a SELECT INTO, INSERT, UPDATE, or DELETE statement. A write operation against a provider refers to an INSERT, UPDATE, or DELETE statement with a remote table as the destination table.

Distributed query occurs	Provider does not support ITransactionLocal	Provider supports ITransactionLocal but not ITransactionJoin	Provider supports both ITransactionLocal and ITransactionJoin
In a transaction by itself (no user transaction).	By default, only read operations are allowed. When the provider level option **Nontransacted Updates** is enabled, write operations are allowed. (When this option is enabled, SQL Server cannot guarantee atomicity and consistency on the provider's data. This can cause partial effects of a write operation to be reflected in the remote data source without the ability to undo them.)	All statements are allowed against remote data. Keyset cursors are read-only. The local transaction is started on the provider with the current SQL Server session's isolation level and is committed at the end of successful statement evaluation. (The default isolation level for a SQL Server session is READ COMMITTED unless it is modified with the SET TRANSACTION ISOLATION LEVEL statement. The provider must support the requested isolation level.)	All statements are allowed. Keyset cursors are read-only. The local transaction is started on the provider with the current SQL Server session's isolation level and is committed at the end of a successful statement evaluation.
In a user transaction (that is, between BEGIN TRAN or BEGIN DISTRIBUTED TRAN and COMMIT).	If the isolation level of the transaction is READ COMMITTED (the default) or below, read operations are allowed. If the isolation level is higher, no distributed queries are allowed.	Only read operations are allowed. New distributed transactions are started on the provider with the current SQL Server session's isolation level.	All statements are allowed. New distributed transaction is started on the provider with the current SQL Server session's isolation level and committed when the user transaction commits. For data modification statements, by default SQL Server starts a nested transaction under the distributed transaction, so that the data modification statement can be stopped under certain error conditions without stopping the surrounding transaction. If the XACT_ABORT SET option is on, SQL Server does not require nested transaction support and stops the surrounding transaction in the case of errors during the data modification statement.

Data Type Handling in Distributed Queries

OLE DB providers expose their data in terms of the OLE DB-defined data types (indicated by DBTYPE in OLE DB). SQL Server processes external data inside the server as native SQL Server types; this results in a mapping of OLE DB data types to SQL Server native types and vice versa as data is consumed by SQL Server or exported by SQL Server, respectively. This mapping is done implicitly unless otherwise noted.

Data types in distributed queries are handled by using one of two mapping methods:

- Consumption-side mapping maps types from OLE DB data types to SQL Server native data types on the consuming side, when remote tables appear in SELECT statements and on the input side of INSERT, UPDATE, and DELETE statements.

- Export-side mapping maps types from SQL Server data types to OLE DB data types on the exporting side, when a remote table appears as the destination table of an INSERT or UPDATE statement.

OLE DB type	DBCOLUMNFLAG	SQL Server data type
DBTYPE_I1*		numeric(3, 0)
DBTYPE_I2		smallint
DBTYPE_I4		int
DBTYPE_UI8		numeric(19,0)
DBTYPE_UI1		tinyint
DBTYPE_UI2*		numeric(5,0)
DBTYPE_UI4*		numeric(10,0)
DBTYPE_UI8*		numeric(20,0)
DBTYPE_R4		float
DBTYPE_R8		real
DBTYPE_NUMERIC		numeric
DBTYPE_DECIMAL		decimal
DBTYPE_CY		money
DBTYPE_BSTR	DBCOLUMNFLAGS_ISFIXEDLENGTH =true or Max Length > 4000 characters	ntext
DBTYPE_BSTR	DBCOLUMNFLAGS_ISFIXEDLENGTH =true	nchar
DBTYPE_BSTR	DBCOLUMNFLAGS_ISFIXEDLENGTH =false	nvarchar

(continued)

OLE DB type	DBCOLUMNFLAG	SQL Server data type
DBTYPE_IDISPATCH		Error
DBTYPE_ERROR		Error
DBTYPE_BOOL		bit
DBTYPE_VARIANT*		**nvarchar**
DBTYPE_IUNKNOWN		Error
DBTYPE_GUID		**uniqueidentifier**
DBTYPE_BYTES	DBCOLUMNFLAGS_ISLONG=true or Max Length > 8000	**image**
DBTYPE_BYTES	DBCOLUMNFLAGS_ISROWVER=true, DBCOLUMNFLAGS_ISFIXEDLENGTH =true, Column size = 8	**timestamp**
DBTYPE_BYTES	DBCOLUMNFLAGS_ISFIXEDLENGTH =true	**binary**
DBTYPE_BYTES	DBCOLUMNFLAGS_ISFIXEDLENGTH =true	**varbinary**
DBTYPE_STR	DBCOLUMNFLAGS_ISFIXEDLENGTH =true	**char**
DBTYPE_STR	DBCOLUMNFLAGS_ISFIXEDLENGTH =true	**varchar**
DBTYPE_STR	DBCOLUMNFLAGS_ISLONG=true or Max Length > 8000 characters	**text**
DBTYPE_WSTR	DBCOLUMNFLAGS_ISFIXED=true	**nchar**
DBTYPE_WSTR	DBCOLUMNFLAGS_ISFIXEDLENGTH =true	**nvarchar**
DBTYPE_WSTR	DBCOLUMNFLAGS_ISLONG=true or Max Length >4000 characters	**ntext**
DBTYPE_UDT		Error
DBTYPE_DATE*		**datetime**
DBTYPE_DBDATE		**datetime** (explicit conversion required)
DBTYPE_DBTIME		**datetime** (explicit conversion required)
DBTYPE_DBTIMESTAMP*		**datetime**
DBTYPE_ARRAY		Error
DBTYPE_BYREF		Ignored

(continued)

OLE DB type	DBCOLUMNFLAG	SQL Server data type
DBTYPE_VECTOR		Error
DBTYPE_RESERVED		Error

* Indicates some form of translation to the SQL Server type's representation, as there is no exact equivalent data type in SQL Server. Such conversions could result in loss of precision, overflow, or underflow. The default implicit mappings can be changed in the future if the corresponding data types are supported by future SQL Server releases.

Note **numeric(p,s)** indicates SQL Server data type **numeric** with precision p and scale s. The maximum allowed precision for DBTYPE_NUMERIC and DBTYPE_DECIMAL is 38. The provider must support binding to the DBTYPE_BSTR column as DBTYPE_WSTR while creating an accessor. DBTYPE_VARIANT columns are consumed as Unicode character strings **nvarchar**. This requires support for conversion from DBTYPE_VARIANT to DBTYPE_WSTR from the provider. The provider is expected to implement this conversion as defined in OLE DB. For more information, see "OLE DB Interfaces Consumed by SQL Server" later in this chapter.

How to Interpret the Table

The mapping to a SQL Server type is determined by the OLE DB data type and the DBCOLUMNFLAGS values that describe the column or scalar value. In the case of the COLUMNS schema rowset, the DATA_TYPE and COLUMN_FLAGS columns represent these values. In the case of the **IColumnsInfo::GetColumnInfo** interface, the wType and dwFlags members of the DBCOLUMNINFO structure represent this information.

To use consumption-side mapping for a given column with a specific DBTYPE and DBCOLUMNFLAG value, look for the corresponding SQL Server type in the table. The type rules for columns from remote tables in expressions can be described by the following simple rule:

A given remote column value is legal in a Transact-SQL expression if the corresponding mapped SQL Server type in the table is legal in the same context.

The table and the rule define:

- Comparisons and expressions.

  In general, X <op> <remote-column> is a valid expression if <op> is a valid operator on the data type of X and the data type that <remote-column> maps to.

- Explicit conversions.

  Convert(X, <remote-column>) is allowed if the DBTYPE of <remote-column> maps to native data type Y (as per table above) and explicit conversion from Y to X is allowed.

If users want remote data to be converted to a nondefault native data type, they must use an explicit conversion.

To use export-side mapping in the case of UPDATE and INSERT statements against remote tables, map native SQL Server data types to OLE DB data types using the same table. A mapping from a SQL Server type S1 to a given OLE DB type T is allowed if either of these exist:

- The corresponding mapping can be found in Table 2 directly.
- There is an allowed implicit conversion of S1 to another SQL Server type S2 such that S2 maps to type T in Table 2.

Large Object Handling

As indicated in the table, if columns of the type DBTYPE_STR, DBTYPE_WSTR, or DBTYPE_BSTR also report DBCOLUMNFLAGS_ISLONG, or if their maximum length exceeds 4,000 characters, SQL Server treats them as a **text** or **ntext** column as appropriate. Similarly, for DBTYPE_BYTES columns, if DBCOLUMNFLAGS_ISLONG is set or if the maximum length is higher than 8,000 bytes, the columns are treated as **image** columns.

SQL Server does not expose the full text and image functionality on large objects from an OLE DB provider. TEXTPTRS are not supported on large objects from an OLE DB provider; hence, none of the related functionality is supported, for example, the TEXTPTR system function and READTEXT, WRITETEXT, and UPDATETEXT statements. SELECT statements that retrieve entire large object columns are supported, as are UPDATE and INSERT statements for entire large object columns in remote tables.

For SQL Server to access large object columns through a distributed query, the provider must support at least one of the following structured storage interfaces on the large object in increasing order of preference and functionality: **ISequentialStream**, **Istream**, or **ILockBytes**. Accordingly, the provider must return DBPROPVAL_OO_BLOB as the value of the DBPROP_OLEOBJECTS property when it is queried through the **IDBProperties** interface. Also, the provider must indicate support for at least one of these interfaces in the DBPROP_STRUCTUREDSTORAGE property.

Accessing Large Object Columns

At query execution, SQL Server performs the following steps to retrieve large object columns:

Before opening the rowset through **IOpenRowset::OpenRowset**, SQL Server requests support for one or more of the structured storage interfaces (**ISequentialStream**, **Istream**, and **ILockBytes**) on the large object columns. The first interface supported by the provider is required; additional interfaces are requested as "set if cheap" by setting the *dwOptions* element of the corresponding DBPROP structure to DBPROPOPTIONS_SETIFCHEAP. For example, if a provider supports both **ISequentialStream** and **ILockBytes**, **ISequentialStream** is required and **ILockBytes** is requested as "set if chcap."

After the rowset is opened, SQL Server uses **IRowsetInfo::GetProperties** to identify the actual interfaces available in the rowset. The last or most preferable interface that the provider returned is used. When SQL Server creates an accessor against the large object column, the column is bound as DBTYPE_IUNKNOWN with the *iid* element of the DBOBJECT structure in the binding set to the interface.

Reading from Large Object Columns

Use the interface pointer for the requested structured storage interface returned in the row buffer from **IRowset::GetData** to read from the large object column. If the provider does not support multiple open large objects at the same time (that is, if it does not support DBPROP_MULTIPLE_STORAGEOBJECTS) and if the row has multiple large object columns, SQL Server copies the large object columns into a local work table.

UPDATE and INSERT Statements on Large Object Columns

SQL Server passes to the provider a pointer to a new storage object rather than using the provider-supplied interface to modify the storage object. For each large object column, the value that is updated or inserted on a storage object is created with the chosen structured storage interface. Depending on whether it is an UPDATE or an INSERT operation, a pointer to the storage object is passed to the provider through **IRowsetChange::SetData** or **IRowsetChange::InsertRow**, respectively.

Error Handling

When a specific method invocation against an OLE DB provider returns an error code, SQL Server looks for the provider's extended error information before returning information about the error condition to the user.

SQL Server uses the OLE DB error object as specified by OLE DB. Some of the high-level steps are:

- When a method invocation returns an error code from the provider, SQL Server looks for the **ISupportErrorInfo** interface. If this interface is supported, SQL Server calls **ISupportErrorInfo::InterfaceSupportsErrorInfo** to verify whether error objects are supported by the interface that produced the error code.

- If error objects are supported by the interface, SQL Server calls the **GetErrorInfo** function to get an **IErrorInfo** interface pointer on the current error object.

- SQL Server uses the **IErrorInfo** interface to get a pointer to the **IErrorRecords** interface.

- SQL Server uses **IErrorRecords** to loop through all the error records in the object and get the error message text corresponding to each record.

For more information about how the provider's error object is used, see your OLE DB documentation.

Security

When a consumer connects to an OLE DB provider, the provider typically requires a user ID and a password, unless the consumer wants to be authenticated as an integrated security user. In the case of distributed queries, SQL Server acts as the OLE DB provider's consumer on behalf of the SQL Server login that executes the distributed query. SQL Server maps the current SQL Server login to a user ID and password on the linked server.

These mappings can be specified by the user for a given linked server and can be set up and managed by the system stored procedures **sp_addlinkedsrvlogin** and **sp_droplinkedsrvlogin**. By setting the initialization group properties DBPROP_AUTH_USERID and DBPROP_AUTH_PASSWORD through **IDBProperties::SetProperties**, the user ID and password determined by the mapping are passed to the provider during connection establishment.

When a client connects to SQL Server through Windows NT Authentication, SQL Server does not propagate the Windows NT Authentication to a provider. In this case, the Windows NT authenticated logins must map to a specific user ID and password to access a linked server.

After the security context used for the connection is determined, the authentication of this security context and the permission checking for that context against data objects in the data source are entirely up to the OLE DB provider.

For more information about **sp_addlinkedsrvlogin** and **sp_droplinkedsrvlogin**, see SQL Server Books Online.

Query Execution Scenarios

When evaluating a distributed query, SQL Server interacts with the OLE DB provider in one or more of these scenarios:

- Remote query
- Indexed access
- Pure table scans
- UPDATE and DELETE statements
- INSERT statement
- Pass-through queries

Remote Query

SQL Server generates a SQL query that evaluates a portion of the original query that can be evaluated in its entirety by the provider. This scenario is possible only against SQL Command providers. For the subset of the SQL grammar that is used by SQL Server to generate remote queries, see "Transact-SQL Subset Used for Generating Remote Queries" later in this chapter.

When SQL Server generates the SQL text to be executed remotely, the table and column names are quoted with the quoting character of the provider as reported through the DBLITERAL_QUOTE literal of the **IDBInfo** interface. If this literal is not supported, table and column names are not quoted.

If the provider supports parameterized query execution, SQL Server considers a parameterized query execution strategy to evaluate a join of a remote table with a local table. The parameterized query is executed repeatedly for parameter values generated from each row of the local table. This strategy reduces the number of rows that are retrieved from the provider and is beneficial when a local table with a small number of rows is joined with a remote table with a large number of rows. This remote join strategy can be enforced by the REMOTE join optimizer hint. For more information about parameterized query execution, see SQL Server Books Online.

The following are the higher-level steps against the provider in the remote query scenario:

- SQL Server creates a **Command** object from the **Session** object by using **IDBCreateCommand::CreateCommand**.
- If the **Remote Query Timeout** server configuration option is set to a value > 0, SQL Server sets the DBPROP_COMMANDTIMEOUT property on the **Command** object to the same value by using **ICommandProperties::SetProperties**; **ICommand::SetCommandText** must be called to set the command text to the generated Transact-SQL string.

- SQL Server calls **ICommandPrepare::Prepare** to prepare the command. If the provider does not support this interface, SQL Server continues with Step 4.

- If the generated query is parameterized, SQL Server uses **ICommandWithParameters::SetParameterInfo** to describe the parameters and **IAccessor::CreateAccessor** to create accessors for the parameters.

- SQL Server calls **ICommand::Execute** to execute the command and create the rowset.

- SQL Server uses the **IRowset** interface to navigate and consume rows from the table. Use **IRowset::GetNextRows** to fetch rows, **IRowset::RestartPosition** to reposition to the beginning of the rowset, and **IRowset::ReleaseRows** to release rows.

Provider Properties of Interest for Remote Query Execution

The Transact-SQL grammar supported by the provider determines the extent to which SQL Server can delegate query execution.

In many cases, SQL Server uses nested SELECT statements in the FROM clause of a query when it generates the query strings to be executed remotely. Because nested SELECT support is not required by SQL-92 entry level, SQL Server does not delegate queries with nested SELECT statements to the provider by default. However, the provider can support a SQL Server specific property called SQLPROP_NESTEDQUERIES through **IDBProperties**, which enables SQL Server to take advantage of nested queries. Alternatively, the administrator can also set the **Nested Queries** provider option on a particular provider to make SQL Server generate nested queries against the provider.

SQL Server uses parameterized query execution with a question mark (?) as the parameter marker in the Transact-SQL string. Parameterized query execution is used against the SQL Server, Jet, and Oracle OLE DB providers. Against other providers, parameterized query execution is used if the provider supports **ICommandWithParameters** on the **Command** object and at least one of the following conditions are met:

- The provider indicates the ODBC Core level of SQL Server support through the DBPROP_SQLSUPPORT property.

- The provider indicates support for the question mark (?) parameter marker by supporting the SQLPROP_DYNAMICSQL SQL Server-specific property through **IDBProperties**. For more information, see "SQL Server-Specific Properties" later in this chapter.

- The administrator sets the **Dynamic Parameters** provider option on the provider to make SQL Server generate parameterized queries.

Character Set and Sort Order Implications

SQL Server has a server-wide, character-set code page for non-Unicode (based on ANSI code pages) string data. There are also server-wide sort orders defined for both Unicode and non-Unicode character data. The sort order used to evaluate string comparisons and sorting in a distributed query is always the local sort order of the server. Similarly, non-Unicode string data from a remote table is interpreted in the code page defined in the local SQL Server.

SQL Server delegates string comparisons to the provider only if the character set (for non-Unicode data), sort order, and string comparison semantics used by the linked server are the same as those used by the local server.

In the case of SQL Server linked servers, SQL Server automatically determines character set and sort order compatibility. For other providers, the administrator must indicate to SQL Server whether the linked server has the same character set, sort order, and string comparison semantics as the local SQL Server. If the semantics are the same, the **Collation Compatible** linked server option can be set to true by using the **sp_serveroption** stored procedure. This option should be set to true only if both of the following conditions are met:

- The remote sort order and character set are the same as the local SQL Server.

- The string comparison semantics used by the OLE DB provider follow that of SQL-92 standard specifications or equivalently the comparison semantics of SQL Server.

Indexed Access

SQL Server uses an index exposed by the provider to evaluate certain predicates of the distributed query. This scenario is possible only against Index providers and when the user sets the **Index as Access Path** provider option. The following are the major high-level steps that SQL Server performs against the provider while using an index to execute a query:

- Opens the index rowset through **IOpenRowset::OpenRowset** with the full table name and index name. The full table and index names are generated as described in the remote queries scenario.

- Opens the base table rowset through **IOpenRowset::OpenRowset** with the full table name.

- Sets ranges on the index rowset based on the query predicate through **IRowsetIndex::SetRange**.

- Scans rows off the index rowset through **IRowset** on the index rowset.

- Uses the bookmark column from the retrieved index rows to fetch corresponding rows from the base table rowset through **IRowsetLocate::GetRowsByBookmark**.

- The rowset properties DBPROP_IRowsetLocate and DBPROP_BOOKMARKS are required on the rowset opened against the base table.

Pure Table Scans

SQL Server scans the entire remote table from the provider and performs all query evaluation locally. The rowset corresponding to the table is opened by calling **IOpenRowset::OpenRowset**. SQL Server constructs the table name supplied to OPENROWSET from the catalog, schema, and object name parts as follows:

1. Each of the name parts are quoted with the provider's quoting character (DBLITERAL_QUOTE) and then concatenated with the DBLITERAL_CATALOG_SEPARATOR character embedded between them.

2. After the rowset object is opened, SQL Server uses the **IColumnsInfo** interface to verify that the execution-time metadata is the same as compile-time metadata for the table.

3. SQL Server uses the **IRowset** interface to navigate and consume rows from the table. Use **IRowset::GetNextRows** to fetch rows, **IRowset::RestartPosition** to reposition to the beginning of the rowset, and **IRowset::ReleaseRows** to release rows.

UPDATE and DELETE Statements

The following conditions must be satisfied for a remote table to be updated or deleted from a SQL Server distributed query:

- The provider must support bookmarks for the rowset opened through **IOpenRowset** on the table being updated or deleted.

- The provider must support the **IRowsetLocate** and **IRowsetChange** interfaces on the rowset opened through **IOpenRowset** for the table being updated or deleted.

- The **IRowsetChange** interface must support update (**SetData**) and delete (**DeleteRows**) methods.

- If the provider does not support **ITransactionLocal**, UPDATE/DELETE statements are allowed only if the **Non-transacted** option is set for that provider and if the statement is not in a user transaction.

- If the provider does not support **ITransactionJoin**, an UPDATE/DELETE statement is allowed only if it is not in a user transaction.

The following rowset properties are required on the rowset opened against the updated table: DBPROP_IRowsetLocate, DBPROP_IRowsetChange, and DBPROP_BOOKMARKS. The DBPROP_UPDATABILITY rowset property is set to DBPROPVAL_UP_CHANGE or DBPROPVAL_UP_DELETE depending on whether the operation performed is an UPDATE or a DELETE, respectively.

The following high-level steps against the provider for processing an UPDATE or DELETE operation are performed:

1. SQL Server opens the base table rowset through the **IOpenRowset** interface. SQL Server requires the above-mentioned properties on the rowset.

2. SQL Server determines the set of qualifying rows to be updated or deleted.

3. SQL Server uses the bookmarks to position on the qualifying rows through the **IRowsetLocate** interface.

4. Use **IRowsetChange::SetData** for UPDATE operations or **IRowsetChange::DeleteRows** for delete operations to perform the required changes on the qualifying rows.

INSERT Statement

The conditions for supporting INSERT statements against a remote table are less stringent than for UPDATE and DELETE statements:

- The provider must support **IRowsetChange::InsertRow** on the rowset opened on the base table being inserted into.

- If the provider does not support **ITransactionLocal**, INSERT statements are allowed only if the **Non-transacted updates** option is set for that linked server and if the statement is not in a user transaction.

- If the provider does not support **ITransactionJoin**, INSERT statements are allowed only if they are not in a user transaction.

SQL Server uses **IOpenRowset::OpenRowset** to open a rowset on the base table and calls **IRowsetChange::InsertRow** to insert new rows into the base rowset.

Pass-through Queries

This scenario is similar to the scenario in "Remote Query" except that the command text given to **ICommand** is a command string submitted by the user and is not interpreted by SQL Server. SQL Server uses DBGUID_DEFAULT as the dialect identifier when it calls **ICommandText::SetCommandText**. DBGUID_DEFAULT indicates that the provider should use its default dialect. If this command text returns more than one result set, for example, if the command invokes a stored procedure that returns multiple result sets, SQL Server would use only the first result set from the command.

For a list of all OLE DB interfaces that SQL Server uses, see "OLE DB Interfaces Consumed by SQL Server" later in this chapter.

OLE DB Interfaces Consumed by SQL Server

The following table lists all of the OLE DB interfaces used by SQL Server. The Required column indicates whether the interface is part of the bare minimum OLE DB functionality that SQL Server needs or whether it is optional. If a given interface is not marked as required, SQL Server can still access the provider, but some specific SQL Server functionality or optimization is not possible against the provider.

In the case of the optional interfaces, the Scenarios column indicates one or more of the scenarios that use the specified interface. For example, the **IRowsetChange** interface on base table rowsets is an optional interface; this interface is used in the UPDATE and DELETE statements and INSERT statement scenarios. If this interface is not supported, UPDATE, DELETE, and INSERT statements cannot be supported against that provider. Some of the other optional interfaces are marked "performance" in the Scenarios column, indicating that the interface results in better general performance. For example, if the **IDBSchemaRowset** interface is not supported, SQL Server must open the rowset twice: once for its metadata and once for query execution. By supporting **IDBSchemaRowset**, SQL Server performance is improved.

Object	Interface	Required	Comments	Scenarios
Data Source	**IDBInitialize**	Yes	Initialize and set up data and security context.	
	IDBCreateSession	Yes	Create DB session object.	
	IDBProperties	Yes	Get information about capabilities of provider, set initialization properties, required property: DBPROP_INIT_TIMEOUT.	
	IDBInfo	No	Get quoting literal, catalog, name, part, separator, character, and so on.	Remote query.

(continued)

Object	Interface	Required	Comments	Scenarios
DB Session	**IDBSchemaRowset**	No	Get table/column metadata. Rowsets needed: TABLES, COLUMNS, PROVIDER_TYPES; others that are used if available: INDEXES.	Performance, indexed access.
	IOpenRowset	Yes	Open a rowset on a table/index.	
	IGetDataSource	Yes	Use to get back to the DSO from a DB session object.	
	IDBCreateCommand	No	Use to create a command object (query) for providers that support querying.	Remote query, pass-through query.
	ITransactionLocal	No	Use for transacted updates.	UPDATE and DELETE, INSERT statements.
	ITransactionJoin	No	Use for distributed transaction support.	UPDATE and DELETE, INSERT statements if in a user transaction.
Rowset	**IRowset**	Yes	Scan rows.	
	IAccessor	Yes	Bind to columns in a rowset.	
	IColumnsInfo	Yes	Get information about columns in a rowset.	
	IRowsetInfo	Yes	Get information about rowset properties.	
	IRowsetLocate	No	Needed for UPDATE/DELETE operations and to do index-based lookups; used to look up rows by bookmarks.	Indexed access, UPDATE and DELETE statements.

(continued)

Object	Interface	Required	Comments	Scenarios
	IRowsetChange	No	Needed for INSERTS/UPDATES / DELETES on a rowset. Rowsets against base tables should support this interface for INSERT, UPDATE and DELETE statements.	UPDATE and DELETE, INSERT statements.
	IConvertType	Yes	Use to verify whether the rowset supports specific data type conversions on its columns.	
Index	IRowset	Yes	Scan rows.	Indexed access, performance.
	IAccessor	Yes	Bind to columns in a rowset.	Indexed access, performance.
	IColumnsInfo	Yes	Get information about columns in a rowset.	Indexed access, performance.
	IRowsetInfo	Yes	Get information about rowset properties.	Indexed access, performance.
	IRowsetIndex	Yes	Needed only for rowsets on an index; used for indexing functionality (set range, seek).	Indexed access, performance.
Command	ICommand	Yes		Remote query, pass-through query.
	ICommandText	Yes	Use for defining the query text.	Remote query, pass-through query.
	IColumnsInfo	Yes	Use for getting column metadata for query results.	Remote query, pass-through query.
	ICommandProperties	Yes	Use to specify required properties on rowsets returned by the command.	Remote query, pass-through query.

(continued)

Object	Interface	Required	Comments	Scenarios
	ICommandWithParameters	No	Use for parameterized query execution.	Remote query, performance.
	ICommandPrepare	No	Use for preparing a command to get metadata (used in pass-through queries if available).	Remote query, performance.
Error	IErrorRecords	Yes	Use for getting a pointer to an IErrorInfo interface corresponding to a single error record.	
	IErrorInfo	Yes	Use for getting a pointer to an IErrorInfo interface corresponding to a single error record.	
Any object	ISupportErrorInfo	No	Use to verify whether a given interface supports error objects.	

Note The Index object, Command object, and Error object are not mandatory. However, if they are supported, the listed interfaces are mandatory as specified in the Required column.

Transact-SQL Subset Used for Generating Remote Queries

SQL Server uses the following subset of the Transact-SQL language for queries evaluated by SQL command providers:

- SELECT statements with SELECT, FROM, WHERE, GROUP BY, UNION, UNION ALL, ORDER BY DESC, ASC, and HAVING clauses. UNION and UNION ALL are generated only against providers that support SQL-92 entry level, not against those supporting ODBC Core.
- SELECT clause:
- Scalar subqueries in the SELECT list.

- Column aliases without the AS keyword.
- FROM clause:
  - Explicit join keywords are not used; comma-separated table names are used to specify inner joins, and outer joins are not specified in remote queries.
  - Nested queries of the form FROM (<nested query>) <alias>.
  - Table aliases without the AS keyword.
- WHERE clause uses subqueries with [NOT] EXISTS, ANY, ALL.
- Expressions:
  - Aggregate functions used: MIN([DISTINCT]), MAX([DISTINCT]), COUNT([DISTINCT]), SUM([DISTINCT]), AVG([DISTINCT]), and COUNT(*).
  - Comparison Operators: <, =, <=, >, <>, >=, IS NULL, and IS NOT NULL.
  - Boolean operators: AND, OR, and NOT.
  - Arithmetic operators: +, -, *, and /.
- Constants:
  - Numeric and money literals are always surrounded by ( ).
  - Character literals are quoted with ''.

SQL Server-Specific Properties

The SQL Server-specific properties SQLPROP_DYNAMICSQL and SQLPROP_NESTEDQUERIES are supported by **IDBProperties**. These two properties are part of a SQL Server specific property set called SQLPROPSET_OPTHINTS and have defined PROPID values. The property set SQLPROPSET_OPTHINTS and the two properties are defined by using the following constants:

```
extern const GUID SQLPROPSET_OPTHINTS = { 0x2344480c, 0x33a7, 0x11d1, {
0x9b, 0x1a, 0x0, 0x60, 0x8, 0x26, 0x8b, 0x9e } };
enum SQLPROPERTIES
    {
    SQLPROP_NESTEDQUERIES = 0x4,
    SQLPROP_DYNAMICSQL = 0x5
    };
```

Glossary

access control list (ACL)
A list associated with a file that contains information about which users or groups have permission to access or modify the file.

account operator Windows NT Server operator who manages user accounts.

active data in memory Data being read or written to.

Active Directory Single, network-based storage hierarchy based on X.500 standards and protected by ACLs.

ad hoc name Name based on the OPENROWSET function.

adjective phrasing English Query phrasing that expresses an adjectival relationship, for example, "books are popular."

aggregation Precomputed higher-level (rolled up) value that summarizes low-level (detail) data in a dimension.

alert Microsoft SQLServerAgent service definition matching one or more SQL Server events and a response, should those events occur.

analysis server Server providing the core computational functionality of OLAP services.

article Any grouping of data to be replicated.

auditing The process an operating system uses to detect and record security-related events, for example, an attempt to create, access, or delete objects such as files and directories.

Authentication In a multiuser or network operating system, the process by which the system validates a user's logon information. A user's name and password are compared against an authorized list; if the system detects a match, access is granted to the extent specified in the permission list for that user.

Authenticode A cryptographic feature of Microsoft Internet Explorer.

automatic parameter Parameter resulting from caching a plan created for dynamic SQL and turning the constants into parameters.

backward compatibility mode Mode in which a SQL Server 7.0 application or database functions as it did in SQL Server 6.x.

bidirectional merge replication Merge replication in which updated records on the mobile client are copied to the server and vice versa.

biometric authentication Authentication provided by devices such as fingerprint or retinal scanners.

Certificate Management Process through which public and private encryption keys are securely and reliably managed by a Certification Authority.

chained transactions Sybase System 10 transactions that have implicit starting points but must be explicitly committed.

clock algorithm Data access control method used by SQL Server 7.0.

clustered index Index in which the order of the values is the same as the order of the data in the table.

COM The extension reserved by MS-DOS for a type of executable binary (program) file limited to a single 64-KB segment.

configuration Alternative set of indexes.

console tree Tree of categories and objects relevant to a particular server. This tree is found on the left pane of MMC.

context switching A type of multitasking; the act of turning the central processor's "attention" from one task to another, rather than allocating increments of time to each task in turn.

convergence Transactional consistency level in which all sites can work freely in a disconnected manner; when all the nodes have synchronized, all sites converge to the same value.

correlated queries Nested queries. (*See* nested queries.)

cost threshold value Value used to assess the first potential operation plan. If the latter's value is less than cost threshold, no further cost optimization takes place and execution begins immediately.

cost-based query optimizer Query optimizer that chooses a SQL Server procedural plan on a cost-effective basis.

covered query Query handled by an explicitly declared covering index or index intersection.

covering index Nonclustered index built upon all of the columns required to satisfy a SQL Server query, both in the selection criteria and in the WHERE clause.

CryptoAPI Microsoft's cryptographic application programming interface (APIs); a set of software libraries with high-level APIs that manage the details of key management, formatting, and cipher algorithms.

cryptography Security feature that protects the privacy and integrity of data, especially data in transit across a network.

cube Information container in the OLAP data model, for example, the cube of sales information. (*See* dimension; hierarchy; measure; level; virtual cube.)

Custom Conflict Resolution Merge replication conflict resolution method that makes use of custom resolvers.

custom resolver A COM-object or stored procedure written to the public resolver interface and invoked during reconciliation by the Merge Agent to support business rules.

DA controller Internal SCSI controllers that connect all of the internal disk drives within the Symmetrix storage system into the 4-GB internal cache.

Data Access Object (DAO) Connectivity tool designed for desktop access to data and based on the Microsoft Jet database engine technology.

data consumer Any component that needs to access data from the OLE DB provider.

data explosion Dramatic increase of the volume of stored data due to excessive preaggregation.

data mart A scaled-down version of a data warehouse that is tailored to contain only information likely to be used by the target group. (*See* dependent data mart; independent data mart.)

data page Page containing all the data associated with the rows of a table, except **text** and **image** data.

data provider OLE DB component that owns the data it exposes to the outside world.

data sparsity Relative lack of data values in a cube, which can waste data storage space and system resources.

data warehouse Subject-oriented, integrated, time-variant, non-volatile store of data collected from other systems that becomes the foundation for decision support and data analysis.

Decision Support Objects Object model allowing programmatic access to administrative functions in the OLAP Services Analysis Server.

default result sets Set-based operations.

defined table Table in which the number and types of columns are either known in advance or specified as part of the query.

degree of parallelism Actual number of threads used by a parallel query.

dependent data mart Data mart containing a subset of enterprise-wide data.

Desktop OLAP (DOLAP) Enables the user to analyze a data slice multidimensionally while disconnected from the corporate network, for example, a traveling sales manager viewing revenue summary for a particular region.

details pane Right pane of MMC detailing a selected item on the console tree.

dimension Descriptive category in a cube within the data warehousing paradigm, for example, the dimensions of time, geography, product, and so on in a sales cube.

dirty page Any buffer cache page modified after being brought into the buffer cache.

Distributed COM (DCOM) The version of Microsoft's Component Object Model (COM) specification that stipulates how components communicate over Windows-based networks. It permits the distribution of different components for a single application across two or more networked computers and allows an application to run distributed across a network so that the distribution of components is not apparent to the user.

Distributed Password Protocol A password-based authentication protocol.

distributed query Any SELECT, INSERT, UPDATE, or DELETE statement that references tables and rowsets from one or more external OLE DB data sources.

Distribution Agent Agent that moves the transactions and snapshot jobs held in distribution database tables to Subscribers.

DNA architecture Windows Distributed interNet Applications architecture.

drive pool methodology A technique for creating disk I/O parallelism.

DTS Data Pump High-speed, in-process COM server that moves and transforms OLE DB rowsets between heterogeneous data stores.

DTS package Complete description of all the work to be performed as part of the transformation process.

DTS step object Object coordinating the flow of control and execution of tasks in the DTS package.

dynamic locking Low-cost locking determined at run time by the storage engine and query processor based on the characteristics of the schema and query.

enabling technology Set of software libraries that encapsulates certain algorithms or procedures, which the operating system makes available to other applications and system services.

enterprise data warehouse Data warehouse containing enterprise-wide data for consolidated data analysis.

exchange operator Operator in a query execution plan that provides process management, data redistribution, and flow control.

exclusive lock Lock preventing concurrent transactions from updating the same resource at the same time. (*See* update lock.)

explicit transaction Transaction that issues BEGIN TRANSACTION, COMMIT or ROLLBACK statements.

extended memory size option SQL Server 7.0 Enterprise Edition memory configuration parameter that indicates the number of megabytes of memory to use as a disk cache in addition to the conventional buffer pool.

extent Basic unit in which space is allocated to tables and indexes. An extent is a contiguous group of eight pages, or 64 KB.

fact Numeric data that is the core of what is being analyzed.

FASMI test Refinement of Codd's definition of OLAP, stating that OLAP applications should deliver Fast Analysis of Shared Multidimensional Information.

fiber Windows NT lightweight thread scheduled within a single OS thread.

file content search Type of search that supports property textual searches and full-text searches, and can incorporate such searches into a query that includes relational operations against database data.

file grow Automatic space allocation to a file to prevent logs or databases from running out of space.

file shrink Automatic size reduction of a file carried out by moving rows from pages at the end of a file to pages allocated earlier in the file.

firewall A security system intended to protect an organization's network against external threats, such as hackers, coming from another network, such as the Internet.

first-wins conflict resolution Merge replication conflict resolution method in which the winner is the one who first submitted the change.

flattening Conversion of nested queries into semi-joins.

FREETEXT predicate Predicate used to determine whether values in full-text registered columns reflect the meaning, rather than the exact words, specified in the predicate.

full-text catalog Entity holding a collection of full-text indexes.

full-text search A search for one or more documents, records, or strings based on all of the actual text data rather than on an index containing a limited set of keywords.

global temporary table Temporary table that is visible to all sessions.

group Security administrative unit within the Windows NT operating system that contains Windows NT user accounts or other groups. Privileges can be specified for the group, and each member will have those privileges. (*See* role.)

GUID Globally unique identifier. In the Component Object Model (COM), a 16-byte code that identifies an interface to an object across all computers and networks.

hard page fault Memory management problem in which Windows goes to disk to resolve memory references.

hash To be mapped to a numerical value by a transformation known as a hashing function. Hashing is used to convert an identifier or key, meaningful to a user, into a value for the location of the corresponding data in a structure, such as a table.

hash buckets SQL Server 7.0 system configuration parameter consisting of a prime number used as input into a memory-hashing algorithm.

hash join Join that hashes input values, based on a repeatable randomizing function, and compares values in the hash table for matches.

hash team Technique consisting of taking advantage of similar operations across multiple phases.

heap Table that has nonclustered index(es).

heap page Nonclustered index page.

heterogeneous data Data stored in a data store other than SQL Server.

hierarchy Range of levels of data detail within a data warehousing dimension, for example, years, months, and days, in the time dimension.

homogeneous data Data currently stored in SQL Server.

hot plug Ability of a RAID controller to provide a failed drive replacement while remaining online.

hot spot Area on a disk where many queries try to read or write data at the same time, which creates a disk I/O bottleneck.

Hybrid OLAP (HOLAP) Combines the best features of the ROLAP and MOLAP architectures: superior performance and extensive scalability.

hyper-volume The logical division of an EMC hard disk drive.

immediate guaranteed consistency Transactional consistency level in which all participating sites are guaranteed to have the same data values at the same time, and the data is in the state that would have been achieved had all the work been done at the publishing site.

impersonation Process in which remote server applications can assume the identity of your user account.

implicit transaction Transaction that has an implicit starting point but must be explicitly committed.

incremental repopulation Writing only data changes to the table since the last population.

independent data mart Data mart containing data coming directly from the operational data sources.

Index Allocation Map (IAM) SQL Server 7.0 method of recording the location of extents.

index intersection Process in which the query processor considers multiple indexes from a given table, builds a hash table based on them, and uses the hash table to reduce I/O for a query.

index join A variation on index intersection, consisting of joining multiple indexes to form a covering index.

index page Page that contains only data from columns that comprise a particular index.

index provider Provider that supports and exposes indexes according to OLE DB and allows index-based lookup of base tables.

indexing components Components that manage the initial population and subsequent updating of the full-text indexes.

inflectional forms Changes undergone by a word to reflect change of number, gender, voice, mood, and so on, for example, "child" and "children", "drive," "drives," "drove," "driving," and "driven."

inflectional stem A word's basic inflectional form, from which all the inflectional forms derive; for example, "do" is the stem of "does," "did," and "done."

insertion hot spots Hot spot created by inserting data in the same disk area, for example, the end of a busy table.

integrity Completeness and accuracy of data stored in a computer, especially after it has been manipulated in some way.

intent lock Lock indicating that SQL Server is attempting to acquire a shared or exclusive lock on some of the resources lower in the hierarchy.

interesting ordering Avoiding sort operations by keeping track of the ordering of intermediate results that move from operator to operator.

interface Object consisting of a collection of methods that a client application can call, which are assembled and exposed to the system in the same way, regardless of the language used to create the object.

inter-query parallelism Ability to assign different queries to different processors.

intra-query parallelism Ability to break a single query into multiple subtasks and execute them on multiple processors in an SMP computer.

join Referencing together in a query multiple tables from a relational database.

key A row lock within an index.

key management The process of distributing keys between sender and receiver.

last checked Value stored in each buffer representing the last time the clock came by to check on this buffer.

last touched Value stored in each buffer page representing the last time this buffer page was active.

latent guaranteed consistency Transactional consistency level in which all participating sites are guaranteed to have the same data values that were achieved at the publishing site at some point in time.

leaf node Lowest level of the index tree of a clustered index; storage location of the index entry of a nonclustered index.

level Rung on the hierarchical ladder of a dimension.

linguistic search Word search, phrase search, or prefix search.

linked server-based name Four-part name of the form <linked-server>.<catalog>.<schema>.<object>.

local temporary table Temporary table that is visible only in the current session.

log file　Operating system file that holds all the transaction log information used to recover a database.

Log Reader Agent　Agent that moves transactions marked for replication from the transaction log on the Publisher to the distribution database.

loose consistency　Latent guaranteed consistency.

major entity　Semantic entity normally used in English Query to correspond to an entire table.

mallet　Traditional name of the nefarious intermediary blocked by cryptography.

measure　Quantitative value found in a cube, for example, dollar sales, unit sales, and so on in a sales cube.

Merge Agent　Agent that moves and reconciles incremental data changes that occurred after the initial snapshot was created.

merge join　Join that simultaneously passes over two sorted inputs to perform inner joins, outer joins, semi-joins, intersections, and unions.

merge replication　Mode of replication in which Publishers and Subscribers can work independently and reconnect periodically to merge their results, with automatic conflict resolution.

message digest　Small value (usually 16 bytes) produced by a hashing algorithm from an arbitrarily long stream of data.

metadata　Descriptive information about software components and their relationships.

minor entity　English Query semantic entity associated with a major entity. (*See* name; trait.)

mirroring　Method of fault tolerance to hard disk failure implemented by writing the same information onto two sets of drives.

mixed extent　Extent that allows allocation of a single page to a small table or index.

model　Database used as the template for all the databases created on the SQL Server system.

MSSQLServer service　Primary service responsible for SQL Server.

multiphase optimization　Form of optimization using a cost threshold value to prevent over-optimization.

name　Type of English Query minor entity that indicates how its associated major entity is identified in questions and statements, for example, "book" refers to the major entity Books table.

name phrasing　English Query phrasing that expresses a name relationship, for example, "author names are the names of authors."

nested queries　Queries that are created on top of other queries in a nested fashion.

nested views　Views that are created on top of other views in a nested fashion.

Network Library　Microsoft SQL Server Net-Library used by the client to connect to the aliased server.

noise word　Extremely common word of no interest to a full-text search, for example, "a," "but," and "the."

non-SQL Command Providers　Provider that supports the Command object and its mandatory interfaces but does not support a SQL standard dialect recognized by SQL Server.

nonclustered indexes　B-trees formed out of 8-KB index pages.

nonleaf level　Upper part of an index B-tree structure.

nonrelational data Data not stored in relational databases, for example, audio and video clips and e-mail messages.

one-computer upgrade Upgrading to SQL Server 7.0 on your existing hardware.

online RAID expansion RAID feature allowing disks to be added dynamically to a physical RAID array while online, as long as there are hot-plug slots available.

Open Database Connectivity (ODBC)
A C/C++ API designed to target different sources from the same source code by substituting different drivers.

Open Information Model Object models for specific types of information, flexible enough to support new information types.

over-optimization Occurs when the query optimizer uses more resources to determine the best plan than are required to execute the plan.

Open Databases Configuration parameter in SQL Server version 6.5 and earlier consisting of the number of SQL Server databases allowed to be active at any one time.

Open Objects Configuration parameter consisting of the number of objects SQL Server allows to have actively open at any point in time.

optimistic concurrency control Form of concurrency control that does not place shared locks on tables.

page Fundamental unit of data storage in SQL Server, consisting of 8 KB.

page chain Sequence of pages in which each page has a pointer to the next page holding data for the table.

page splitting Creation of two nonsequential pages from one page lacking the space to accept new data that must be inserted into the page because of the logical ordering of data defined in that page.

parallel data scanning Reading sequential data in parallel.

parallel query Parallel execution of a single query across multiple processors.

parallel utilities Utilities run in parallel.

parameterized query Query in which the application identifies the parameters.

parity Error-checking procedure in which the number of 1s must be the same—either even or odd—for each group of bits transmitted without error. Method of fault tolerance.

partial preaggregation Optimal preaggregation that computes only the optimum set of aggregations from which all other aggregations can be derived at run time.

partitioned cube Logical cube that is spread over multiple physical cubes and even separate physical servers.

PASSFILT Enabling technology that lets an administrator install a trusted program that is called every time a user changes a password.

permissions validation stage Security stage that controls the activities the user is allowed to perform in the SQL Server database.

Personal Information Exchange A protocol that securely transfers the contents of a P-Store from one location to another.

pessimistic concurrency control Form of concurrency control that places shared locks on tables.

phrase search Search for two or more words following one another immediately, after noise words have been disregarded.

phrasing English Query syntactical expression of a relationship. (*See* adjective phrasing; name phrasing; preposition phrasing; subset phrasing; trait phrasing; verb phrasing.)

pool methodology *See* drive pool methodology.

preaggregation The precomputing of aggregations.

prefetch hint Message from the query processor to the storage engine listing which records the query processor will soon need.

prefix Any character or group of characters used to specify a prefix search.

prefix search Search for all words that begin with a given prefix, for example, "geo*" finds "geophysics" and "geography."

preposition phrasing English Query phrasing that expresses a prepositional relationship, for example, "publishers are in cities."

primary file Starting point of the database; contains the pointers to the rest of the files in the database.

priority-based conflict resolution
Merge replication conflict resolution method in which every publication is assigned a priority number so that in case of conflict, the publication with the highest number wins.

Private Communication Technology (PCT)
An improved version of Secure Sockets Layer.

processor affinity Association between a processor and a thread.

property textual search Search done on document properties such as author, subject, type, word count, printed page count, and time last written.

Protected Store (P-Store) A set of software libraries that allows applications to fetch and retrieve security and other information from a personal storage location, hiding the implementation and details of the storage itself.

proximity search A search for words or phrases found near one another, but not following one another immediately even after noise words are disregarded.

public key encryption Asymmetric scheme that uses a pair of keys for encryption: the public key encrypts data, and a corresponding secret key decrypts it. For digital signatures, the process is reversed: the sender uses the secret key to create a unique electronic number that can be read by anyone possessing the corresponding public key, which verifies the message is from the sender.

publication Collection of one or more articles.

Publisher Server that makes data available for replication to other servers.

pull subscription Subscription in which the Subscriber asks for periodic updates of all changes at the Publisher.

push subscription Subscription in which the Publisher propagates the changes to the Subscriber without a specific request from the Subscriber.

query cost Estimated elapsed time, in seconds, required to execute a query on a specific hardware configuration.

query execution Major phase in query processing consisting of executing the plan chosen during query optimization.

query governor SQL Server 7.0 feature that prevents a query from running if its query cost is greater than an administrator-specified upper cost limit.

query optimization Major phase in query processing consisting of choosing the fastest execution plan.

query processor Major SQL Server component that accepts, selects, and then executes the plan chosen for executing the syntax.

random I/O Form of disk I/O in which data is read in random order.

recovery Restoration of lost data or the reconciliation of conflicting or erroneous data after a system failure. Recovery is often achieved using a disk or tape backup and transaction logs.

referential integrity The way in which an RDBMS manages relationships between tables.

relationship English Query semantic relationship between entities, for example, "publishers publish books" is a relationship between the major entities "publishers" and "books." (*See* phrasing.)

Remote Access Service (RAS) Windows software that allows a user to gain remote access to the network server by using a modem.

Remote Data Objects (RDO) Object-oriented data access tool with no native file format of its own. RDO can be used only with databases complying with the most recent ODBC standards.

Remote Data Services (RDS) Client-side component that interfaces with ADO and provides cursors, remote object invocation, and explicit and implicit remote recordset functionality such as fetch and update.

remote table Table stored in an OLE DB data source and external to the server running SQL Server executing the query.

Replication Monitor Component of a Distributor enabling a member of the **sysadmin** fixed server role to view the status of replication agents and troubleshoot potential problems at the Distributor.

role Security administrative unit within SQL Server that contains SQL Server logins, Windows NT logins, groups, or other roles. (*See* group.)

rowset A tabular object used by OLE DB to expose its data.

sandbox Scope of a Java applet.

search engine Program that searches for key words in documents or in a database.

secure channel Communications link that has been protected against unauthorized access, operation, or use by means of isolation from the public network, encryption, or other forms of control.

Secure DCOM DCOM options that automatically use SSPI authentication and message encryption.

Secure RPC RPC options that automatically use SSPI authentication and message encryption.

Secure Sockets Layer (SSL) Proposed open standard developed by Netscape Communications for establishing a secure communications channel to prevent the interception of critical information.

security principals Users and groups of users, from the point of view of the SQL Server 7.0 security system architecture.

Security Support Provider A library that manages a particular authentication or cryptographic scheme.

selectivity　Property that relates to how many rows are typically identified by a key value. A unique key value has high selectivity; a nonunique key value (for example, one found in 1,000 rows) has poor selectivity.

semantic entity　English Query entity used to establish semantic relationships between tables, table elements, and so on, allowing the user to type database queries in English language phrases, which are then translated into SQL statements. (*See* major entity; minor entity.)

sequential I/O　Form of disk I/O in which data is read in the same order as it is stored on the disk.

serial execution plan　Execution plan used by a nonparallel query.

server alias　Label by which the entry will be referenced at connect time.

service component　Logical OLE DB object that encapsulates a piece of DBMS functionality, for example, query processors, cursor engines, or transaction managers.

shared lock　Lock that allows concurrent transactions to read a resource.

simple table provider　Provider that exposes the opening of a rowset against a base table through the **IOpenRowset** interface.

simulated configuration　Configuration that is not actually created and is used only to estimate the costs if it were created.

singleton SELECT　SELECT statement that returns one row based on the criteria defined in the WHERE clause of the statement.

site autonomy　State of affairs in which all sites operate independently.

Snapshot Agent　Agent that prepares the schema and initial data files of published tables and stored procedures, stores the snapshot on the Distributor, and records information about the synchronization status in the distribution database.

snapshot replication　Type of replication that takes a picture, or snapshot, of the published data in the database at one moment in time and does a total refresh of the Subscriber data.

soft page fault　Memory management problem in which an application requests memory pages still inside RAM but outside of the application's **Working Set**.

sort pages　Amount of memory allocated per user for sorting operations in SQL Server 6.5.

spindle　Axle for mounting a disk or reel of magnetic tape.

spoofing　Practice of making a transmission appear to come from an authorized user.

star index　Multicolumn index on a star-schema's fact table used in conjunction with the Cartesian product strategy.

star schema　Type of database schema designed to allow a user to intuitively navigate information in the database.

static structures　SQL Server 6.5 preallocation of SQL Server memory to SQL Server components such as user connections, locks, open objects and worker thread.

storage engine　Major SQL Server component that writes data to and reads data from the disk. It manages records, controls concurrency, and maintains log files.

storage location　Position at which a particular item can be found—either an addressed location or a uniquely identified location on a disk, tape, or similar medium.

stored procedure Procedure that is actually stored within a database.

stored procedure cache SQL Server 6.5 fixed segment of memory based on the procedure cache **sp_configure** parameter.

stored procedure percent SQL Server 6.5 configuration parameter that sets what percentage of the available memory left goes to procedure cache.

Subscriber Server that stores replicas and receives updates from a publisher.

subset phrasing English Query phrasing that expresses a subset relationship, for example, "some books are bestsellers."

syntax-based query optimizer Query optimizer that creates its SQL procedural plan on the basis of the exact syntax of the query and the order of the clauses within the query.

system integrity Security feature that ensures the underlying security software cannot be tampered with.

temporary table Table that creates a snapshot of data for a connected user's session.

text search catalog Catalog in which Index Services stores indexes and property values.

thread In programming, a process that is part of a larger process or program.

tight consistency Immediate guaranteed consistency.

torn page Page that is written only partially, due to a power failure or another problem.

torn page detection Detection of incomplete I/O.

trait Type of English Query minor entity that identifies what its associated major entity has; for example, "books have titles," "books have authors." A trait is a kind of relationship. (*See* relationship.)

trait phrasing English Query phrasing that expresses a trait relationship, for example, "books have royalties."

Transact-SQL Simple programming language that provides basic conditional processing and simple repetition control, included in Microsoft SQL Server.

transaction log File that records transactional changes occurring in a database, providing a basis for updating a master file and establishing an audit trail.

Transport Layer Security An upcoming Internet standard that merges SSL and the ideas in PCT.

transactional consistency State of affairs in which all sites are guaranteed to have the same data values at the same time.

transactional replication Replication method in which transactions (INSERT, UPDATE, or DELETE statements) executed on one computer are replicated to another computer.

transformation Sequence of procedural operations that is applied to the information in a data source before it can be stored in the specified destination.

trigger Action that causes a procedure to be carried out automatically when a user attempts to modify data.

trust Unilateral access of the accounts of one domain to another domain.

trusted path Windows NT security feature that prevents spoofing.

two-computer upgrade Upgrading to SQL Server 7.0 on a new computer.

two-phase commit Process that ensures transactions applying to more than one server are completed on either all servers or none.

uniform extent Extent owned by a single object; all pages in the extent can be used only by the owning object.

universal server approach Approach in which all data must exist in a single repository and must be accessed using a single access language.

update lock Lock allowing only one transaction at a time to update a resource, thus preventing the deadlocks due to concurrent attempts to obtain an exclusive lock.

user-defined filegroup Filegroup defined by the user.

user rights Special capabilities that administrators assign to accounts that can use a given computer.

verb phrasing English Query phrasing that expresses a verbal relationship, for example, "authors write books."

view Logical table created through the specification of one or more relational operations on one or more tables.

virtual cube Cube consisting of two or more physical, logical, or partitioned cubes linked at query time along one or more common dimensions.

virtual directory Directory that references one or more physical directories and, optionally, other virtual directories.

virtual log file Logical segment of a log file; unit of truncation for the transaction log.

virtual memory Memory that appears to an application to be larger and more uniform than it is.

width threshold Limit beyond which the Cost Evaluation module of the Index Tuning Wizard ceases to consider wider indexes.

worker thread Windows operating system threads used to service batches of SQL Server commands submitted to the database server.

wrapper DLL DLL that intercepts external library function calls made to an application to control the application or process that instantiated the DLL.

Index

X

COMPREND 1 CD

DATE DE RETOUR		L.-Brault
0 2 FEV. 2001		

Microsoft Press offers *comprehensive* learning solutions to help new users, power users, and professionals get the most from *Microsoft technology.*

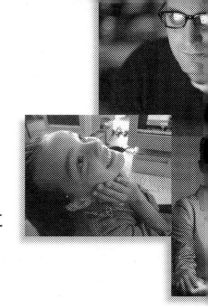

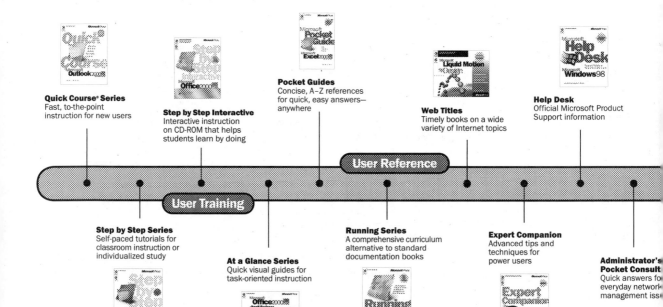

Quick Course® Series
Fast, to-the-point instruction for new users

Step by Step Interactive
Interactive instruction on CD-ROM that helps students learn by doing

Pocket Guides
Concise, A–Z references for quick, easy answers—anywhere

Web Titles
Timely books on a wide variety of Internet topics

Help Desk
Official Microsoft Product Support information

User Reference

User Training

Step by Step Series
Self-paced tutorials for classroom instruction or individualized study

At a Glance Series
Quick visual guides for task-oriented instruction

Running Series
A comprehensive curriculum alternative to standard documentation books

Expert Companion
Advanced tips and techniques for power users

Administrator's Pocket Consult
Quick answers for everyday network management issue

With **over 200** print, *multimedia, and online resources*—

whatever your information
need or learning style,

we've got a solution to help

you *start faster and go farther.*

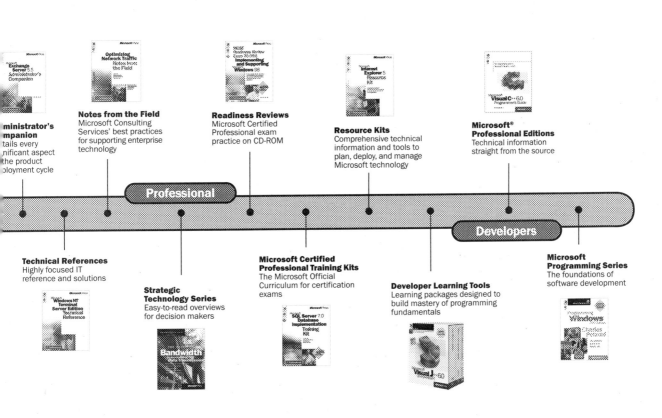

Notes from the Field
Microsoft Consulting
Services' best practices
for supporting enterprise
technology

Readiness Reviews
Microsoft Certified
Professional exam
practice on CD-ROM

Resource Kits
Comprehensive technical
information and tools to
plan, deploy, and manage
Microsoft technology

**Microsoft®
Professional Editions**
Technical information
straight from the source

ministrator's
mpanion
tails every
nificant aspect
the product
ployment cycle

Professional

Technical References
Highly focused IT
reference and solutions

**Strategic
Technology Series**
Easy-to-read overviews
for decision makers

**Microsoft Certified
Professional Training Kits**
The Microsoft Official
Curriculum for certification
exams

Developers

Developer Learning Tools
Learning packages designed to
build mastery of programming
fundamentals

**Microsoft
Programming Series**
The foundations of
software development

*Look for them at your bookstore
or computer store today!*

mspress.microsoft.com

The **intelligent** way
to practice for the
MCP exam.

If you took the Microsoft, Certified Professional (MCP) exam today, would you pass? With the READINESS REVIEW MCP exam simulation on CD-ROM, you get a low-risk, low-cost way to find out! Use this electronic assessment tool to take randomly generated, 60-question practice tests covering actual MCP objectives. Test and retest with different question sets each time, then consult the companion study guide to review all featured exam items and identify areas for further study. READINESS REVIEW—it's the smart way to prep!

Microsoft Press® products are available worldwide wherever quality computer books are sold. For more information, contact your book or computer retailer, software reseller, or local Microsoft® Sales Office, or visit our Web site at mspress.microsoft.com. To locate your nearest source for Microsoft Press products, or to order directly, call 1-800-MSPRESS in the U.S. (in Canada, call 1-800-268-2222).

Prices and availability dates are subject to change.

Microsoft®

mspress.microsoft.com